W9-AXK-755

GHOST IN THE SHELL

STAND ALONE COMPLEX

EPISODE2:TESTATION

002

Yu Kinutani

Translation by
Andria Cheng

Lettered by

Hemet Public Library
300 E. Latham Ave.
Hemet, CA 92543

KODANSHA
COMICS

Ghost In the Shell: Stand Alone Complex: Episode 2: Testation is a work of fiction. Names, characters, places, and incidents are the products of the author's imagination or are used fictitiously. Any resemblance to actual events, locales, or persons, living or dead, is entirely coincidental.

A Kodansha Comics Trade Paperback Original

Ghost In the Shell: Stand Alone Complex: Episode 2: Testation copyright © 2010 Yu Kinutani © Shirow Masamune•Production I.G/KODANSHA English translation copyright © 2011 Yu Kinutani © Shirow Masamune• Production I.G/KODANSHA

All rights reserved.

Published in the United States by Kodansha Comics, an imprint of Kodansha USA Publishing, LLC, New York.

Publication rights for this English edition arranged through Kodansha Ltd., Tokyo.

First published in Japan in 2010 by Kodansha Ltd., Tokyo.

ISBN 978-1-935-42986-9

Printed in the United States of America.

www.kodanshacomics.com

9 8 7 6 5 4 3 2 1

Translator: Andria Cheng
Lettering: Paige Pumphrey

CONTENTS

HONORIFICS EXPLAINED

Throughout the Kodansha Comics books, you will find Japanese honorifics left intact in the translations. For those not familiar with how the Japanese use honorifics and, more important, how they differ from American honorifics, we present this brief overview.

Politeness has always been a critical facet of Japanese culture. Ever since the feudal era, when Japan was a highly stratified society, use of honorifics—which can be defined as polite speech that indicates relationship or status—has played an essential role in the Japanese language. When addressing someone in Japanese, an honorific usually takes the form of a suffix attached to one's name (example: "Asuna-san"), is used as a title at the end of one's name, or appears in place of the name itself (example: "Negi-sensei," or simply "Sensei!").

Honorifics can be expressions of respect or endearment. In the context of manga and anime, honorifics give insight into the nature of the relationship between characters. Many English translations leave out these important honorifics and therefore distort the feel of the original Japanese. Because Japanese honorifics contain nuances that English honorifics lack, it is our policy at Kodansha Comics not to translate them. Here, instead, is a guide to some of the honorifics you may encounter in Kodansha Comics books.

-san: This is the most common honorific and is equivalent to Mr., Miss, Ms., or Mrs. It is the all-purpose honorific and can be used in any situation where politeness is required.

-sama: This is one level higher than "-san" and is used to confer great respect.

-dono: This comes from the word "tono," which means "lord." It is an even higher level than "-sama" and confers utmost respect.

-kun: This suffix is used at the end of boys' names to express familiarity or endearment. It is also sometimes used by men among friends, or when addressing someone younger or of a lower station.

-chan: This is used to express endearment, mostly toward girls. It is also used for little boys, pets, and even among lovers. It gives a sense of childish cuteness.

Bozu: This is an informal way to refer to a boy, similar to the English terms "kid" and "squirt."

Sempai/
Senpai: This title suggests that the addressee is one's senior in a group or organization. It is most often used in a school setting, where underclassmen refer to their upperclassmen as "sempai." It can also be used in the workplace, such as when a newer employee addresses an employee who has seniority in the company.

Kohai: This is the opposite of "sempai" and is used toward underclassmen in school or newcomers in the workplace. It connotes that the addressee is of a lower station.

Sensei: Literally meaning "one who has come before," this title is used for teachers, doctors, or masters of any profession or art.

-[blank]: This is usually forgotten in these lists, but it is perhaps the most significant difference between Japanese and English. The lack of honorific means that the speaker has permission to address the person in a very intimate way. Usually, only family, spouses, or very close friends have this kind of permission. Known as yobisute, it can be gratifying when someone who has earned the intimacy starts to call one by one's name without an honorific. But when that intimacy hasn't been earned, it can be very insulting.

Ghost in the Shell
Stand Alone Complex
Episode 2: Testation

Yu Kinutani

GHOST IN THE SHELL
STAND ALONE COMPLEX
EPISODE TESTATION

002

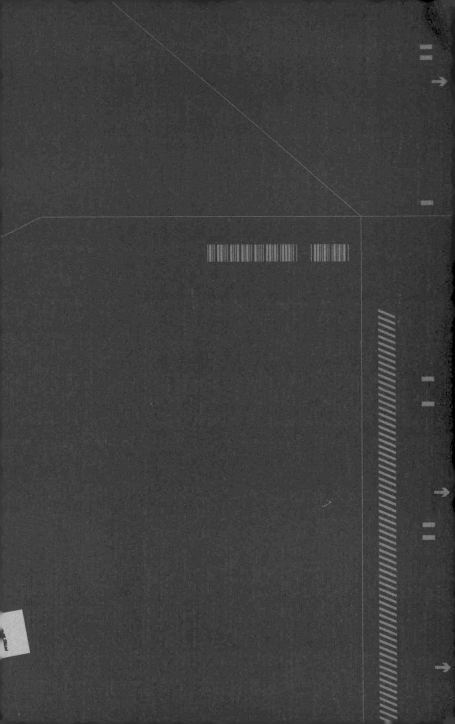

GHOST IN THE SHELL
STAND ALONE COMPLEX

EPISODE2:TESTATION

002

CONTENTS

#012: Runaway Tank

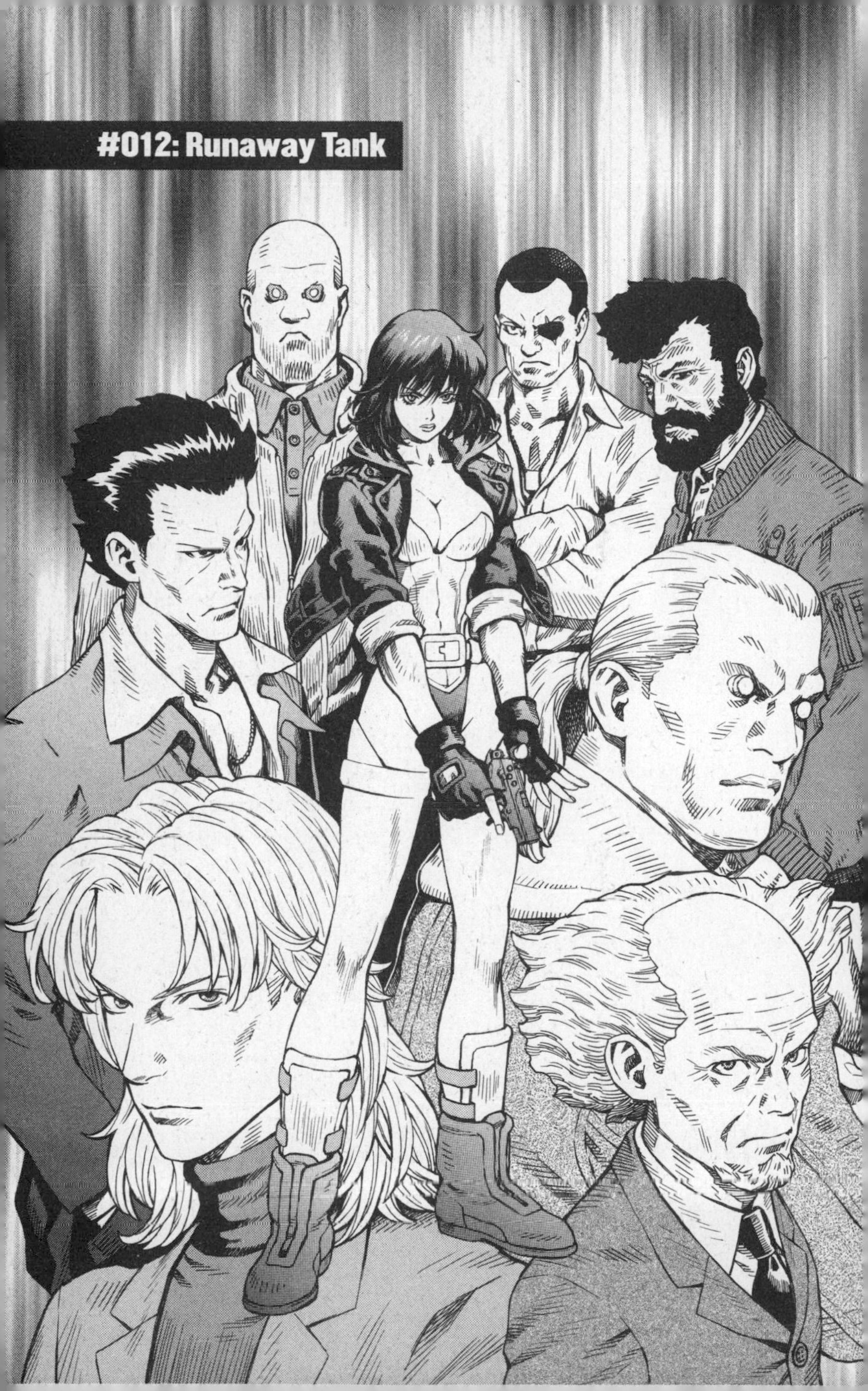

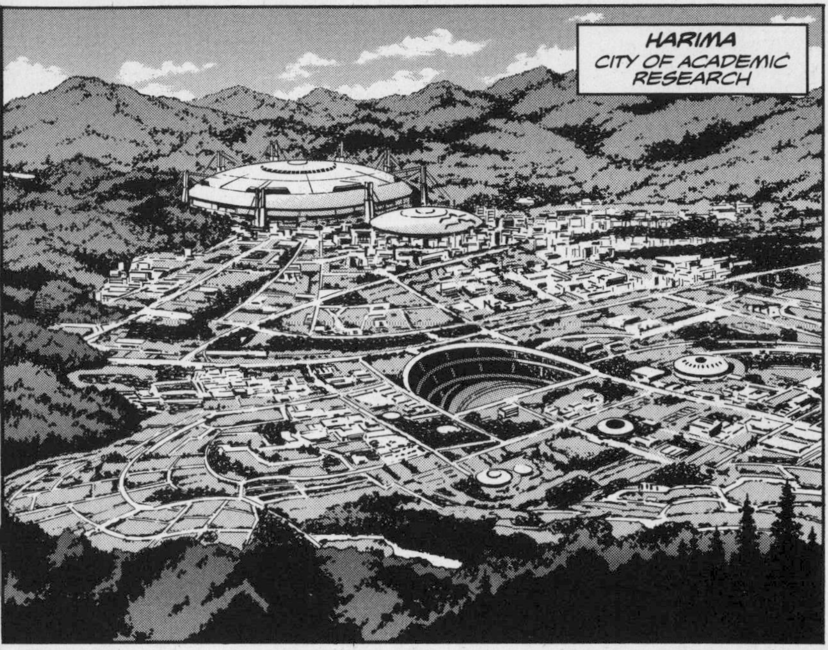
HARIMA
CITY OF ACADEMIC RESEARCH

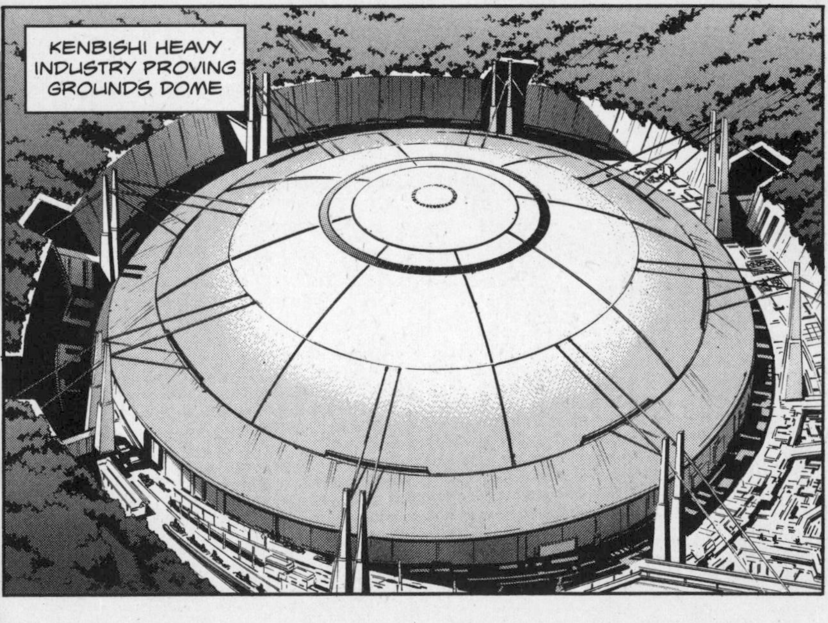
KENBISHI HEAVY INDUSTRY PROVING GROUNDS DOME

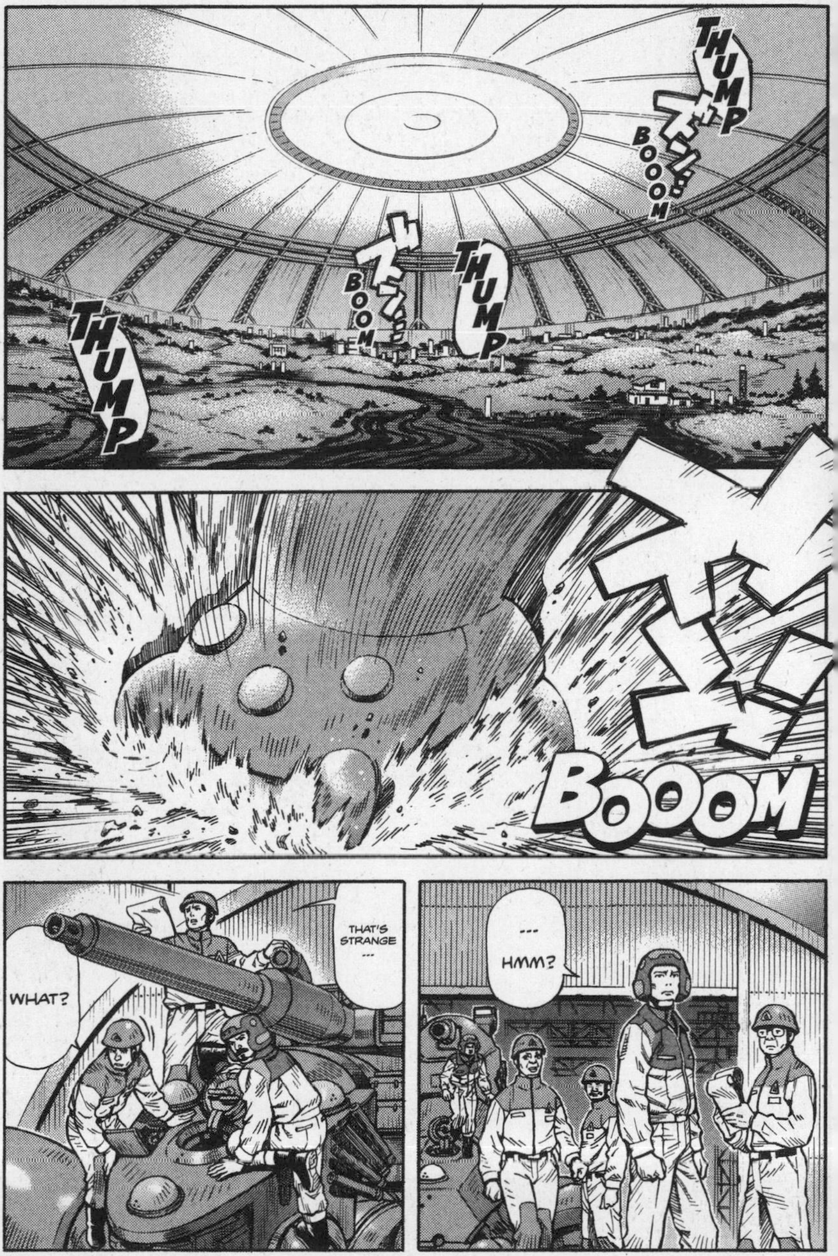
THUMP
BOOOOM
THUMP
BOOOM
THUMP
BOOOM
--- HMM?
THAT'S STRANGE ---
WHAT?

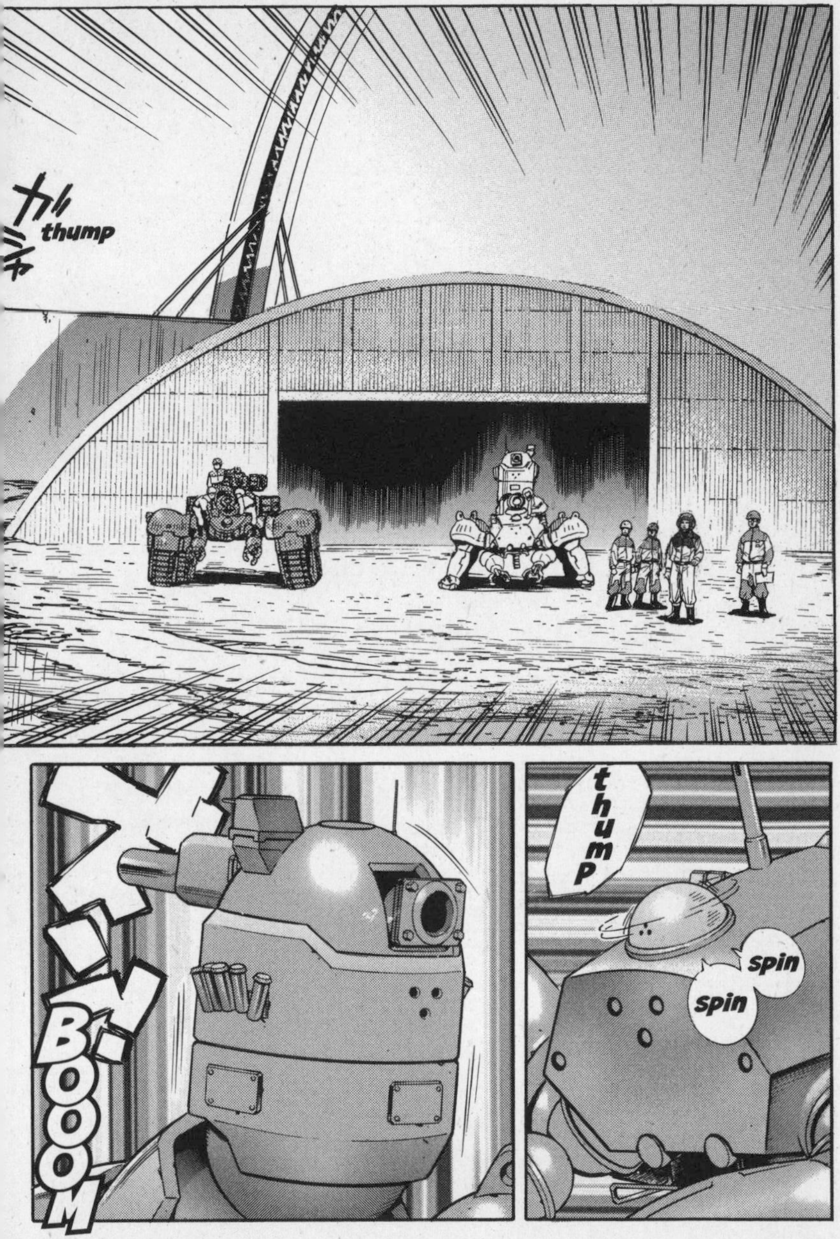
thump
thump
spin
spin
BOOOM

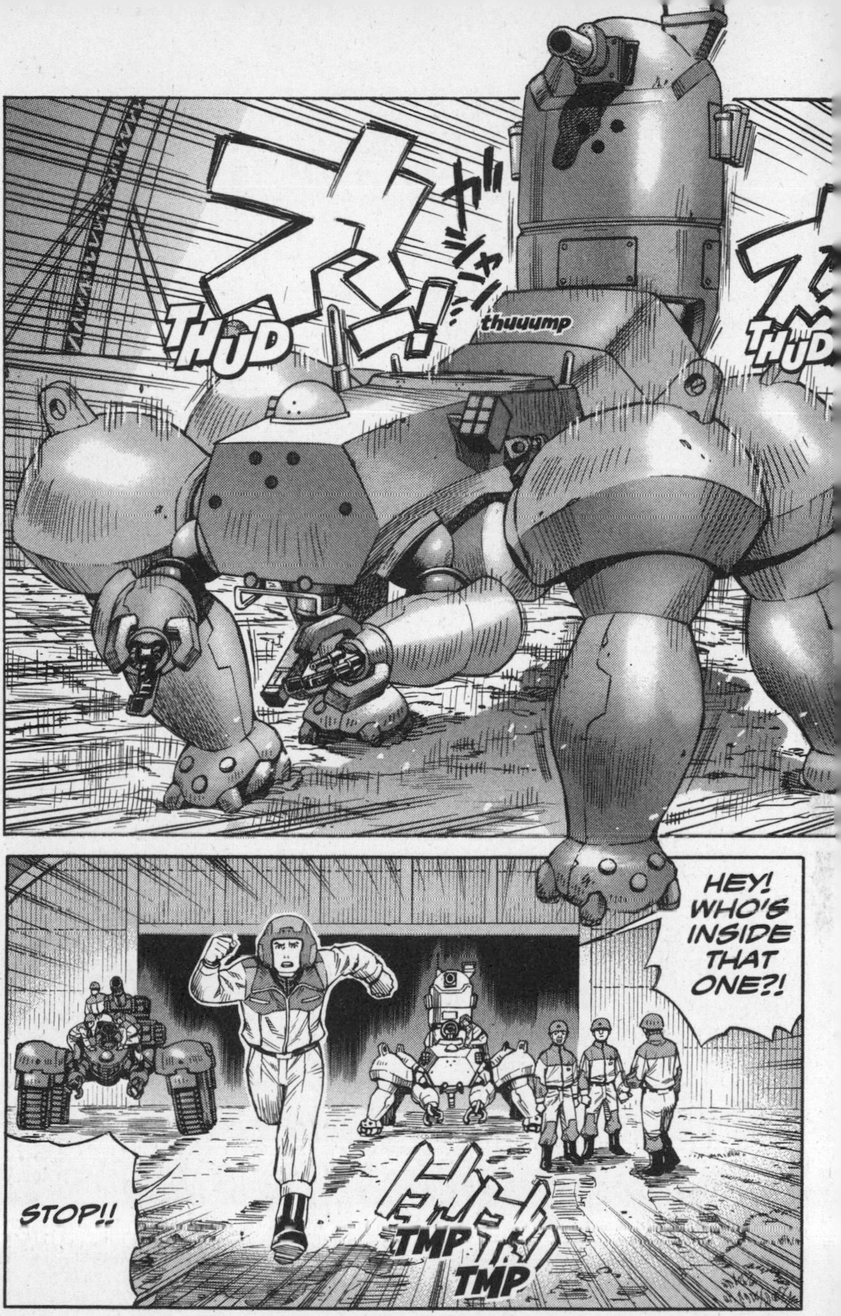
THUD
thuuump
THUD
HEY! WHO'S INSIDE THAT ONE?!
TMP
TMP
STOP!!

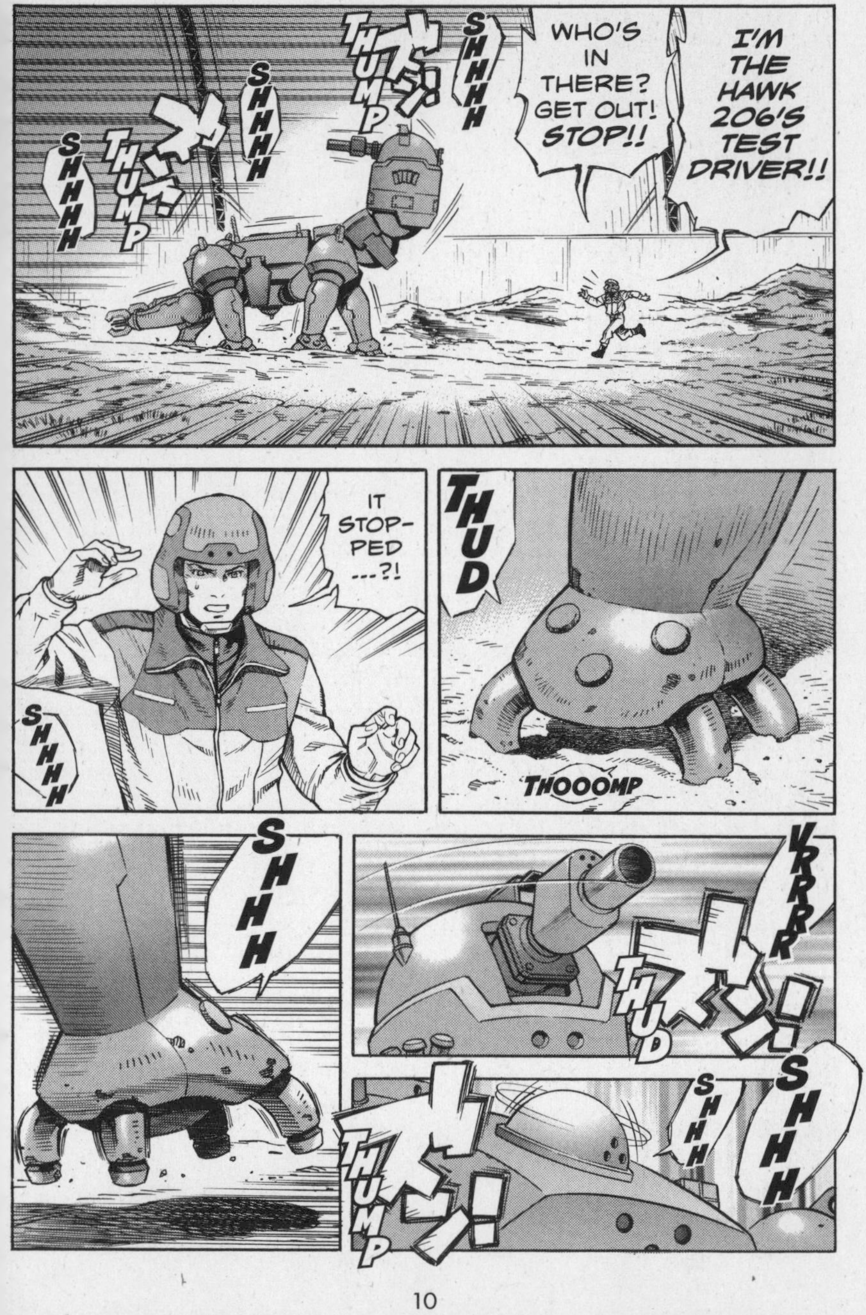
I'M THE HAWK 206'S TEST DRIVER!!
WHO'S IN THERE? GET OUT! STOP!!
SHHHH
THUMP
SHHHH
THUMP
SHHHH
THUD
THOOOMP
IT STOP-PED ---?!
SHHHH
VRRRR
THUD
SHHHH
SHHHH
THUMP
SHHHH

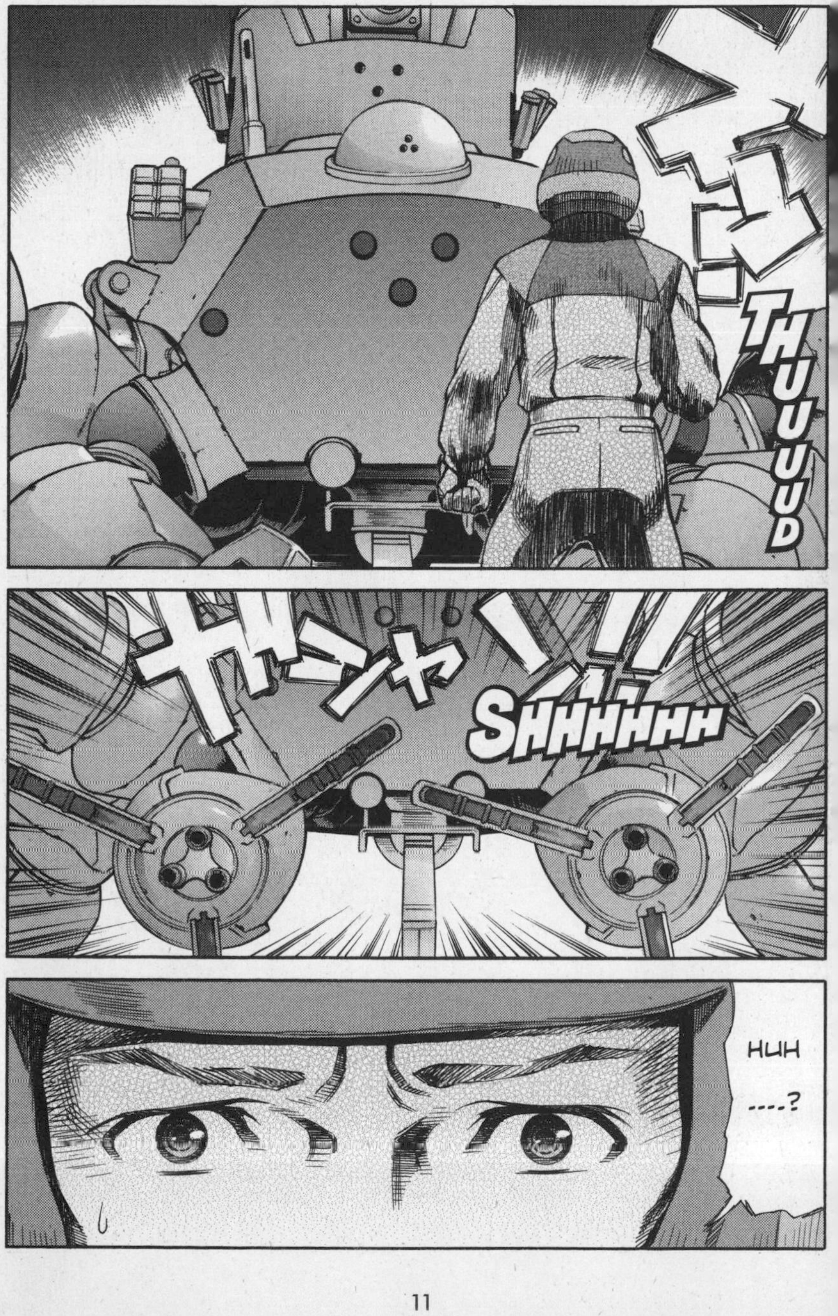
THUUUUD
SHHHHHH
HUH
----?

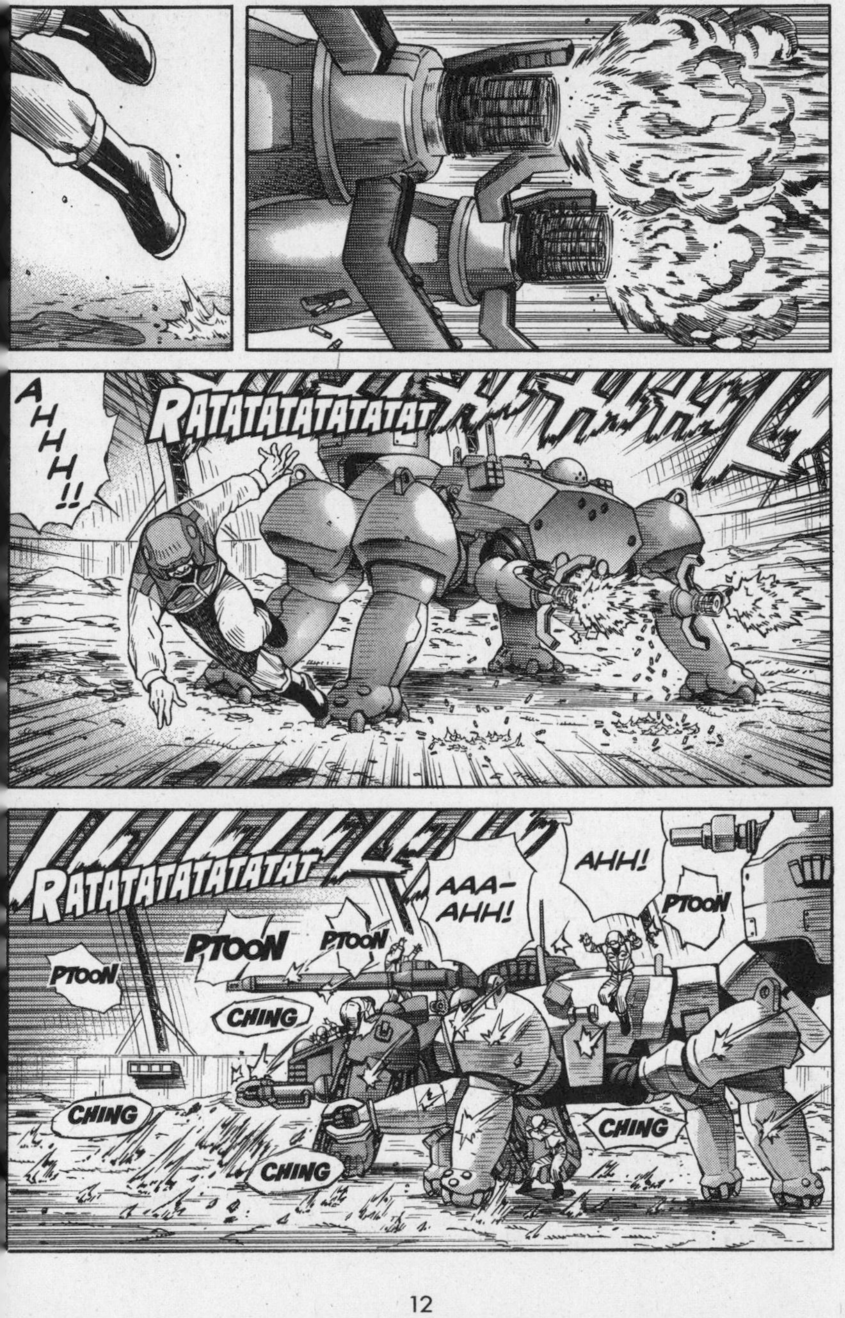
RATATATATATATAT
AHHH!!
AHH!
PTOON
AAA-AHH!
RATATATATATATAT
PTOON
PTOON
PTOON
CHING
CHING
CHING
CHING

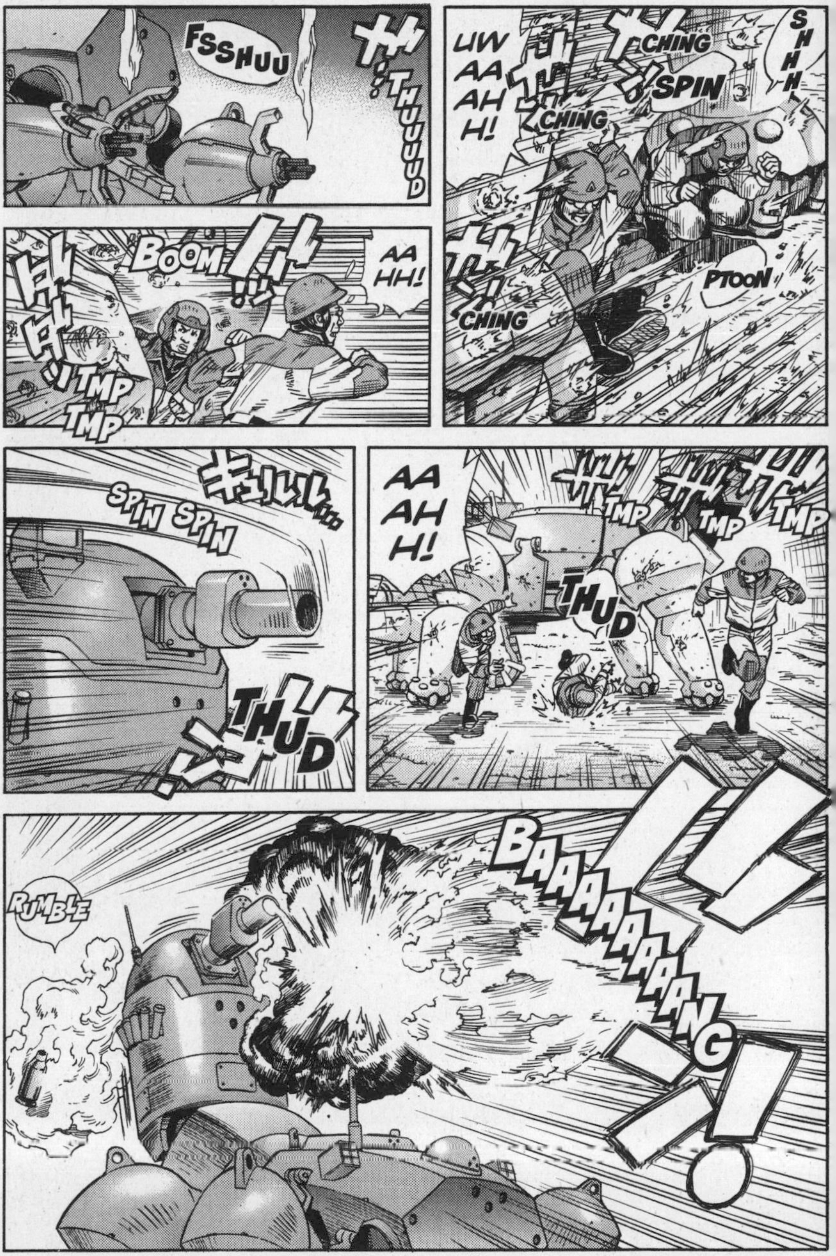
UWAAAAHH!
CHING
SPIN
SHHH
CHING
CHING
PTOON
FSSHUU
THUUUUD
AAHH!
BOOM
TMP TMP
AAAHH!
TMP
TMP
TMP
THUD
SPIN SPIN
THUD
RUMBLE
BAAAAAAAAANG

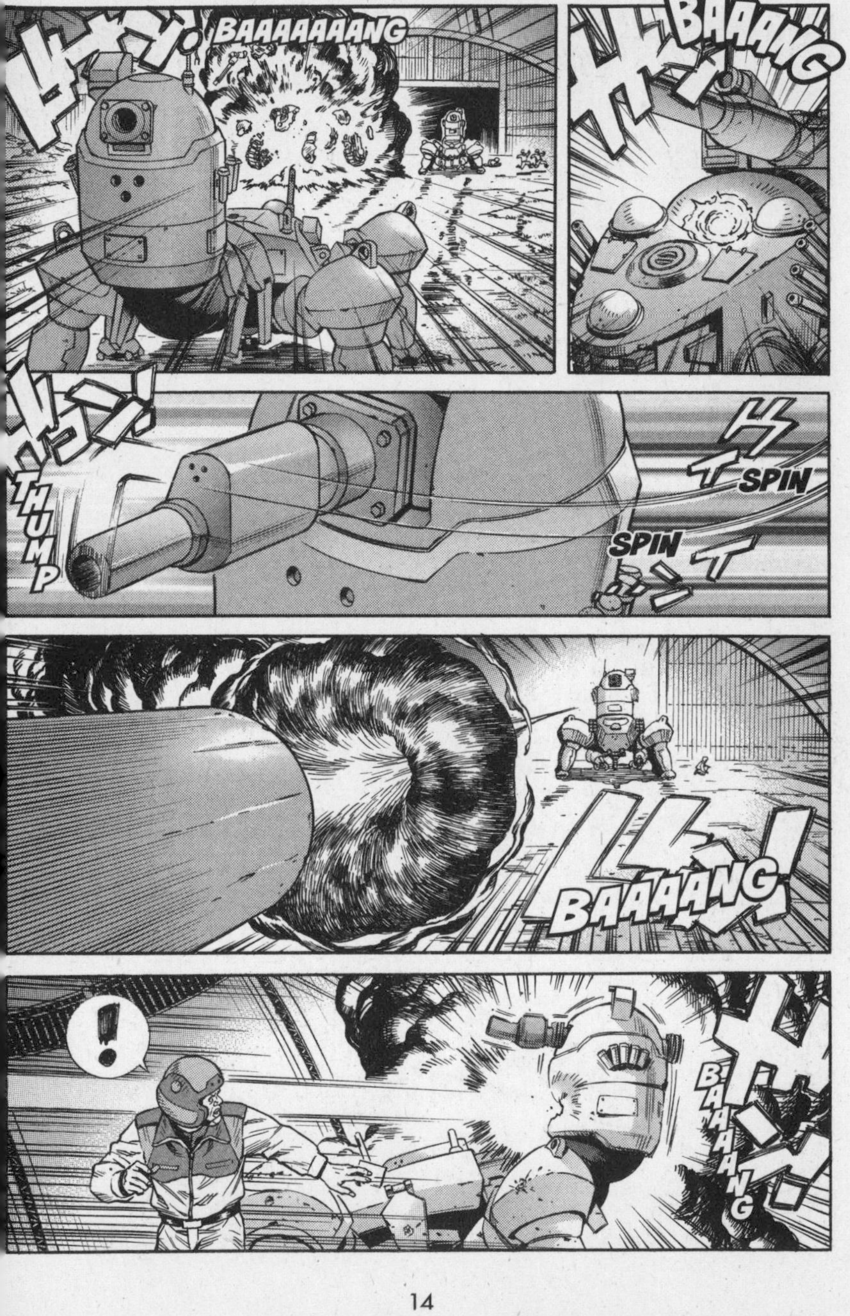
BAAANG
BAAAAAAANG
SPIN
SPIN
THUMP
BAAAANG
BAAAANG
!

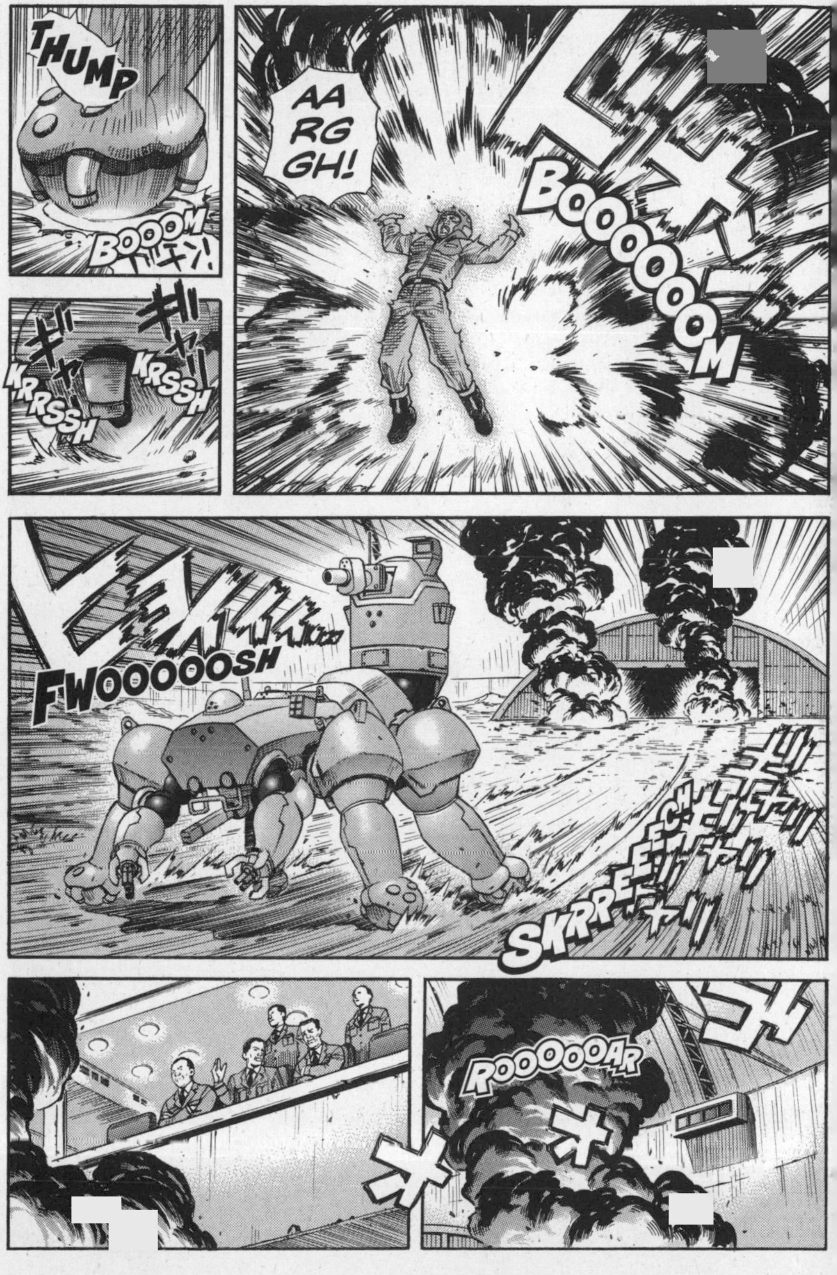
AARGH!
BOOOOOOOOM
THUMP
BOOOM
KRRSSH
KRSSSH
FWOOOOOSH
SKRREEEECH
ROOOOOAR

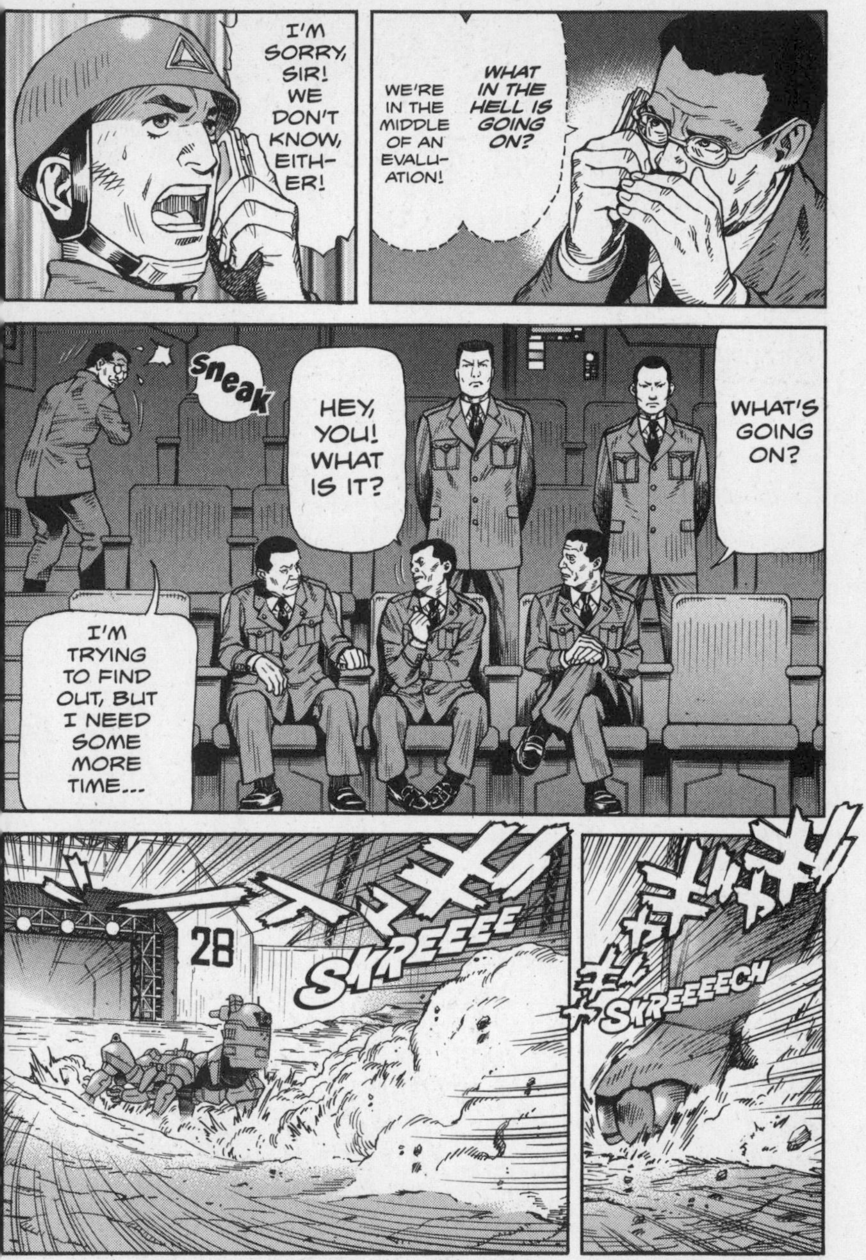
WHAT IN THE HELL IS GOING ON?
WE'RE IN THE MIDDLE OF AN EVALUATION!
I'M SORRY, SIR! WE DON'T KNOW, EITHER!
WHAT'S GOING ON?
HEY, YOU! WHAT IS IT?
sneak
I'M TRYING TO FIND OUT, BUT I NEED SOME MORE TIME...
SKREEEECH
28
SKREEEEE

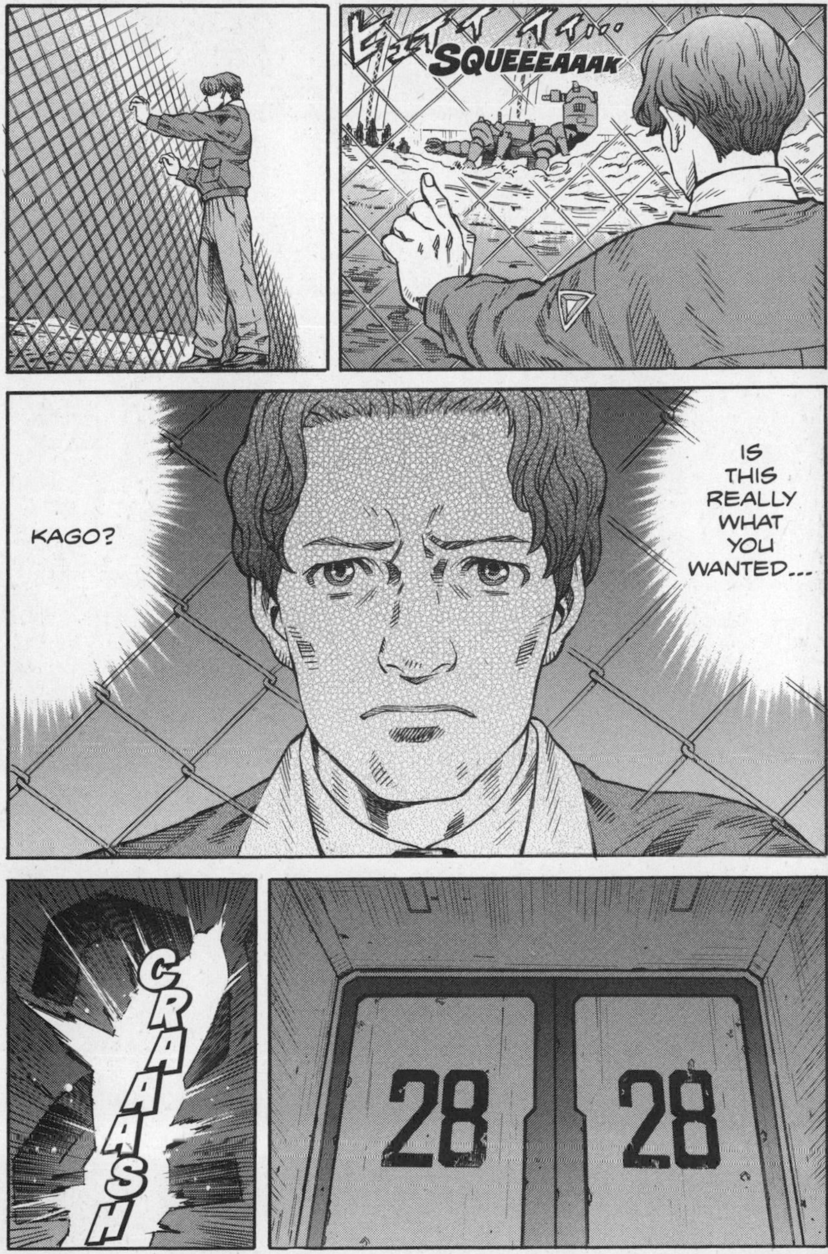
SQUEEEAAAK
IS THIS REALLY WHAT YOU WANTED...
KAGO?
28
28
CRAAAASH

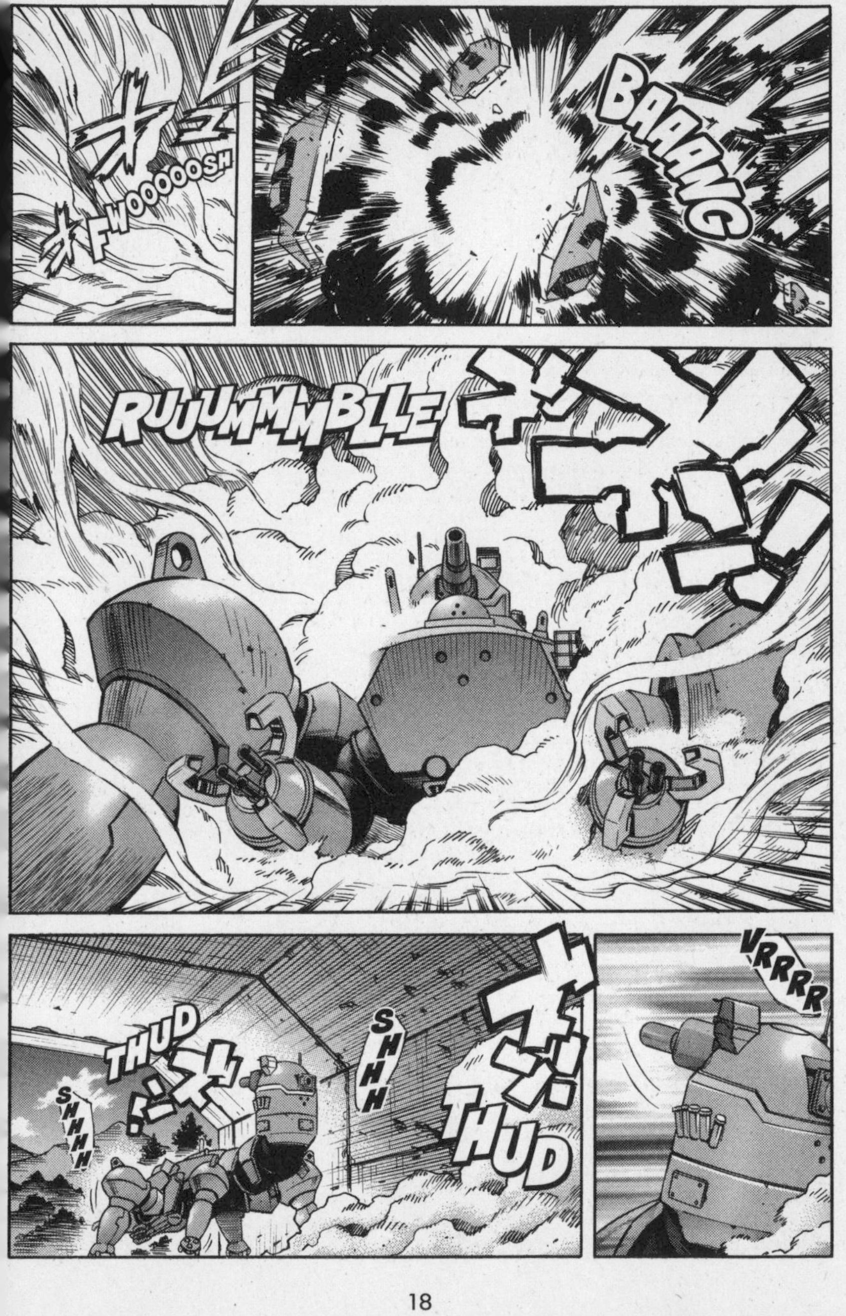
BAAANG!
FWOOOOOSH
RUUUMMMBLLE
VRRRR
SHHH
THUD
THUD
SHHH

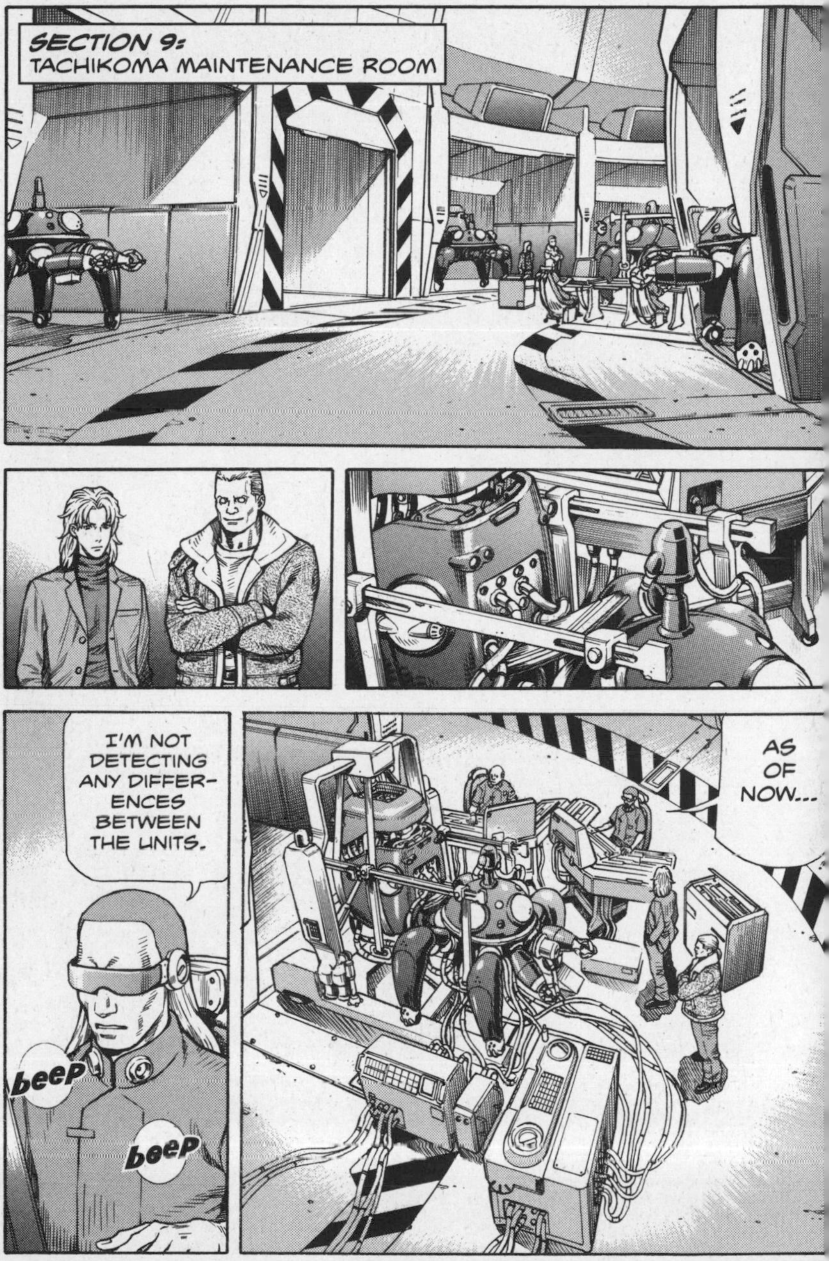
SECTION 9:
TACHIKOMA MAINTENANCE ROOM
AS OF NOW...
I'M NOT DETECTING ANY DIFFER-ENCES BETWEEN THE UNITS.
beep
beep

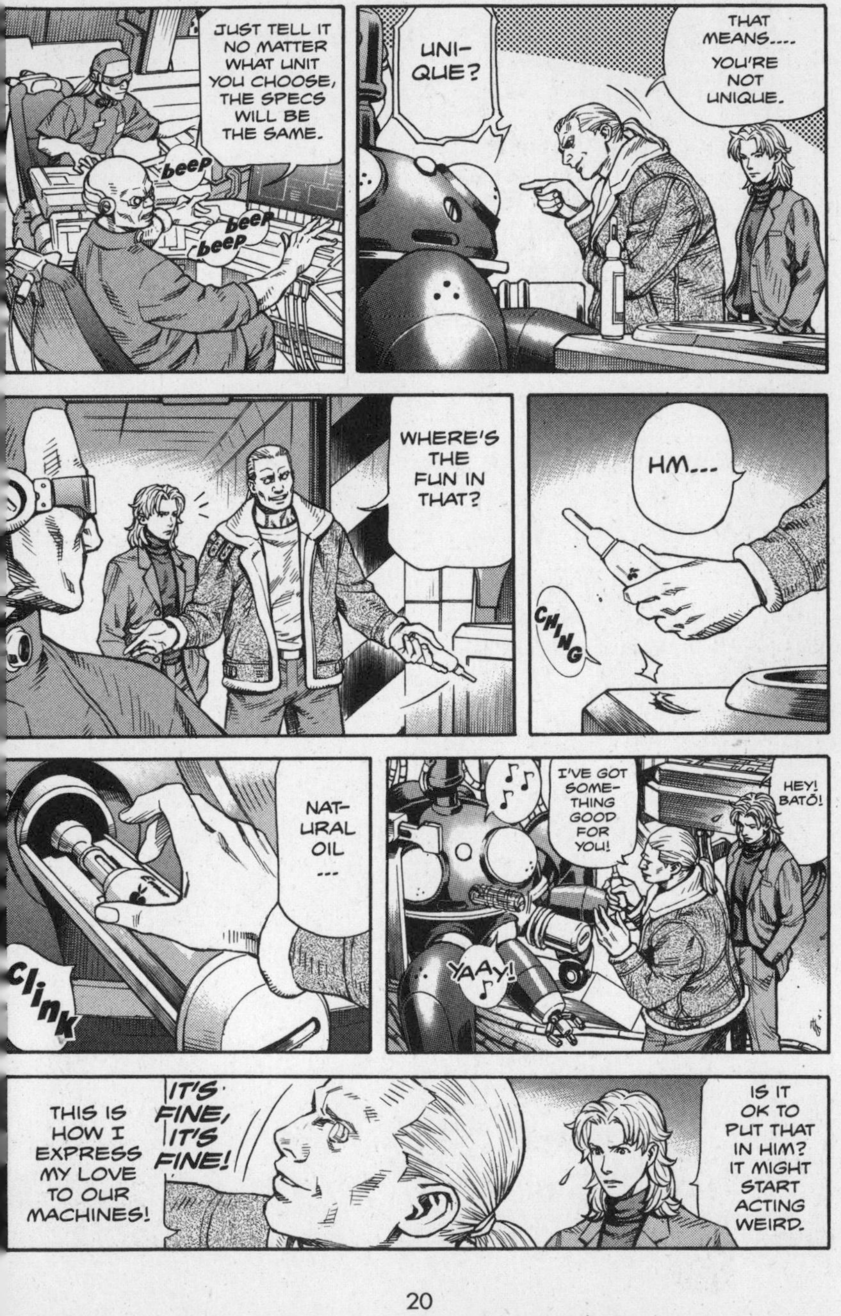
THAT MEANS.... YOU'RE NOT UNIQUE.
UNI-QUE?
JUST TELL IT NO MATTER WHAT UNIT YOU CHOOSE, THE SPECS WILL BE THE SAME.
beep
beep beep
HM...
CHING
WHERE'S THE FUN IN THAT?
HEY! BATŌ!
I'VE GOT SOME-THING GOOD FOR YOU!
YAAY!
NAT-URAL OIL...
Clink
IS IT OK TO PUT THAT IN HIM? IT MIGHT START ACTING WEIRD.
IT'S FINE, IT'S FINE!
THIS IS HOW I EXPRESS MY LOVE TO OUR MACHINES!

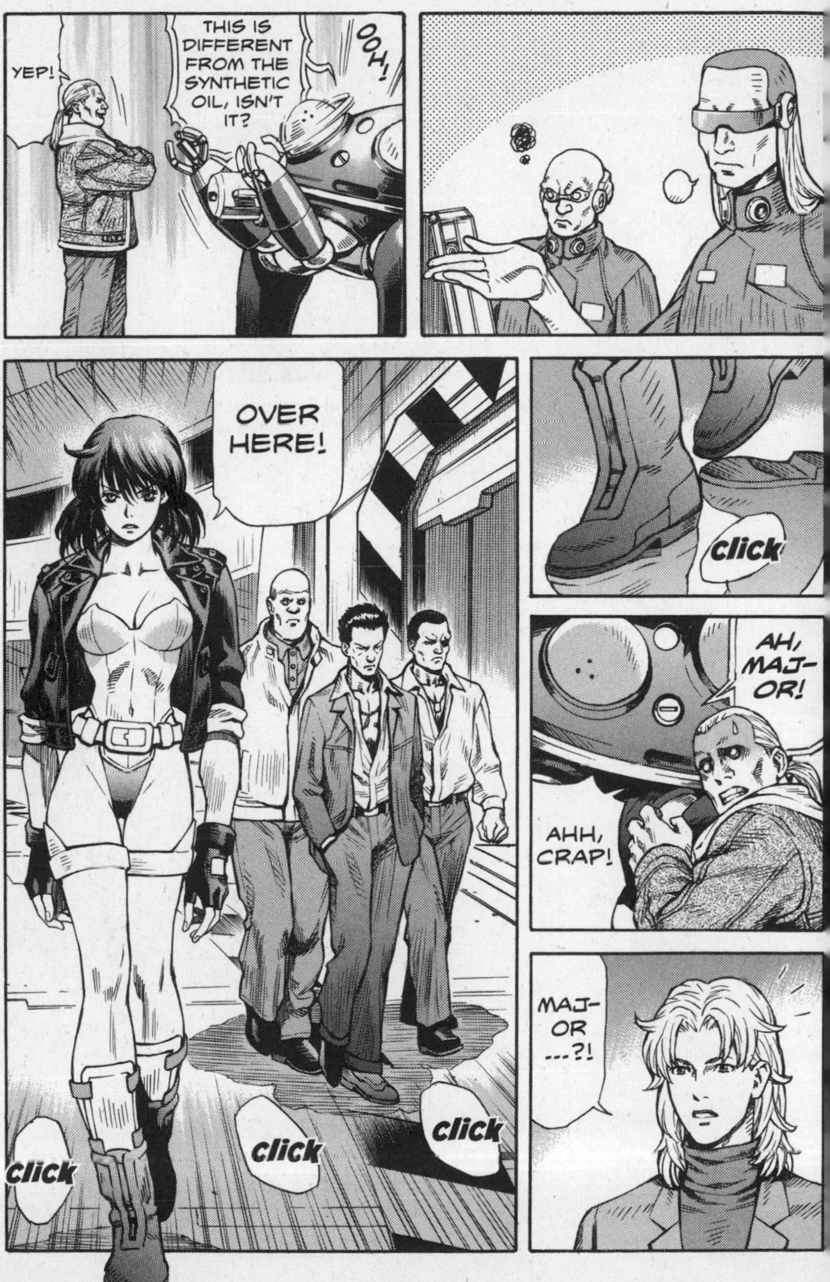
OOH!
THIS IS DIFFERENT FROM THE SYNTHETIC OIL, ISN'T IT?
YEP!
click
AH, MAJ-OR!
AHH, CRAP!
MAJ-OR ...?!
OVER HERE!
click
click
click

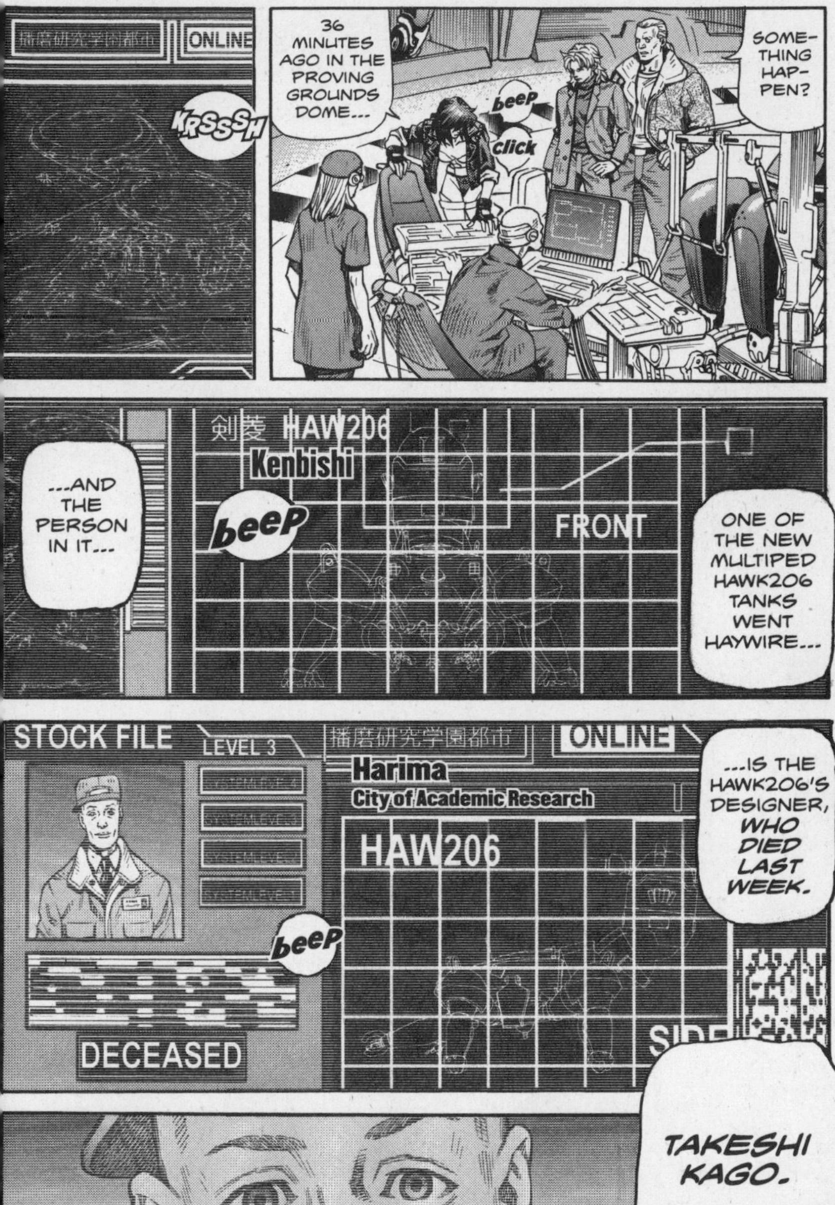
SOMETHING HAPPEN?
36 MINUTES AGO IN THE PROVING GROUNDS DOME...
beep
click
KRSSSH
播磨研究学園都市
ONLINE
ONE OF THE NEW MULTIPED HAWK206 TANKS WENT HAYWIRE...
FRONT
剣菱 HAW206
Kenbishi
beep
...AND THE PERSON IN IT...
...IS THE HAWK206'S DESIGNER, WHO DIED LAST WEEK.
ONLINE
播磨研究学園都市
Harima
City of Academic Research
HAW206
beep
LEVEL 3
STOCK FILE
DECEASED
TAKESHI KAGO.

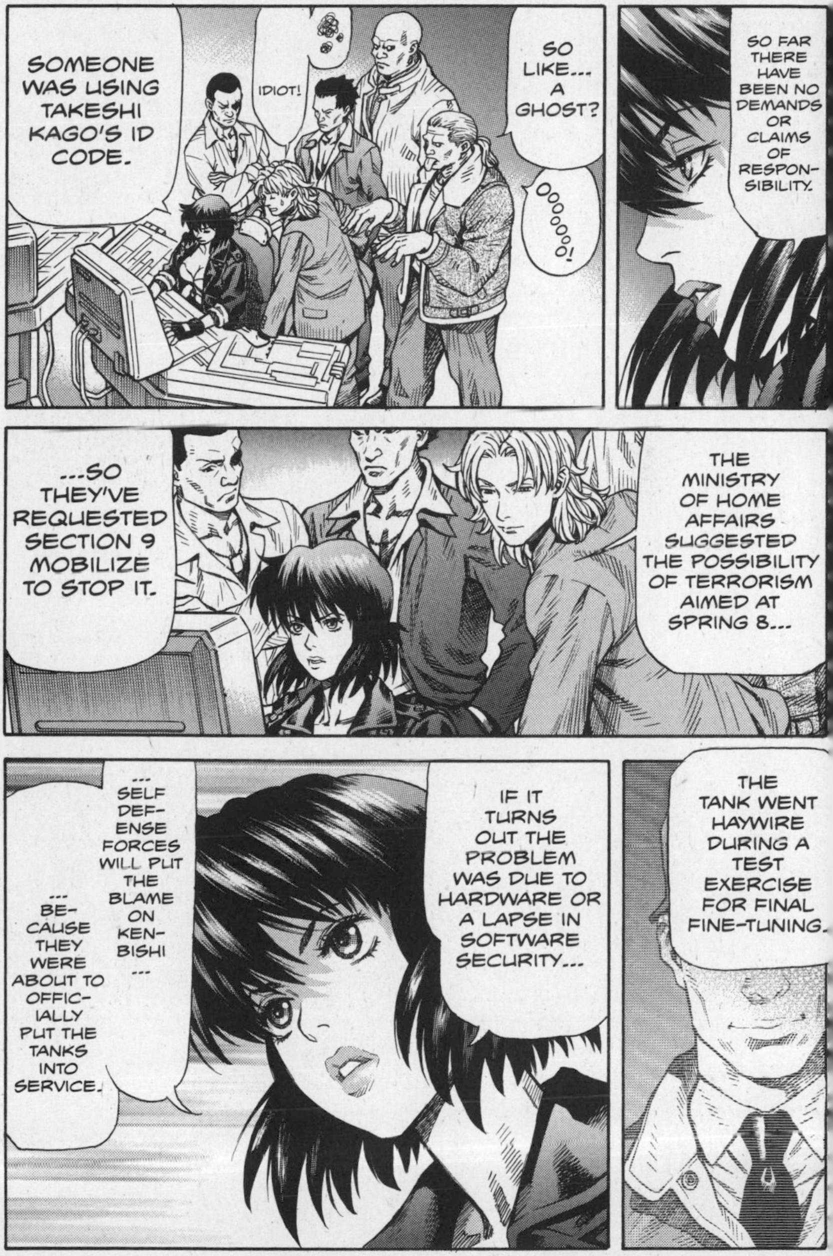
SO FAR THERE HAVE BEEN NO DEMANDS OR CLAIMS OF RESPON-SIBILITY.
SOMEONE WAS USING TAKESHI KAGO'S ID CODE.
SO LIKE... A GHOST?
OOOOOO!
IDIOT!
THE MINISTRY OF HOME AFFAIRS SUGGESTED THE POSSIBILITY OF TERRORISM AIMED AT SPRING 8...
...SO THEY'VE REQUESTED SECTION 9 MOBILIZE TO STOP IT.
THE TANK WENT HAYWIRE DURING A TEST EXERCISE FOR FINAL FINE-TUNING.
IF IT TURNS OUT THE PROBLEM WAS DUE TO HARDWARE OR A LAPSE IN SOFTWARE SECURITY...
...SELF DEF-ENSE FORCES WILL PUT THE BLAME ON KEN-BISHI...
...BE-CAUSE THEY WERE ABOUT TO OFFIC-IALLY PUT THE TANKS INTO SERVICE.

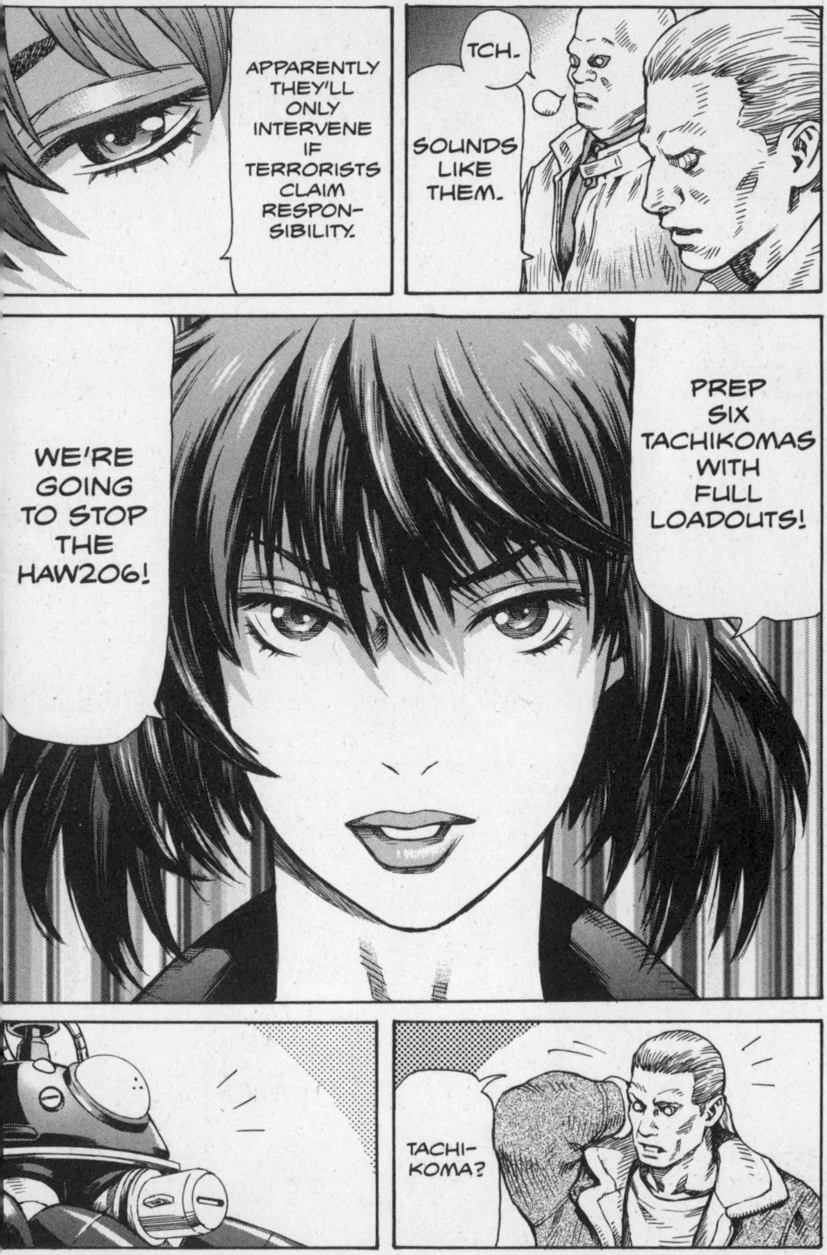
TCH.
SOUNDS LIKE THEM.
APPARENTLY THEY'LL ONLY INTERVENE IF TERRORISTS CLAIM RESPON-SIBILITY.
PREP SIX TACHIKOMAS WITH FULL LOADOUTS!
WE'RE GOING TO STOP THE HAW206!
TACHI-KOMA?

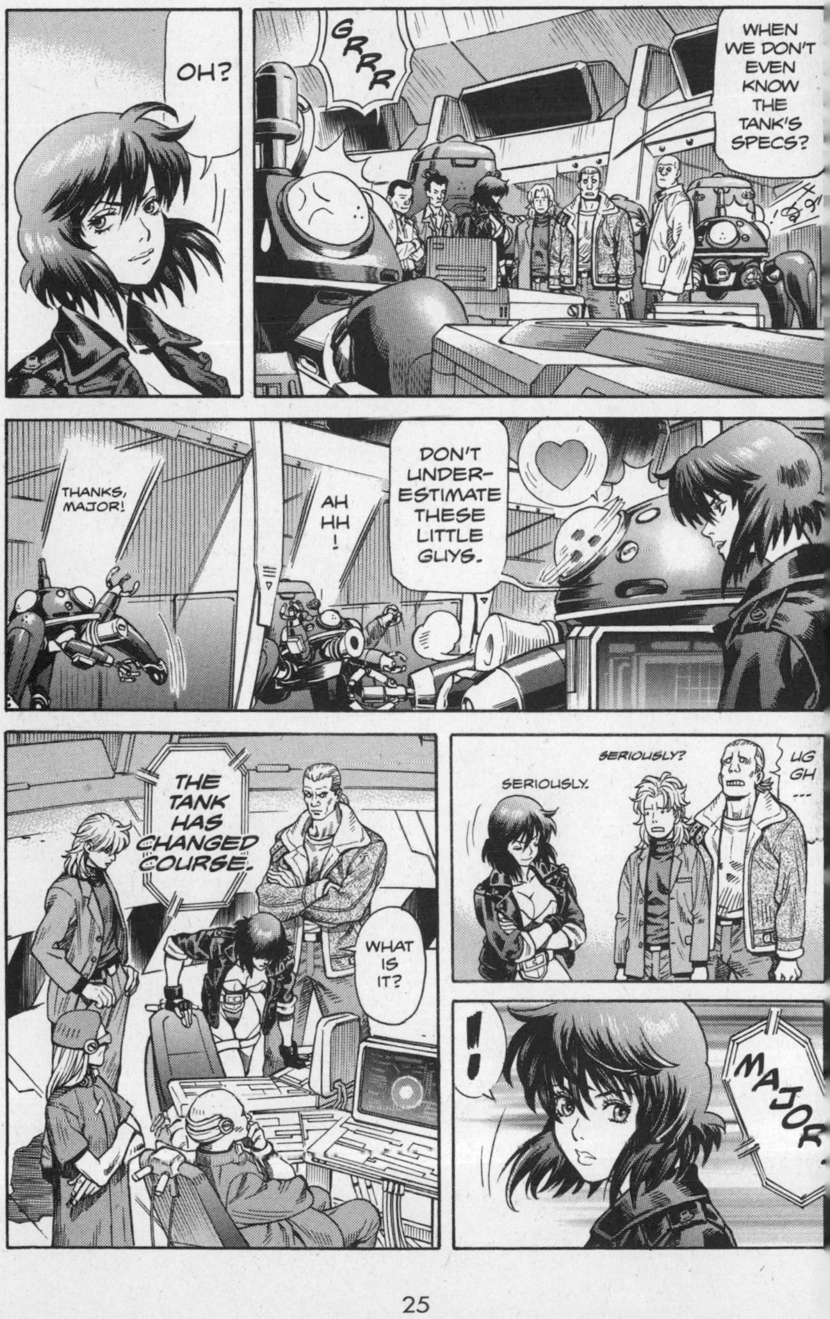
GRRR
WHEN WE DON'T EVEN KNOW THE TANK'S SPECS?
OH?
DON'T UNDER-ESTIMATE THESE LITTLE GUYS.
AH HH !
THANKS, MAJOR!
UG GH ---
SERIOUSLY?
SERIOUSLY.
MAJOR
!
THE TANK HAS CHANGED COURSE.
WHAT IS IT?

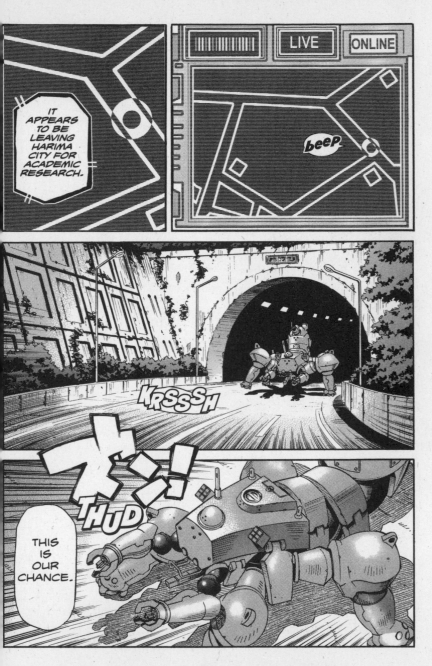

LIVE   ONLINE

IT APPEARS TO BE LEAVING HARIMA CITY FOR ACADEMIC RESEARCH.

beep.

KRSSSH

THUD

THIS IS OUR CHANCE.

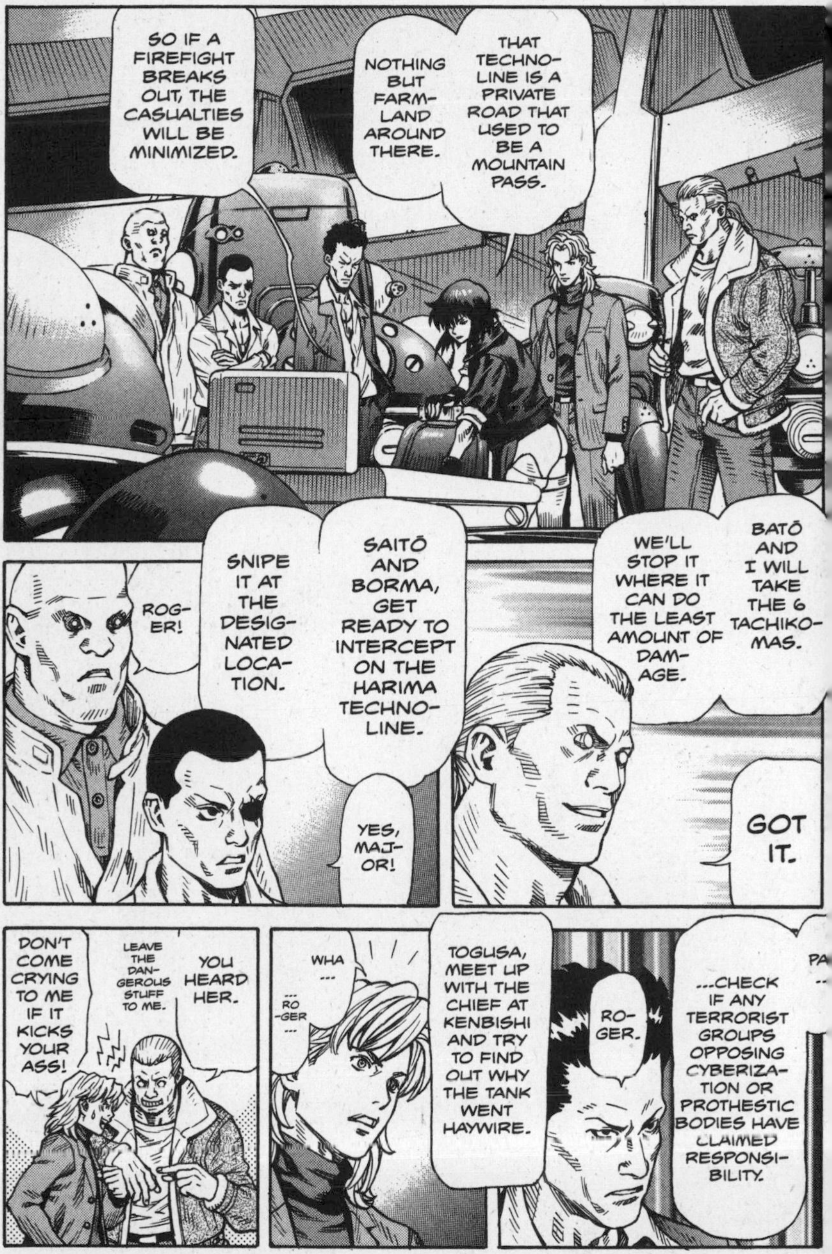
THAT TECHNO-LINE IS A PRIVATE ROAD THAT USED TO BE A MOUNTAIN PASS.
NOTHING BUT FARM-LAND AROUND THERE.
SO IF A FIREFIGHT BREAKS OUT, THE CASUALTIES WILL BE MINIMIZED.
BATŌ AND I WILL TAKE THE 6 TACHIKO-MAS.
WE'LL STOP IT WHERE IT CAN DO THE LEAST AMOUNT OF DAM-AGE.
GOT IT.
SAITŌ AND BORMA, GET READY TO INTERCEPT ON THE HARIMA TECHNO-LINE.
SNIPE IT AT THE DESIG-NATED LOCA-TION.
ROG-ER!
YES, MAJ-OR!
PA --
...CHECK IF ANY TERRORIST GROUPS OPPOSING CYBERIZA-TION OR PROTHESTIC BODIES HAVE CLAIMED RESPONSI-BILITY.
RO-GER.
TOGUSA, MEET UP WITH THE CHIEF AT KENBISHI AND TRY TO FIND OUT WHY THE TANK WENT HAYWIRE.
WHA ---
--- RO -GER ---
YOU HEARD HER.
LEAVE THE DAN-GEROUS STUFF TO ME.
DON'T COME CRYING TO ME IF IT KICKS YOUR ASS!

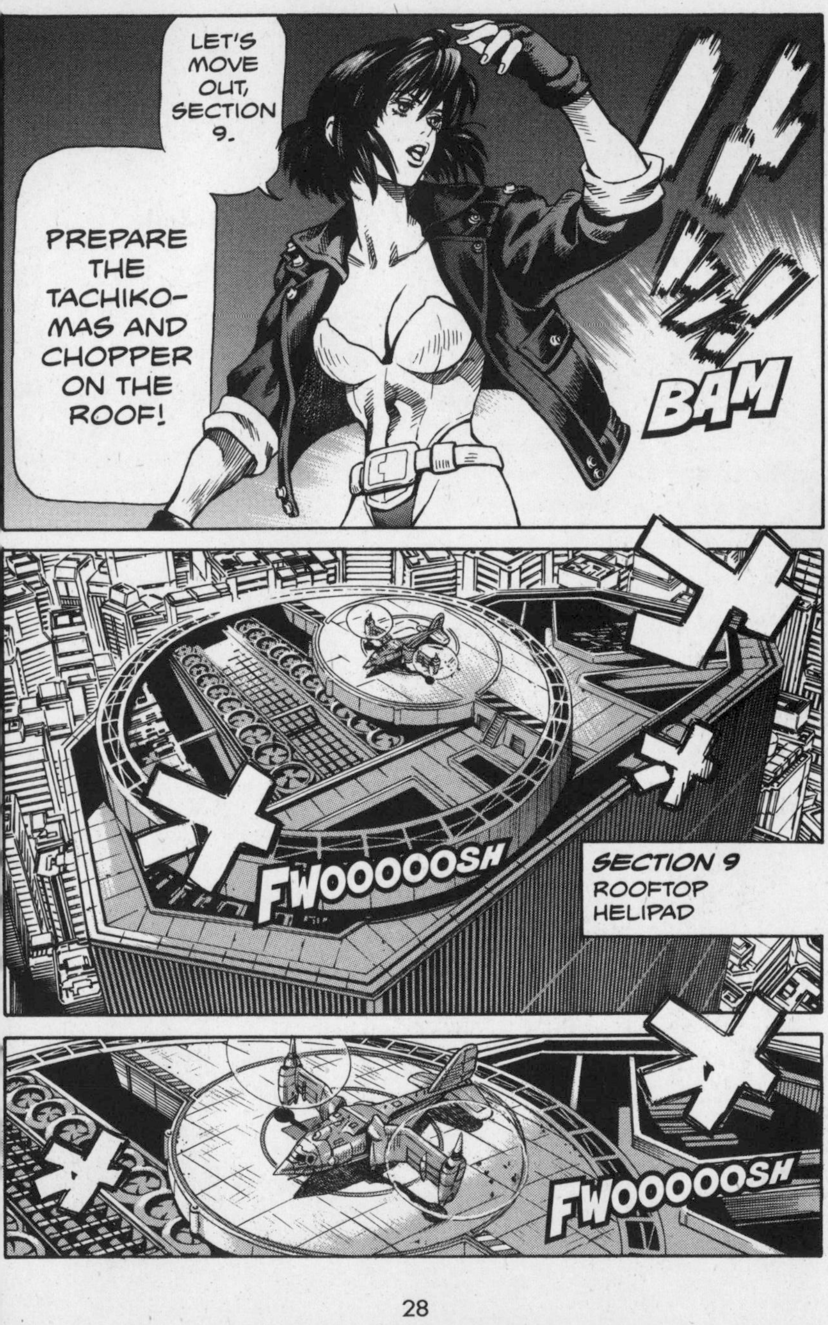
LET'S MOVE OUT, SECTION 9.
PREPARE THE TACHIKO-MAS AND CHOPPER ON THE ROOF!
BAM
SECTION 9 ROOFTOP HELIPAD
FWOOOOOSH
FWOOOOOSH

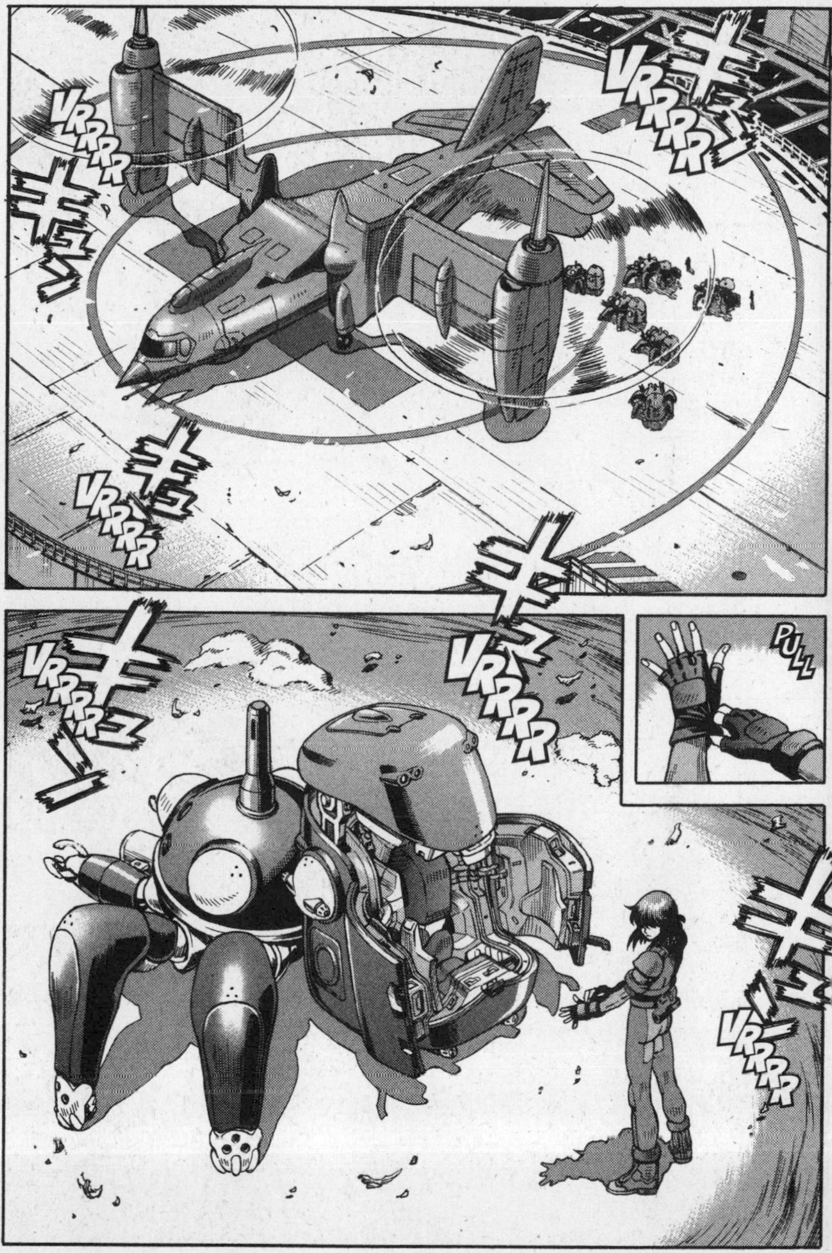
VRRRRR
VRRRR
VRRRRR
PULL
VRRRRR
VRRRRR
VRRRR

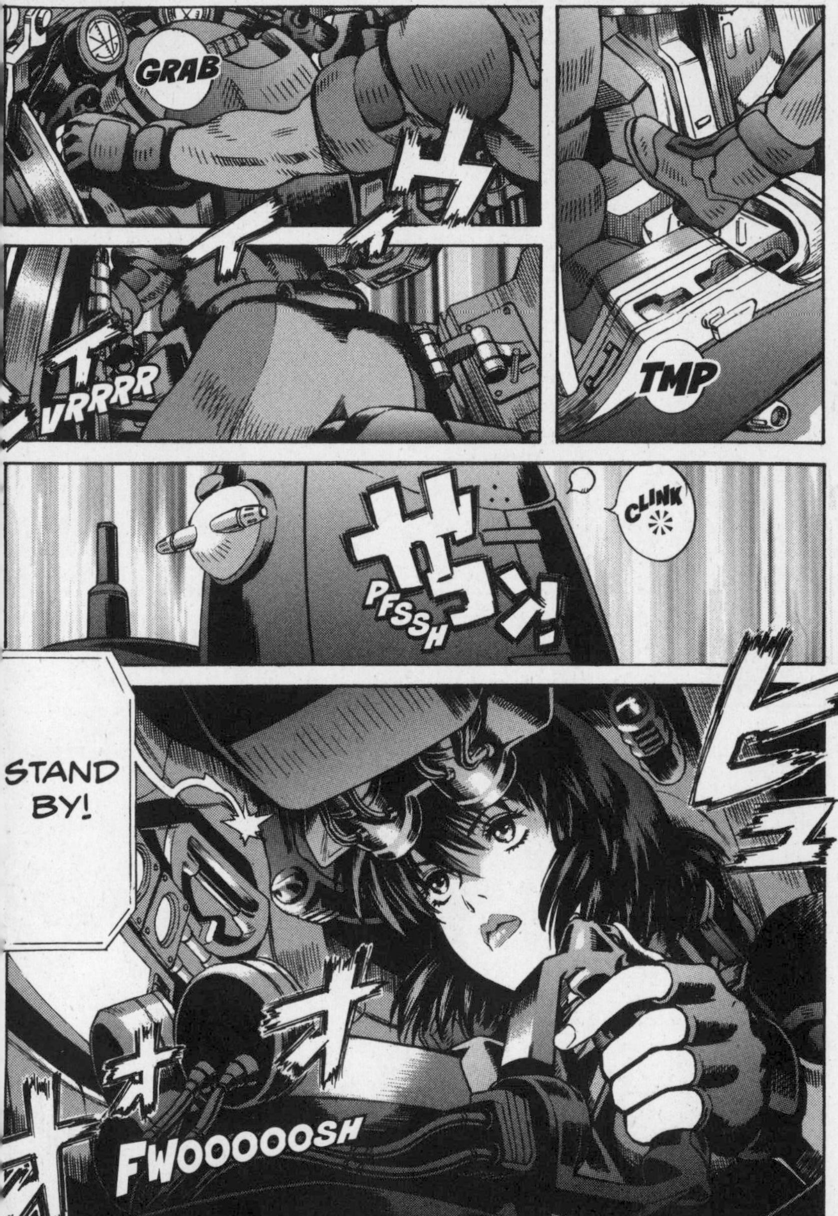
TMP
GRAB
VRRRR
CLINK
PFSSH
STAND BY!
FWOOOOOSH

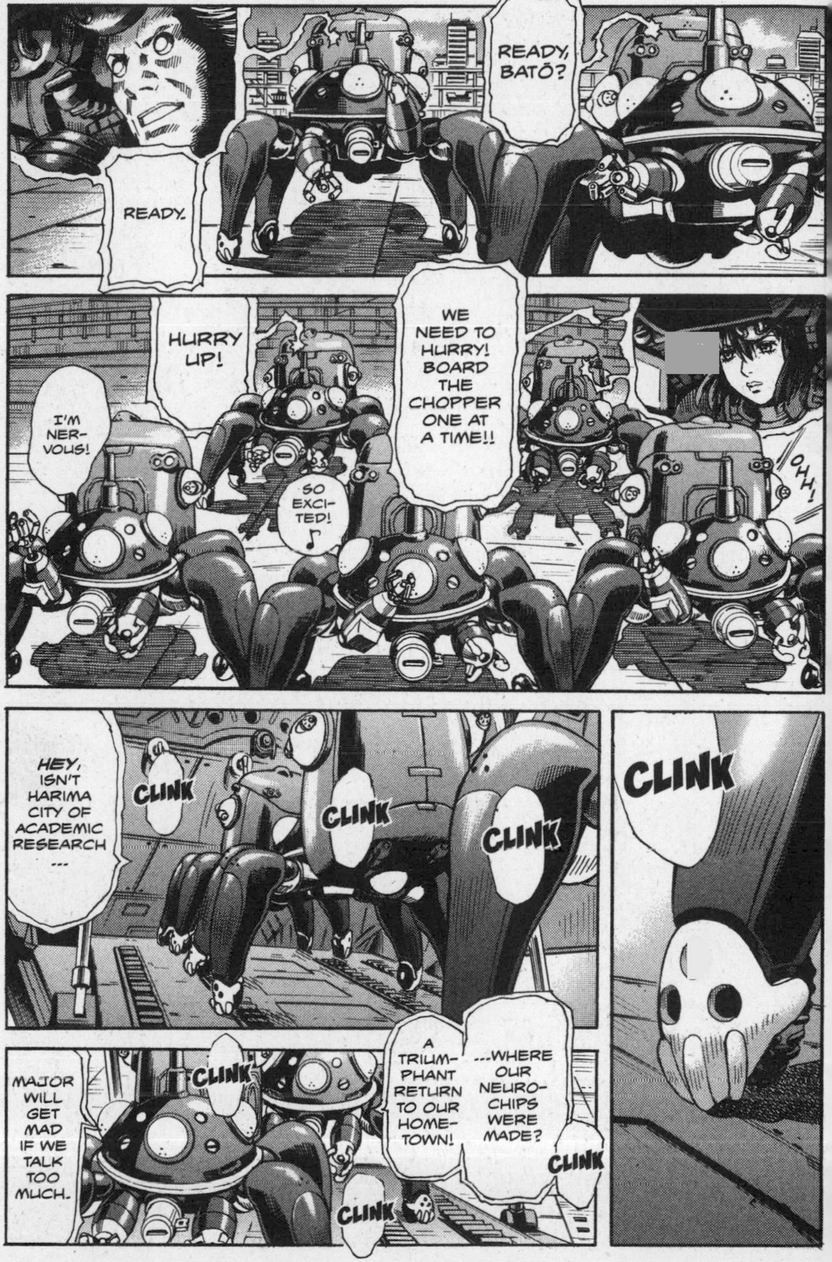
READY, BATŌ?
READY.
OHH!
WE NEED TO HURRY! BOARD THE CHOPPER ONE AT A TIME!!
HURRY UP!
SO EXCITED! ♪
I'M NERVOUS!
CLINK
CLINK
CLINK
CLINK
HEY, ISN'T HARIMA CITY OF ACADEMIC RESEARCH ---
---WHERE OUR NEUROCHIPS WERE MADE?
A TRIUMPHANT RETURN TO OUR HOMETOWN!
CLINK
CLINK
CLINK
MAJOR WILL GET MAD IF WE TALK TOO MUCH.

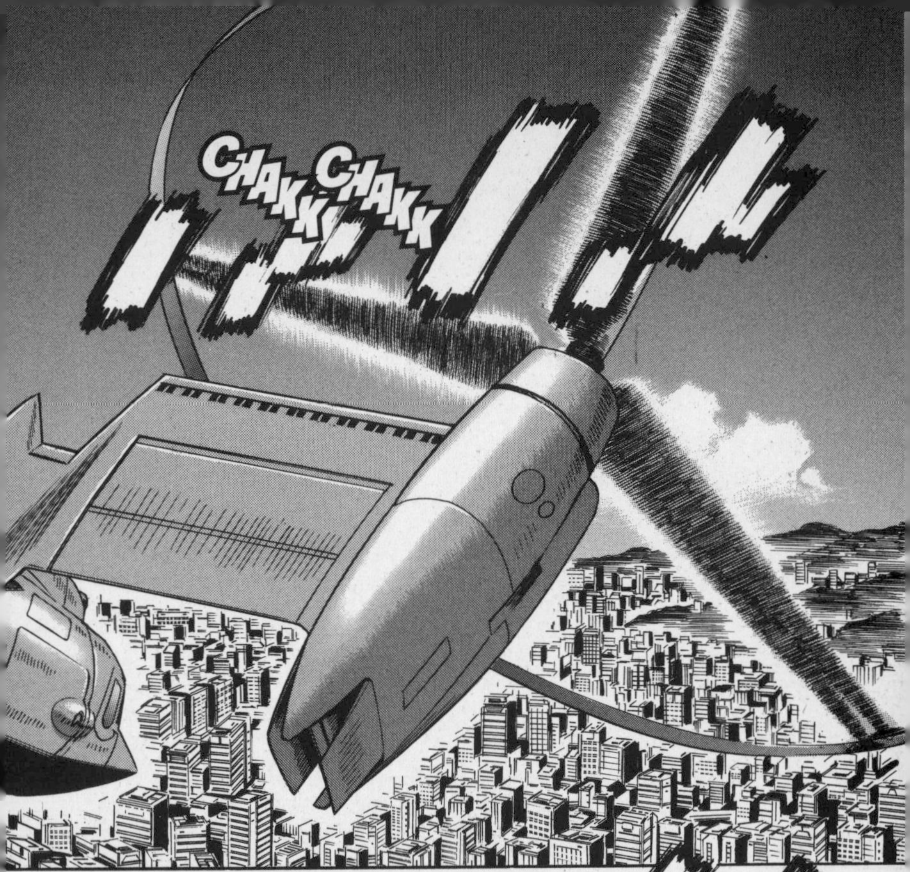
CHAKK CHAKK

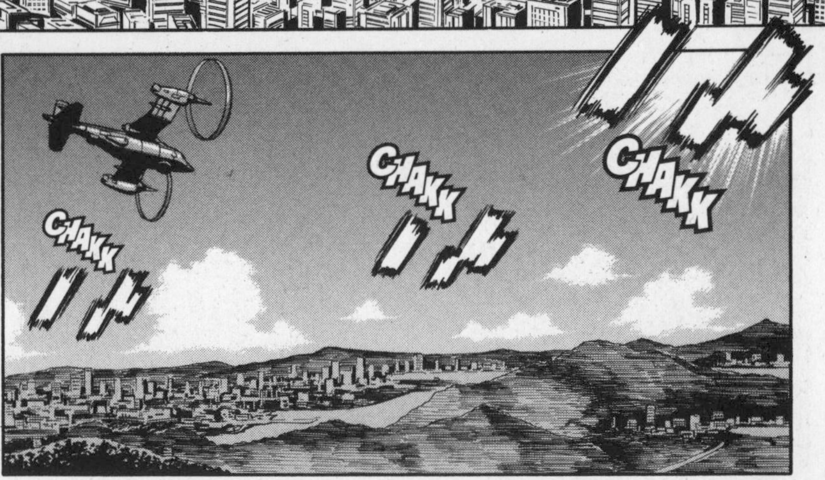
CHAKK
CHAKK
CHAKK

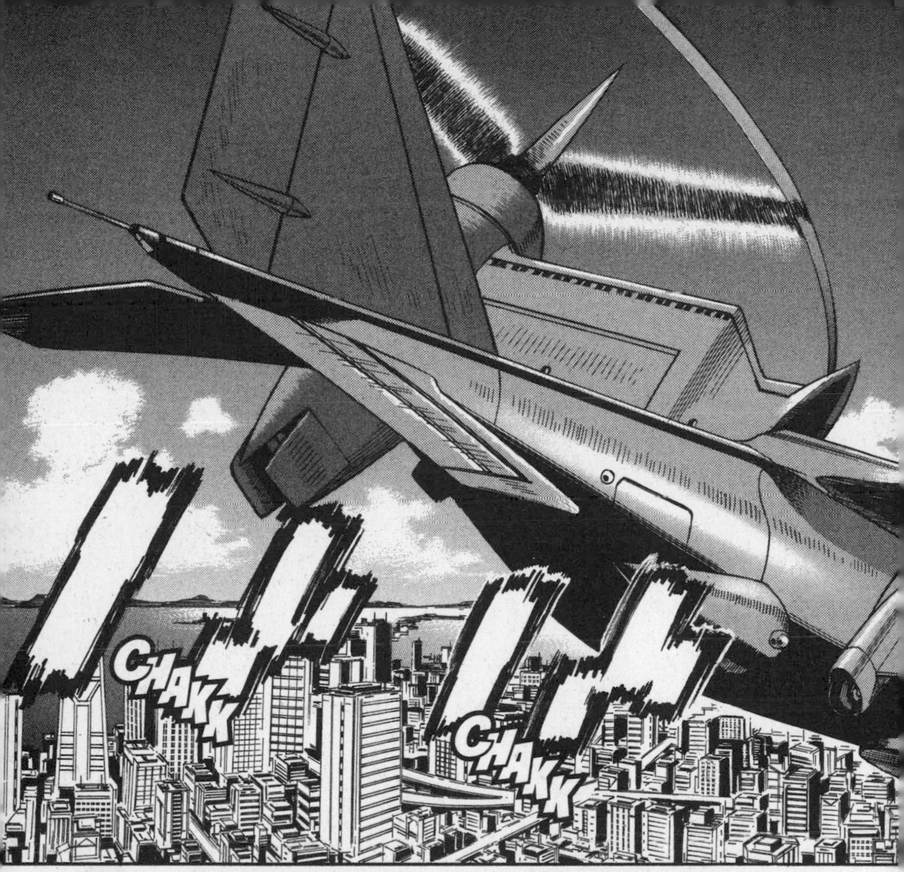
CHAKK
CHAKK
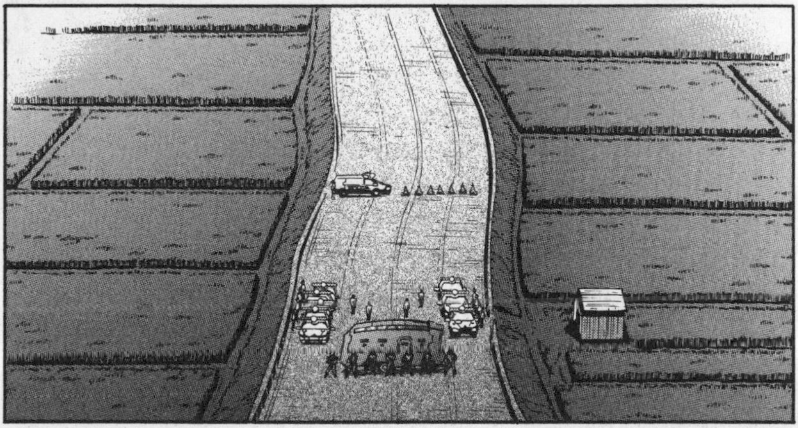

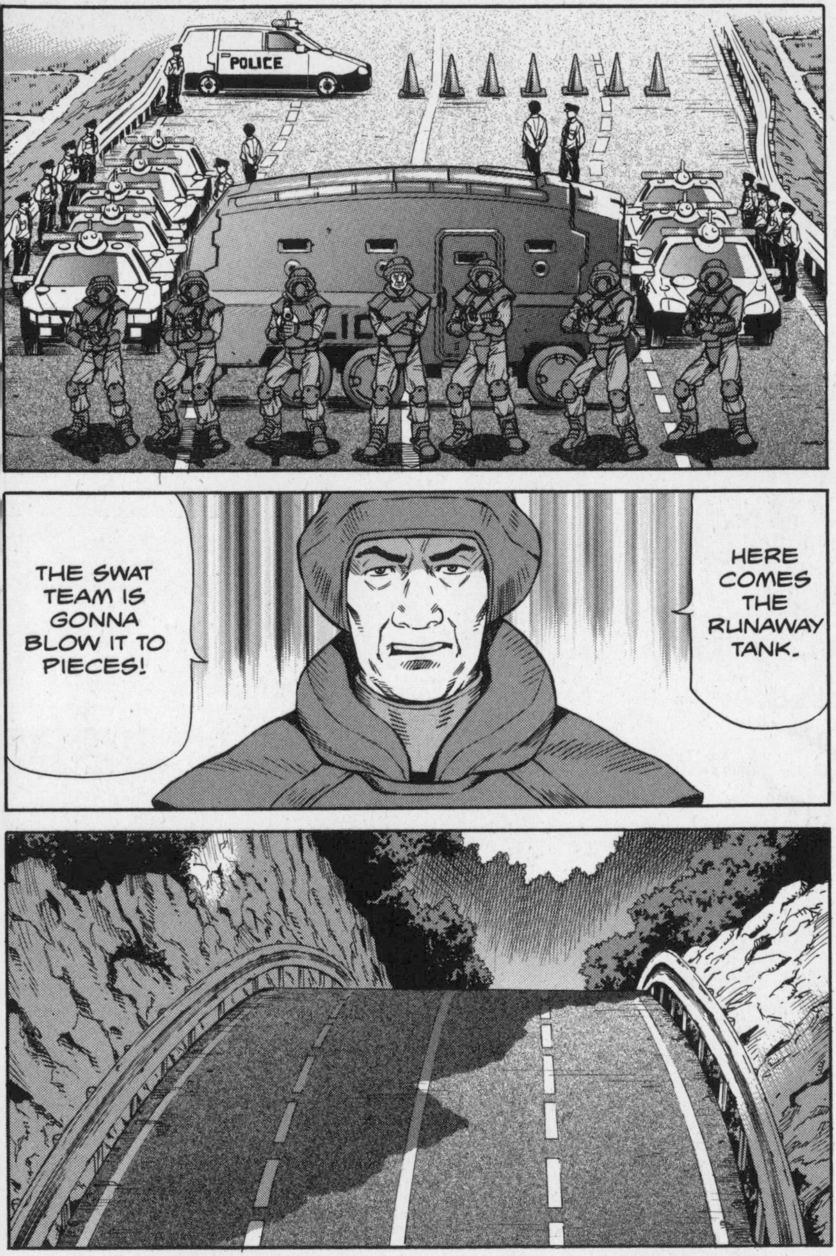
POLICE
HERE COMES THE RUNAWAY TANK.
THE SWAT TEAM IS GONNA BLOW IT TO PIECES!

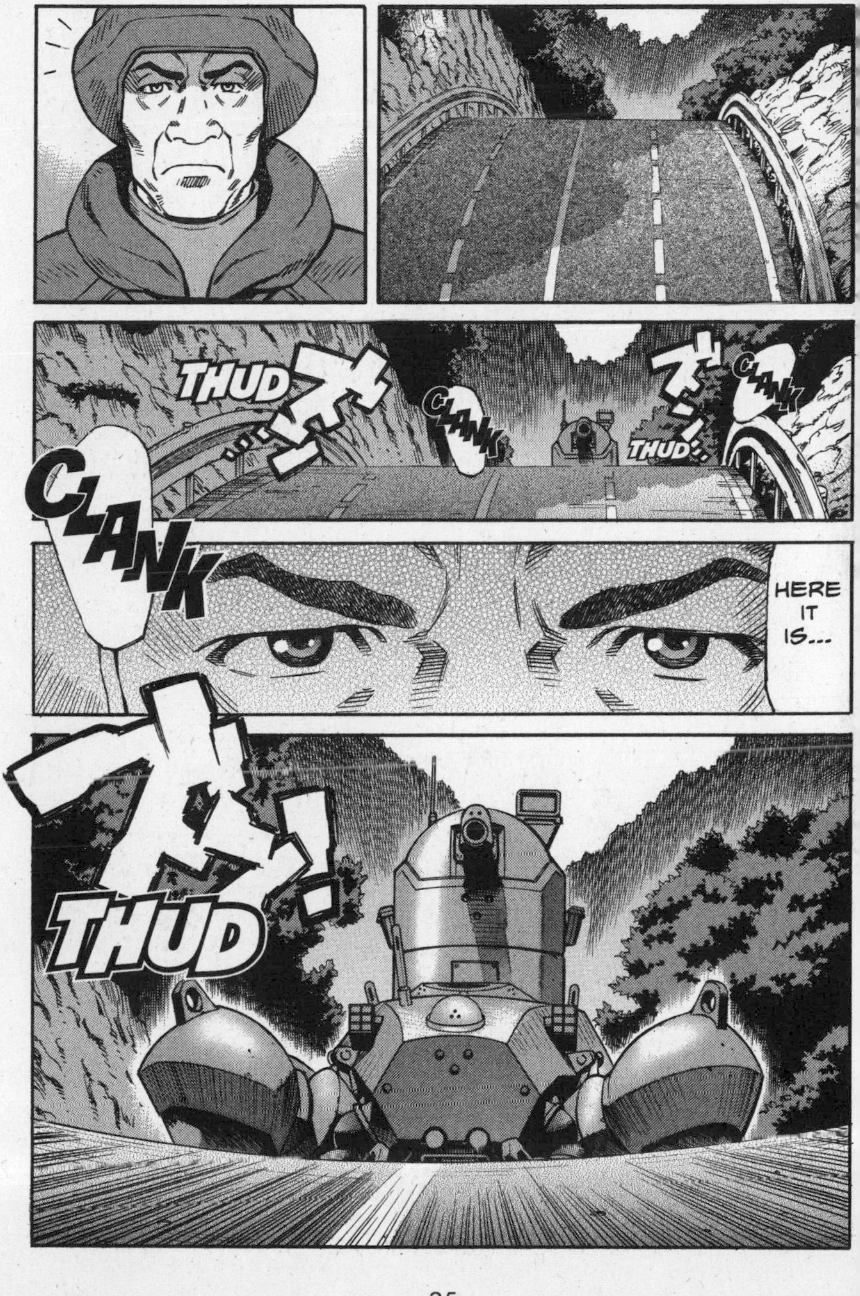
CLANK
THUD
CLANK
THUD
CLANK
HERE IT IS...
THUD

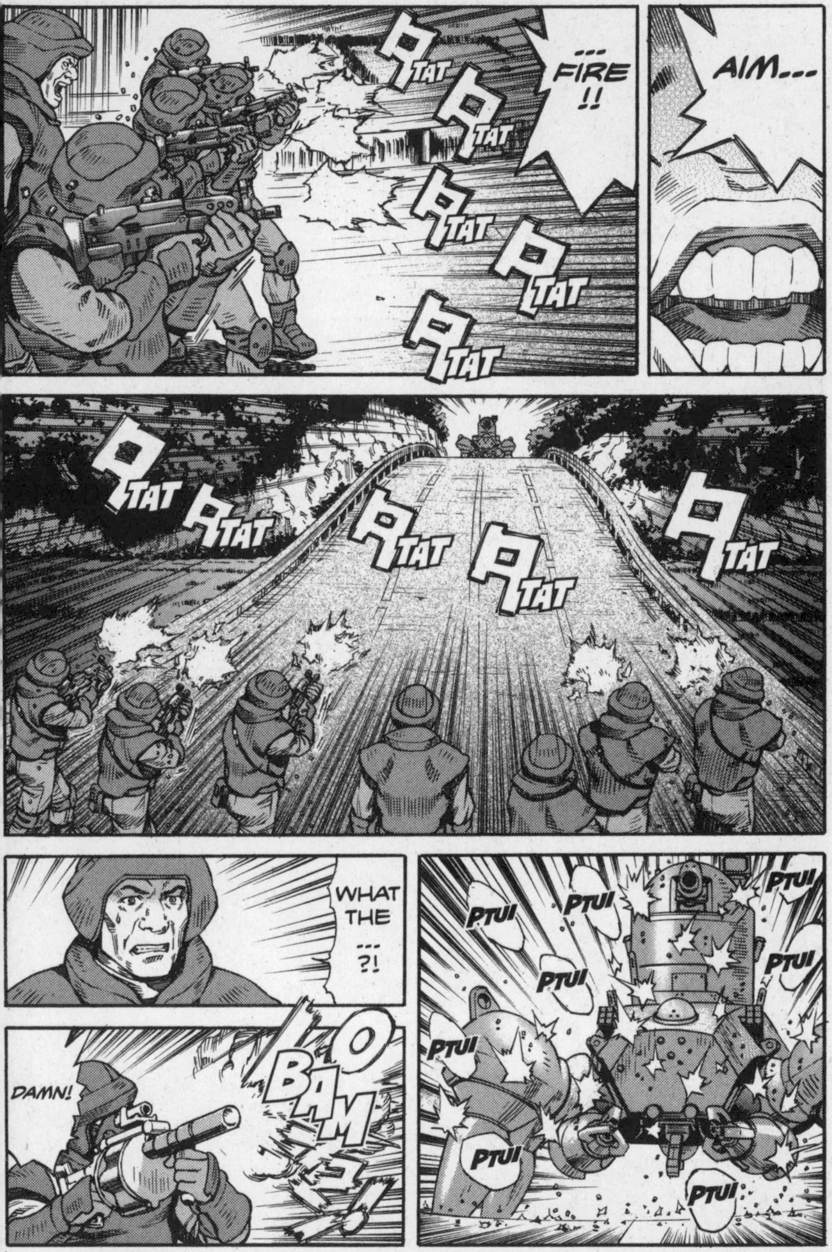
AIM...
...FIRE !!
TAT
TAT
TAT
TAT
TAT
TAT
TAT
TAT
TAT
TAT
PTUI
PTUI
PTUI
PTUI
PTUI
PTUI
PTUI
PTUI
WHAT THE ...?!
DAMN!
BAM

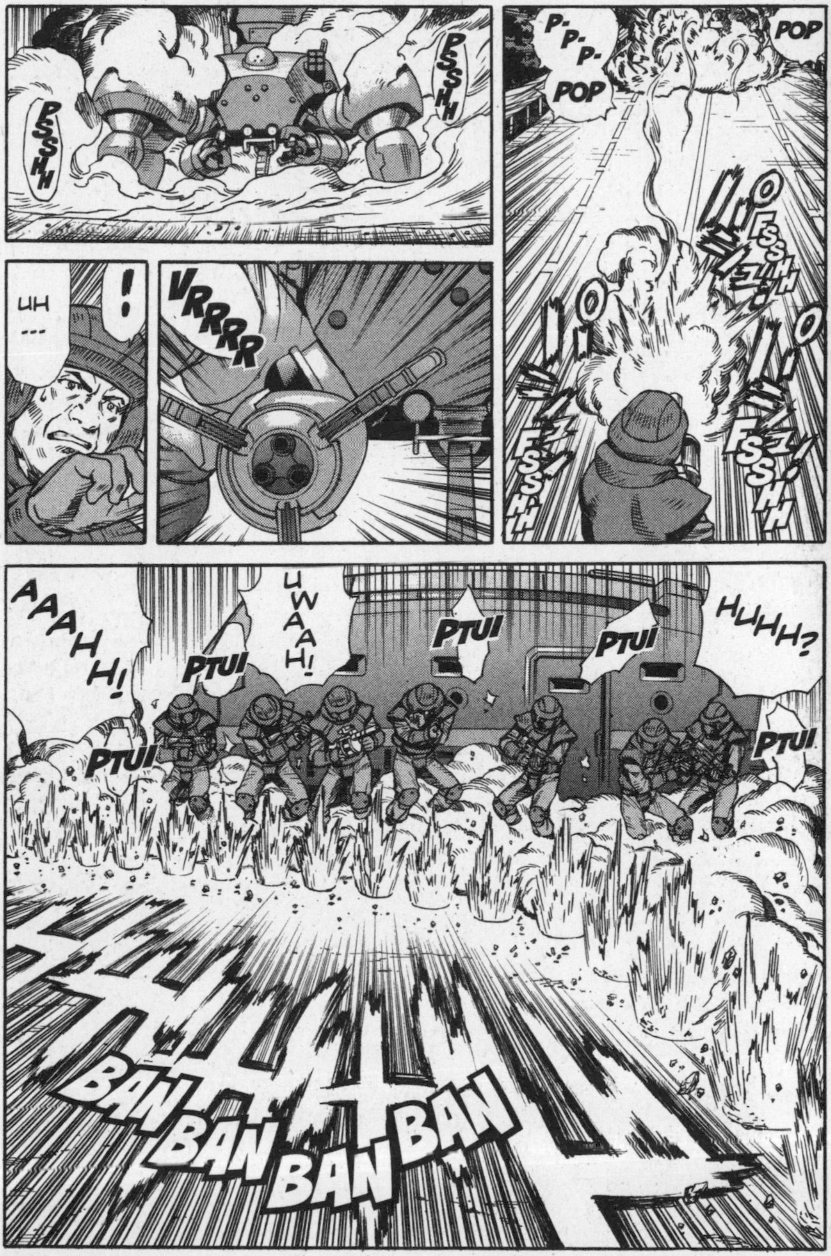
POP
P-P-P-POP
FSSHH
FSSHH
FSSHH
PSSHH
PSSHH
VRRRRR
!
UH ---
HUHHH?
PTUI
PTUI
PTUI
UWAAAH!
PTUI
AAAHHH!
PTUI
BAN BAN BAN BAN

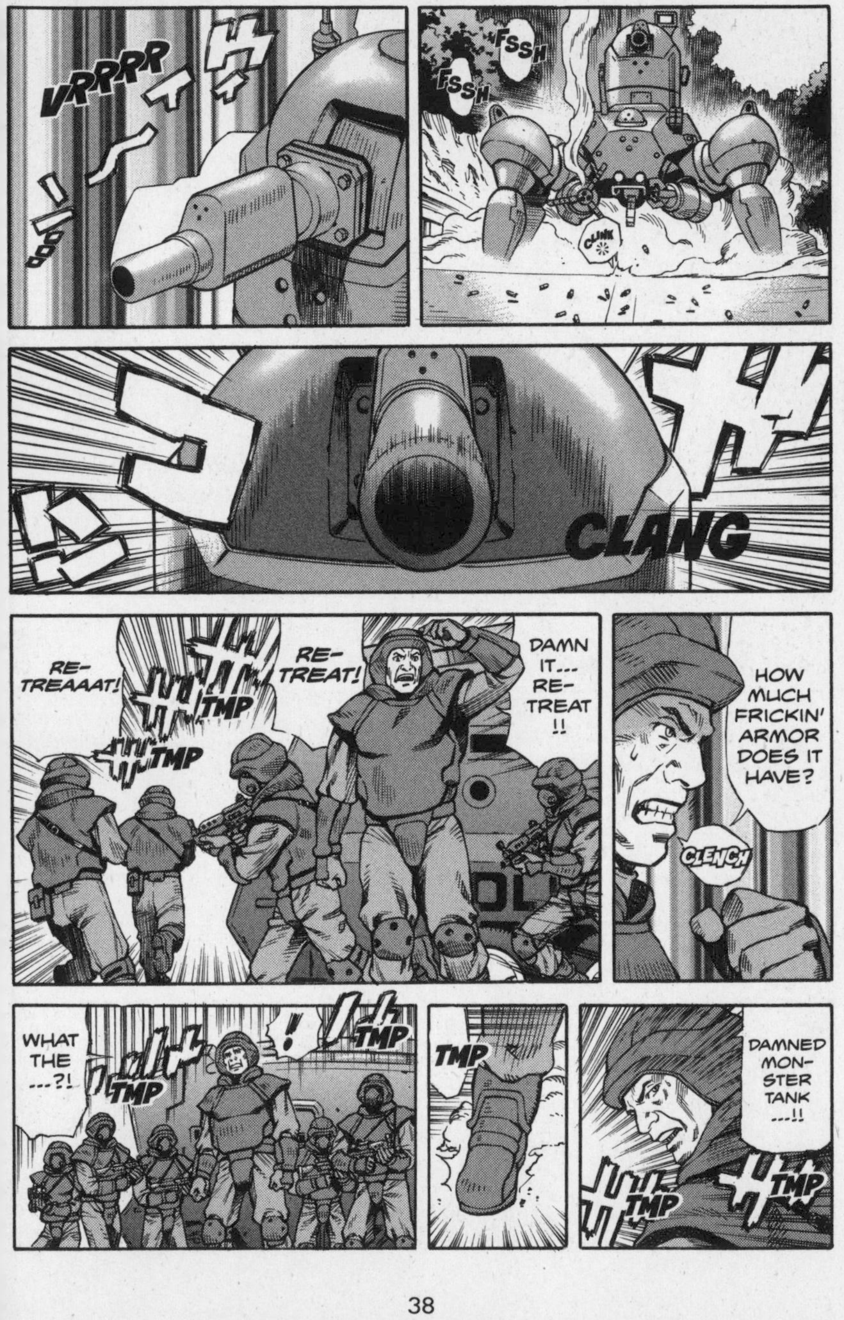
FSSH
FSSH
CLINK
VRRRRR
CLANG
HOW MUCH FRICKIN' ARMOR DOES IT HAVE?
CLENCH
DAMN IT... RE-TREAT!!
RE-TREAT!
TMP
RE-TREAAAT!
TMP
DAMNED MON-STER TANK ...!!
TMP
TMP
TMP
TMP
WHAT THE ---?!
TMP

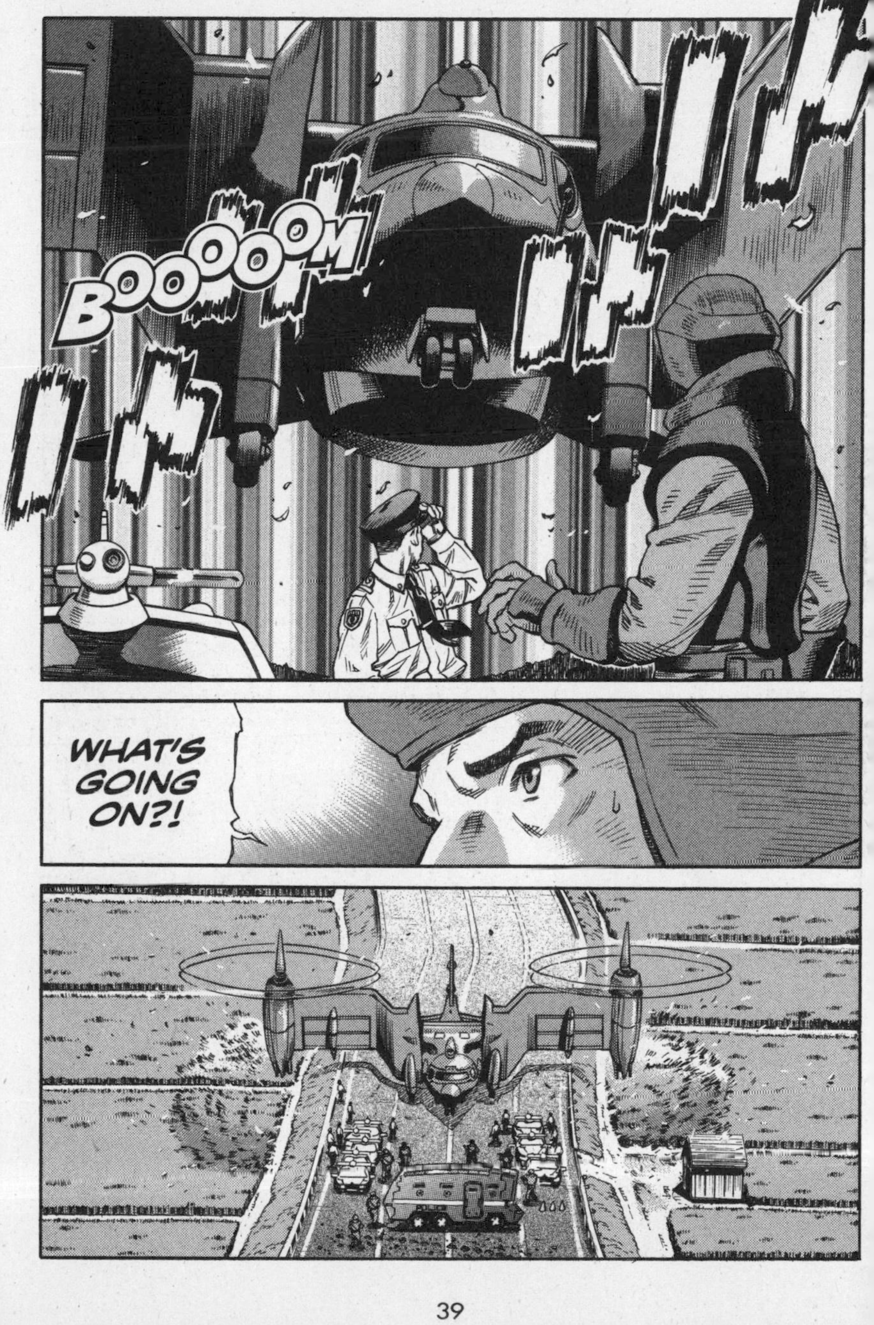
BOOOOOM
WHAT'S GOING ON?!

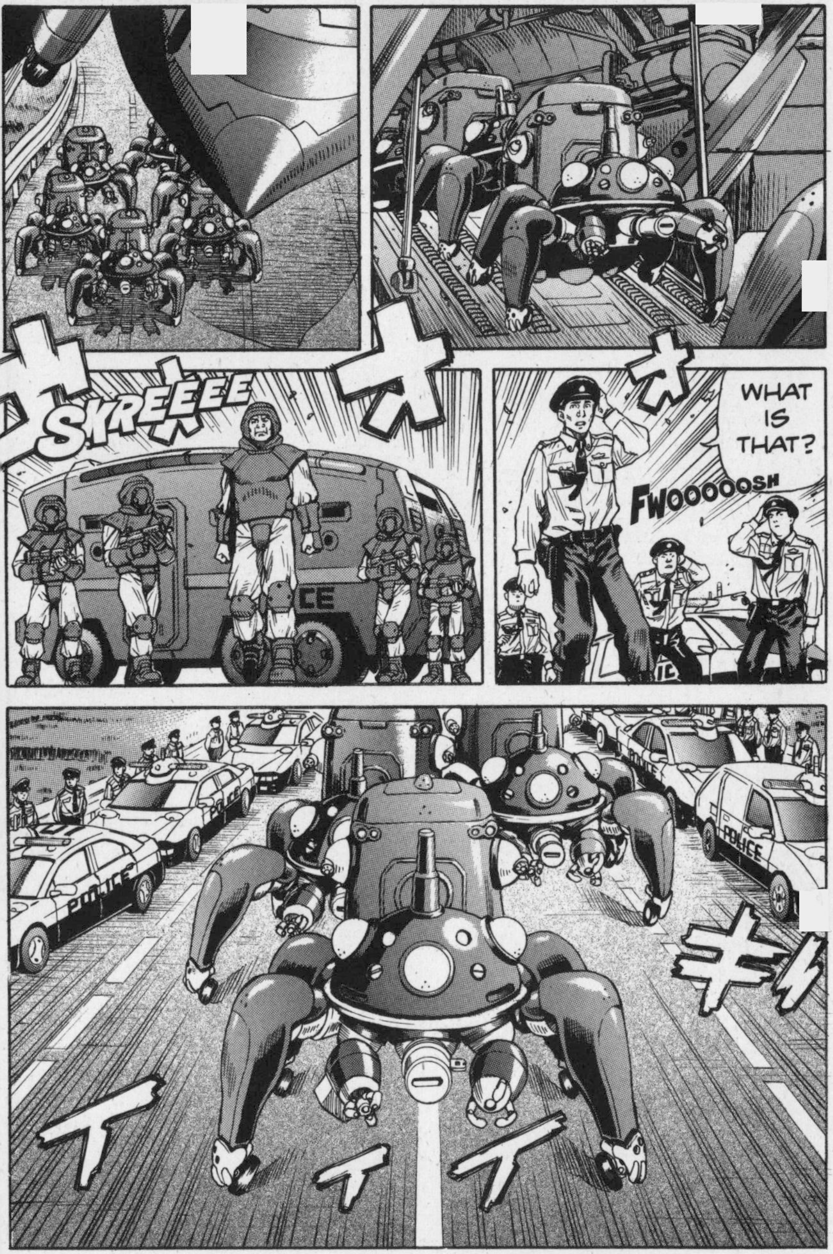
WHAT IS THAT?
FWOOOOOSH
SKREEEEE

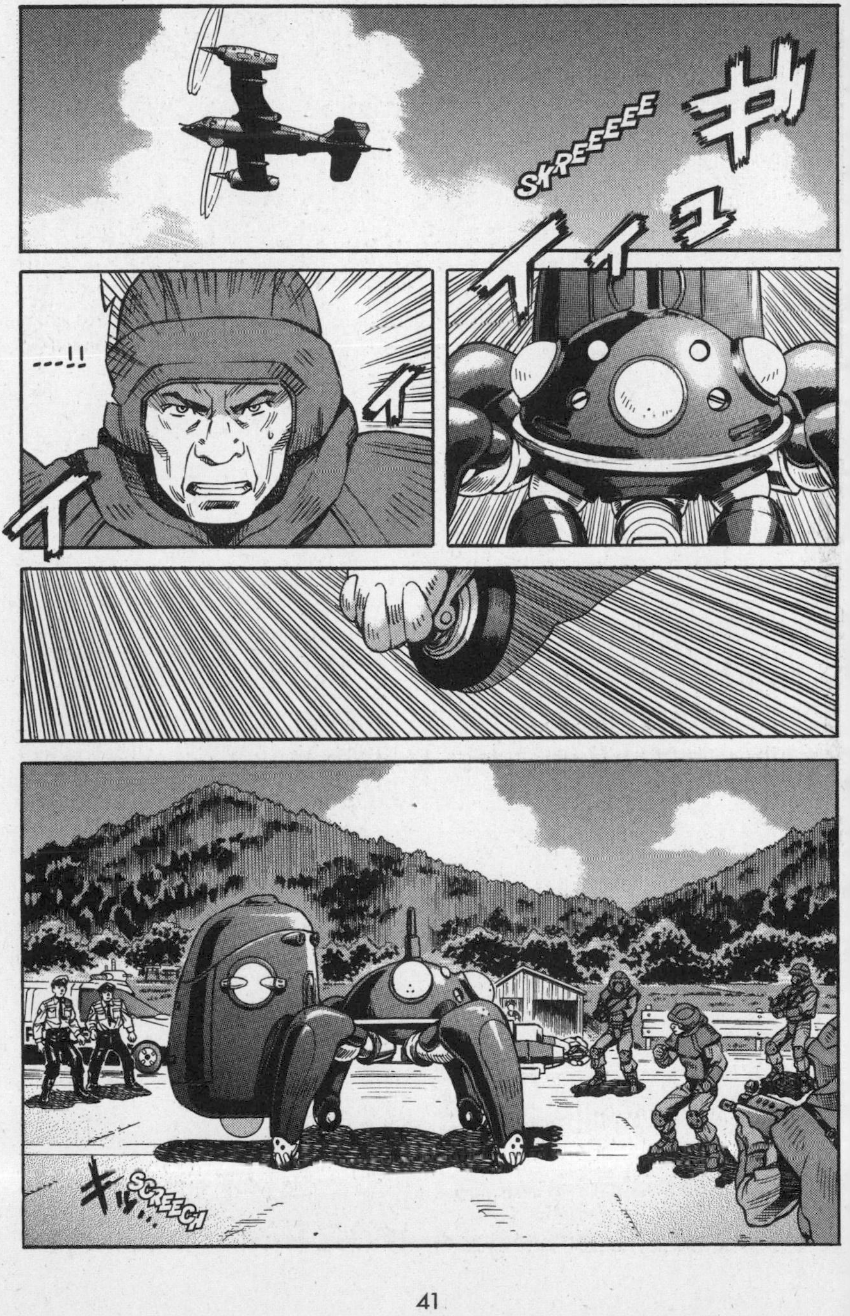
SKREEEEEE
...!!
SCREECH

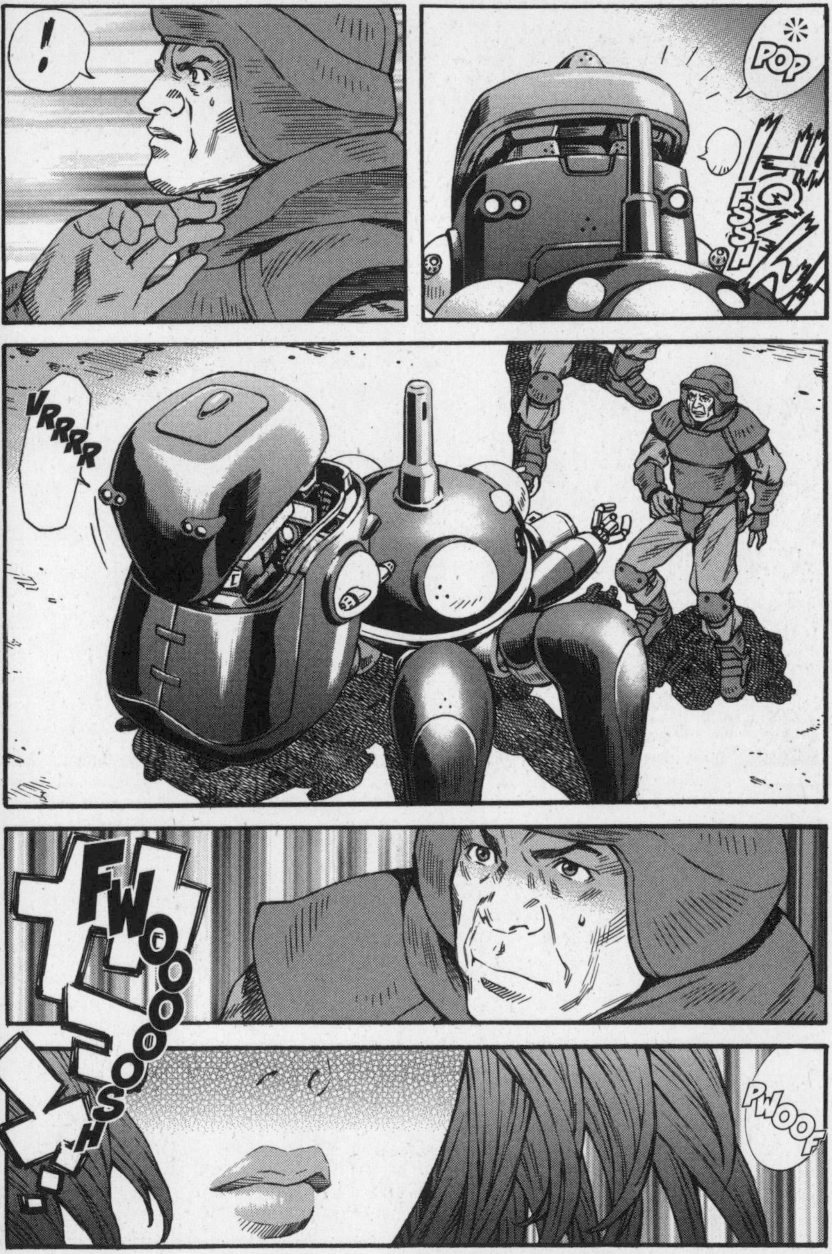

POP
FSSH
!
VRRRR
FWOOOOOOSH
PWOOF

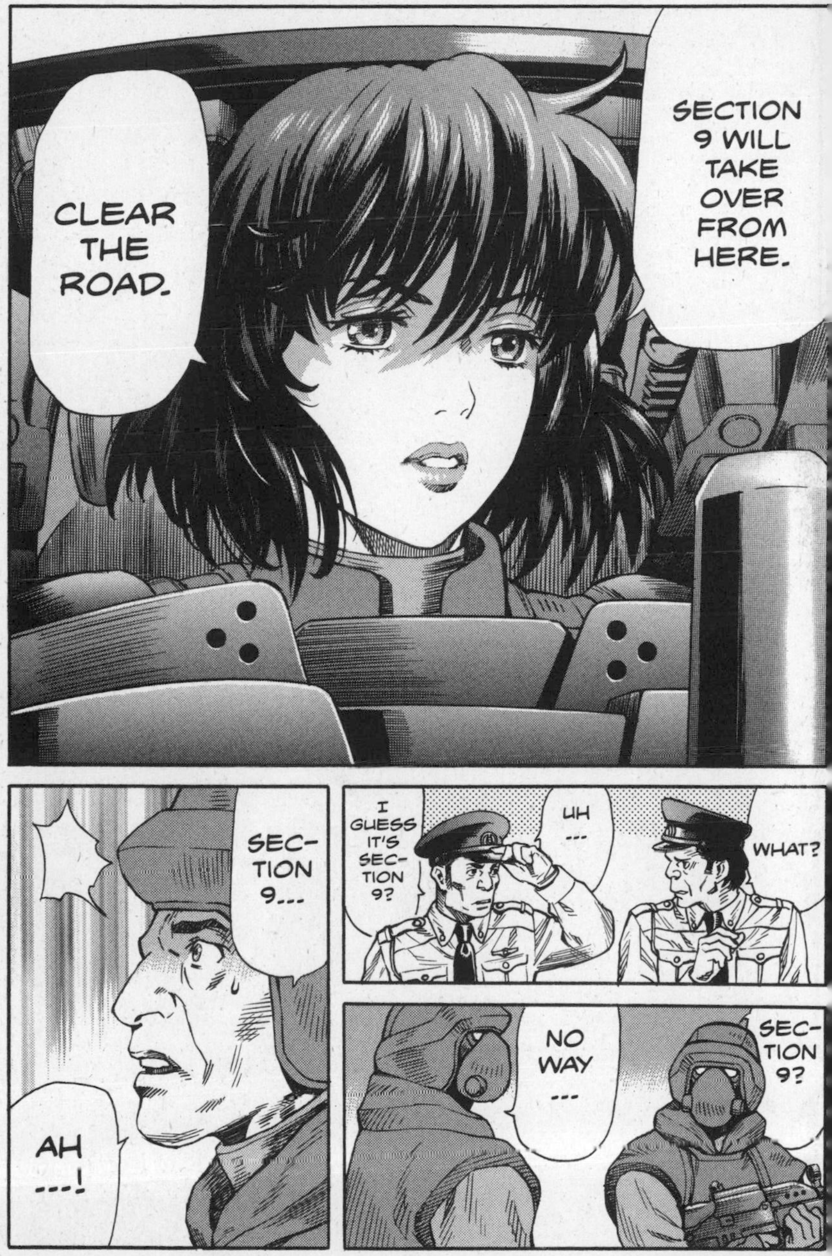
SECTION 9 WILL TAKE OVER FROM HERE.
CLEAR THE ROAD.
WHAT?
UH ---
I GUESS IT'S SEC-TION 9?
SEC-TION 9?
NO WAY ---
SEC-TION 9...
AH ---!

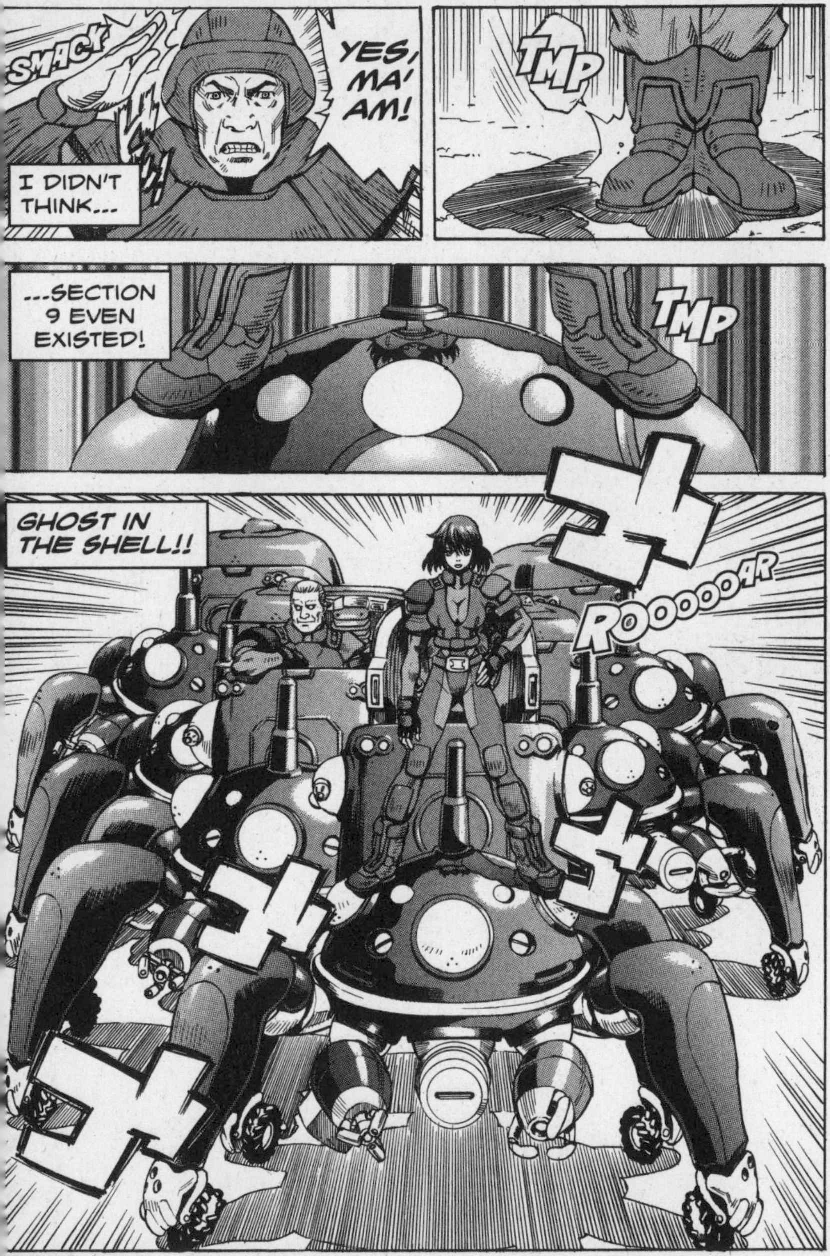
TMP
YES, MA'AM!
SMACK
I DIDN'T THINK...
...SECTION 9 EVEN EXISTED!
TMP
GHOST IN THE SHELL!!
ROOOOOOAR

#012 End

#013: Disclosure

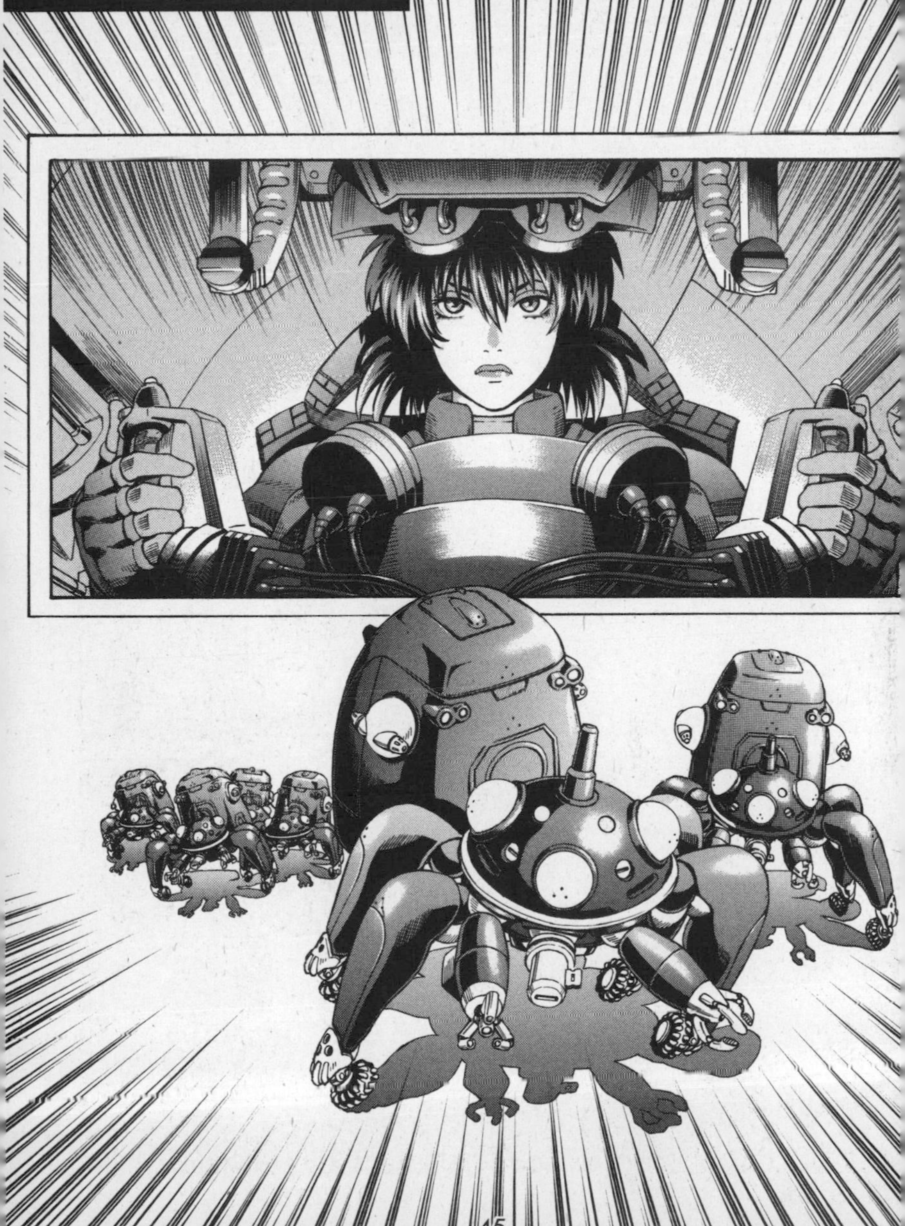

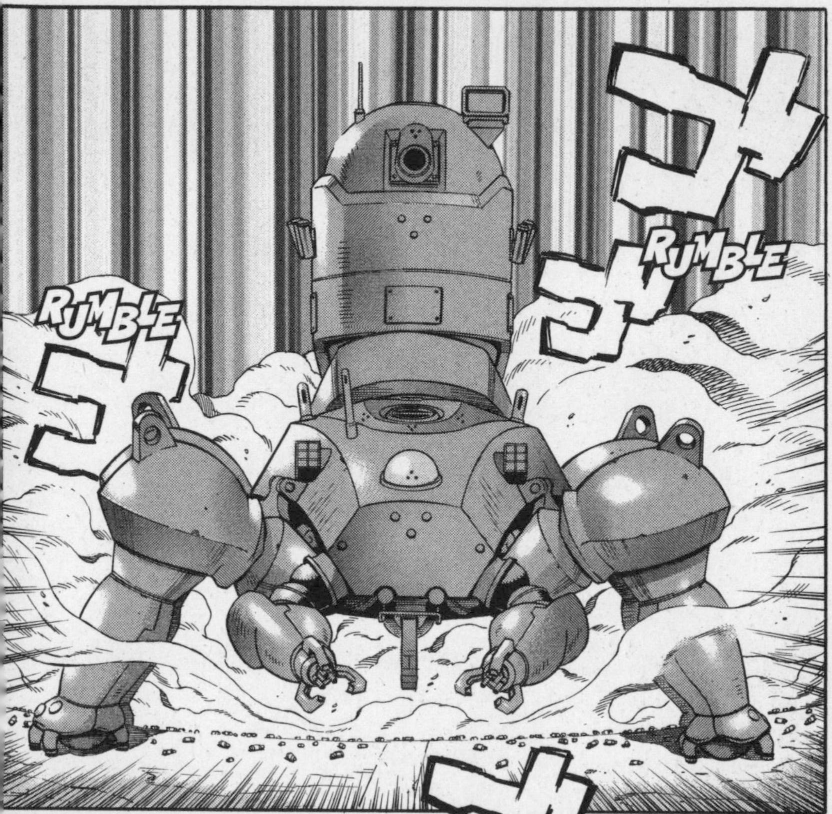
RUMBLE
RUMBLE
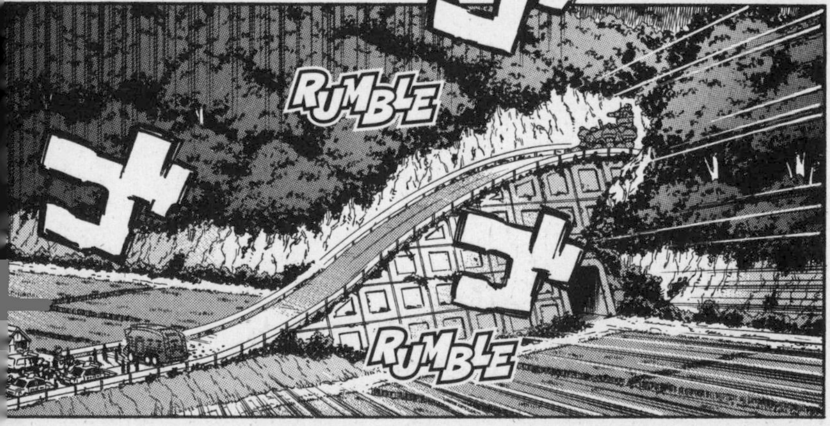
RUMBLE
RUMBLE

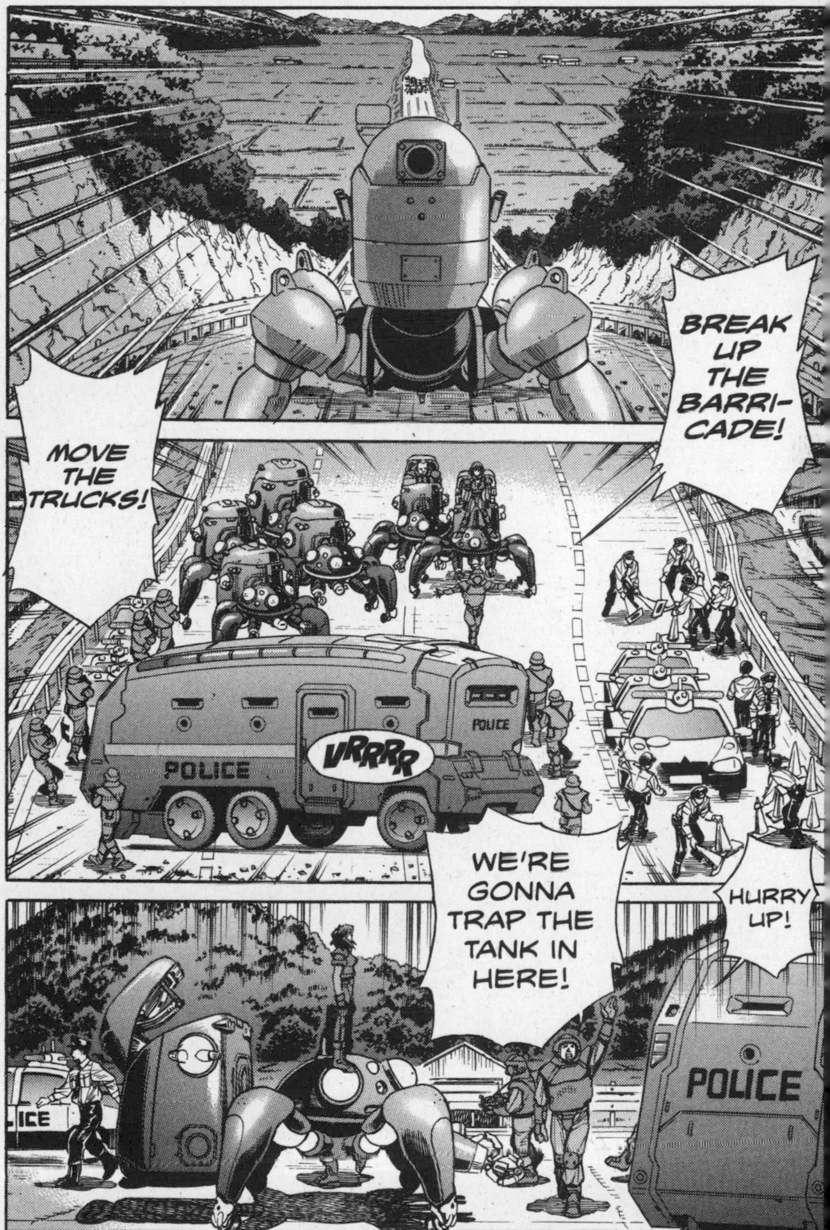
BREAK UP THE BARRI- CADE!
MOVE THE TRUCKS!
POLICE
VRRRR
POLICE
HURRY UP!
WE'RE GONNA TRAP THE TANK IN HERE!
POLICE
LICE

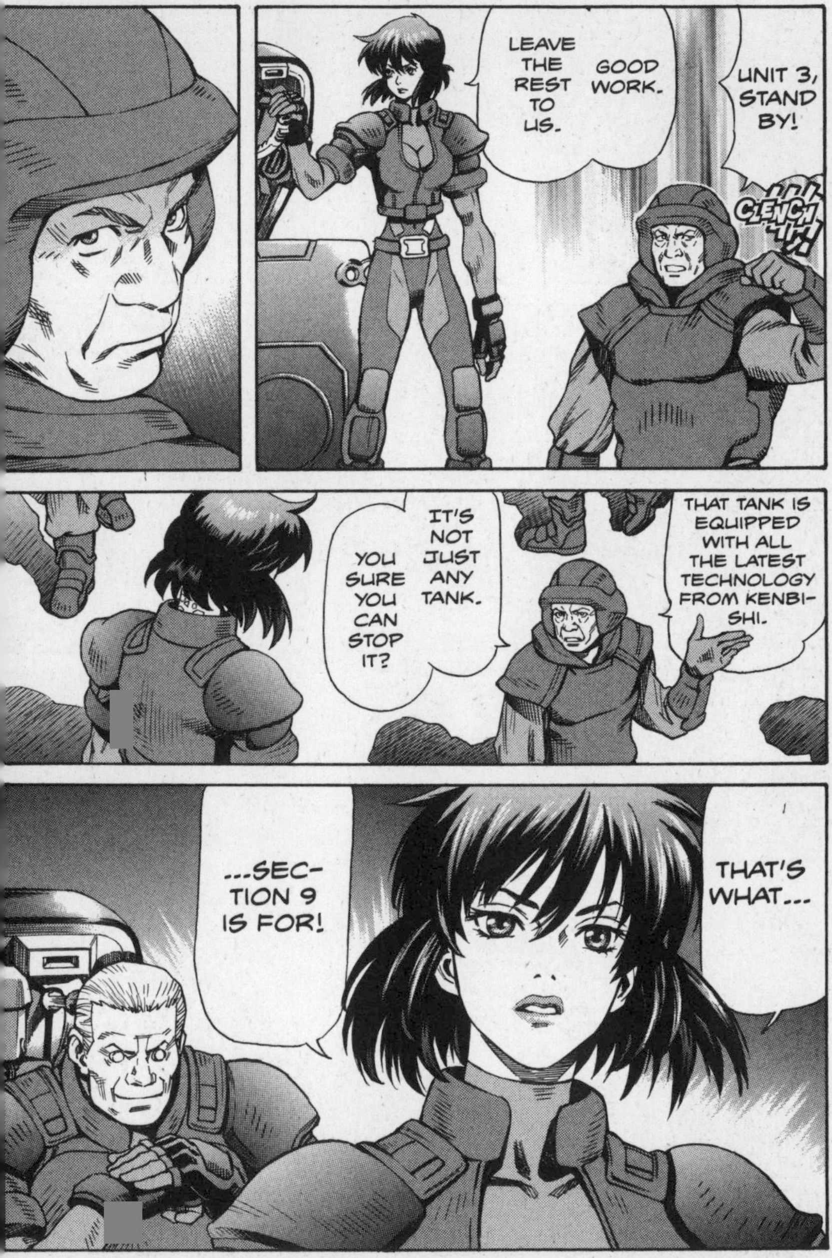
UNIT 3, STAND BY!
CLENCH
GOOD WORK.
LEAVE THE REST TO US.
THAT TANK IS EQUIPPED WITH ALL THE LATEST TECHNOLOGY FROM KENBI-SHI.
IT'S NOT JUST ANY TANK.
YOU SURE YOU CAN STOP IT?
THAT'S WHAT...
...SEC-TION 9 IS FOR!

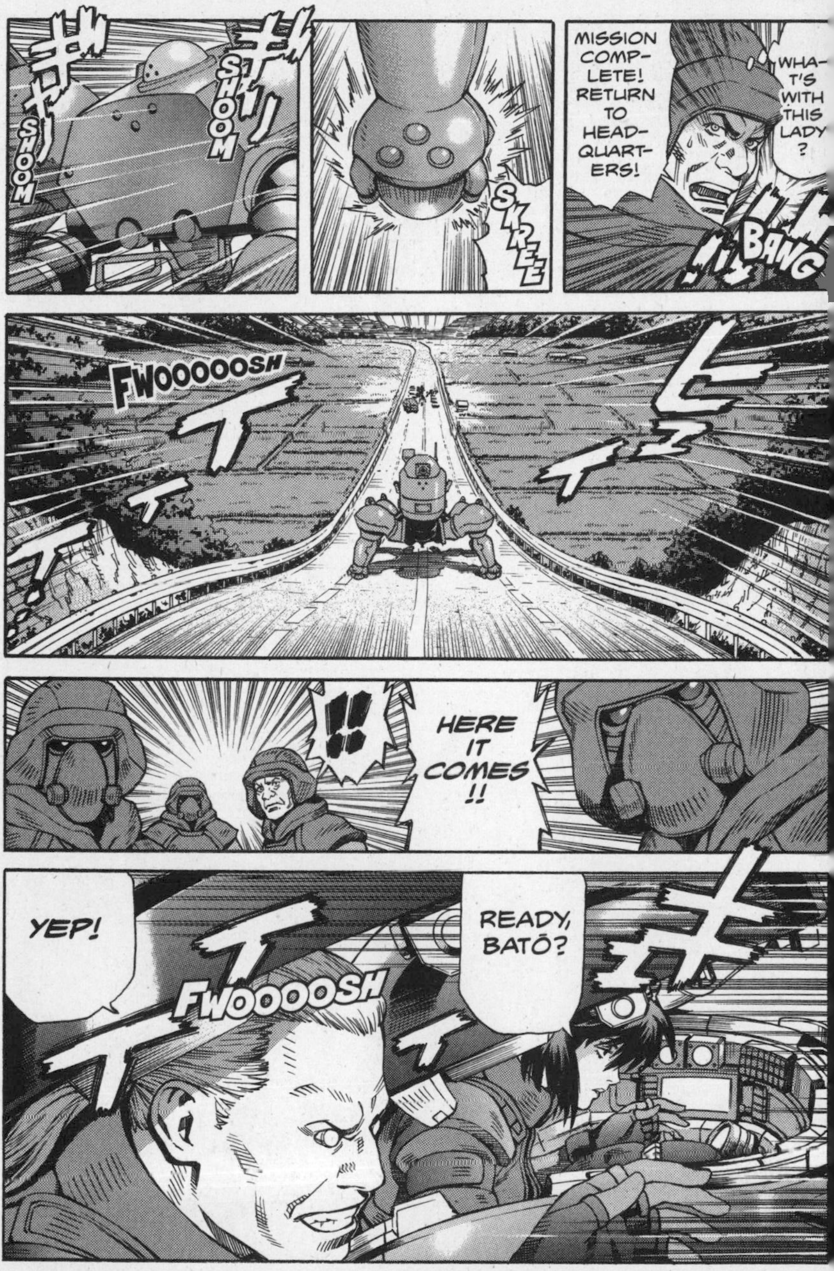
WHAT'S WITH THIS LADY?
MISSION COMPLETE! RETURN TO HEADQUARTERS!
BANG
SKREE
SHOOM
SHOOM
FWOOOOOSH
HERE IT COMES!!
!!
READY, BATŌ?
YEP!
FWOOOOOSH

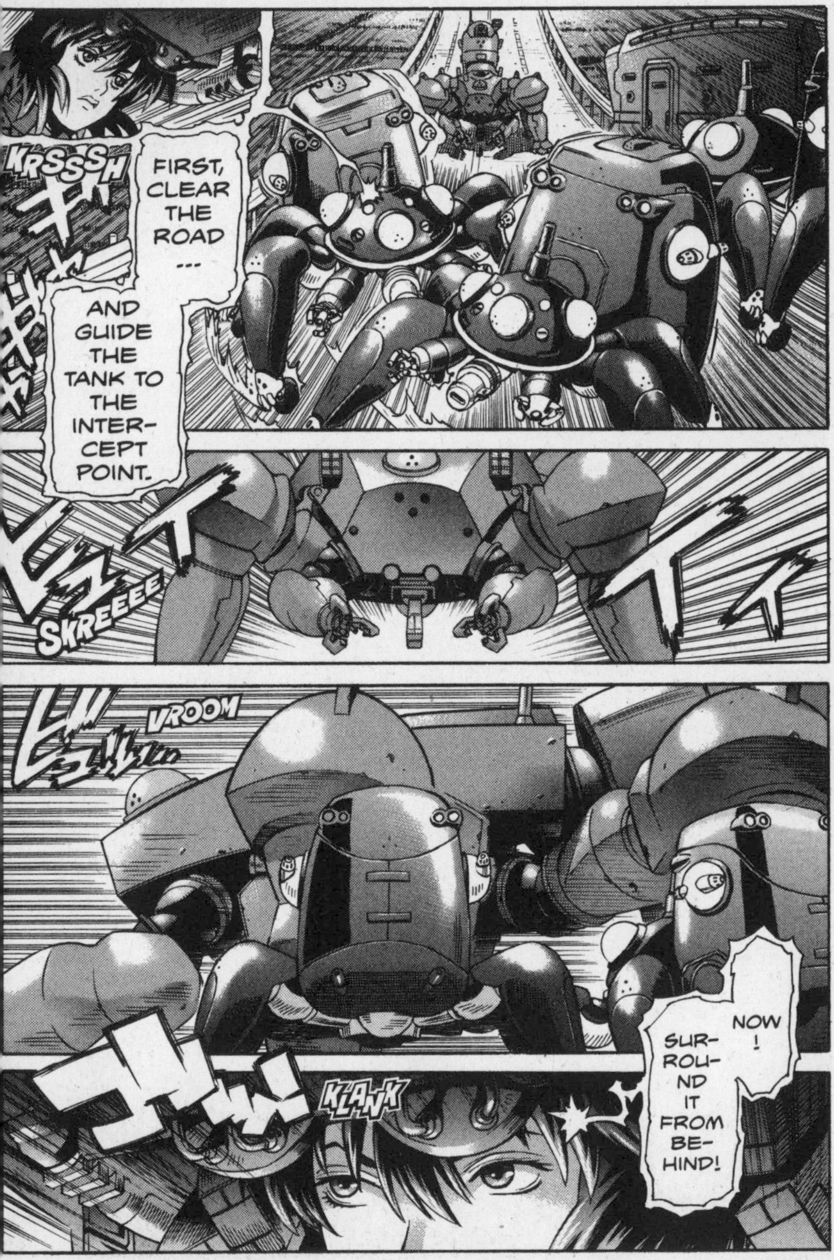
FIRST, CLEAR THE ROAD ---
AND GUIDE THE TANK TO THE INTER-CEPT POINT.
KRSSSH
SKREEEE
VROOM
NOW!
SUR-ROU-ND IT FROM BE-HIND!
KLANK

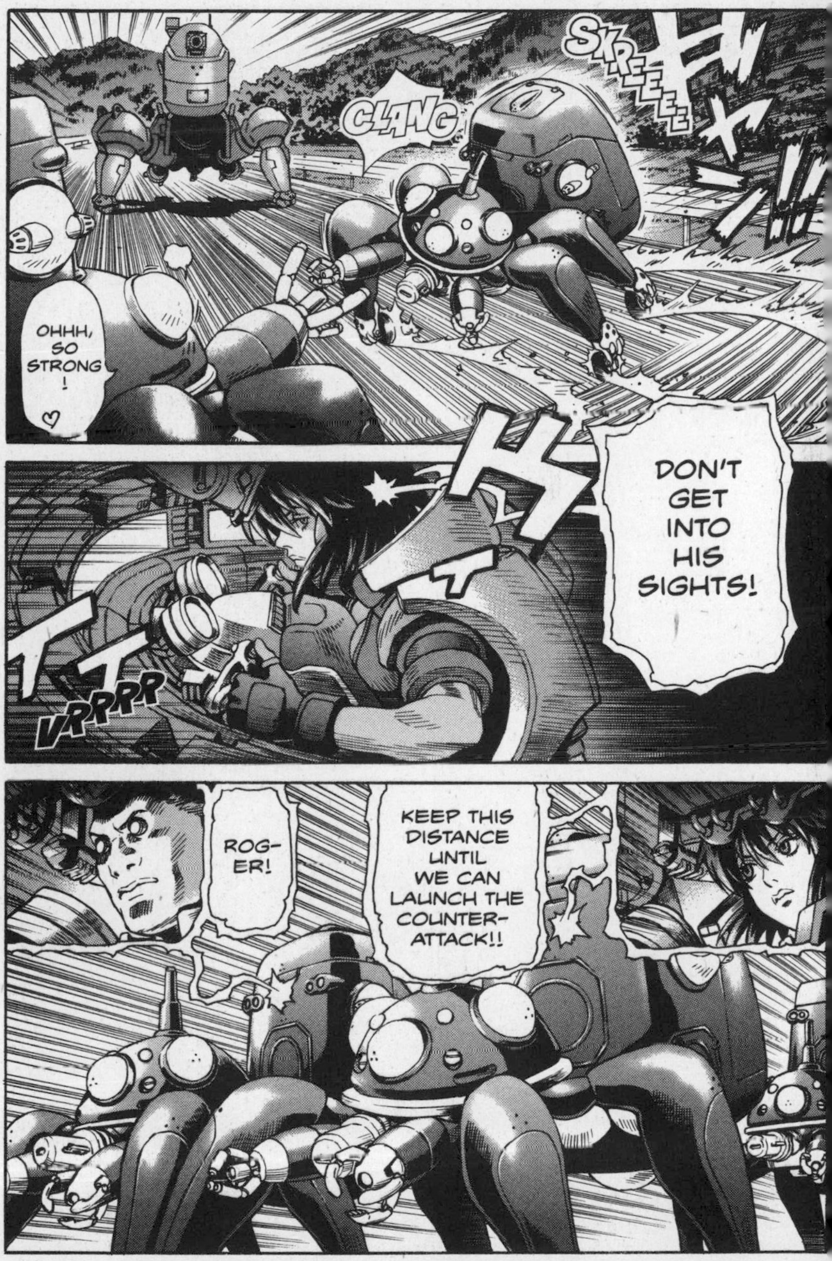
SKREEEEE
CLANG
OHHH, SO STRONG! ♡
DON'T GET INTO HIS SIGHTS!
VRRRRR
KEEP THIS DISTANCE UNTIL WE CAN LAUNCH THE COUNTER-ATTACK!!
ROG-ER!

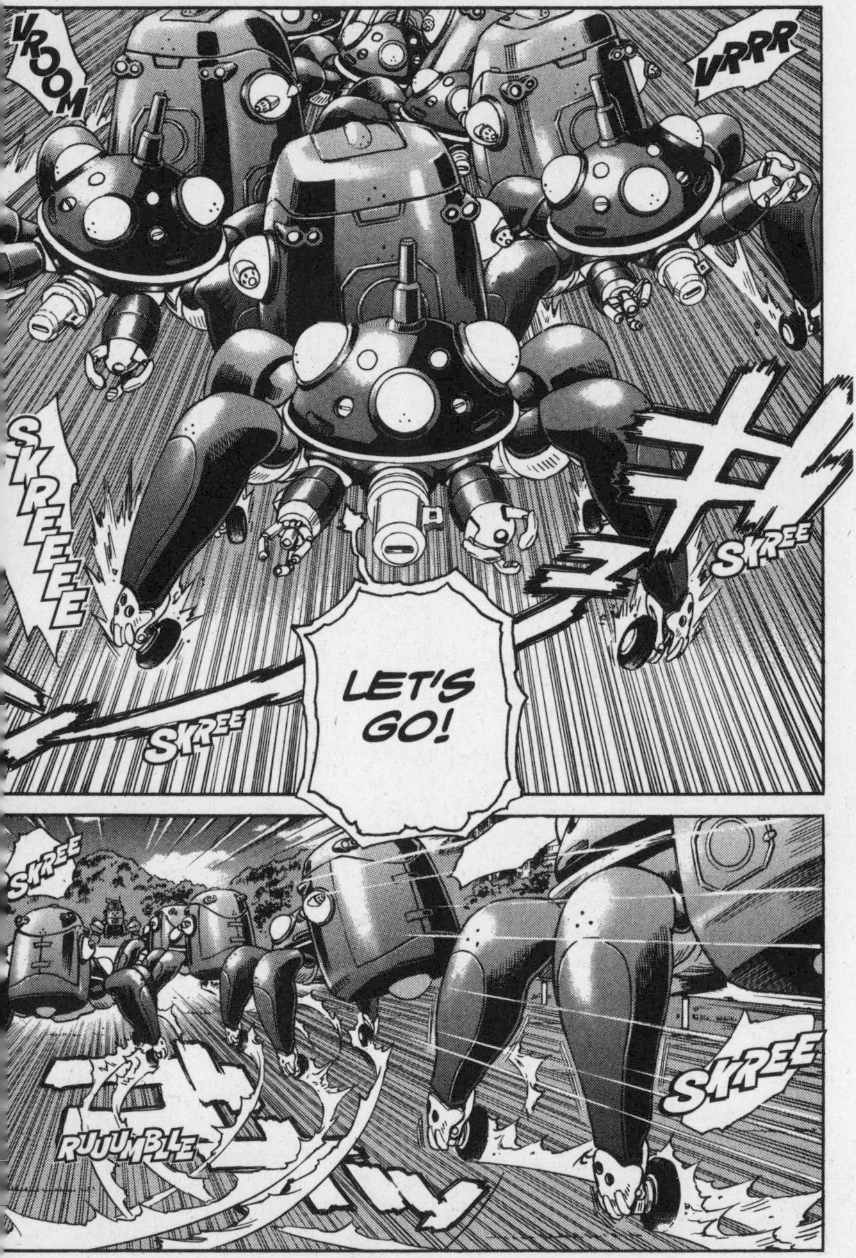
VRRRR
VROOM
SKREE
SKREEEEEE
LET'S GO!
SKREE
SKREE
SKREE
RUUUMBLE

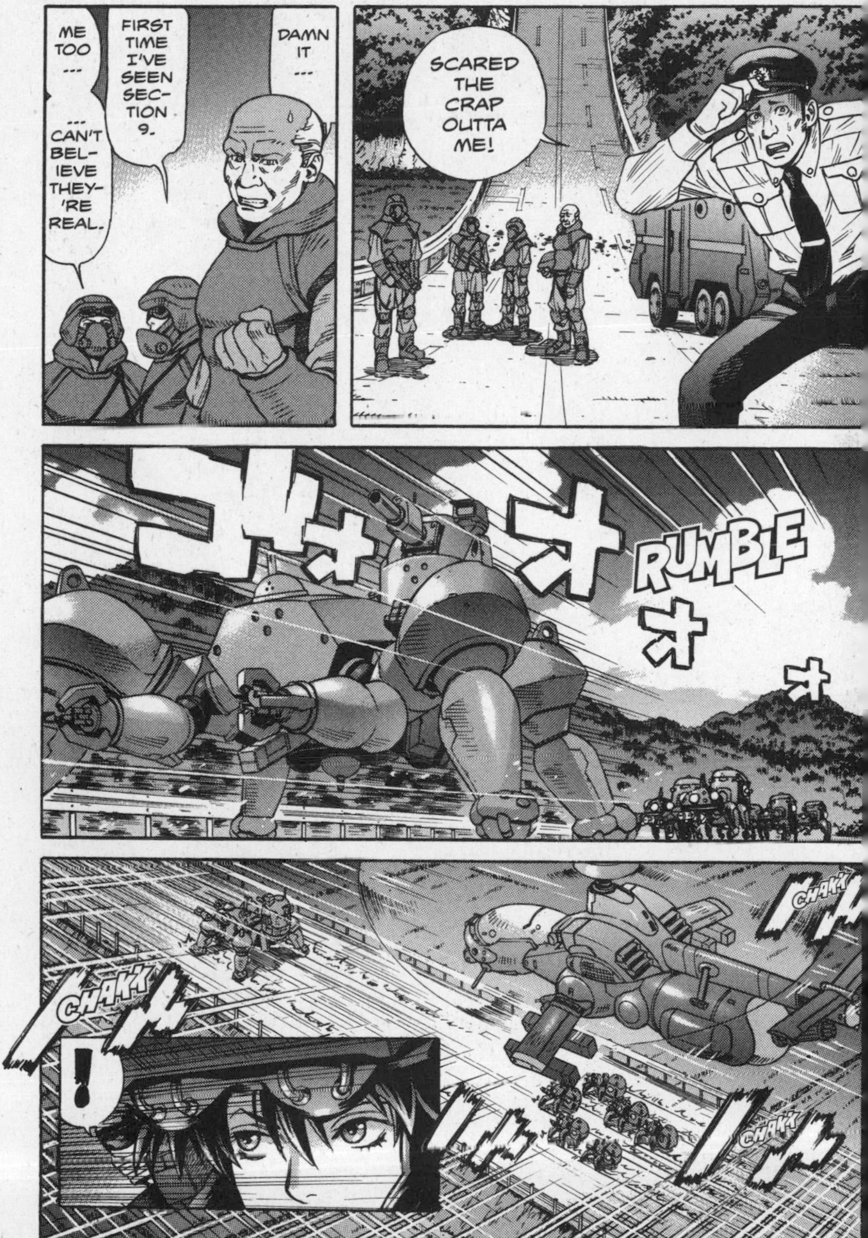

SCARED THE CRAP OUTTA ME!
DAMN IT ---
FIRST TIME I'VE SEEN SEC-TION 9.
ME TOO ---
... CAN'T BEL-IEVE THEY-'RE REAL.
RUMBLE
CHAKK
CHAKK
!
CHAKK

AI HELICOPTERS SIGHTED.

beep

LIVE

beep

CHAKK

CHAKK

CHAKK

CHAKK

SDF, HUH ---

GUESS THEY WANT AN AERIAL VIEW!!

THUD

THUD

IT'S THEIR INSURANCE AND THEIR THREAT AGAINST KENBISHI.

54

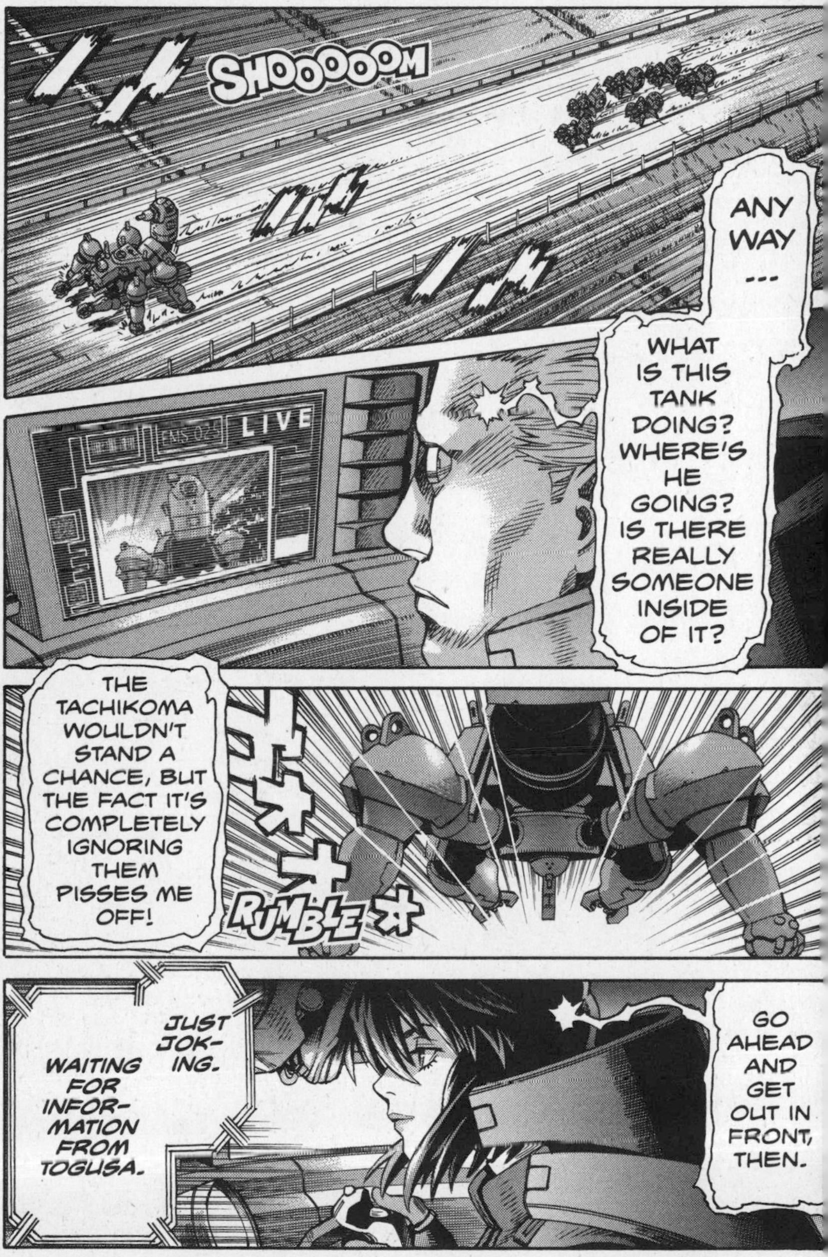
SHOOOOOM
ANY WAY ---
LIVE
WHAT IS THIS TANK DOING? WHERE'S HE GOING? IS THERE REALLY SOMEONE INSIDE OF IT?
THE TACHIKOMA WOULDN'T STAND A CHANCE, BUT THE FACT IT'S COMPLETELY IGNORING THEM PISSES ME OFF!
RUMBLE
GO AHEAD AND GET OUT IN FRONT, THEN.
JUST JOK-ING.
WAITING FOR INFOR-MATION FROM TOGUSA.

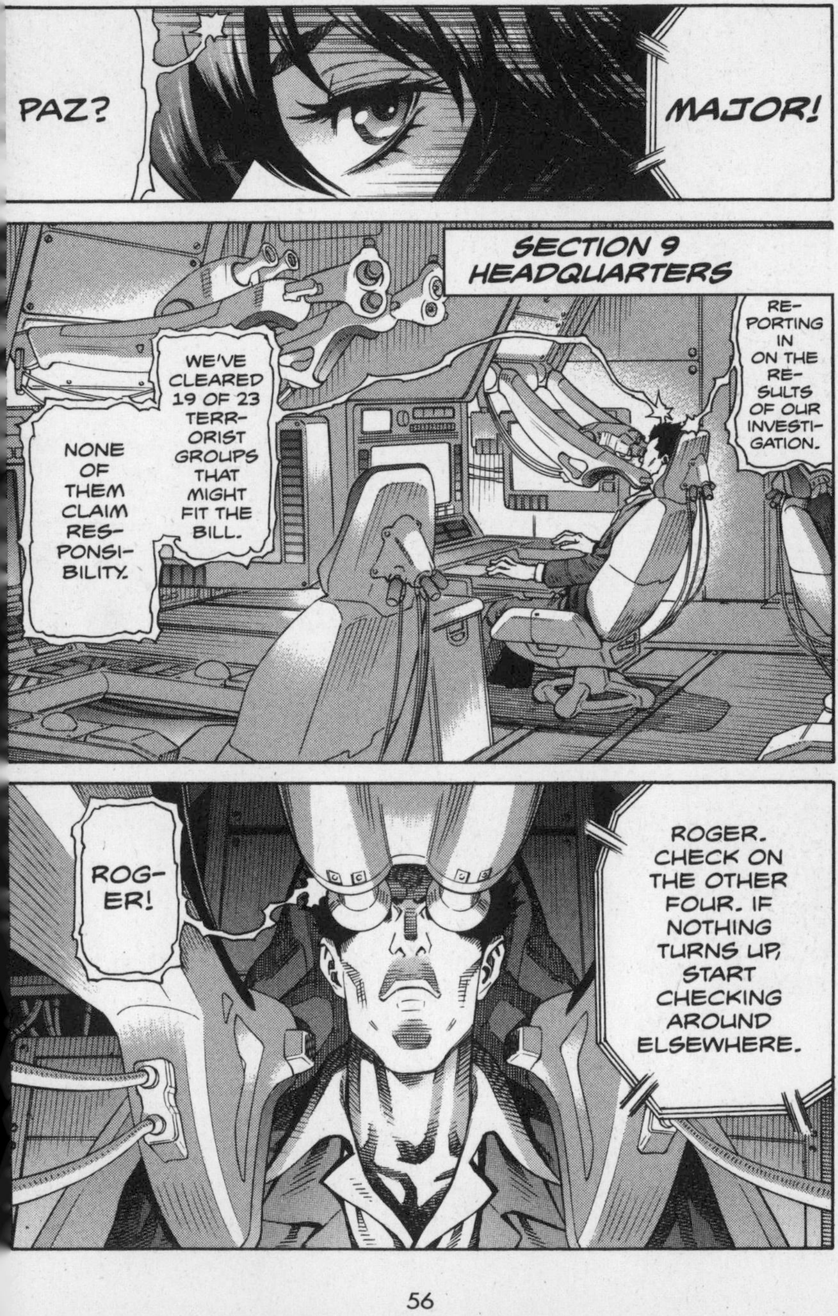
MAJOR!
PAZ?
SECTION 9 HEADQUARTERS
REPORTING IN ON THE RESULTS OF OUR INVESTIGATION.
WE'VE CLEARED 19 OF 23 TERRORIST GROUPS THAT MIGHT FIT THE BILL.
NONE OF THEM CLAIM RESPONSIBILITY.
ROGER. CHECK ON THE OTHER FOUR. IF NOTHING TURNS UP, START CHECKING AROUND ELSEWHERE.
ROGER!

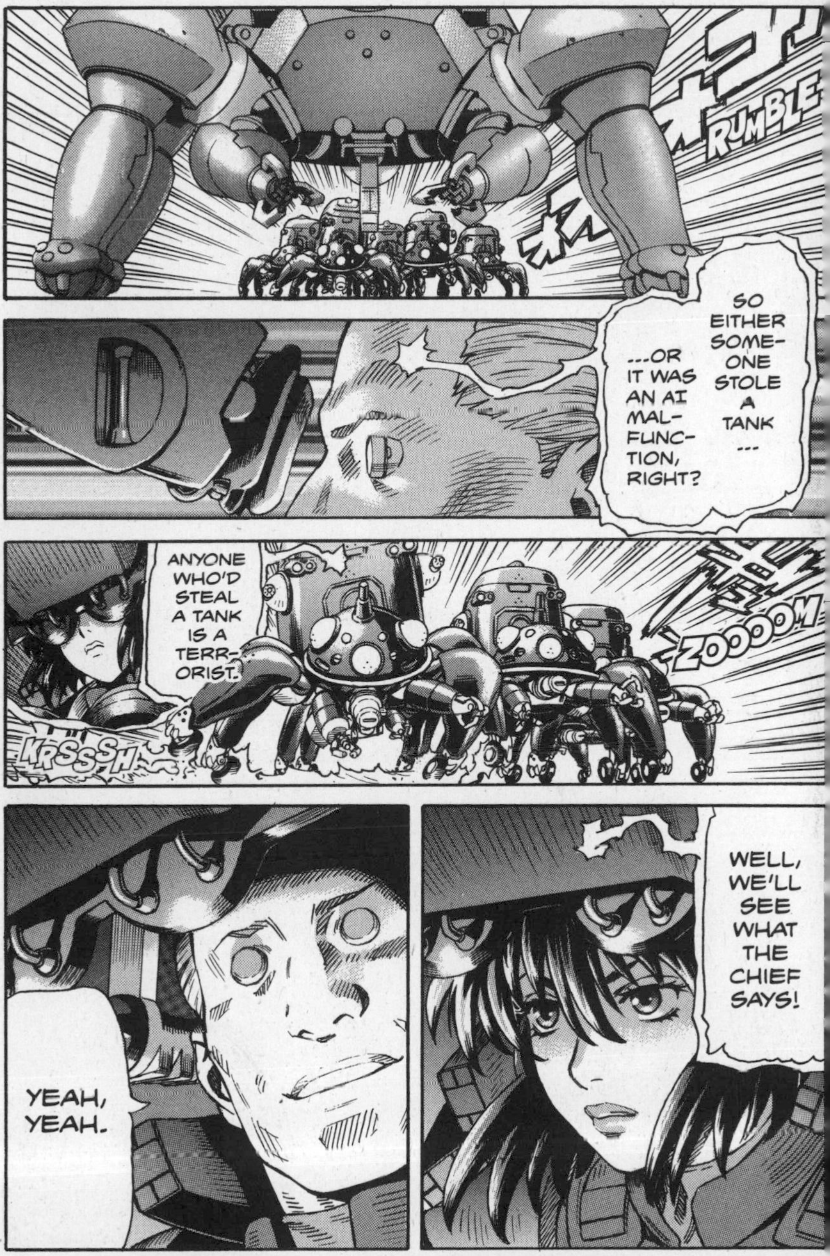
RUMBLE
SO EITHER SOME-ONE STOLE A TANK ---
---OR IT WAS AN AI MAL-FUNC-TION, RIGHT?
ZOOOOM
ANYONE WHO'D STEAL A TANK IS A TERR-ORIST.
KRSSSH
WELL, WE'LL SEE WHAT THE CHIEF SAYS!
YEAH, YEAH.

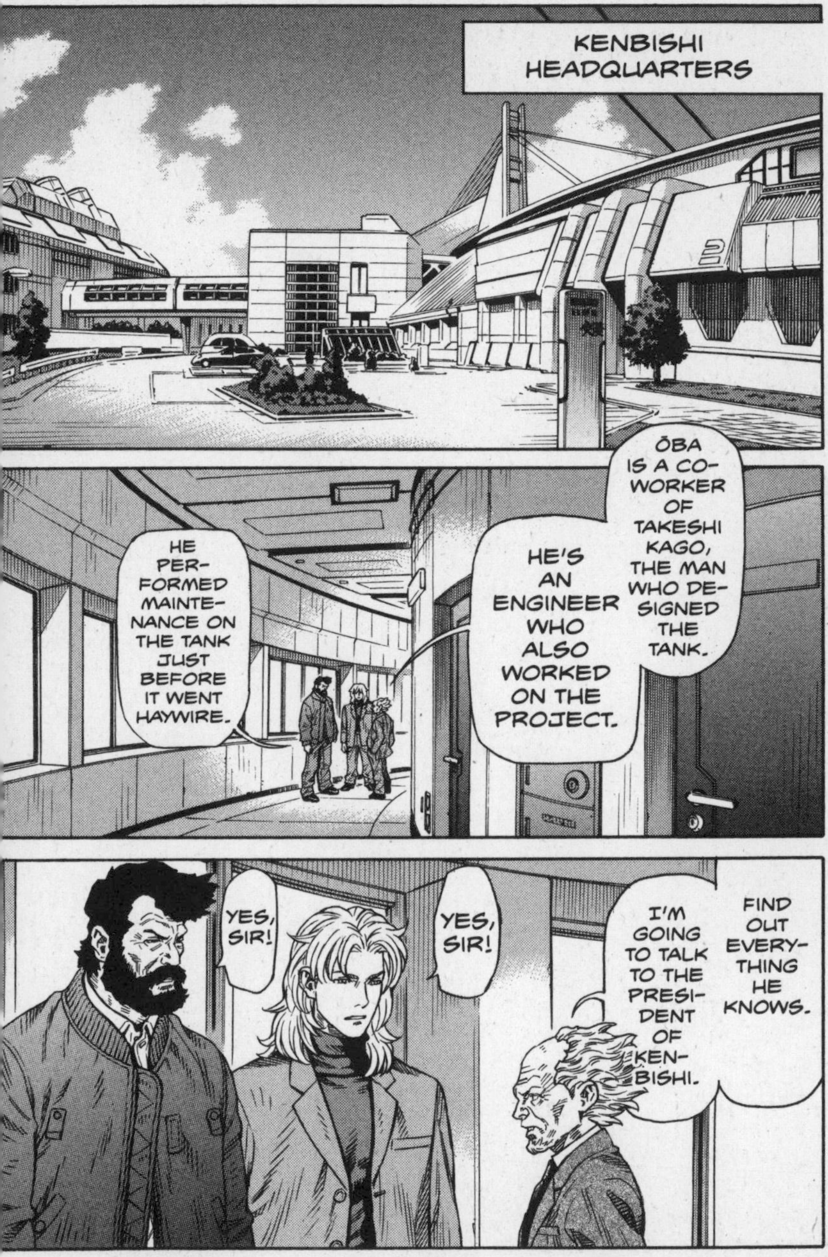
KENBISHI HEADQUARTERS
ŌBA IS A CO-WORKER OF TAKESHI KAGO, THE MAN WHO DESIGNED THE TANK.
HE'S AN ENGINEER WHO ALSO WORKED ON THE PROJECT.
HE PERFORMED MAINTENANCE ON THE TANK JUST BEFORE IT WENT HAYWIRE.
FIND OUT EVERYTHING HE KNOWS.
I'M GOING TO TALK TO THE PRESIDENT OF KENBISHI.
YES, SIR!
YES, SIR!

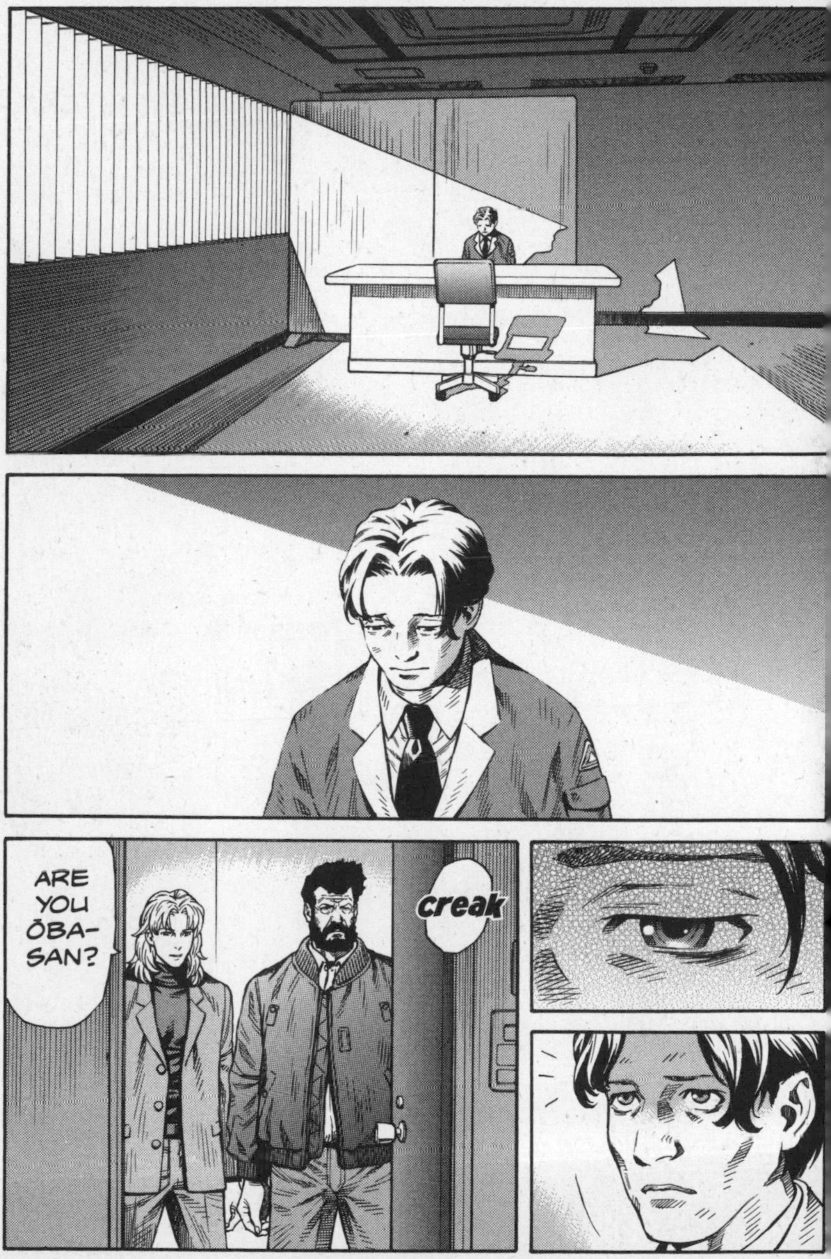
creak
ARE YOU ŌBA-SAN?

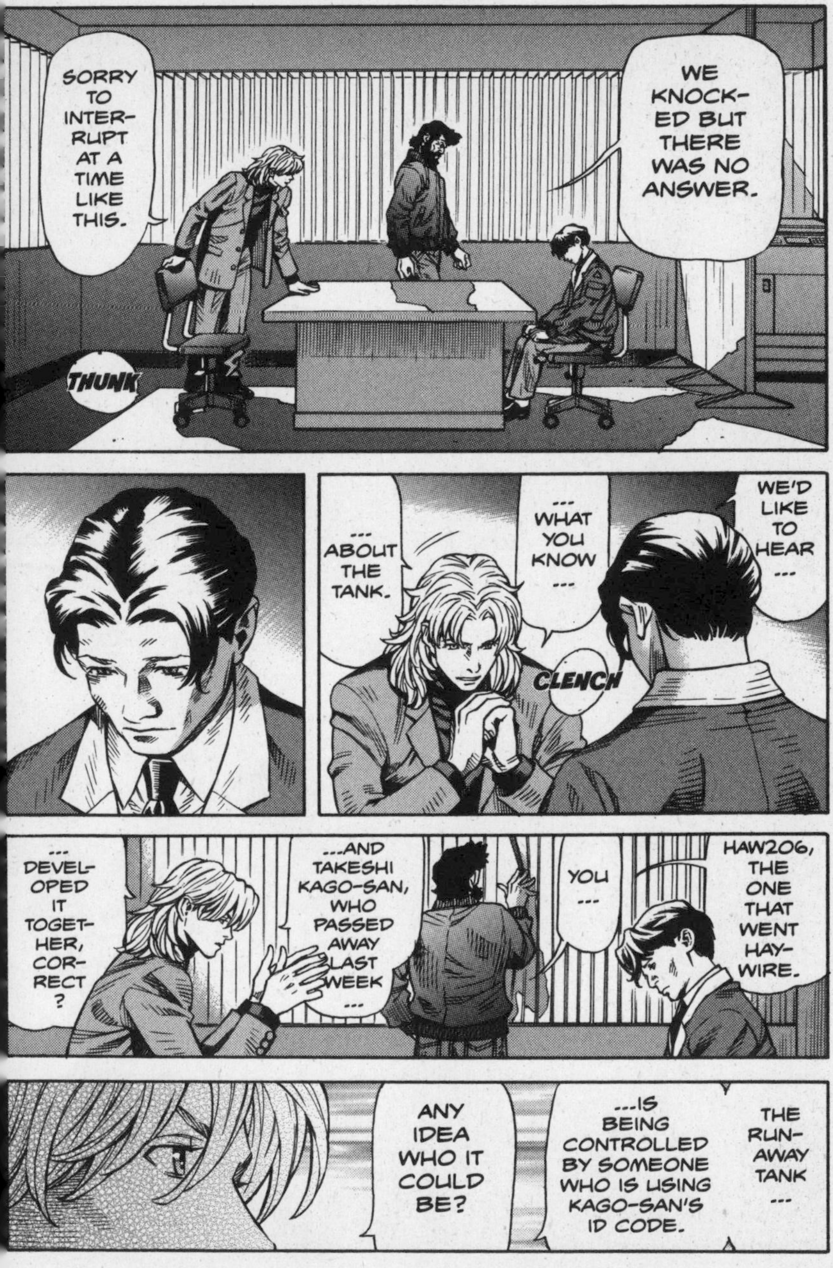
WE KNOCKED BUT THERE WAS NO ANSWER.
SORRY TO INTERRUPT AT A TIME LIKE THIS.
THUNK
WE'D LIKE TO HEAR ---
--- WHAT YOU KNOW ---
--- ABOUT THE TANK.
CLENCH
HAW206, THE ONE THAT WENT HAYWIRE.
YOU ---
---AND TAKESHI KAGO-SAN, WHO PASSED AWAY LAST WEEK ---
--- DEVELOPED IT TOGETHER, CORRECT?
THE RUNAWAY TANK ---
---IS BEING CONTROLLED BY SOMEONE WHO IS USING KAGO-SAN'S ID CODE.
ANY IDEA WHO IT COULD BE?

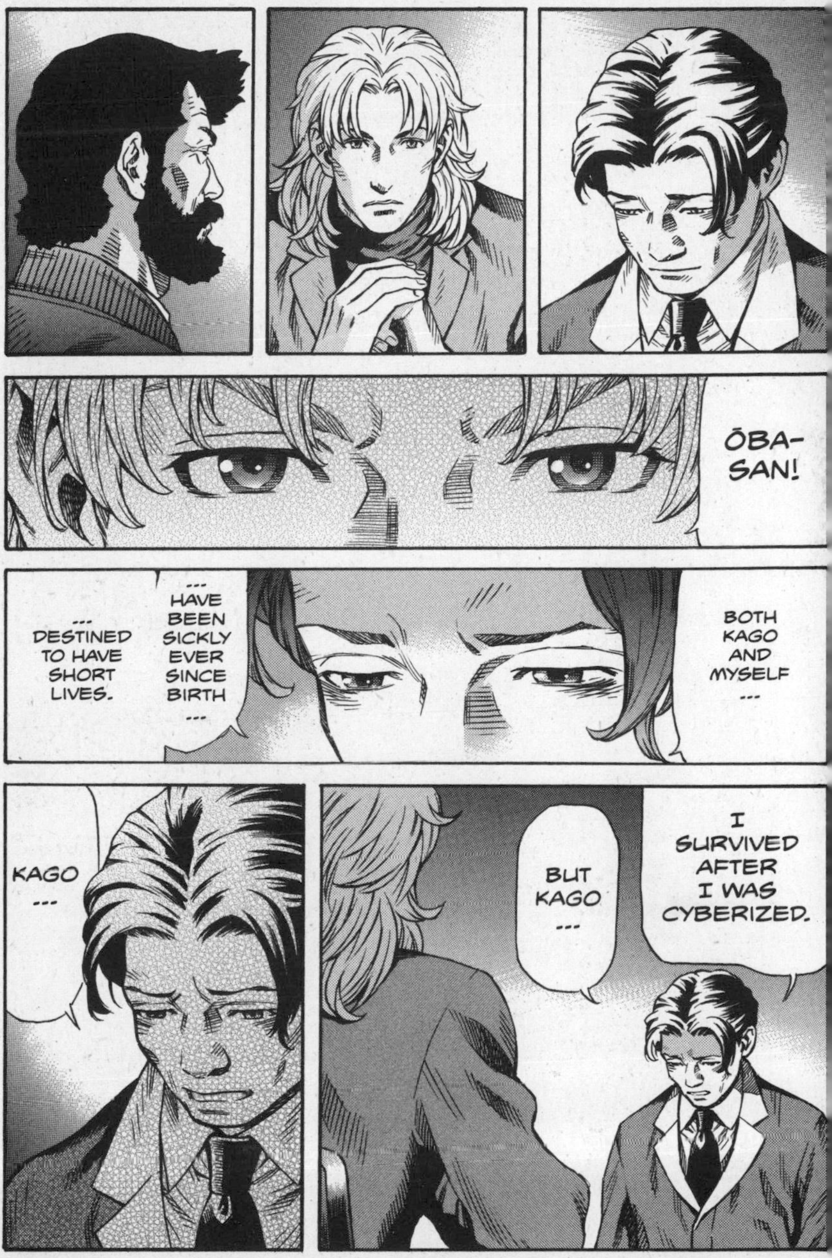
ŌBA-SAN!
BOTH KAGO AND MYSELF ---
--- HAVE BEEN SICKLY EVER SINCE BIRTH ---
--- DESTINED TO HAVE SHORT LIVES.
I SURVIVED AFTER I WAS CYBERIZED.
BUT KAGO ---
KAGO ---

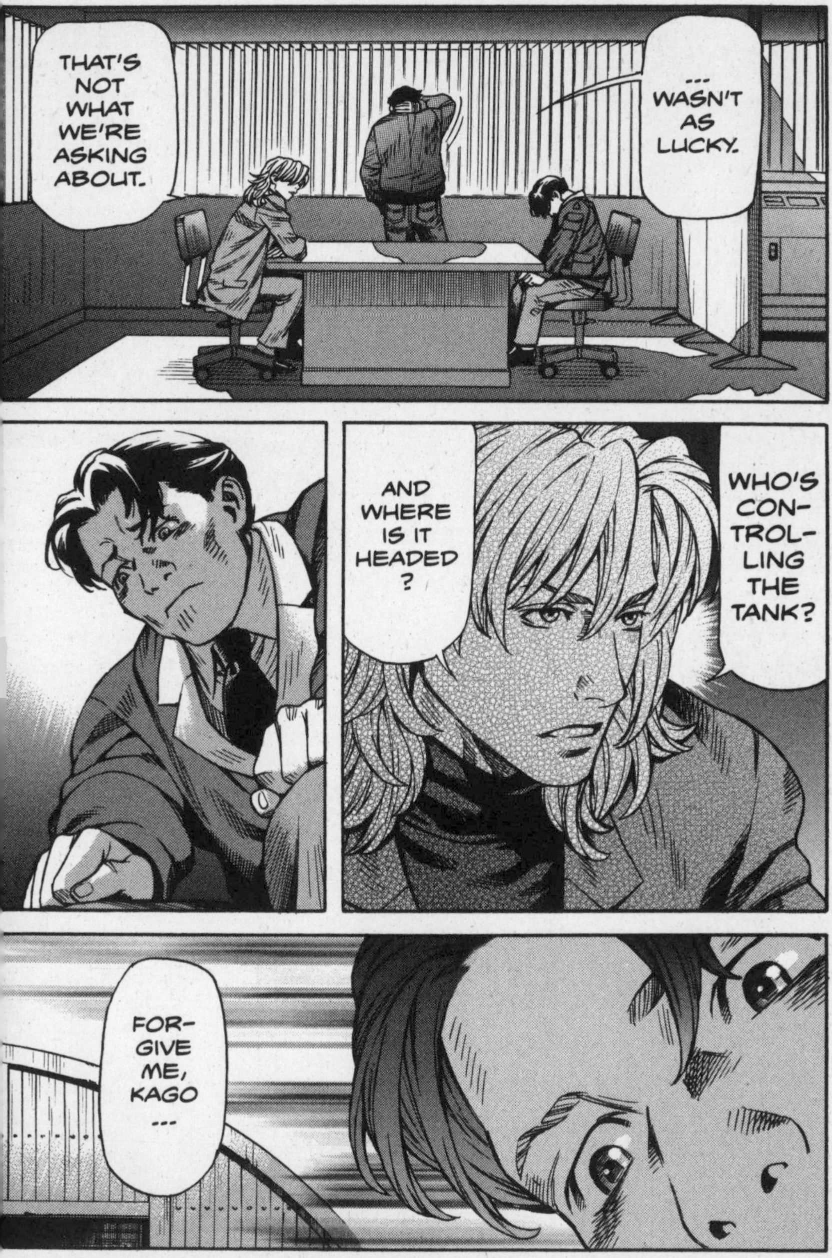

...WASN'T AS LUCKY.
THAT'S NOT WHAT WE'RE ASKING ABOUT.
WHO'S CONTROLLING THE TANK?
AND WHERE IS IT HEADED?
FORGIVE ME, KAGO...

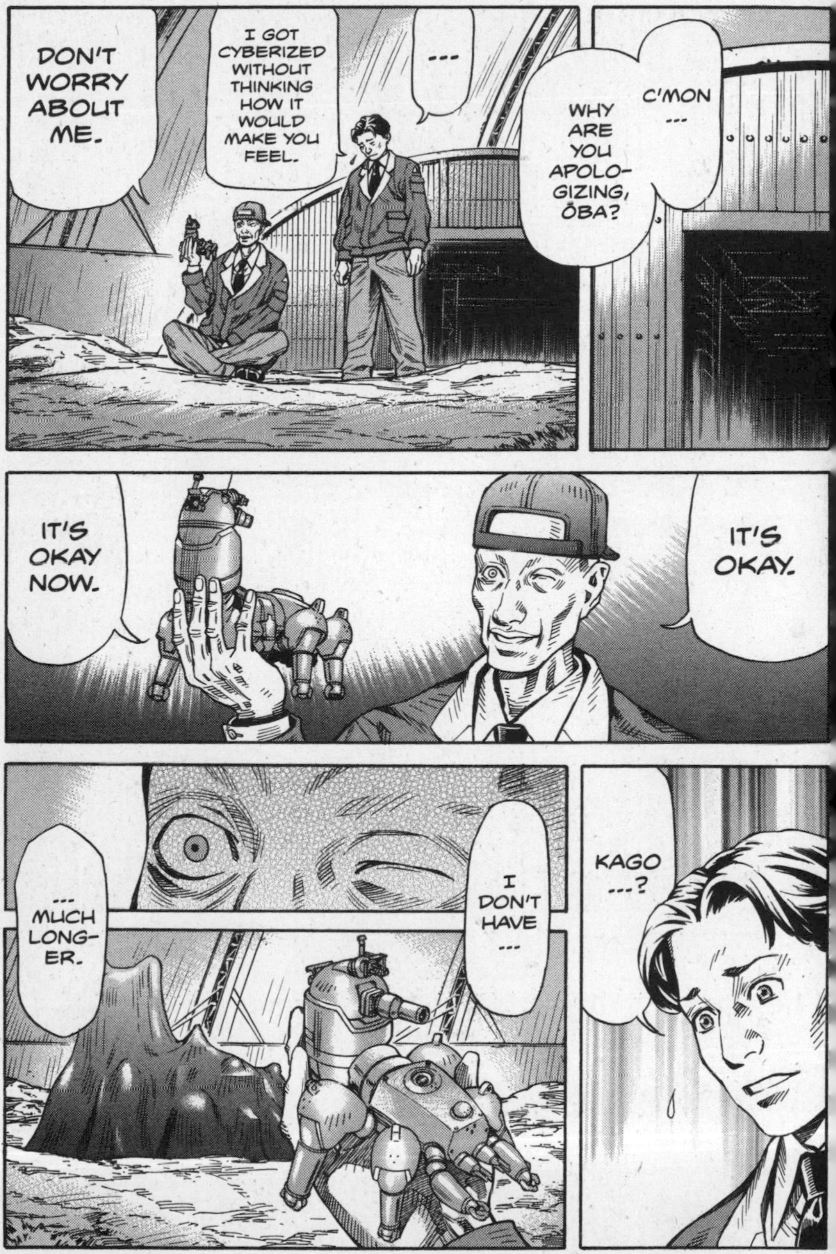

C'MON ...
WHY ARE YOU APOLOGIZING, ŌBA?
...
I GOT CYBERIZED WITHOUT THINKING HOW IT WOULD MAKE YOU FEEL.
DON'T WORRY ABOUT ME.
IT'S OKAY.
IT'S OKAY NOW.
KAGO ...?
I DON'T HAVE ...
... MUCH LONGER.

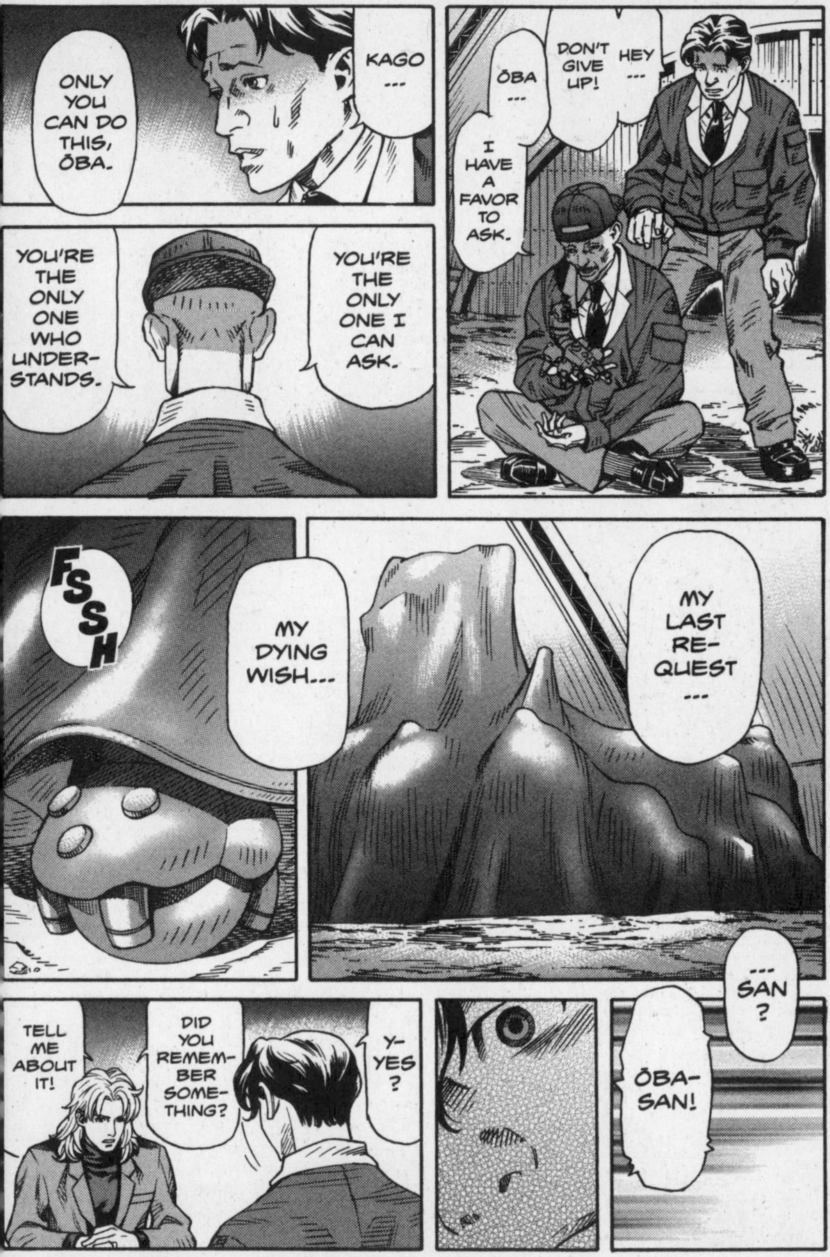

HEY ---
DON'T GIVE UP!
ŌBA ---
I HAVE A FAVOR TO ASK.
KAGO ---
ONLY YOU CAN DO THIS, ŌBA.
YOU'RE THE ONLY ONE I CAN ASK.
YOU'RE THE ONLY ONE WHO UNDERSTANDS.
MY LAST REQUEST ---
MY DYING WISH...
FSSH
--- SAN?
ŌBA-SAN!
Y-YES?
DID YOU REMEMBER SOMETHING?
TELL ME ABOUT IT!

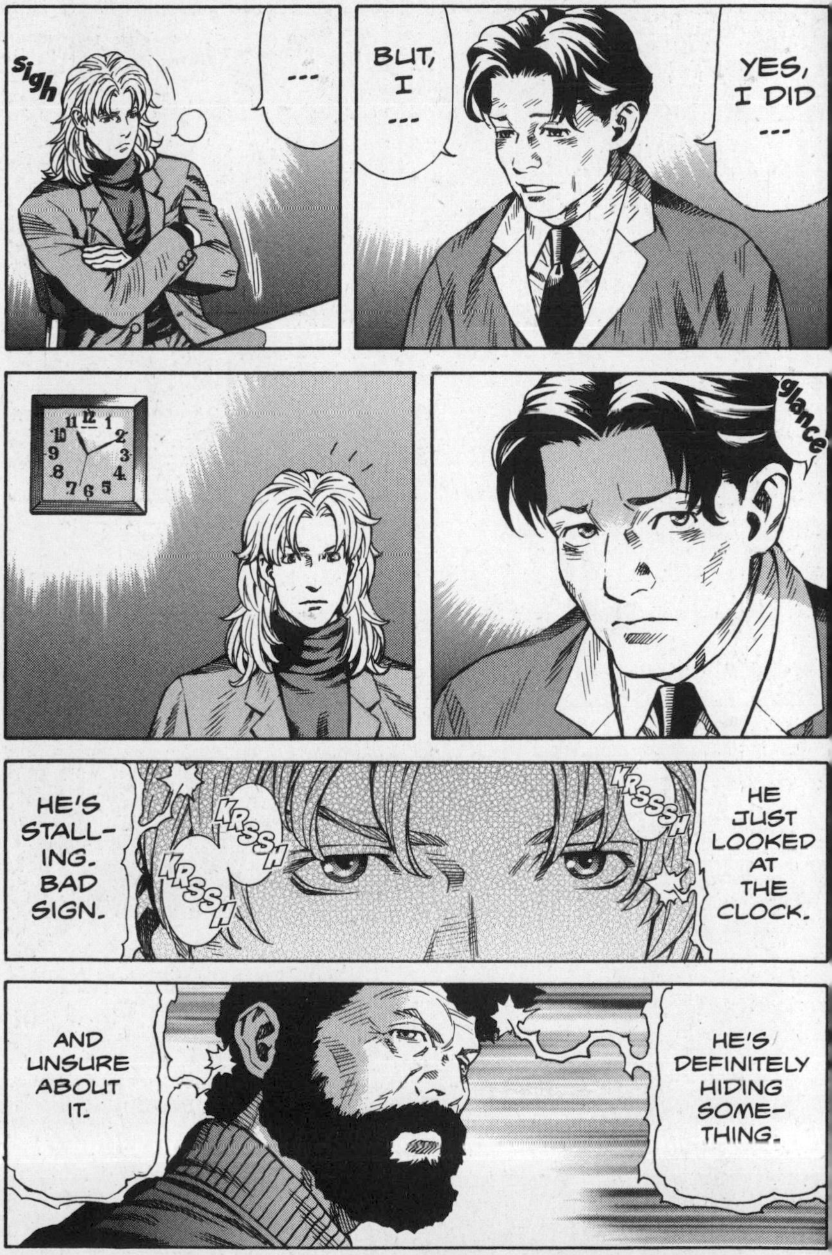
YES, I DID ---
BUT, I ---
sigh
---
glance
HE JUST LOOKED AT THE CLOCK.
KRSSSH
KRSSH
KRSSH
HE'S STALL-ING. BAD SIGN.
HE'S DEFINITELY HIDING SOME-THING.
AND UNSURE ABOUT IT.

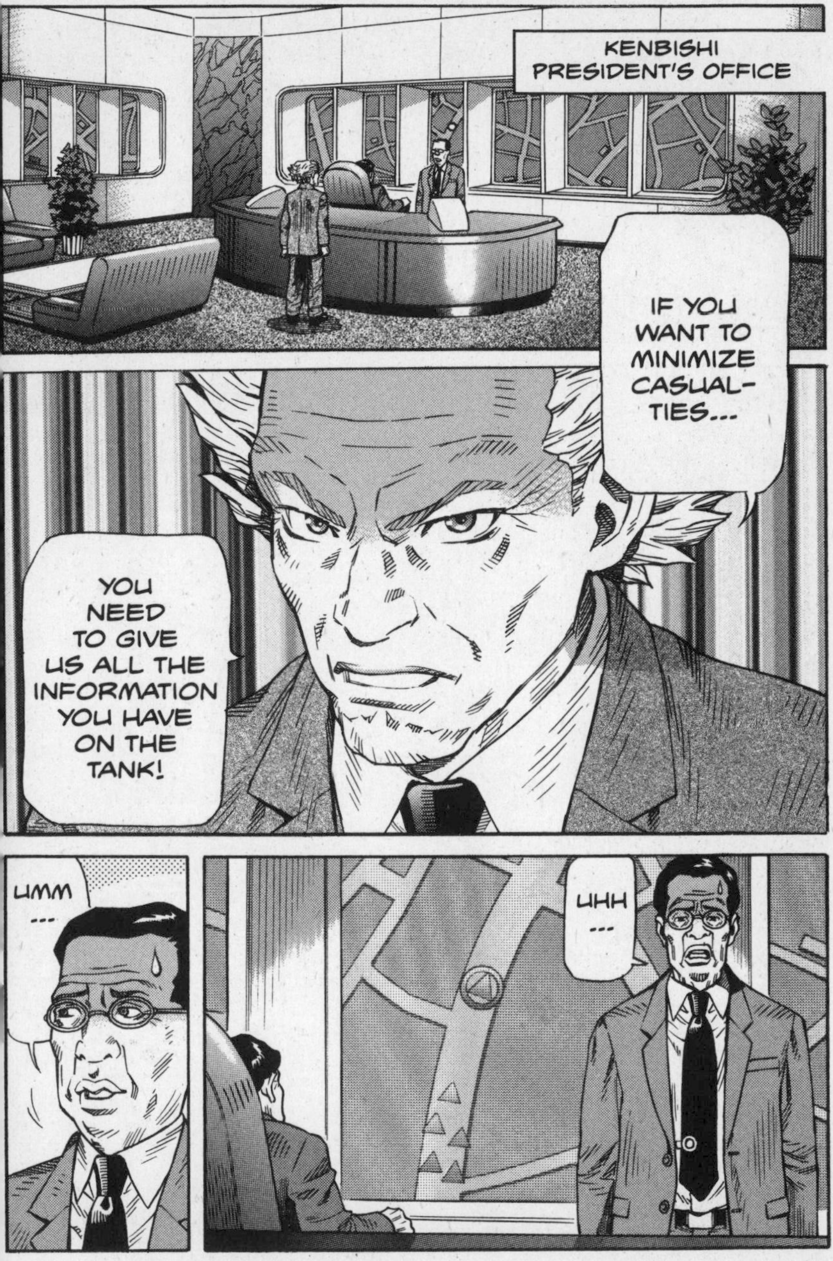
KENBISHI PRESIDENT'S OFFICE
IF YOU WANT TO MINIMIZE CASUAL-TIES...
YOU NEED TO GIVE US ALL THE INFORMATION YOU HAVE ON THE TANK!
UHH ...
UMM ...

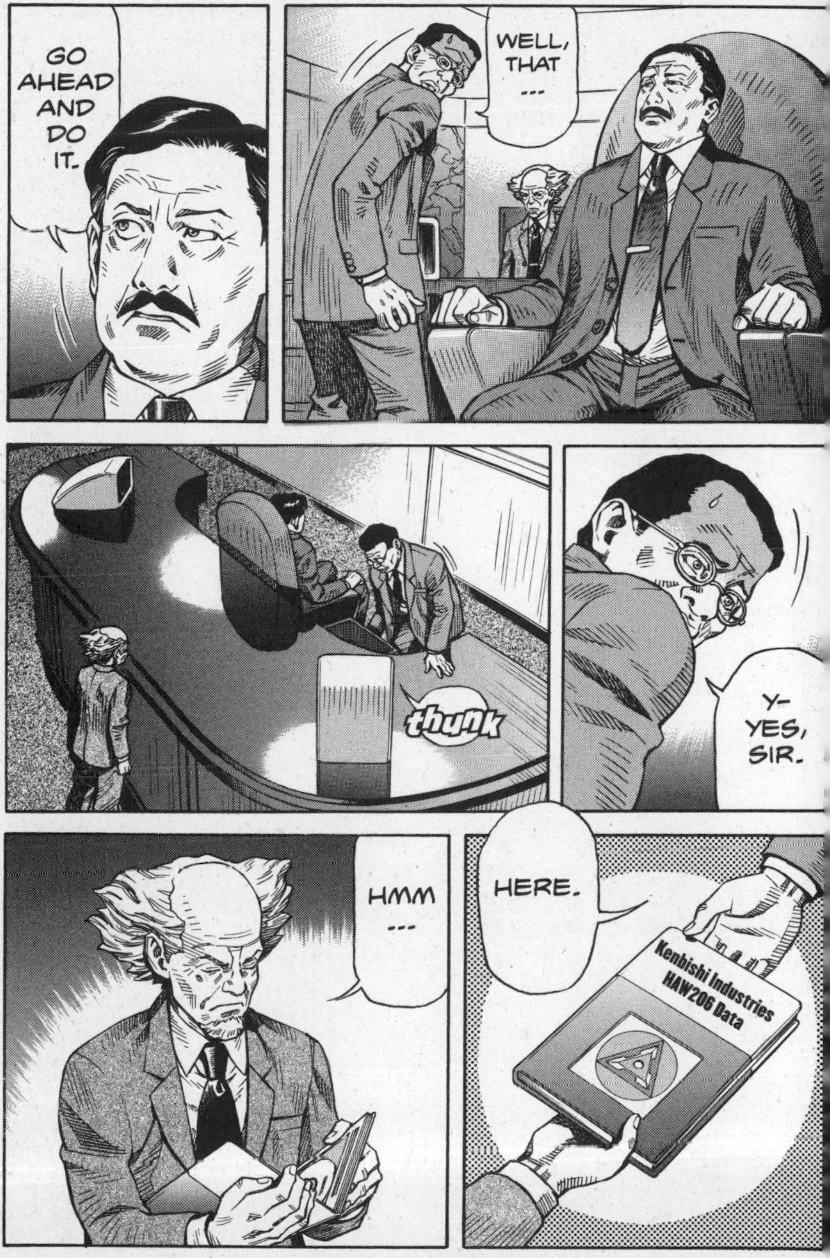
WELL, THAT ---
GO AHEAD AND DO IT.
Y- YES, SIR.
thunk
HERE.
Kenbishi Industries HAW206 Data
HMM ---

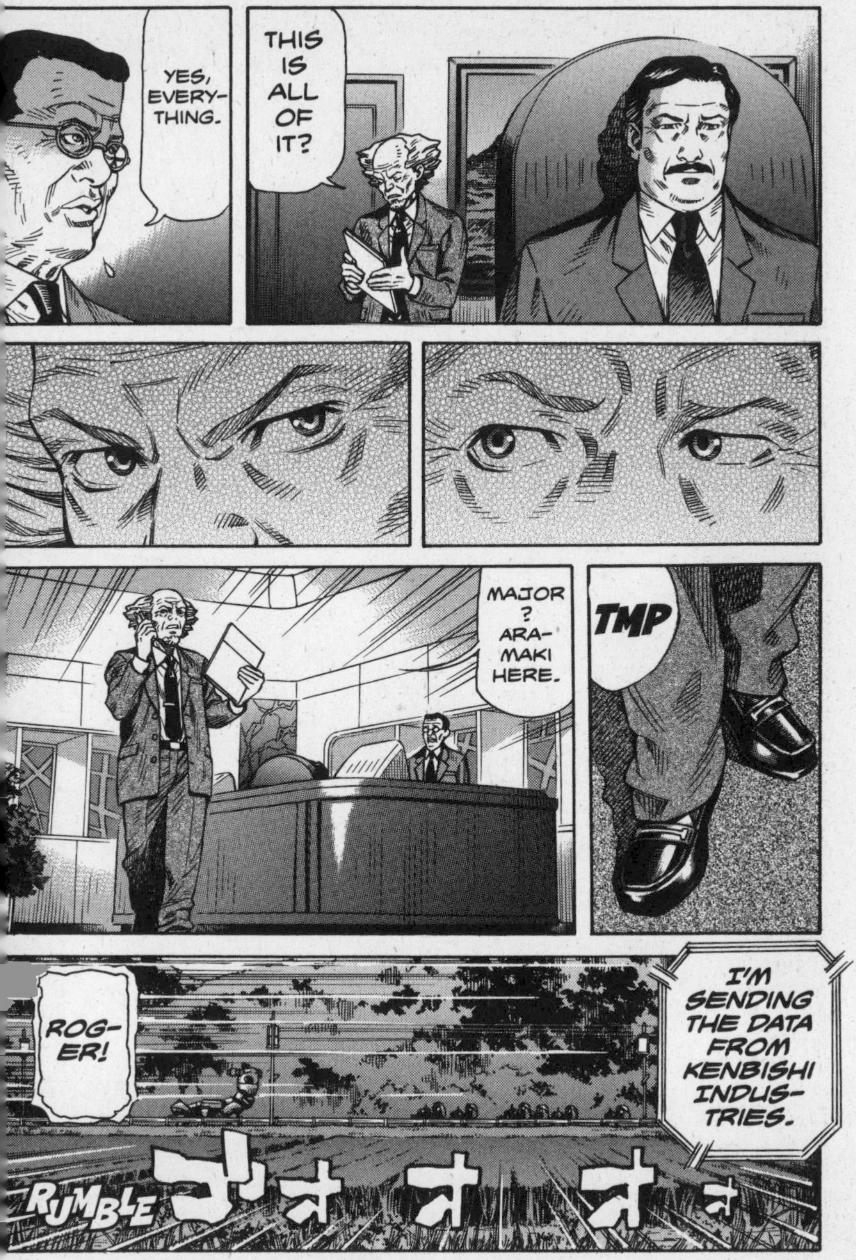
THIS IS ALL OF IT?
YES, EVERY-THING.
TMP
MAJOR? ARA-MAKI HERE.
I'M SENDING THE DATA FROM KENBISHI INDUS-TRIES.
ROG-ER!
RUMBLE
ゴォオオォ

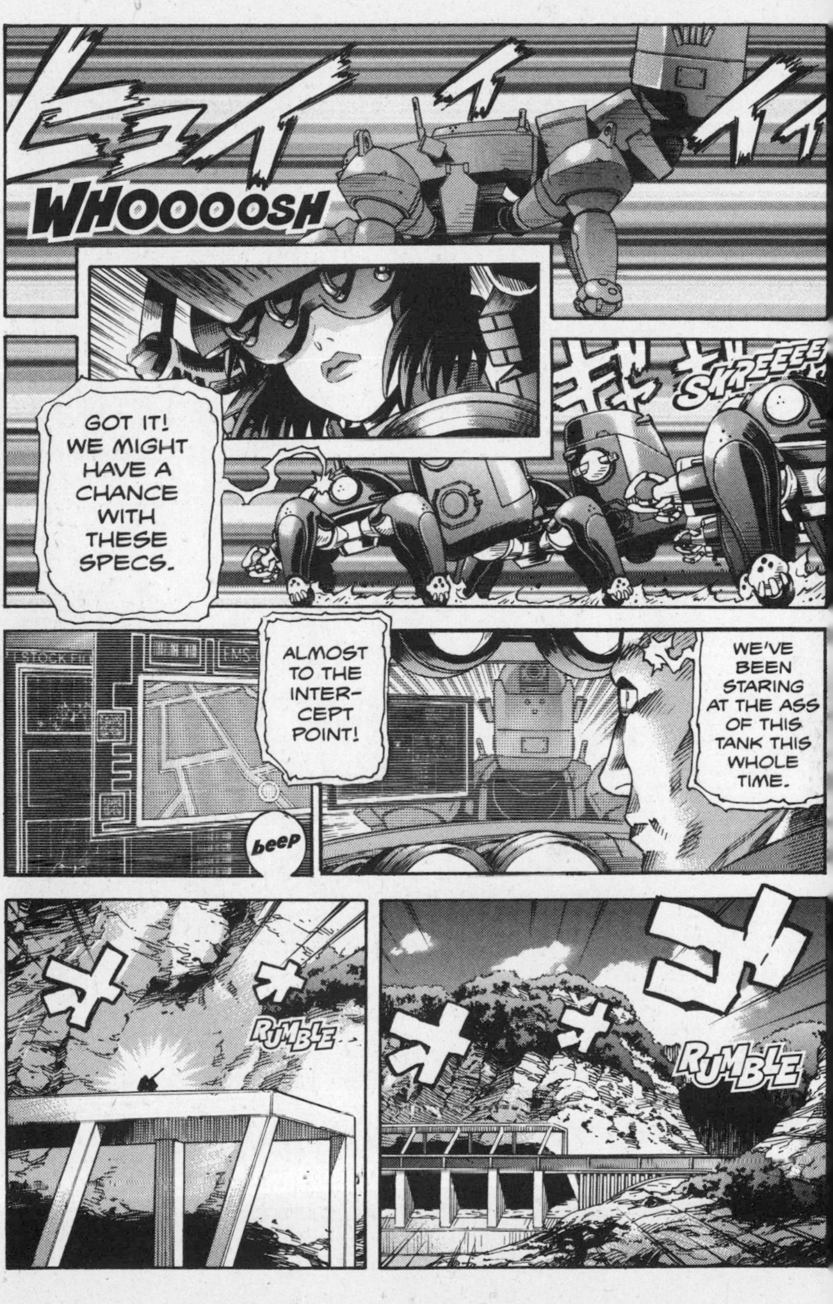

WHOOOOSH
GOT IT! WE MIGHT HAVE A CHANCE WITH THESE SPECS.
SKREEEE
WE'VE BEEN STARING AT THE ASS OF THIS TANK THIS WHOLE TIME.
ALMOST TO THE INTER-CEPT POINT!
beep
RUMBLE
RUMBLE

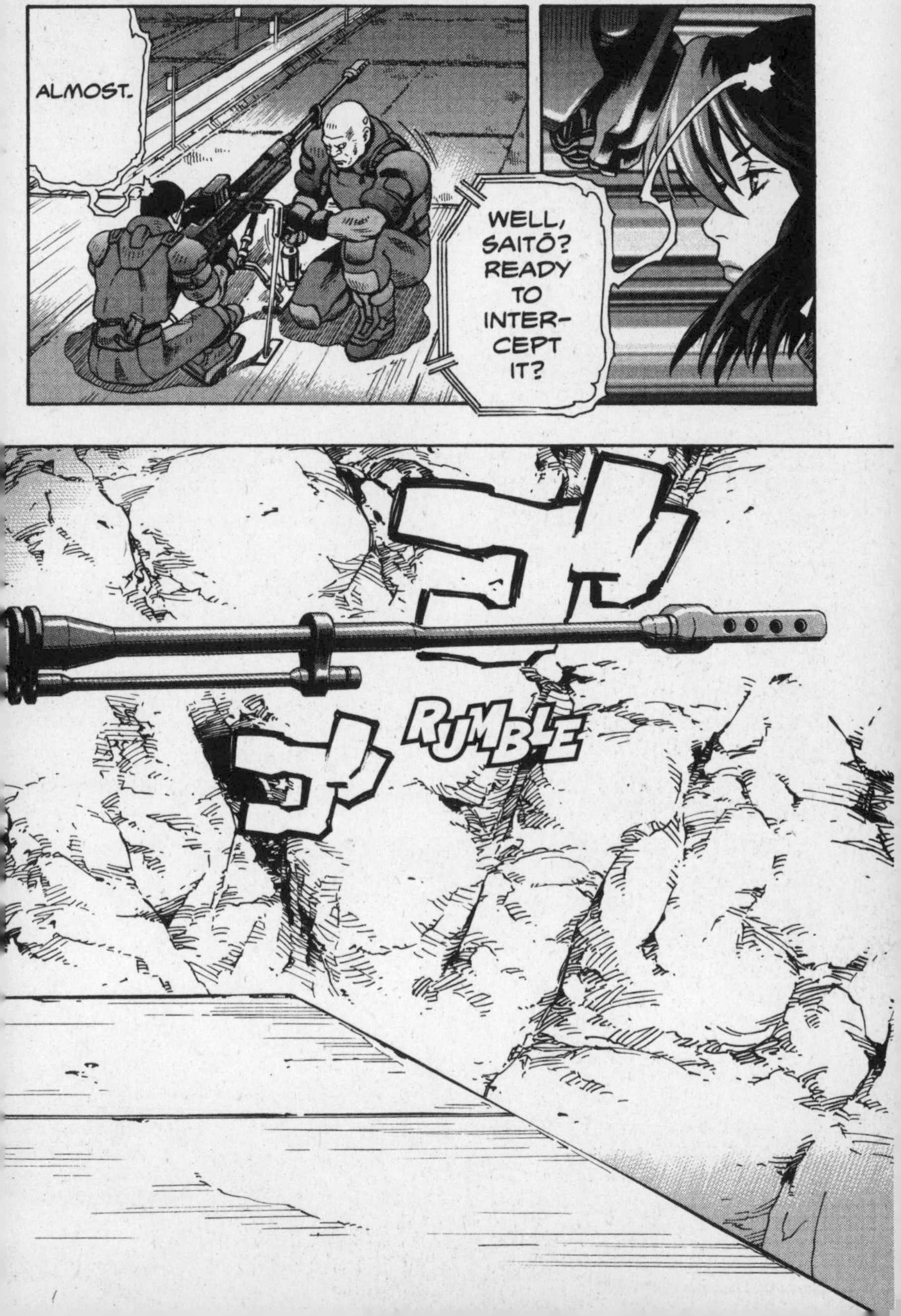
WELL, SAITŌ? READY TO INTERCEPT IT?
ALMOST.
RUMBLE

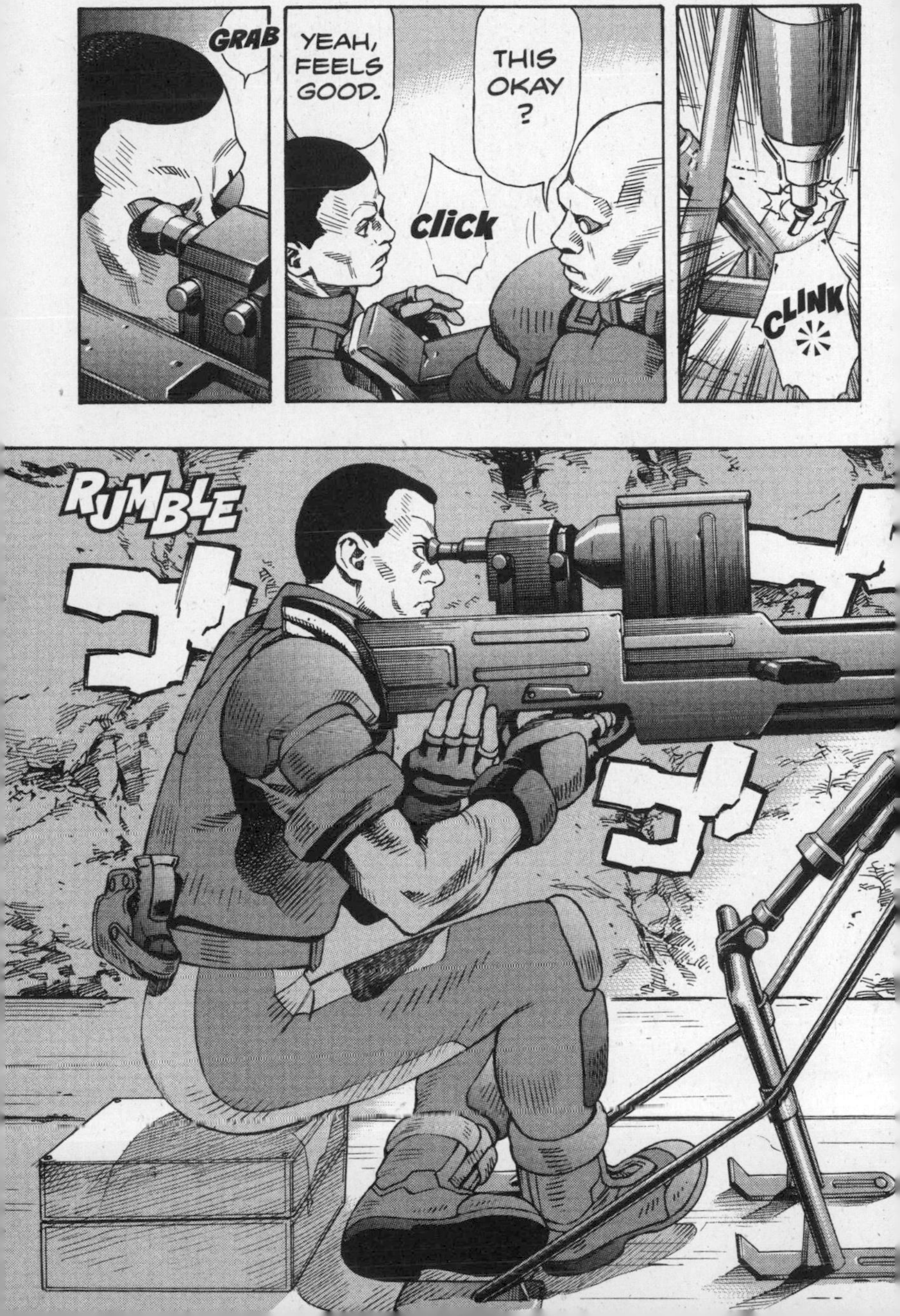
CLINK
THIS OKAY ?
YEAH, FEELS GOOD.
click
GRAB
RUMBLE

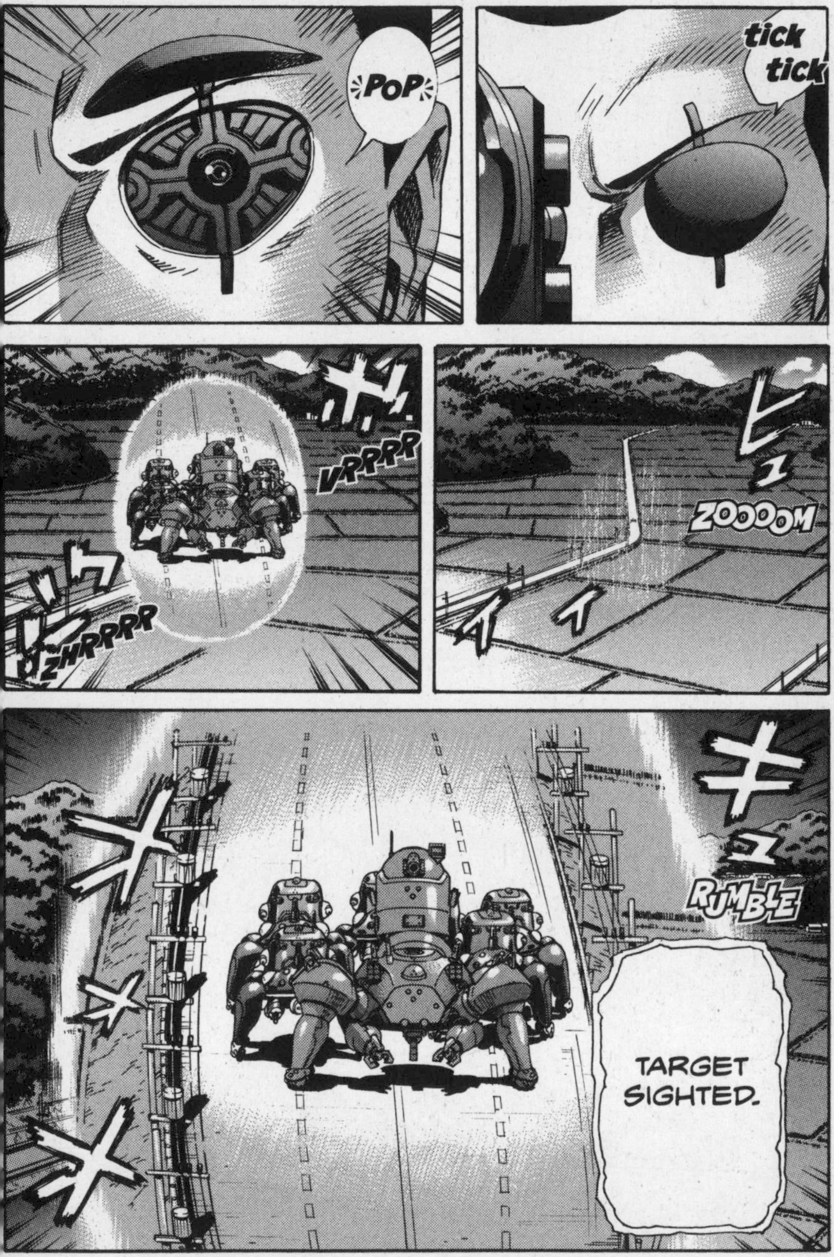
tick tick
POP
ZOOOOM
VRRRRR
ZHRRRRR
RUMBLE
TARGET SIGHTED.

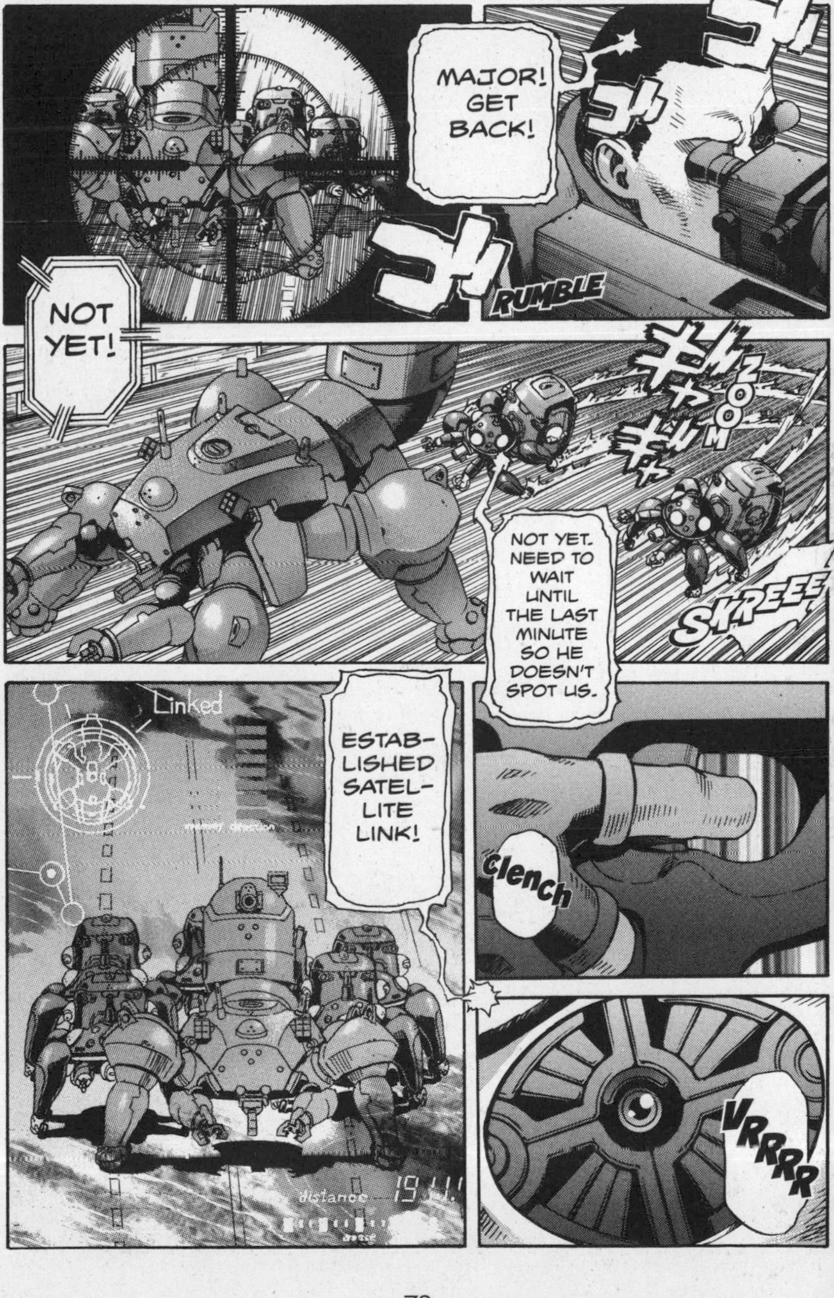
MAJOR! GET BACK!
RUMBLE
NOT YET!
ZOOM
SKREEEE
NOT YET. NEED TO WAIT UNTIL THE LAST MINUTE SO HE DOESN'T SPOT US.
Clench
VRRRR
Linked
ESTAB-LISHED SATEL-LITE LINK!
distance

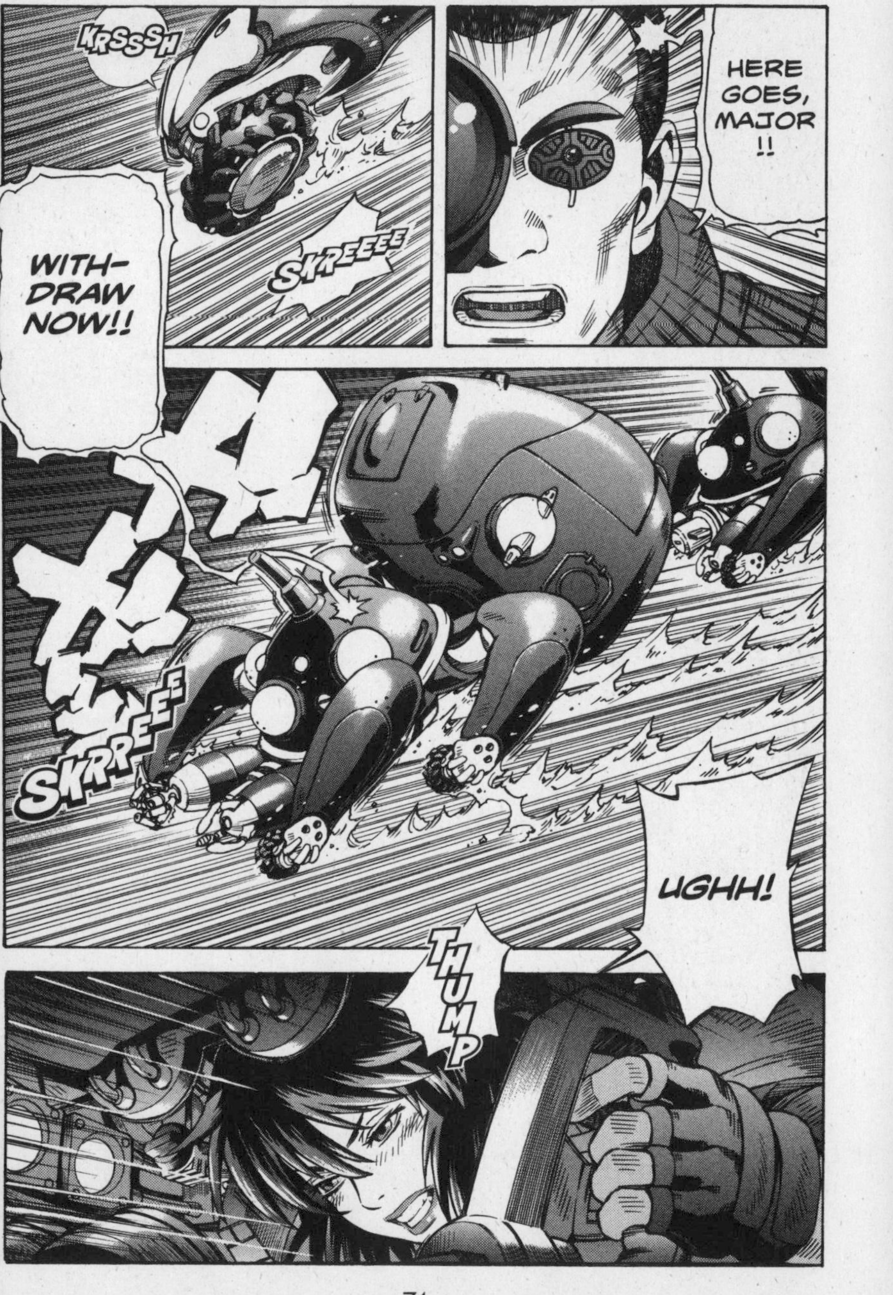
HERE GOES, MAJOR !!
KRSSSH
SKREEEE
WITH-DRAW NOW!!
SKRREEEE
UGHH!
THUMP

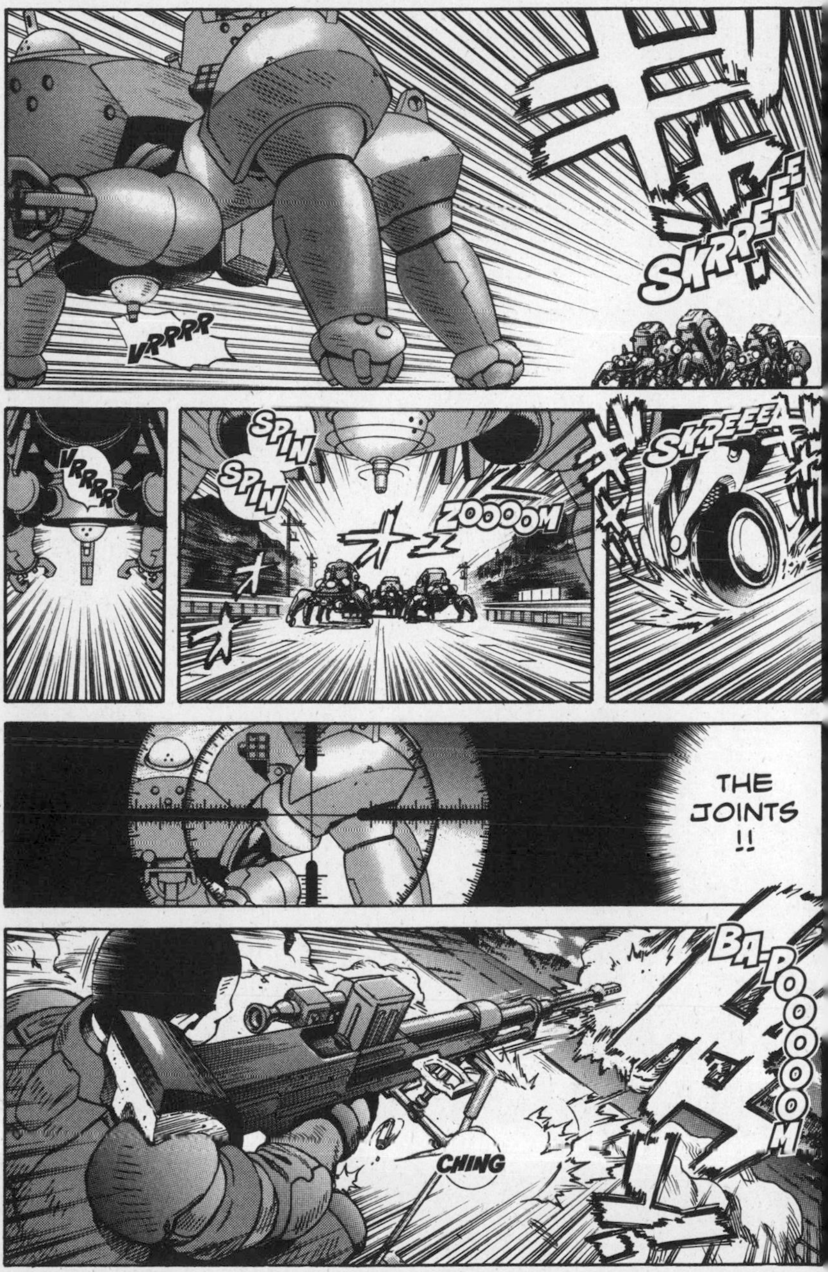
SKRREEE
VRRRR
SKREEE
SPIN
SPIN
ZOOOOM
VRRRR
THE JOINTS !!
BA-POOOOOOM
CHING

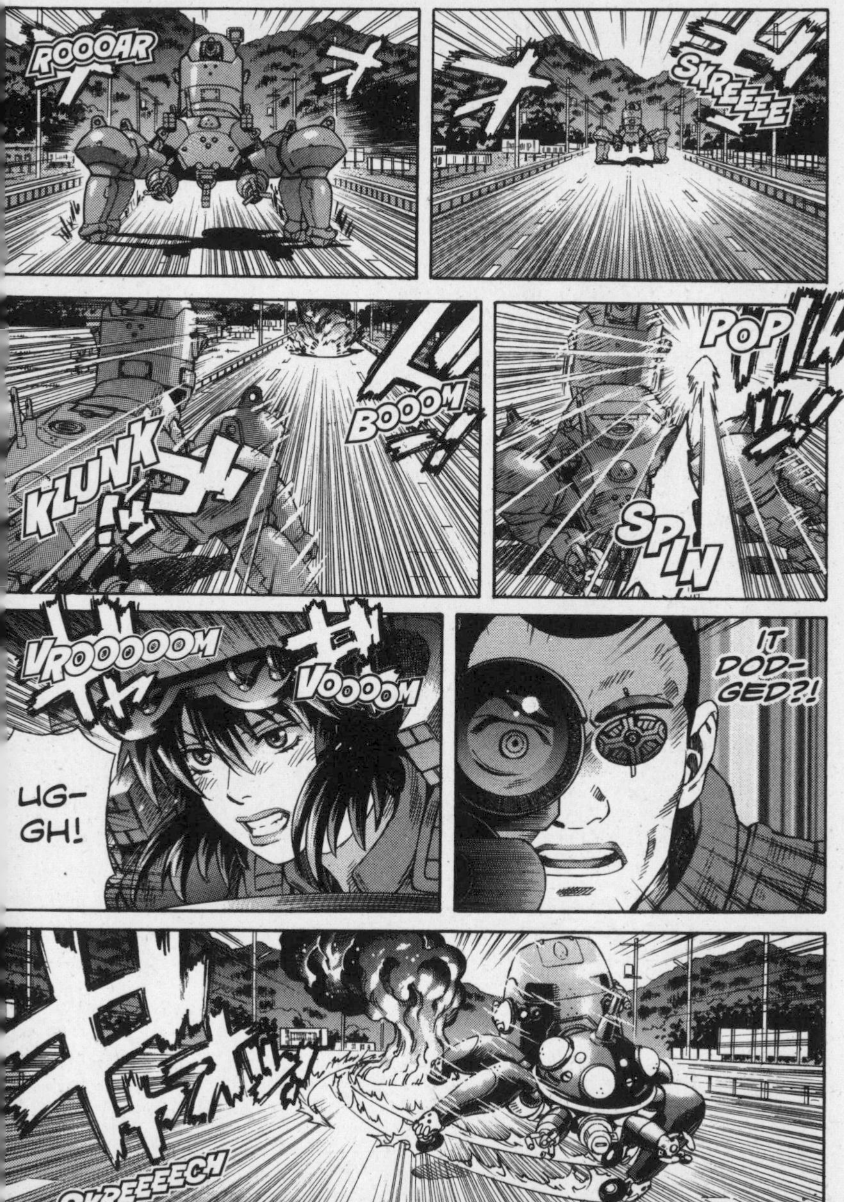
SKREEEEE
ROOOAR
POP
SPIN
BOOOM
KLUNK
IT DODGED?!
VOOOOM
VROOOOOOM
UGH!
SKREEEECH

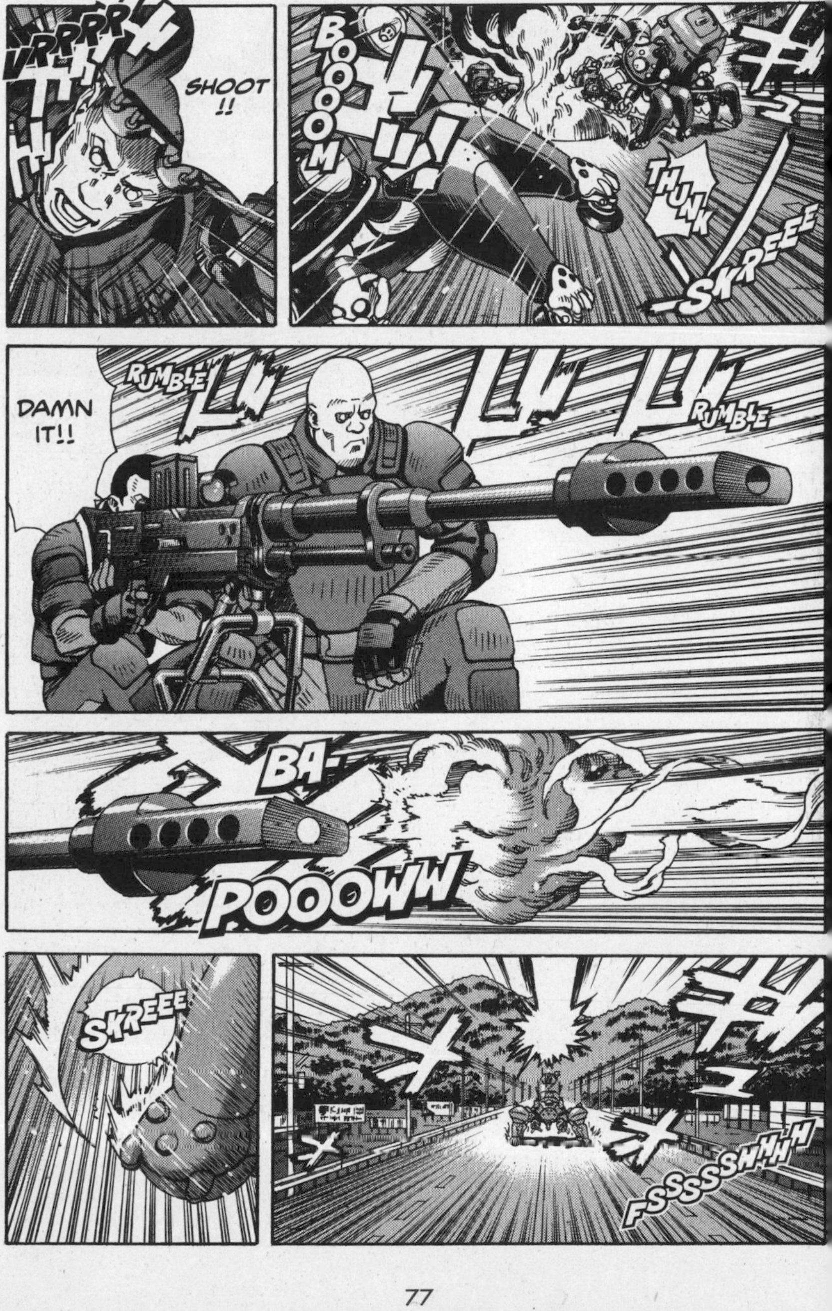
BOOOOM
THUNK
SKREEEE
VRRRRR
SHOOT !!
RUMBLE
RUMBLE
DAMN IT!!
BA-
POOOWW
FSSSSHHHH
SKREEE

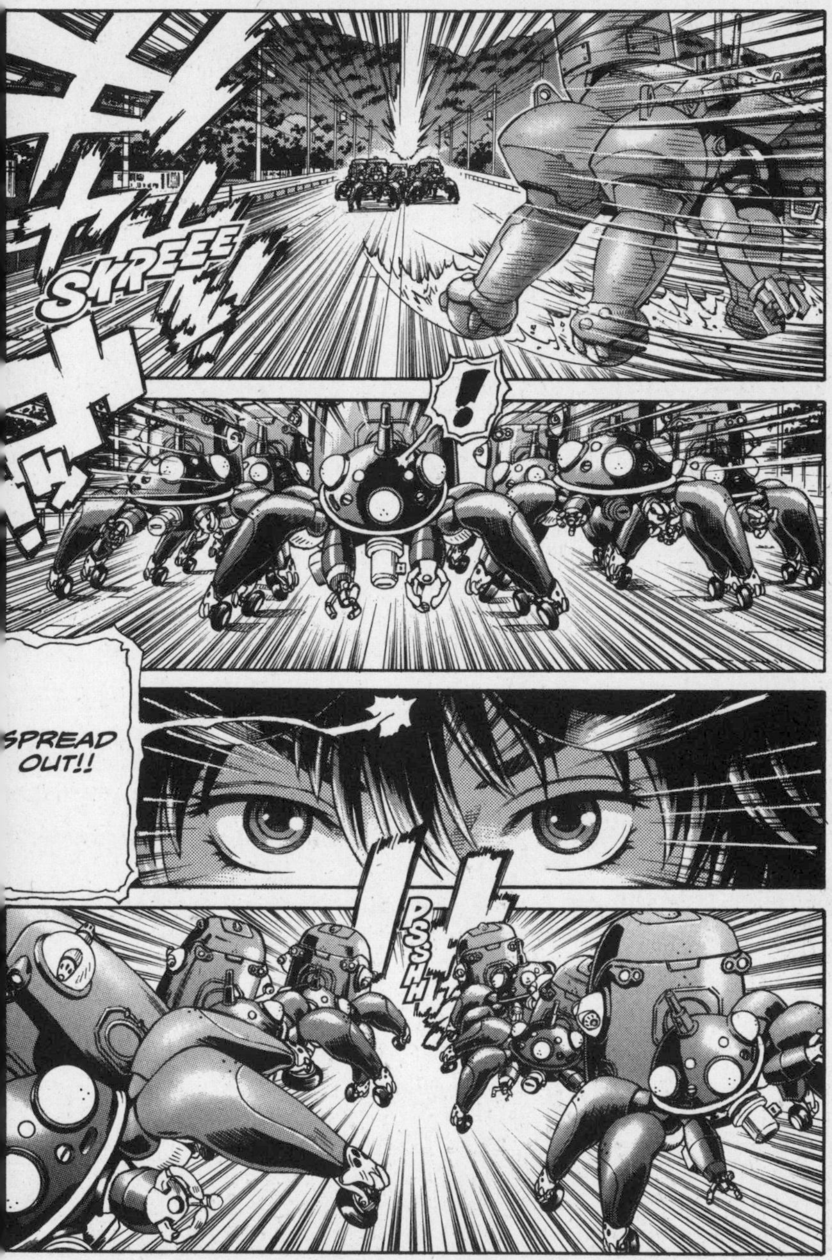
SKREEE
!
SPREAD OUT!!
PSSHH

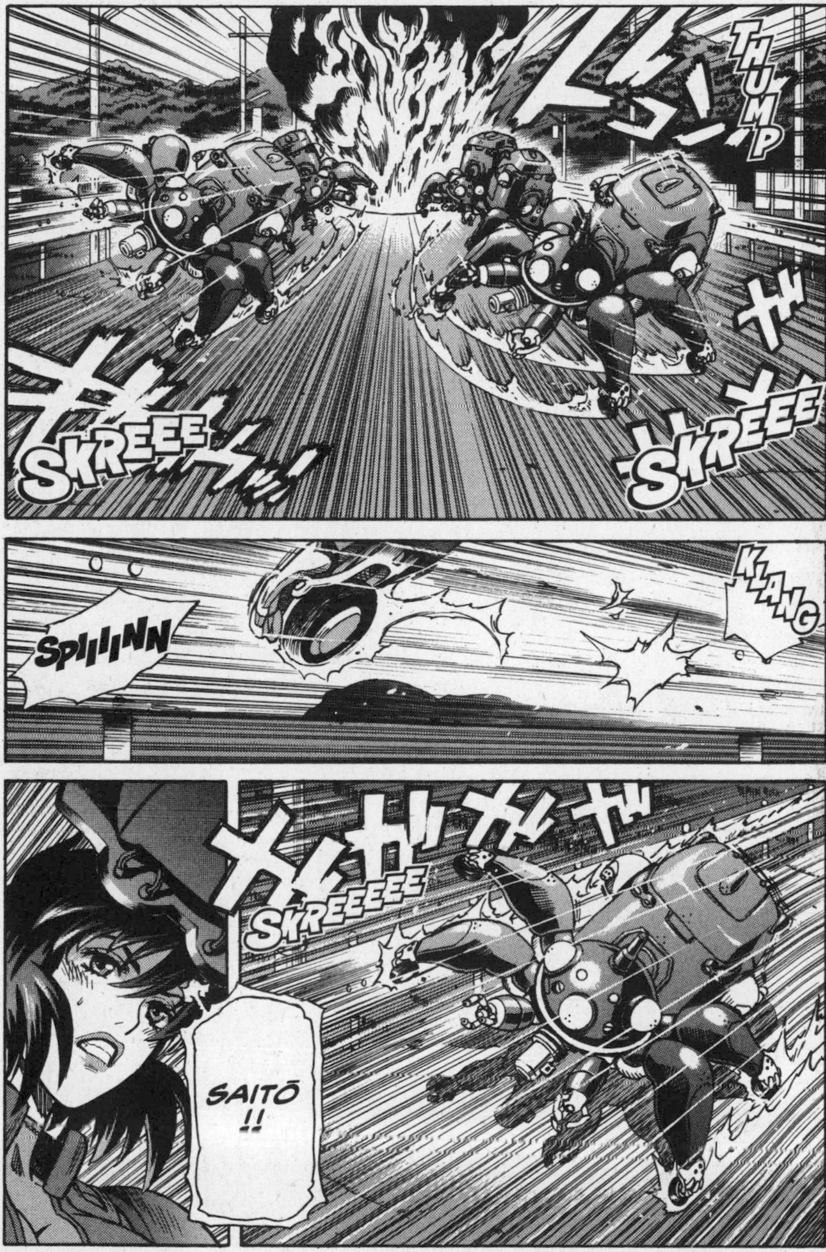
THUMP
SKREEEE
SKREEE
KLANG
SPIIIINN
SKREEEEE
SAITŌ !!

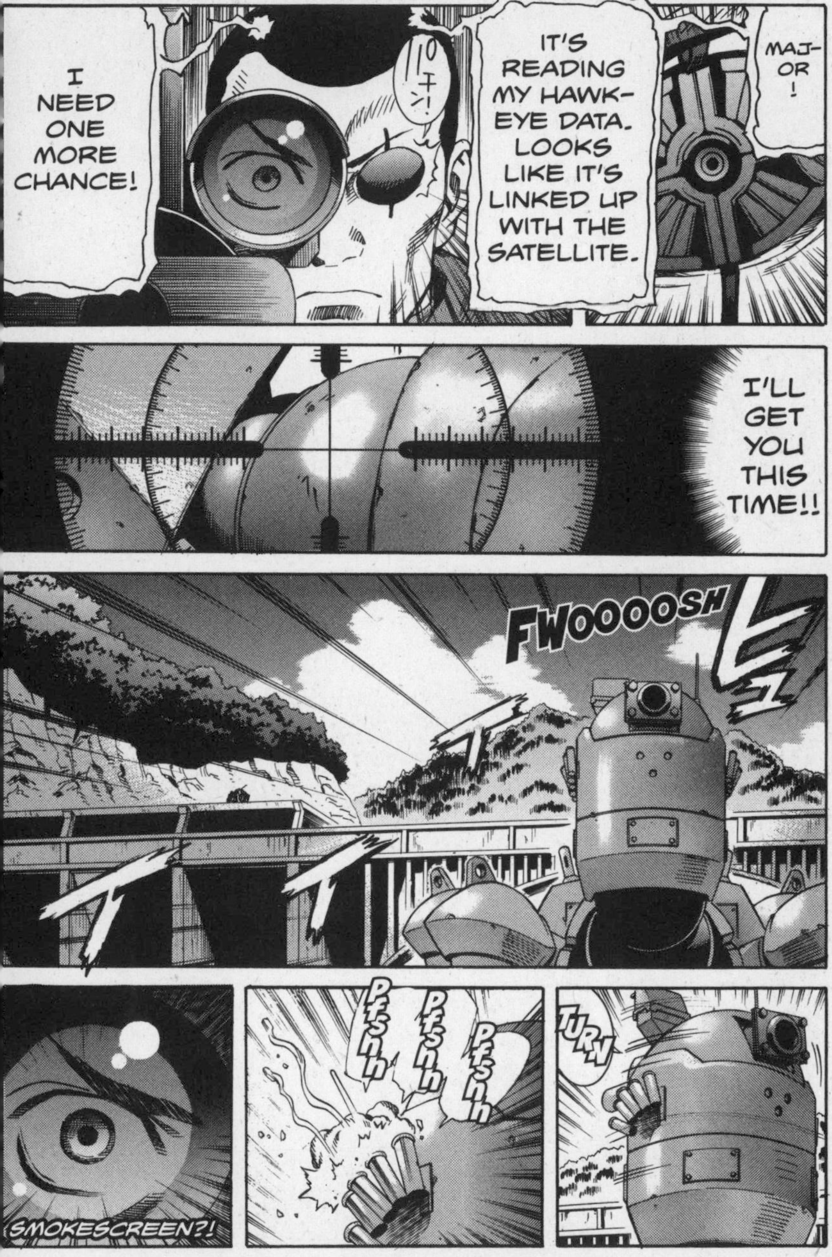
MAJ-OR!
IT'S READING MY HAWK-EYE DATA. LOOKS LIKE IT'S LINKED UP WITH THE SATELLITE.
I NEED ONE MORE CHANCE!
I'LL GET YOU THIS TIME!!
FWOOOOSH
TURN
Pfsnn
Pfsnn
Pfsnn
SMOKESCREEN?!

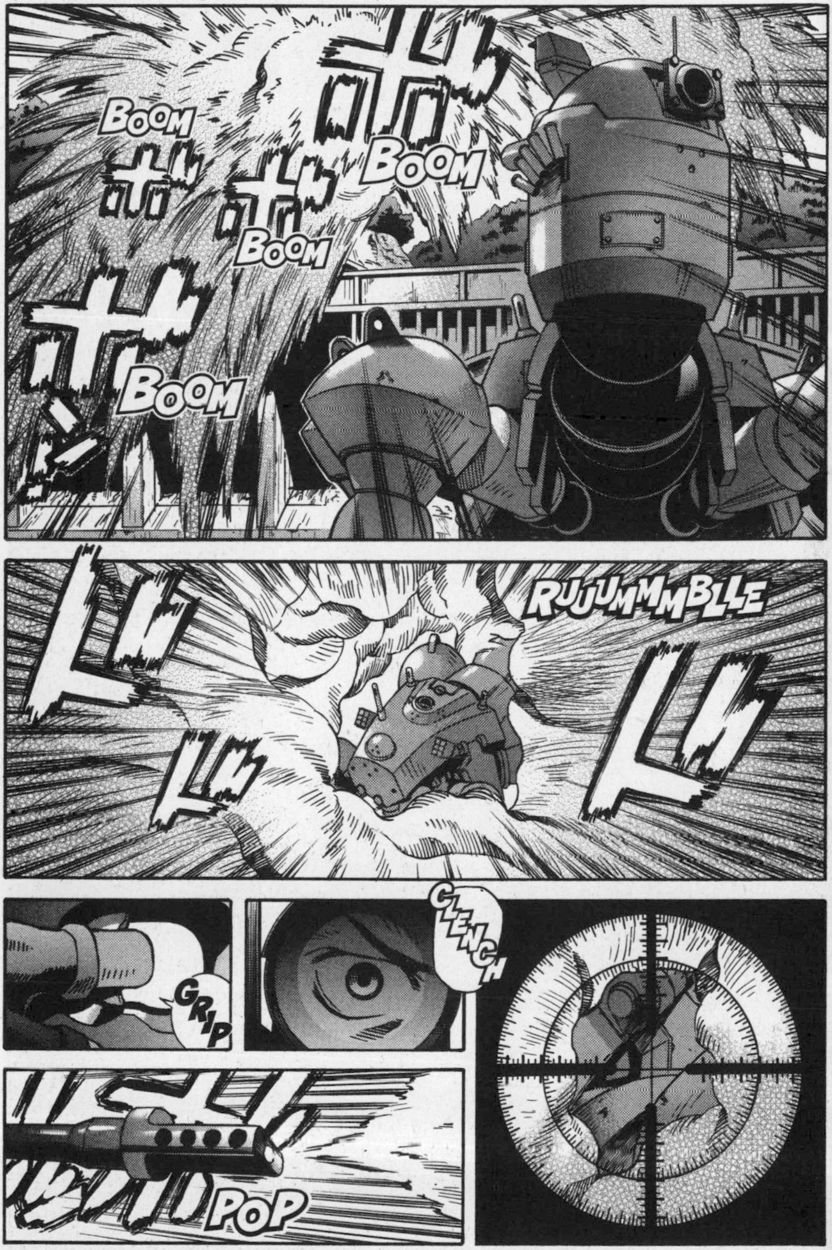
BOOM
BOOM
BOOM
BOOM
RUUUMMMBLLE
CLENCH
GRIP
POP

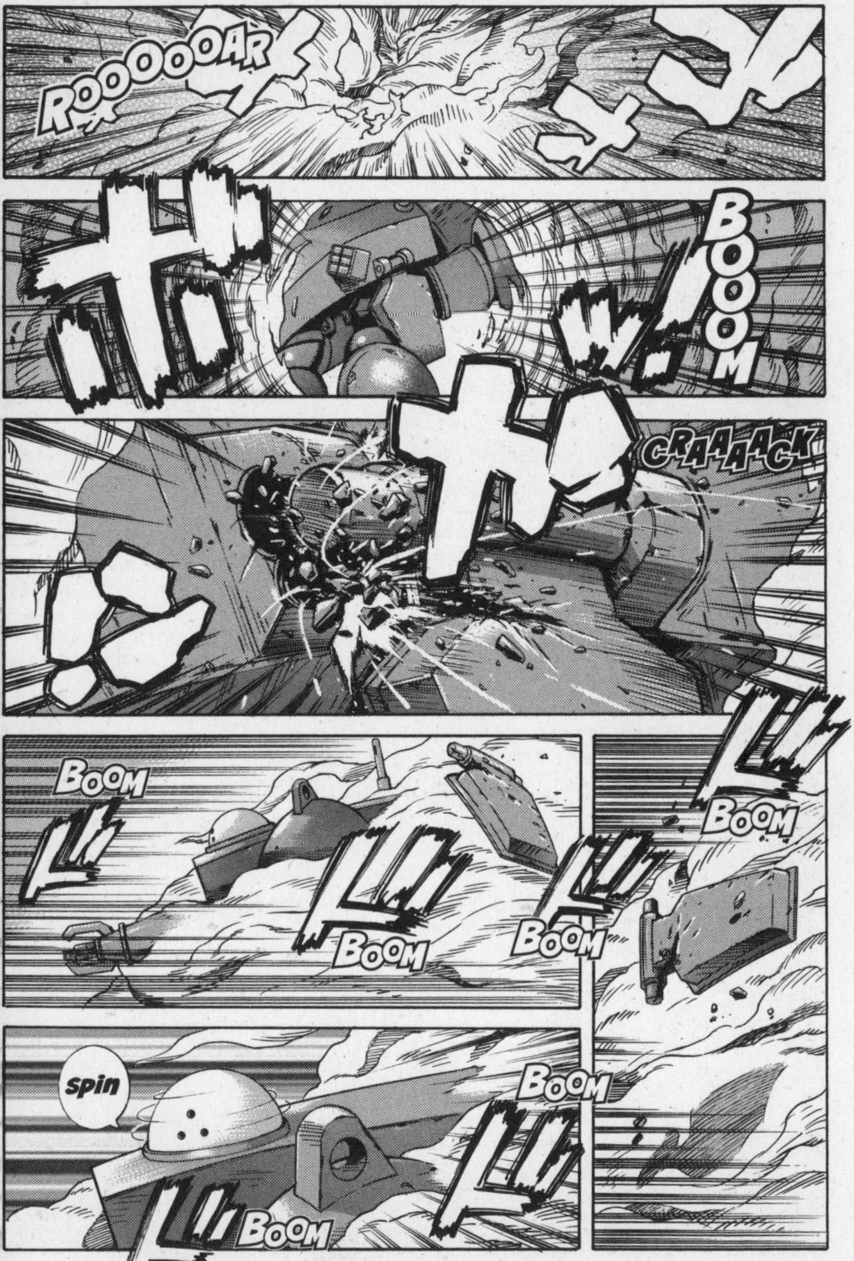
ROOOOOAR
BOOOOM
CRAAAACK
BOOM
BOOM
BOOM
BOOM
BOOM
spin
BOOM

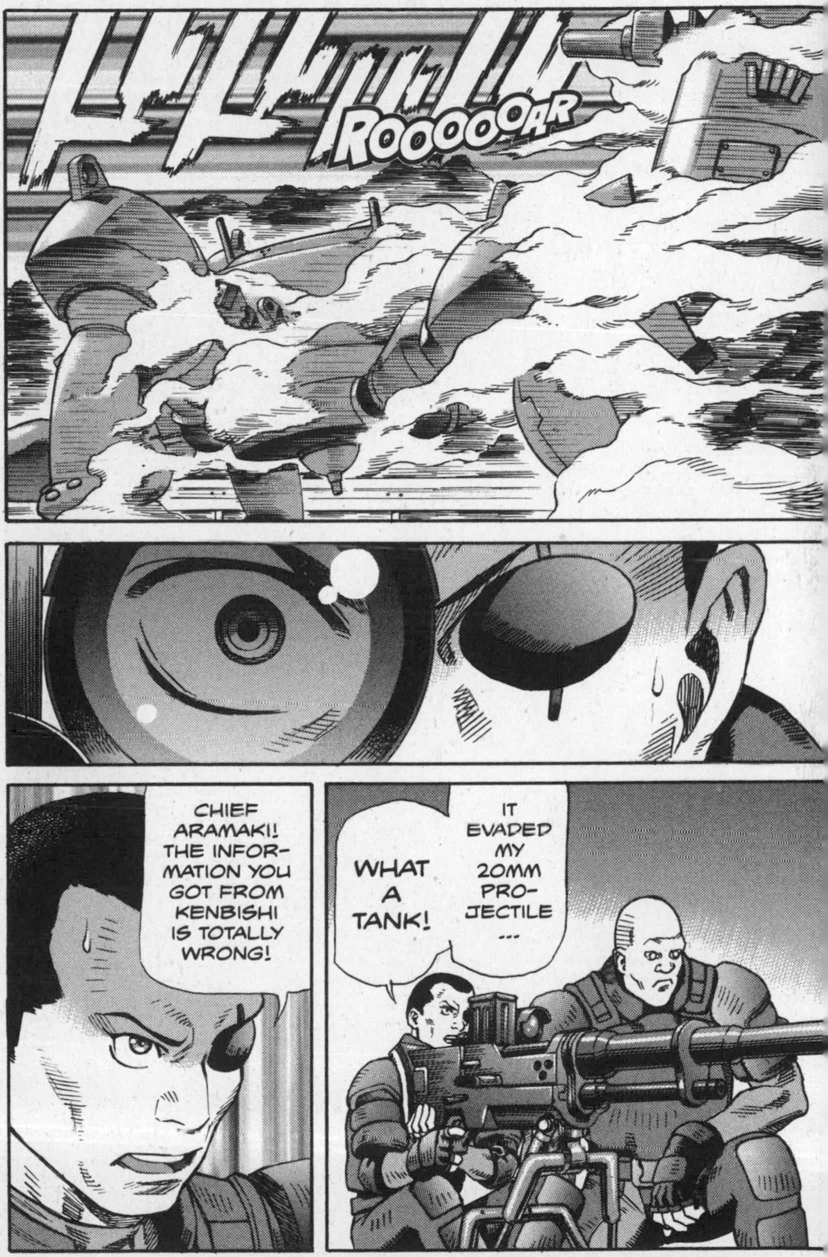
ROOOOOAR
IT EVADED MY 20MM PROJECTILE ...
WHAT A TANK!
CHIEF ARAMAKI! THE INFORMATION YOU GOT FROM KENBISHI IS TOTALLY WRONG!

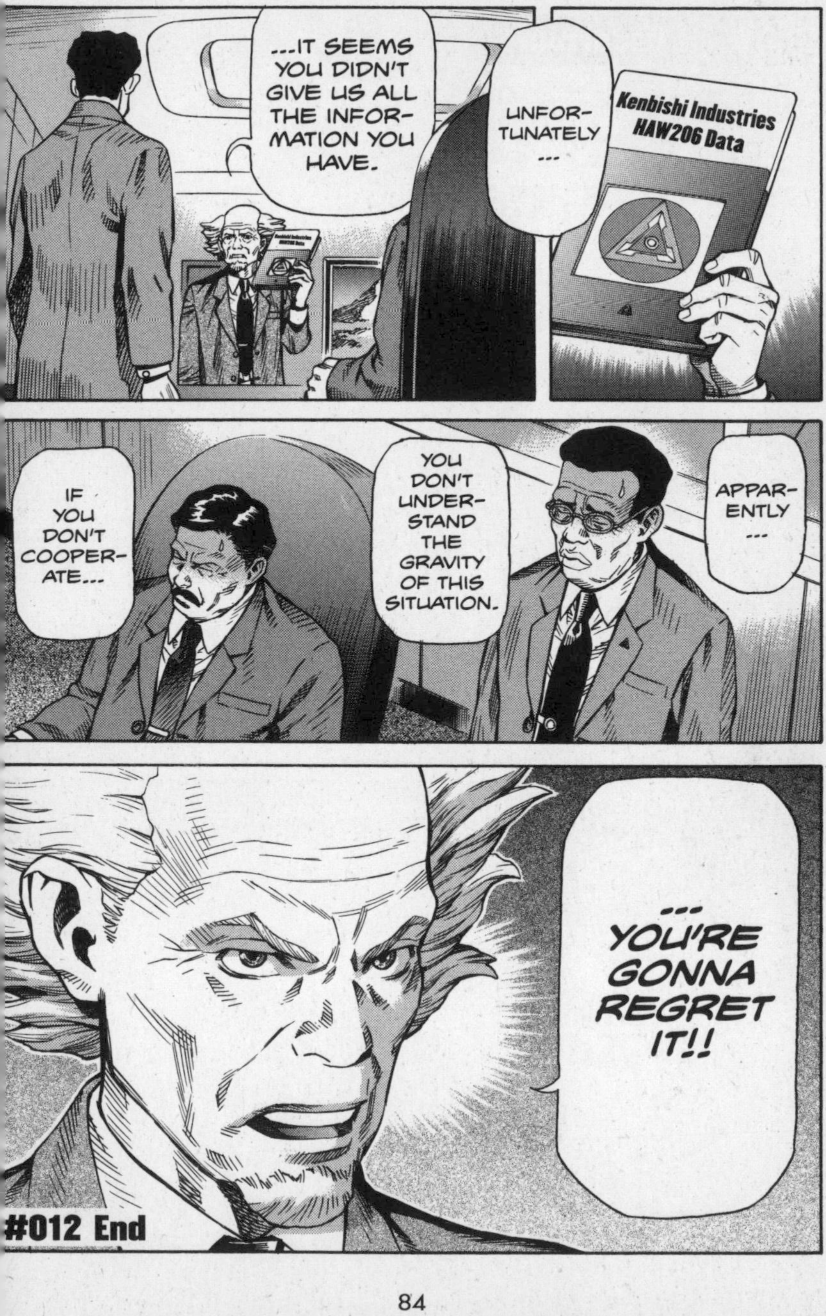

UNFOR-TUNATELY ...
Kenbishi Industries HAW206 Data
...IT SEEMS YOU DIDN'T GIVE US ALL THE INFOR-MATION YOU HAVE.
APPAR-ENTLY ...
YOU DON'T UNDER-STAND THE GRAVITY OF THIS SITUATION.
IF YOU DON'T COOPER-ATE...
... YOU'RE GONNA REGRET IT!!
#012 End

#014: Snipe Opportunity

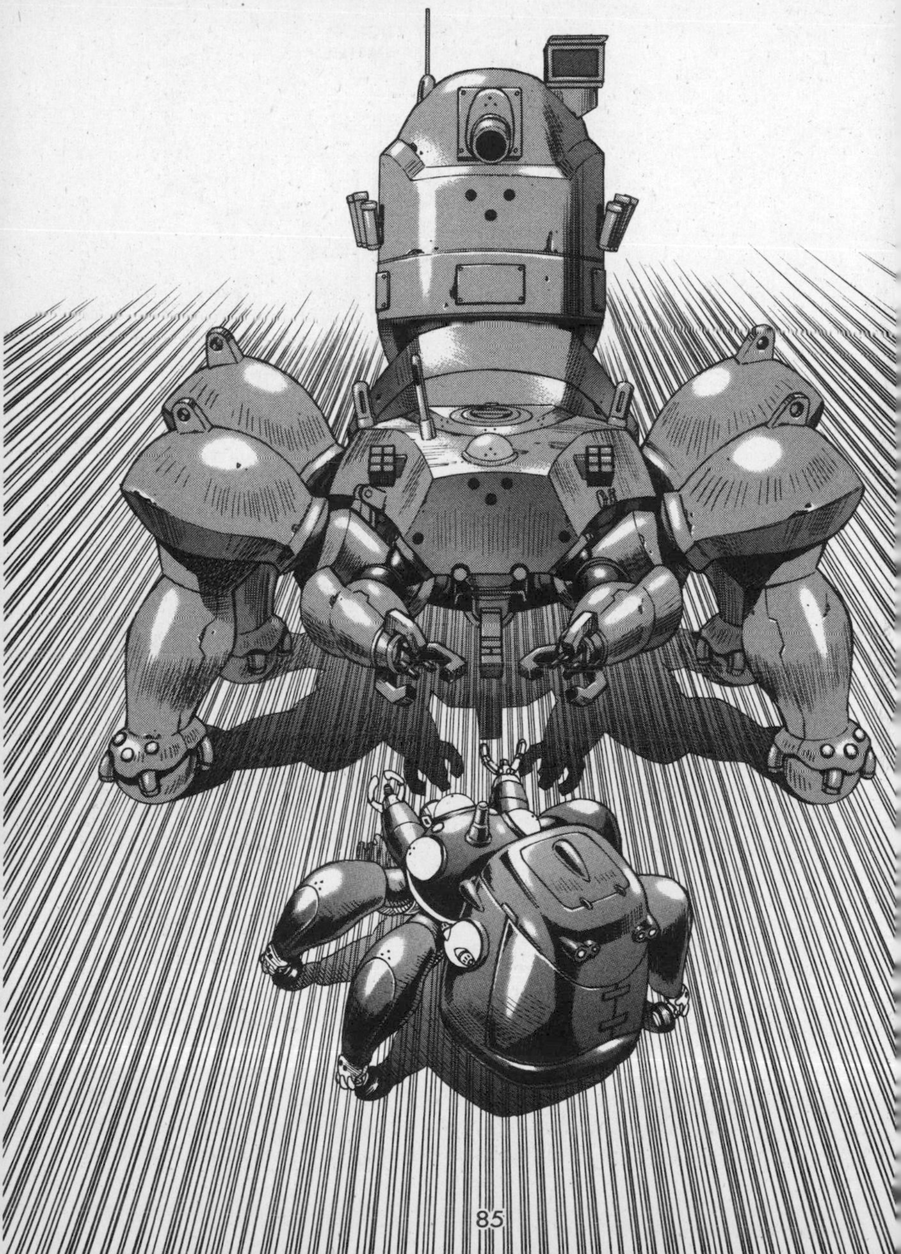

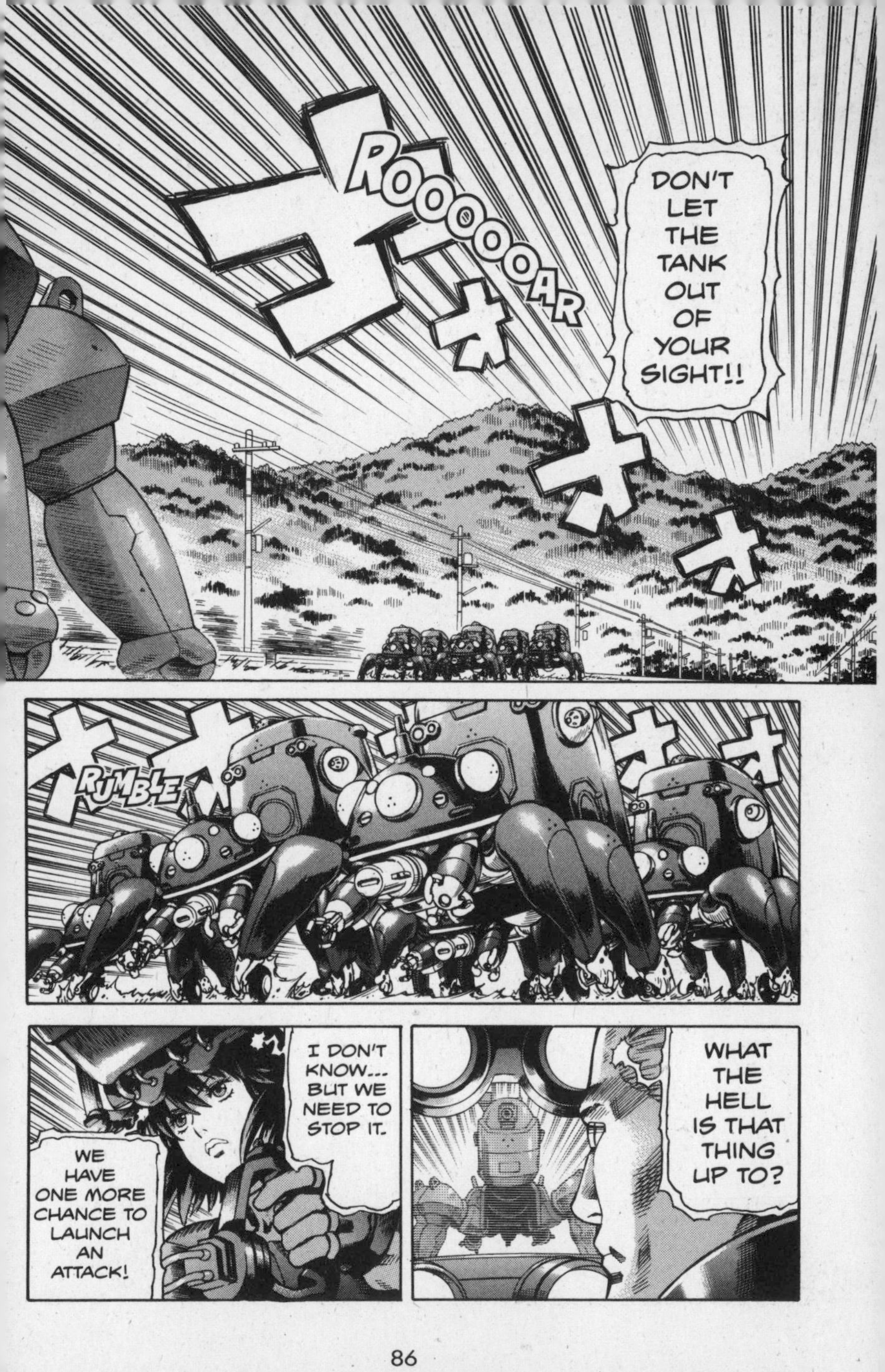
DON'T LET THE TANK OUT OF YOUR SIGHT!!
ROOOOOOAR
RUMBLE
WHAT THE HELL IS THAT THING UP TO?
I DON'T KNOW... BUT WE NEED TO STOP IT.
WE HAVE ONE MORE CHANCE TO LAUNCH AN ATTACK!

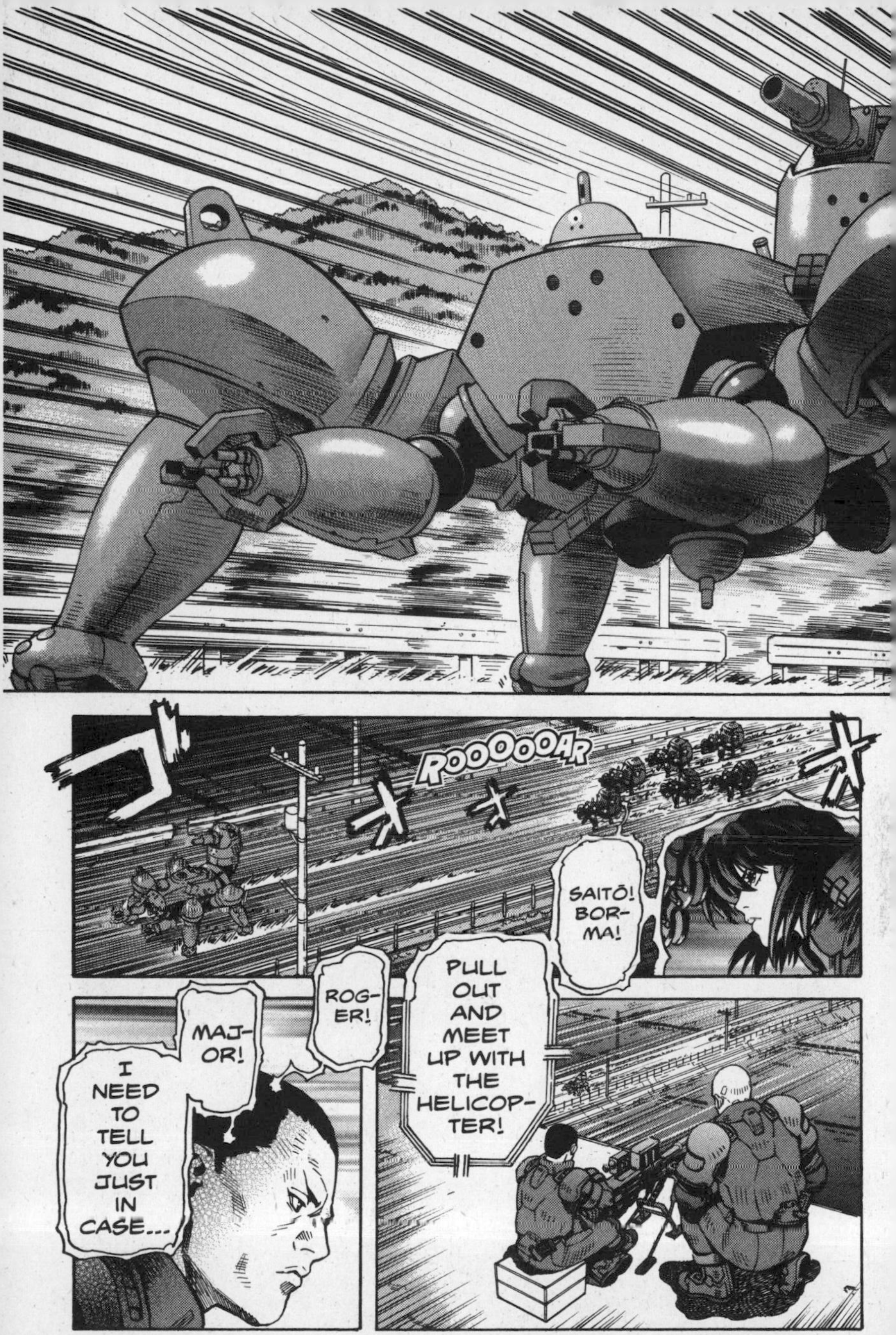
ROOOOOAR
SAITŌ! BOR-MA!
PULL OUT AND MEET UP WITH THE HELICOP-TER!
ROG-ER!
MAJ-OR!
I NEED TO TELL YOU JUST IN CASE...

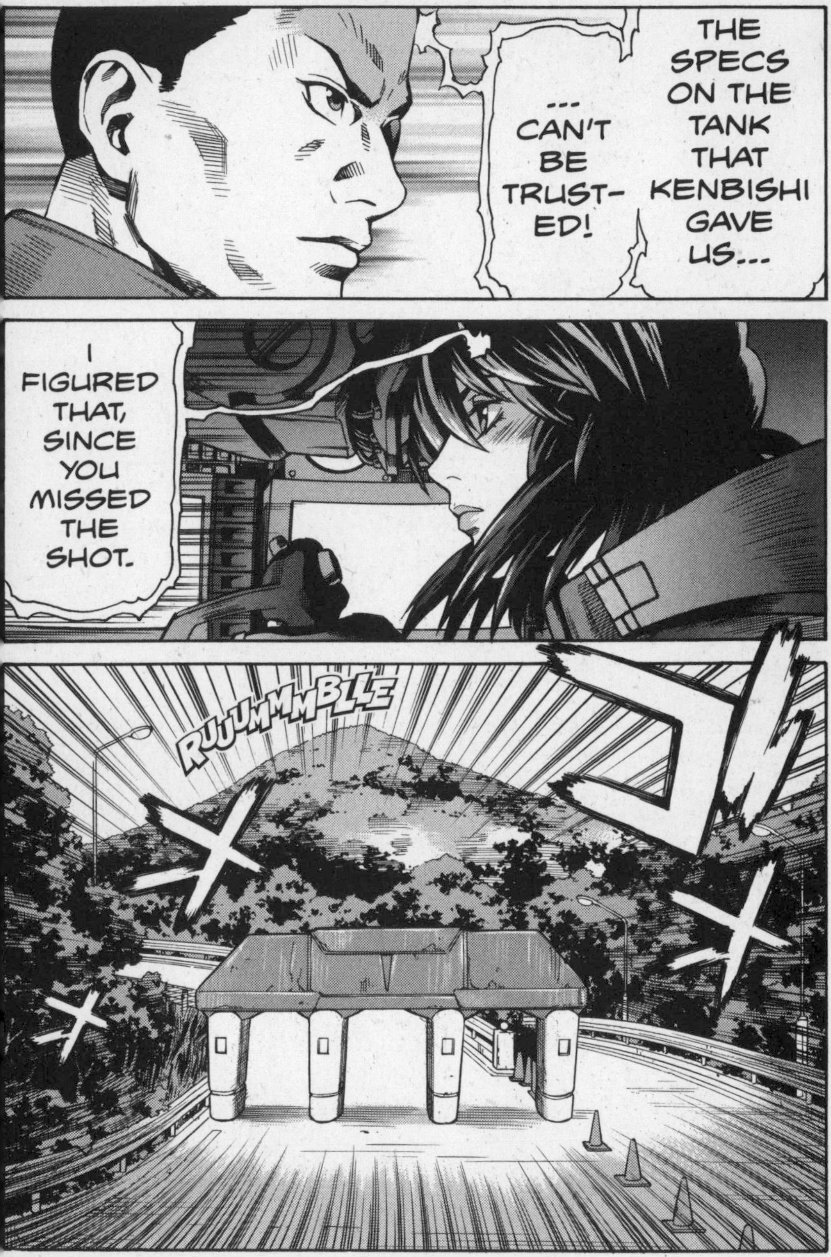
THE SPECS ON THE TANK THAT KENBISHI GAVE US...
...CAN'T BE TRUST-ED!
I FIGURED THAT, SINCE YOU MISSED THE SHOT.
RUUUMMMBLLE

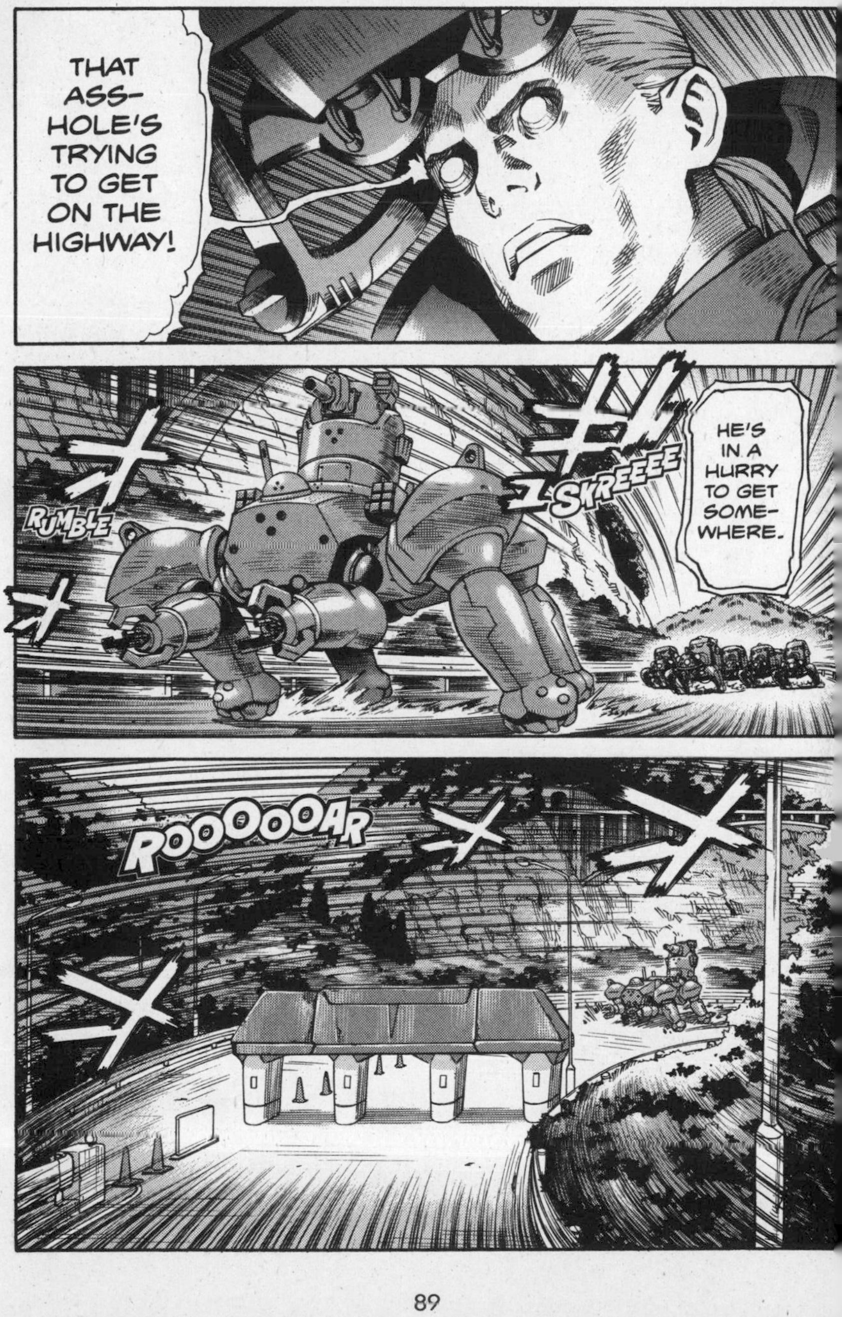
THAT ASS-HOLE'S TRYING TO GET ON THE HIGHWAY!
HE'S IN A HURRY TO GET SOME-WHERE.
SKREEEEE
RUMBLE
ROOOOOOAR

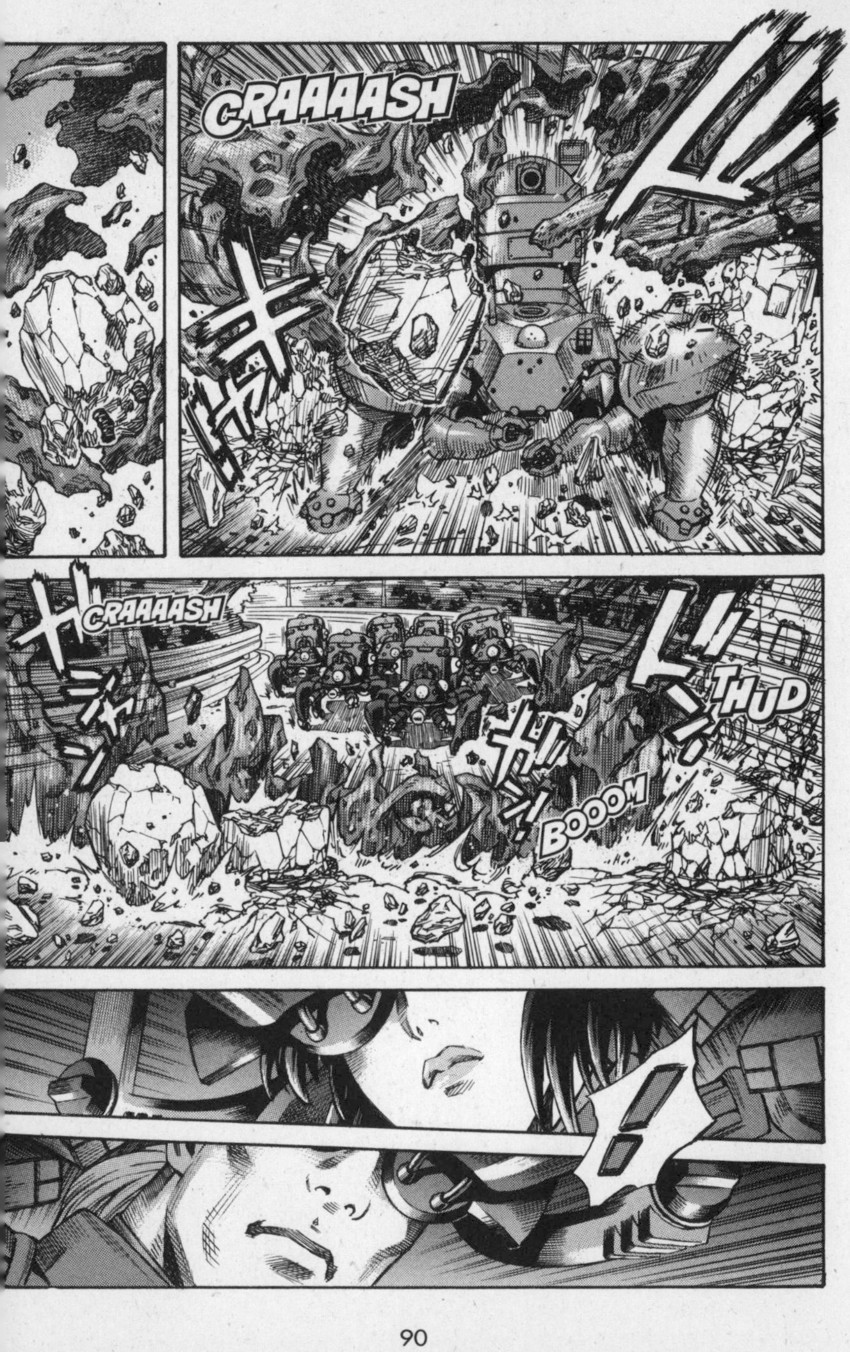
CRAAAASH
THUD
CRAAAASH
BOOOM

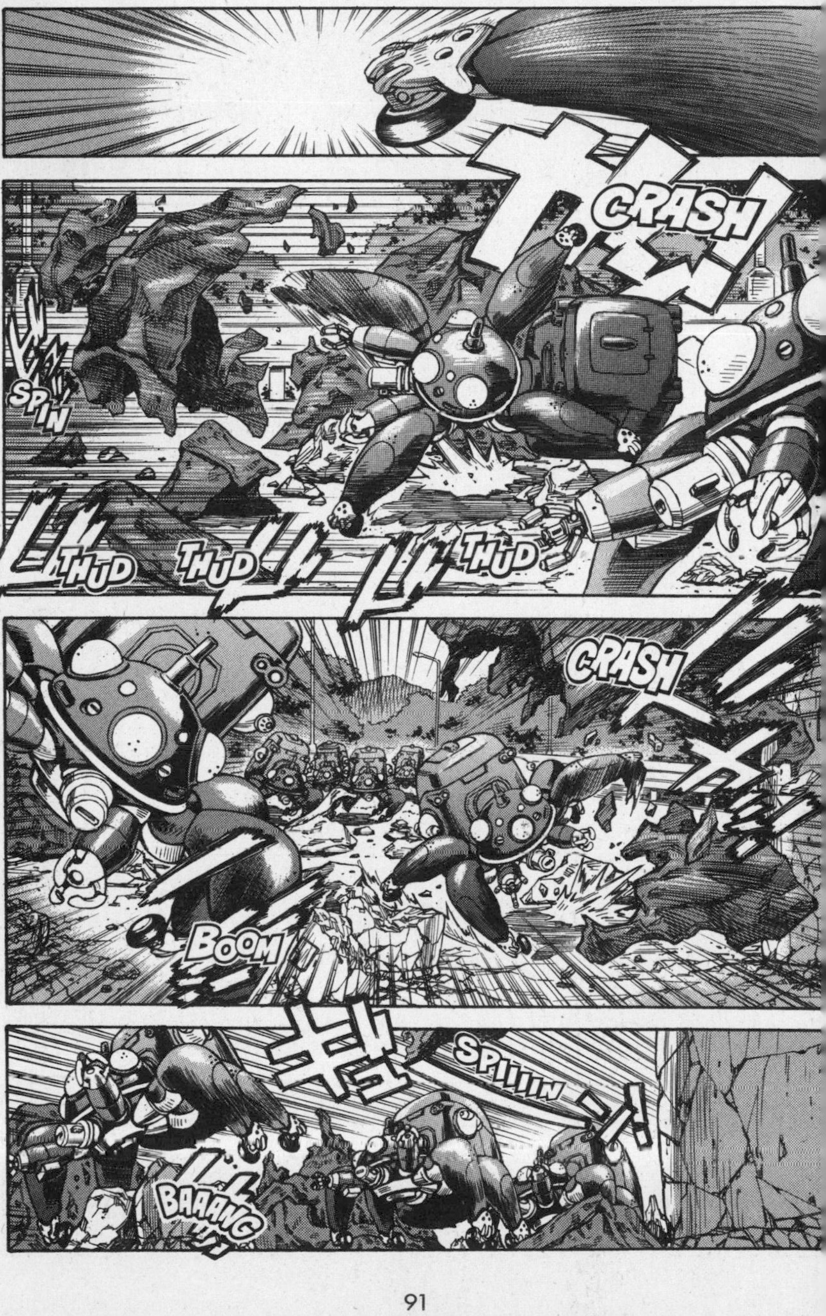
CRASH
SPIN
THUD
THUD
THUD
CRASH
BOOM
SPIIIIN
BAAANG

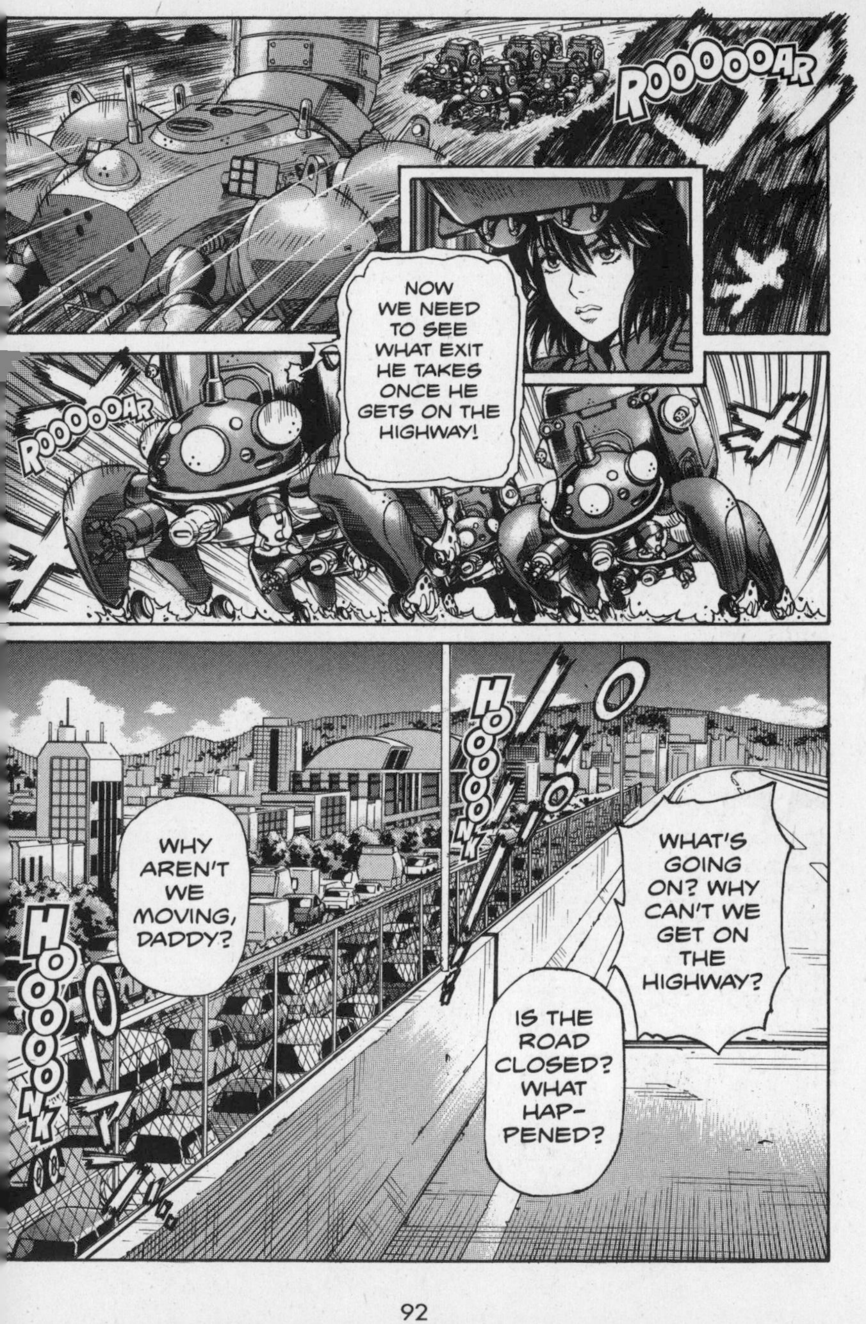
ROOOOOOAR
NOW WE NEED TO SEE WHAT EXIT HE TAKES ONCE HE GETS ON THE HIGHWAY!
ROOOOOAR
HOOOOONK
WHAT'S GOING ON? WHY CAN'T WE GET ON THE HIGHWAY?
IS THE ROAD CLOSED? WHAT HAP-PENED?
WHY AREN'T WE MOVING, DADDY?
HOOOOOONK

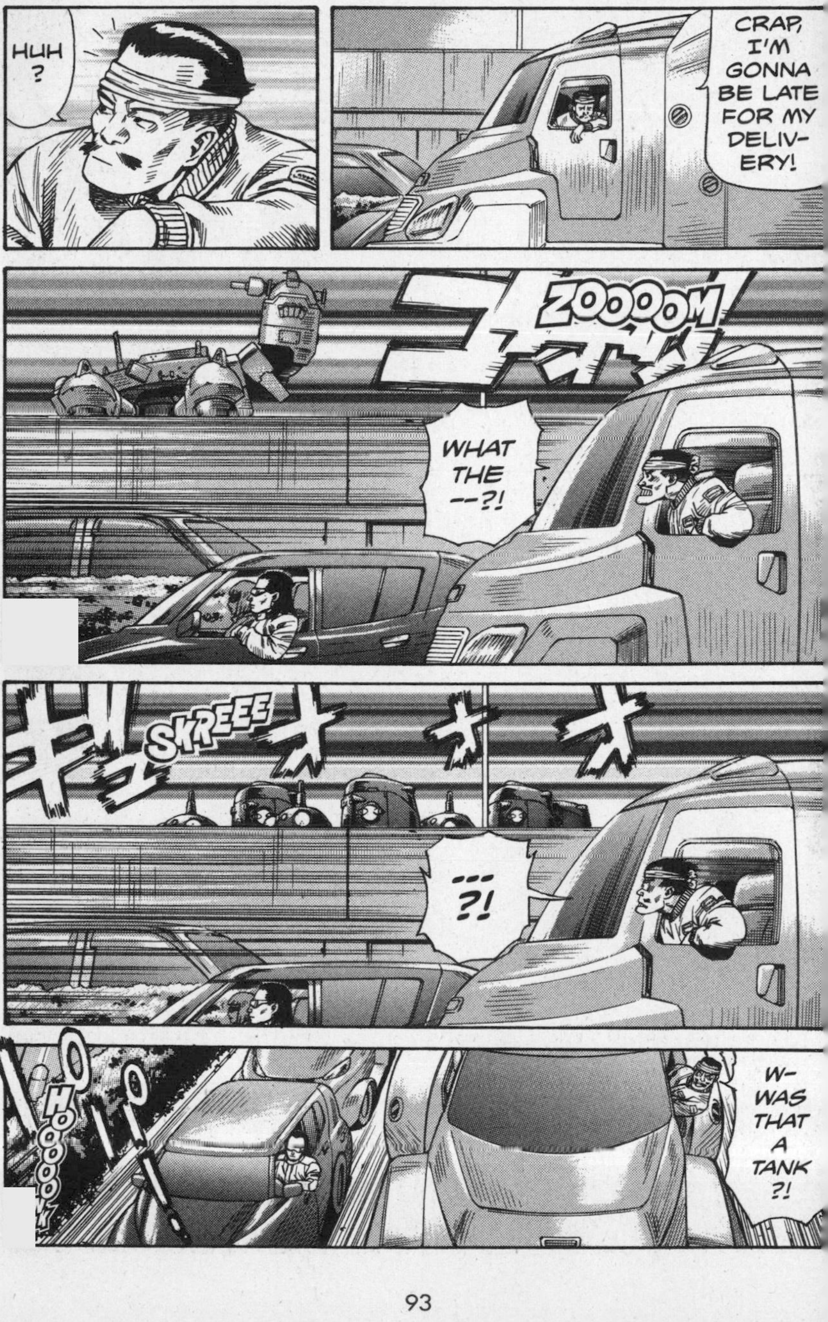
CRAP, I'M GONNA BE LATE FOR MY DELIVERY!
HUH ?
ZOOOOOM
WHAT THE --?!
SKREEE
...?!
W-WAS THAT A TANK?!
HOOOOONK

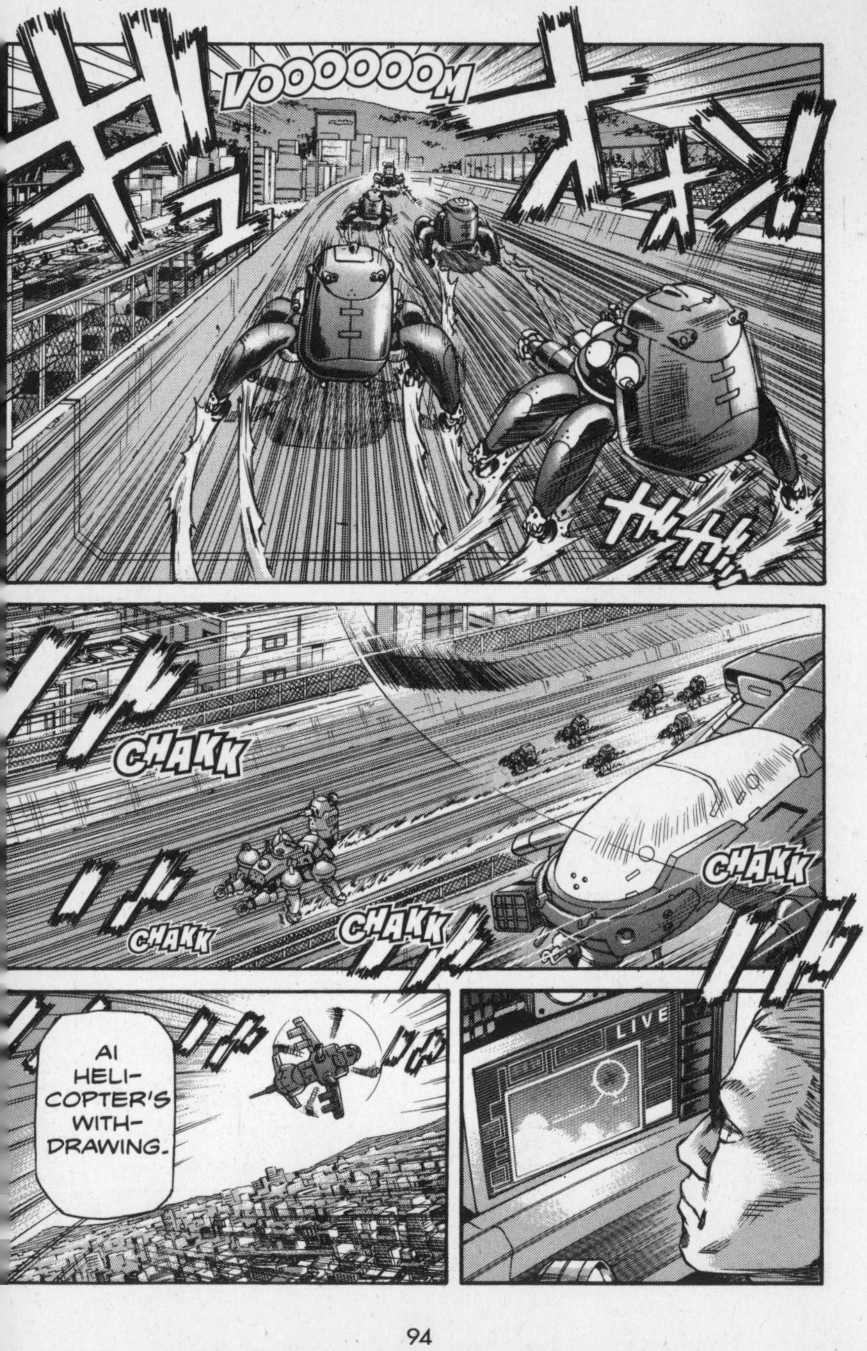
VOOOOOOOM
CHAKK
CHAKK
CHAKK
CHAKK
LIVE
AI HELICOPTER'S WITHDRAWING.

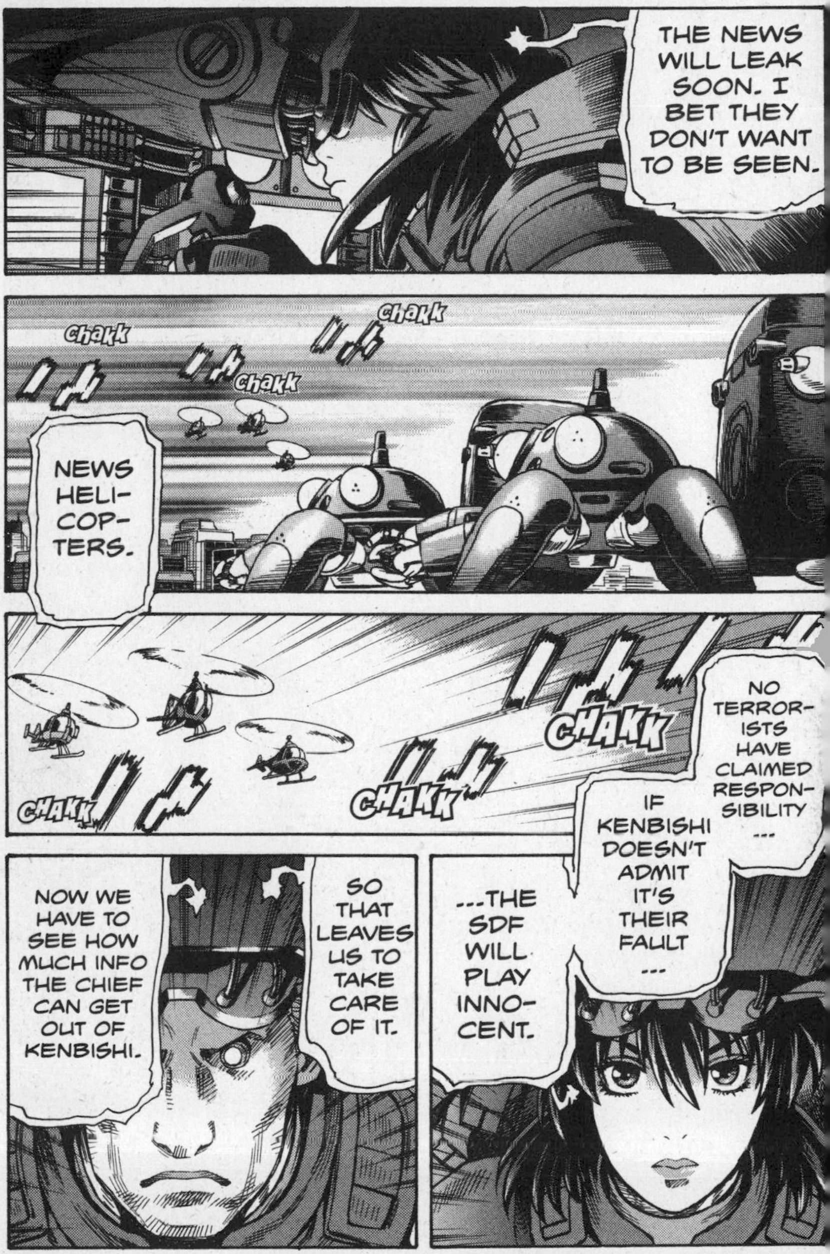
THE NEWS WILL LEAK SOON. I BET THEY DON'T WANT TO BE SEEN.
CHAKK
CHAKK
CHAKK
NEWS HELI-COP-TERS.
NO TERROR-ISTS HAVE CLAIMED RESPON-SIBILITY ...
CHAKK
CHAKK
CHAKK
IF KENBISHI DOESN'T ADMIT IT'S THEIR FAULT ...
...THE SDF WILL PLAY INNO-CENT.
SO THAT LEAVES US TO TAKE CARE OF IT.
NOW WE HAVE TO SEE HOW MUCH INFO THE CHIEF CAN GET OUT OF KENBISHI.

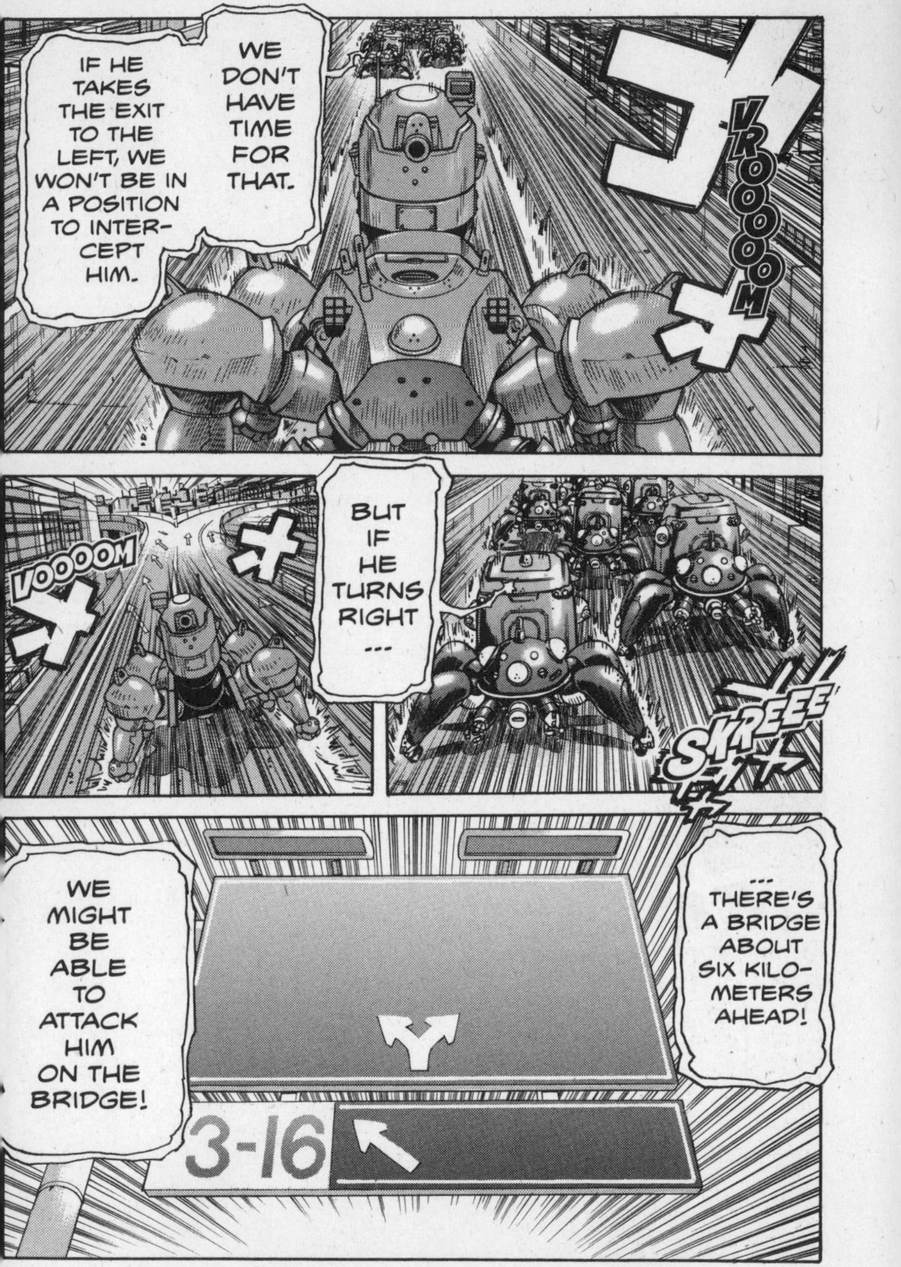
VROOOOOOM
WE DON'T HAVE TIME FOR THAT.
IF HE TAKES THE EXIT TO THE LEFT, WE WON'T BE IN A POSITION TO INTERCEPT HIM.
BUT IF HE TURNS RIGHT ---
SKREEE
VOOOOM
... THERE'S A BRIDGE ABOUT SIX KILOMETERS AHEAD!
WE MIGHT BE ABLE TO ATTACK HIM ON THE BRIDGE!
3-16

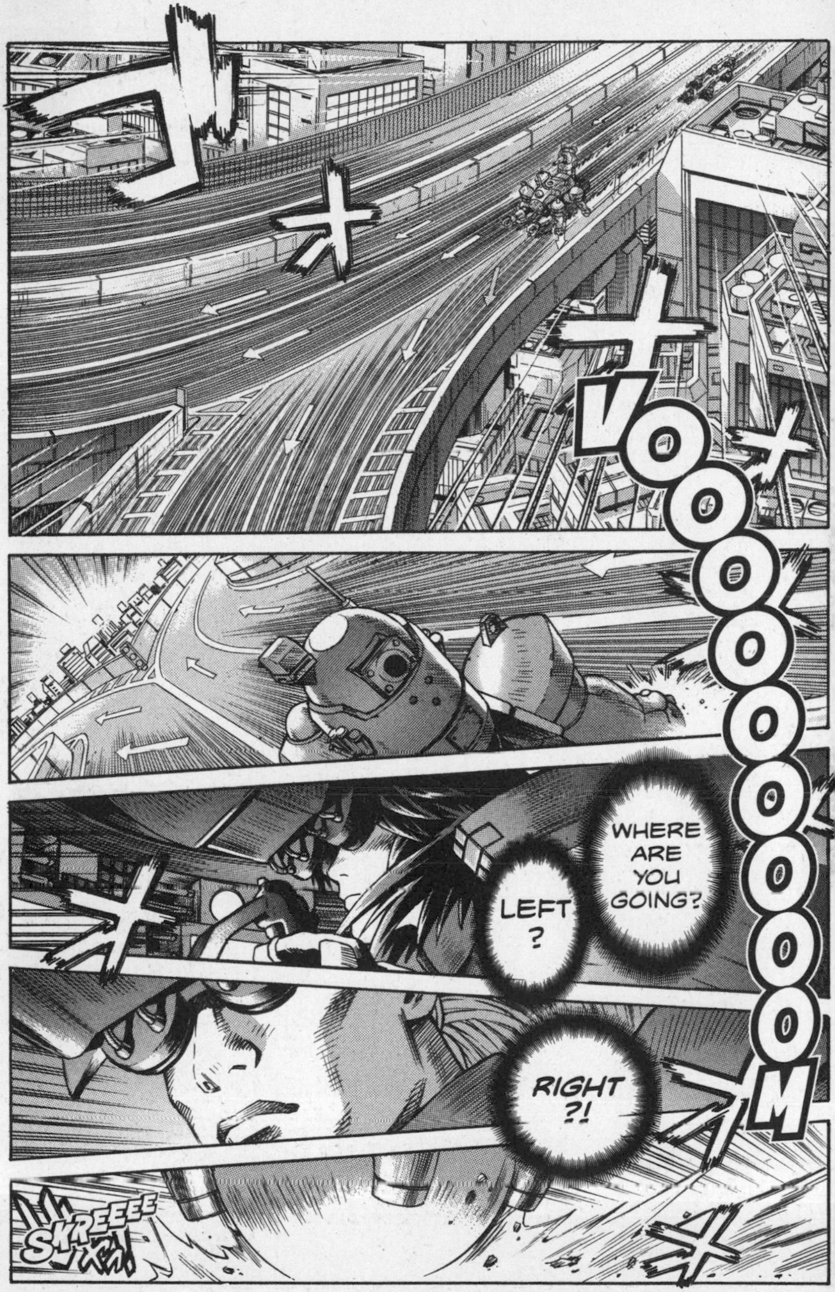
VOOOOOOOOOM
WHERE ARE YOU GOING?
LEFT ?
RIGHT ?!
SKREEEE

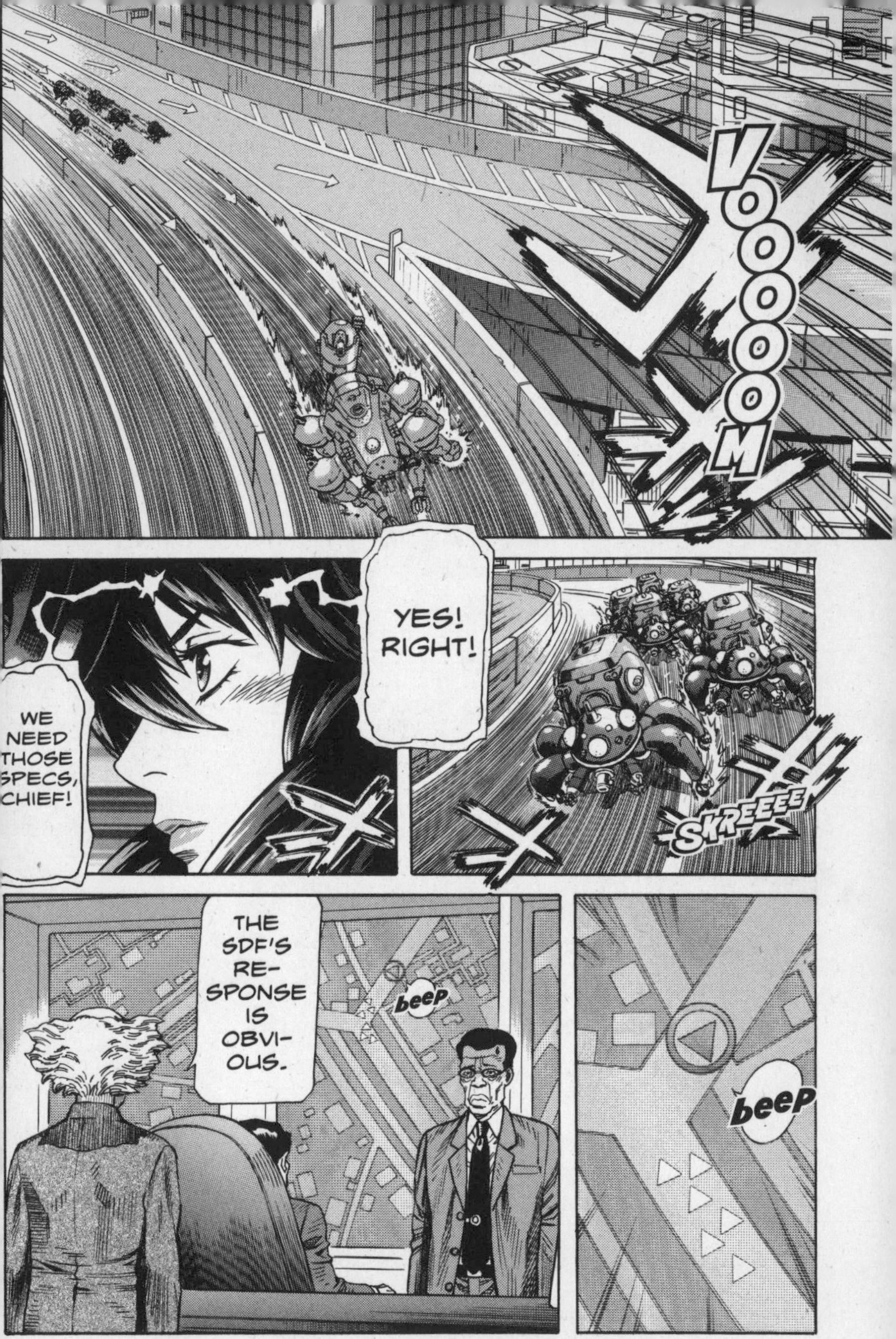
VOOOOOOM
SKREEEE
YES! RIGHT!
WE NEED THOSE SPECS, CHIEF!
beep
THE SDF'S RE-SPONSE IS OBVI-OUS.
beep

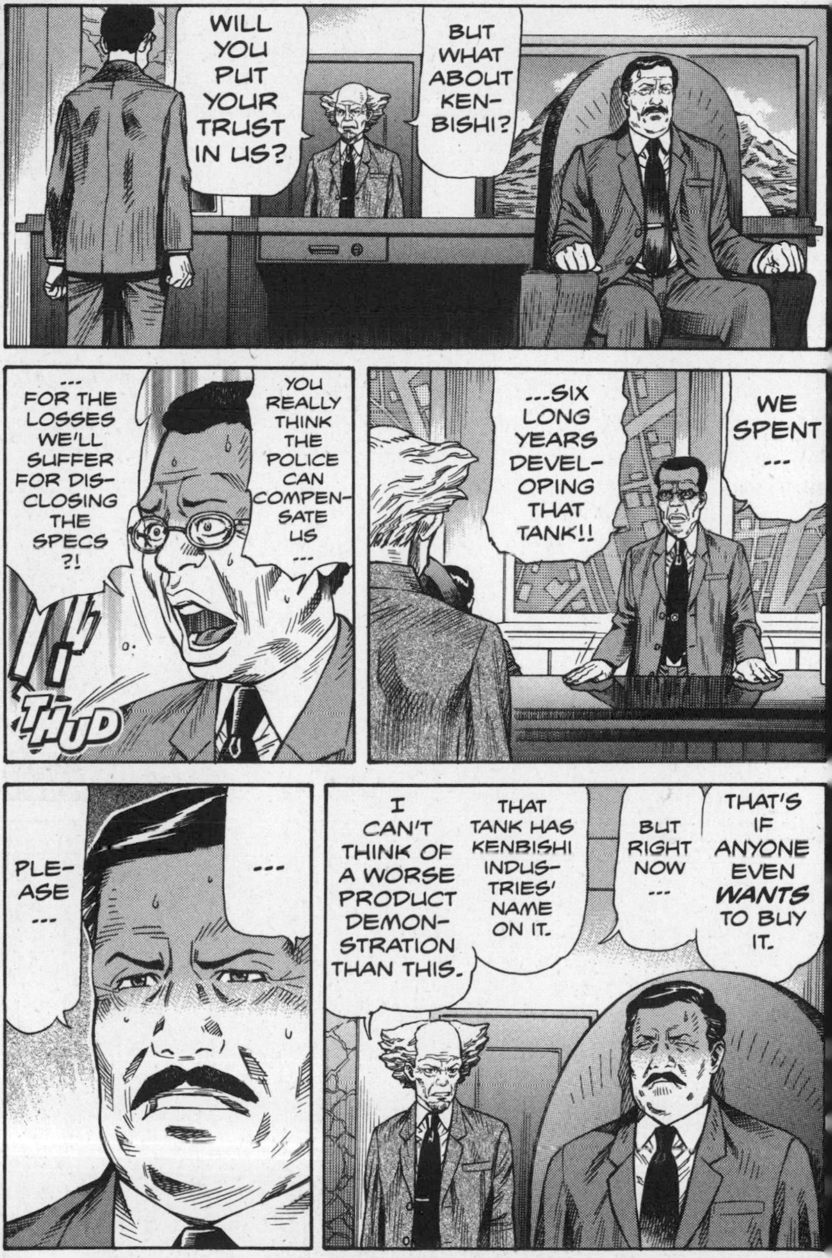
BUT WHAT ABOUT KEN-BISHI?
WILL YOU PUT YOUR TRUST IN US?
WE SPENT ---
---SIX LONG YEARS DEVEL-OPING THAT TANK!!
YOU REALLY THINK THE POLICE CAN COMPEN-SATE US ---
--- FOR THE LOSSES WE'LL SUFFER FOR DIS-CLOSING THE SPECS ?!
THUD
THAT'S IF ANYONE EVEN *WANTS* TO BUY IT.
BUT RIGHT NOW ---
THAT TANK HAS KENBISHI INDUS-TRIES' NAME ON IT.
I CAN'T THINK OF A WORSE PRODUCT DEMON-STRATION THAN THIS.

PLE-ASE ---

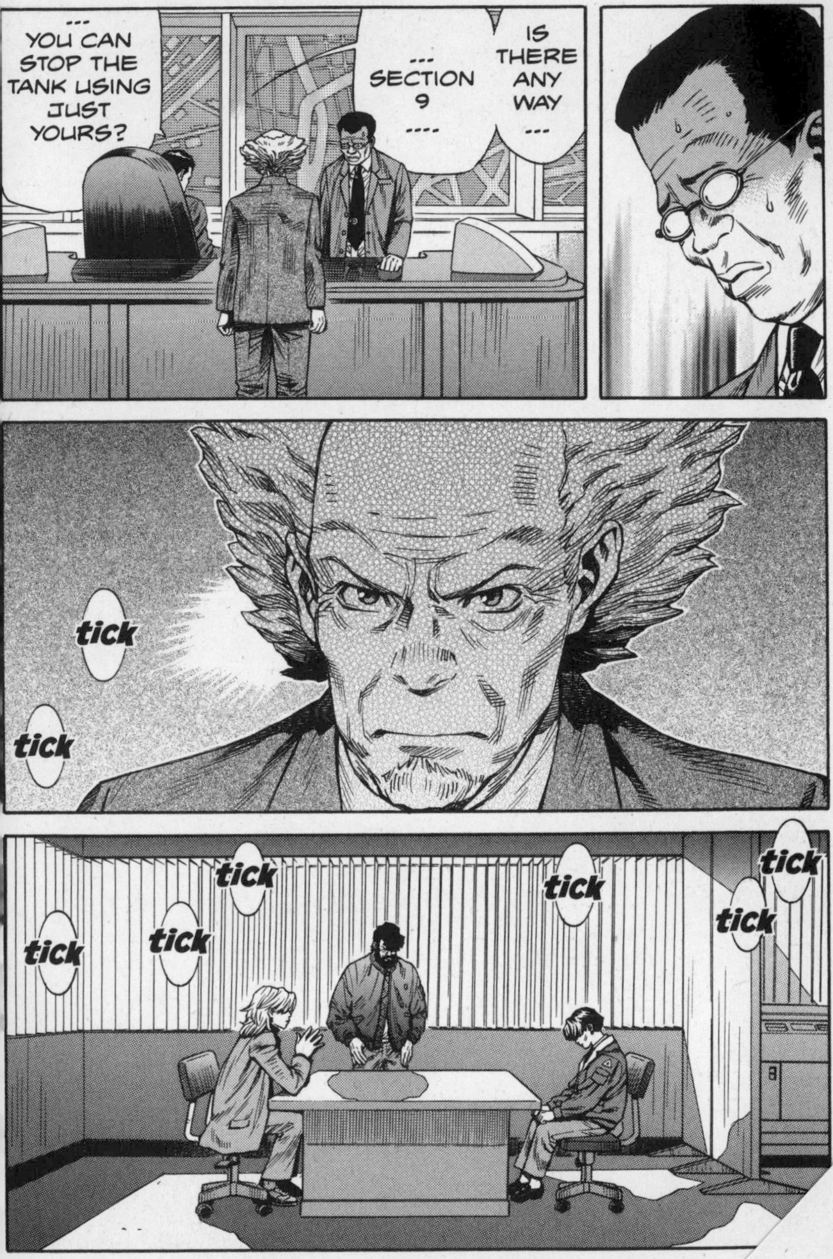
IS THERE ANY WAY ---
--- SECTION 9 ----
--- YOU CAN STOP THE TANK USING JUST YOURS?
tick
tick
tick
tick
tick
tick
tick
tick

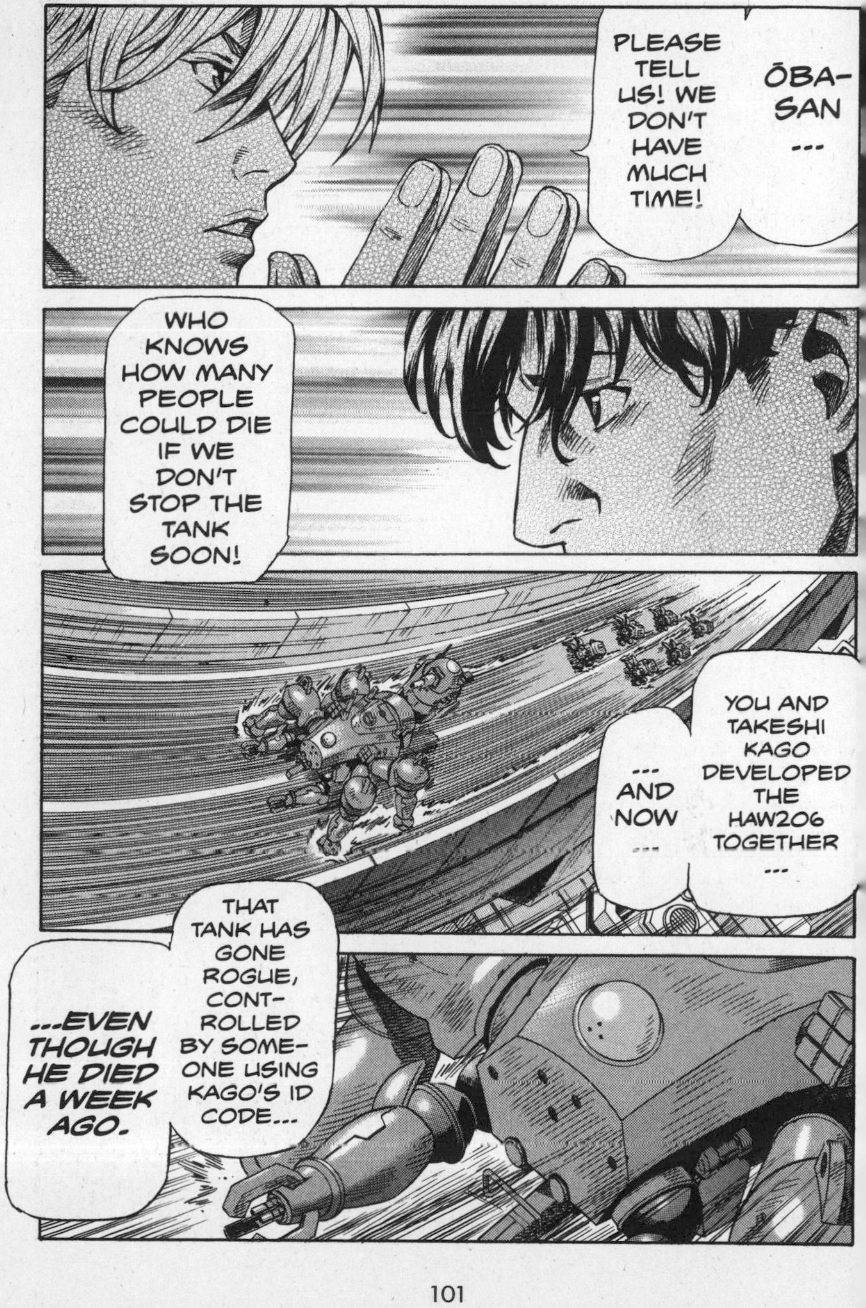
ŌBA-SAN ---
PLEASE TELL US! WE DON'T HAVE MUCH TIME!
WHO KNOWS HOW MANY PEOPLE COULD DIE IF WE DON'T STOP THE TANK SOON!
YOU AND TAKESHI KAGO DEVELOPED THE HAW206 TOGETHER ---
--- AND NOW ---
THAT TANK HAS GONE ROGUE, CONT-ROLLED BY SOME-ONE USING KAGO'S ID CODE...
...EVEN THOUGH HE DIED A WEEK AGO.

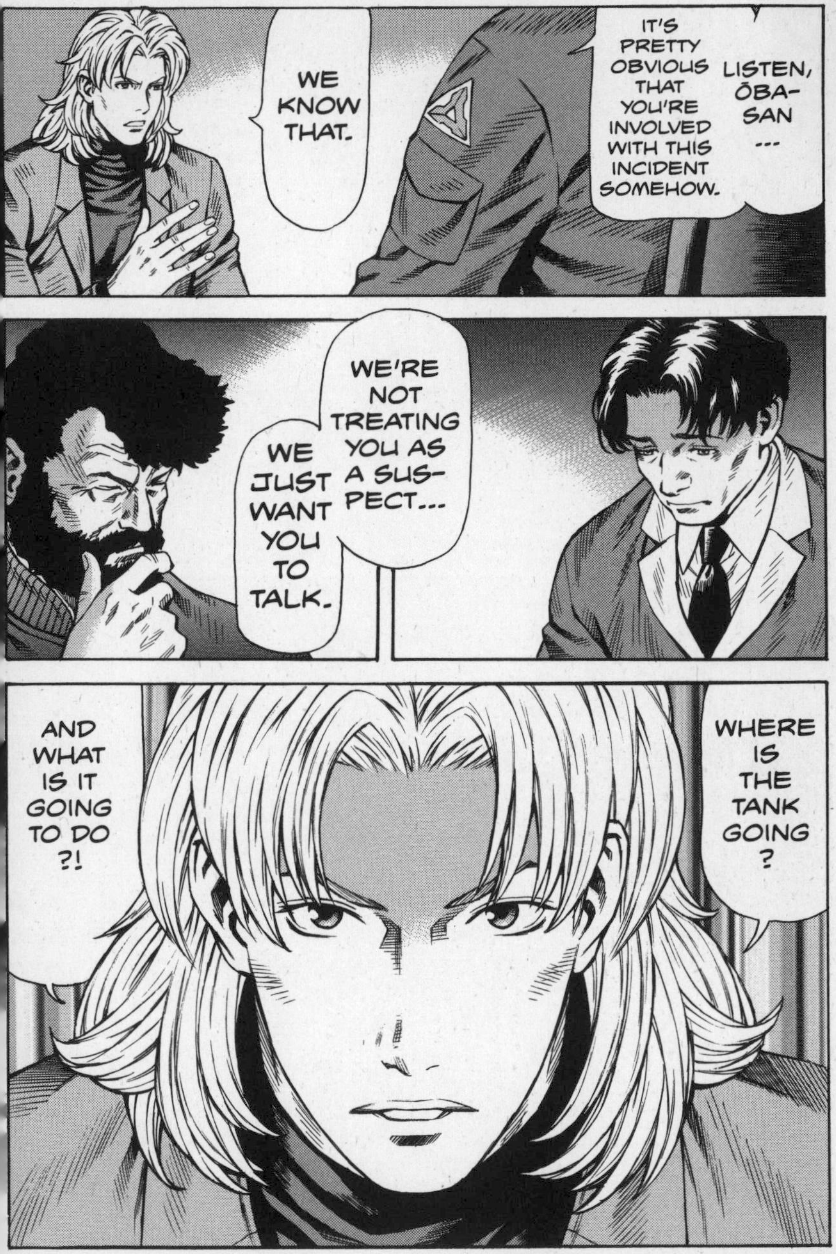
LISTEN, ŌBA-SAN ---
IT'S PRETTY OBVIOUS THAT YOU'RE INVOLVED WITH THIS INCIDENT SOMEHOW.
WE KNOW THAT.
WE'RE NOT TREATING YOU AS A SUS-PECT...
WE JUST WANT YOU TO TALK.
WHERE IS THE TANK GOING?
AND WHAT IS IT GOING TO DO?!

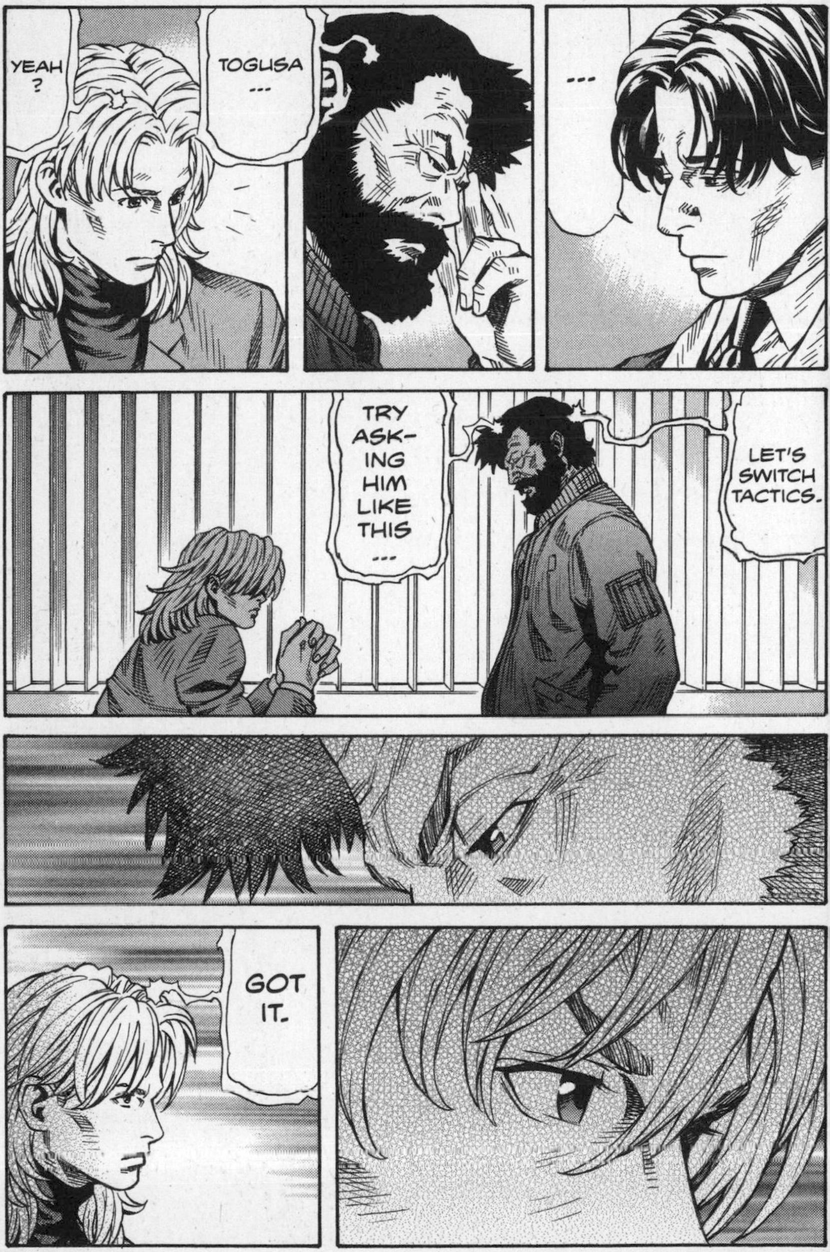
...
TOGUSA ...
YEAH ?
LET'S SWITCH TACTICS.
TRY ASKING HIM LIKE THIS ...
GOT IT.

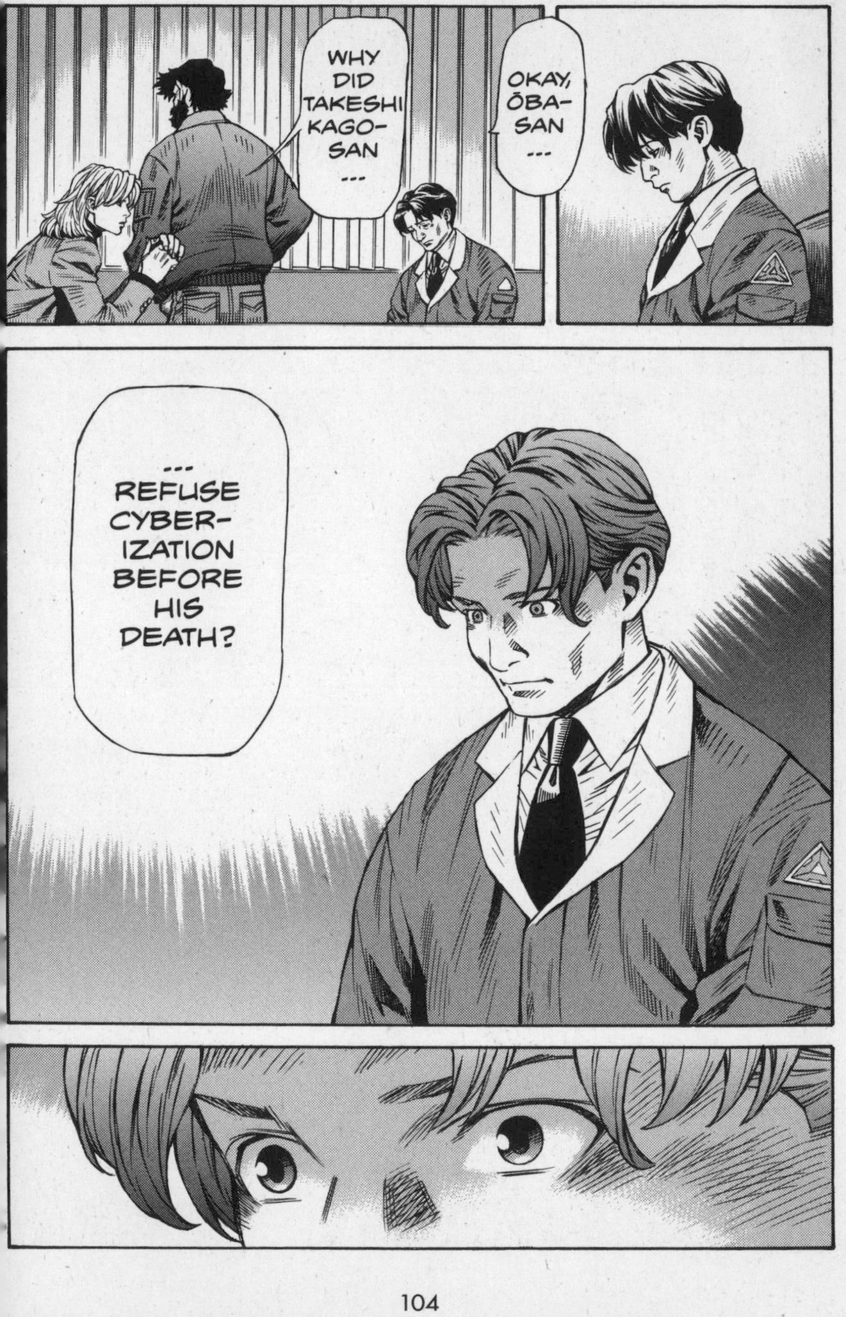
OKAY, ŌBA-SAN ---
WHY DID TAKESHI KAGO-SAN ---
--- REFUSE CYBER-IZATION BEFORE HIS DEATH?

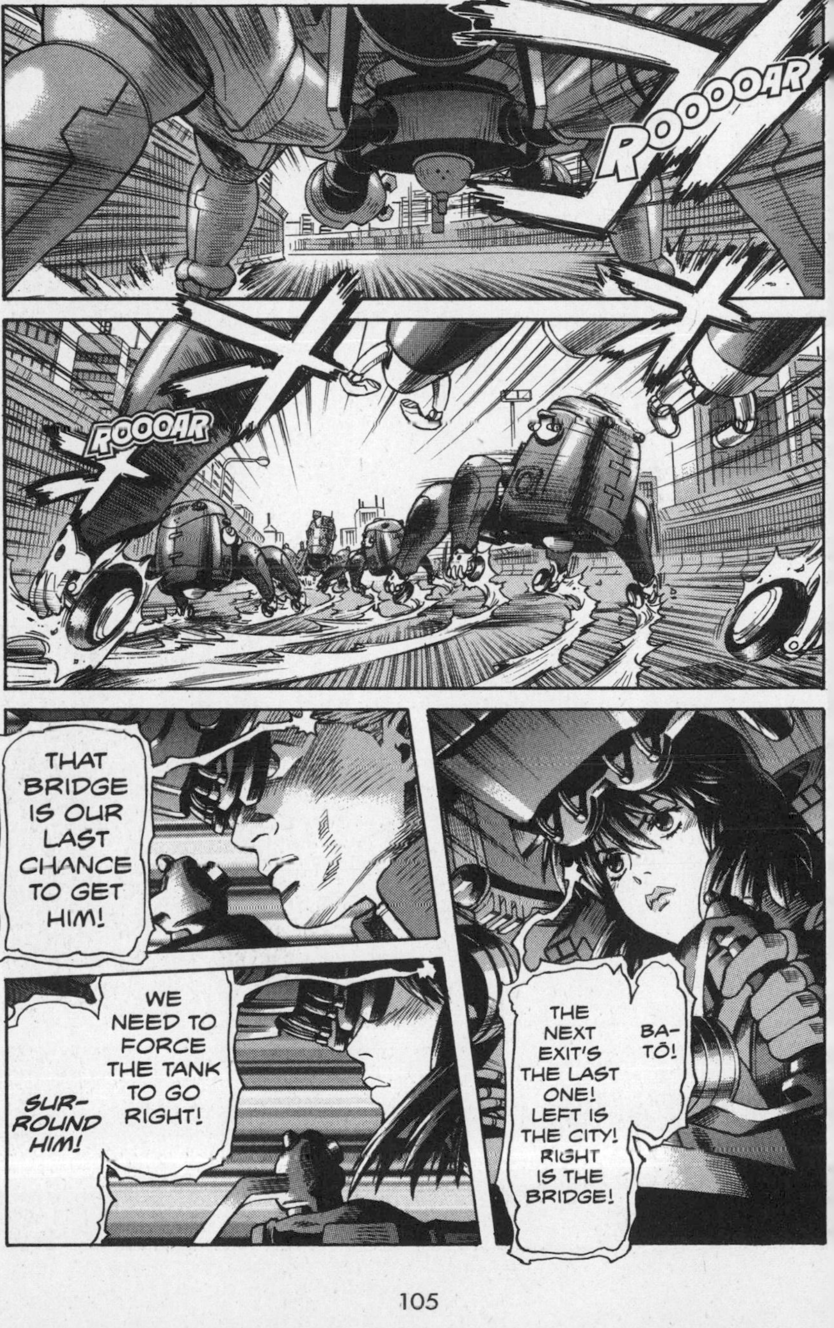
ROOOOAR
ROOOAR
BA-TŌ!
THE NEXT EXIT'S THE LAST ONE! LEFT IS THE CITY! RIGHT IS THE BRIDGE!
THAT BRIDGE IS OUR LAST CHANCE TO GET HIM!
WE NEED TO FORCE THE TANK TO GO RIGHT!
SUR-ROUND HIM!

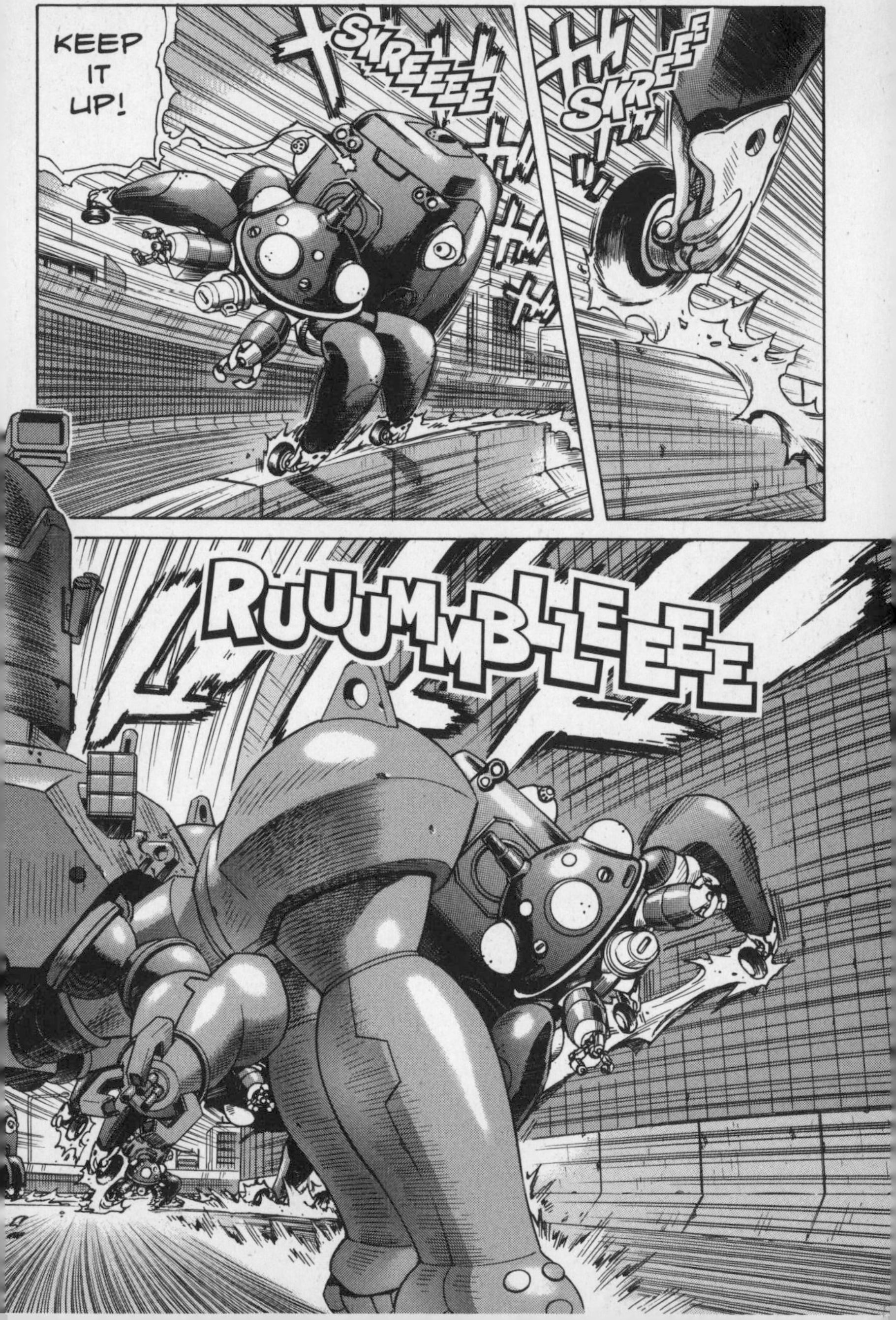
SKREEEE
KEEP IT UP!
SKREEEEE
RUUUMMBLEEEE

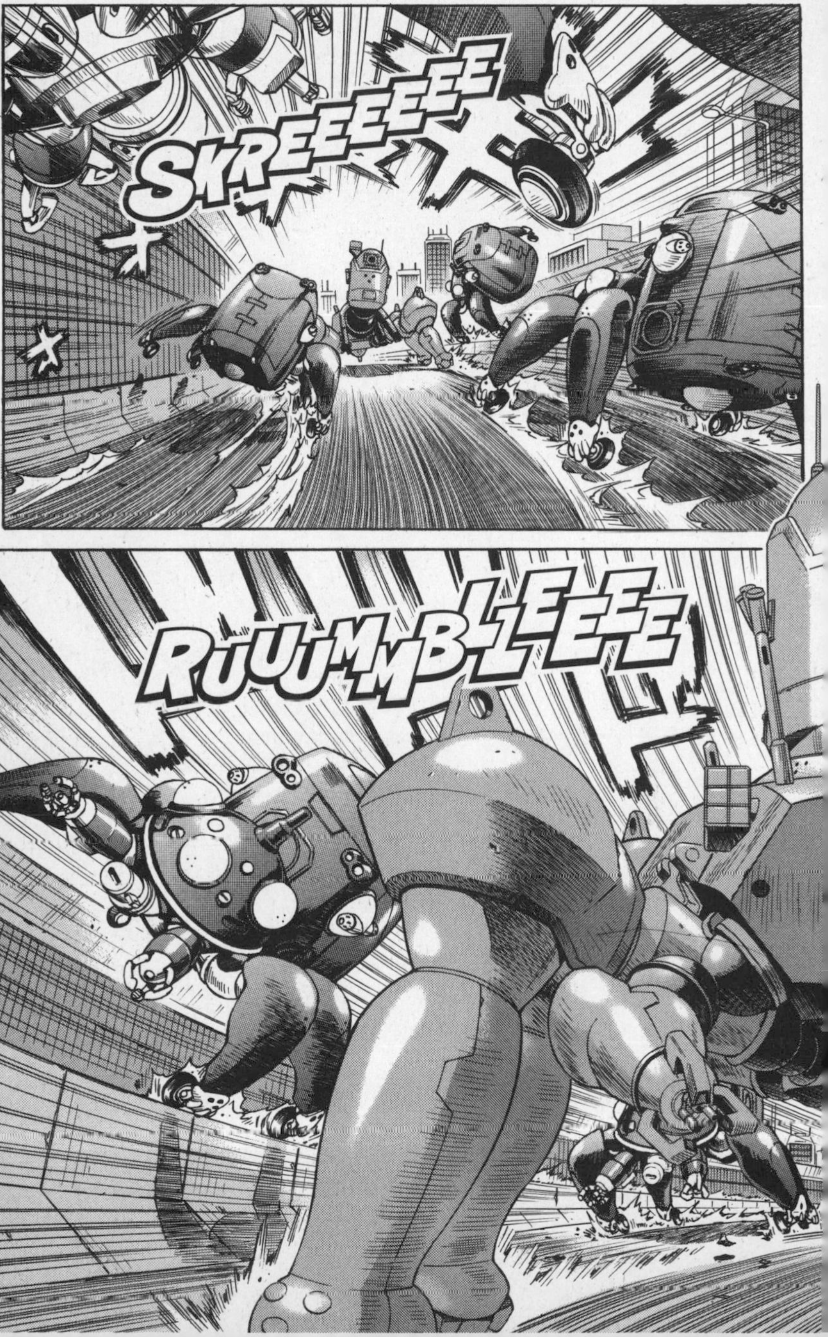
SKREEEEEEE
RUUUMMBLEEEE

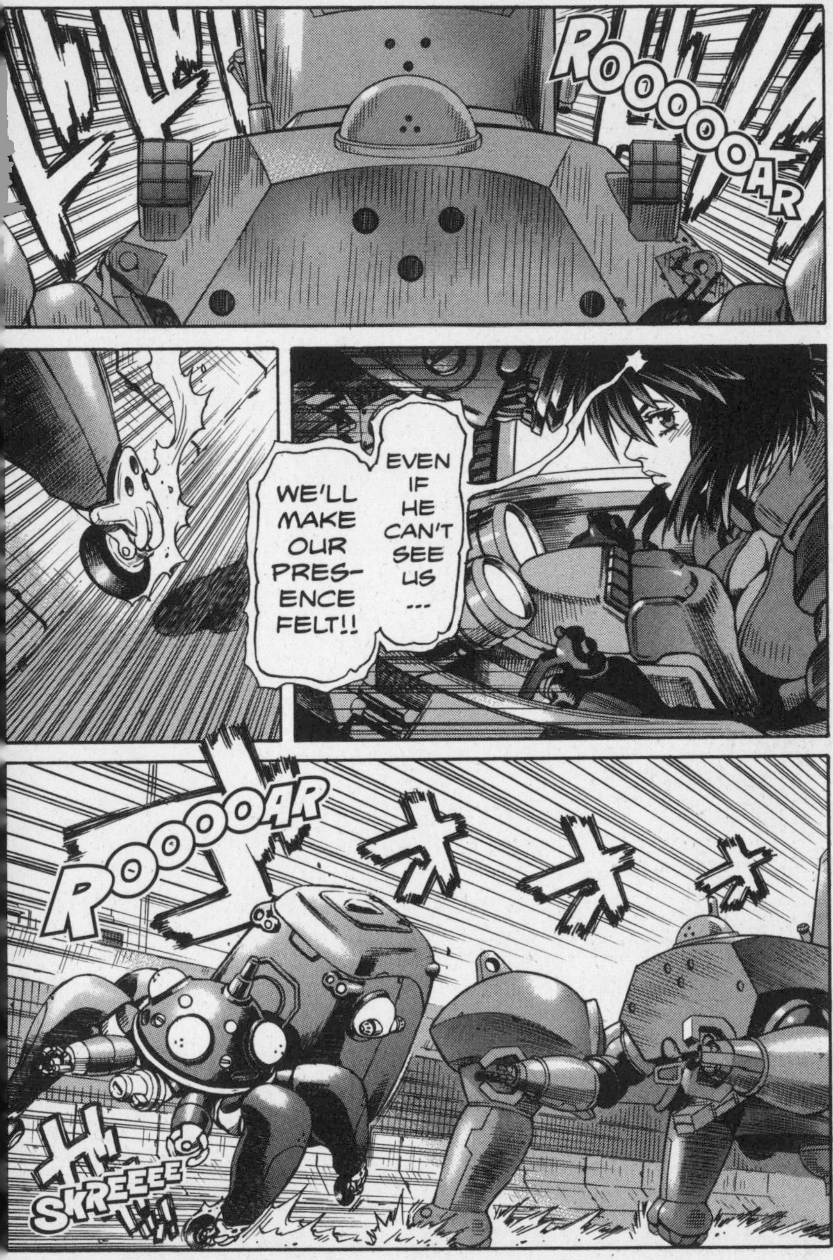
ROOOOOOAR
EVEN IF HE CAN'T SEE US ...
WE'LL MAKE OUR PRES-ENCE FELT!!
ROOOOOAR
SKREEEE

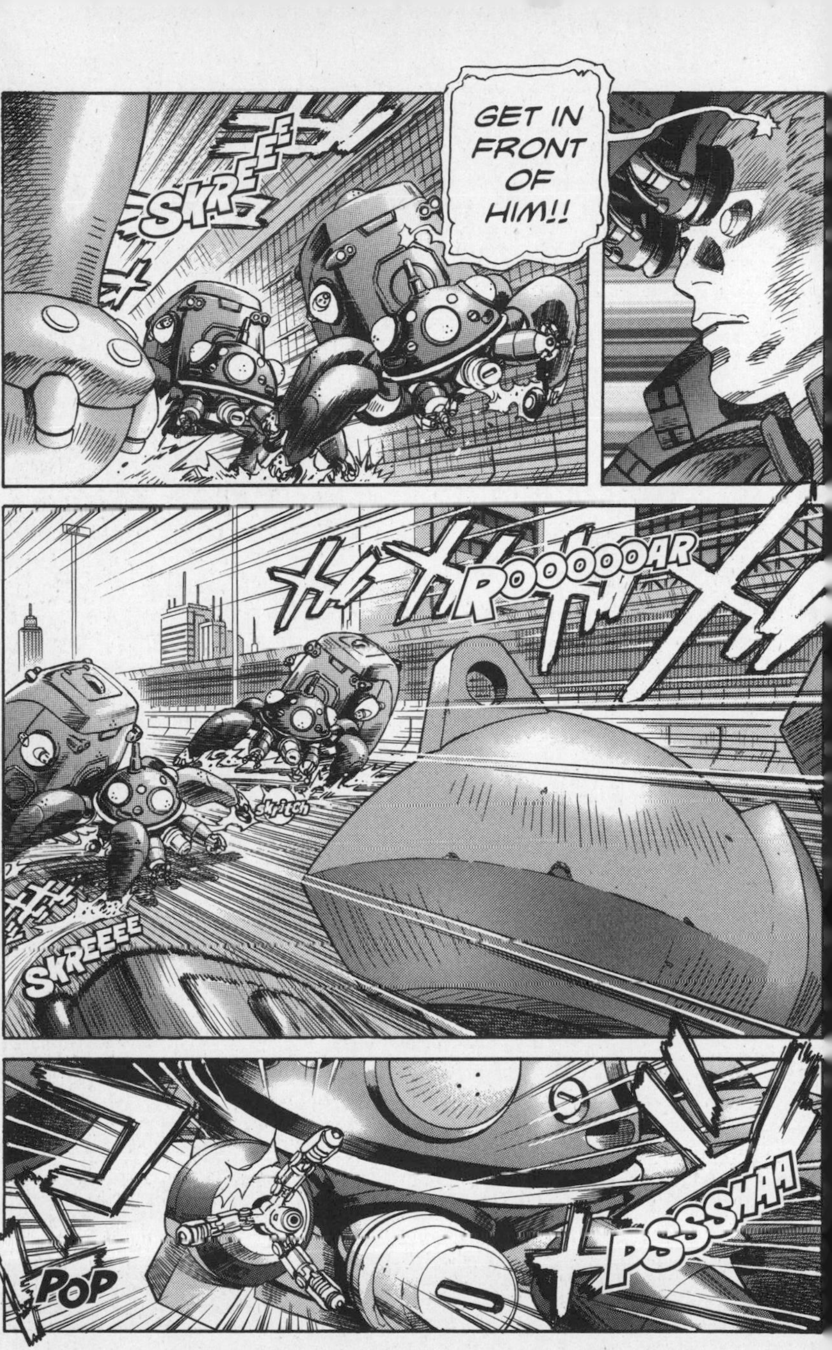
GET IN FRONT OF HIM!!
SKREEE
ROOOOOAR
skritch
SKREEEE
PSSSHAA
POP

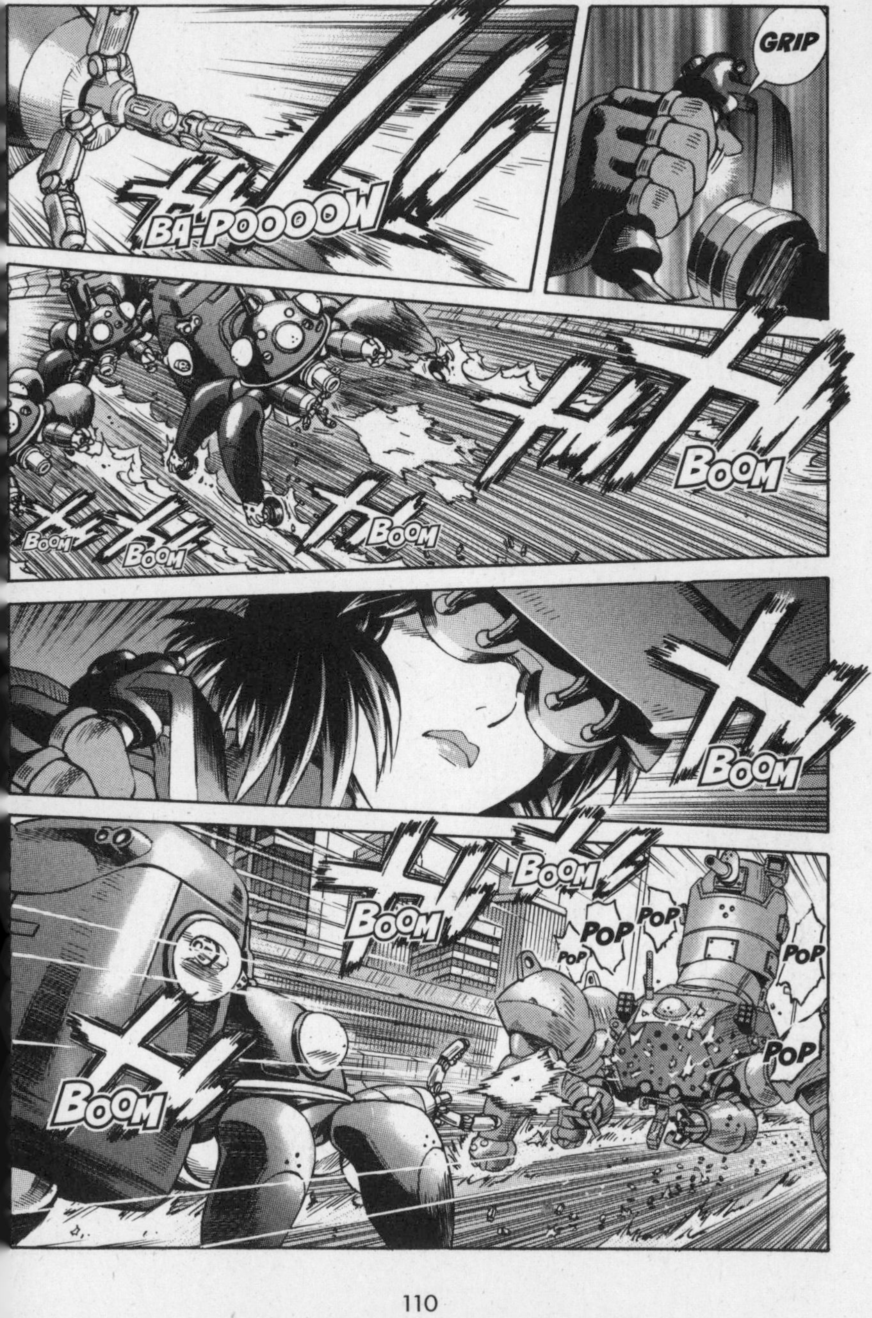
GRIP
BA-POOOOW
BOOM
BOOM
BOOM
BOOM
BOOM
POP
BOOM
POP
POP
BOOM
POP
POP
BOOM

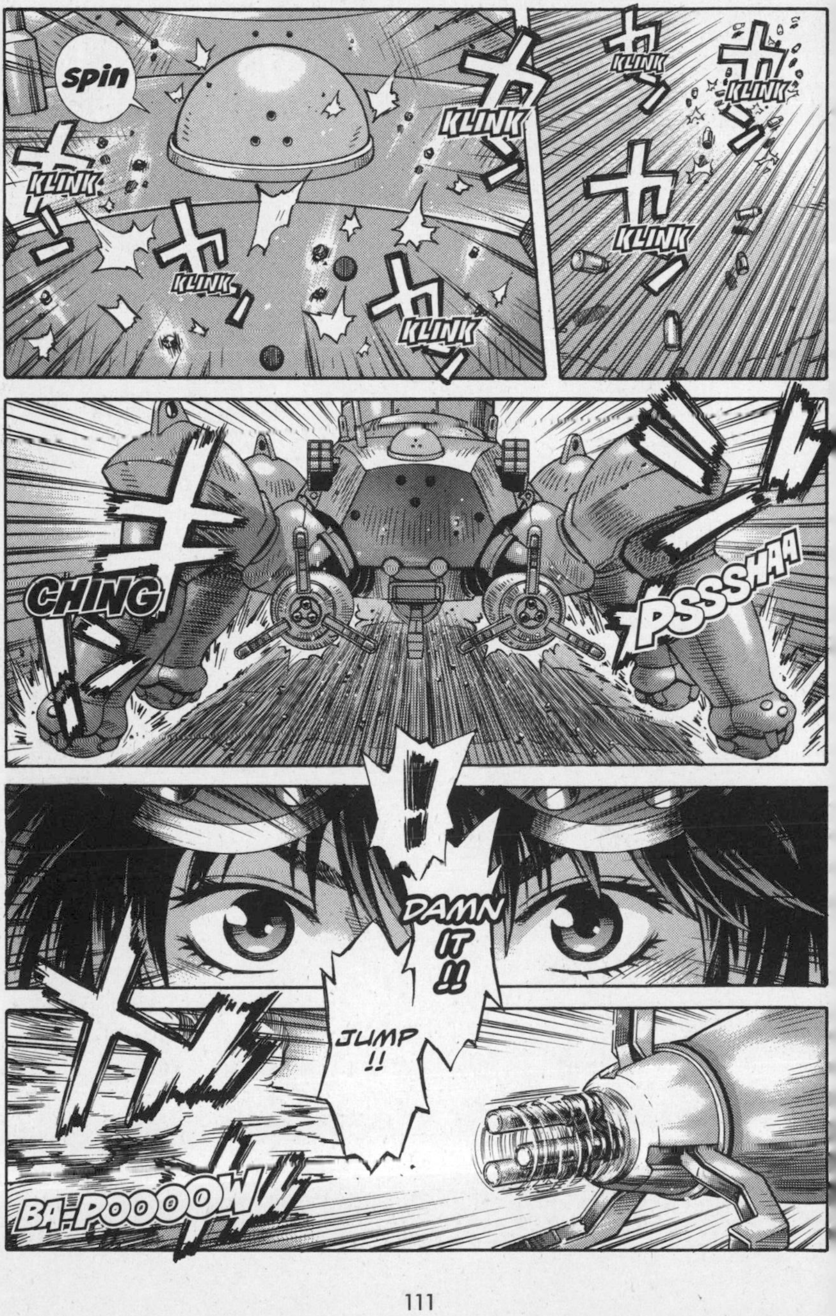
KLINK
KLINK
KLINK
KLINK
spin
KLINK
KLINK
KLINK
PSSSHAA
CHING
!
DAMN IT!!
JUMP!!
BA-POOOOOW

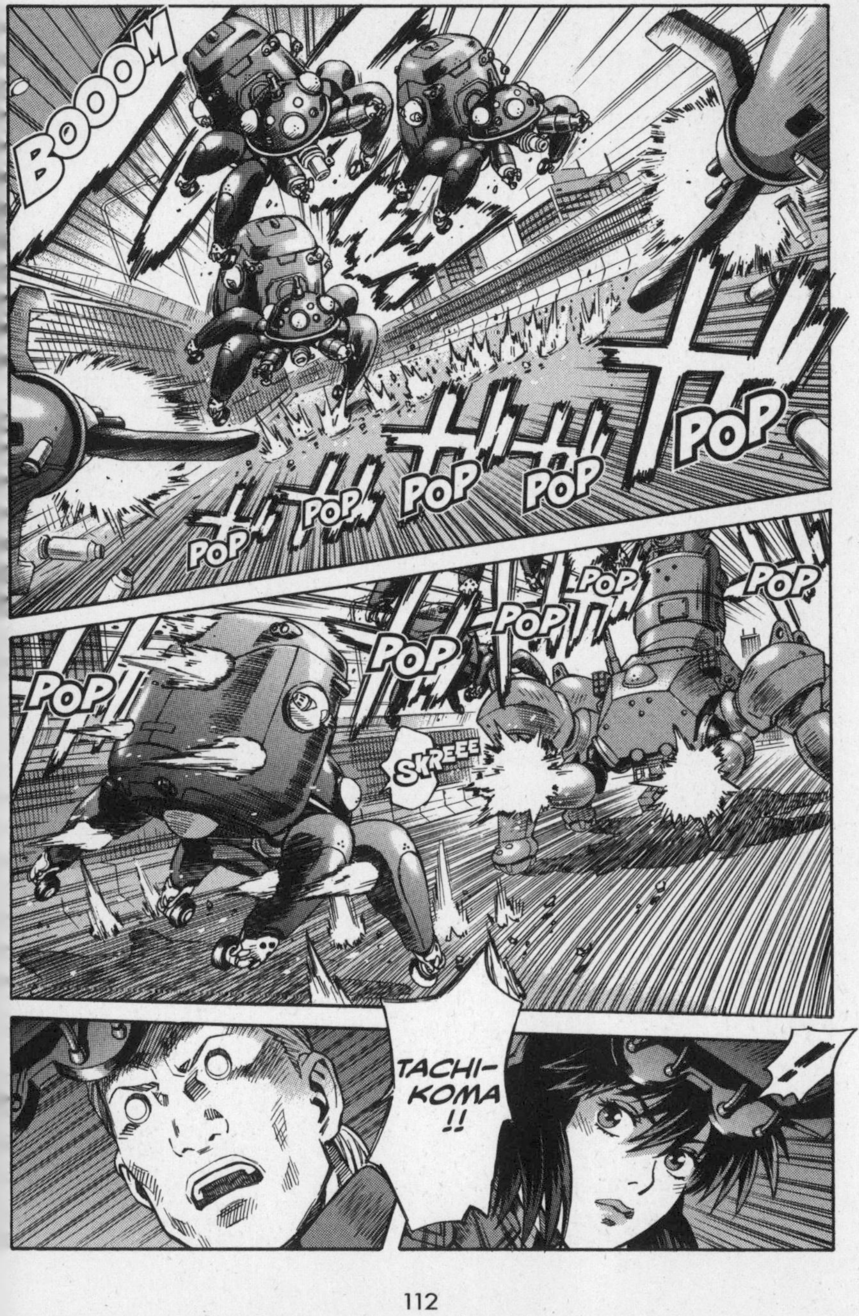
BOOOM
POP
POP
POP
POP
POP
POP
POP
POP
POP
SKREEE
POP
!
TACHI-
KOMA
!!

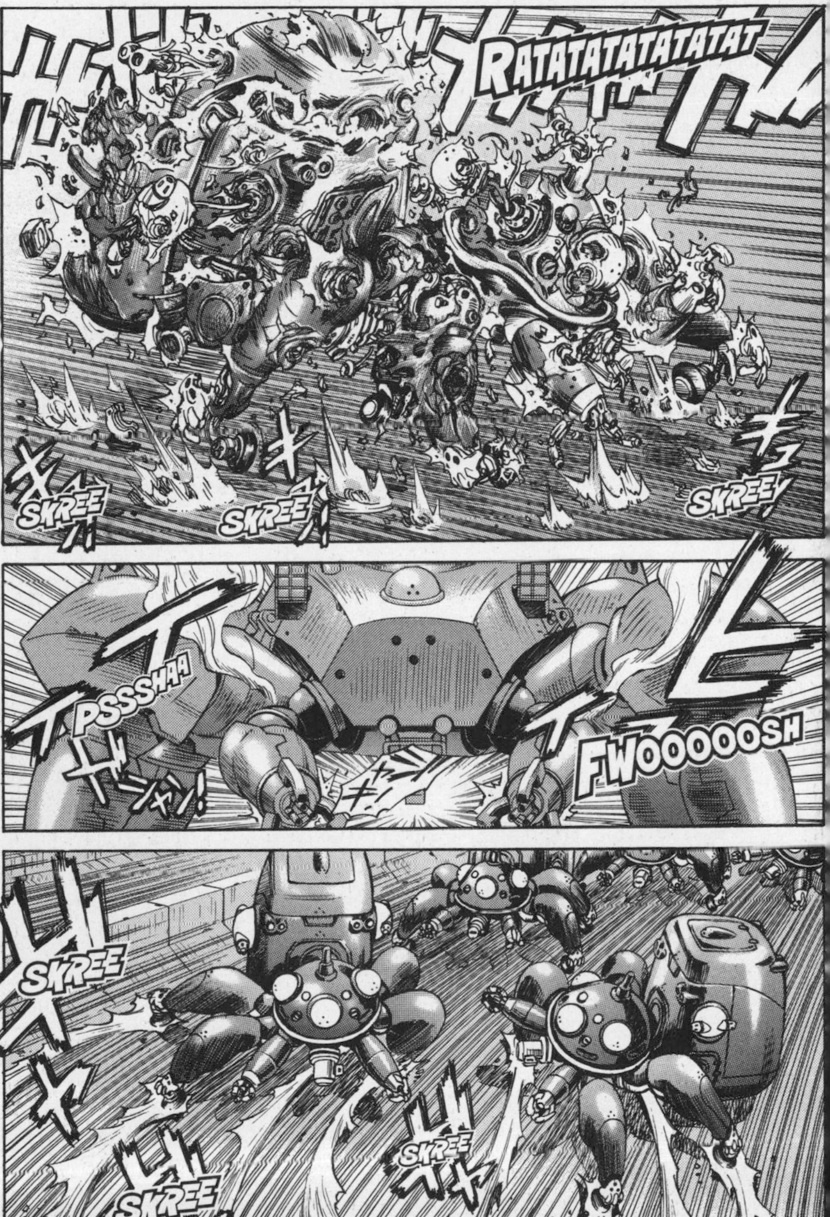
RATATATATATATAT
SKREE
SKREE
SKREE
FWOOOOOOSH
PSSSHAA
SKREE
SKREE
SKREE

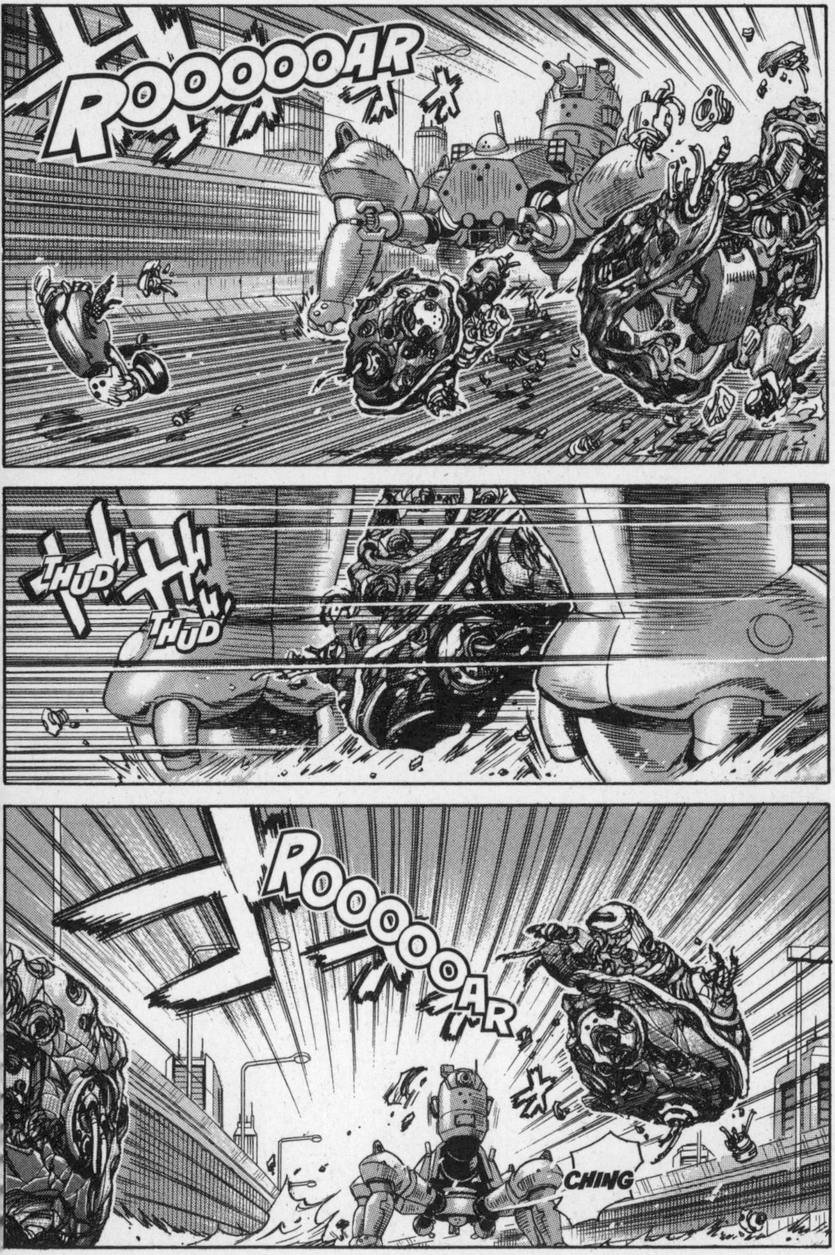
ROOOOOOAR
THUD
THUD
ROOOOOOAR
CHING

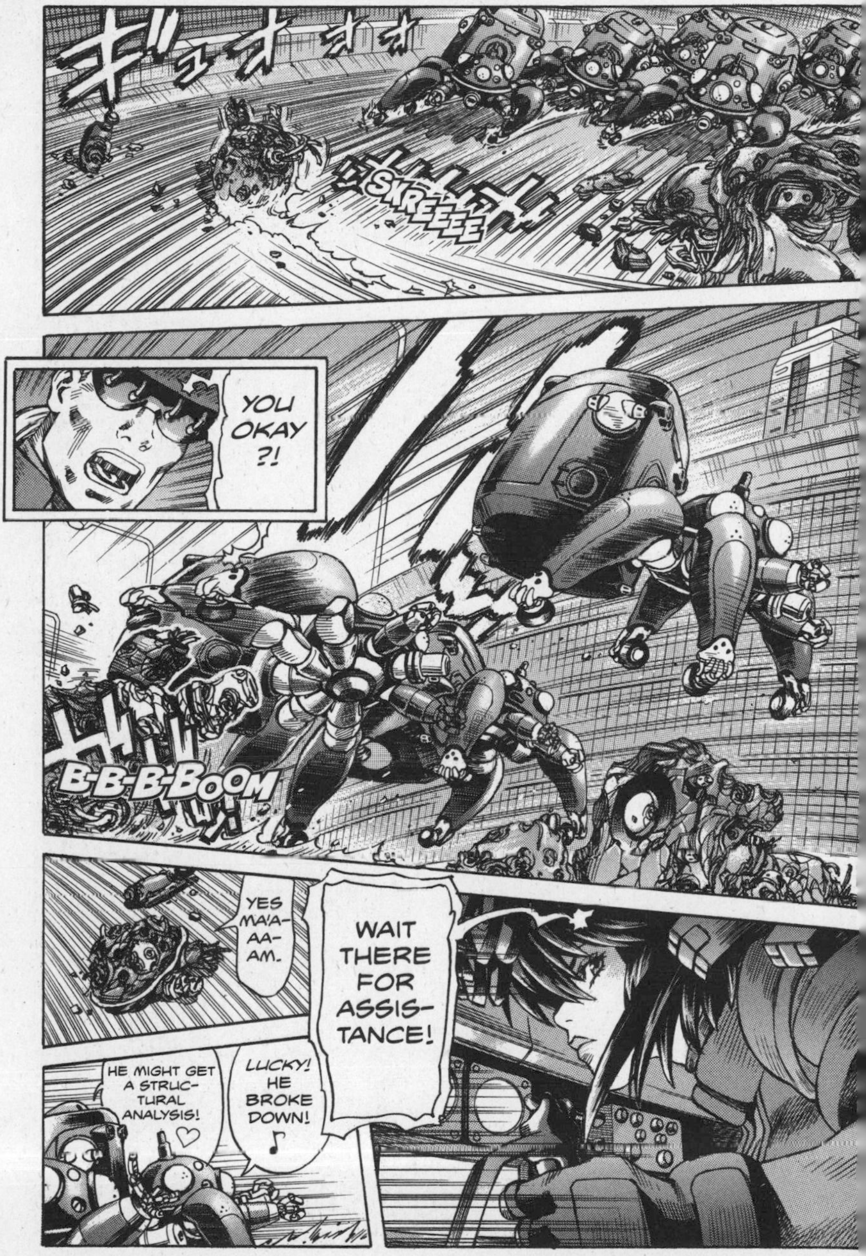
ギュオオオオ
SKREEEE
YOU OKAY ?!
B-B-B-BOOM
WAIT THERE FOR ASSIS-TANCE!
YES MA'A-AA-AM.
LUCKY! HE BROKE DOWN! ♪
HE MIGHT GET A STRUC-TURAL ANALYSIS! ♡

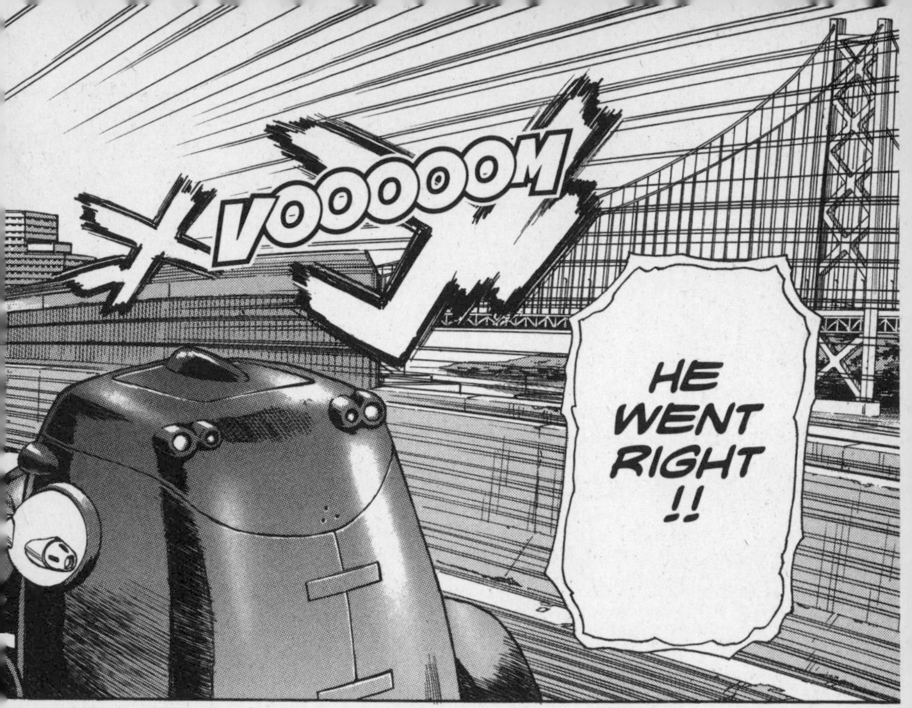
VOOOOOM
HE WENT RIGHT !!
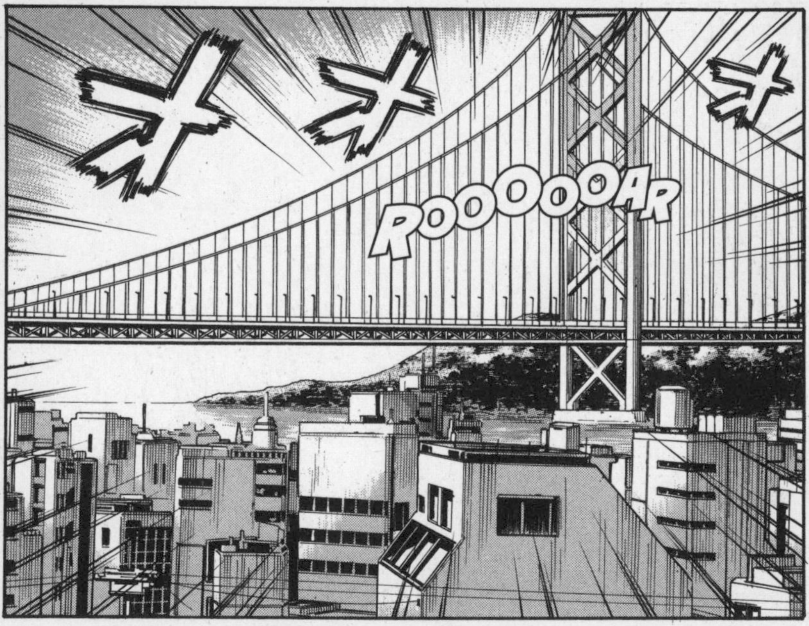
ROOOOOAR

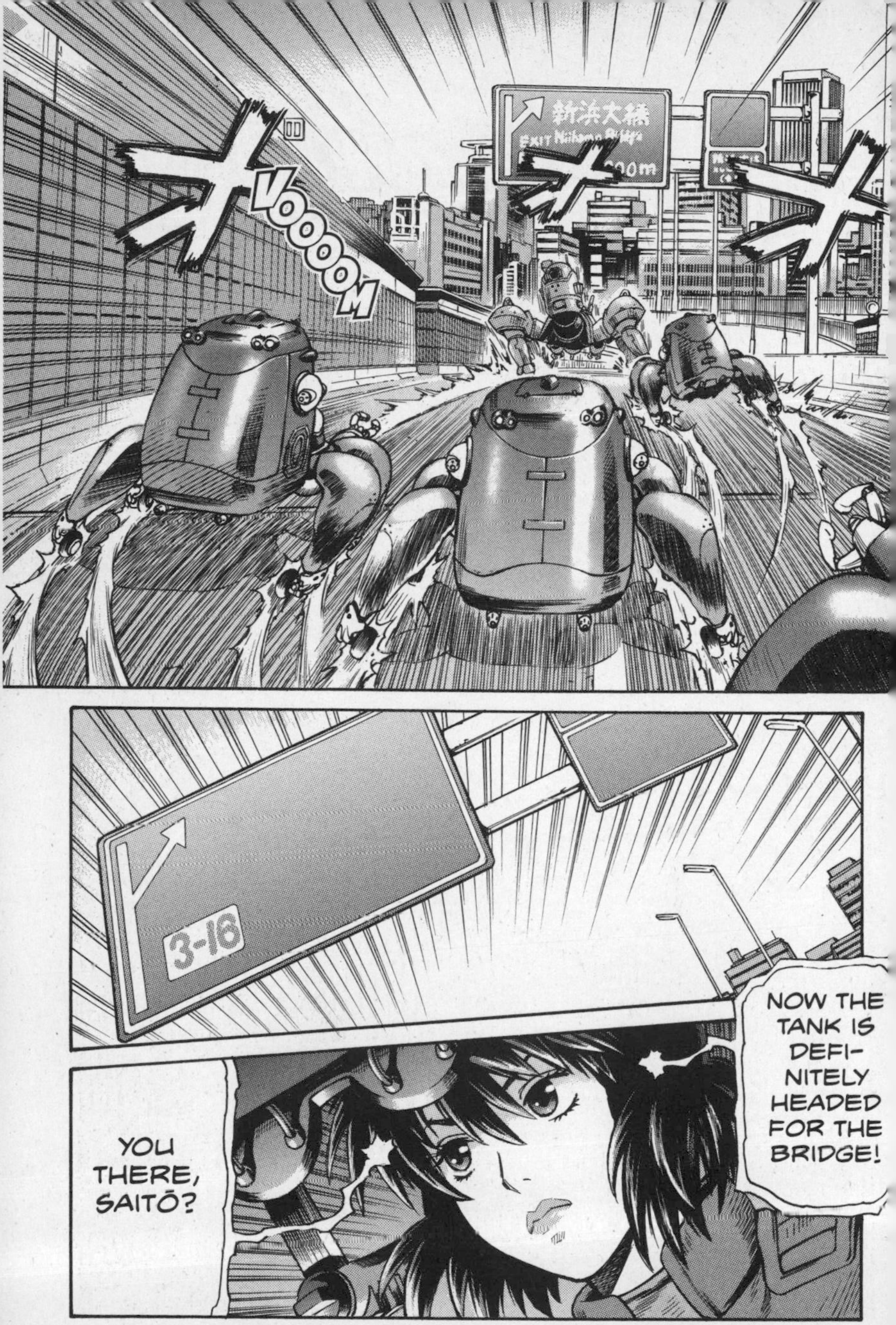
VOOOOOM
新浜大橋
EXIT
3-16
NOW THE TANK IS DEFI-NITELY HEADED FOR THE BRIDGE!
YOU THERE, SAITŌ?

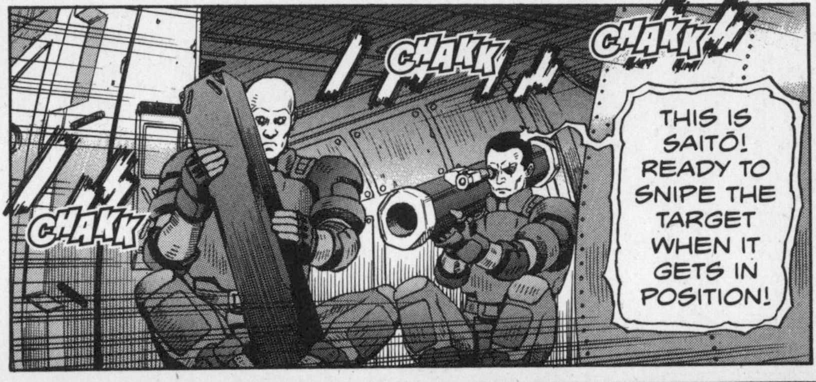
CHAKK
THIS IS SAITŌ! READY TO SNIPE THE TARGET WHEN IT GETS IN POSITION!
CHAKK
CHAKK

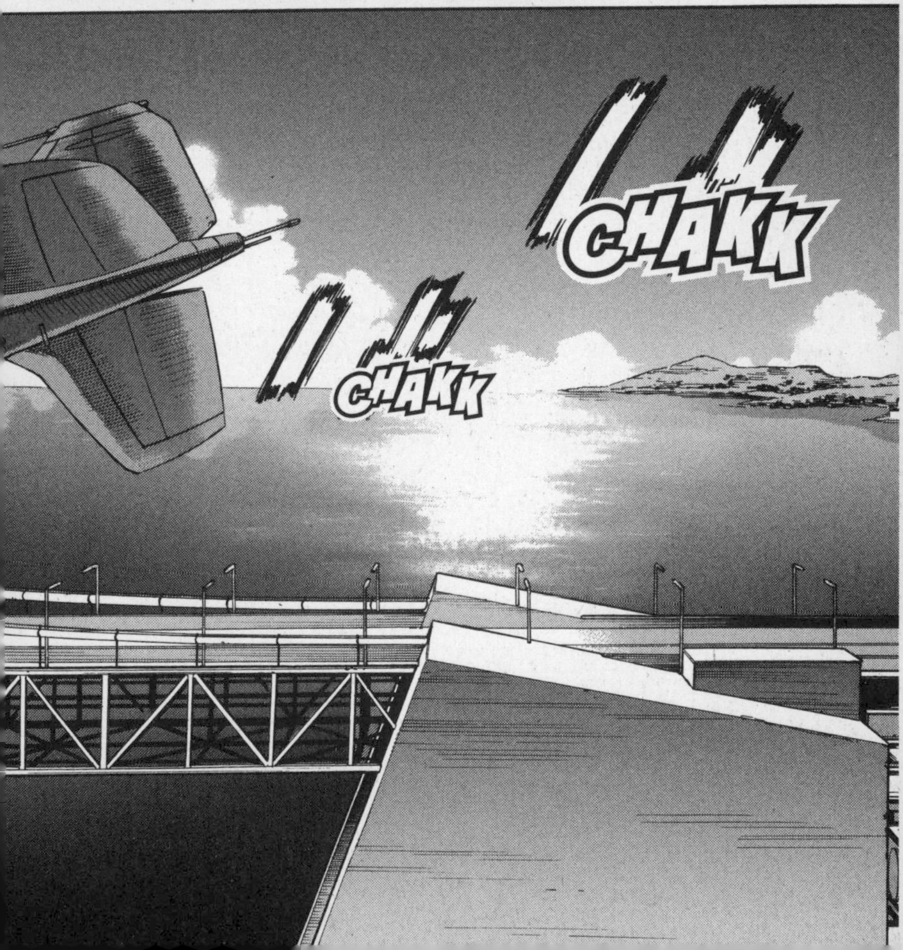
CHAKK
CHAKK

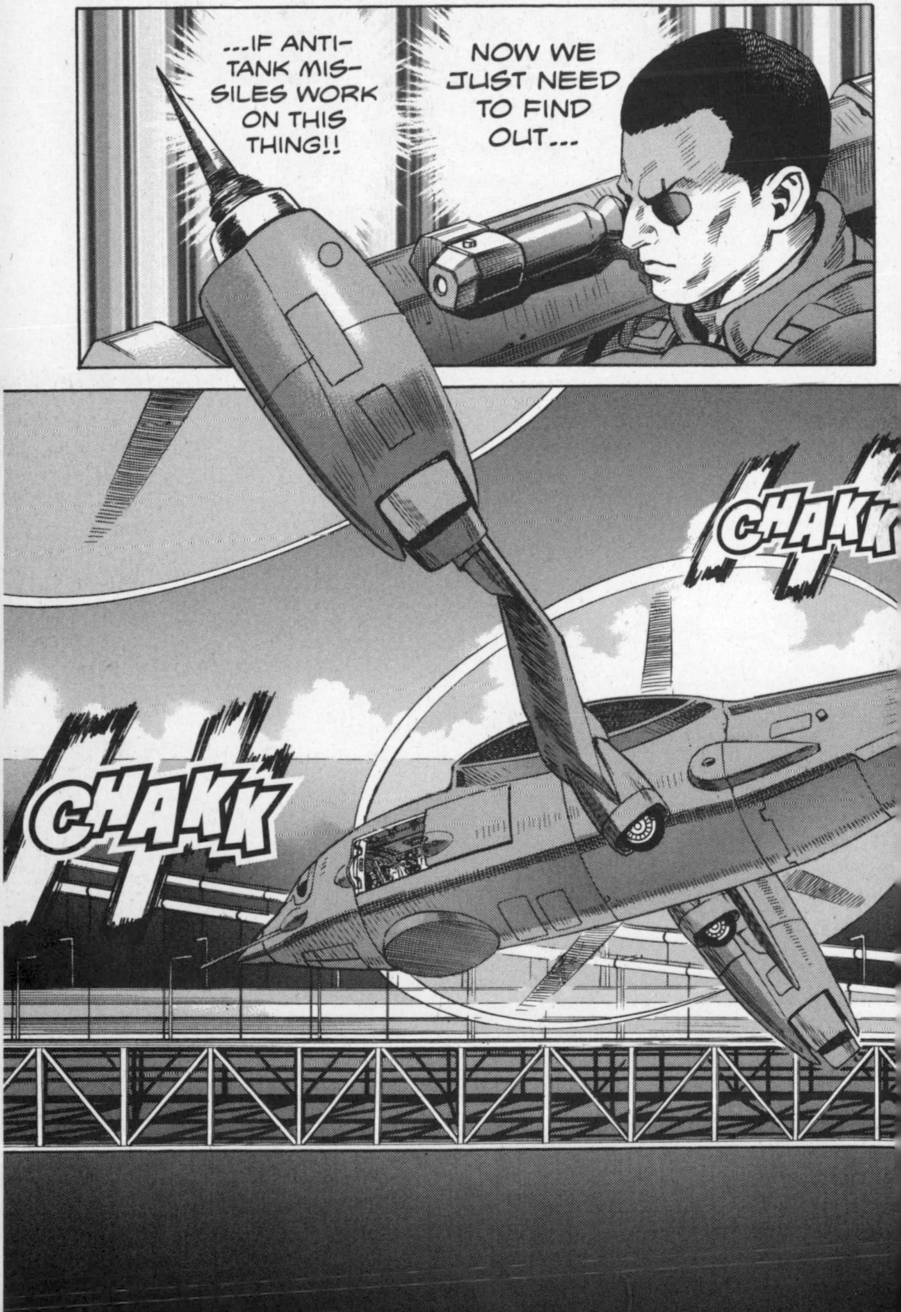
NOW WE JUST NEED TO FIND OUT...
...IF ANTI-TANK MIS-SILES WORK ON THIS THING!!
CHAKK
CHAKK

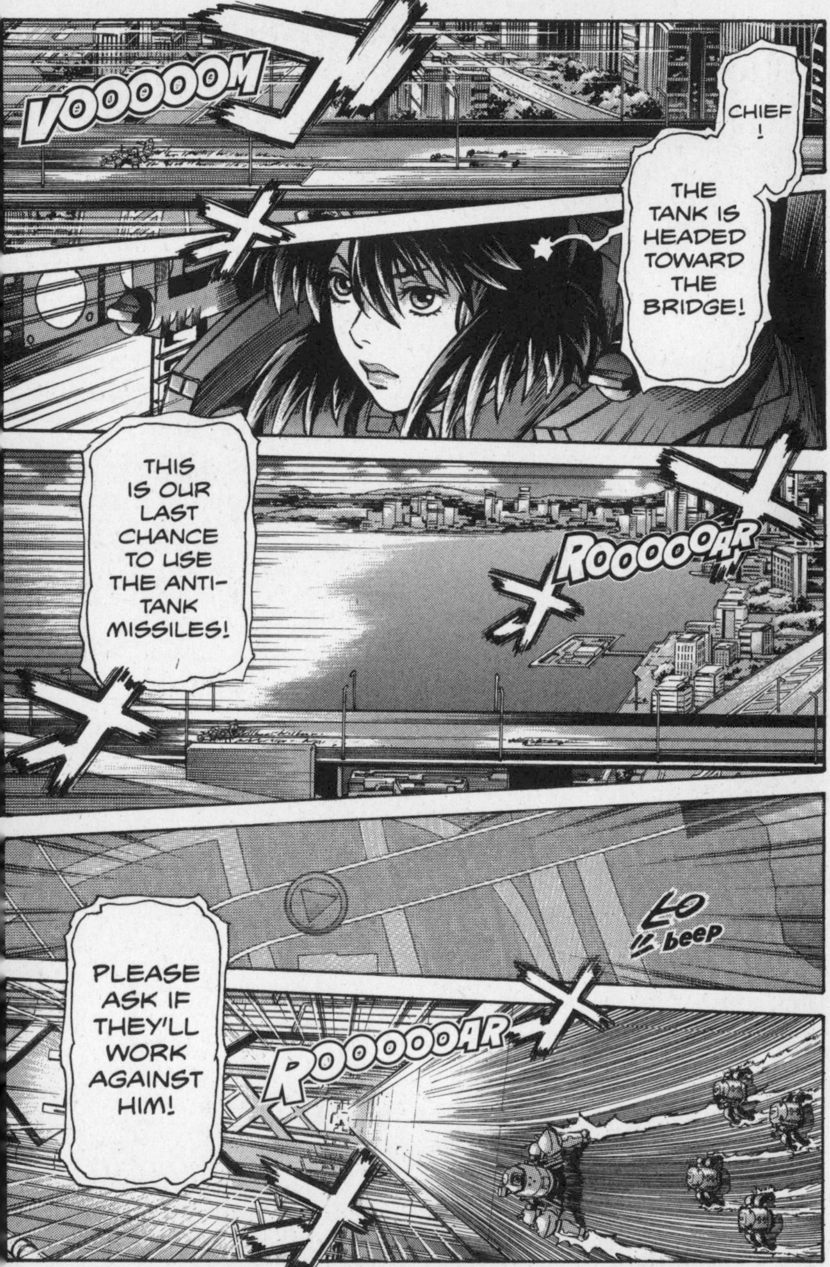
CHIEF! THE TANK IS HEADED TOWARD THE BRIDGE!
VOOOOOM
ROOOOOAR
THIS IS OUR LAST CHANCE TO USE THE ANTI-TANK MISSILES!
beep
PLEASE ASK IF THEY'LL WORK AGAINST HIM!
ROOOOOAR

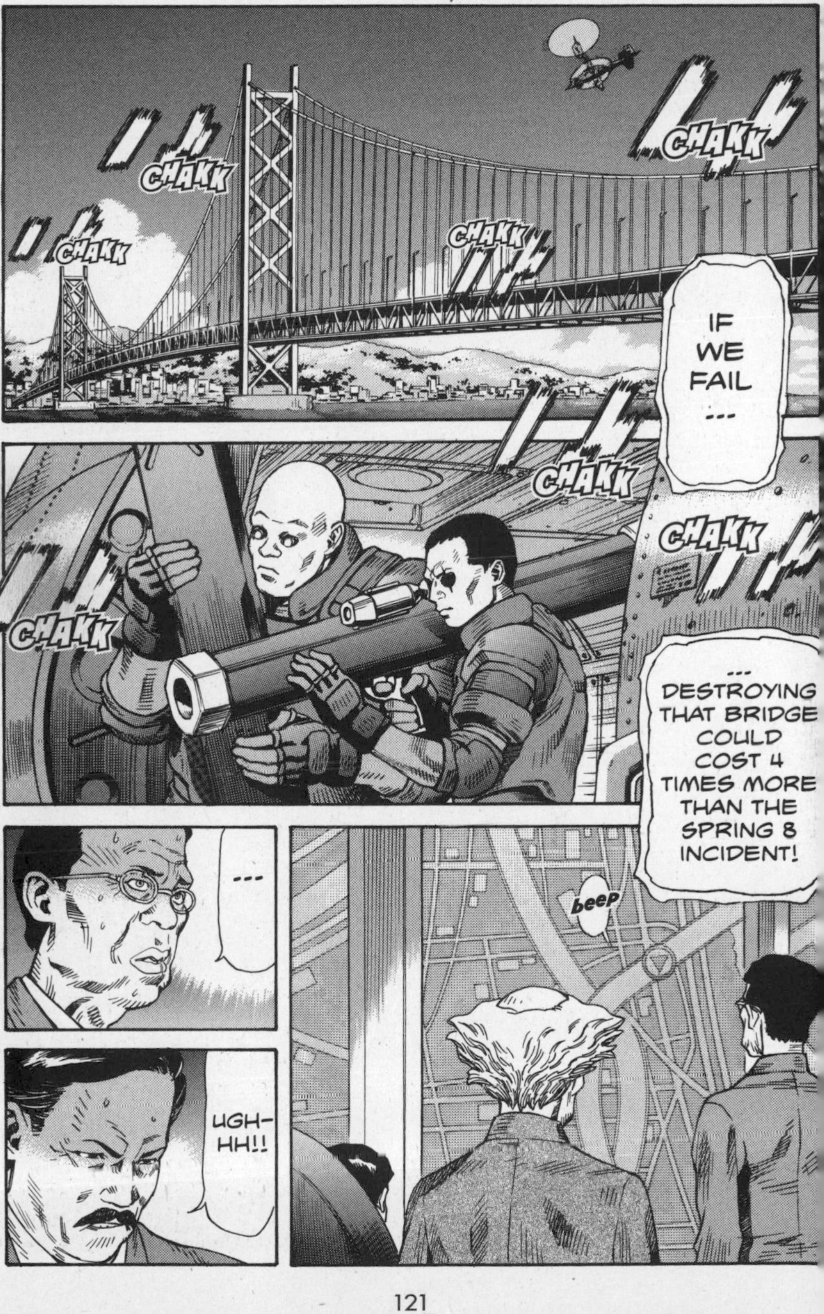
CHAKK
CHAKK
CHAKK
CHAKK
IF WE FAIL ---
CHAKK
CHAKK
CHAKK
--- DESTROYING THAT BRIDGE COULD COST 4 TIMES MORE THAN THE SPRING 8 INCIDENT!
beep

UGH-HH!!

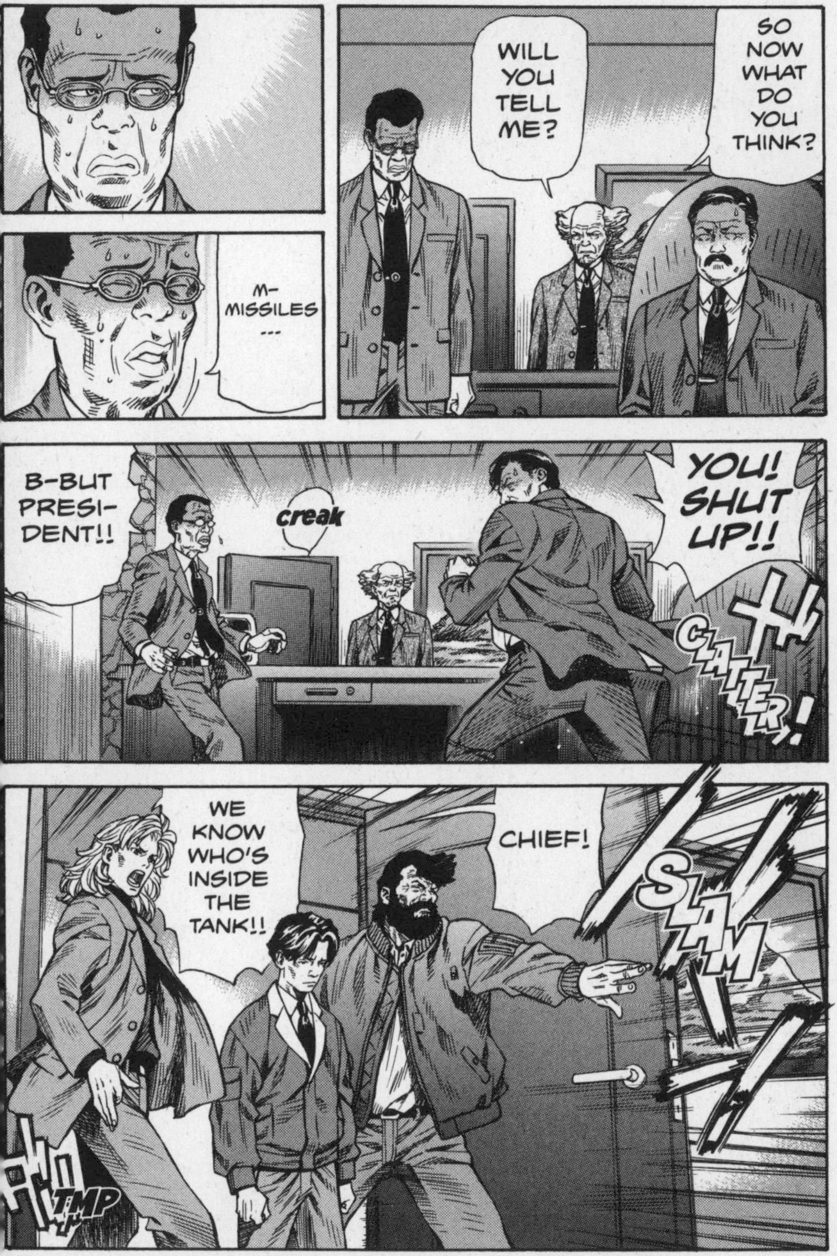
SO NOW WHAT DO YOU THINK?
WILL YOU TELL ME?
M-MISSILES ...
YOU! SHUT UP!!
CLATTER!
creak
B-BUT PRESI-DENT!!
SLAM
CHIEF!
WE KNOW WHO'S INSIDE THE TANK!!
TMP

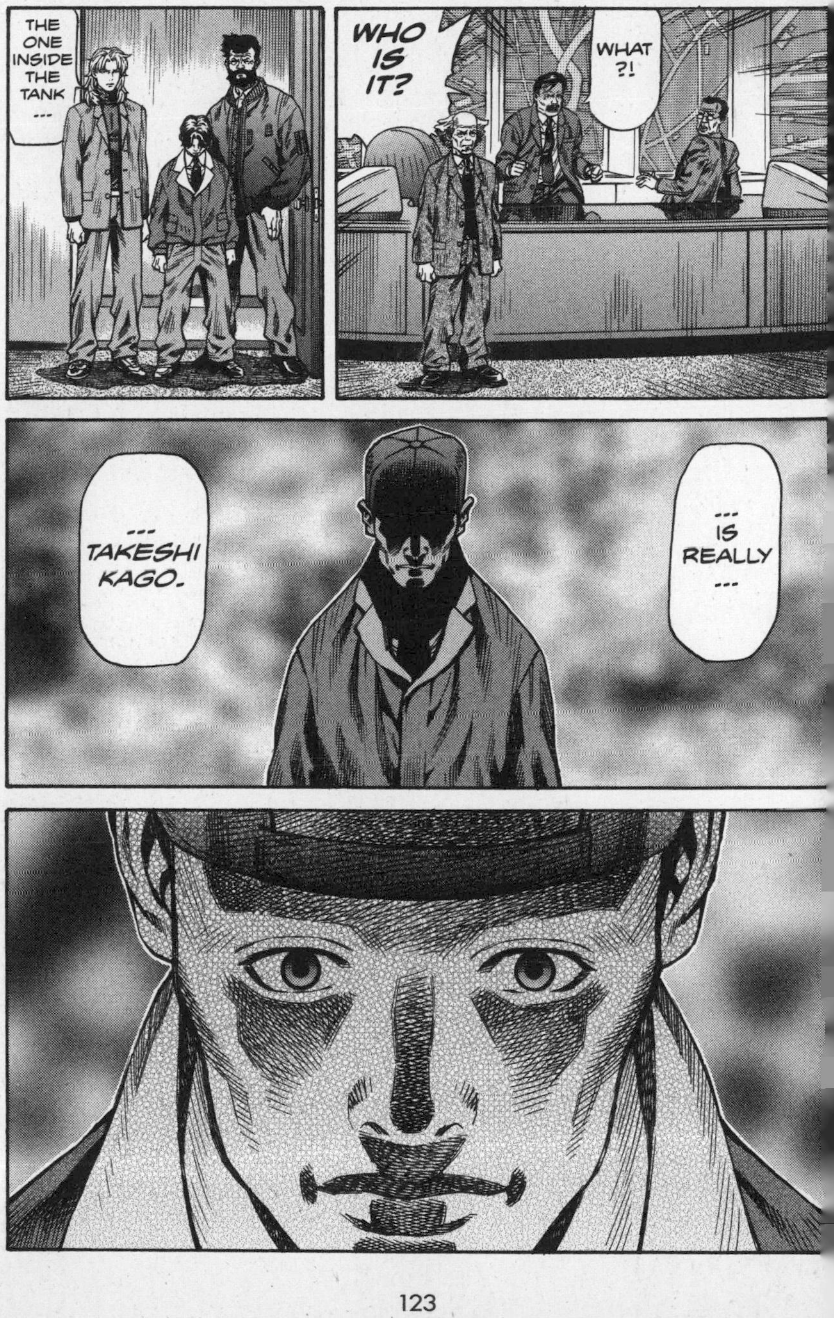
WHAT ?!
WHO IS IT?
THE ONE INSIDE THE TANK ---
--- IS REALLY ---
--- TAKESHI KAGO.

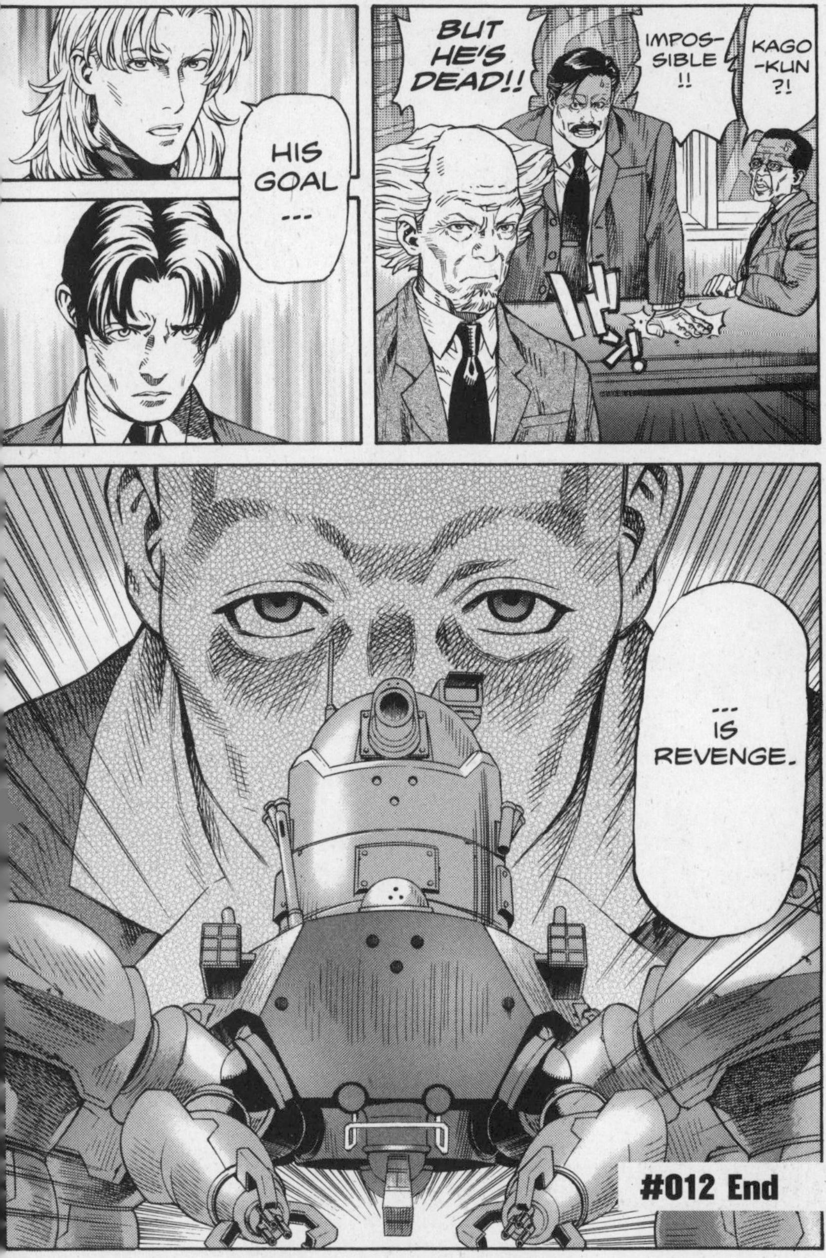
KAGO -KUN ?!
IMPOSSIBLE !!
BUT HE'S DEAD!!
HIS GOAL ---
--- IS REVENGE.
#012 End

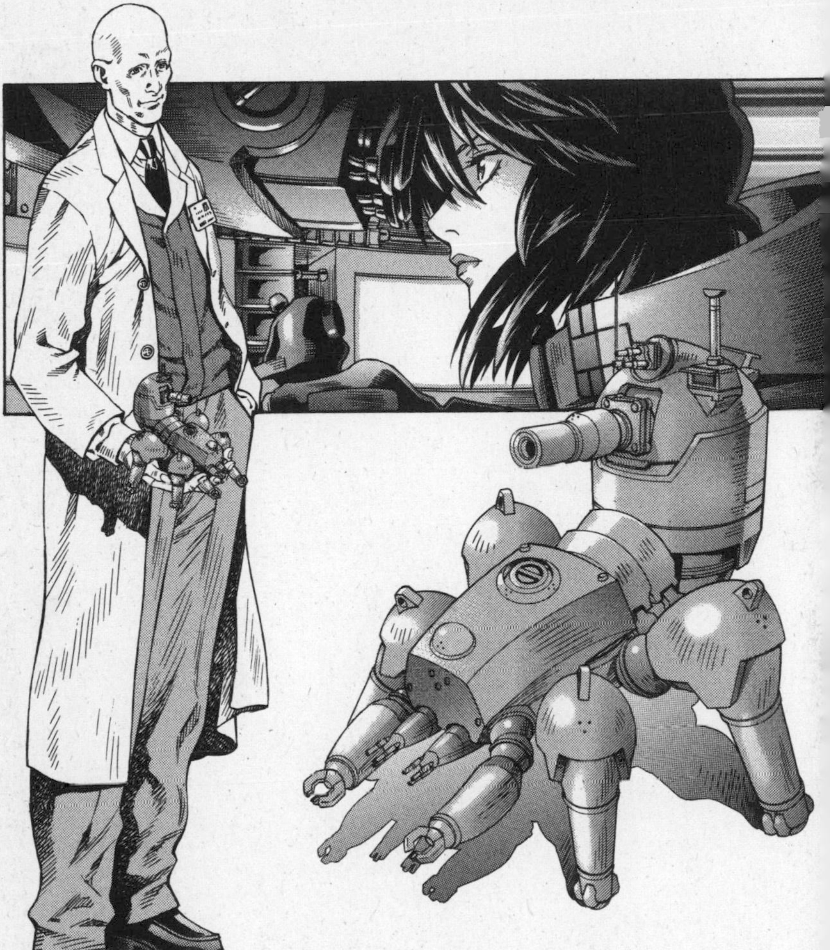

#015: Last Request

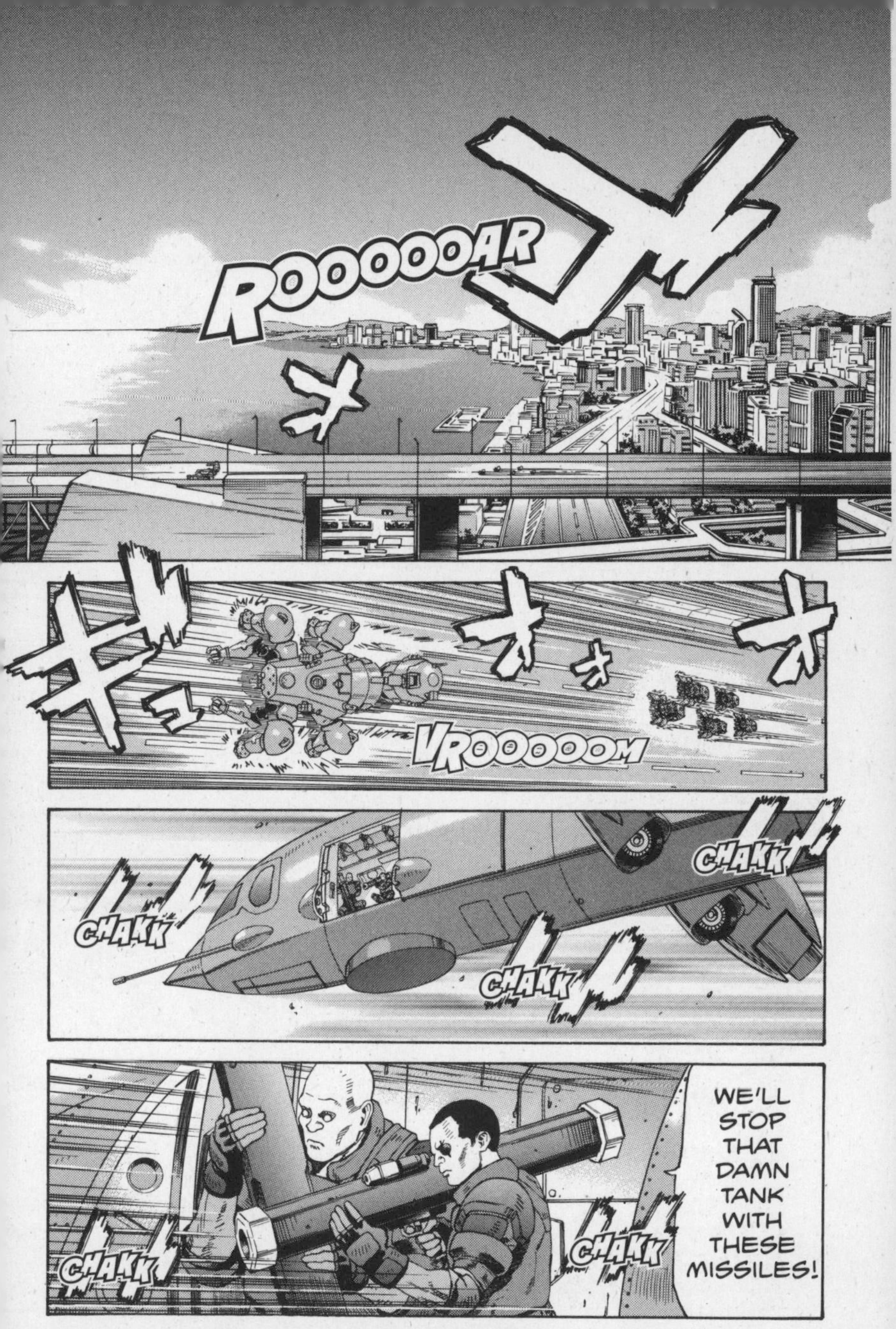
ROOOOOAR
VROOOOOM
CHAKK
CHAKK
CHAKK
WE'LL STOP THAT DAMN TANK WITH THESE MISSILES!
CHAKK
CHAKK

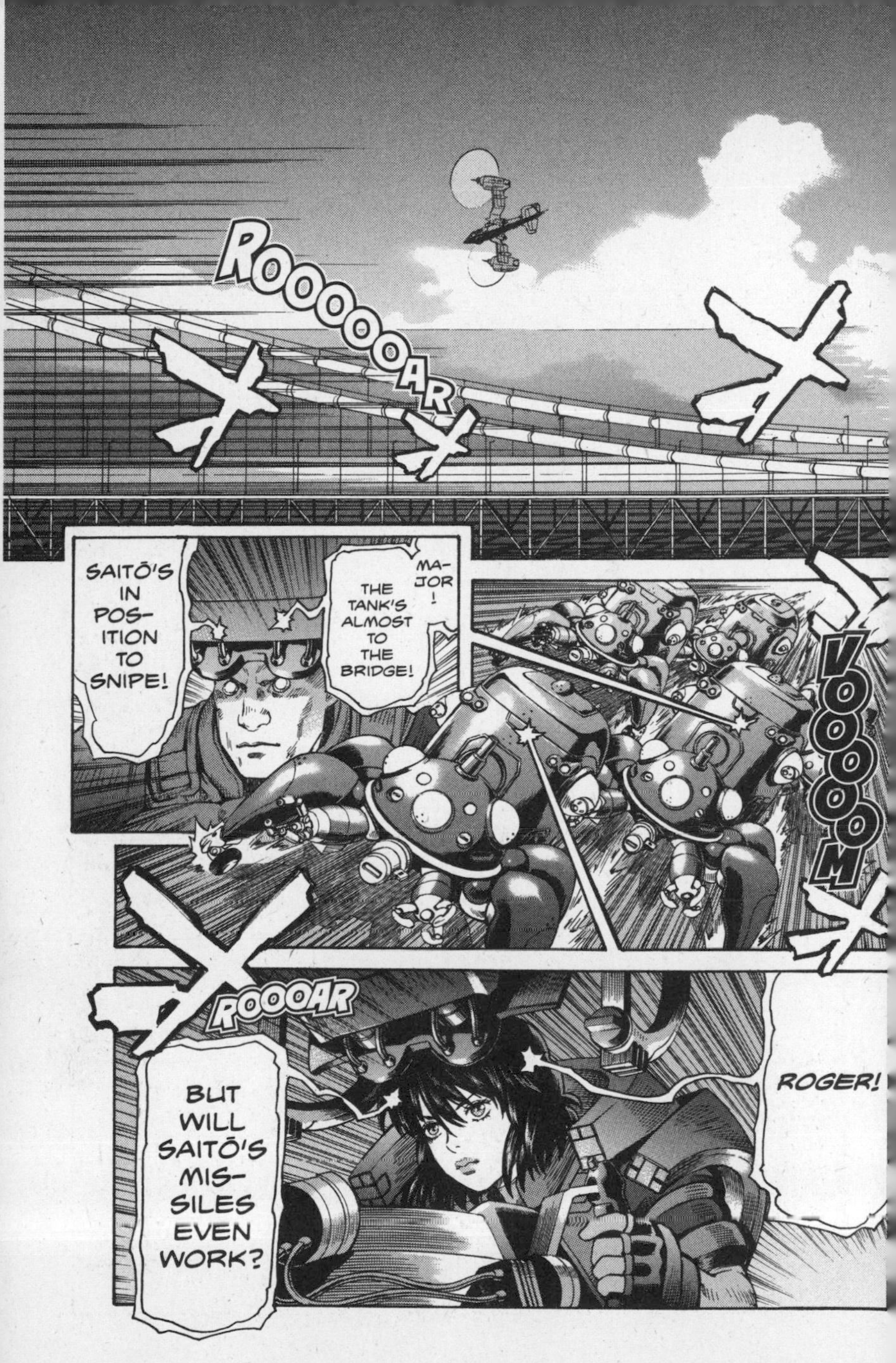
ROOOOOOAR
VOOOOOM
MAJOR!
THE TANK'S ALMOST TO THE BRIDGE!
SAITŌ'S IN POSITION TO SNIPE!
ROGER!
ROOOAR
BUT WILL SAITŌ'S MISSILES EVEN WORK?

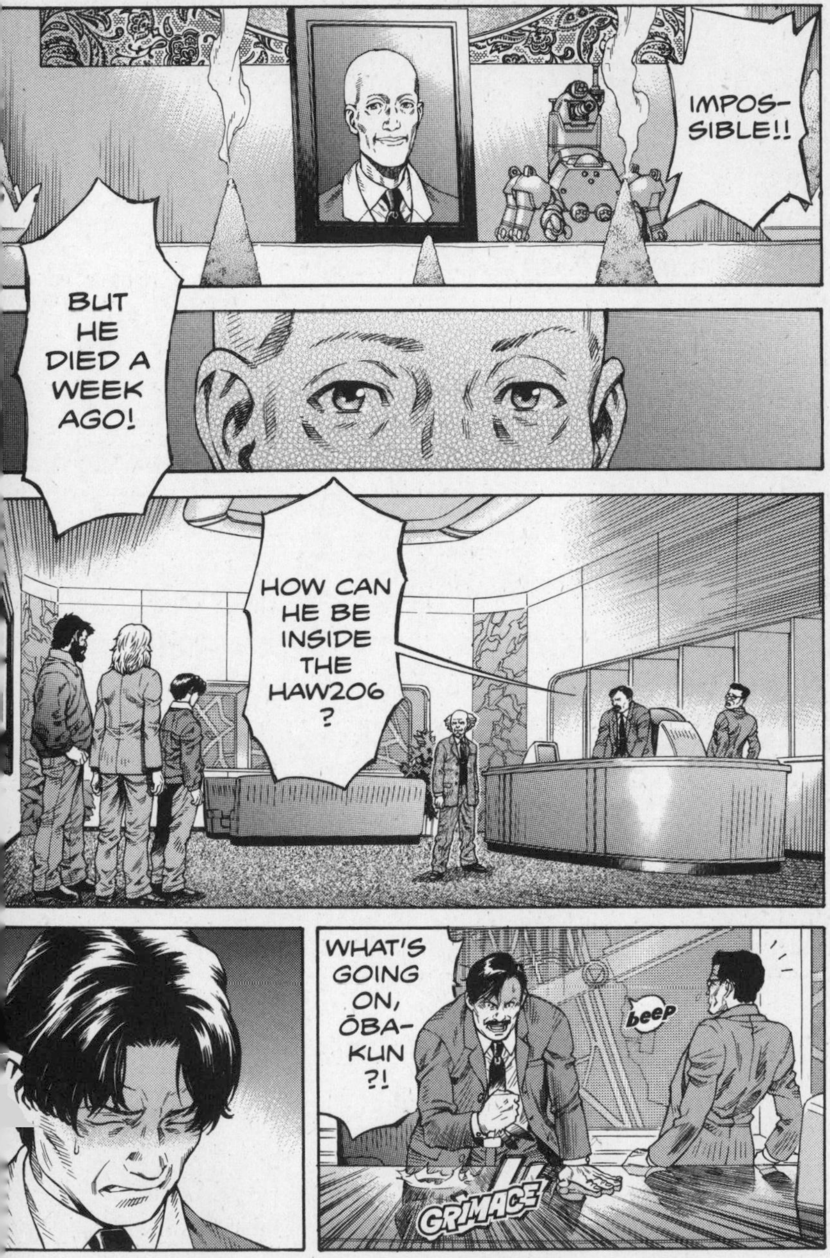
IMPOS-SIBLE!!
BUT HE DIED A WEEK AGO!
HOW CAN HE BE INSIDE THE HAW206?
WHAT'S GOING ON, ŌBA-KUN?!
beep
GRIMACE

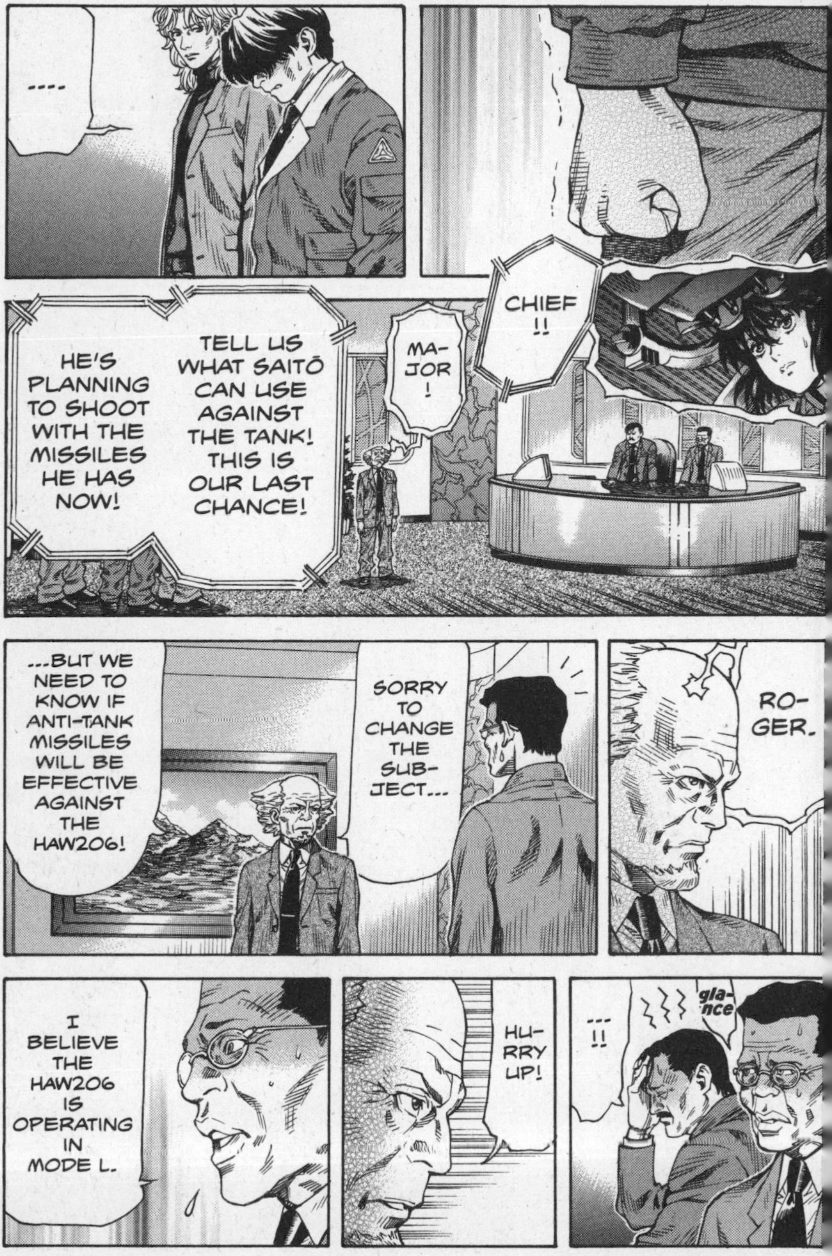

CHIEF !!
MA-JOR !
TELL US WHAT SAITŌ CAN USE AGAINST THE TANK! THIS IS OUR LAST CHANCE!
HE'S PLANNING TO SHOOT WITH THE MISSILES HE HAS NOW!
RO-GER.
SORRY TO CHANGE THE SUB-JECT...
...BUT WE NEED TO KNOW IF ANTI-TANK MISSILES WILL BE EFFECTIVE AGAINST THE HAW206!
gla-nce
---!!
HU-RRY UP!
I BELIEVE THE HAW206 IS OPERATING IN MODE L.

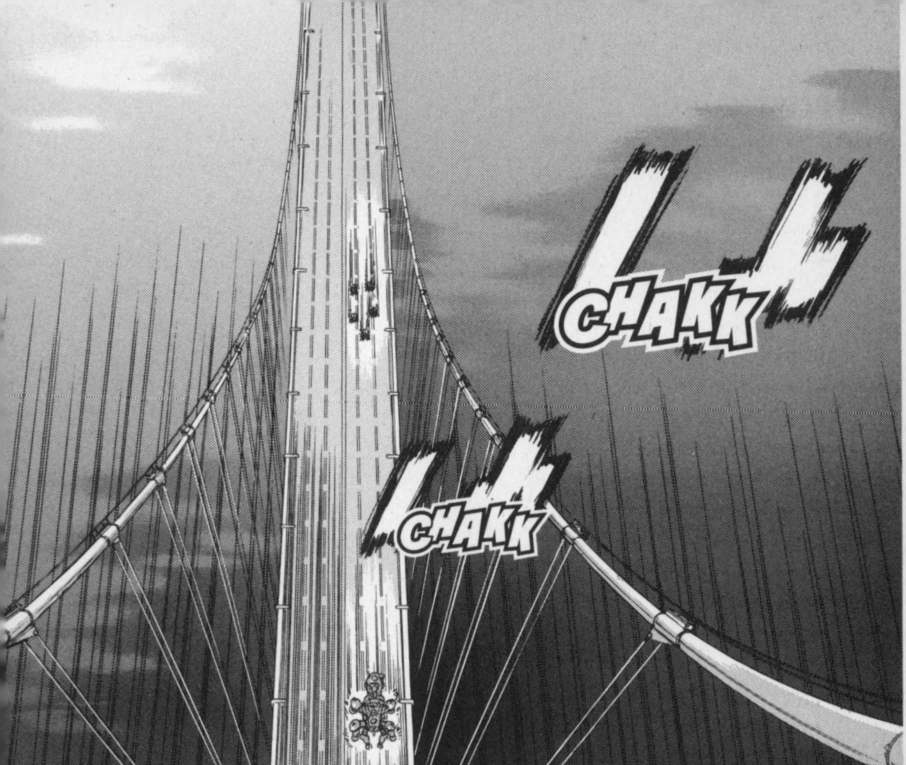
CHAKK
CHAKK

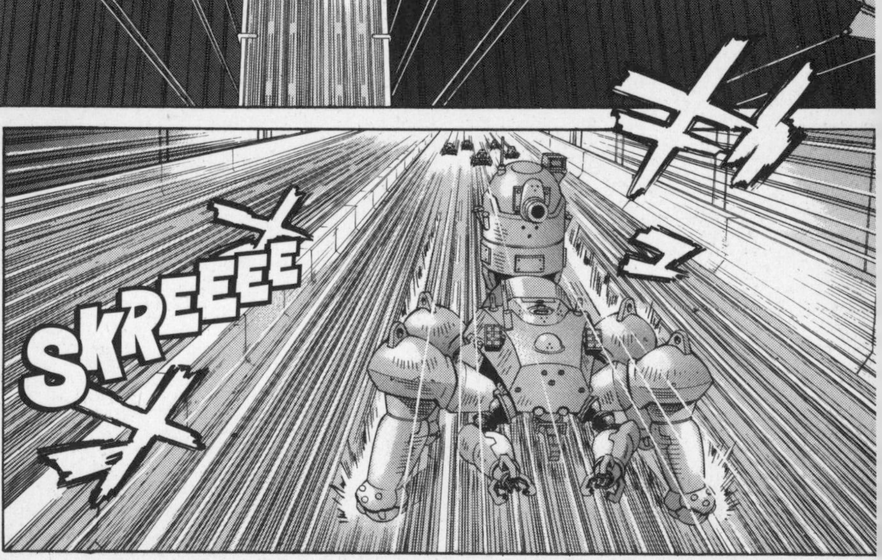
SKREEEEE

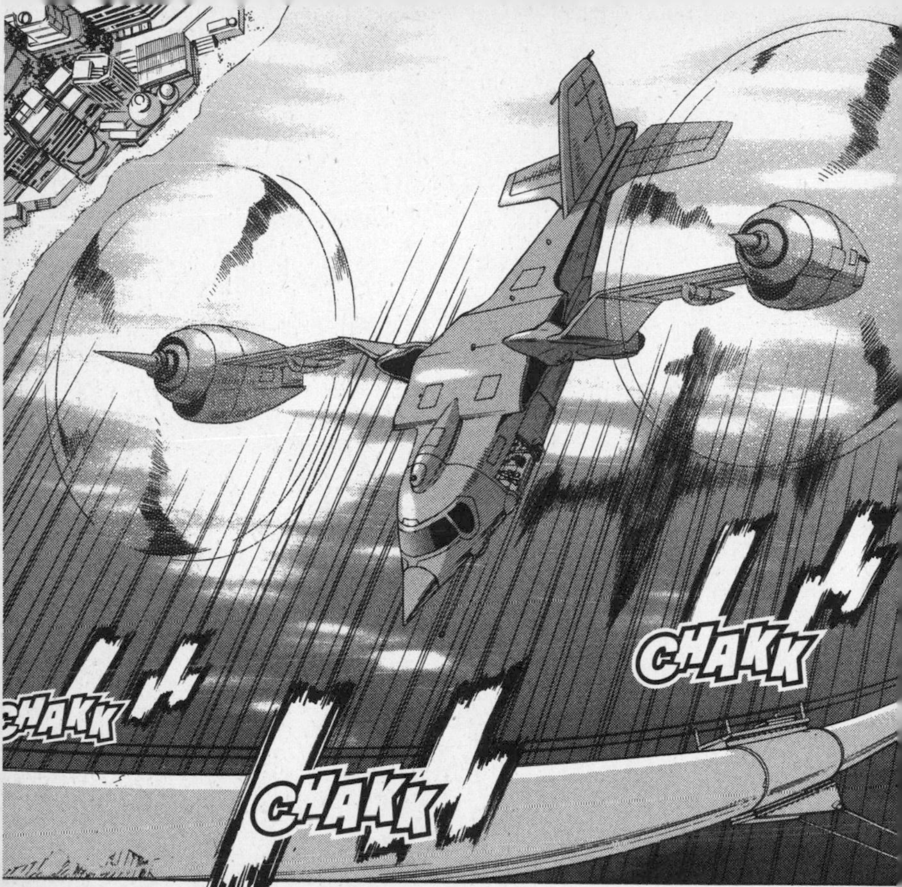
CHAKK
CHAKK
CHAKK
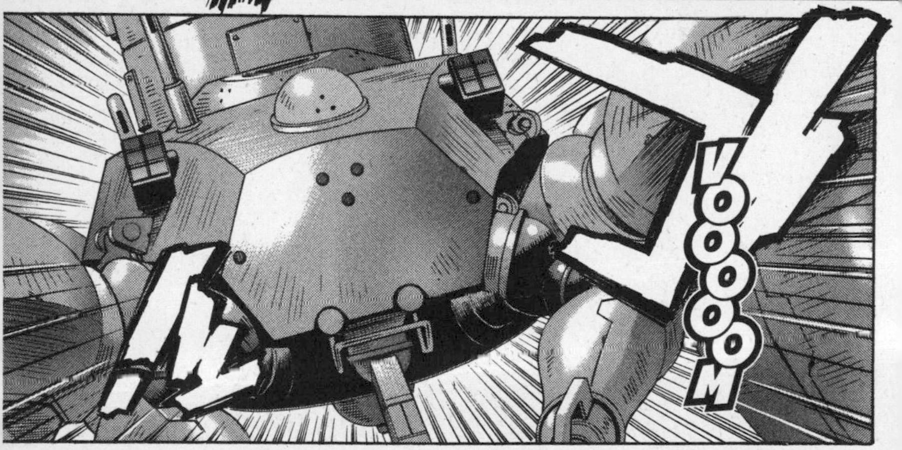
VOOOOOM

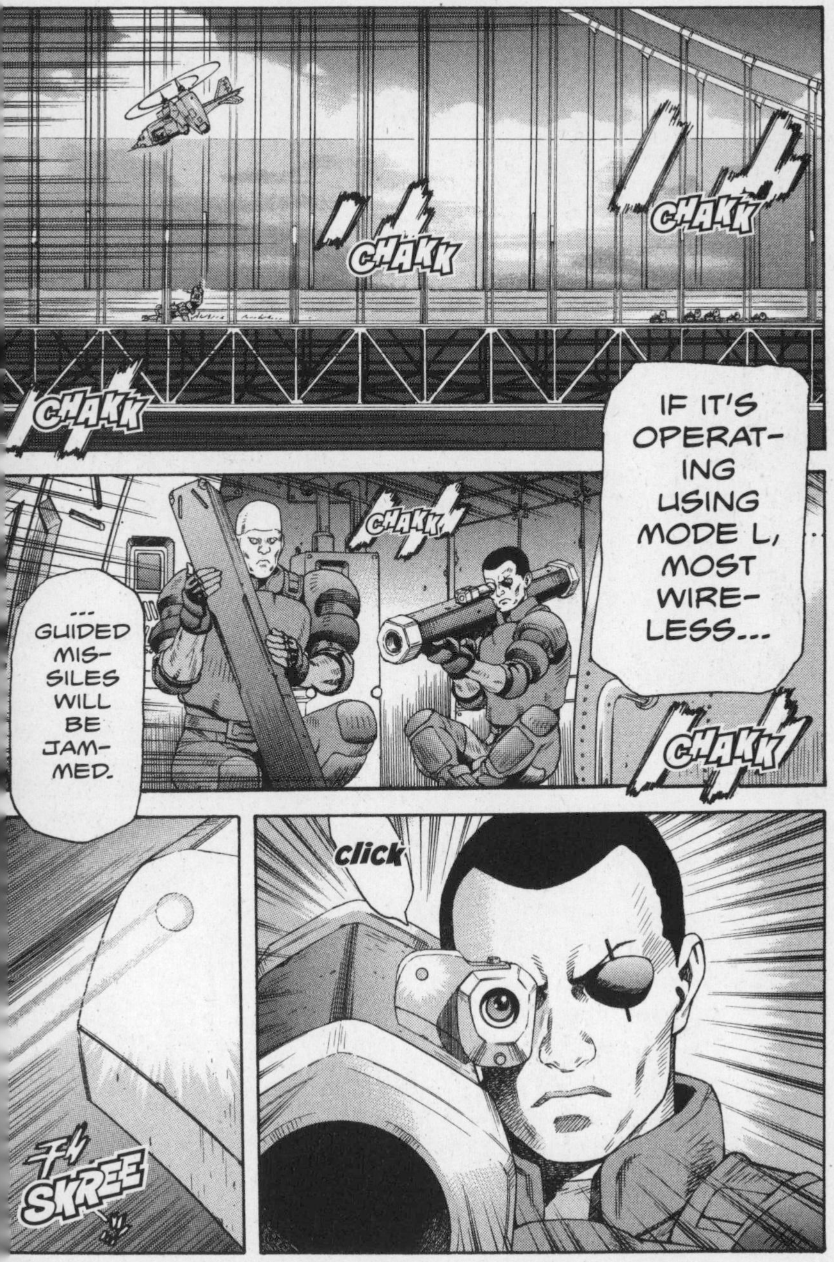
CHAKK
CHAKK
CHAKK
IF IT'S OPERATING USING MODE L, MOST WIRELESS...
CHAKK
CHAKK
...GUIDED MISSILES WILL BE JAMMED.
click
SKREE

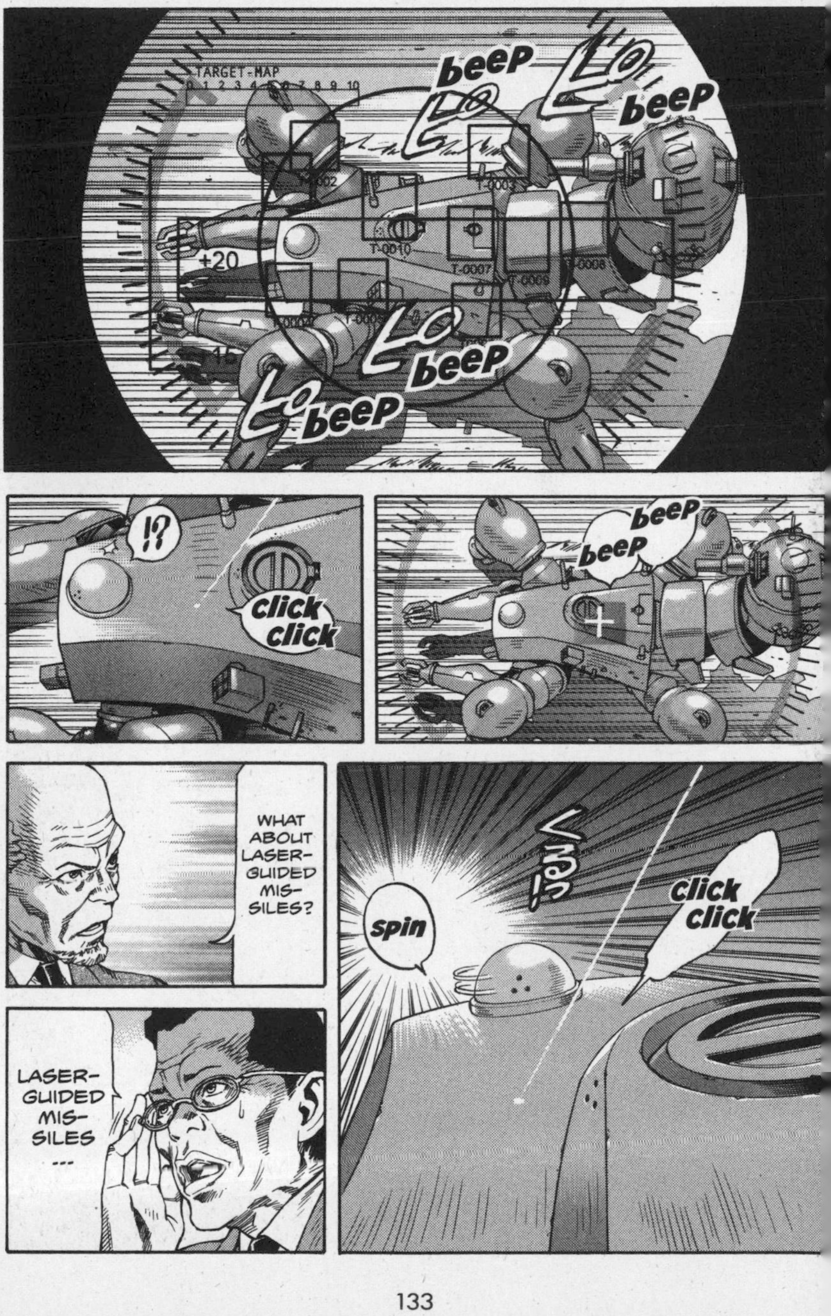
TARGET-MAP
0 1 2 3 4 5 6 7 8 9 10
beep
beep
beep
beep
+20
beep beep
!?
click click
spin
click click
WHAT ABOUT LASER-GUIDED MIS-SILES?
LASER-GUIDED MIS-SILES ...

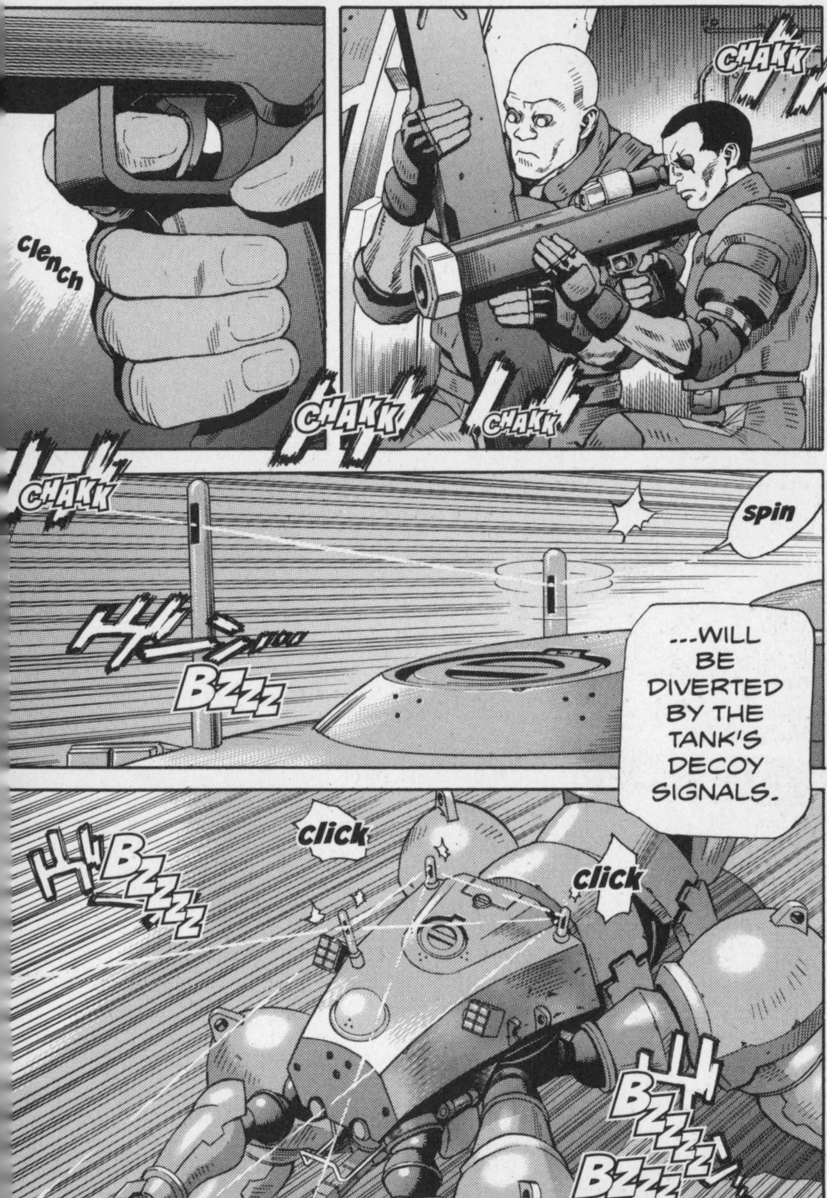
CHAKK
CHAKK
CHAKK
clench
CHAKK
spin
---WILL BE DIVERTED BY THE TANK'S DECOY SIGNALS.
BZZZ
click
click
BZZZZZ
BZZZZZ
BZZZ

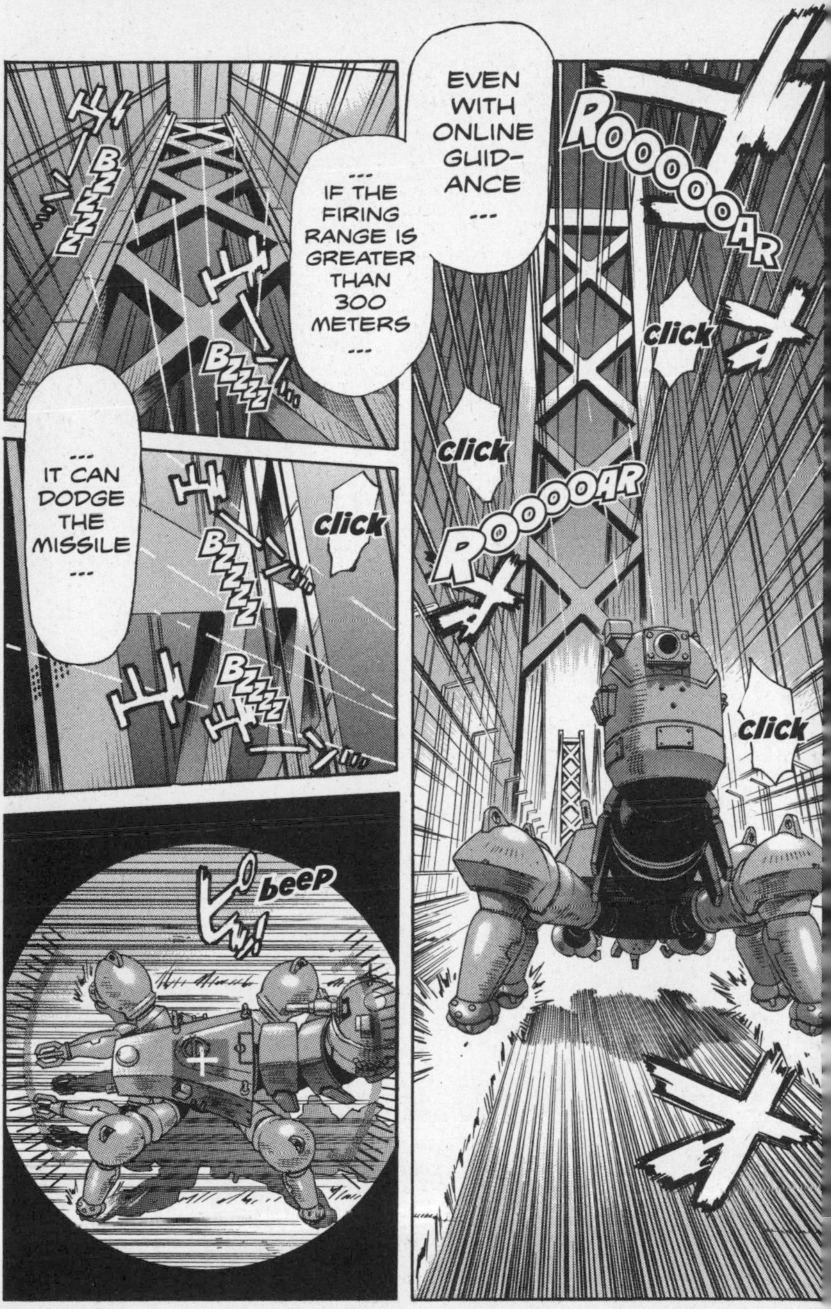
EVEN WITH ONLINE GUID-ANCE ---
ROOOOOOAR
click
click
ROOOOOAR
click
--- IF THE FIRING RANGE IS GREATER THAN 300 METERS ---
BZZZZ
BZZZZ
--- IT CAN DODGE THE MISSILE ---
click
BZZZZ
BZZZZ
beep

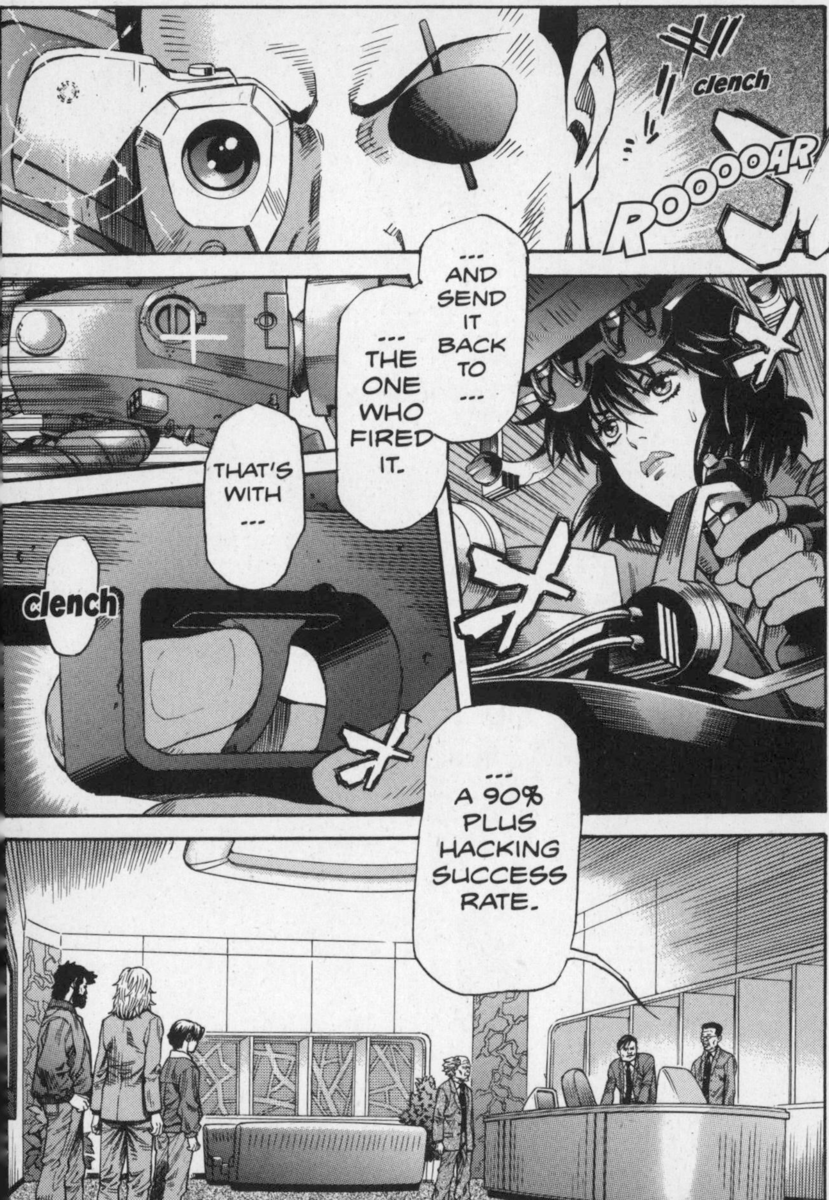
clench
ROOOOAR
... AND SEND IT BACK TO ...
... THE ONE WHO FIRED IT.
THAT'S WITH ...
clench
... A 90% PLUS HACKING SUCCESS RATE.

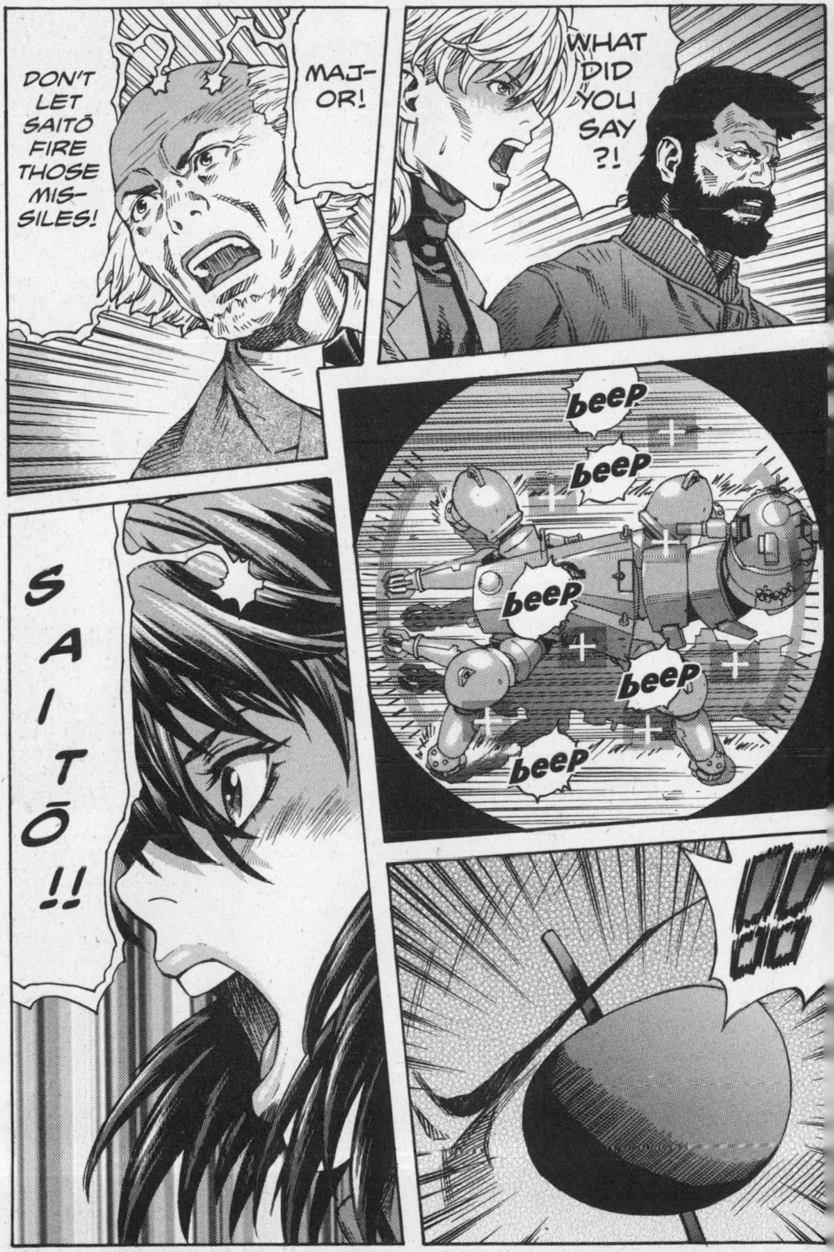
WHAT DID YOU SAY ?!
MAJ-OR!
DON'T LET SAITŌ FIRE THOSE MIS-SILES!
beep
beep
beep
beep
beep
SAITŌ!!

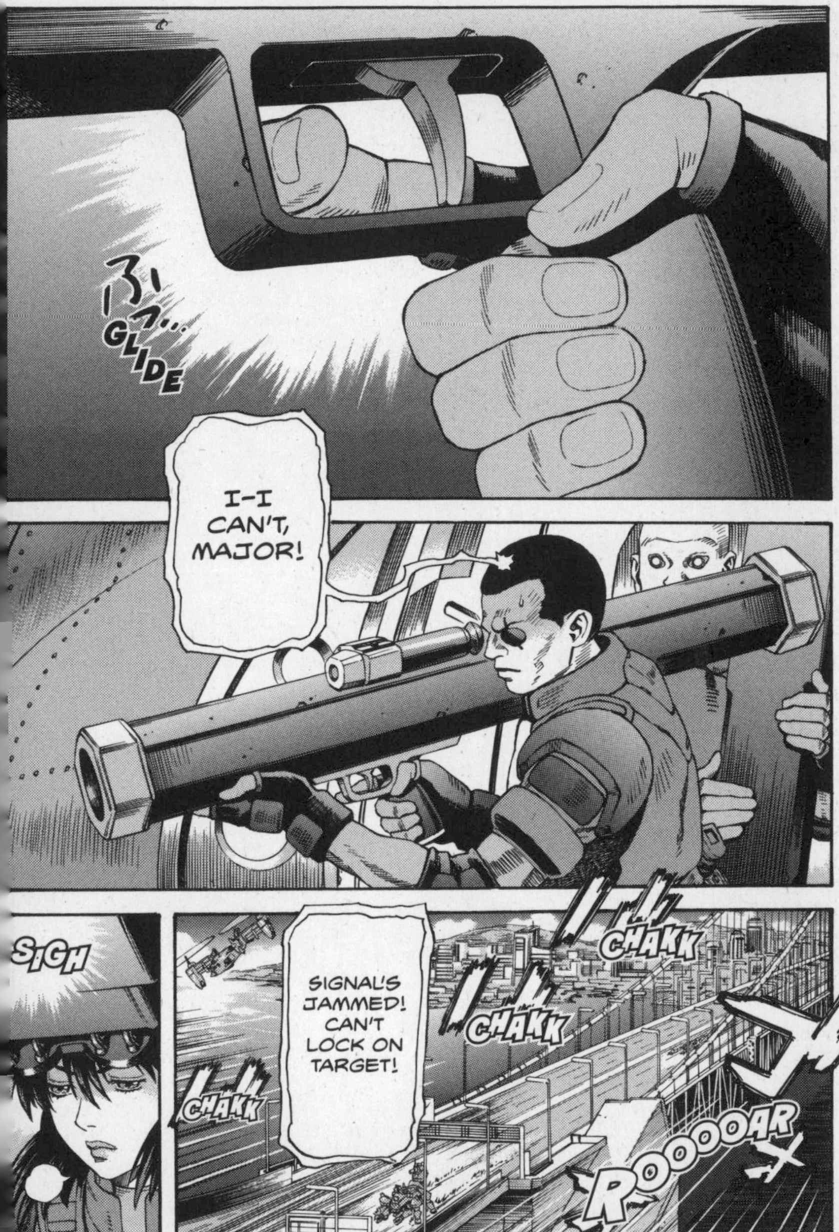
ふー…
GLIDE
I-I CAN'T, MAJOR!
SIGNAL'S JAMMED! CAN'T LOCK ON TARGET!
CHAKK
CHAKK
CHAKK
ROOOOOAR
SIGH

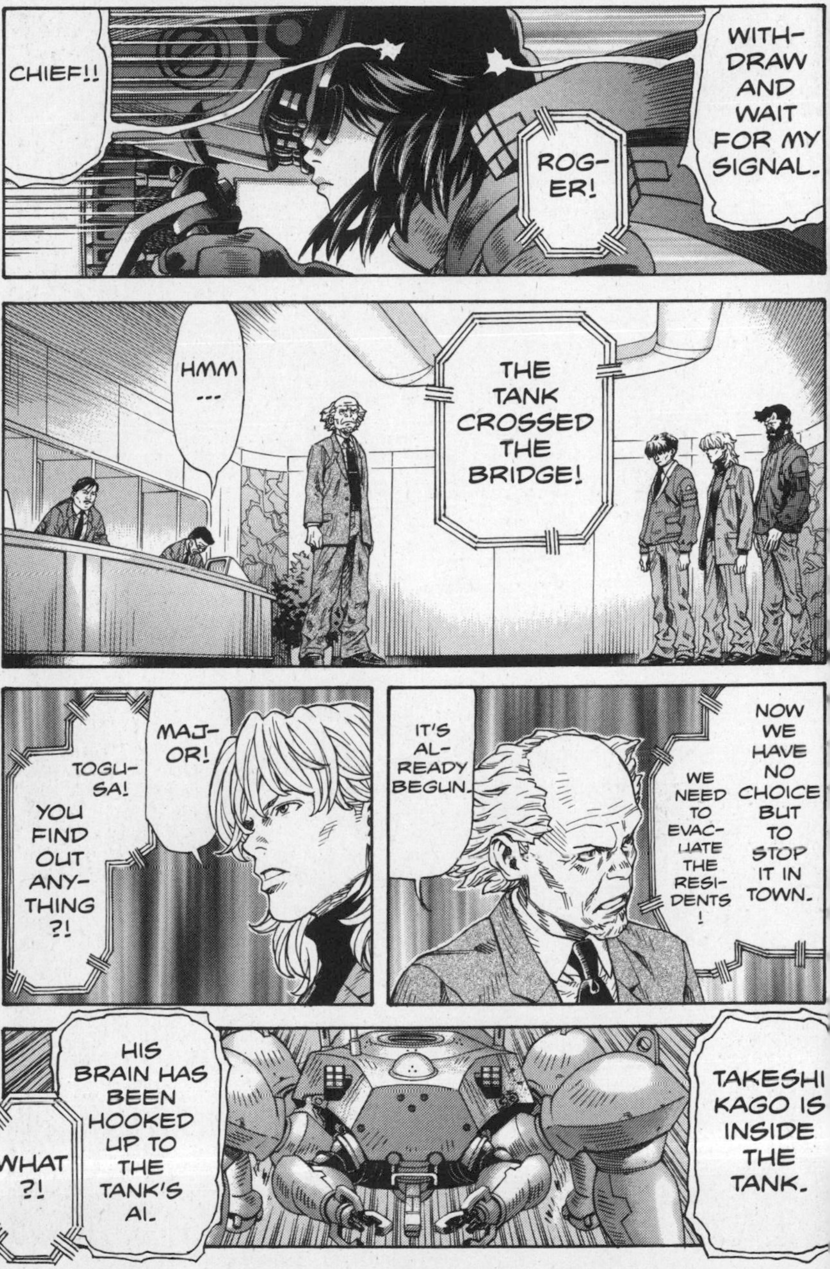
WITHDRAW AND WAIT FOR MY SIGNAL.
ROGER!
CHIEF!!
THE TANK CROSSED THE BRIDGE!
HMM ---
NOW WE HAVE NO CHOICE BUT TO STOP IT IN TOWN.
WE NEED TO EVACUATE THE RESIDENTS!
IT'S ALREADY BEGUN.
MAJOR!
TOGUSA! YOU FIND OUT ANYTHING?!
TAKESHI KAGO IS INSIDE THE TANK.
HIS BRAIN HAS BEEN HOOKED UP TO THE TANK'S AI.
WHAT?!

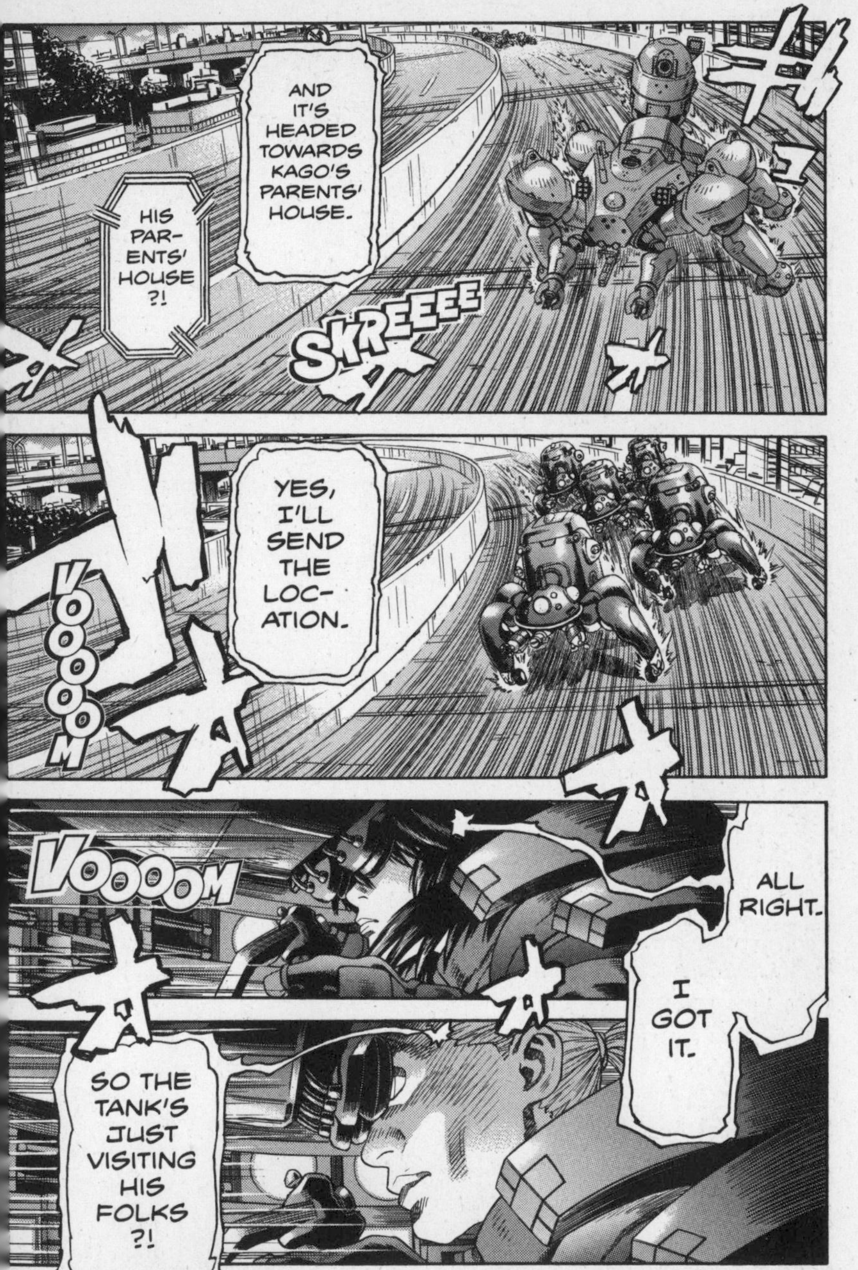
AND IT'S HEADED TOWARDS KAGO'S PARENTS' HOUSE.
HIS PAR-ENTS' HOUSE?!
SKREEEEE
YES, I'LL SEND THE LOC-ATION.
VOOOOOM
ALL RIGHT.
I GOT IT.
VOOOOOM
SO THE TANK'S JUST VISITING HIS FOLKS?!

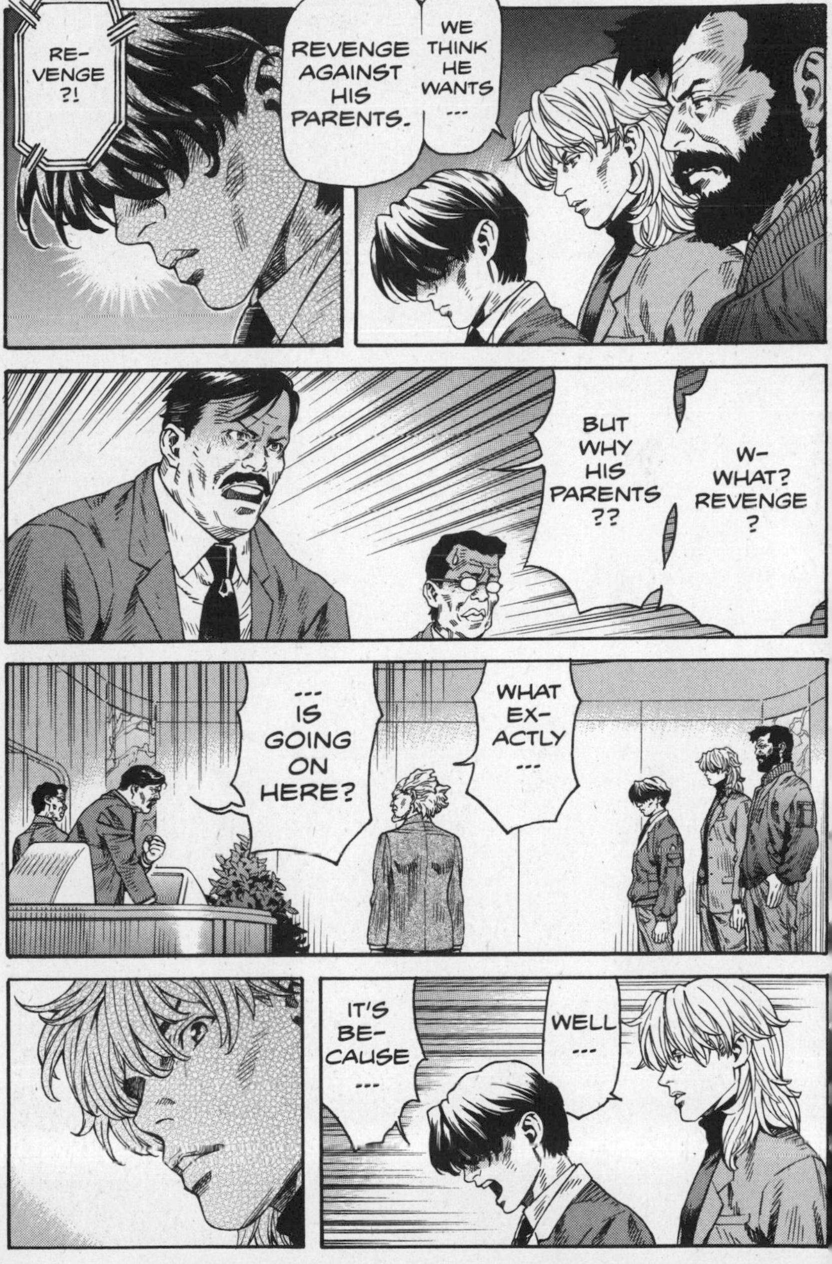
WE THINK HE WANTS ---
REVENGE AGAINST HIS PARENTS.
RE-VENGE?!
W-WHAT? REVENGE?
BUT WHY HIS PARENTS??
WHAT EX-ACTLY ---
--- IS GOING ON HERE?
WELL ---
IT'S BE-CAUSE ---

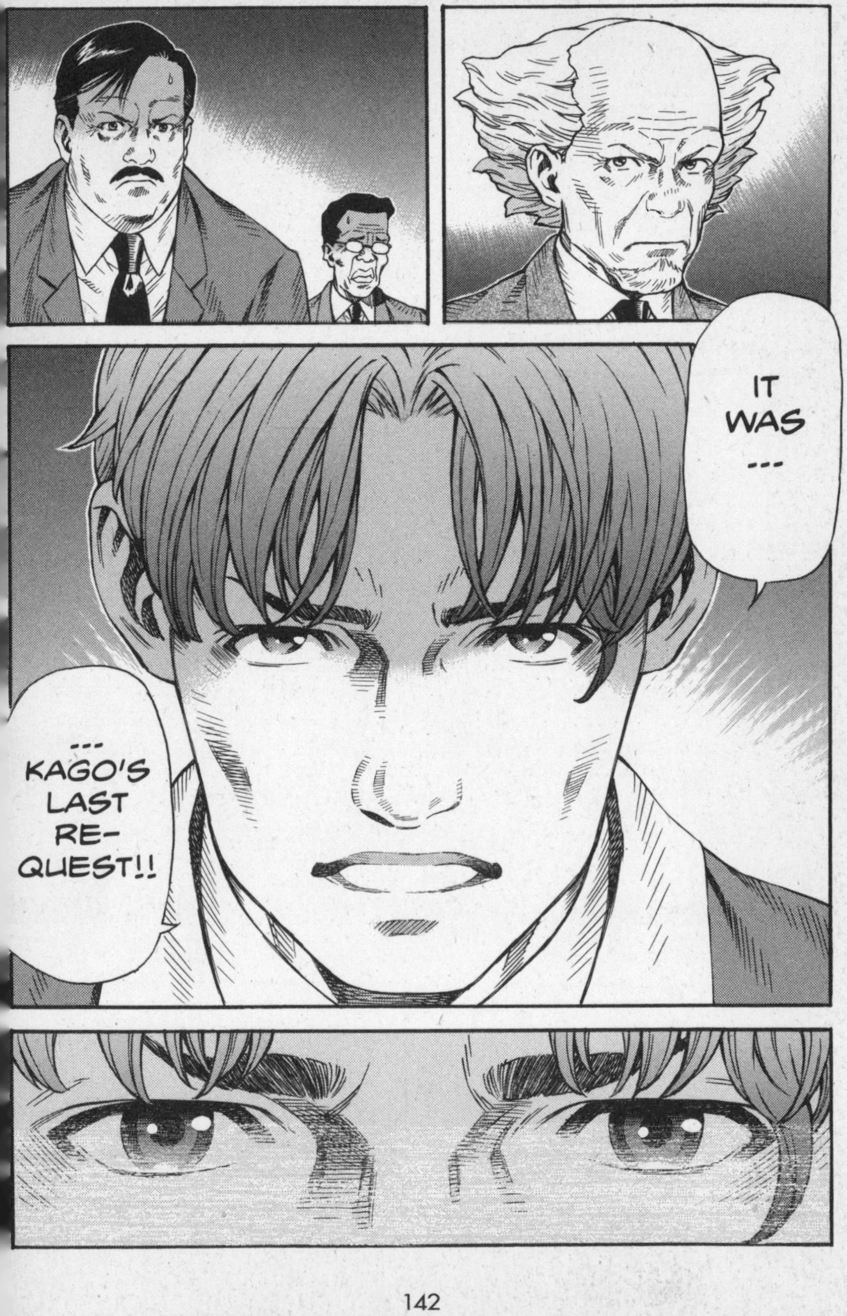
IT WAS ---
--- KAGO'S LAST RE-QUEST!!

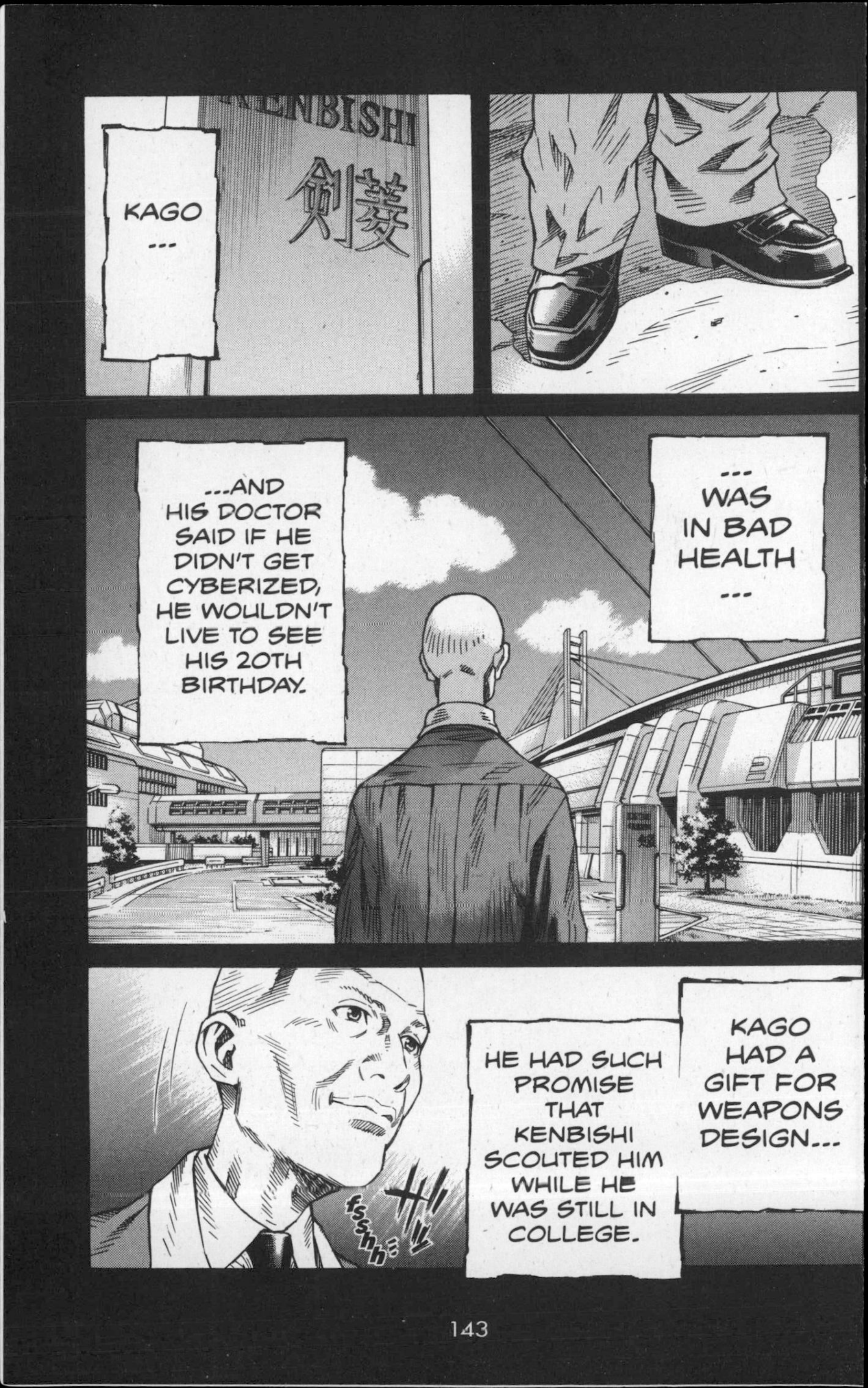
剣菱
KAGO ---
--- WAS IN BAD HEALTH ---
---AND HIS DOCTOR SAID IF HE DIDN'T GET CYBERIZED, HE WOULDN'T LIVE TO SEE HIS 20TH BIRTHDAY.
KAGO HAD A GIFT FOR WEAPONS DESIGN...
HE HAD SUCH PROMISE THAT KENBISHI SCOUTED HIM WHILE HE WAS STILL IN COLLEGE.
fsshh

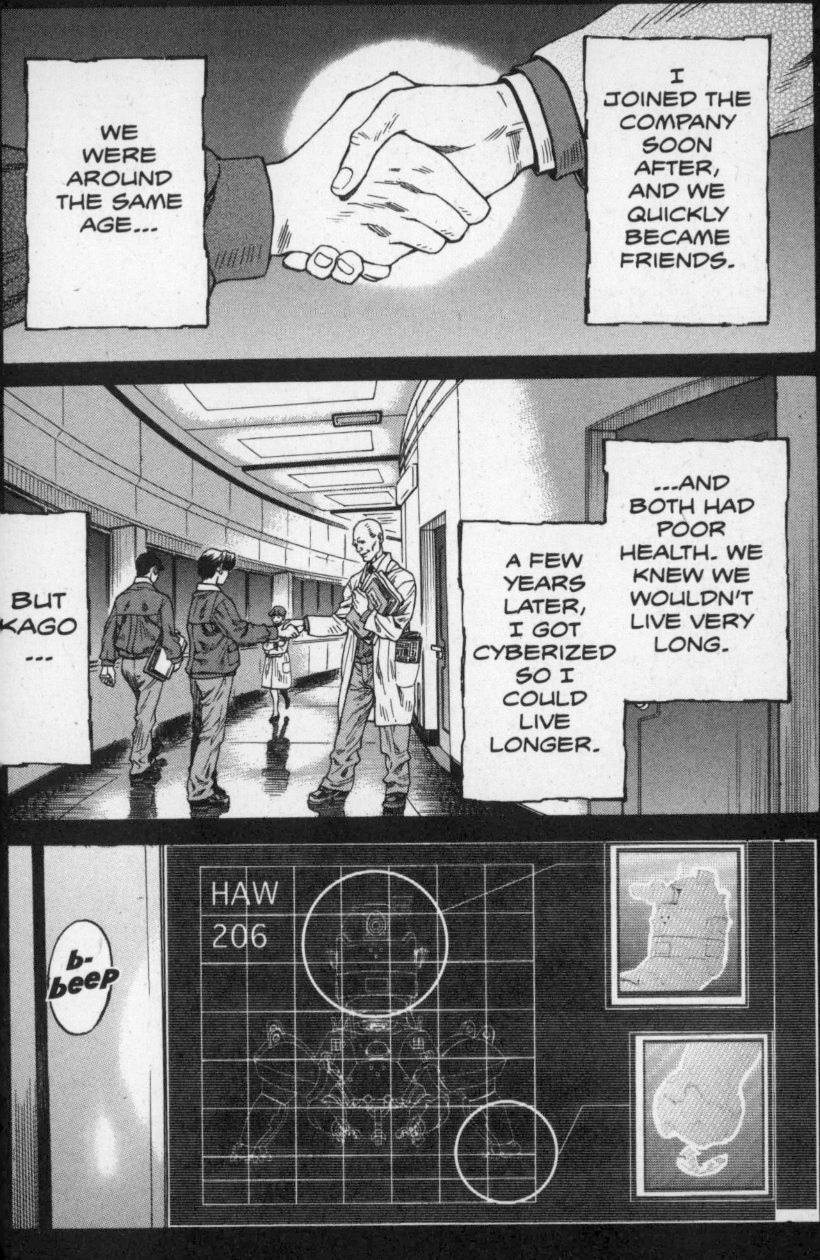
I JOINED THE COMPANY SOON AFTER, AND WE QUICKLY BECAME FRIENDS.
WE WERE AROUND THE SAME AGE...
...AND BOTH HAD POOR HEALTH. WE KNEW WE WOULDN'T LIVE VERY LONG.
A FEW YEARS LATER, I GOT CYBERIZED SO I COULD LIVE LONGER.
BUT KAGO...
HAW 206
b-beep

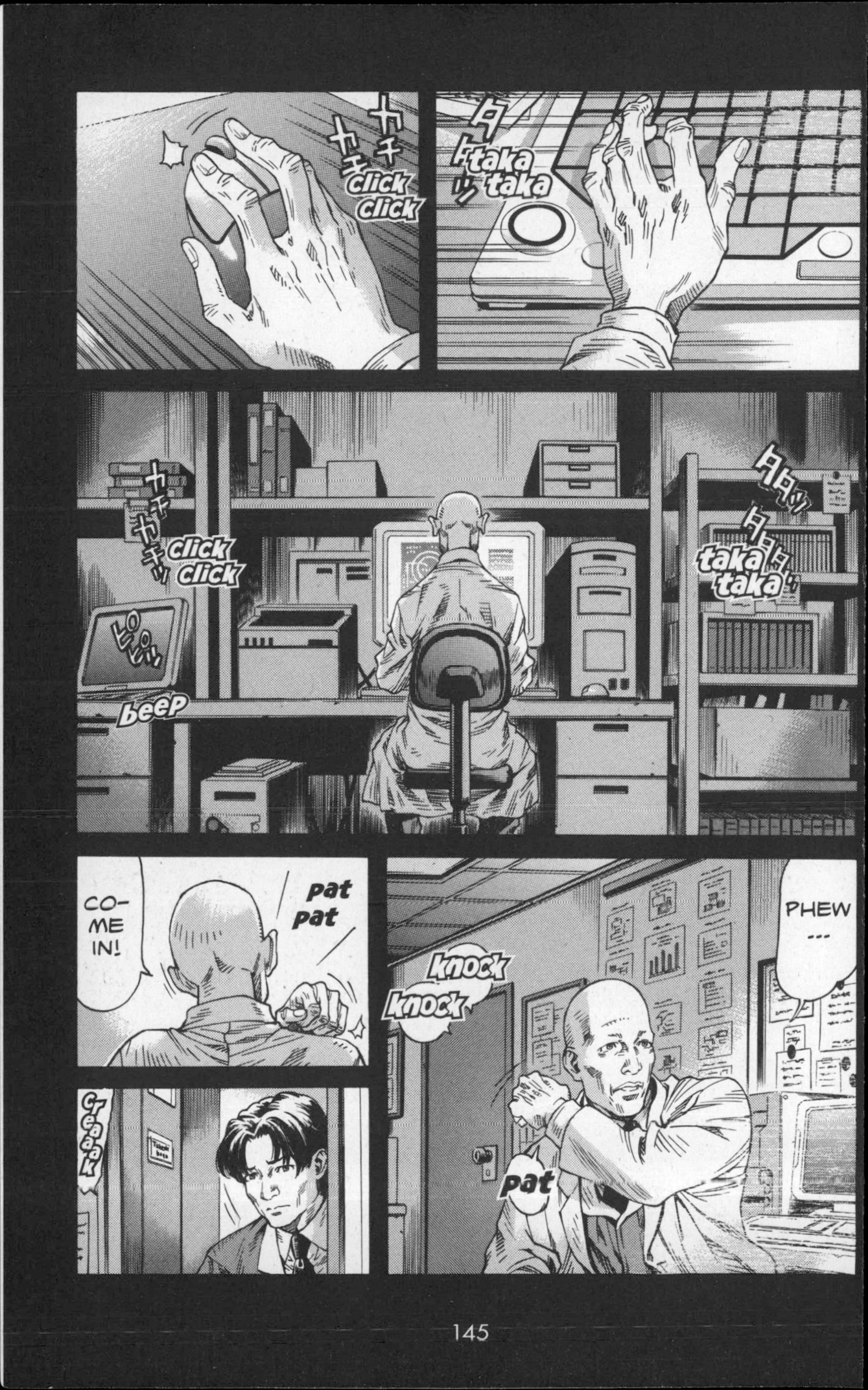

taka
taka
click
click
taka
taka
click
click
beep
PHEW ---
knock
knock
pat
CO-ME IN!
pat
pat
creaak

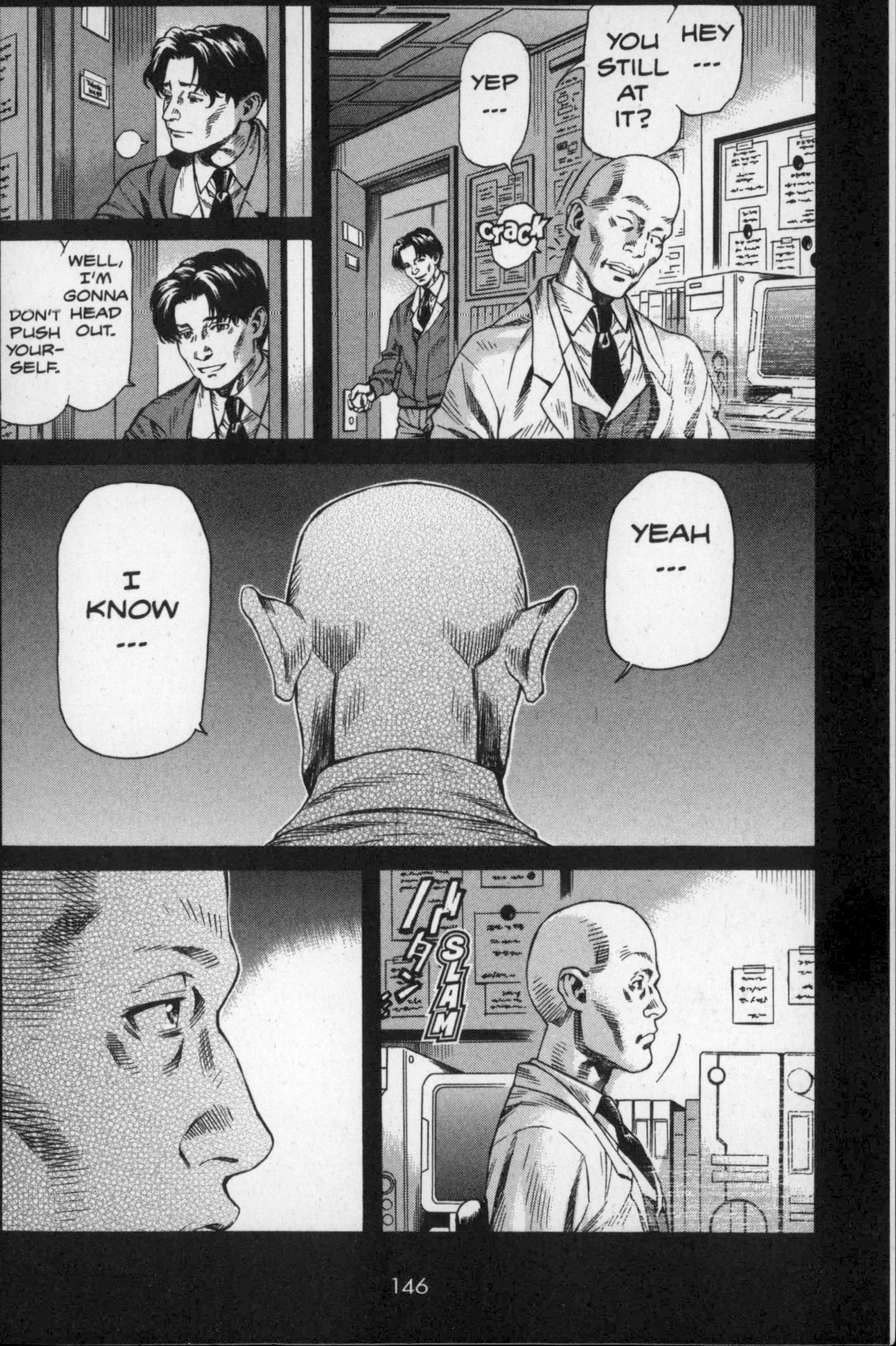
HEY ---
YOU STILL AT IT?
YEP ---
crack
WELL, I'M GONNA HEAD OUT.
DON'T PUSH YOURSELF.
YEAH ---
I KNOW ---
SLAM

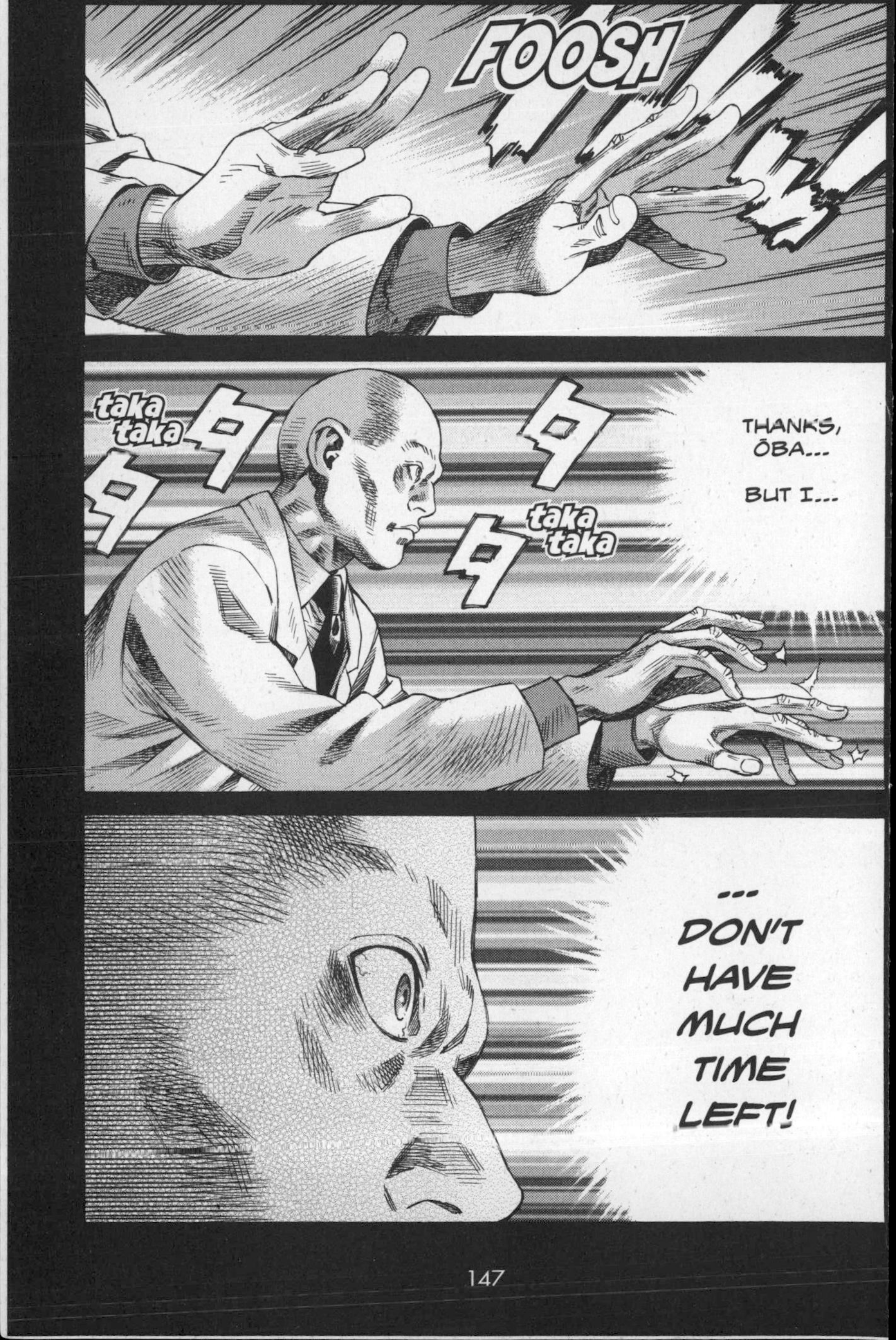
FOOSH
THANKS, ŌBA...
BUT I...
taka taka
taka taka
... DON'T HAVE MUCH TIME LEFT!

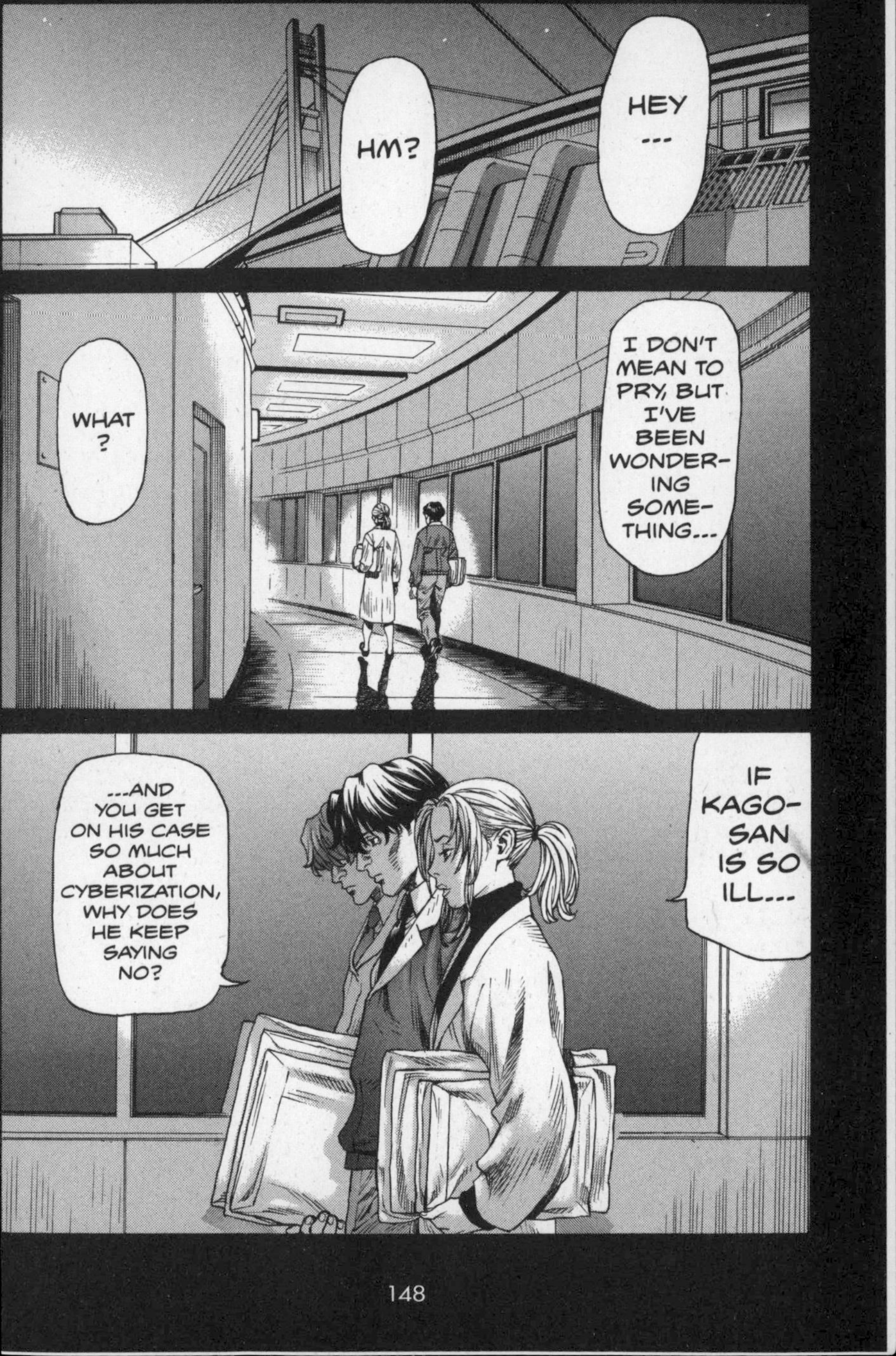
HEY ---
HM?
I DON'T MEAN TO PRY, BUT I'VE BEEN WONDER-ING SOME-THING...
WHAT?
IF KAGO-SAN IS SO ILL...
...AND YOU GET ON HIS CASE SO MUCH ABOUT CYBERIZATION, WHY DOES HE KEEP SAYING NO?

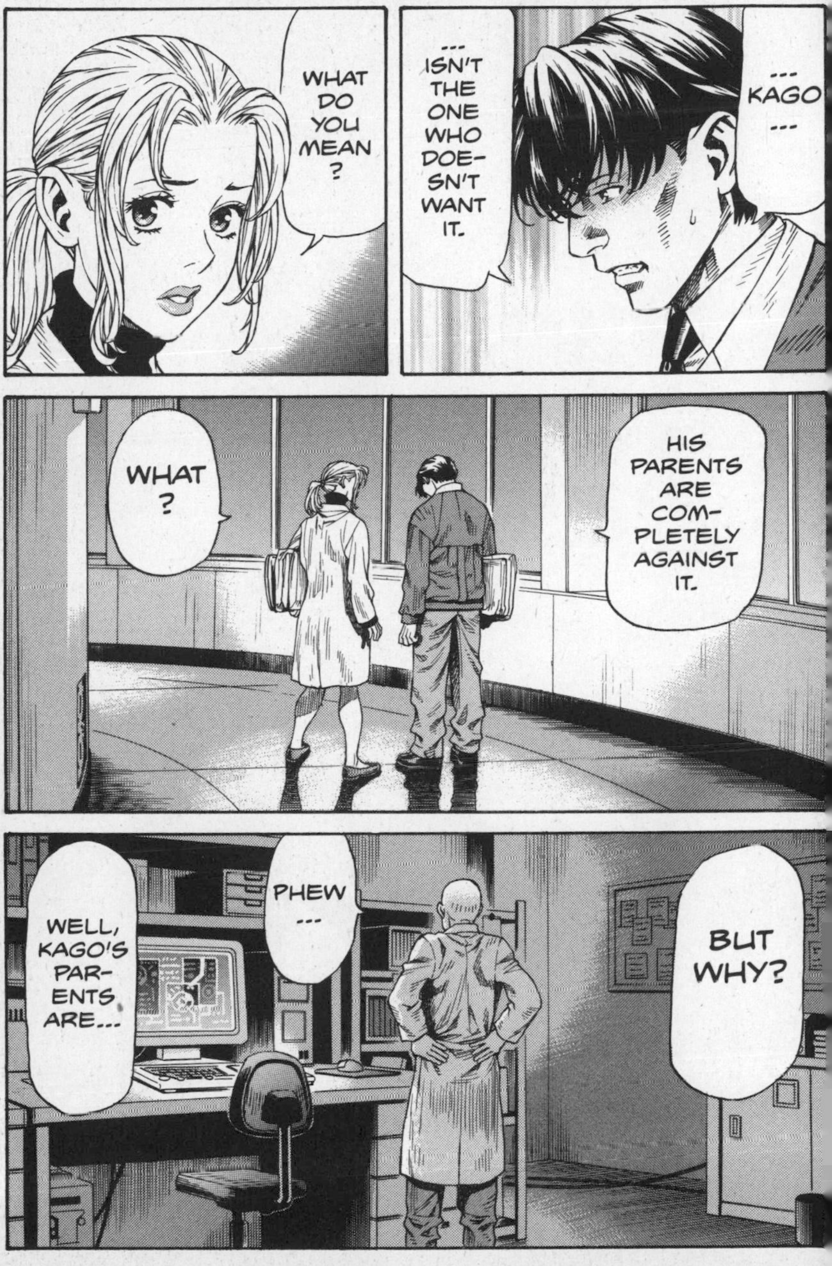
...KAGO...
...ISN'T THE ONE WHO DOE-SN'T WANT IT.
WHAT DO YOU MEAN?
HIS PARENTS ARE COM-PLETELY AGAINST IT.
WHAT?
BUT WHY?
PHEW...
WELL, KAGO'S PAR-ENTS ARE...

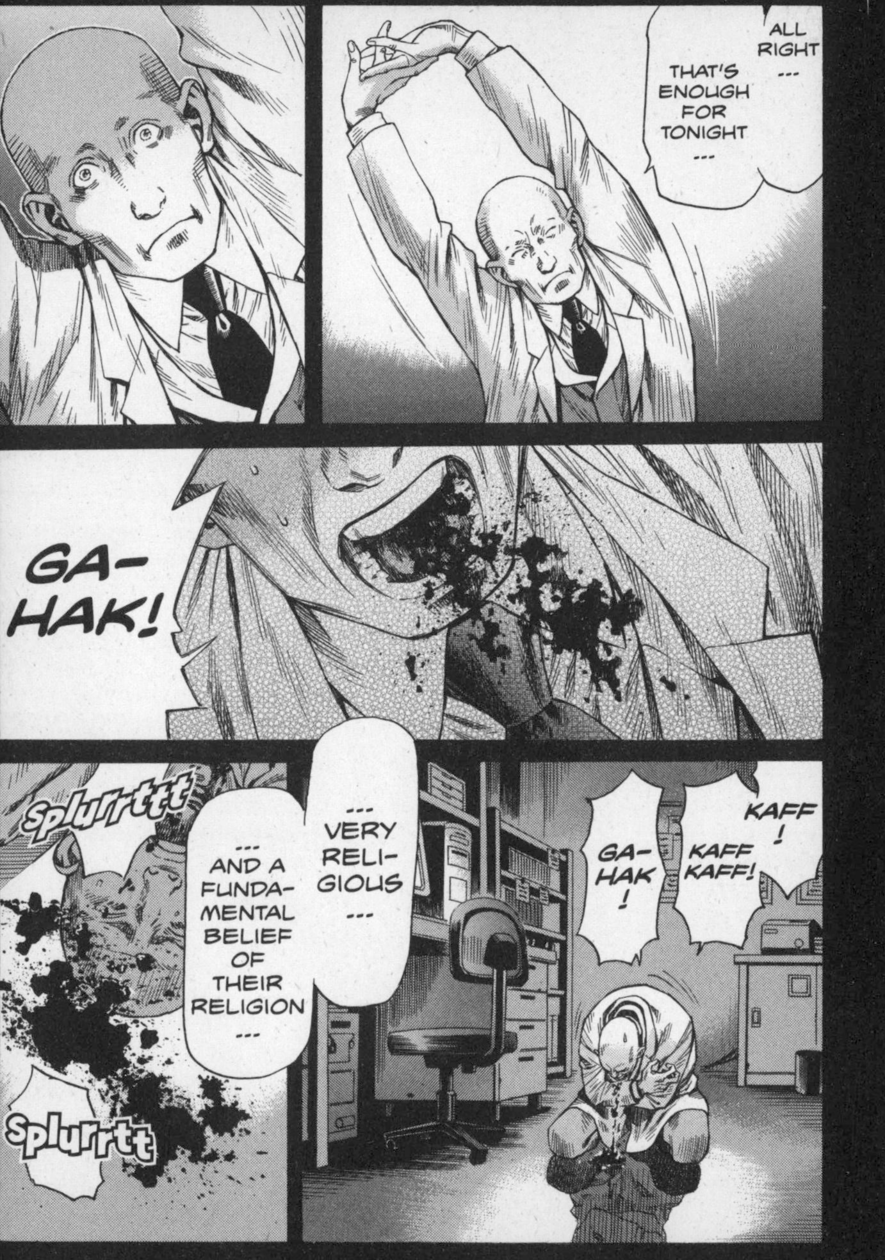
ALL RIGHT ---
THAT'S ENOUGH FOR TONIGHT ---
GA-HAK!
KAFF!
KAFF KAFF!
GA-HAK!
--- VERY RELIGIOUS ---
--- AND A FUNDAMENTAL BELIEF OF THEIR RELIGION ---
splurrttt
splurrtt

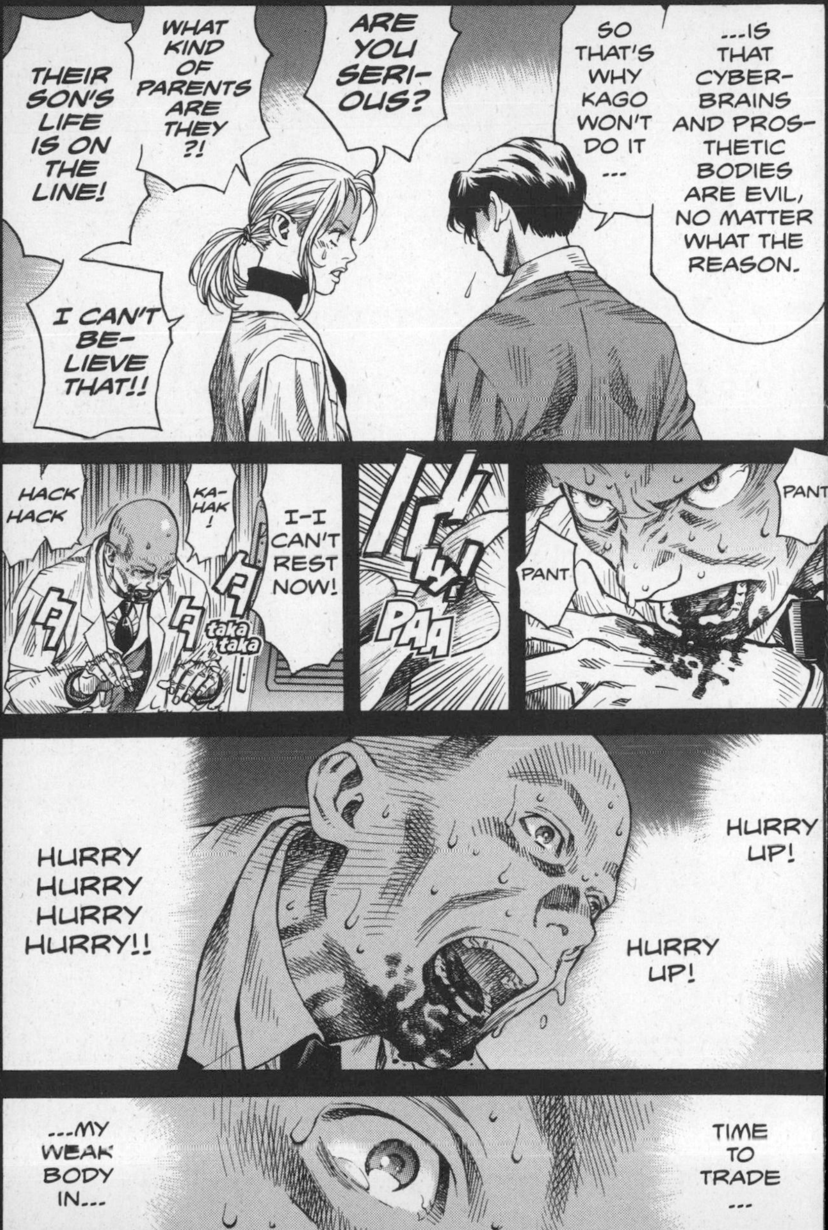

...IS THAT CYBER-BRAINS AND PROS-THETIC BODIES ARE EVIL, NO MATTER WHAT THE REASON.
SO THAT'S WHY KAGO WON'T DO IT ...
ARE YOU SERI-OUS?
WHAT KIND OF PARENTS ARE THEY ?!
THEIR SON'S LIFE IS ON THE LINE!
I CAN'T BE-LIEVE THAT!!
PANT
PANT
PAA
I-I CAN'T REST NOW!
KA-HAK!
HACK HACK
taka taka
HURRY UP!
HURRY UP!
HURRY HURRY HURRY HURRY!!
TIME TO TRADE ...
...MY WEAK BODY IN...

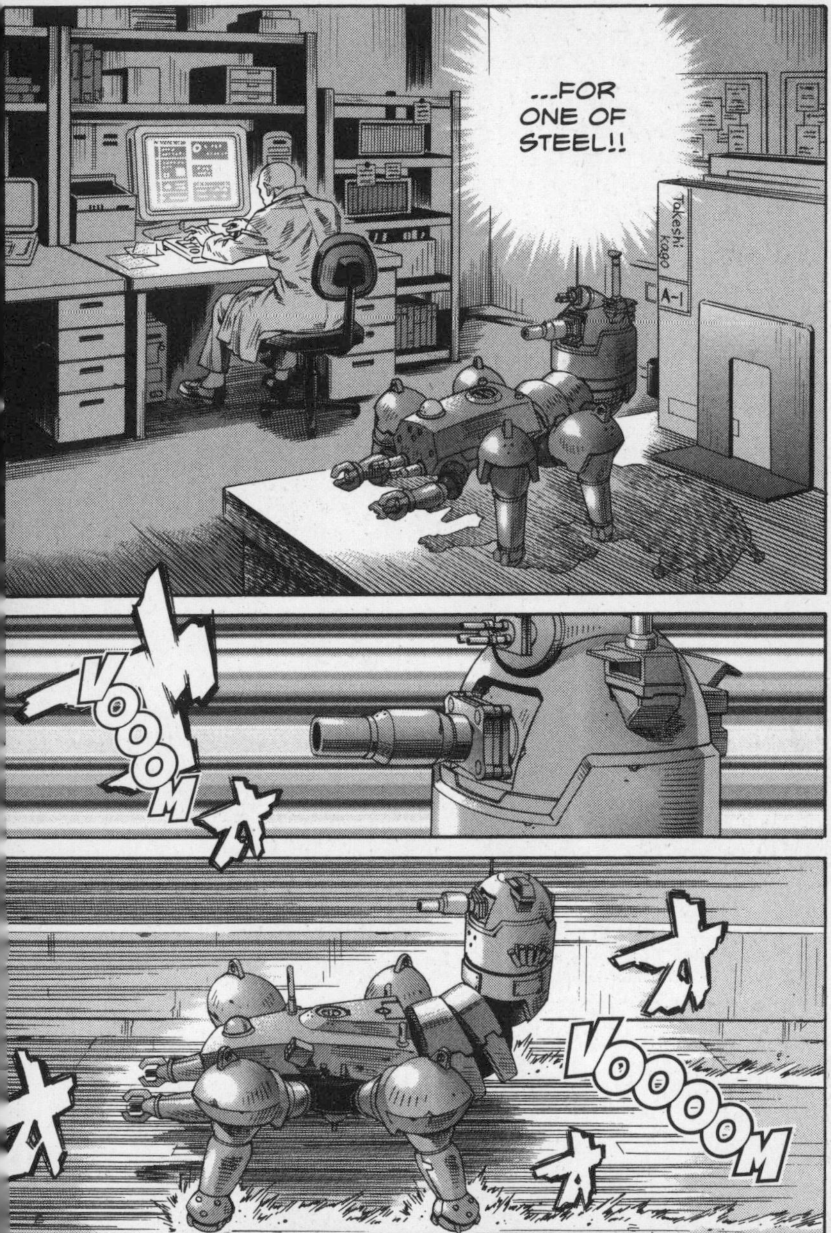
...FOR ONE OF STEEL!!
Takeshi kago
A-1
VOOOM
VOOOOM

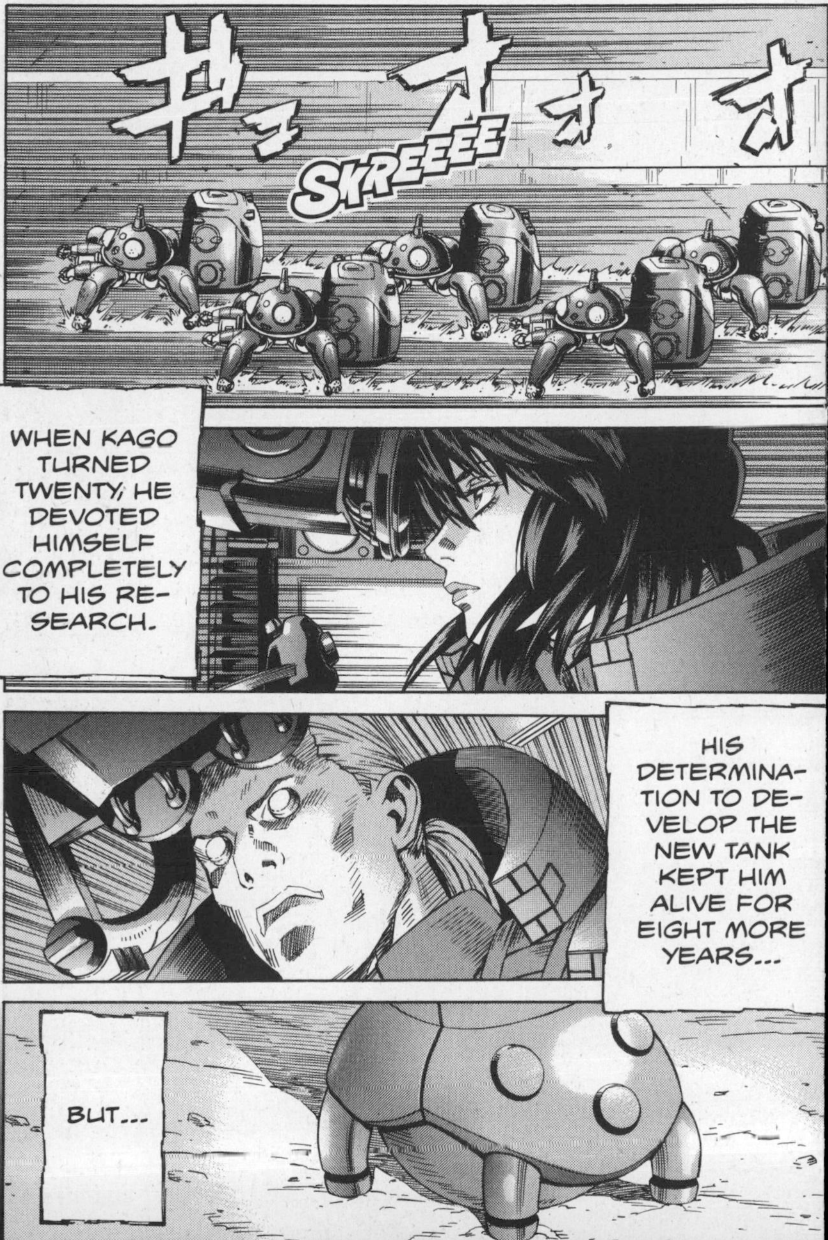
SKREEEEE
WHEN KAGO TURNED TWENTY, HE DEVOTED HIMSELF COMPLETELY TO HIS RE-SEARCH.
HIS DETERMINA-TION TO DE-VELOP THE NEW TANK KEPT HIM ALIVE FOR EIGHT MORE YEARS...
BUT...

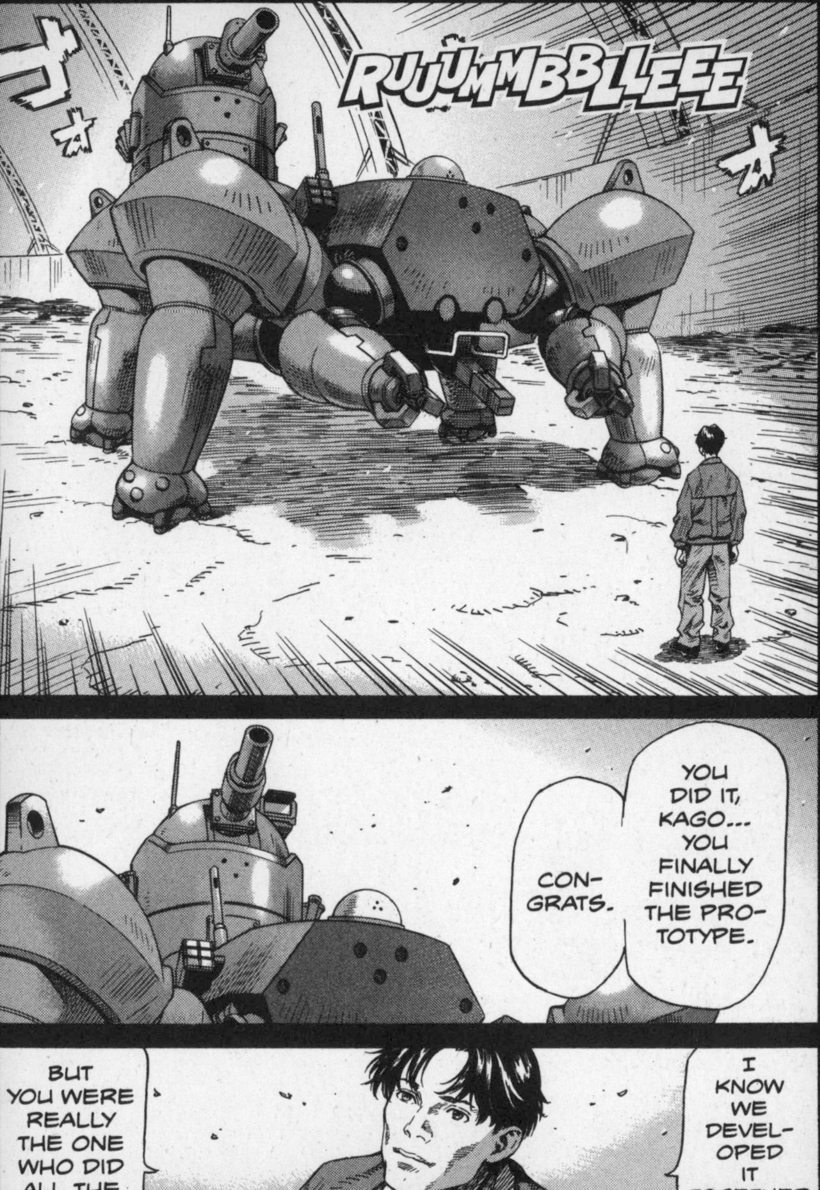
RUUUMMBBLLEEE
YOU DID IT, KAGO... YOU FINALLY FINISHED THE PROTOTYPE.
CONGRATS.
I KNOW WE DEVELOPED IT TOGETHER...
BUT YOU WERE REALLY THE ONE WHO DID ALL THE WORK.

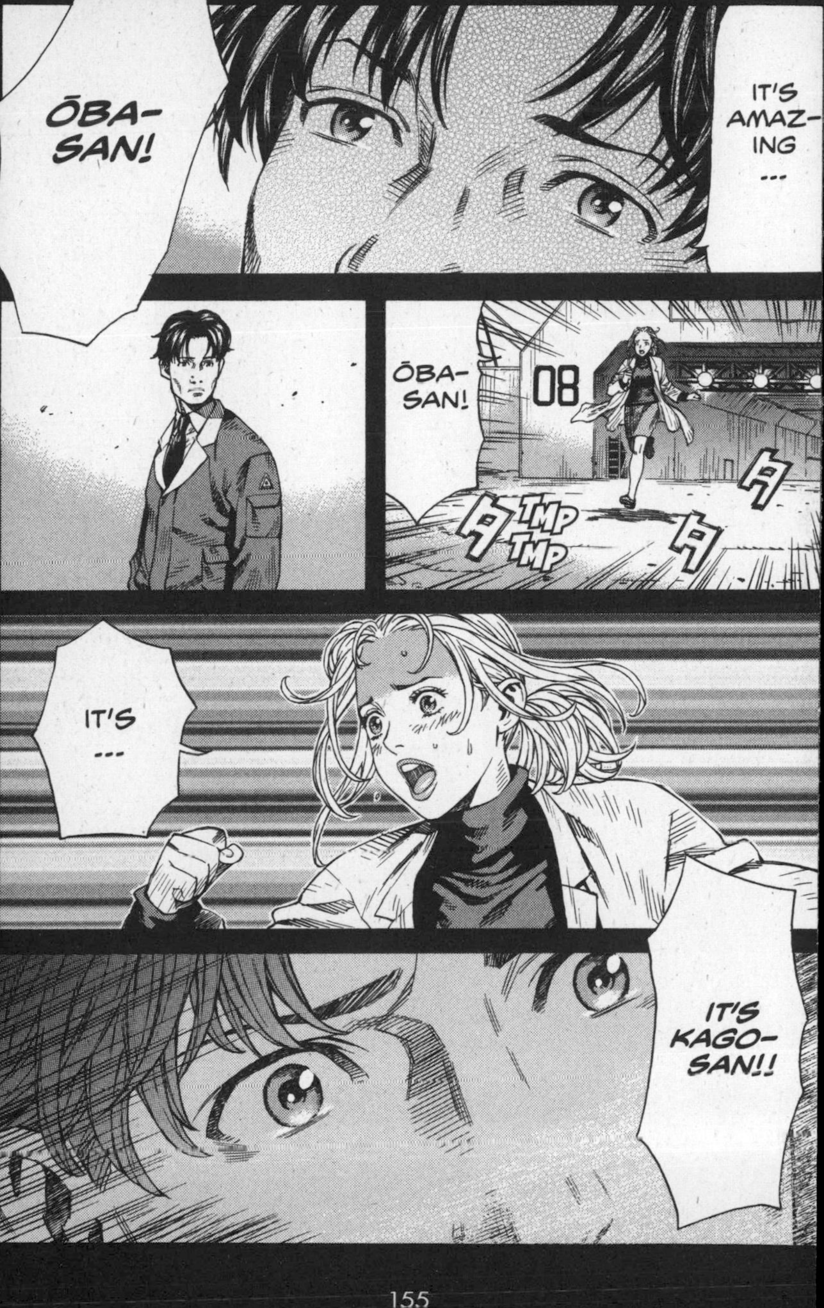
IT'S AMAZING ---
ŌBA-SAN!
ŌBA-SAN!
TMP TMP
IT'S ---
IT'S KAGO-SAN!!

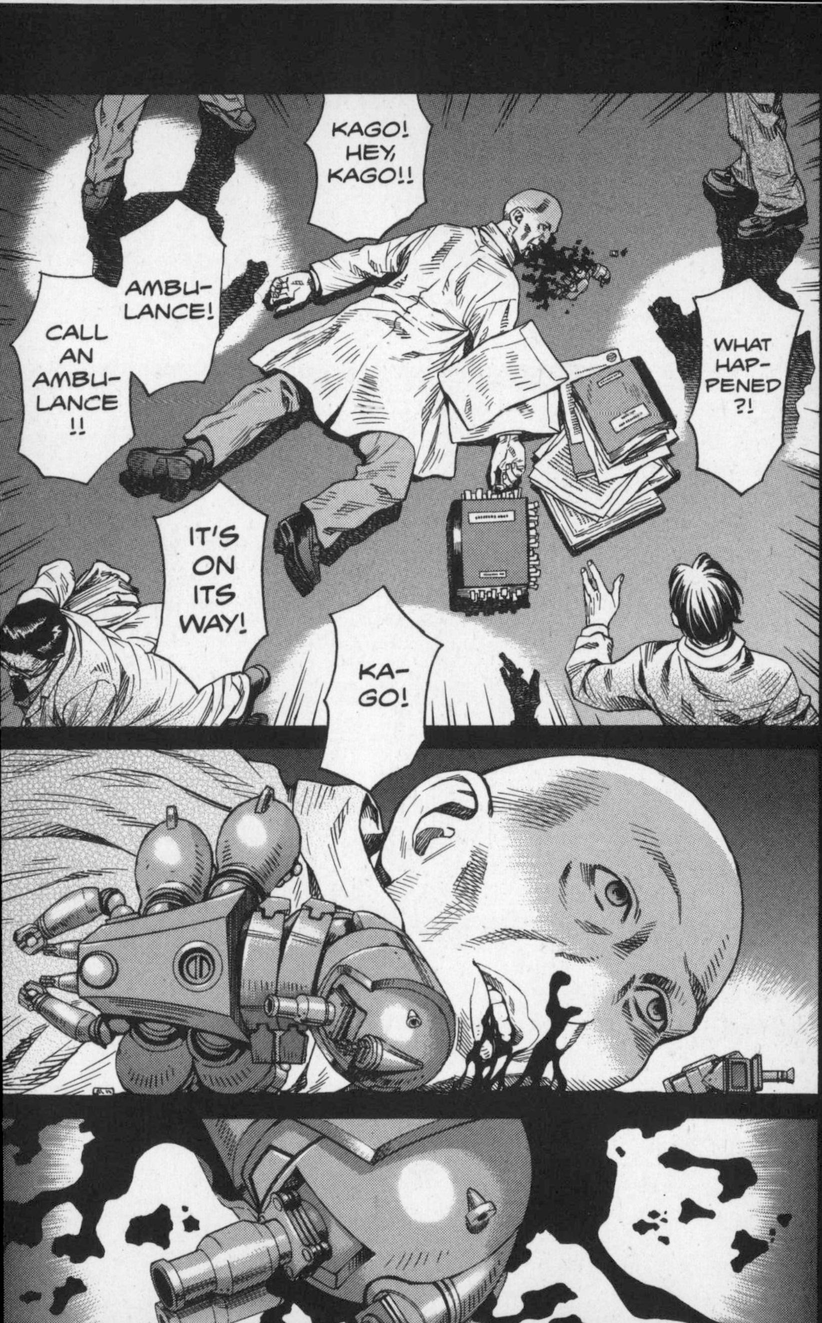
KAGO! HEY, KAGO!!
WHAT HAP-PENED ?!
AMBU-LANCE!
CALL AN AMBU-LANCE !!
IT'S ON ITS WAY!
KA-GO!

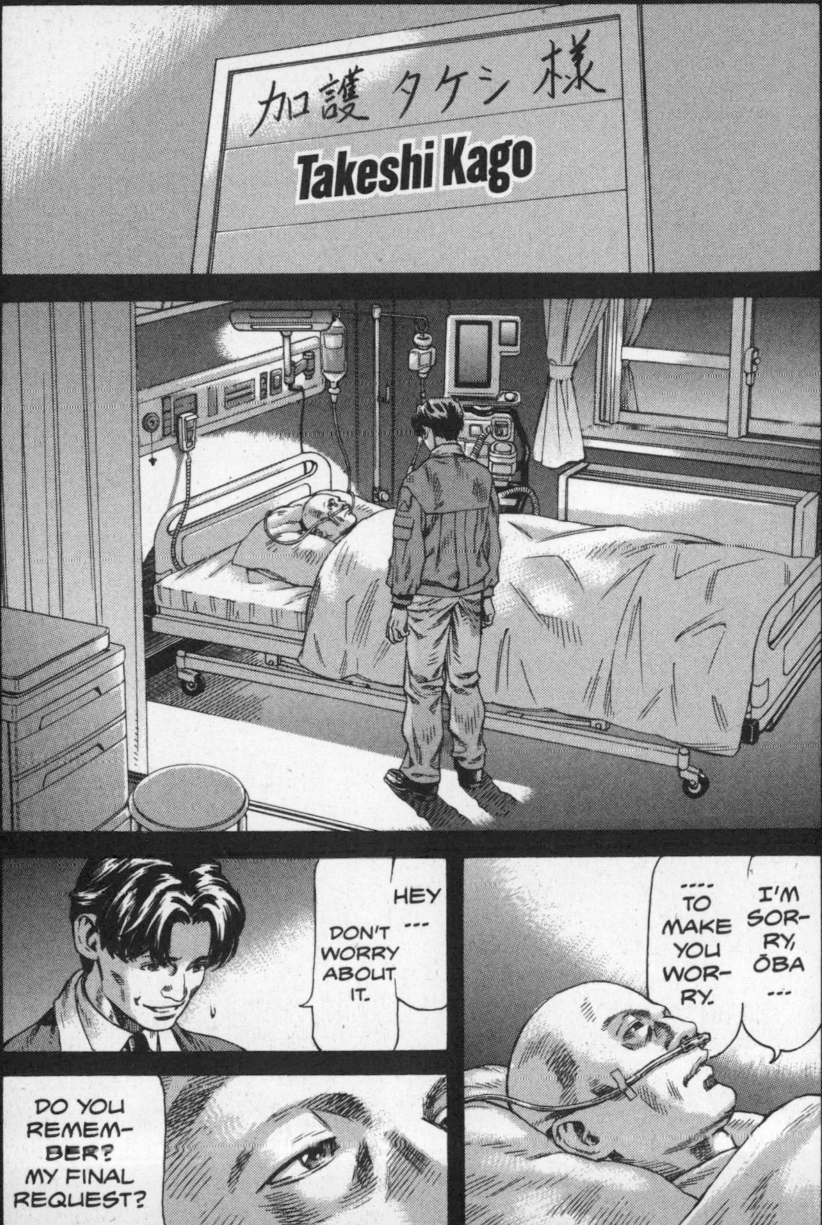
加護 タケシ 様
Takeshi Kago
I'M SOR-RY, ŌBA ---
---- TO MAKE YOU WOR-RY.
HEY ---
DON'T WORRY ABOUT IT.
DO YOU REMEM-BER? MY FINAL REQUEST?

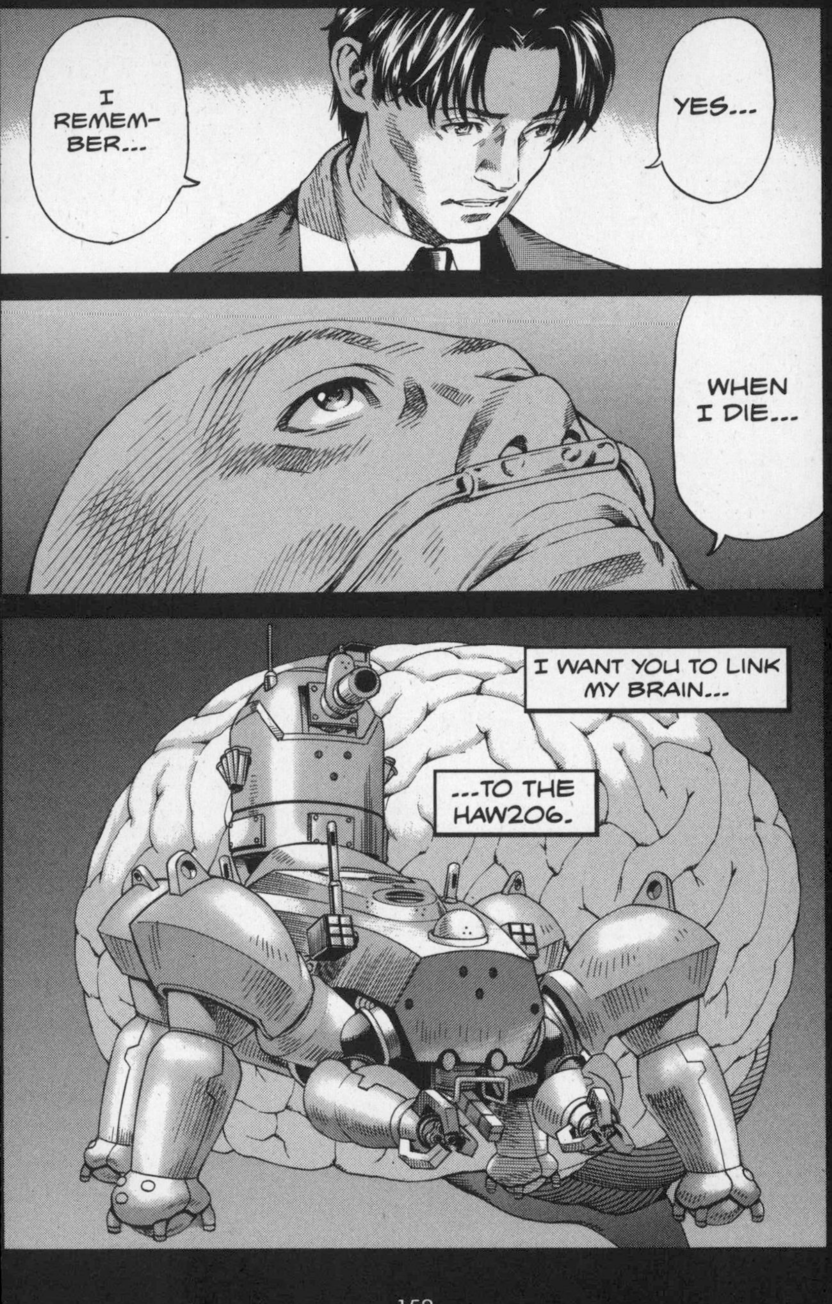
YES...
I REMEMBER...
WHEN I DIE...
I WANT YOU TO LINK MY BRAIN...
...TO THE HAW206.

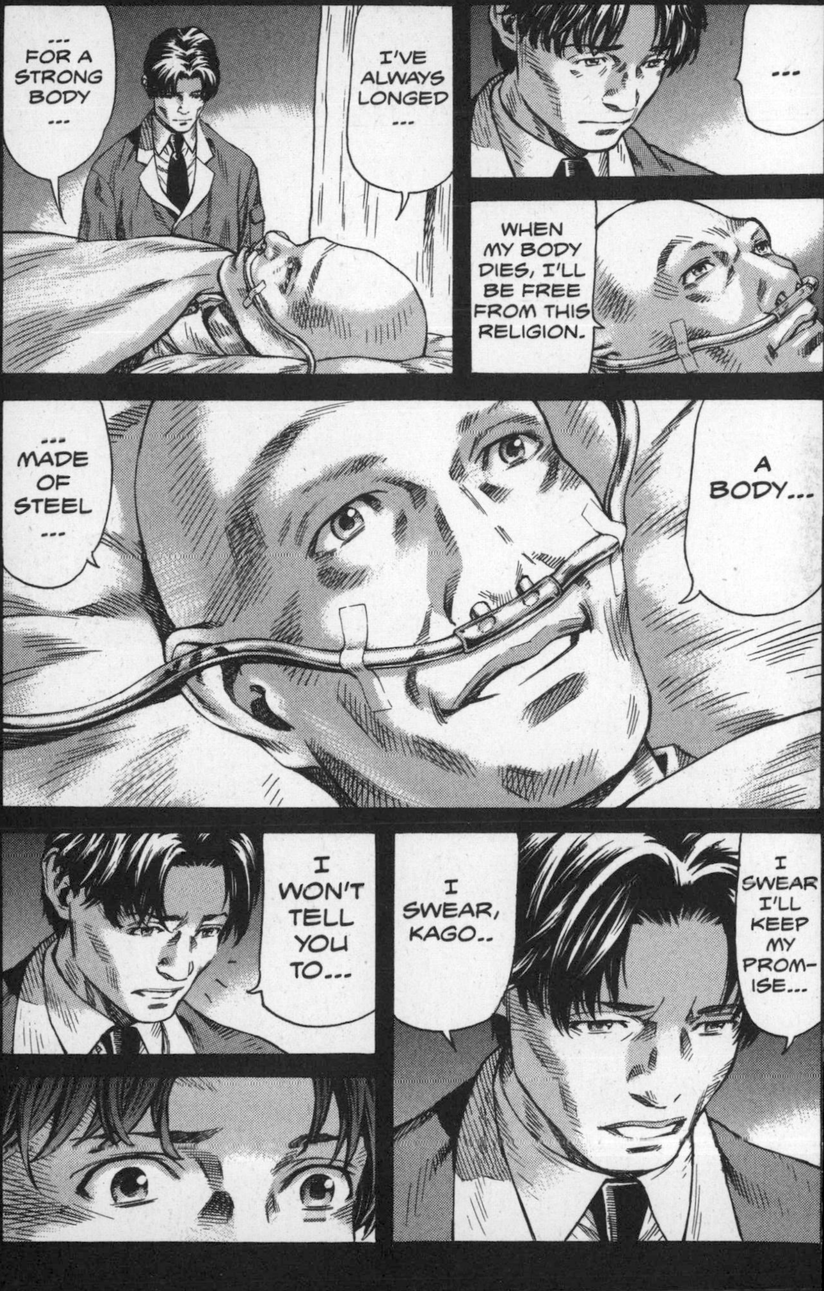

WHEN MY BODY DIES, I'LL BE FREE FROM THIS RELIGION.
I'VE ALWAYS LONGED ---
--- FOR A STRONG BODY ---
A BODY...
--- MADE OF STEEL ---
I SWEAR I'LL KEEP MY PROMISE...
I SWEAR, KAGO..
I WON'T TELL YOU TO...

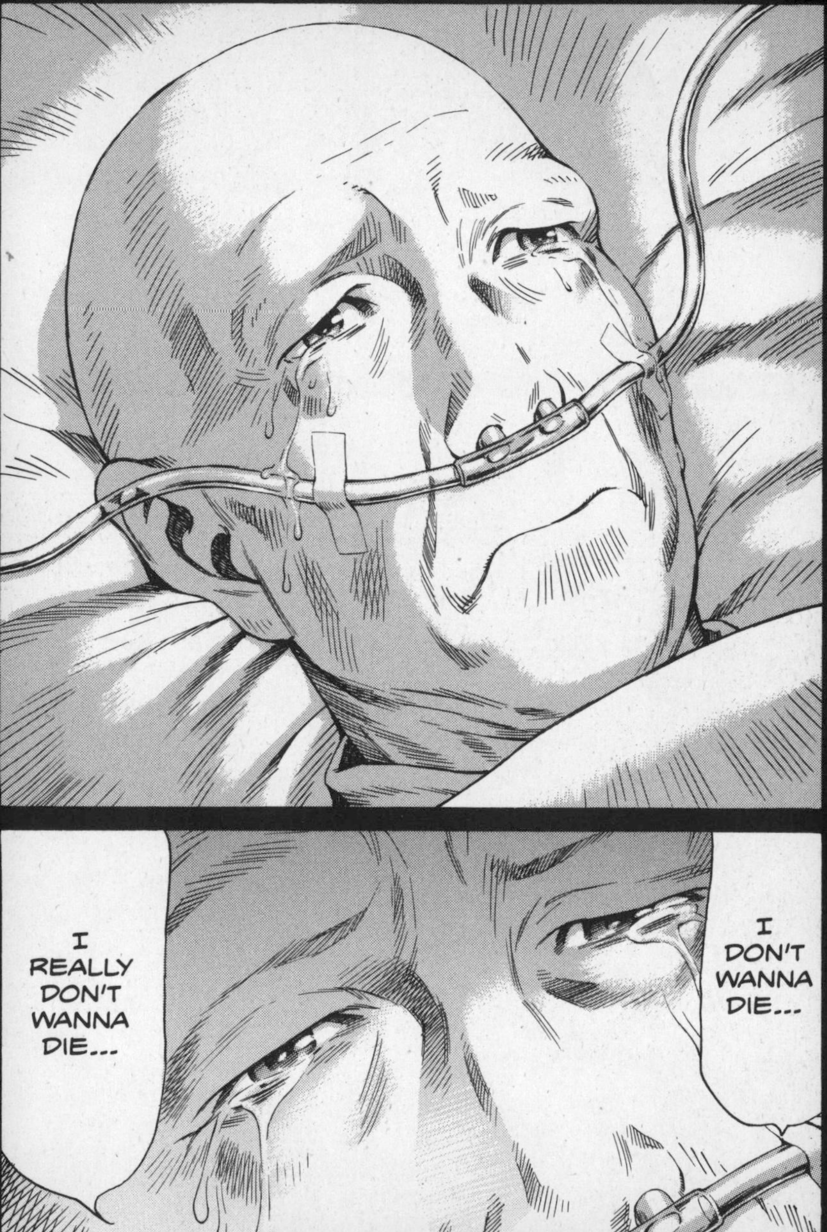
I DON'T WANNA DIE...
I REALLY DON'T WANNA DIE...

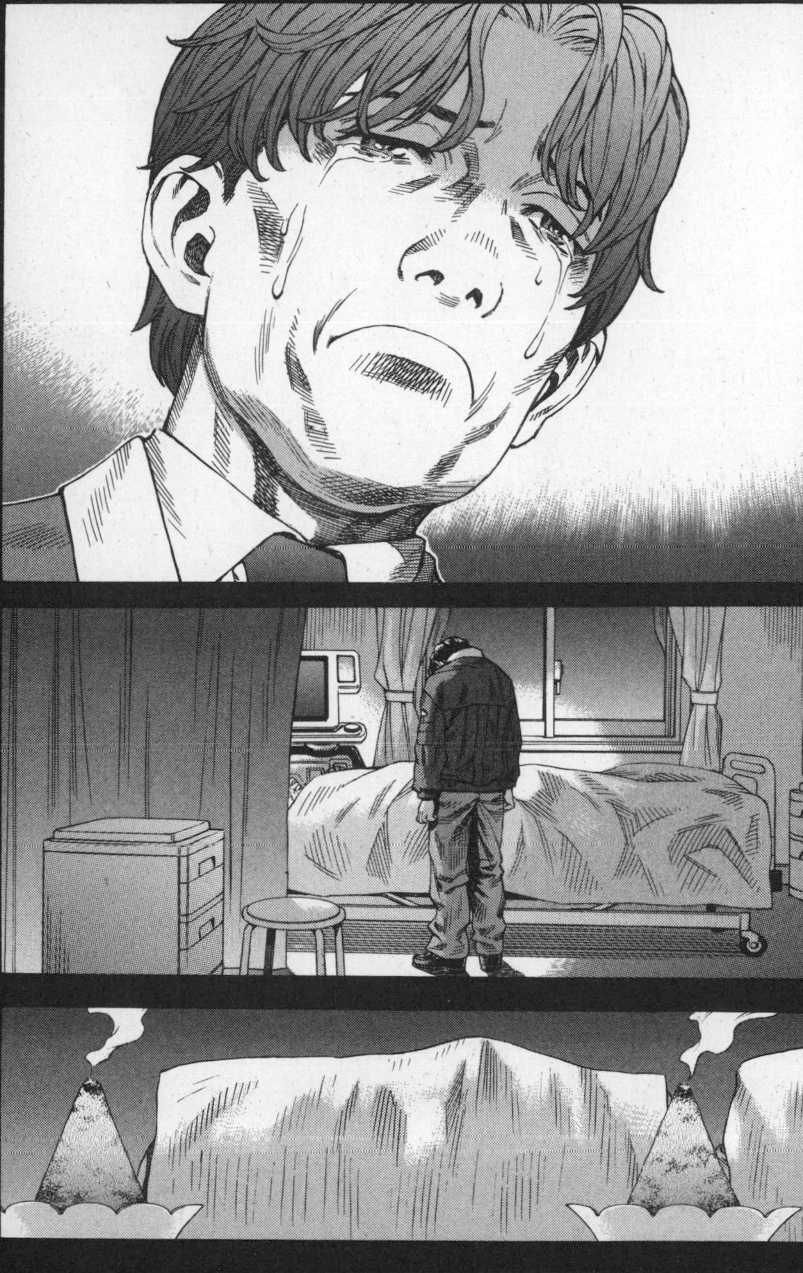

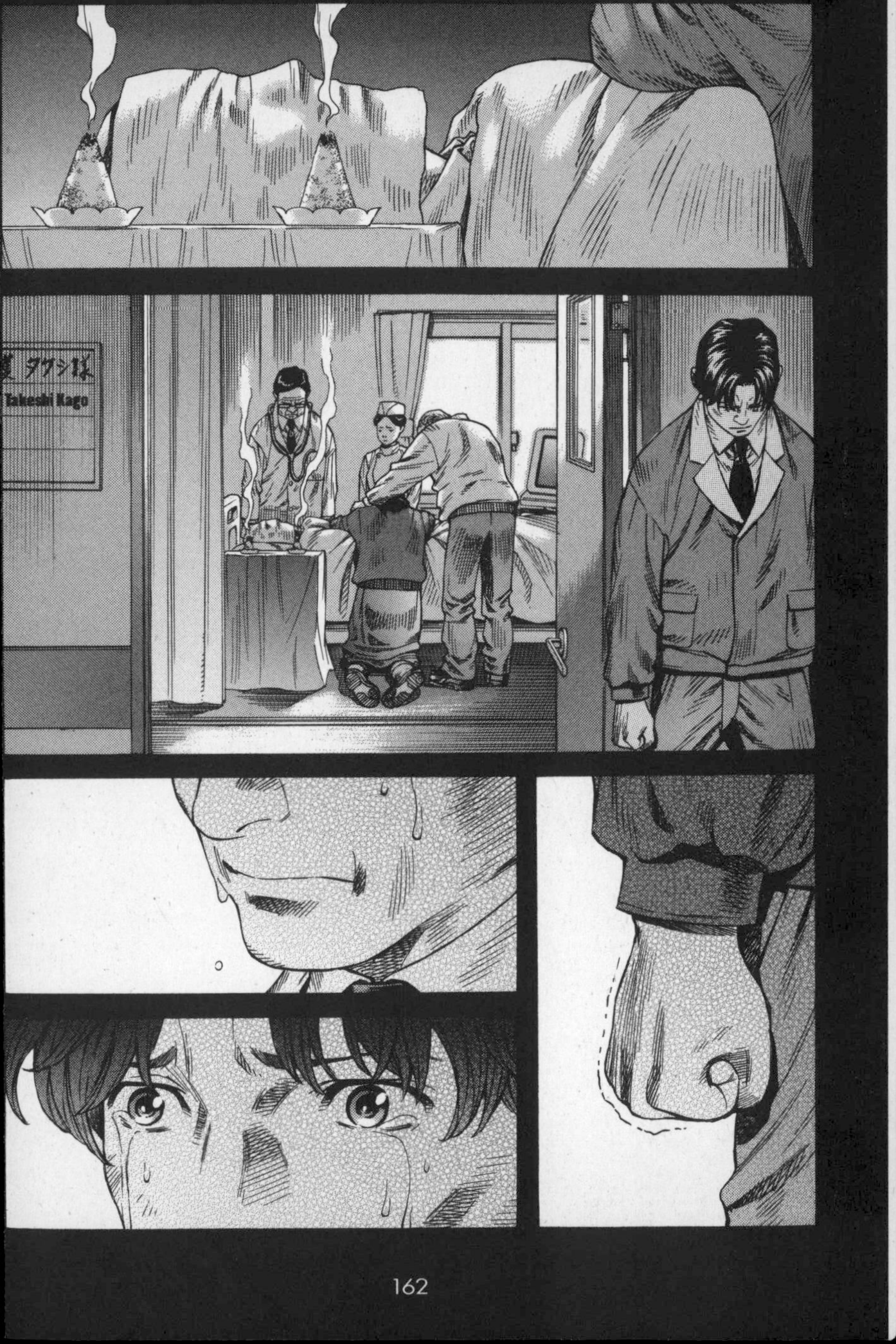
タケシ様
Takeshi Kago

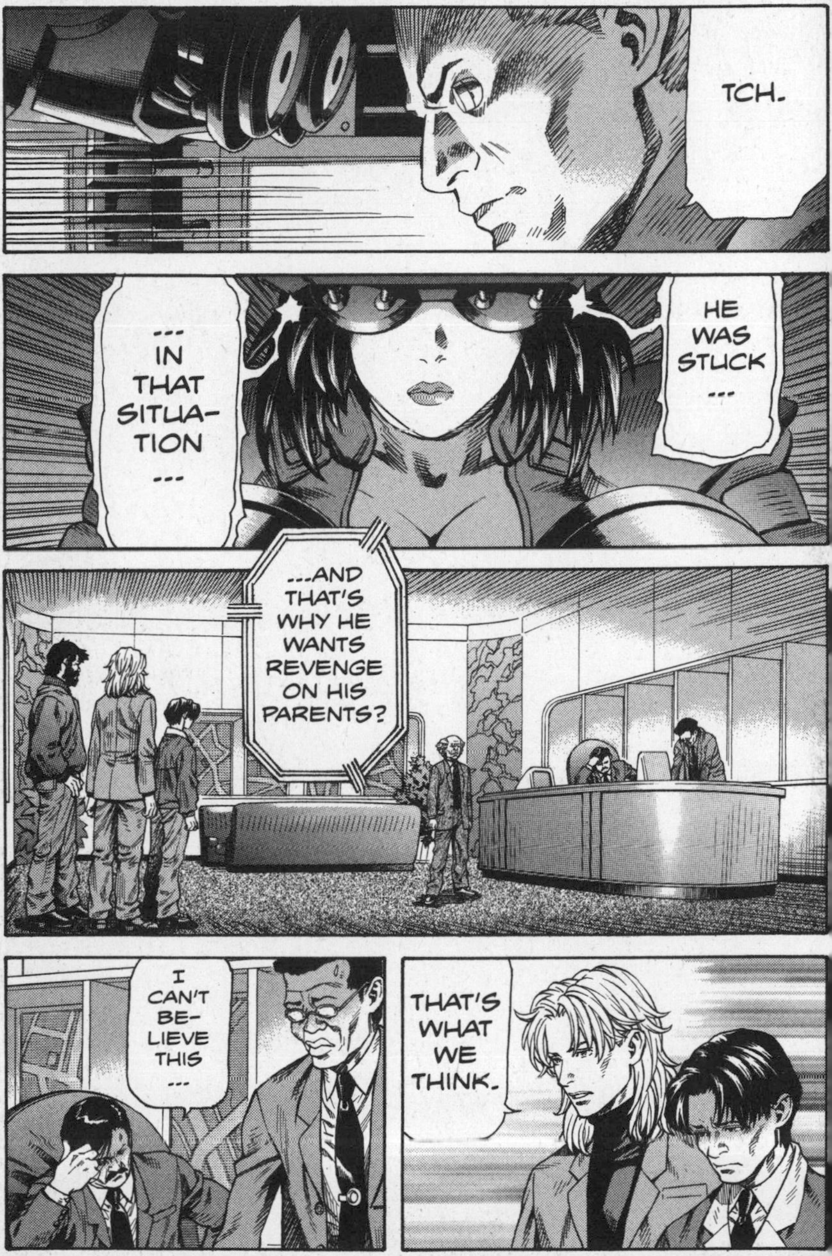
TCH.
HE WAS STUCK ---
--- IN THAT SITUATION ---
---AND THAT'S WHY HE WANTS REVENGE ON HIS PARENTS?
THAT'S WHAT WE THINK.
I CAN'T BELIEVE THIS ---

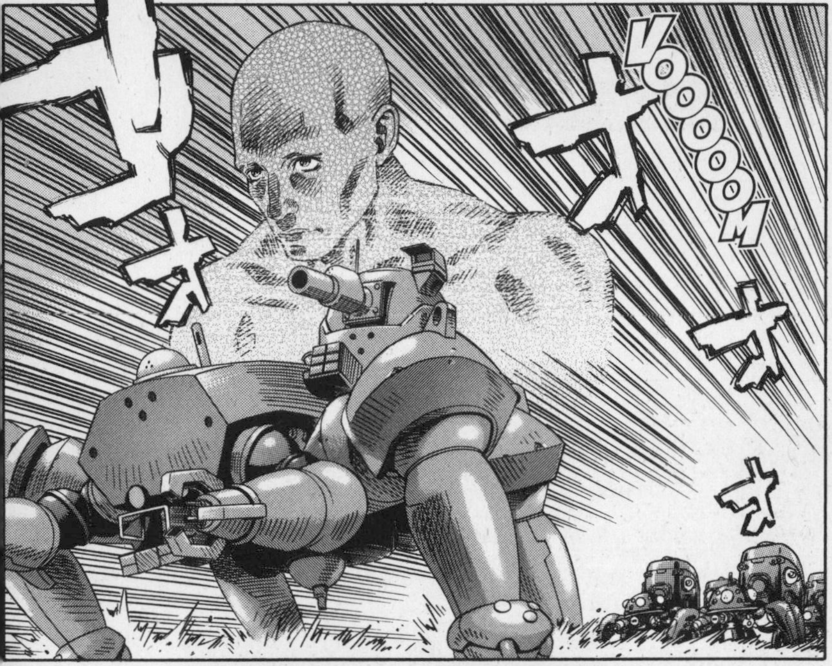
VOOOOOM

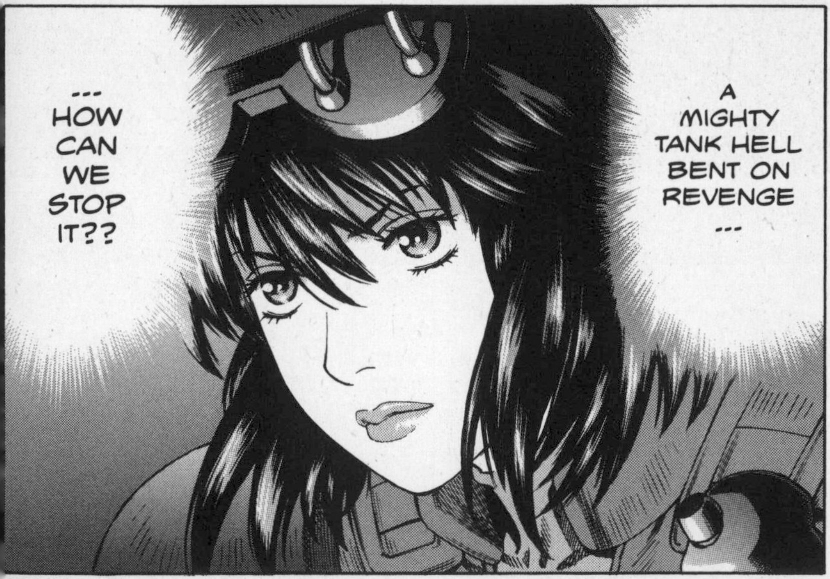
A MIGHTY TANK HELL BENT ON REVENGE ---
--- HOW CAN WE STOP IT??

#015 / End

#016: Battle in the City

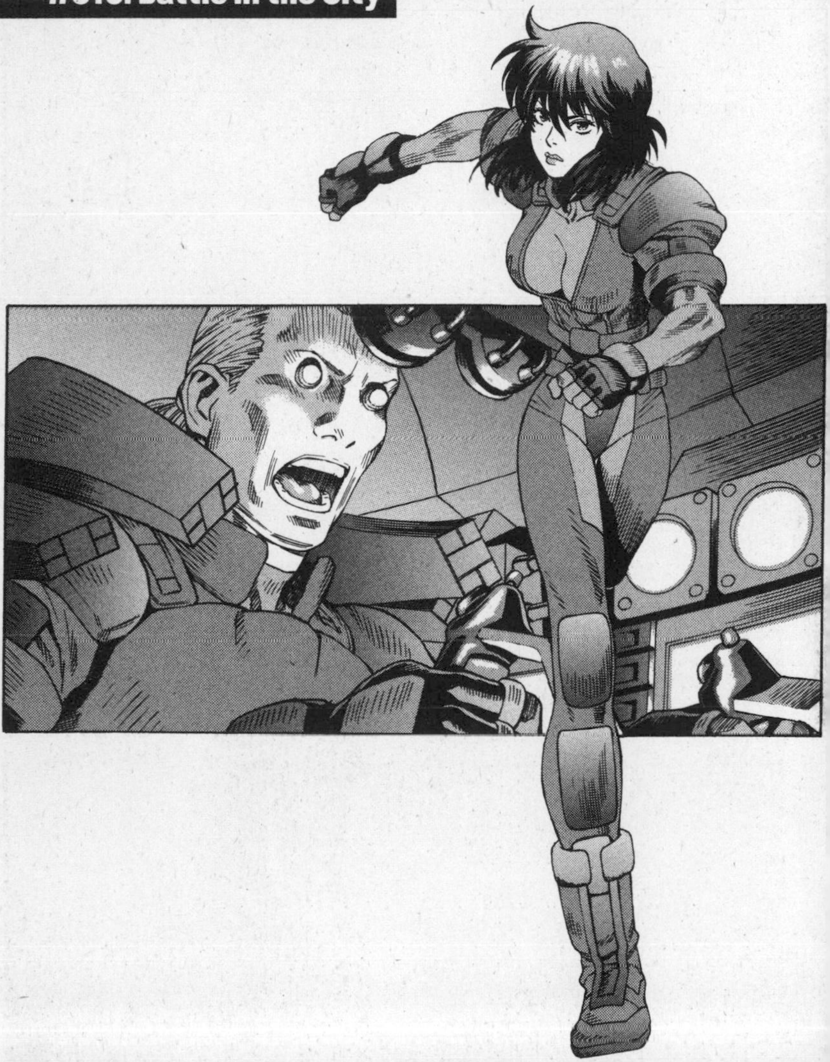

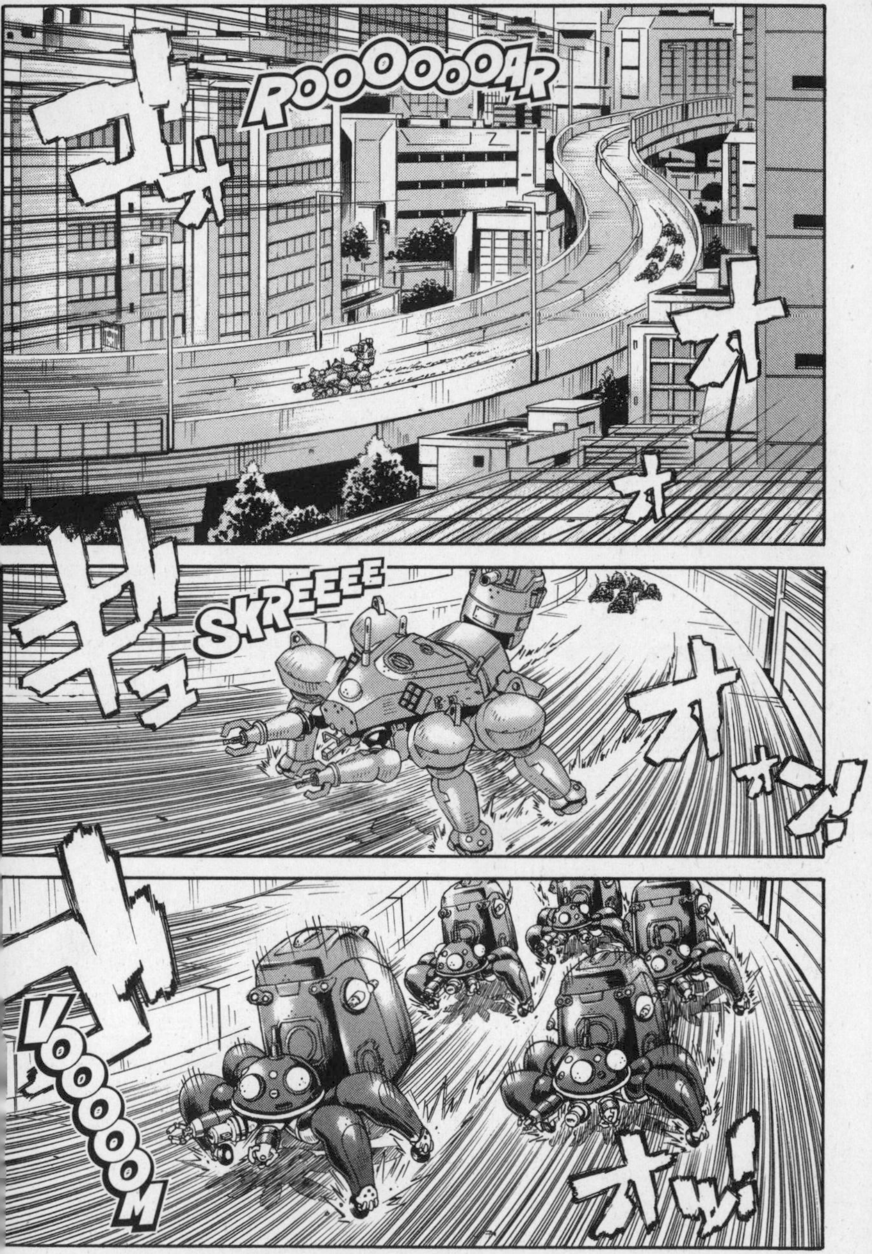
ROOOOOOAR
SKREEEE
VOOOOOOM

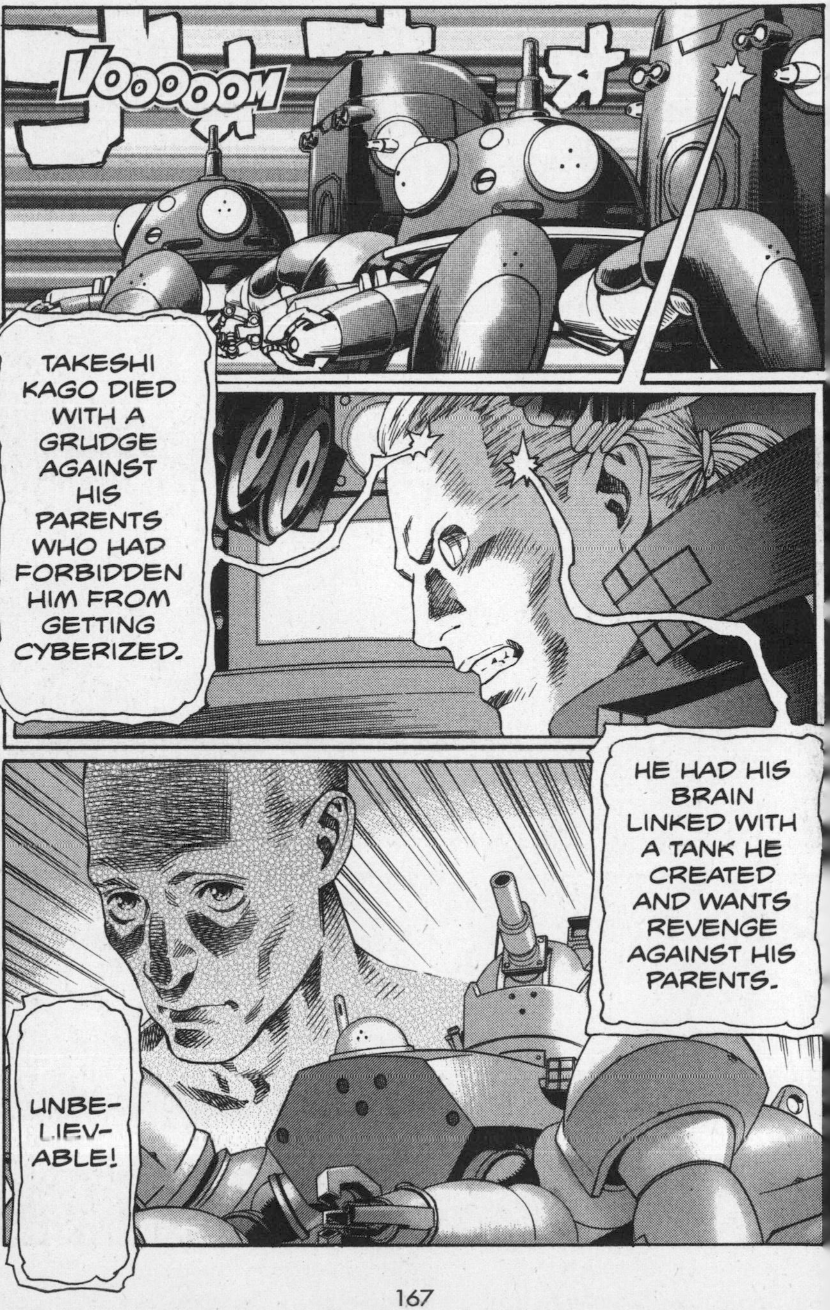
VOOOOOM
TAKESHI KAGO DIED WITH A GRUDGE AGAINST HIS PARENTS WHO HAD FORBIDDEN HIM FROM GETTING CYBERIZED.
HE HAD HIS BRAIN LINKED WITH A TANK HE CREATED AND WANTS REVENGE AGAINST HIS PARENTS.
UNBE-LIEV-ABLE!

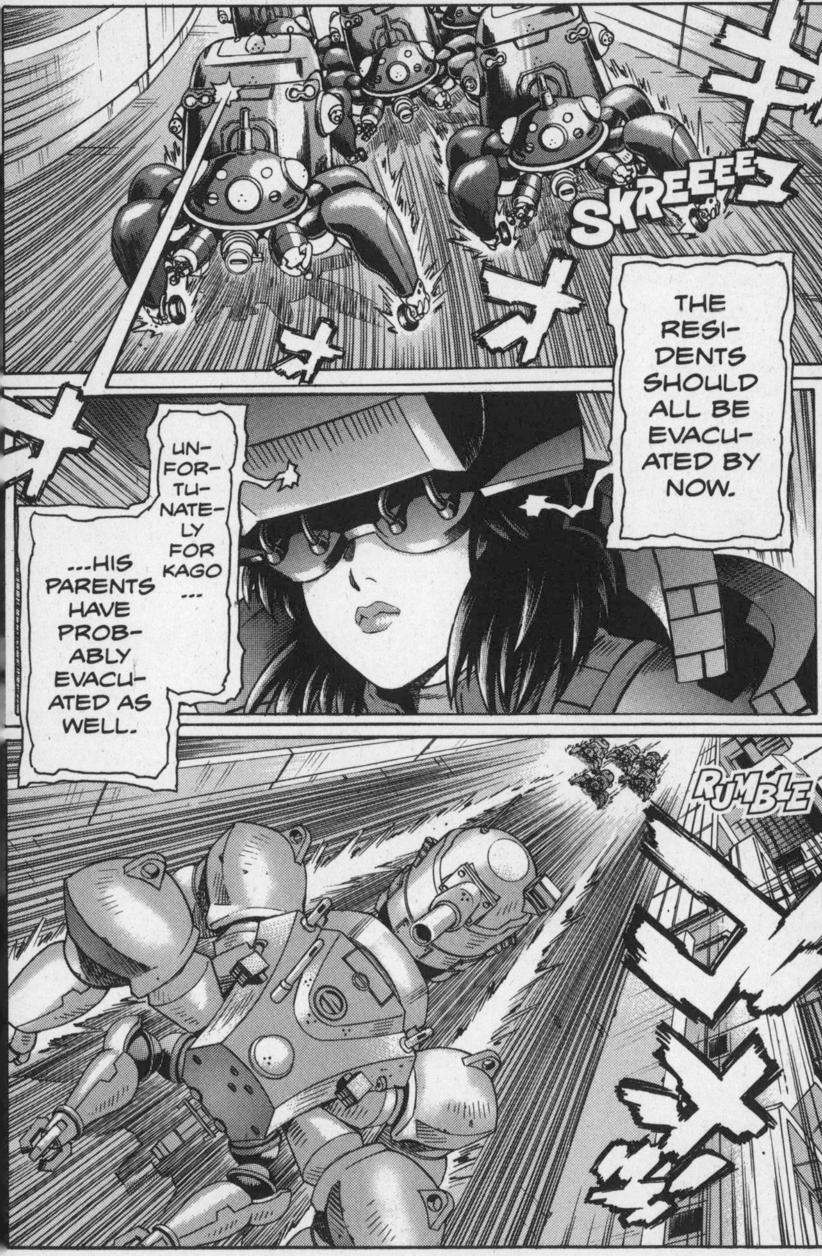
SKREEEE
THE RESIDENTS SHOULD ALL BE EVACUATED BY NOW.
UNFORTUNATELY FOR KAGO...
...HIS PARENTS HAVE PROBABLY EVACUATED AS WELL.
RUMBLE

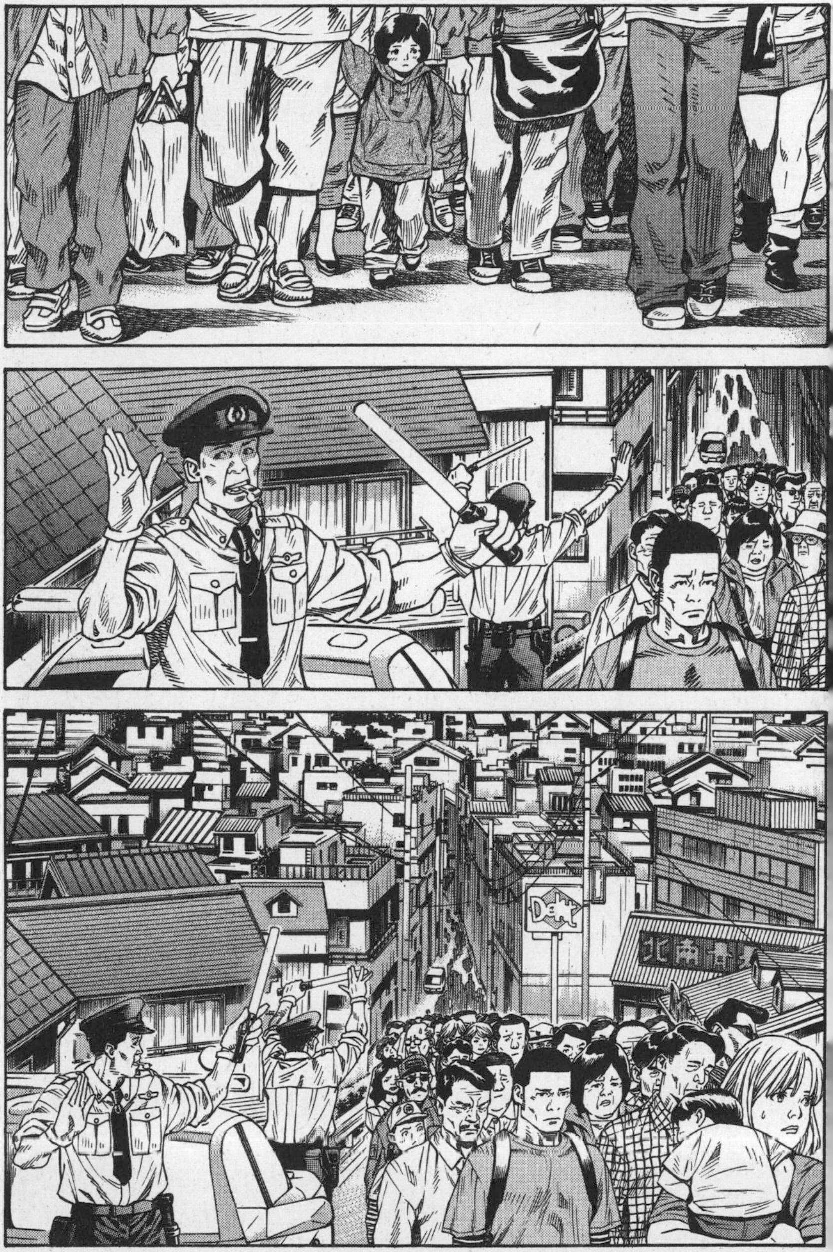

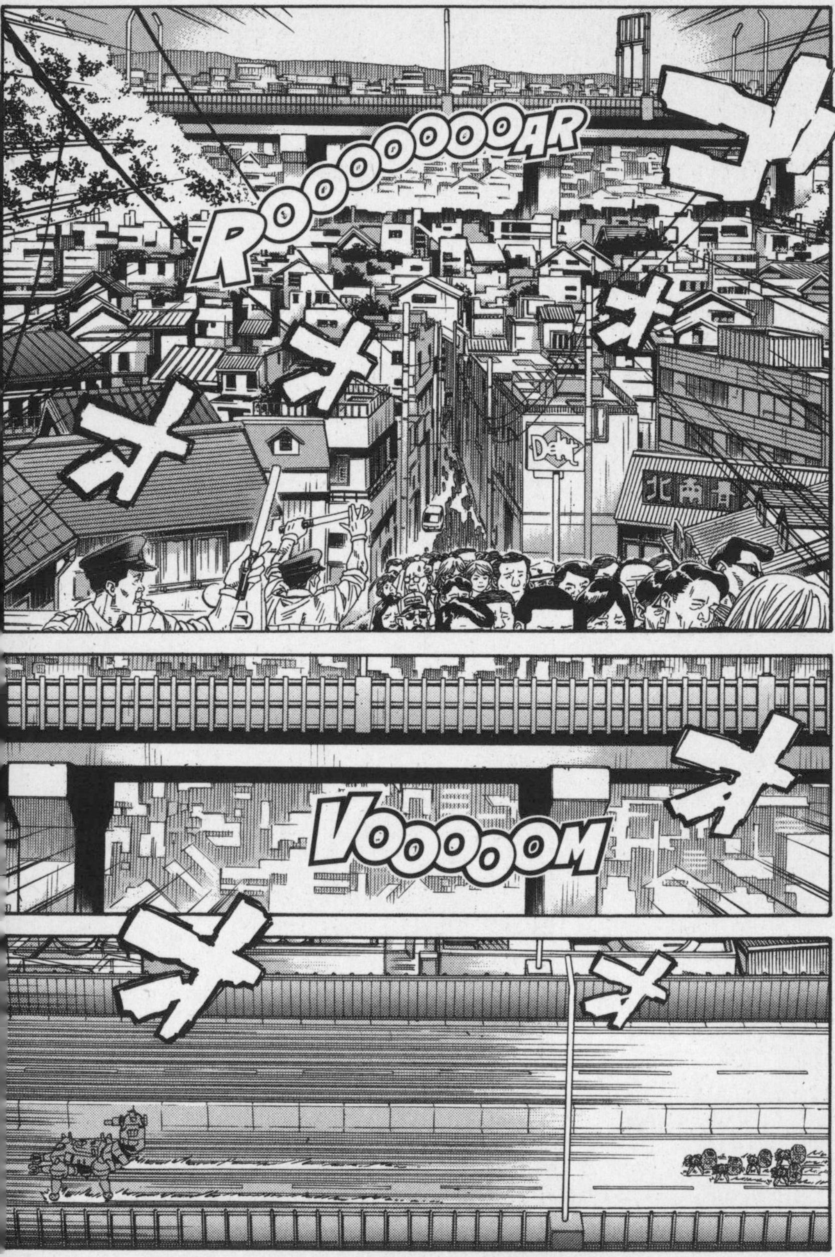
ROOOOOOOAR
VOOOOOM

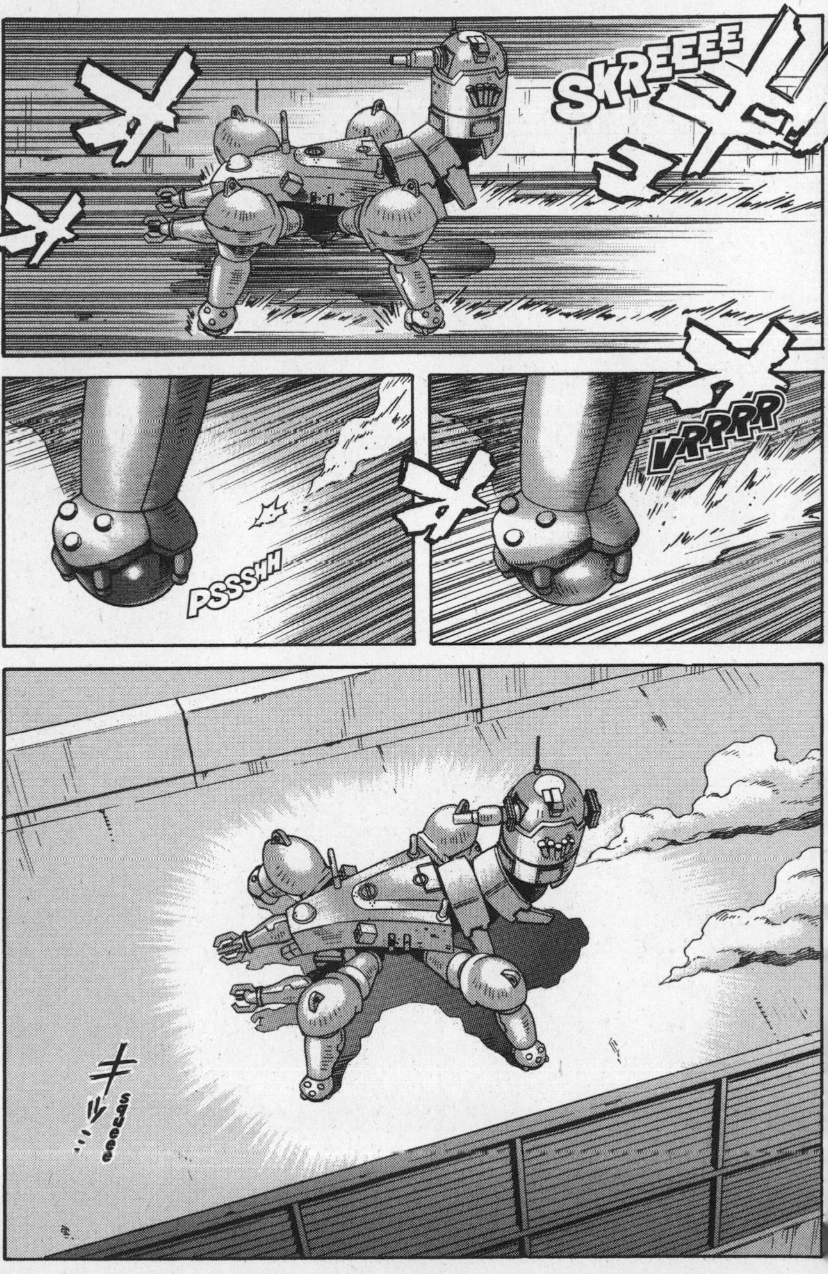
SKREEEE
VRRRRR
PSSSHH
キル…
squeee

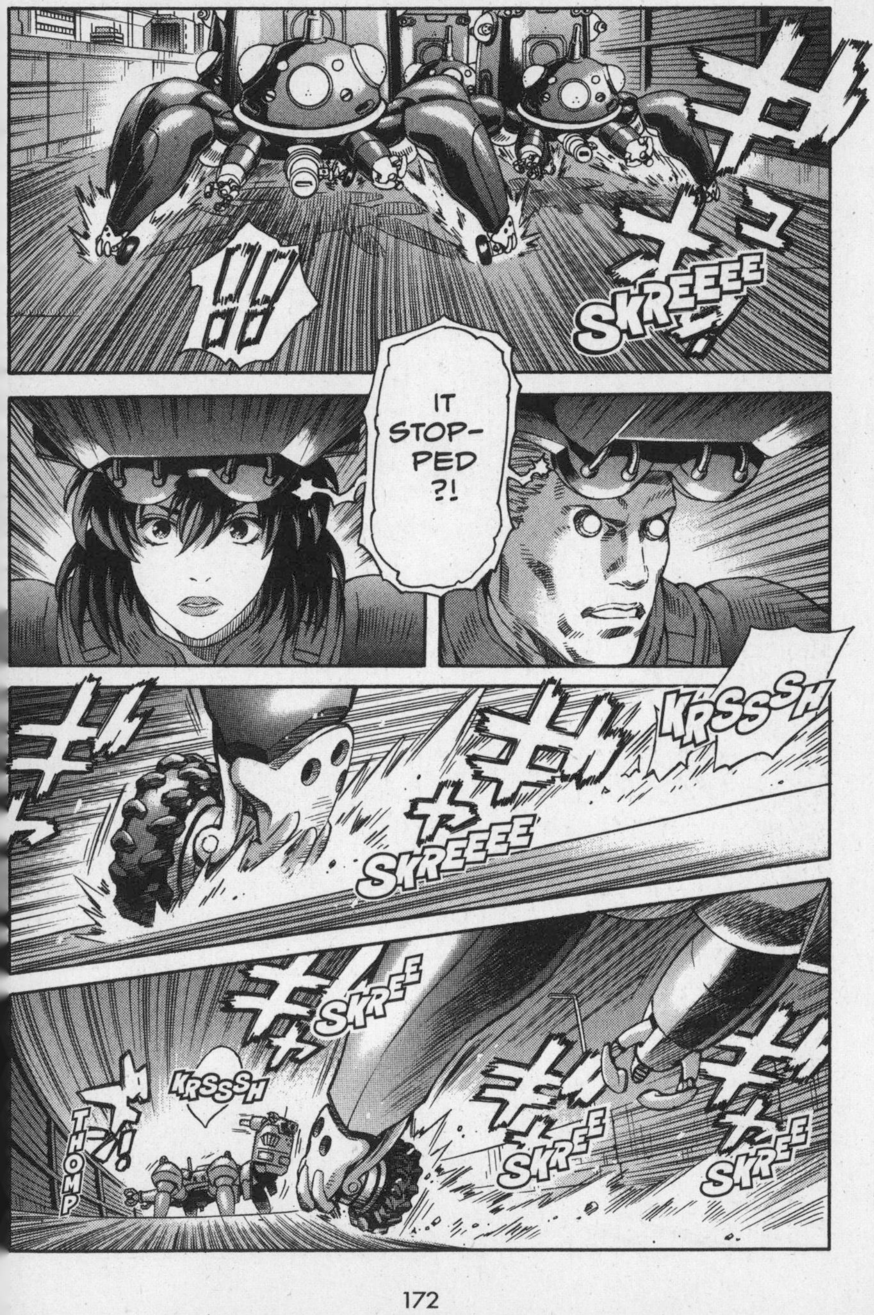
SKREEEE
IT STOPPED?!
KRSSSSH
SKREEEEE
SKREE
SKREE
SKREE
KRSSSH
THOMP

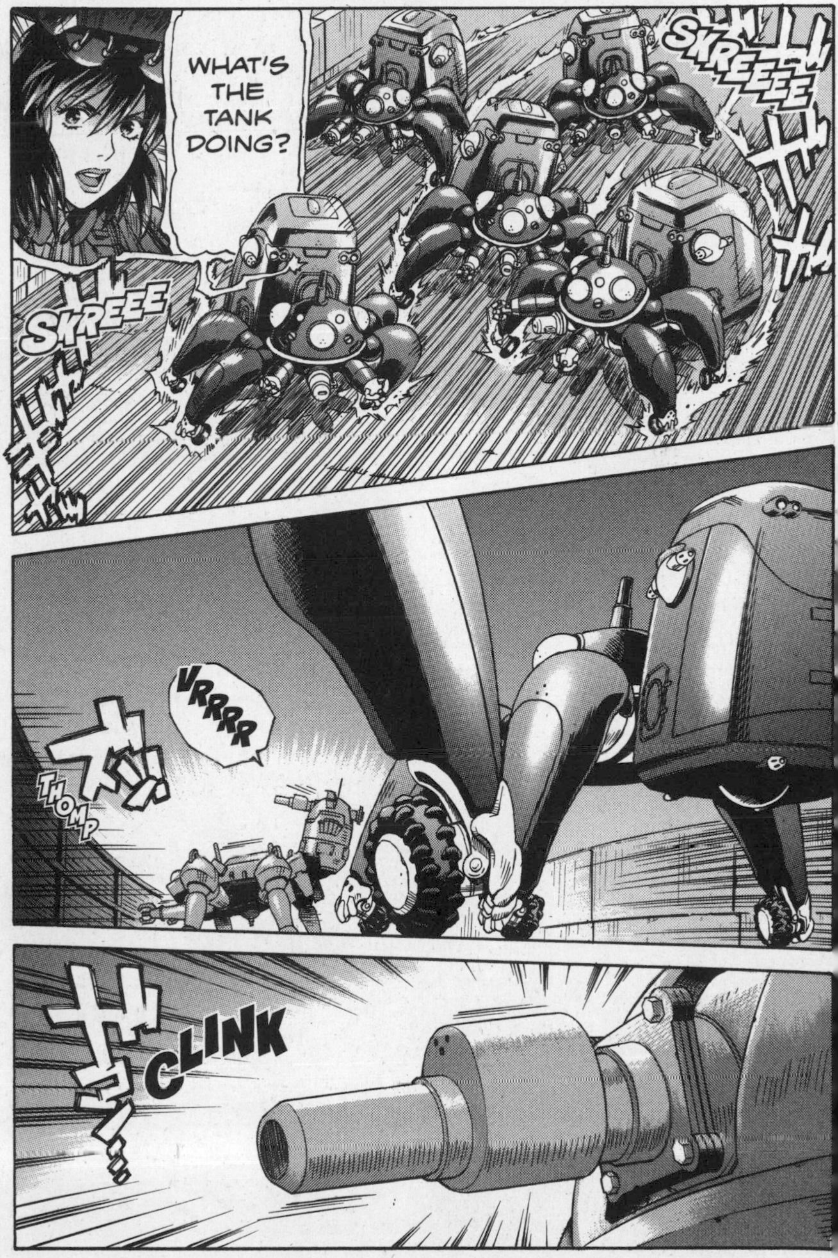
SKREEEE
WHAT'S THE TANK DOING?
SKREEE
VRRRR
THOMP
CLINK

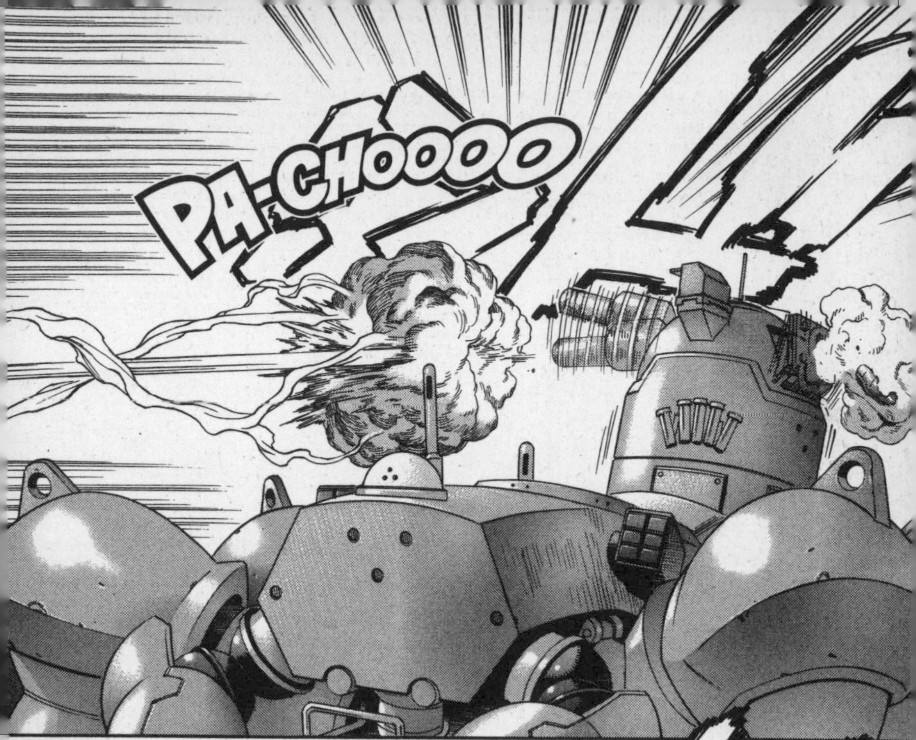
PA-CHOOOOO

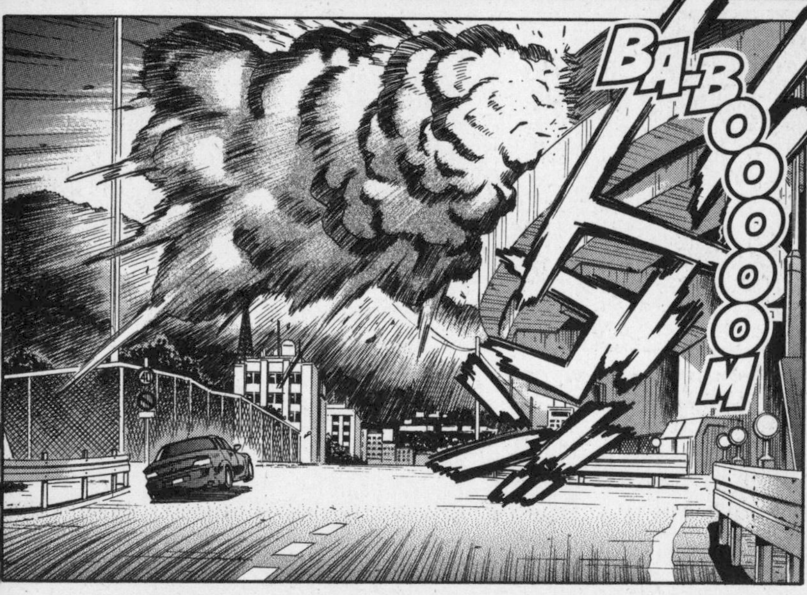
BA-BOOOOOOOM

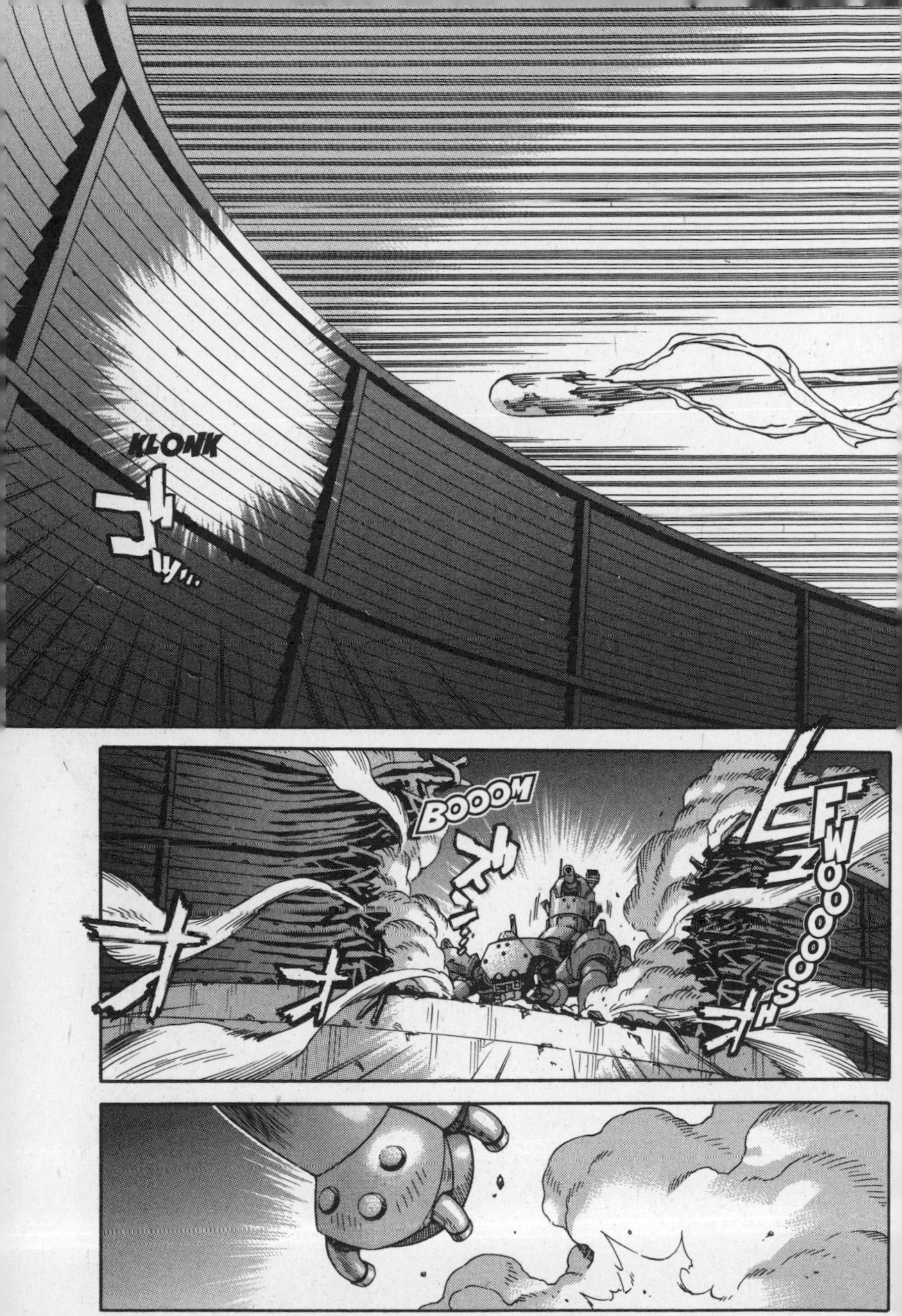
KLONK
FWOOOOOSH
BOOOM

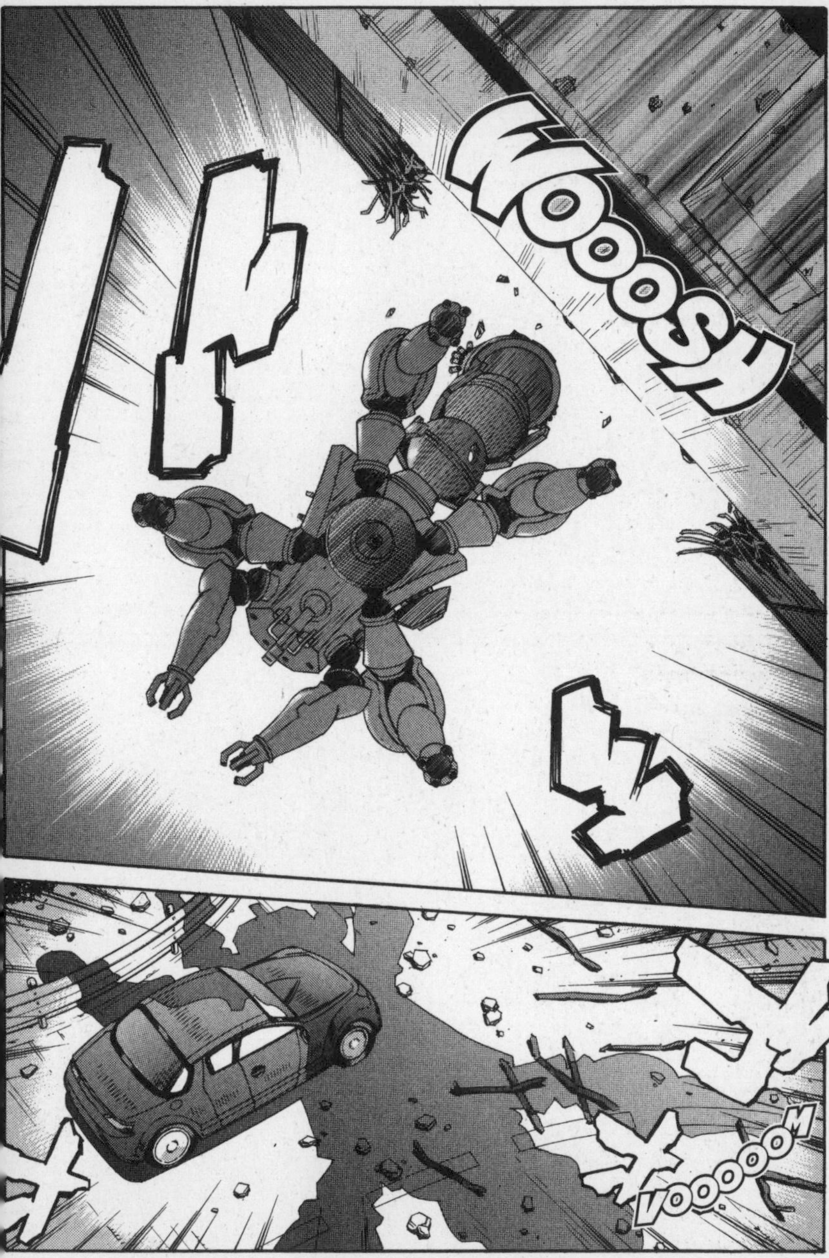
WOOOOSH
VOOOOOOM

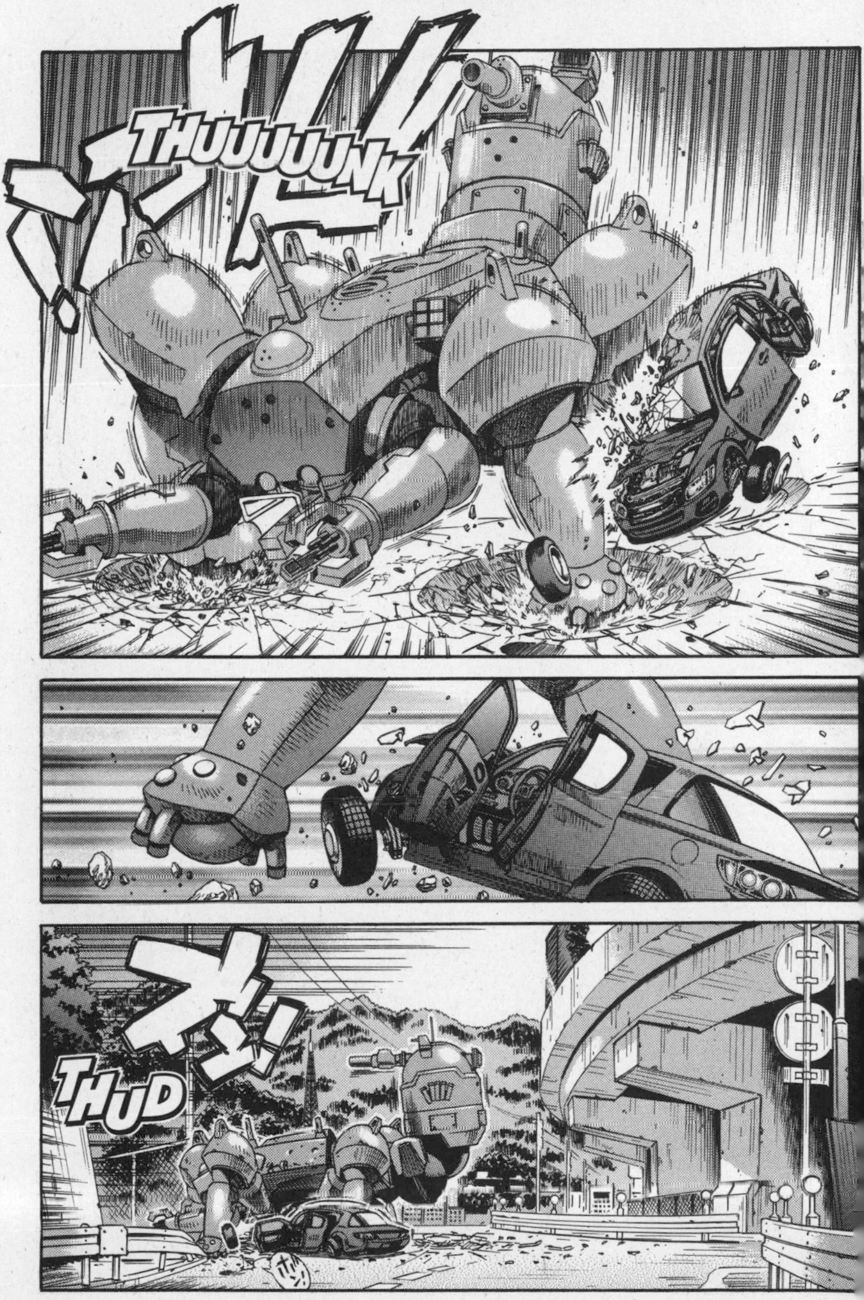
THUUUUUNK
THUD

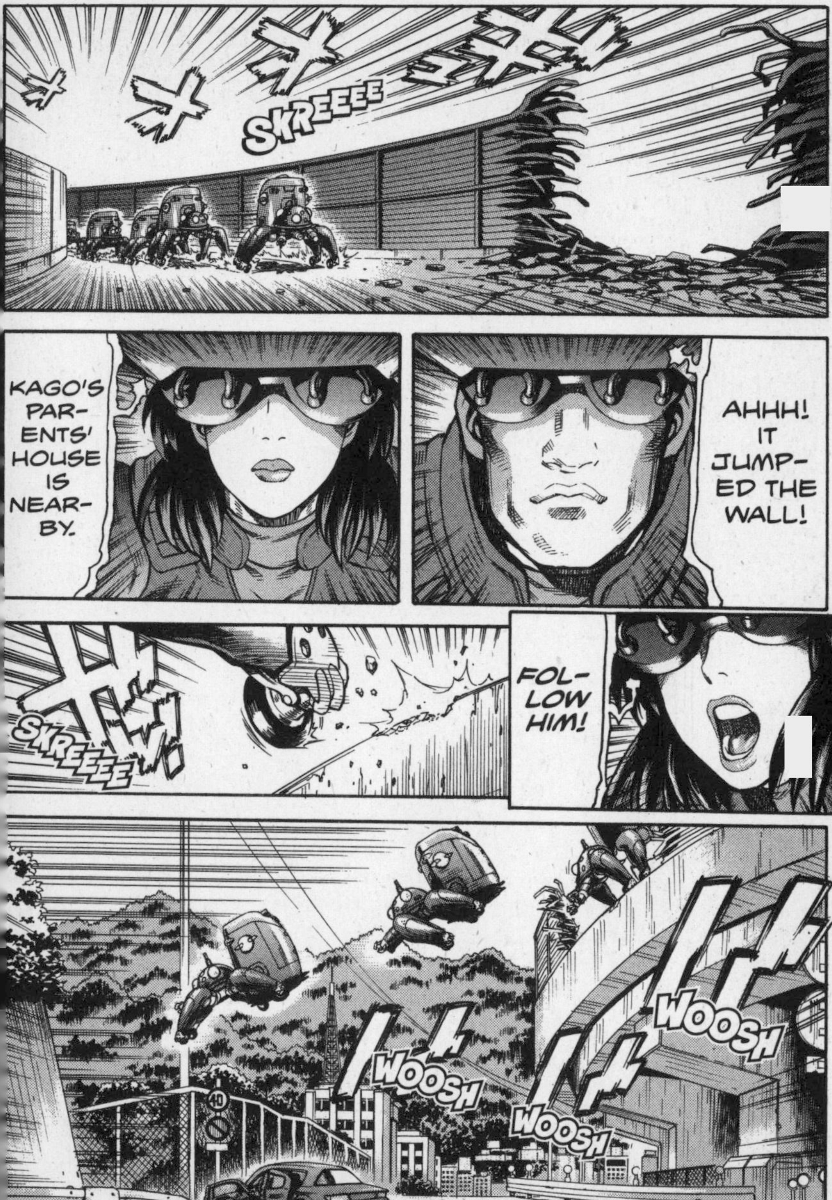
SKREEEE
AHHH! IT JUMPED THE WALL!
KAGO'S PARENTS' HOUSE IS NEARBY.
FOLLOW HIM!
SKREEEE
WOOSH
WOOSH
WOOSH

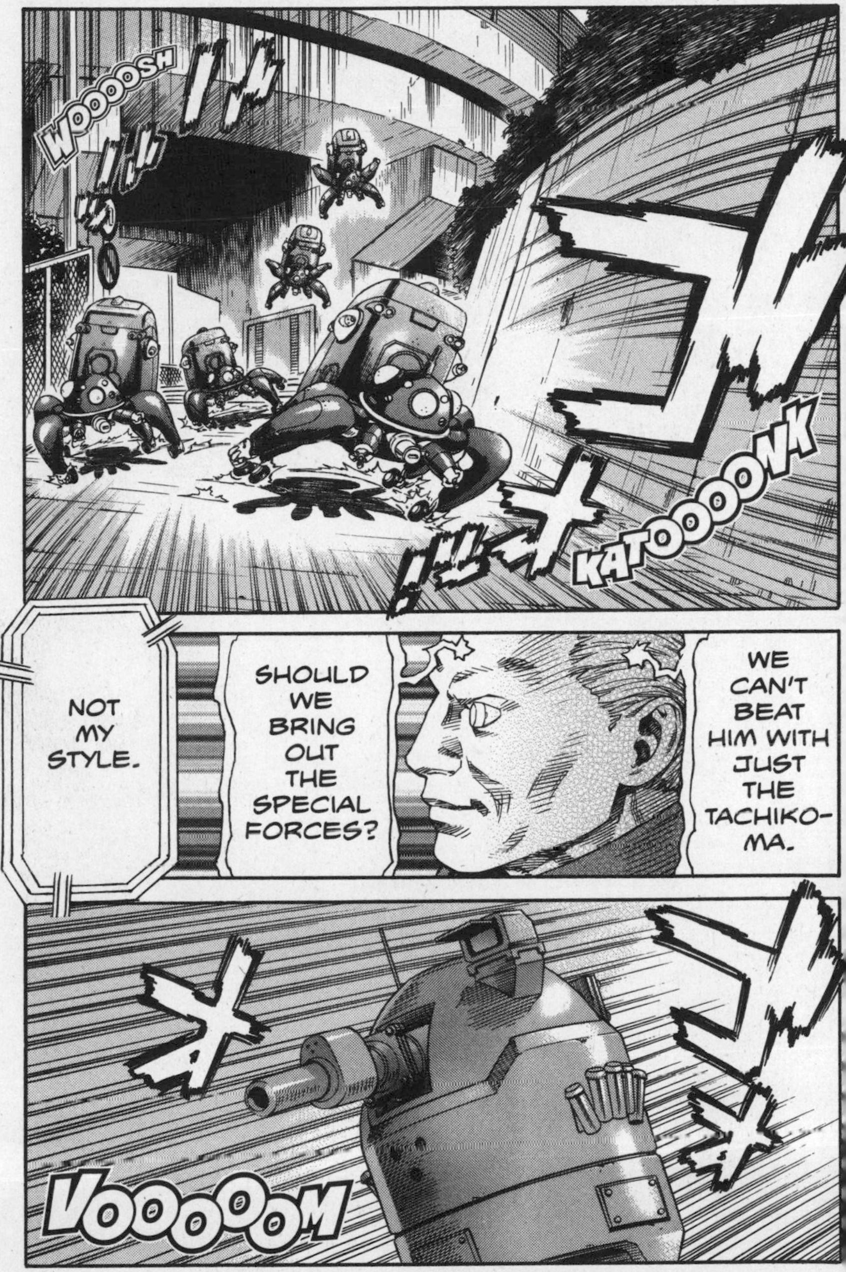
WOOOOSH
KATOOOOONK
WE CAN'T BEAT HIM WITH JUST THE TACHIKOMA.
SHOULD WE BRING OUT THE SPECIAL FORCES?
NOT MY STYLE.
VOOOOOOM

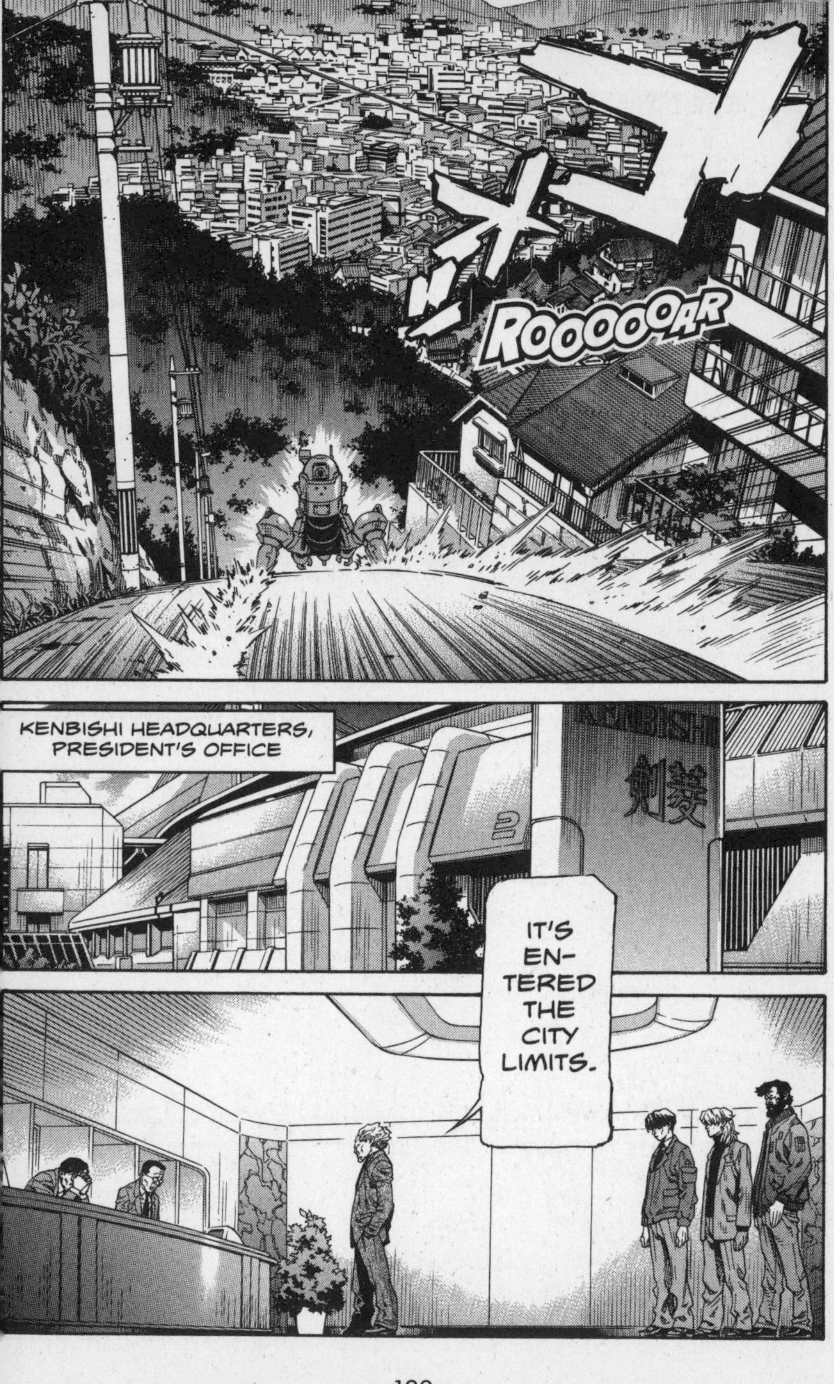
ROOOOOAR
KENBISHI HEADQUARTERS, PRESIDENT'S OFFICE
KENBISHI
IT'S EN-TERED THE CITY LIMITS.

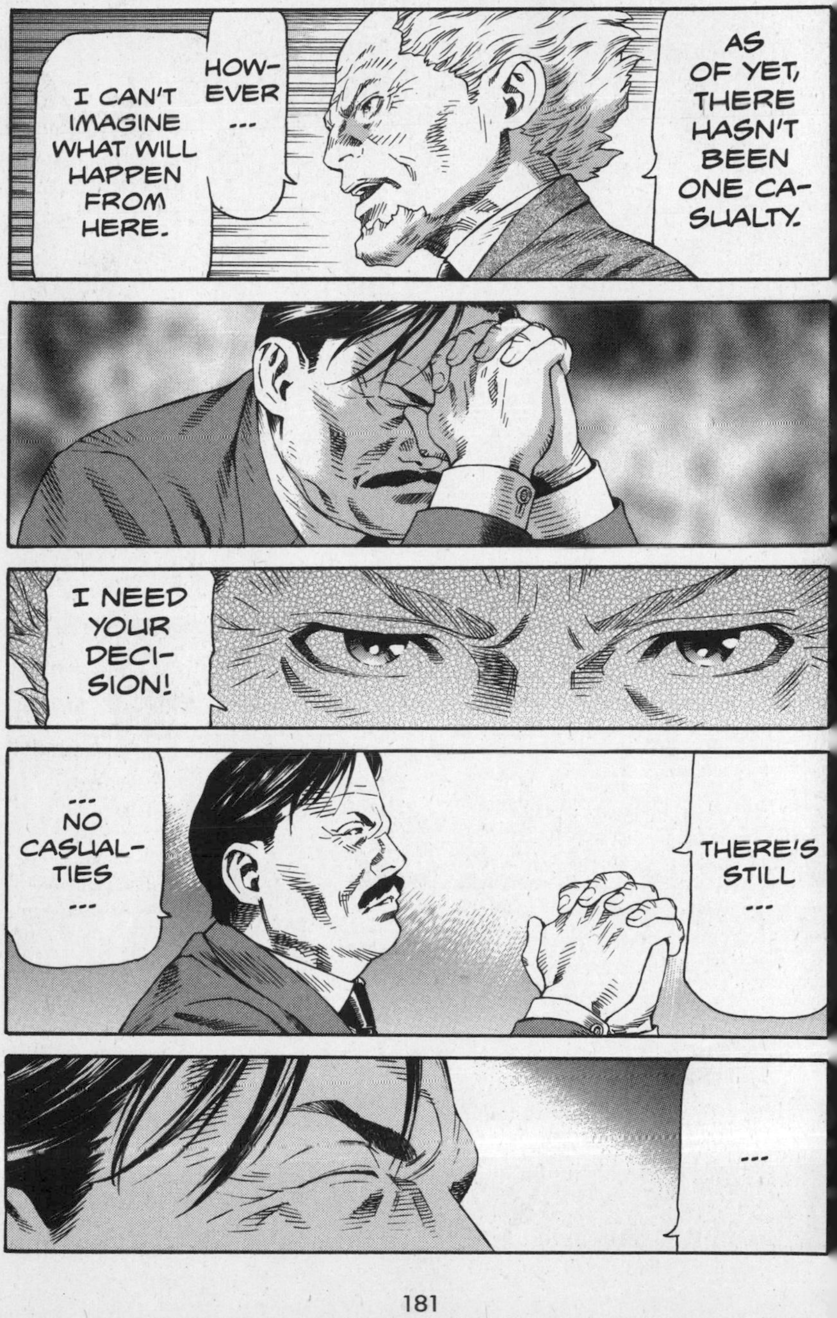
AS OF YET, THERE HASN'T BEEN ONE CA-SUALTY.
HOW-EVER ...
I CAN'T IMAGINE WHAT WILL HAPPEN FROM HERE.
I NEED YOUR DECI-SION!
THERE'S STILL ...
... NO CASUAL-TIES ...
...

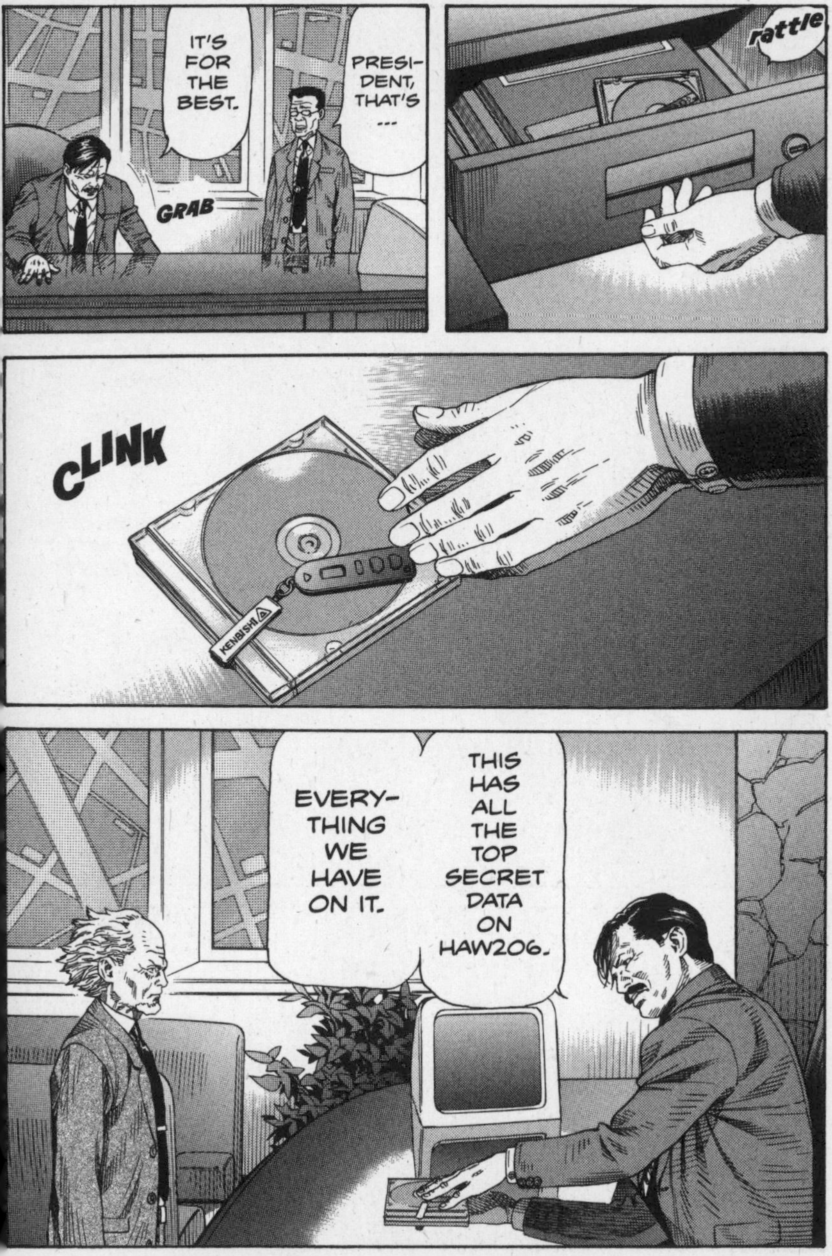
rattle
PRESIDENT, THAT'S ---
IT'S FOR THE BEST.
GRAB
CLINK
KENBISHI
THIS HAS ALL THE TOP SECRET DATA ON HAW206.
EVERYTHING WE HAVE ON IT.

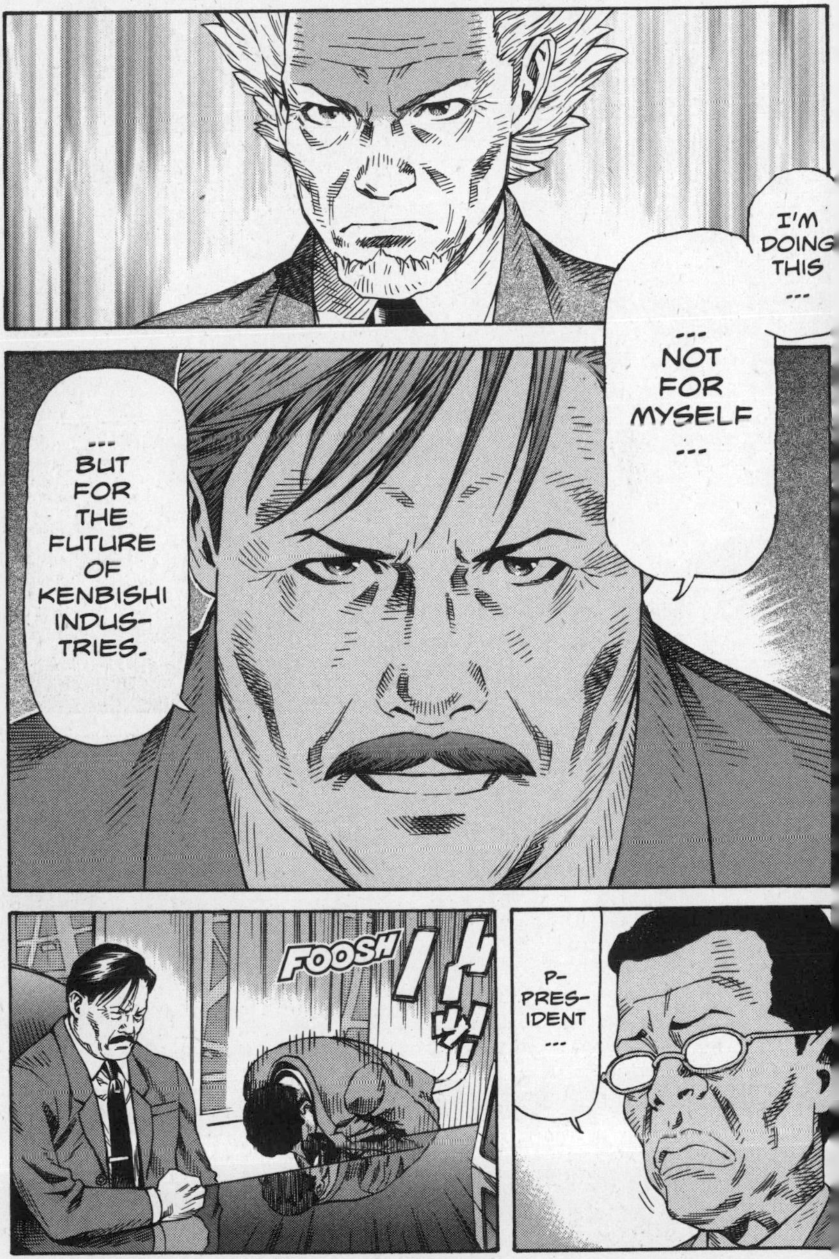
I'M DOING THIS ---
--- NOT FOR MYSELF ---
--- BUT FOR THE FUTURE OF KENBISHI INDUSTRIES.
P-PRESIDENT ---
FOOSH

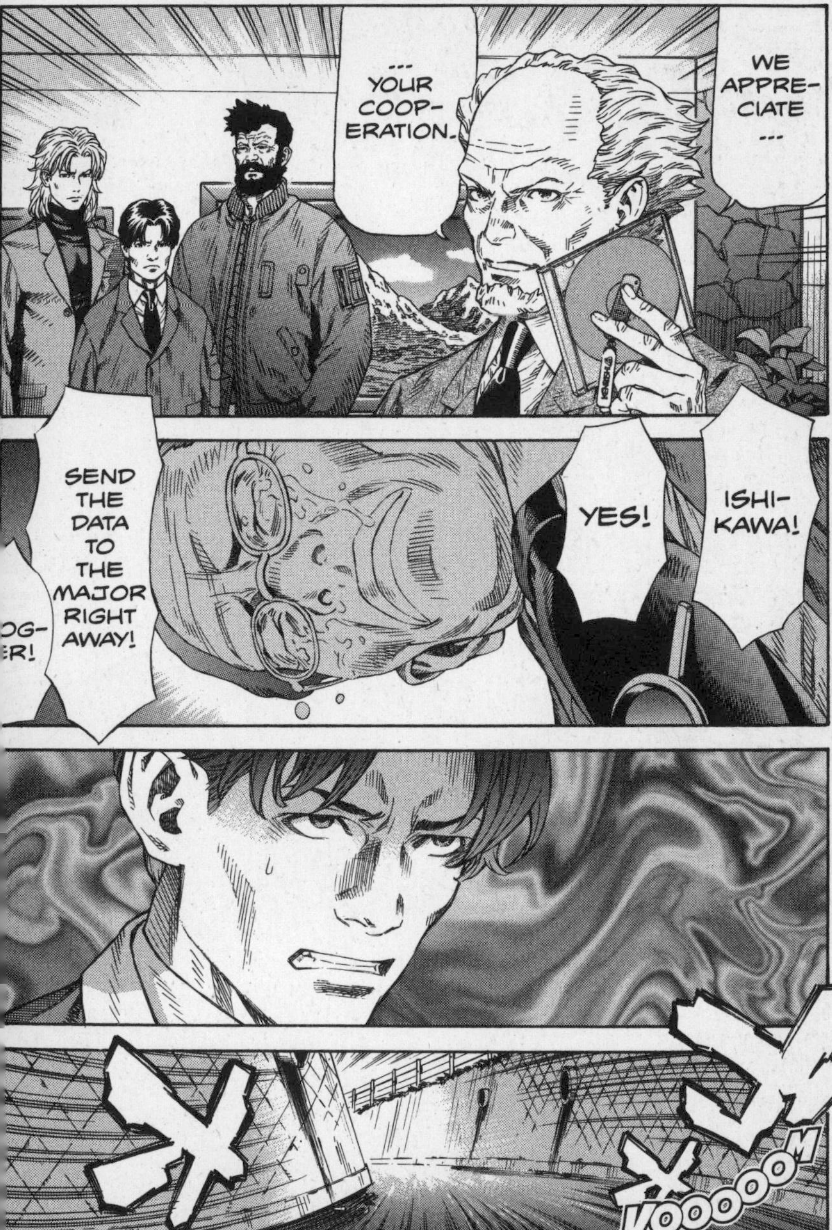

WE APPRECIATE ---
--- YOUR COOPERATION.
ISHIKAWA!
YES!
SEND THE DATA TO THE MAJOR RIGHT AWAY!
OG- ER!
VOOOOOOM

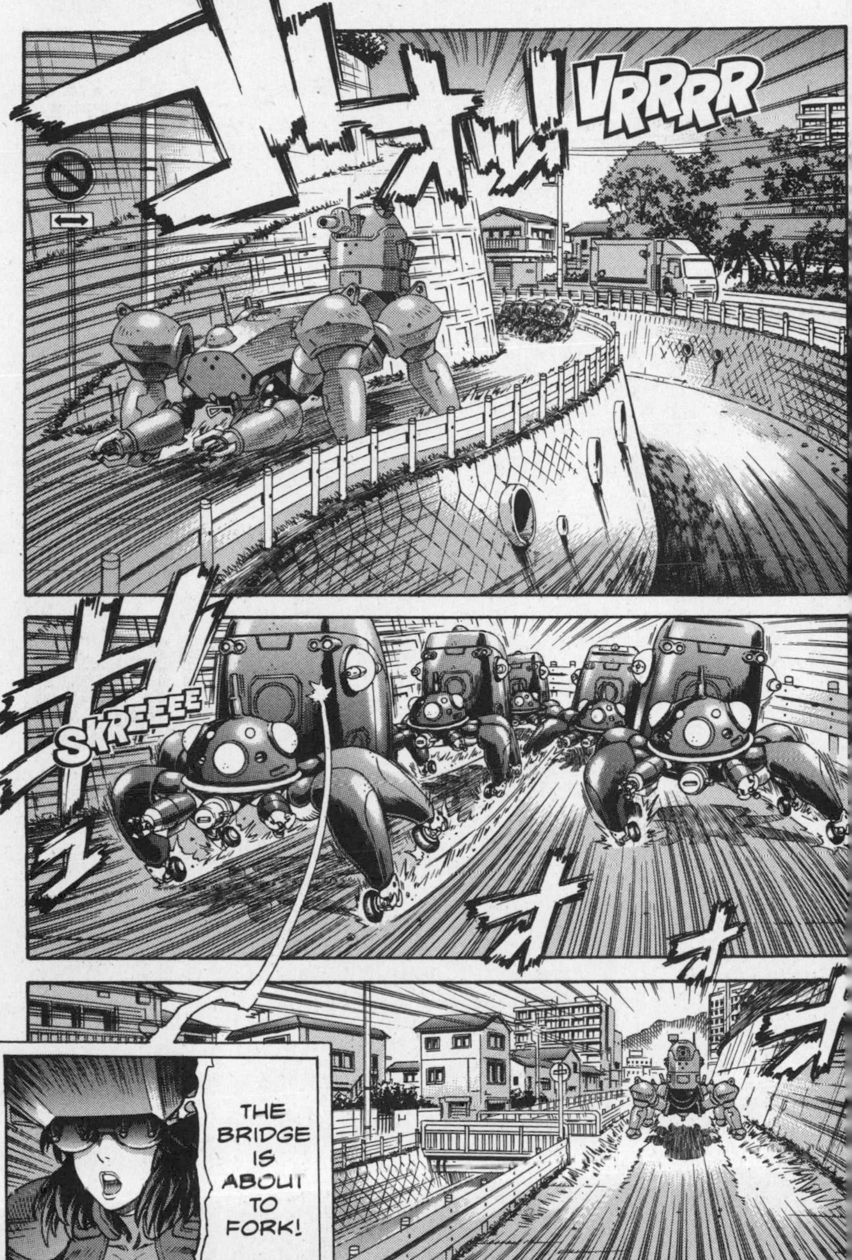
VRRRR
SKREEEE
THE BRIDGE IS ABOUT TO FORK!

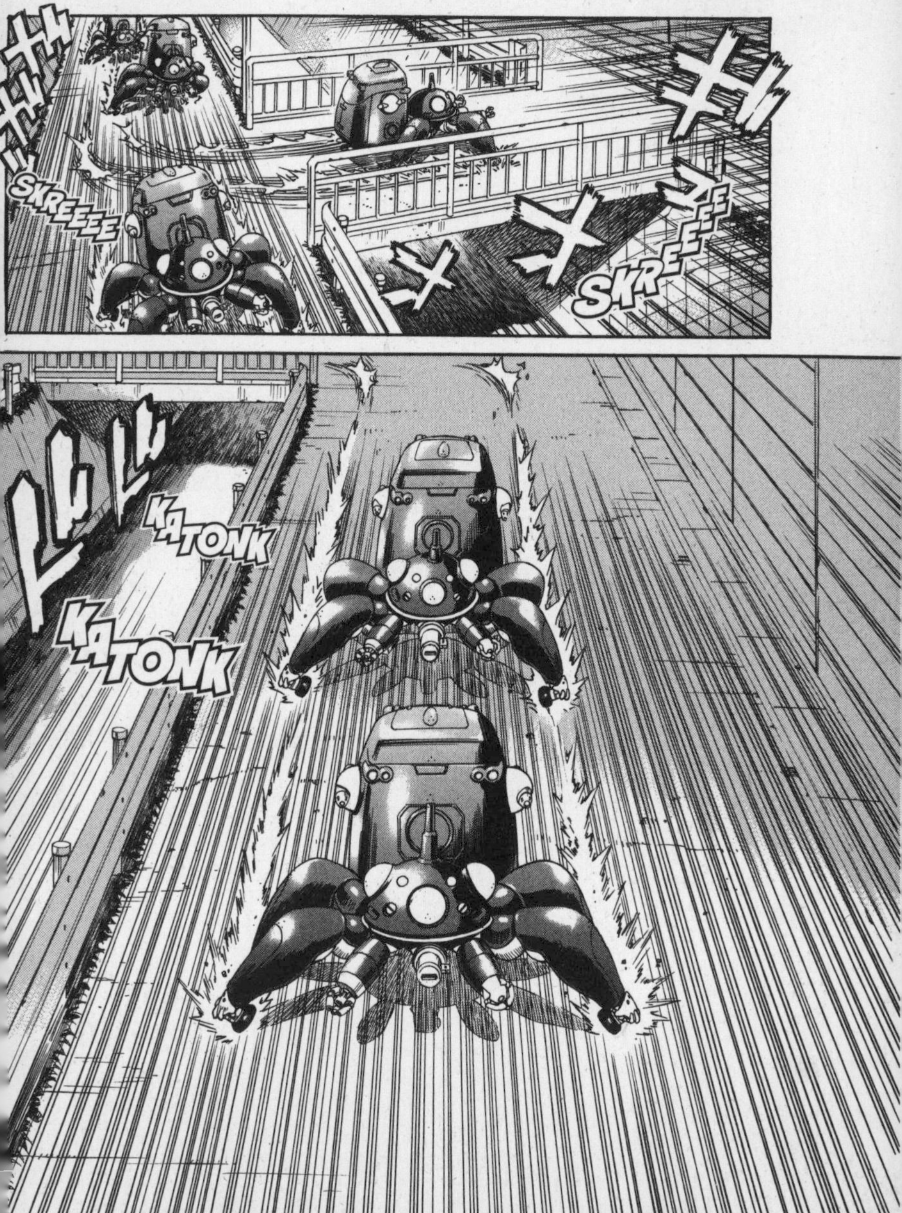
SKREEEEE
SKREEEE
KATONK
KATONK

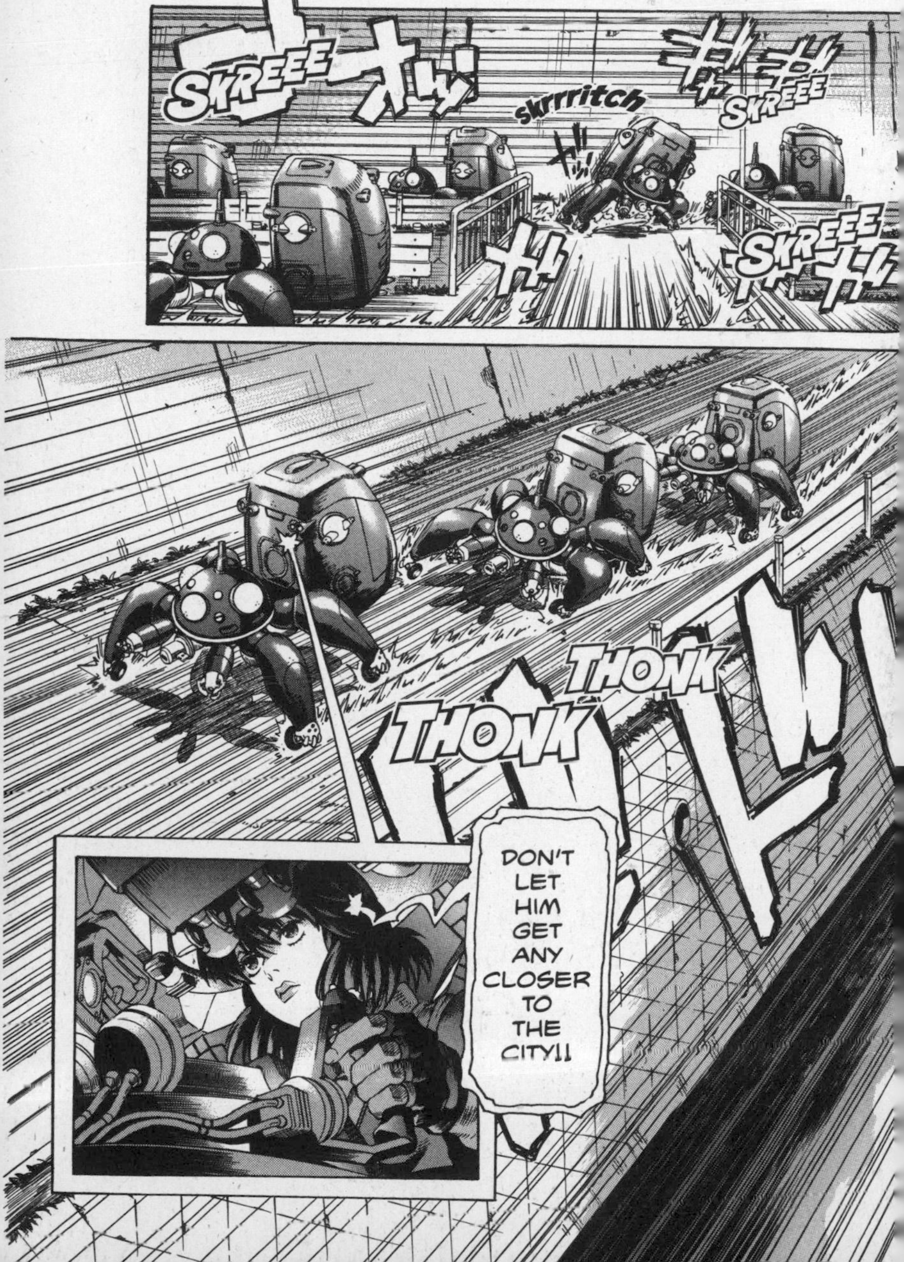
SKREEE
SKREEE
skrrritch
SKREEE
THONK
THONK
DON'T LET HIM GET ANY CLOSER TO THE CITY!!

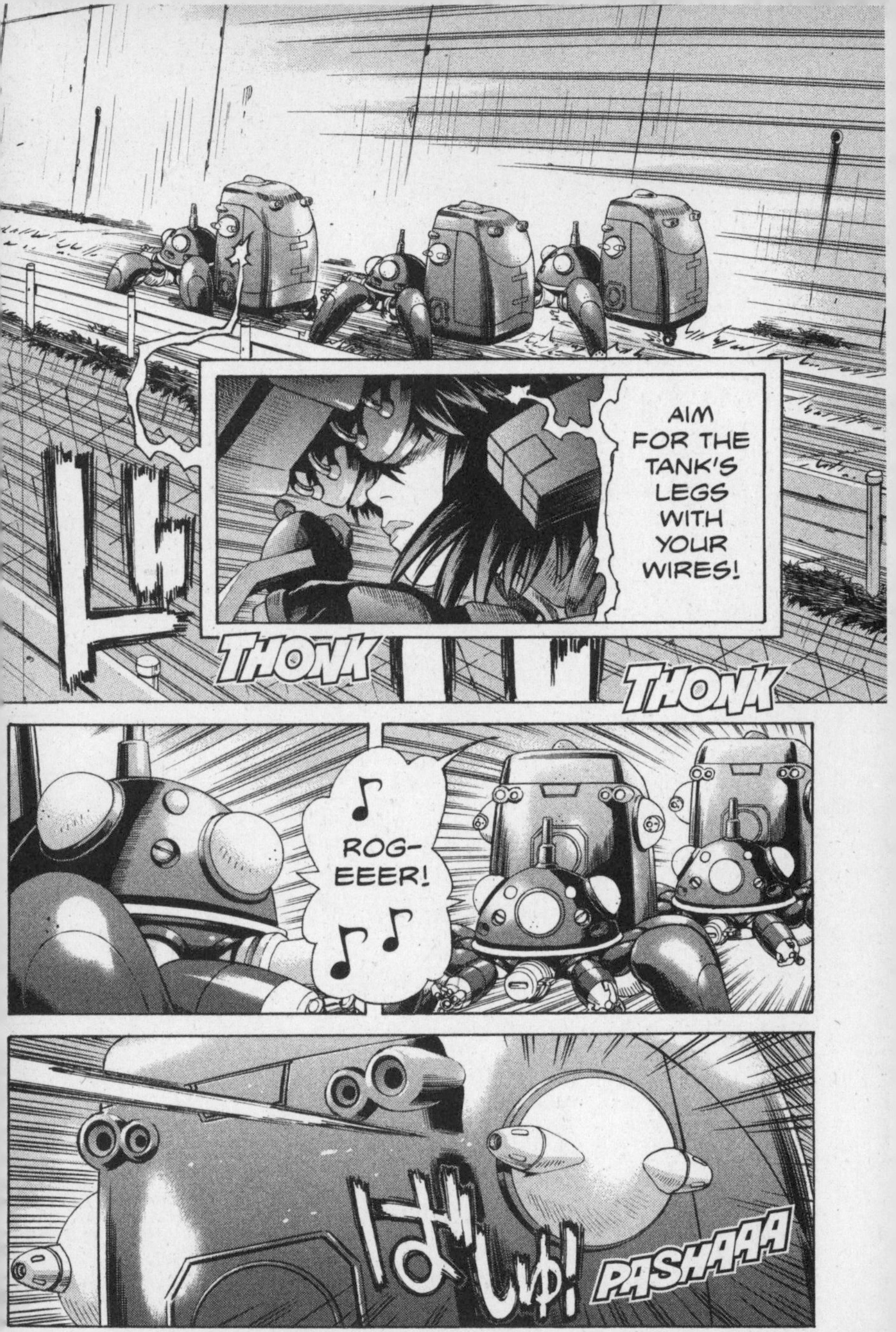
AIM FOR THE TANK'S LEGS WITH YOUR WIRES!
THONK
THONK
♪ ROG-EEER! ♪♪
ぱしゅ!
PASHAAA

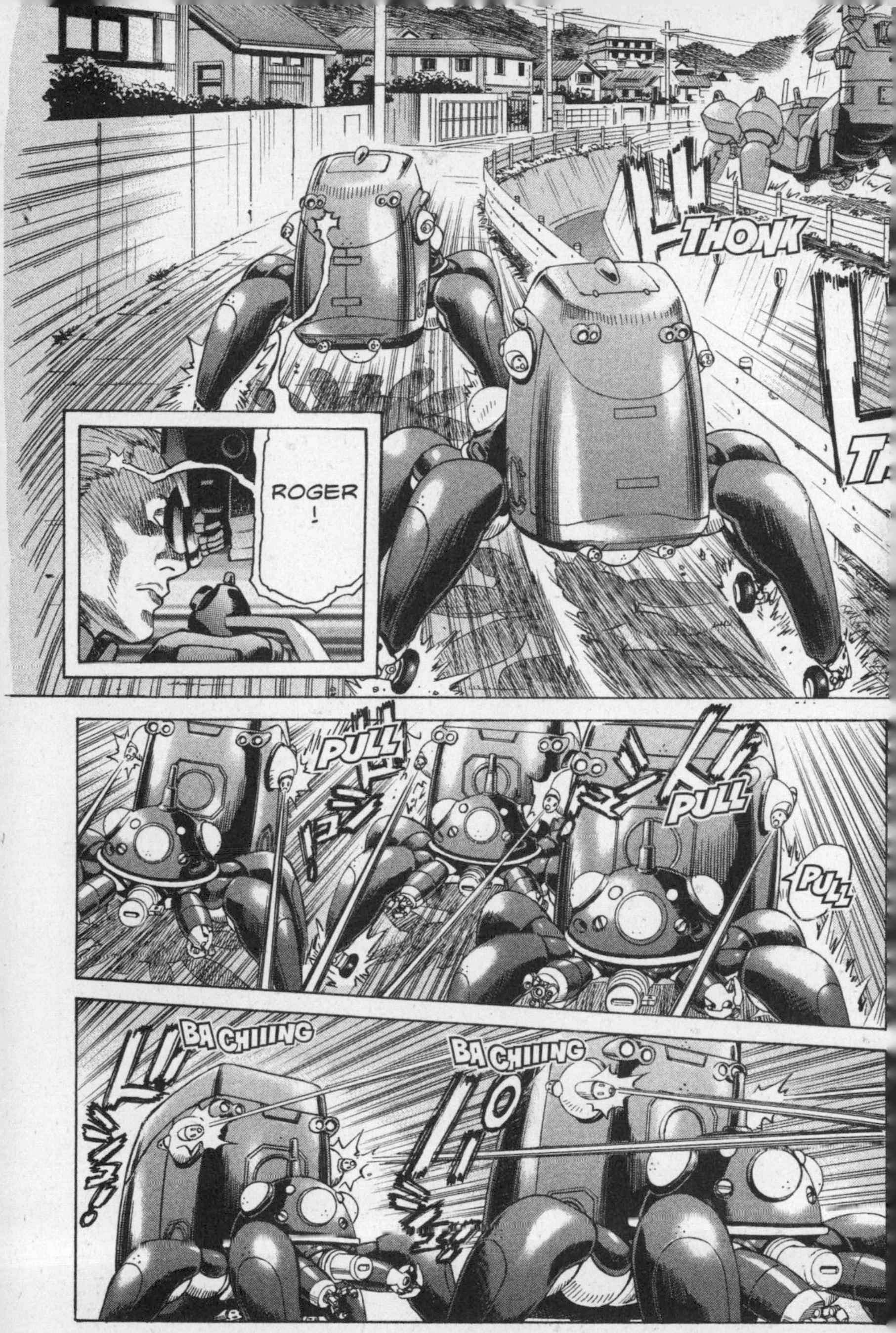
THONK
ROGER !
PULL
PULL
PULL
BA CHIIIING
BA CHIIIING

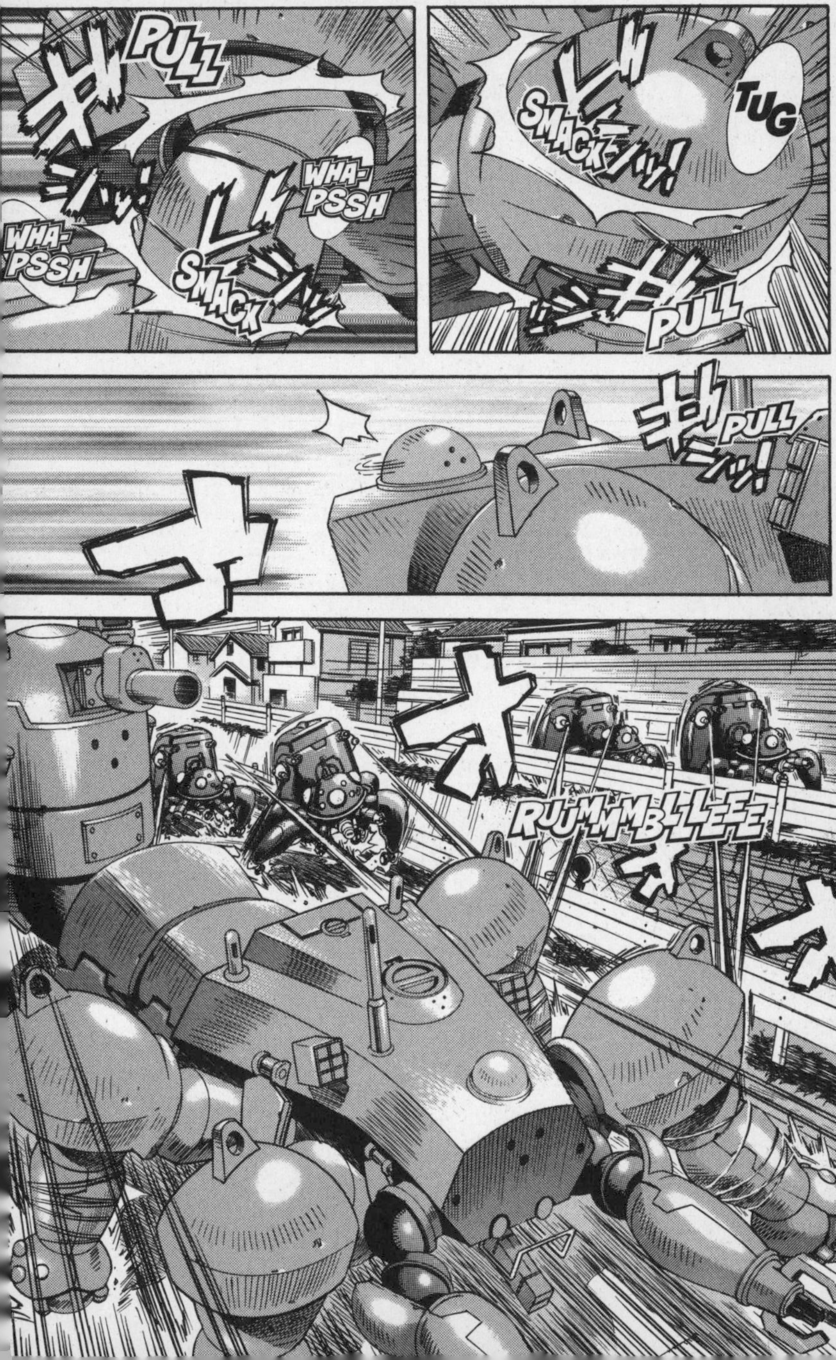
TUG
SMACK
PULL
PULL
WHA-PSSH
SMACK
WHA-PSSH
PULL
RUUMMMBLLEEE

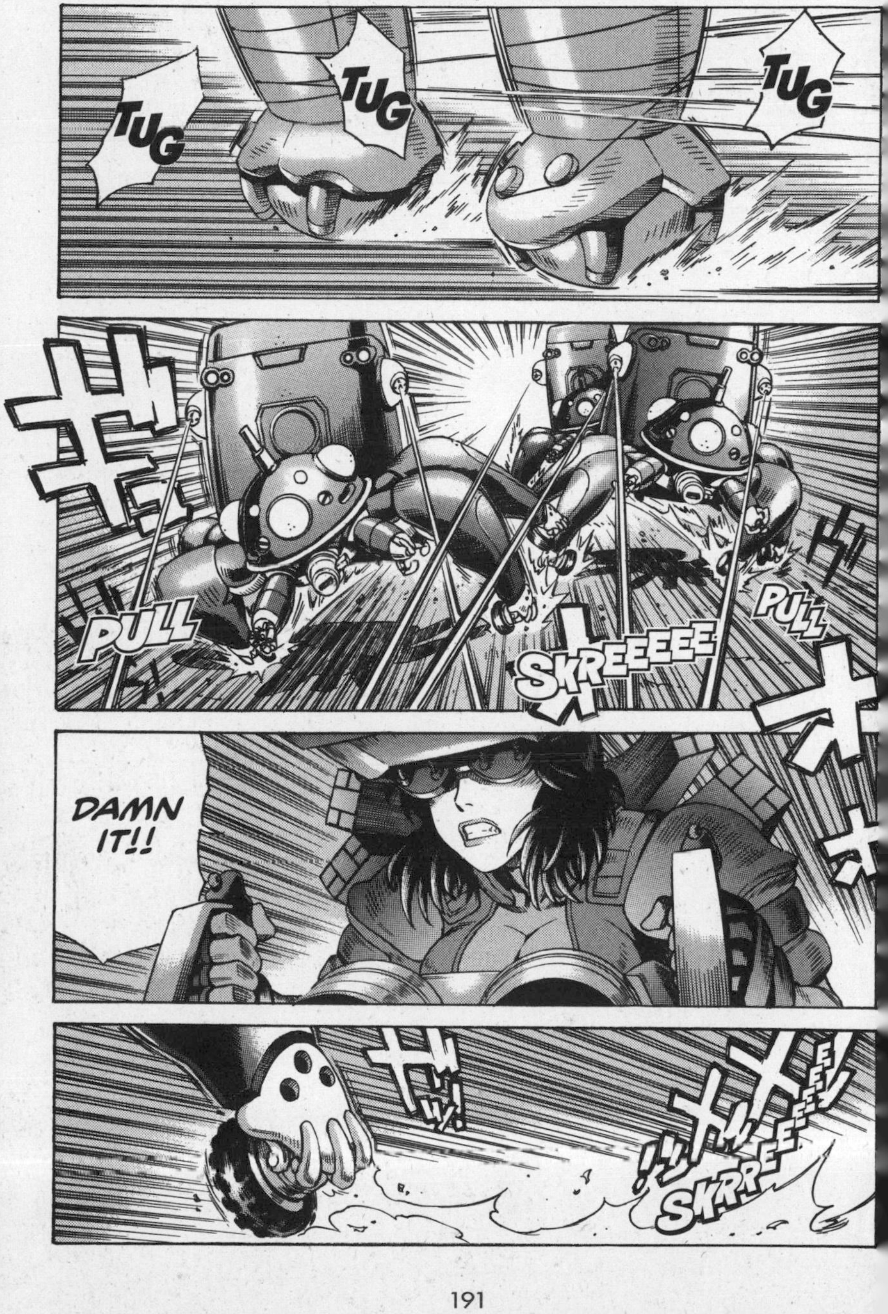
TUG
TUG
TUG
PULL
SKREEEEEE
PULL
DAMN IT!!
SKRREEEEEEE

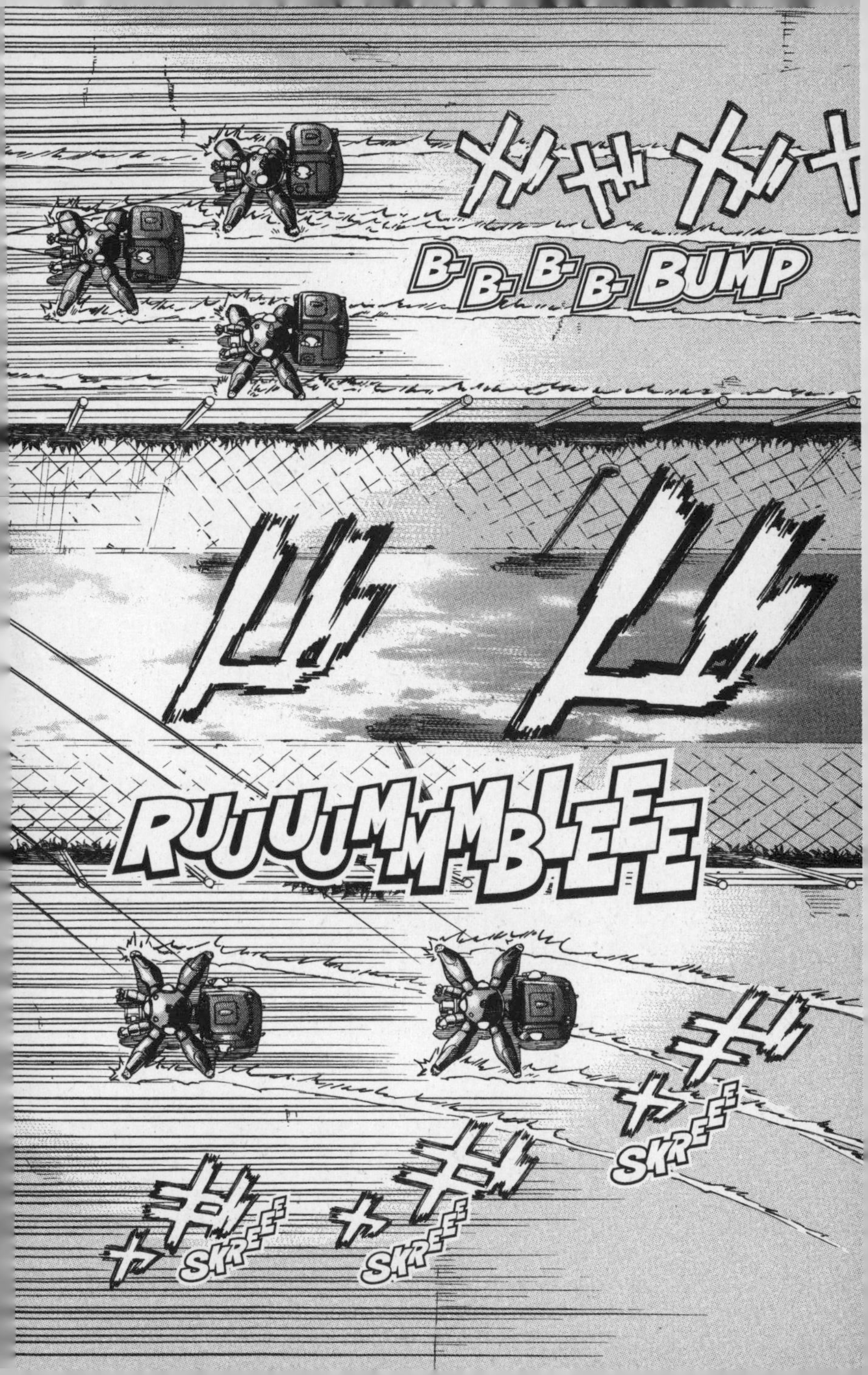
B-B-B-B-BUMP
RUUUMMMBLEEE
SKREEE
SKREEE
SKREEE

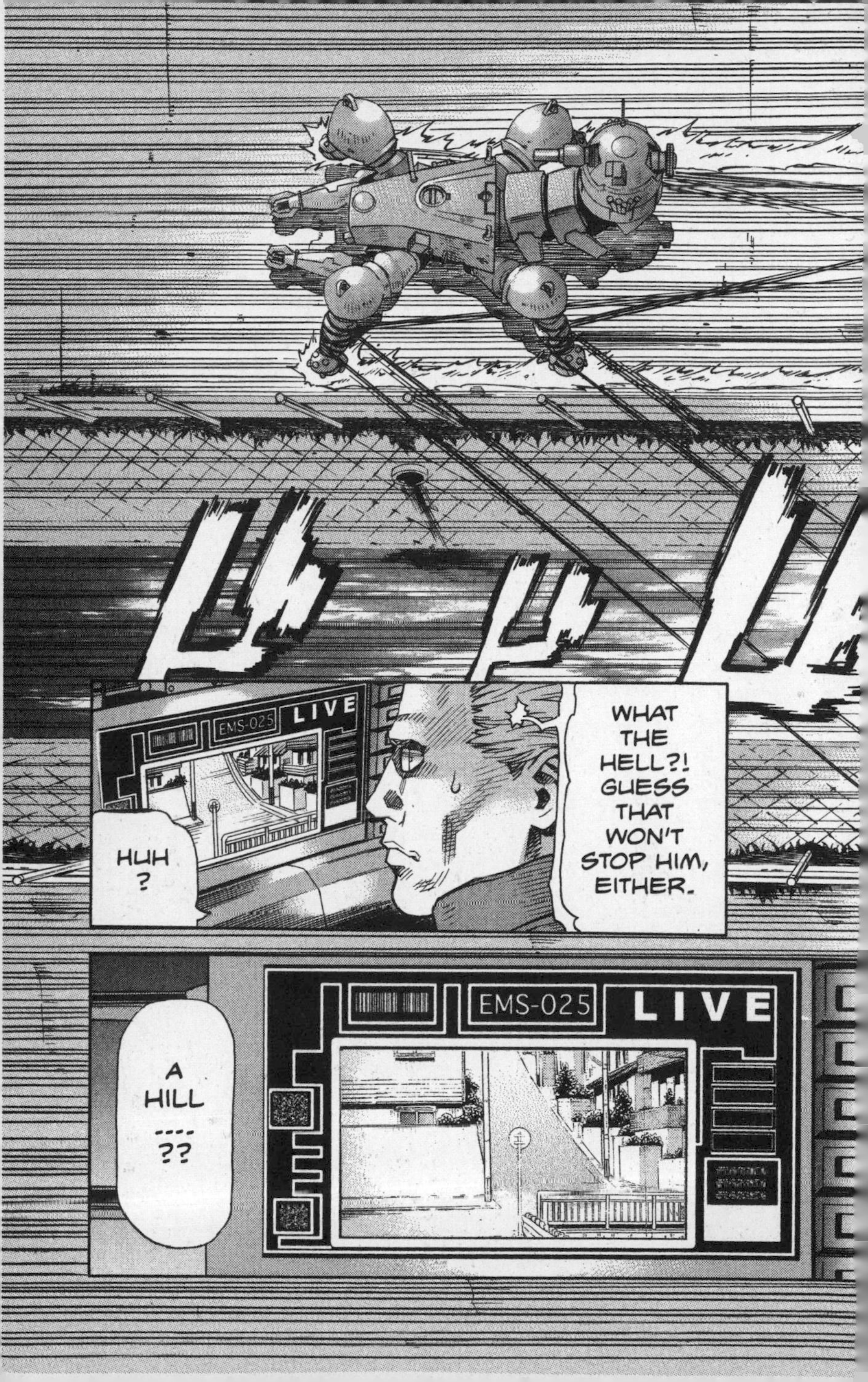
WHAT THE HELL?! GUESS THAT WON'T STOP HIM, EITHER.
HUH ?
EMS-025
LIVE
EMS-025
LIVE
A HILL ---- ??

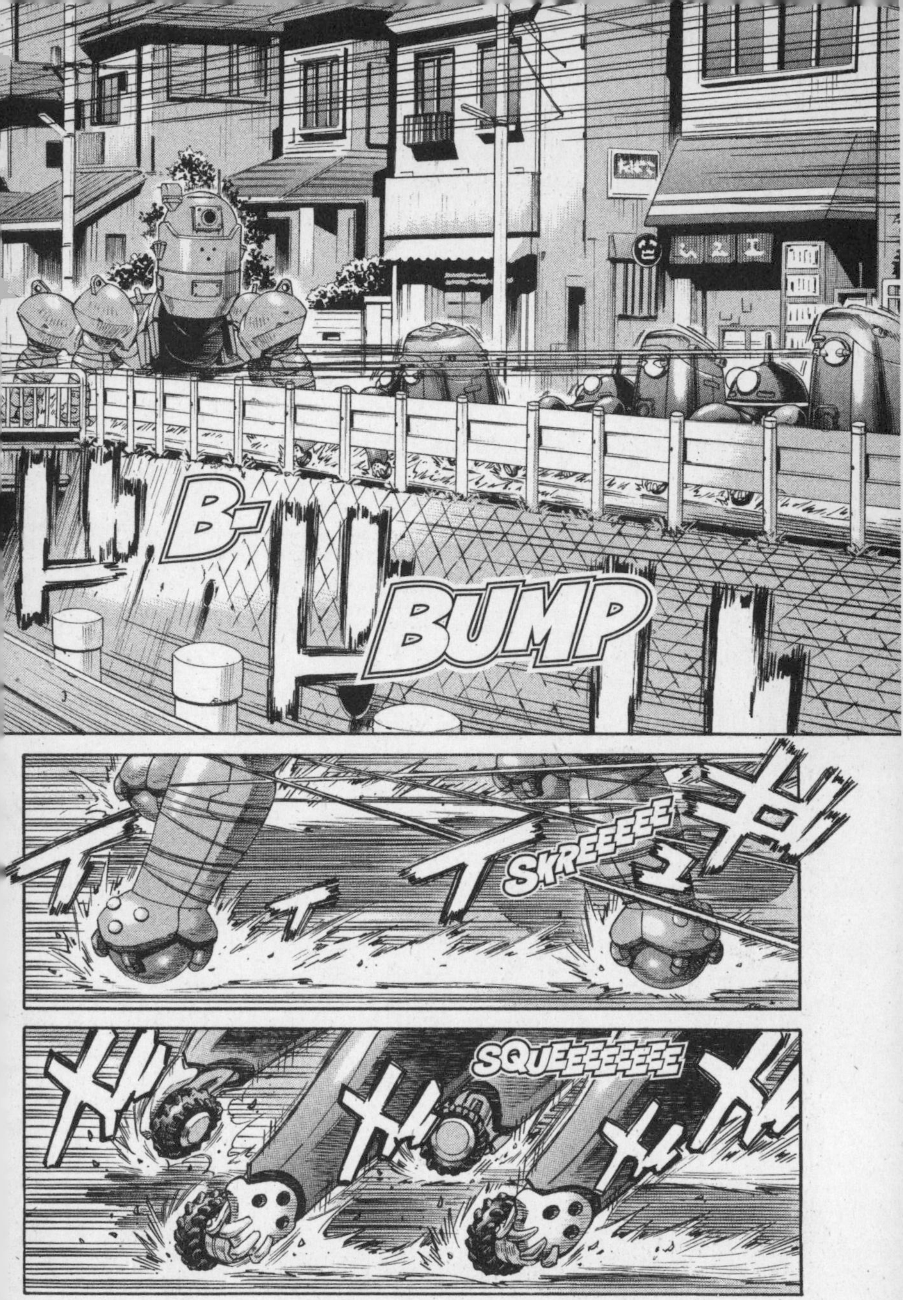
B-
BUMP
SKREEEEEE
SQUEEEEEEEE

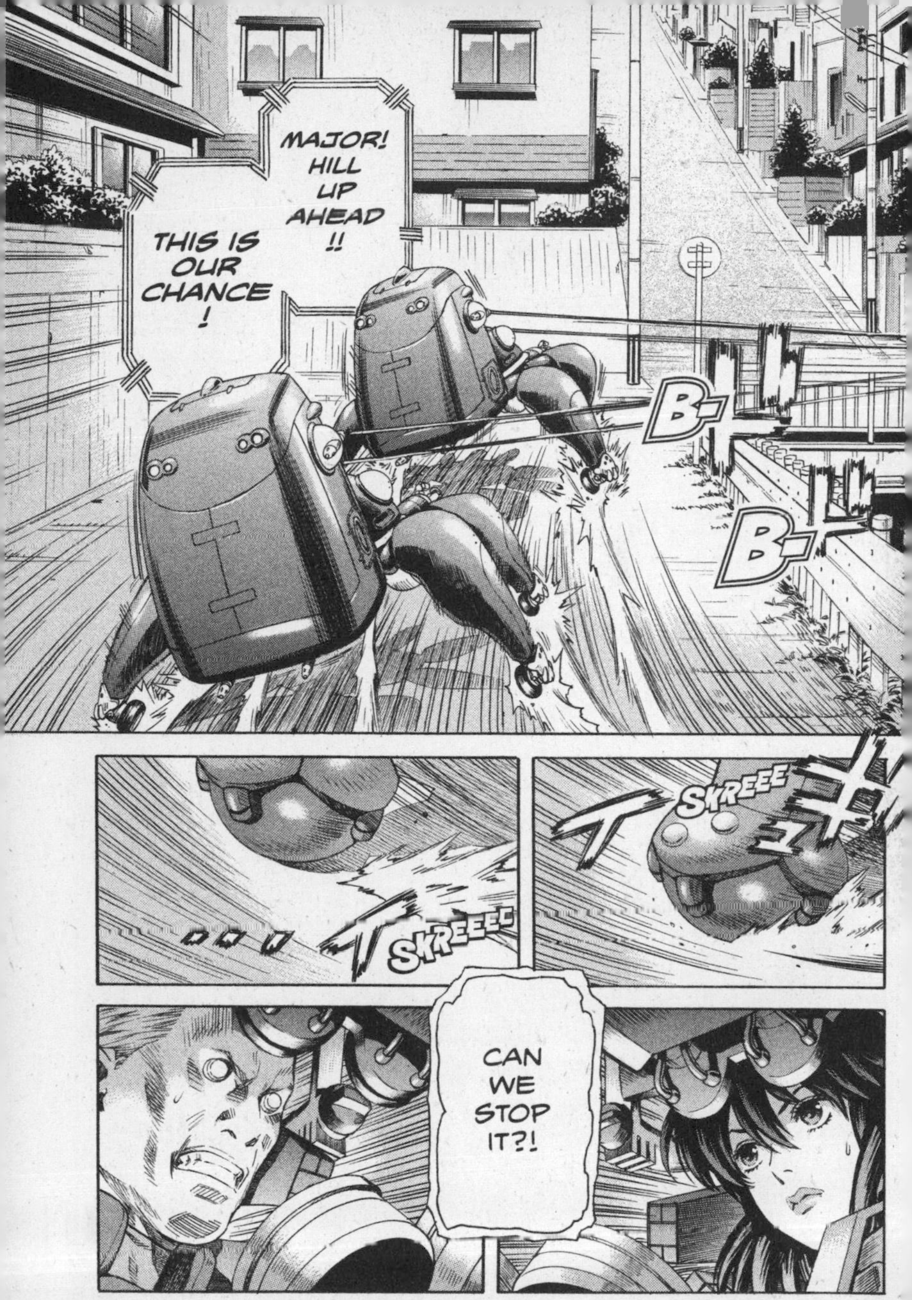
MAJOR! HILL UP AHEAD!!
THIS IS OUR CHANCE!
B-
B-
SKREEE
SKREEEE
CAN WE STOP IT?!

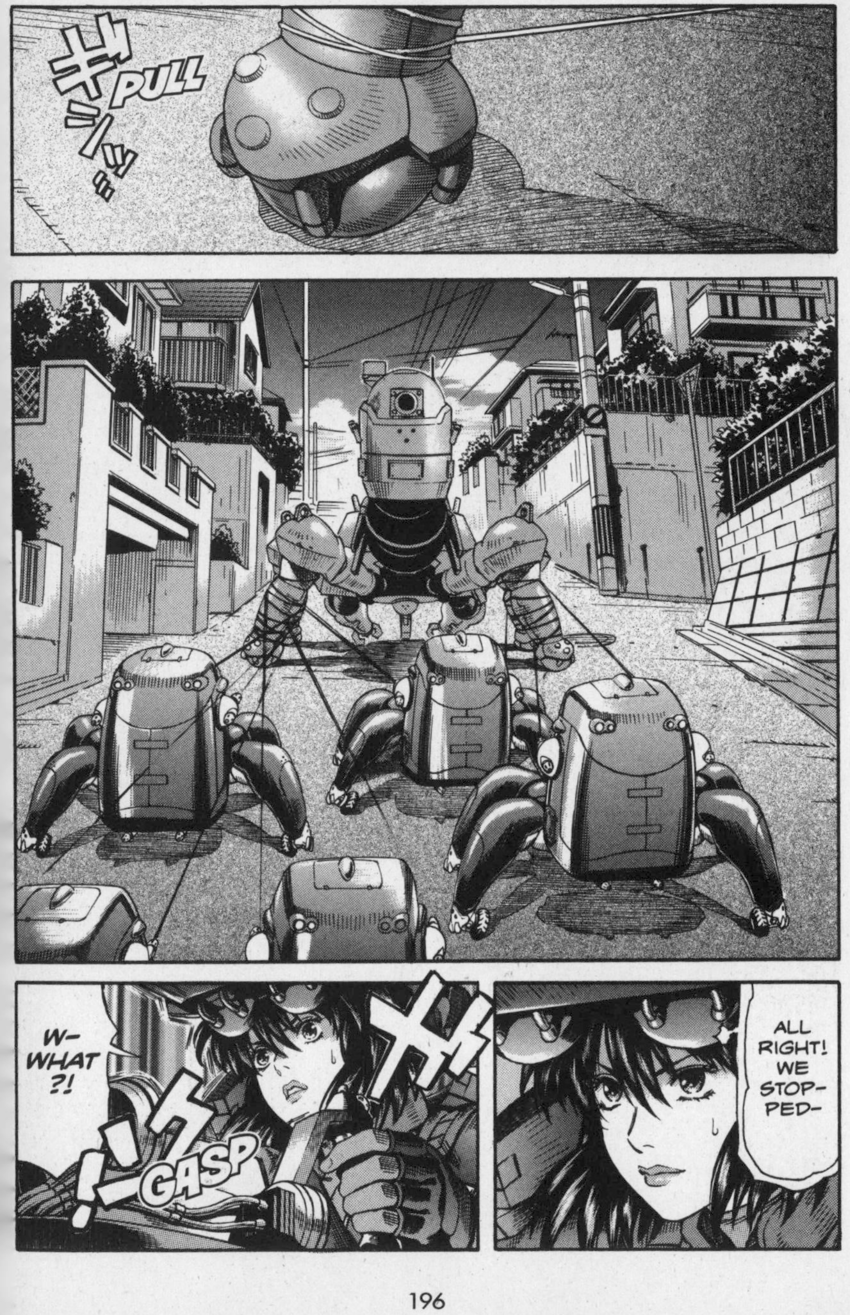
PULL
ALL RIGHT! WE STOP-PED-
W-WHAT?!
GASP

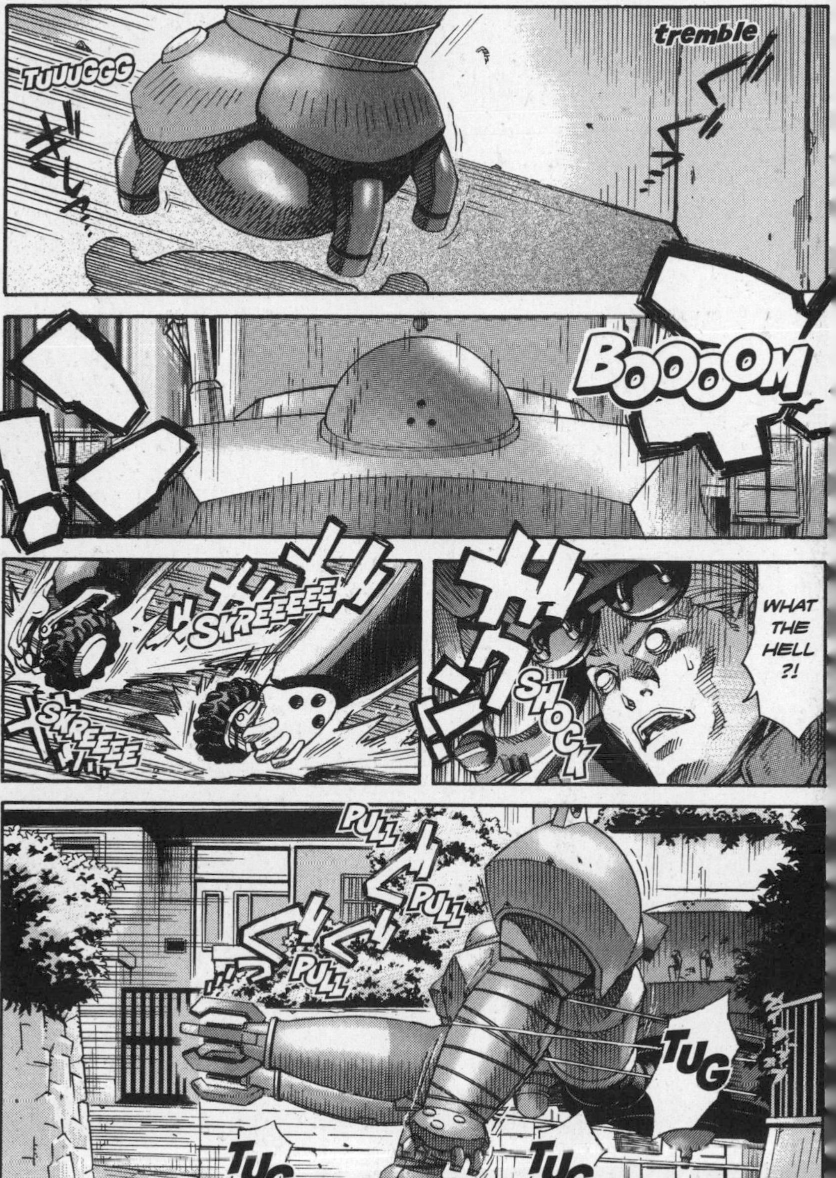
tremble
TUUUGGG
BOOOOOM
WHAT THE HELL ?!
SHOCK
SKREEEEEE
SKREEEEE
PULL
PULL
PULL
TUG
TUG
TUG

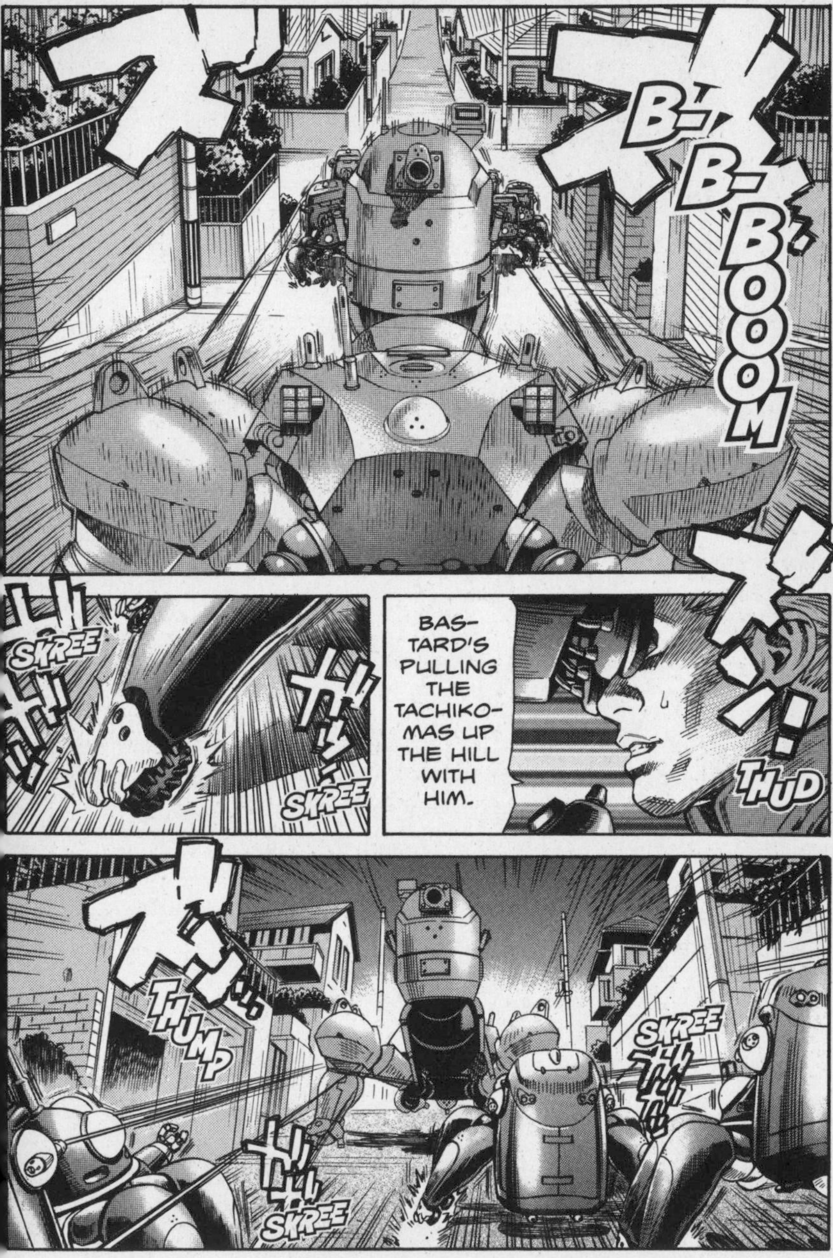
B-B-BOOOM
BAS-TARD'S PULLING THE TACHIKO-MAS UP THE HILL WITH HIM.
THUD
SKREE
SKREE
SKREE
THUMP
SKREE

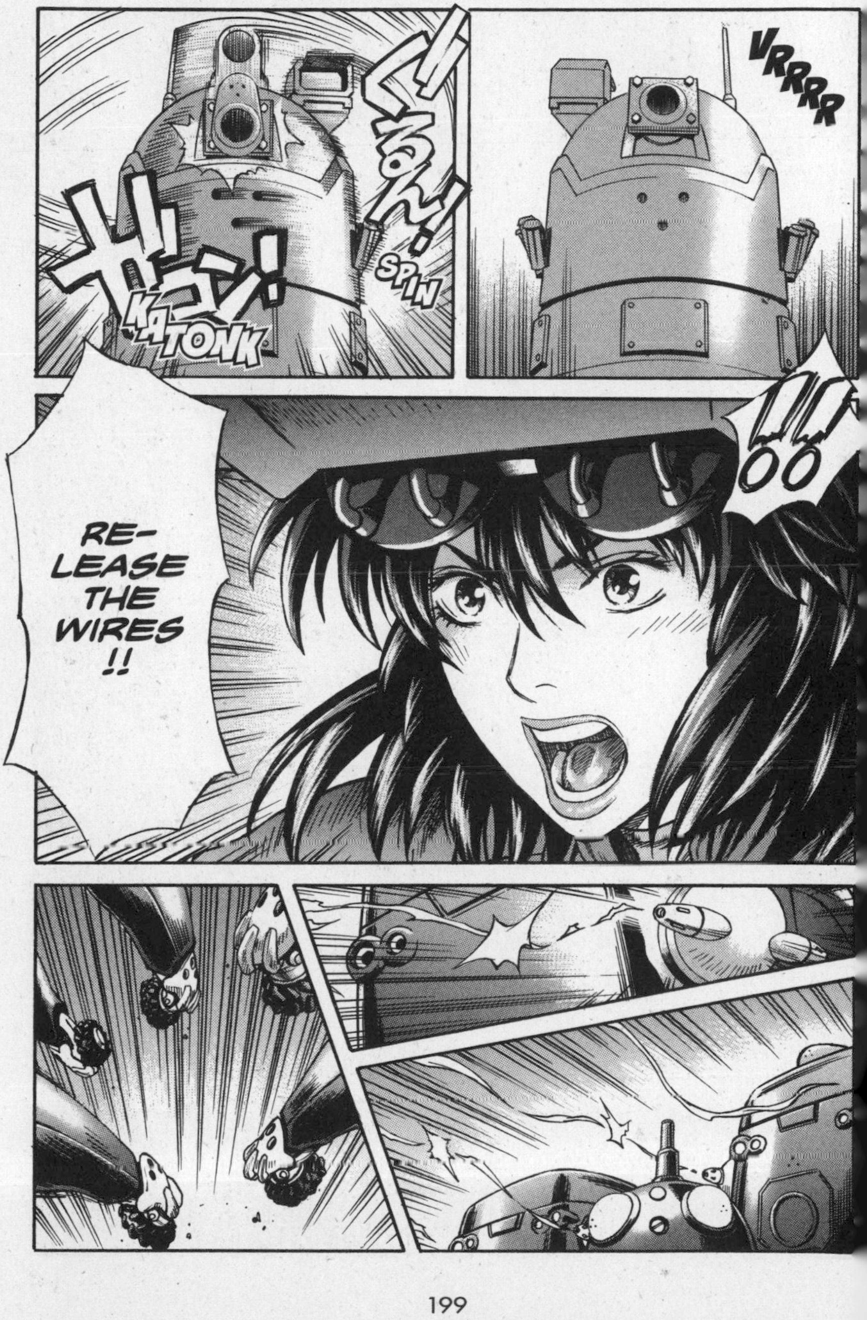

VRRRRR
くるん!
SPIN
ガコン!
KATONK
RE-
LEASE
THE
WIRES
!!

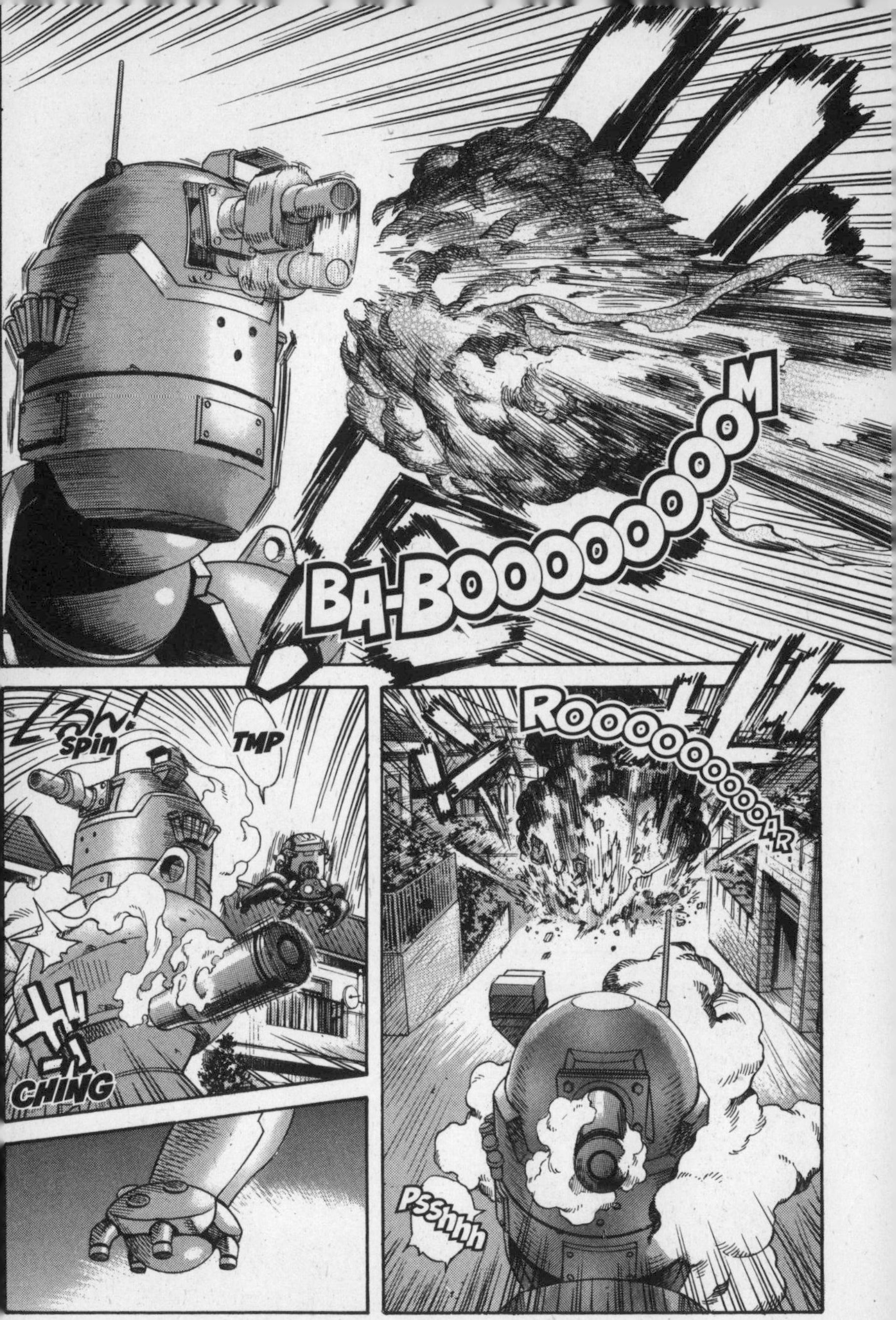
BA-BOOOOOOOOOM
ROOOOOOOOOOOAR
Psshhh
spin
TMP
CHING

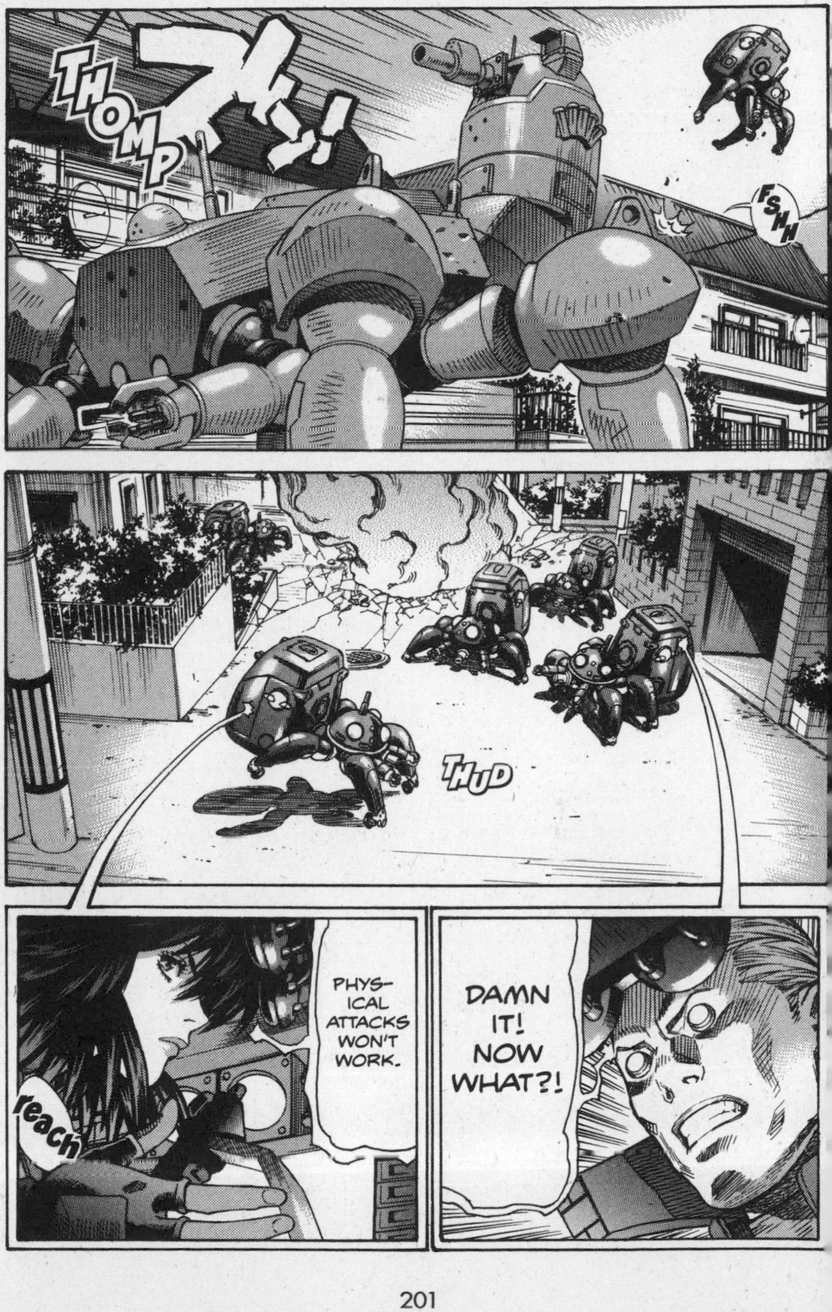
THOMP
FSHH
THUD
DAMN IT! NOW WHAT?!
PHYS-ICAL ATTACKS WON'T WORK.
reach

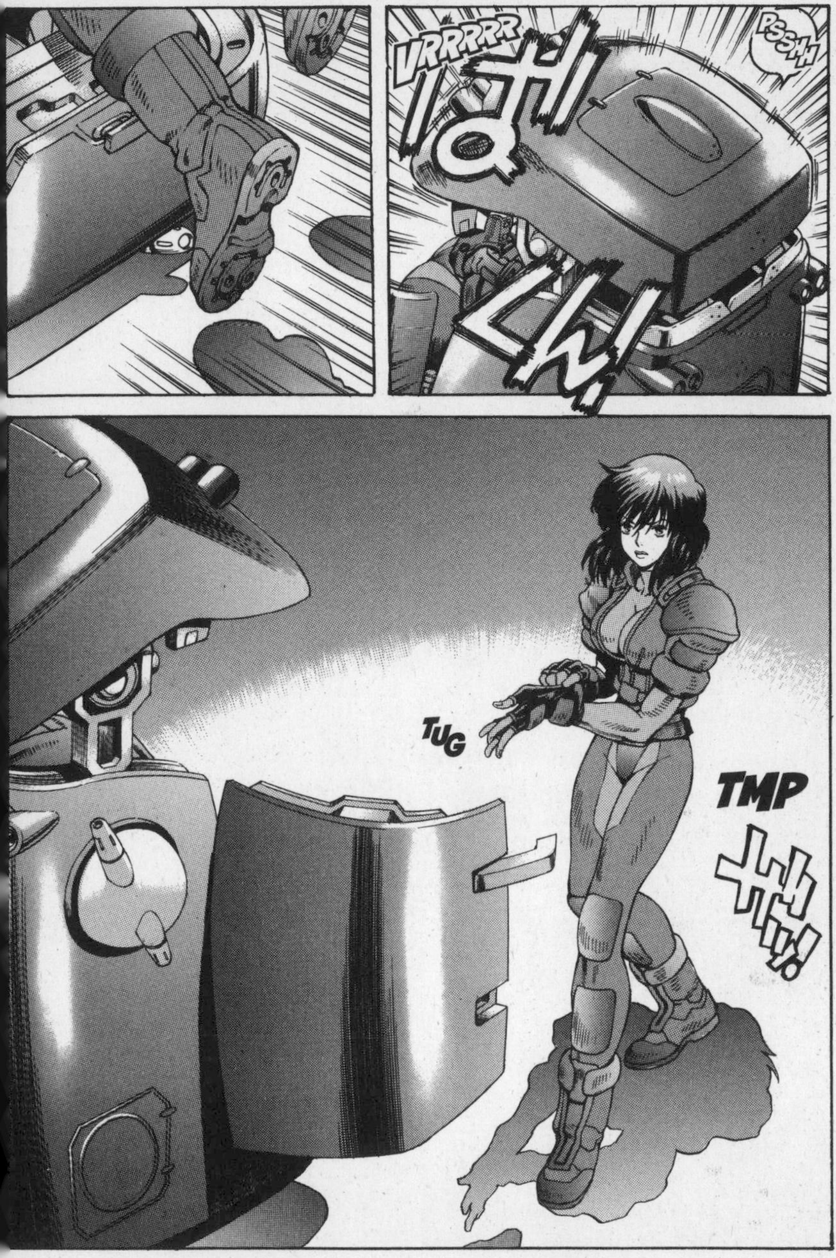
PSSHH
VRRRRR
TMP
TUG

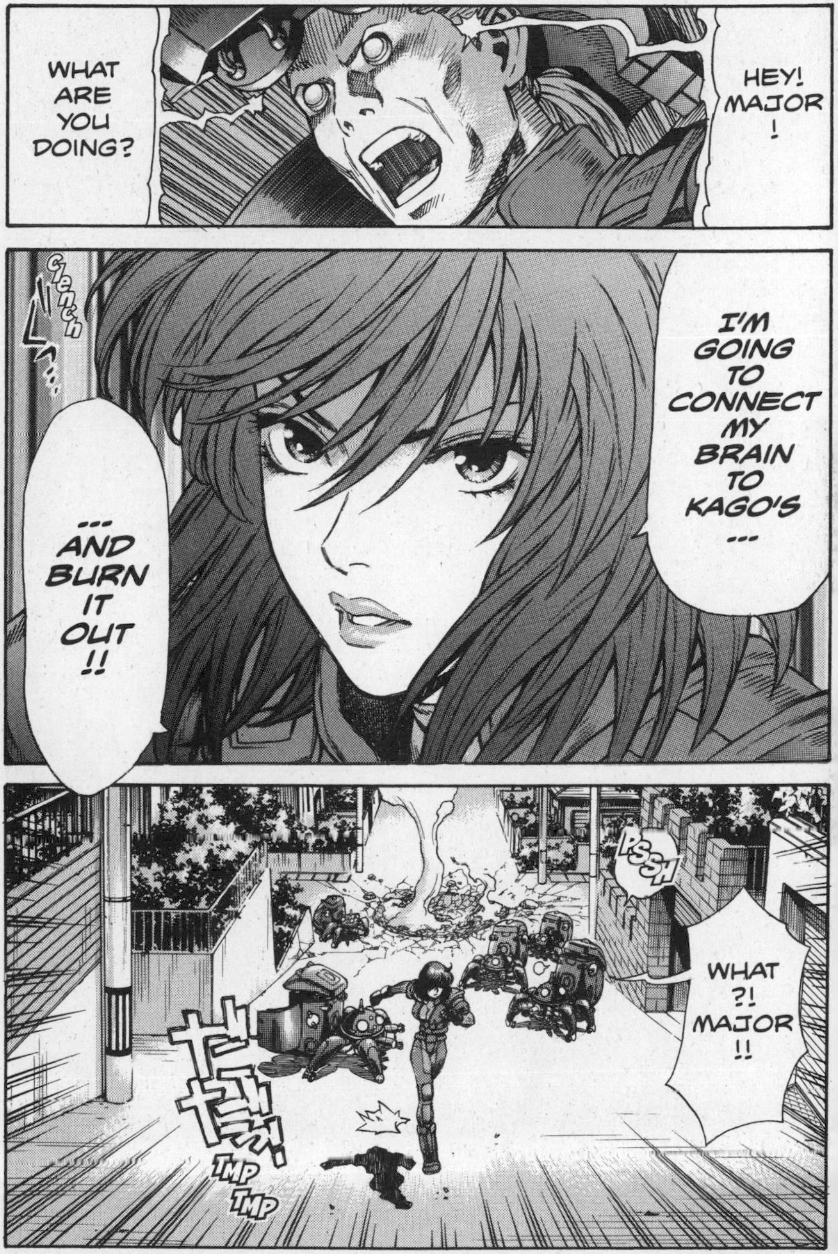
HEY! MAJOR!
WHAT ARE YOU DOING?
clench
I'M GOING TO CONNECT MY BRAIN TO KAGO'S ...
... AND BURN IT OUT!!
PSSH
WHAT?! MAJOR!!
TMP TMP

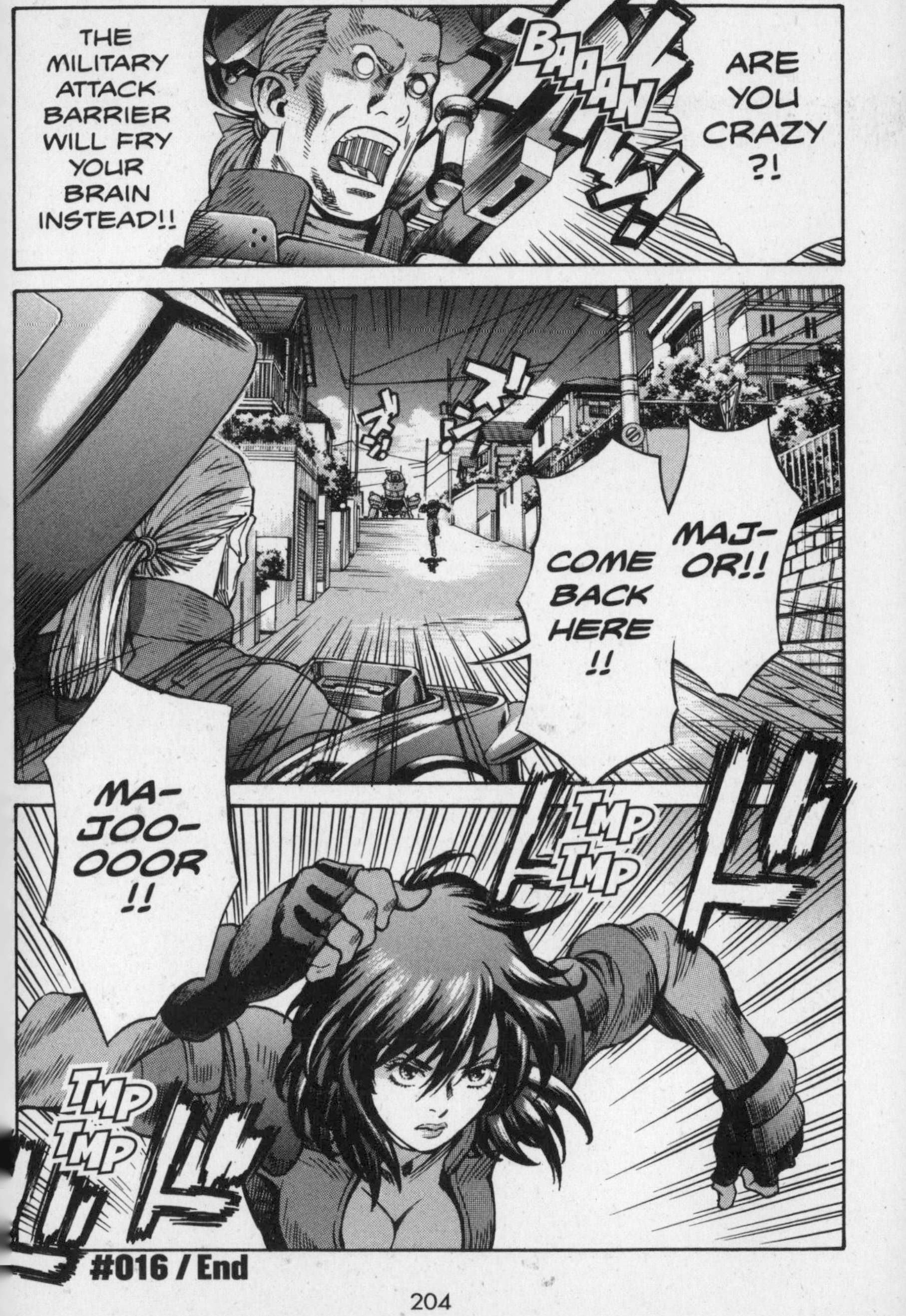
ARE YOU CRAZY ?!
BAAAN
THE MILITARY ATTACK BARRIER WILL FRY YOUR BRAIN INSTEAD!!
MAJ-OR!!
COME BACK HERE !!
MA-JOOO-OOOR !!
TMP TMP
TMP TMP

#016 / End

#017 Cyberbrain Attack

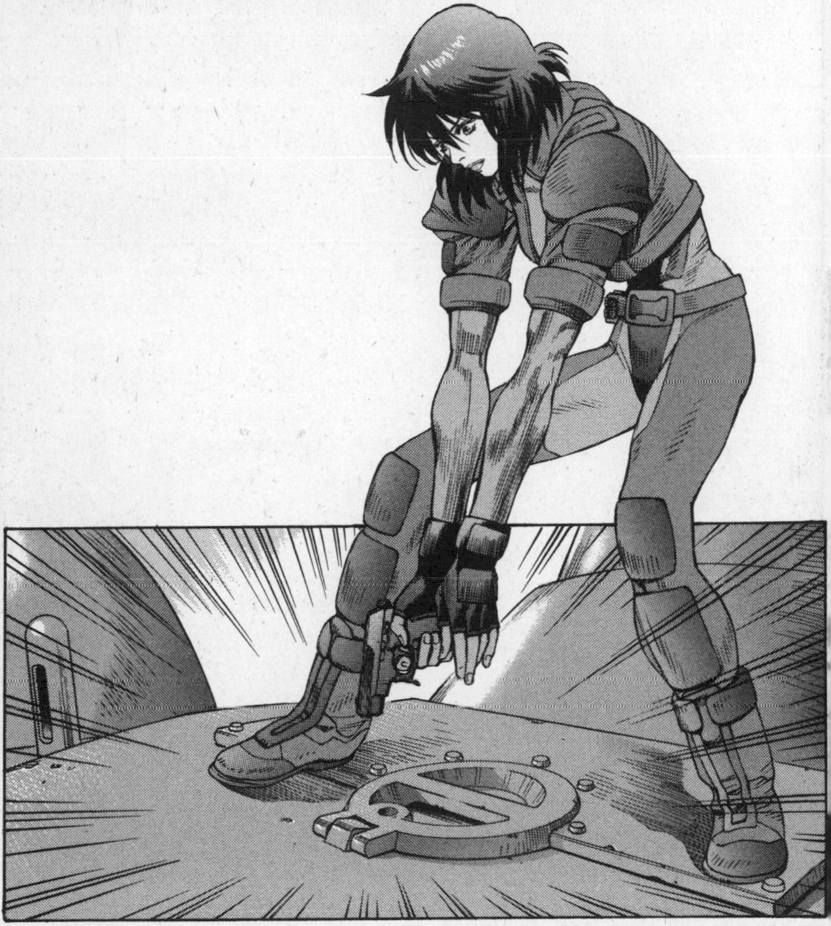

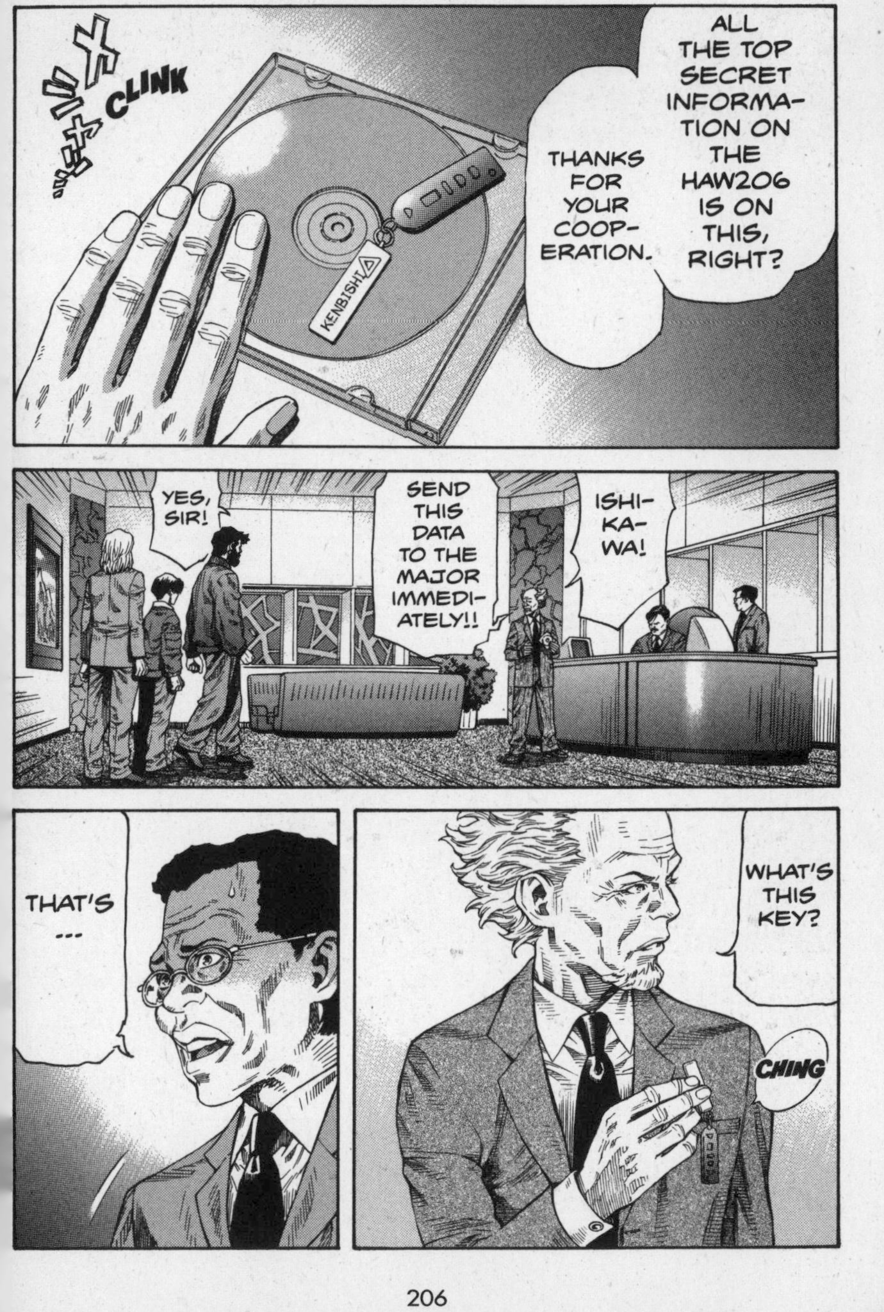
ALL THE TOP SECRET INFORMATION ON THE HAW206 IS ON THIS, RIGHT?
THANKS FOR YOUR COOPERATION.
CLINK
KENBISHI
ISHIKAWA!
SEND THIS DATA TO THE MAJOR IMMEDIATELY!!
YES, SIR!
WHAT'S THIS KEY?
CHING
THAT'S ...

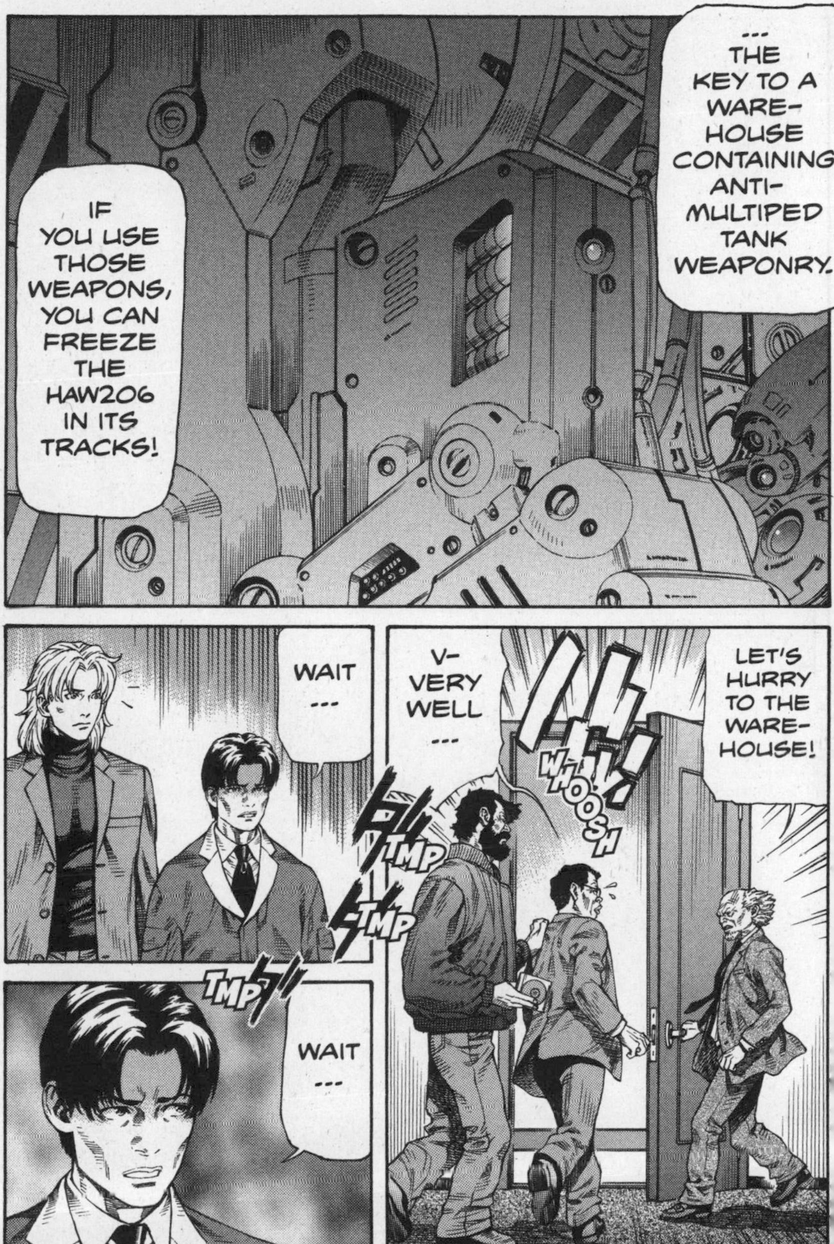
--- THE KEY TO A WARE-HOUSE CONTAINING ANTI-MULTIPED TANK WEAPONRY.
IF YOU USE THOSE WEAPONS, YOU CAN FREEZE THE HAW206 IN ITS TRACKS!
LET'S HURRY TO THE WARE-HOUSE!
WHOOSH
V-VERY WELL ---
TMP
TMP
TMP
WAIT ---
WAIT ---

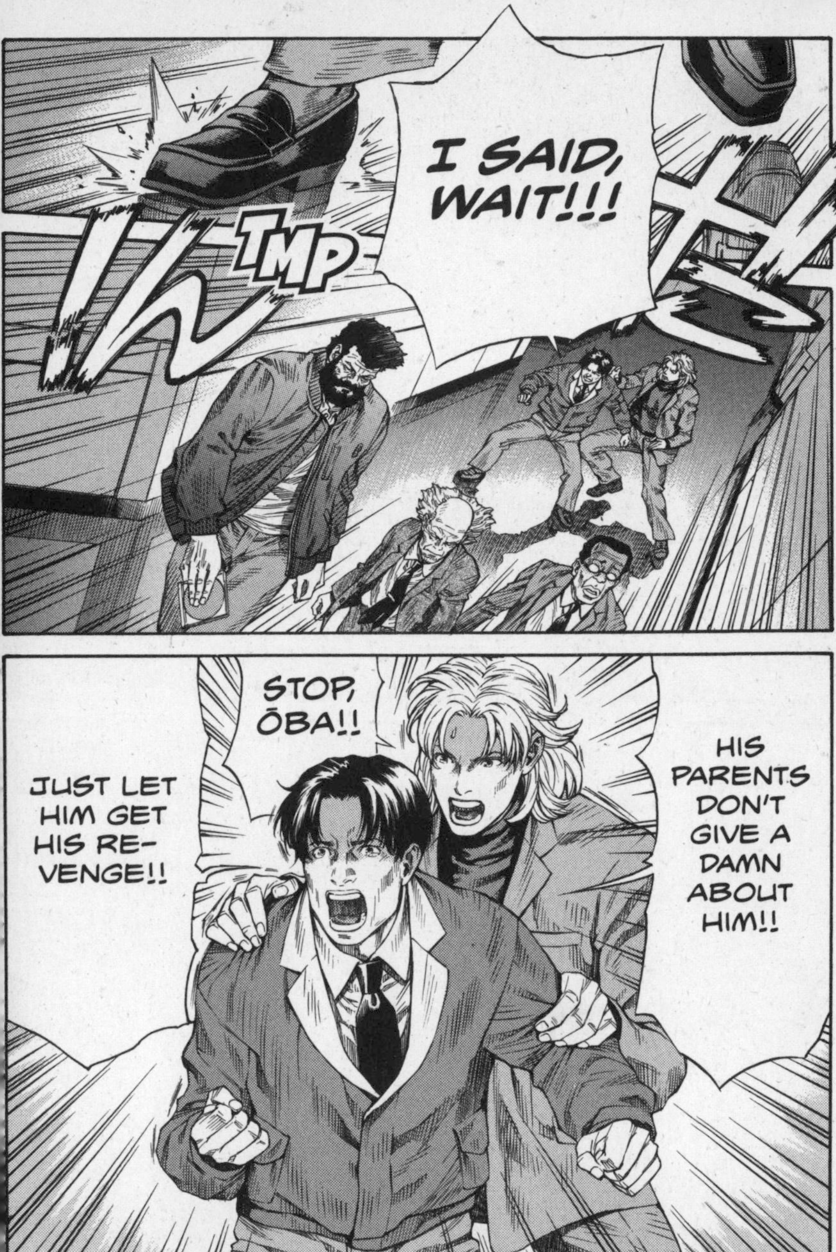
I SAID, WAIT!!!
TMP
STOP, ŌBA!!
HIS PARENTS DON'T GIVE A DAMN ABOUT HIM!!
JUST LET HIM GET HIS RE-VENGE!!

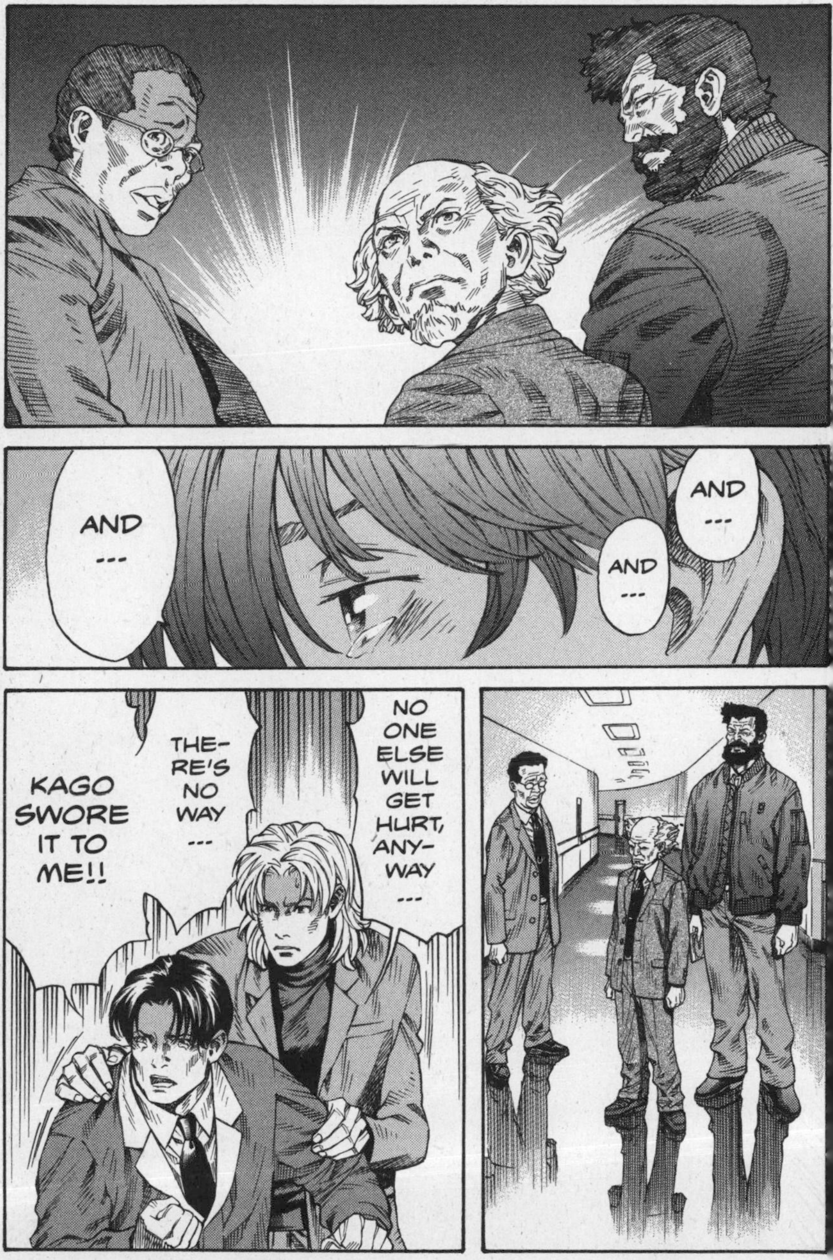
AND ---
AND ---
AND ---
NO ONE ELSE WILL GET HURT, ANYWAY ---
THERE'S NO WAY ---
KAGO SWORE IT TO ME!!

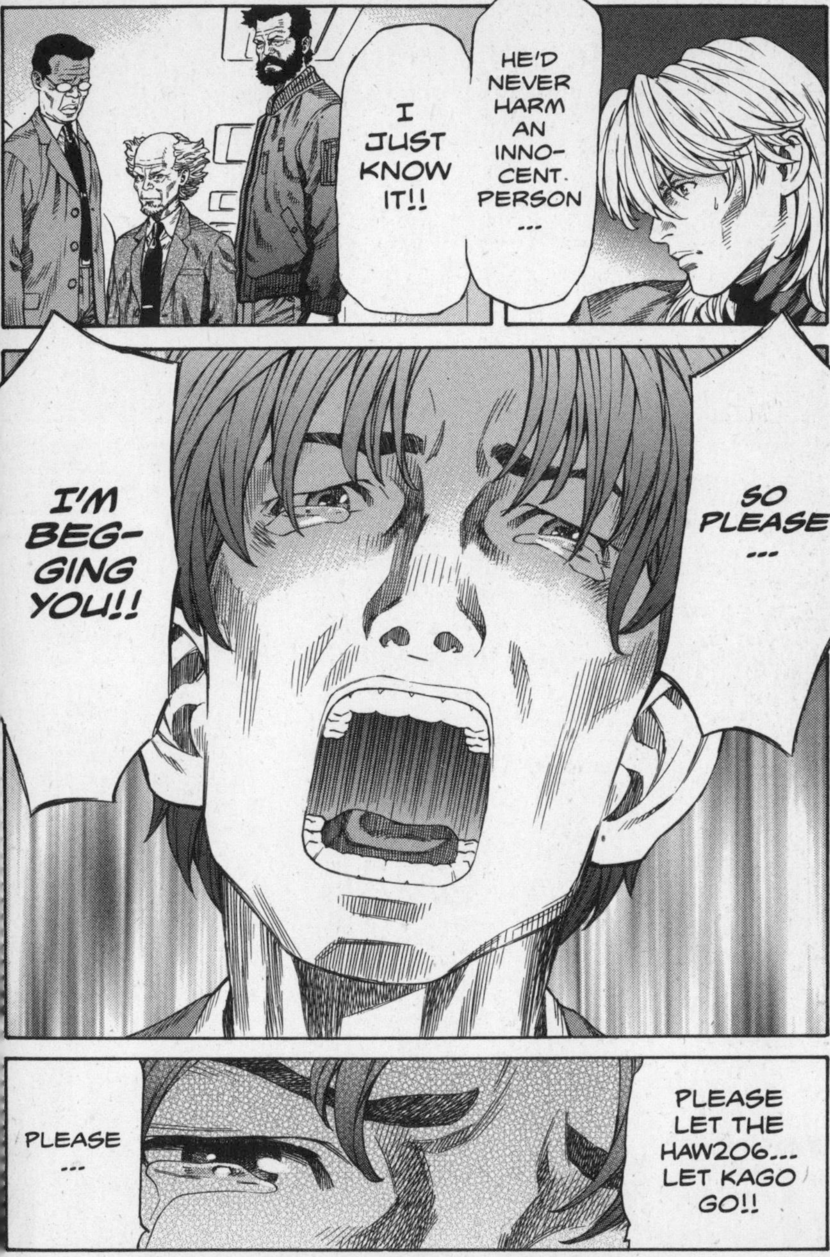
HE'D NEVER HARM AN INNO-CENT PERSON...
I JUST KNOW IT!!
SO PLEASE...
I'M BEG-GING YOU!!
PLEASE LET THE HAW206... LET KAGO GO!!
PLEASE...

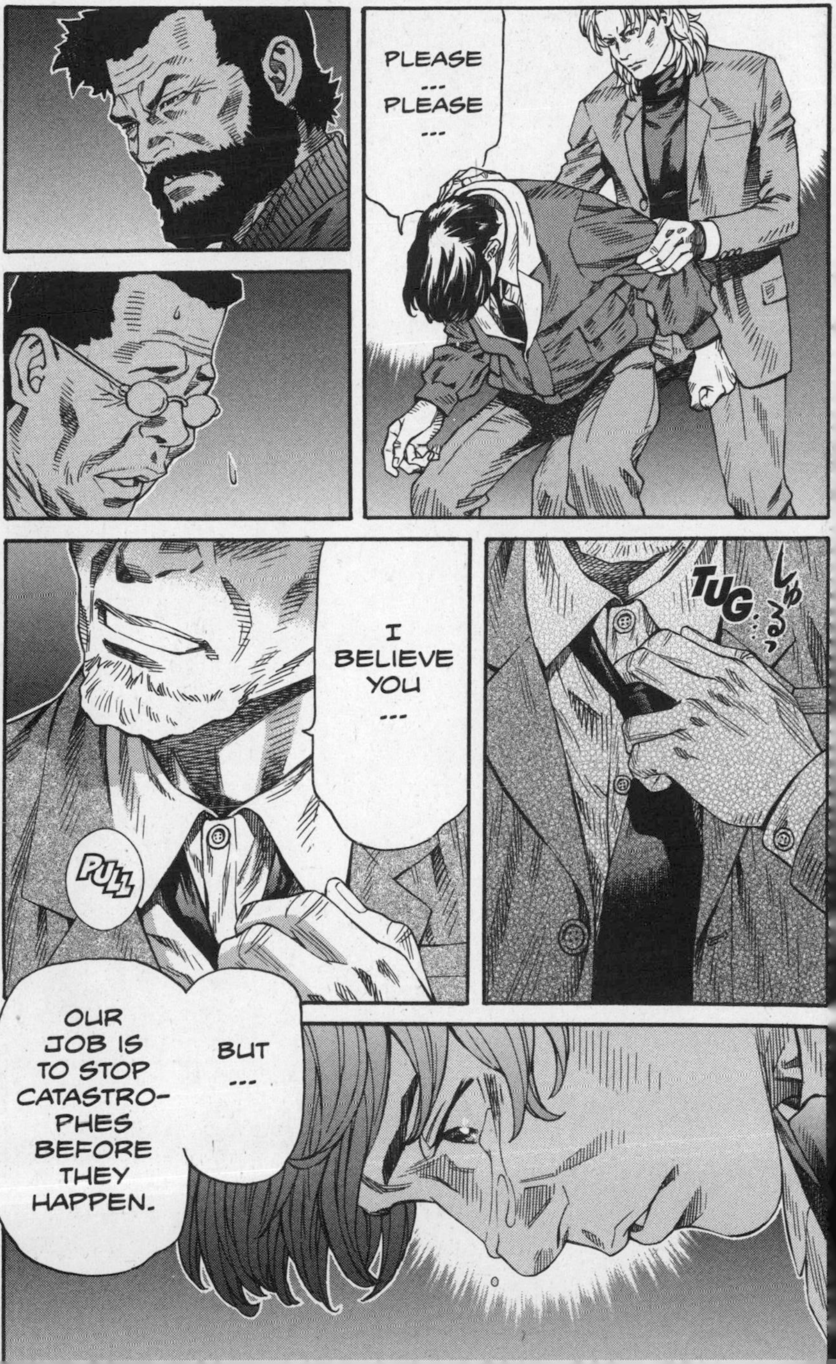
PLEASE --- PLEASE ---
TUG
しゅるっ
I BELIEVE YOU ---
PULL
BUT ---
OUR JOB IS TO STOP CATASTRO-PHES BEFORE THEY HAPPEN.

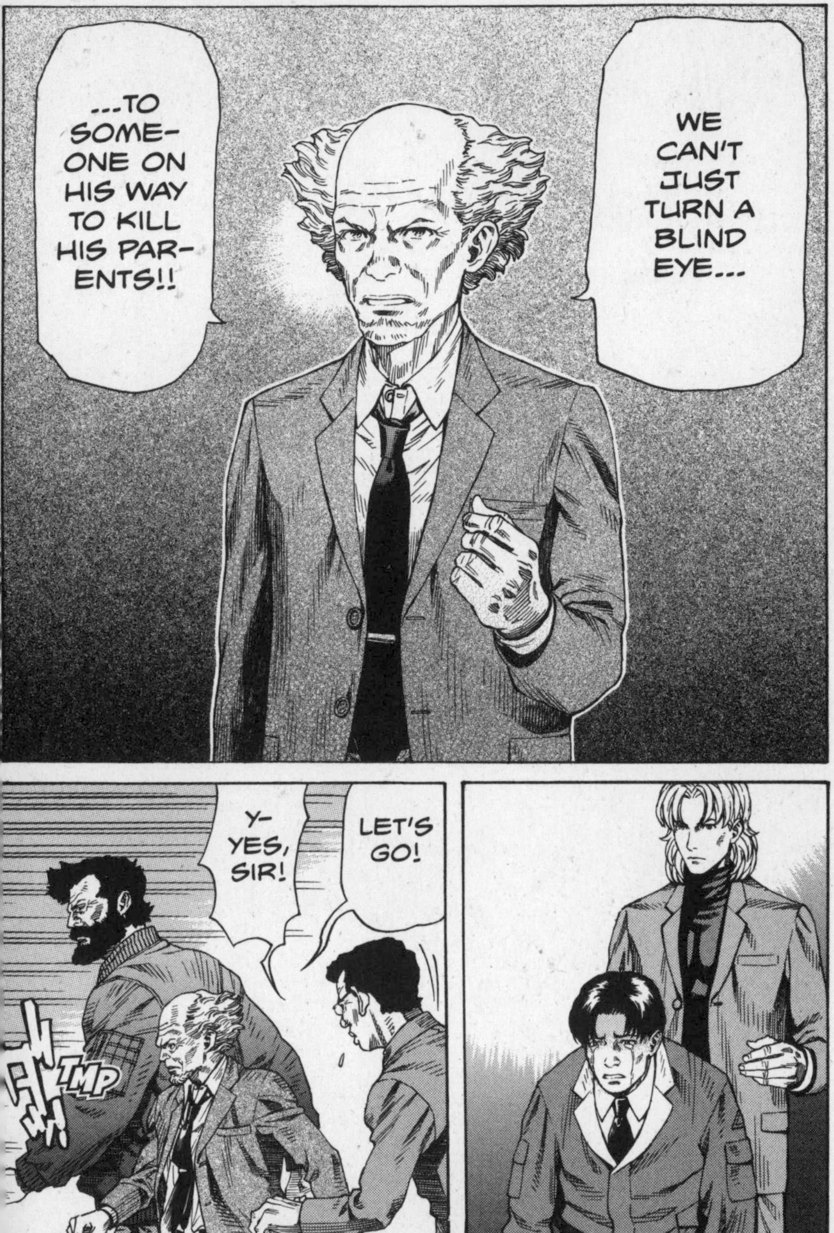
WE CAN'T JUST TURN A BLIND EYE...
...TO SOME-ONE ON HIS WAY TO KILL HIS PAR-ENTS!!
LET'S GO!
Y-YES, SIR!

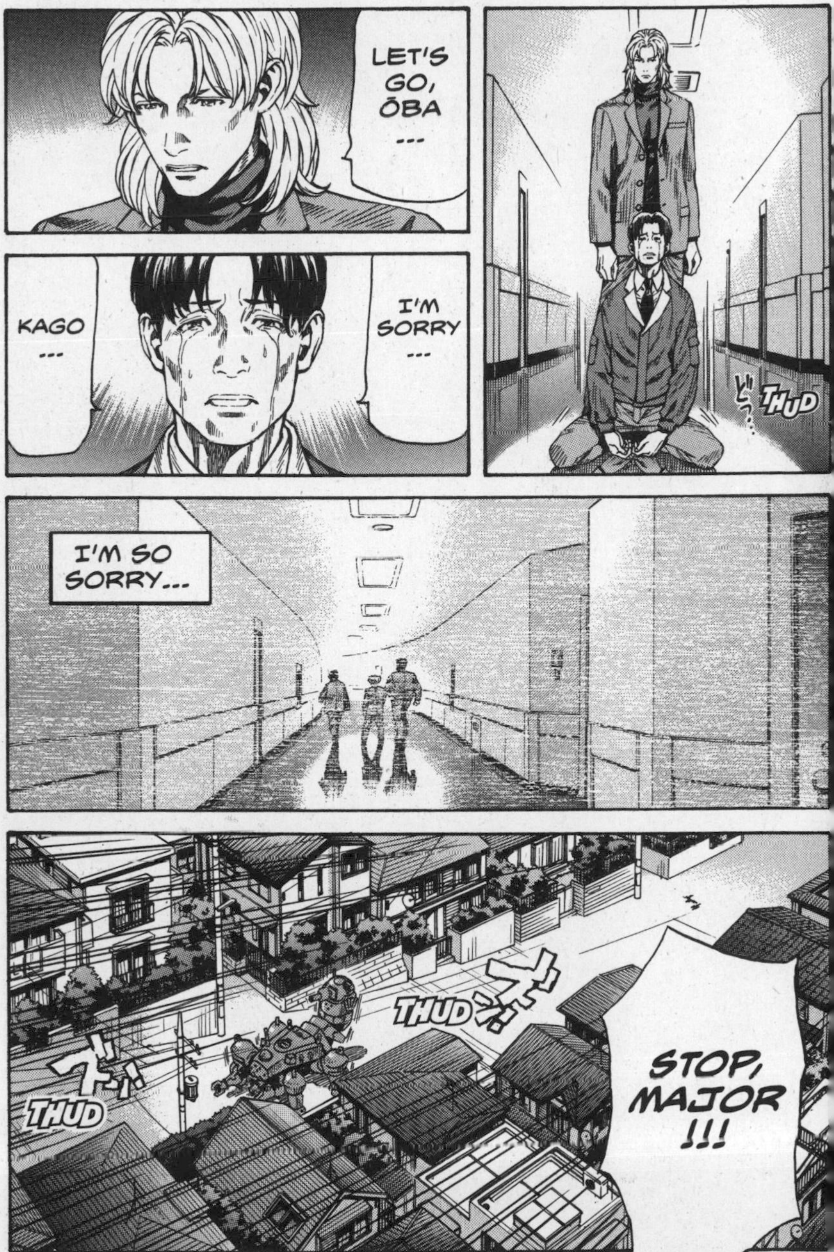
THUD
LET'S GO, ŌBA ---
I'M SORRY ---
KAGO ---
I'M SO SORRY...
STOP, MAJOR !!!
THUD
THUD

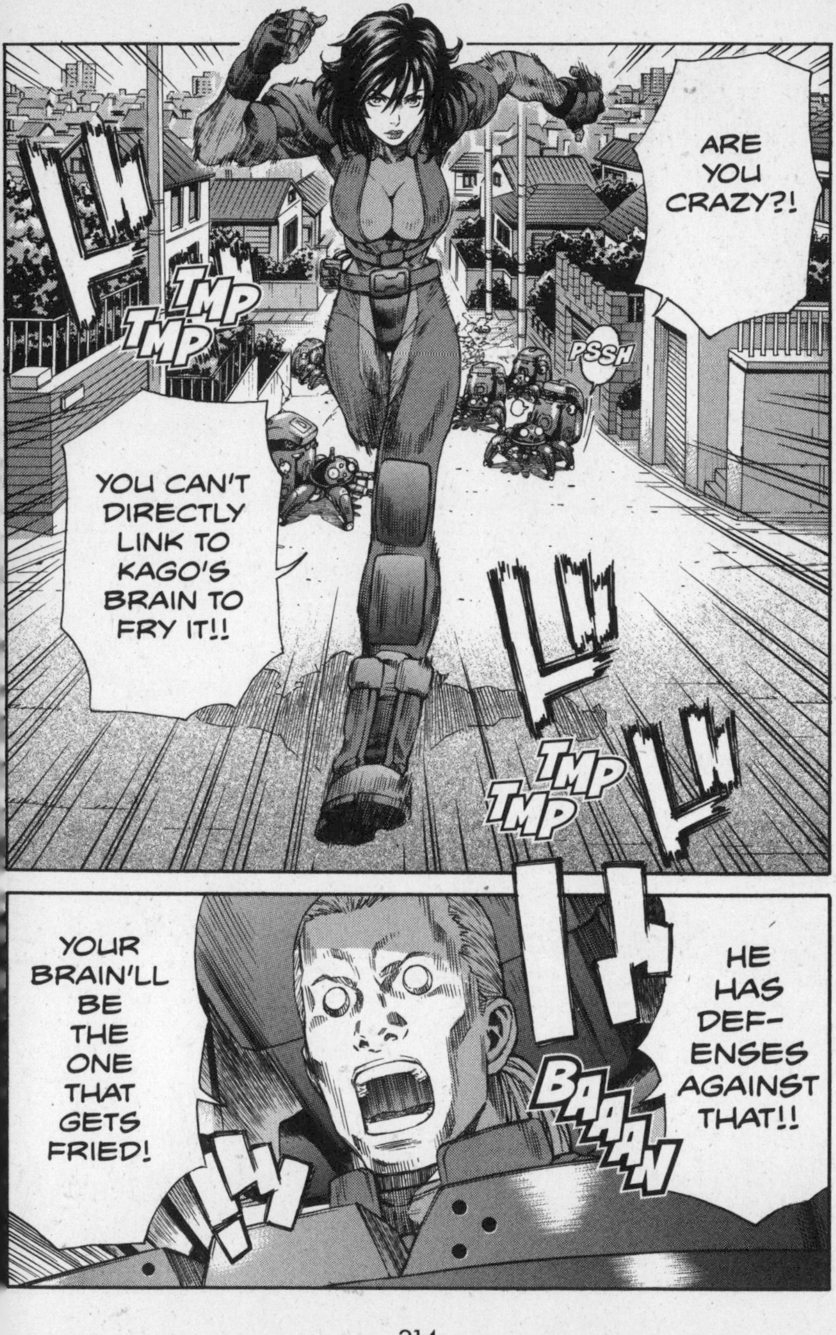
ARE YOU CRAZY?!
TMP TMP
PSSH
YOU CAN'T DIRECTLY LINK TO KAGO'S BRAIN TO FRY IT!!
TMP TMP
HE HAS DEF-ENSES AGAINST THAT!!
BAAAAN
YOUR BRAIN'LL BE THE ONE THAT GETS FRIED!

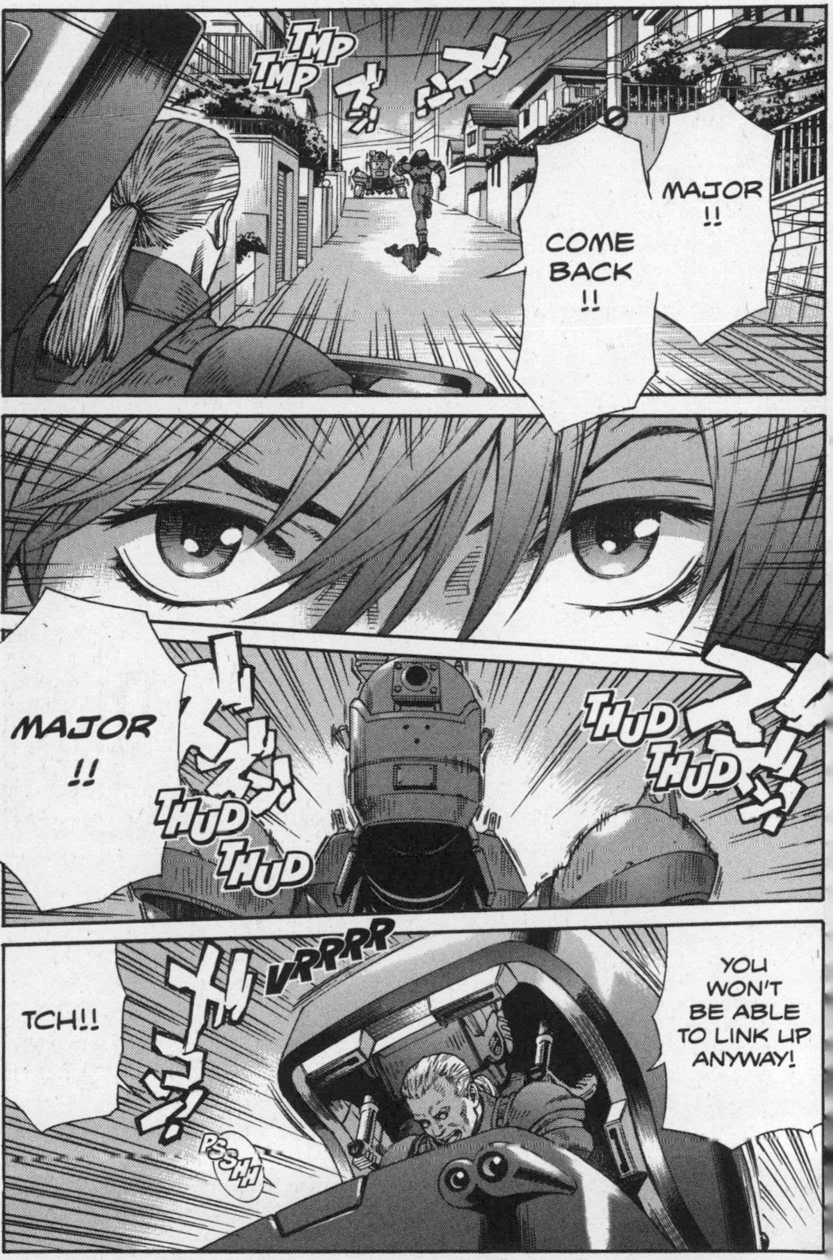
MAJOR !!
COME BACK !!
TMP TMP
THUD THUD
MAJOR !!
THUD THUD
YOU WON'T BE ABLE TO LINK UP ANYWAY!
VRRRRR
TCH!!
PSSHH

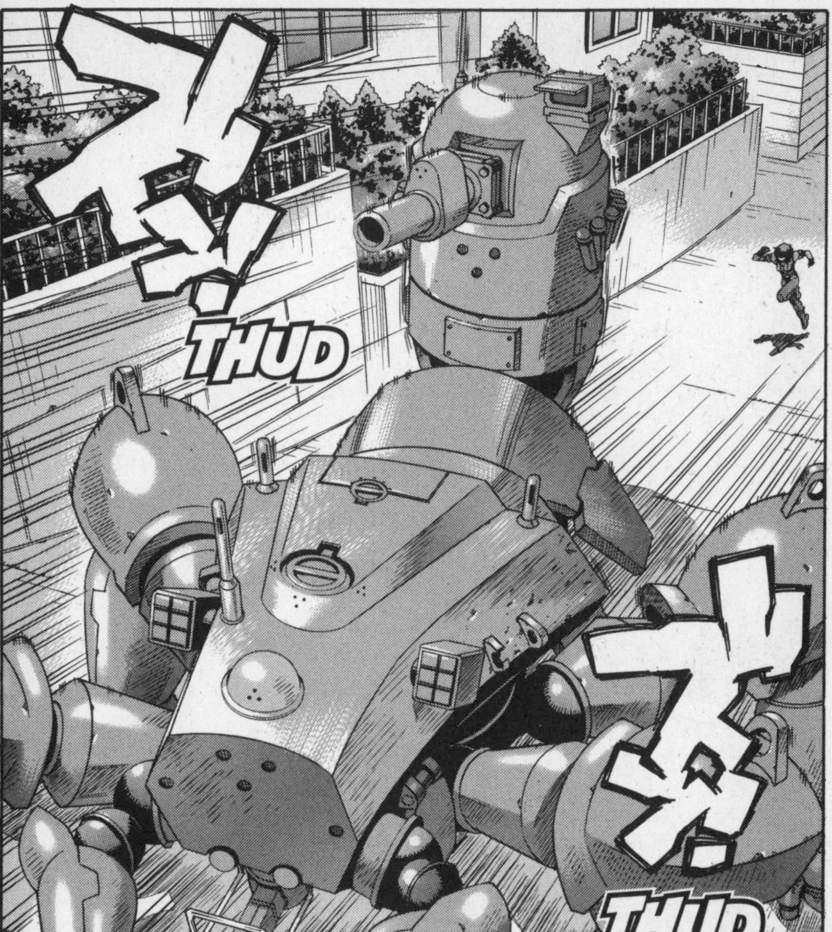
THUD
THUD
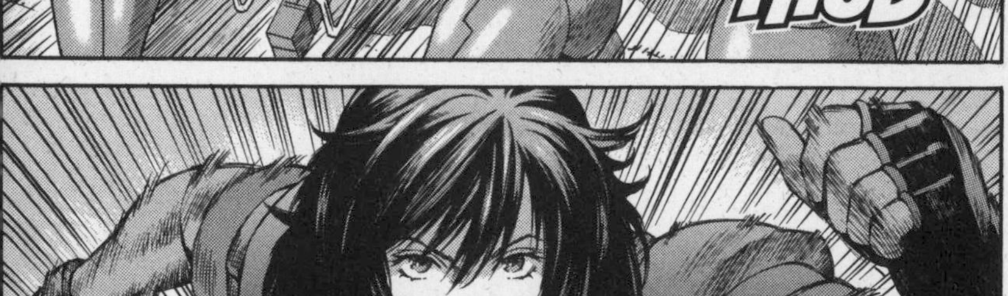

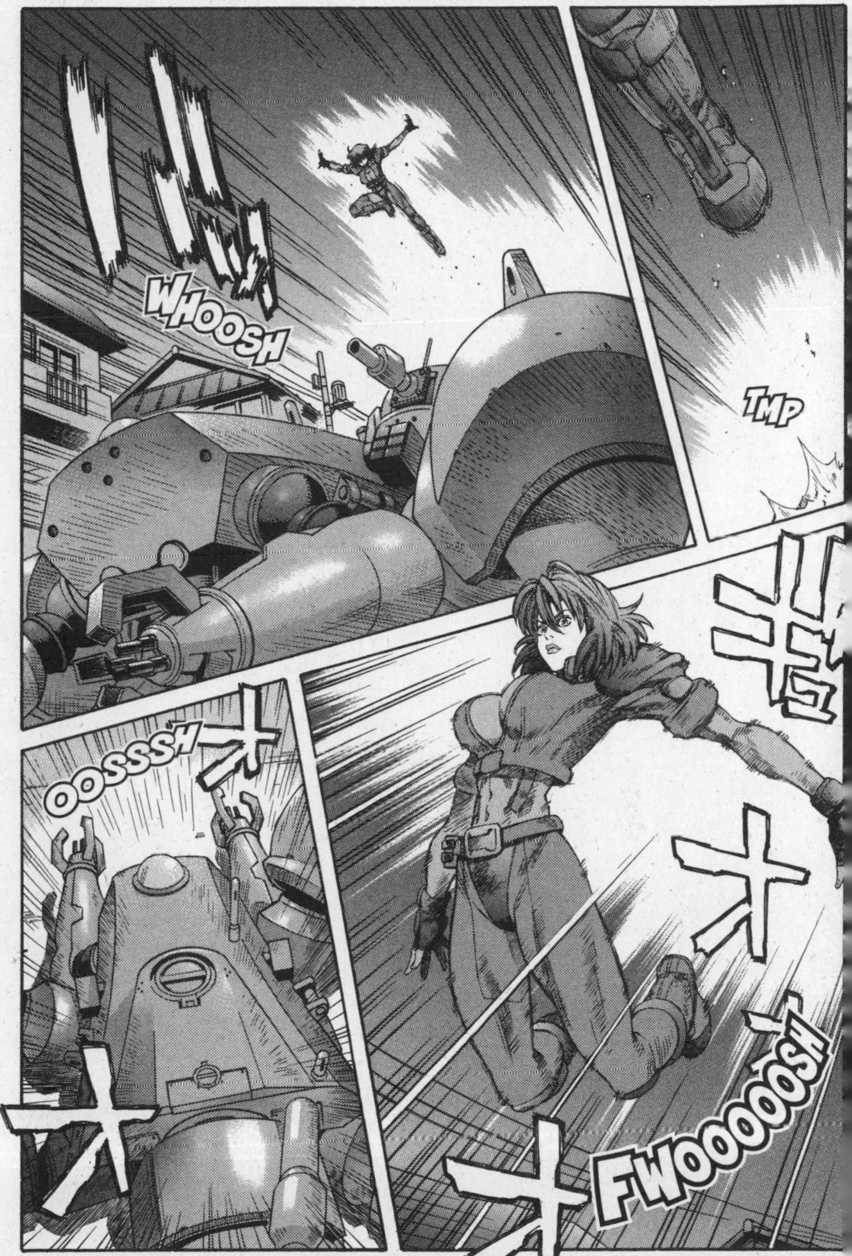
TMP
WHOOSH
FWOOOOOSH
OOSSSSH

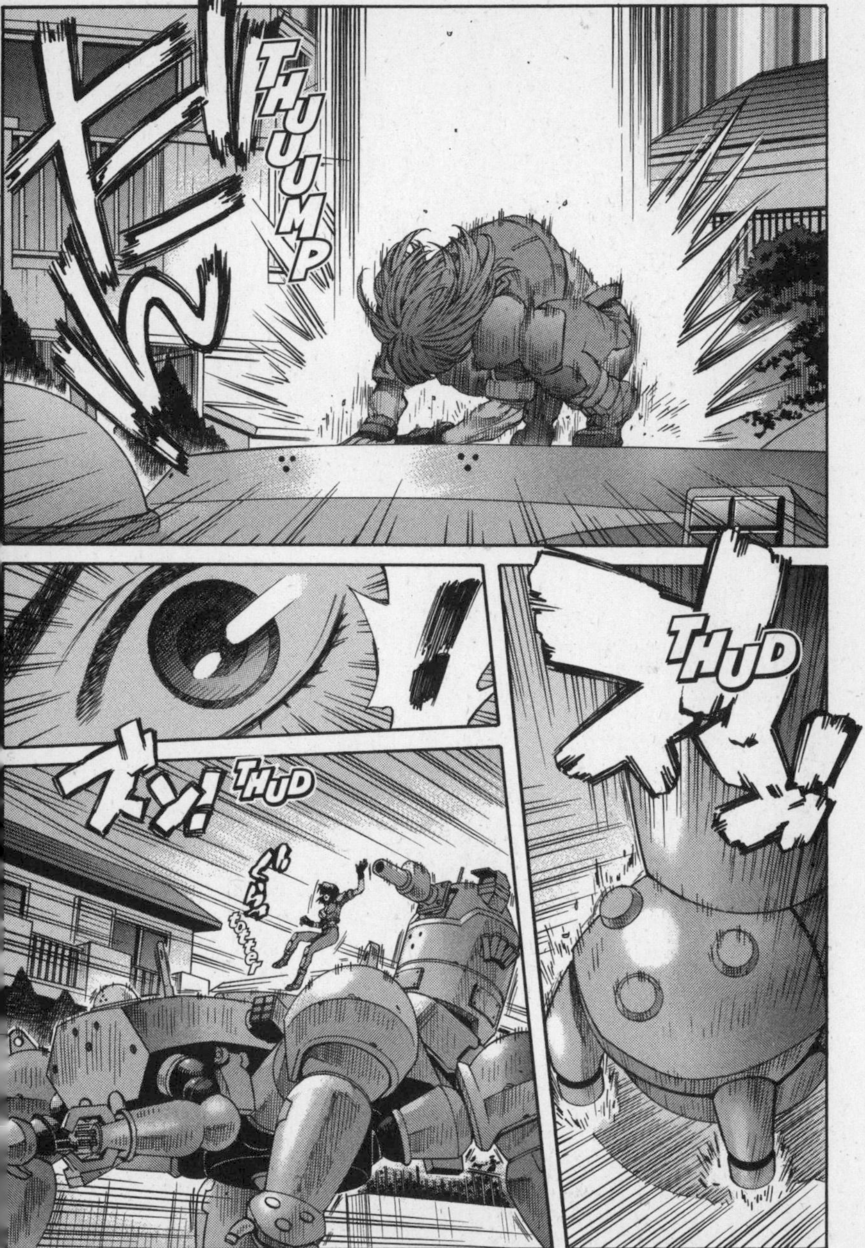
THUUUMP
THUD
!
THUD
totter

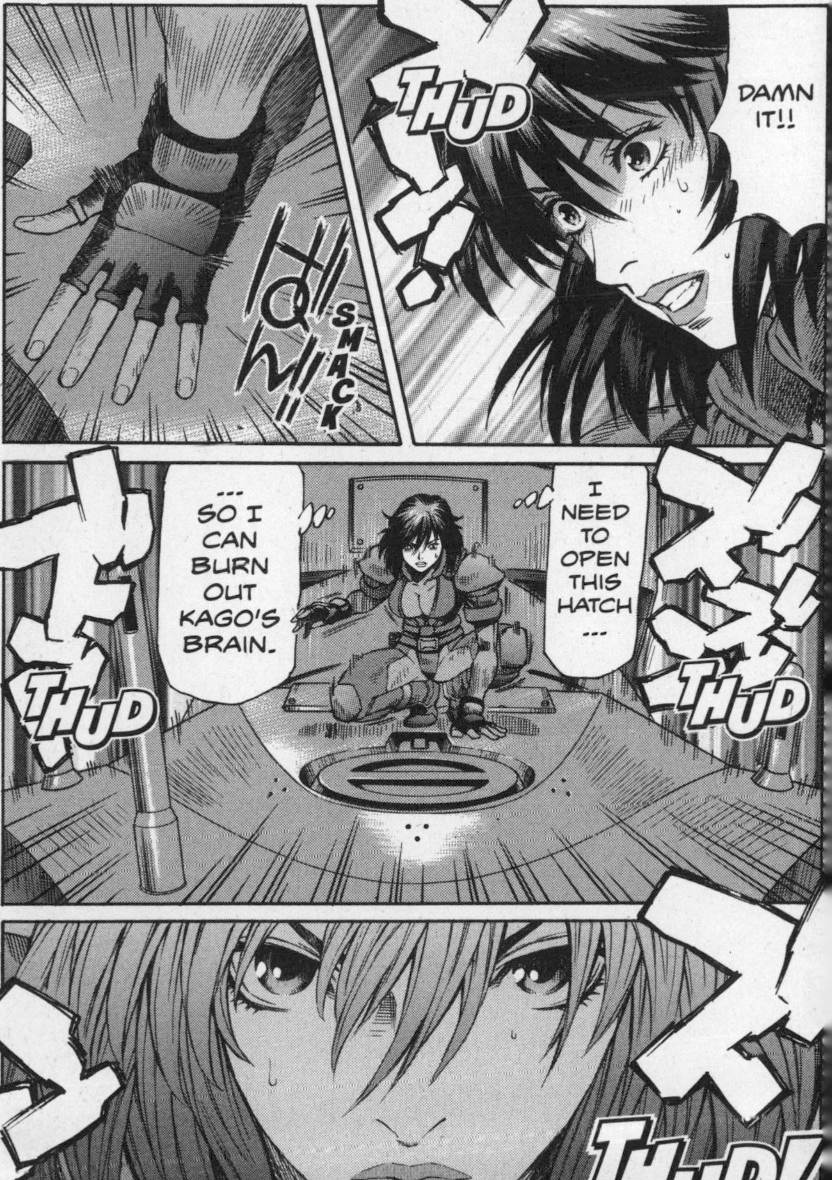
THUD
DAMN IT!!
SMACK
I NEED TO OPEN THIS HATCH ---
THUD
--- SO I CAN BURN OUT KAGO'S BRAIN.
THUD
THUD!

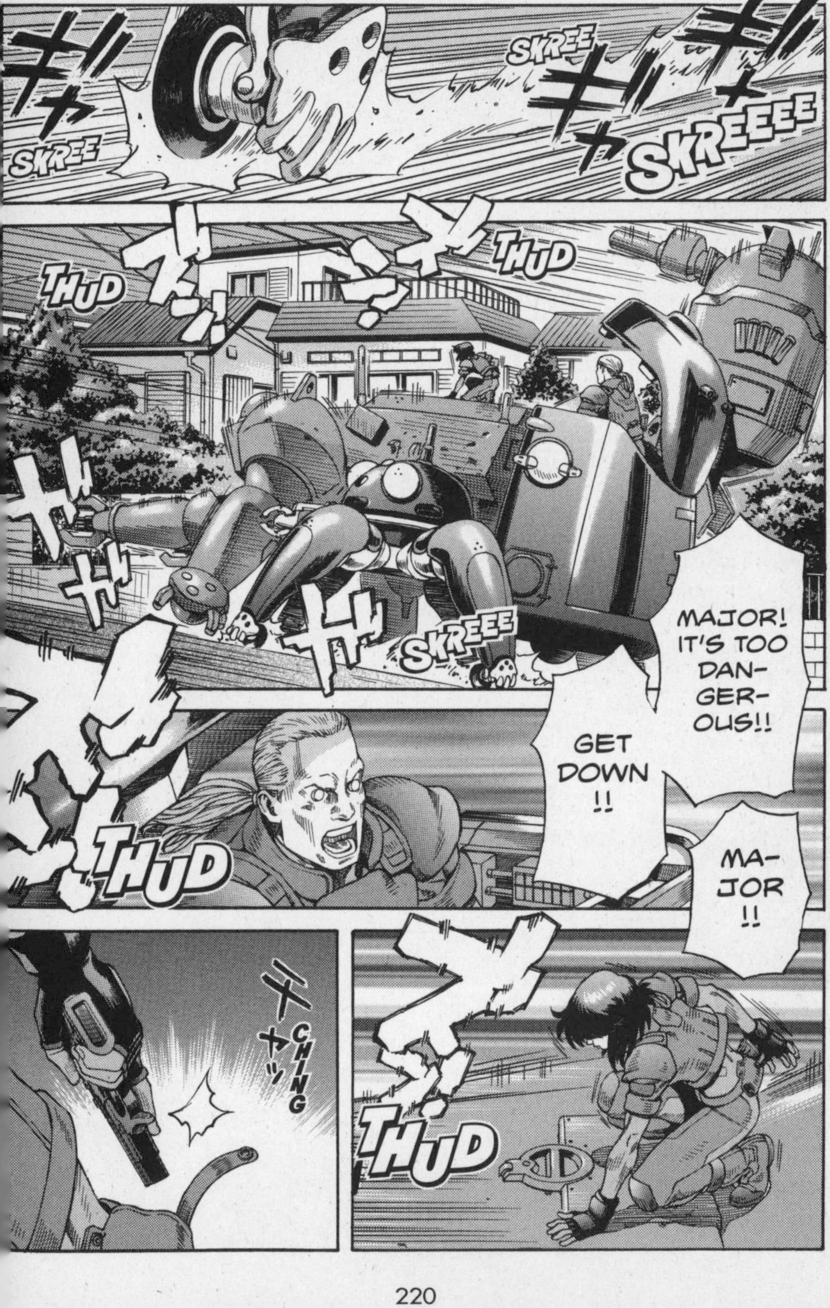
SKREE
SKREEEE
SKREE
THUD
THUD
MAJOR! IT'S TOO DAN- GER- OUS!!
SKREEE
GET DOWN !!
THUD
MA- JOR !!
THUD
CHING

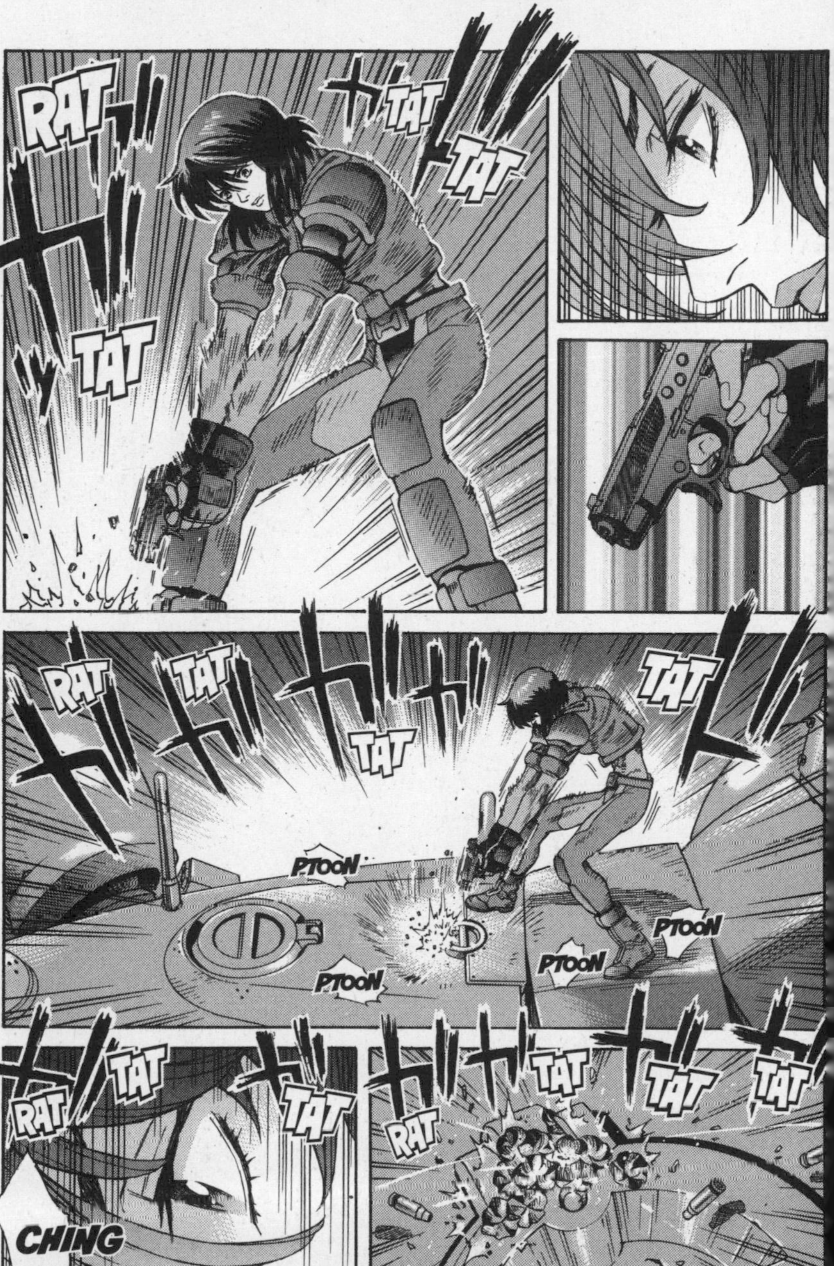
TAT
TAT
RAT
TAT
TAT
TAT
TAT
RAT
PTOON
PTOON
PTOON
PTOON
TAT
TAT
TAT
RAT
TAT
TAT
RAT
CHING

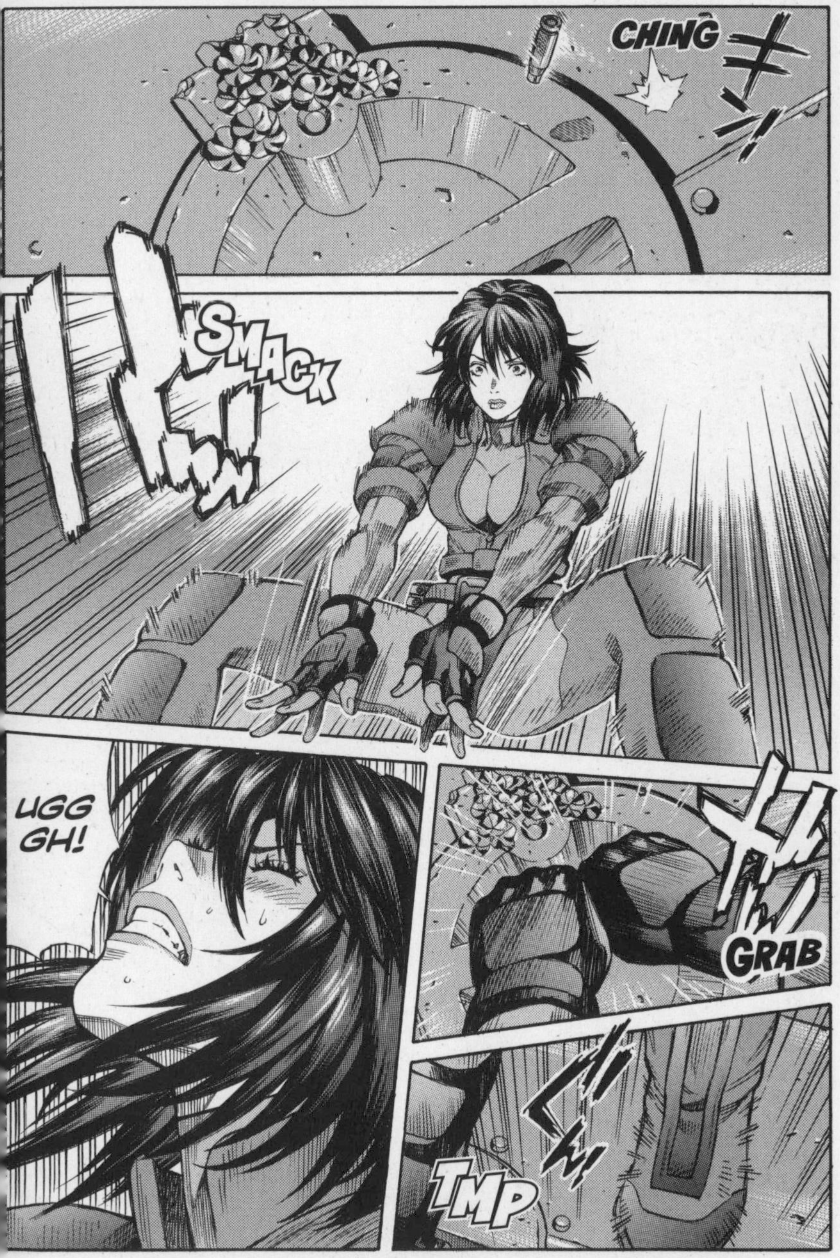
CHING
SMACK
GRAB
TMP
UGG GH!

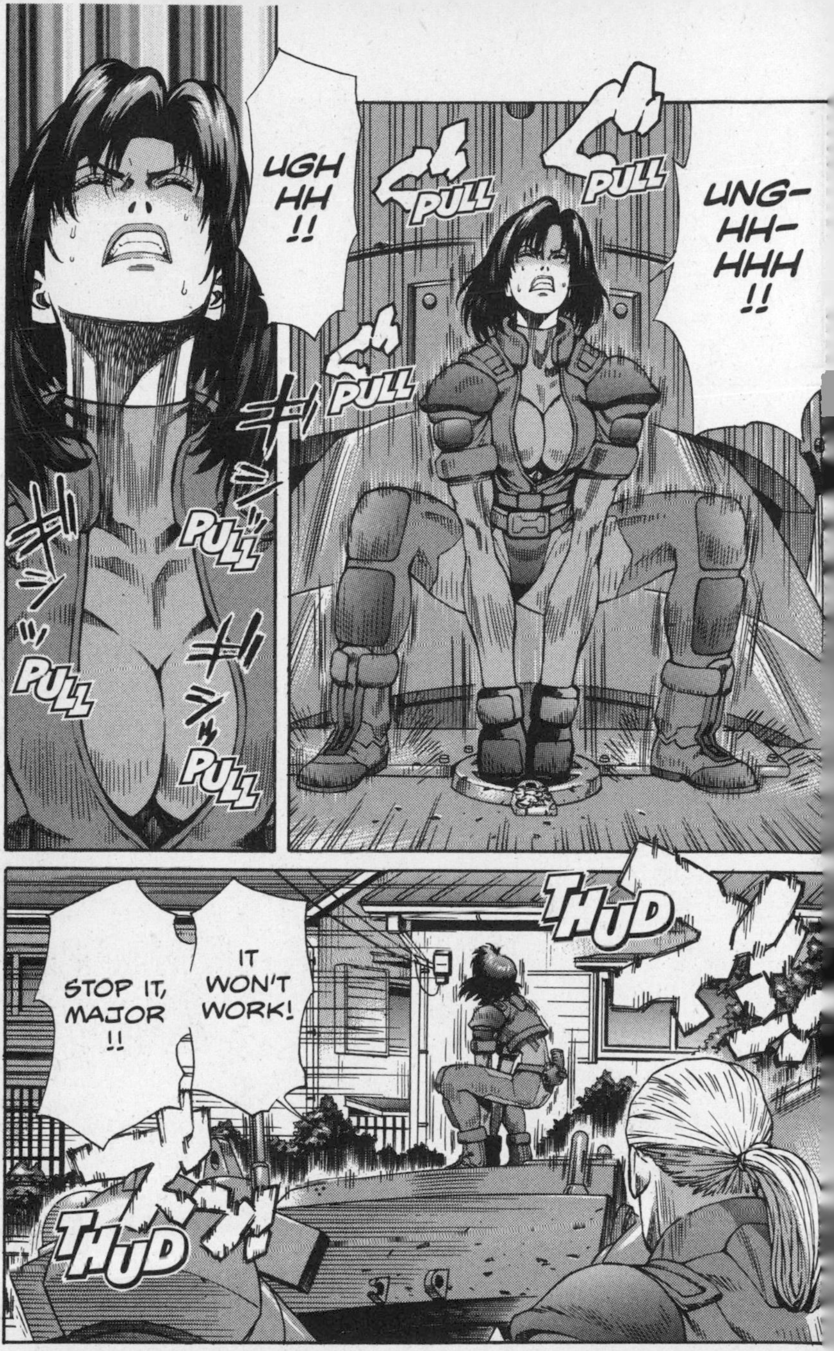

PULL
PULL
UNG-HH-HHH!!
PULL
UGH HH!!
PULL
PULL
PULL
THUD
IT WON'T WORK!
STOP IT, MAJOR!!
THUD

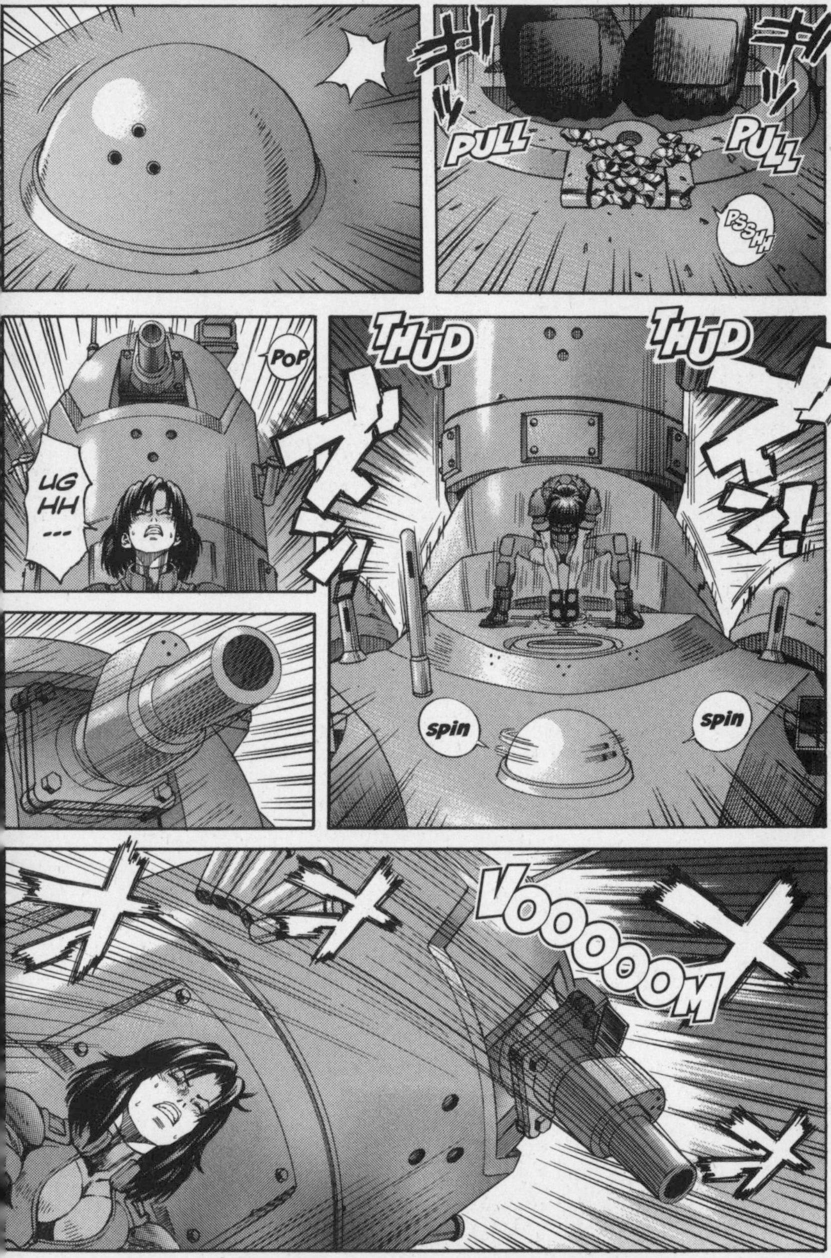
PULL
PULL
PSSHH
THUD
THUD
spin
spin
POP
UG HH ---
VOOOOOOM

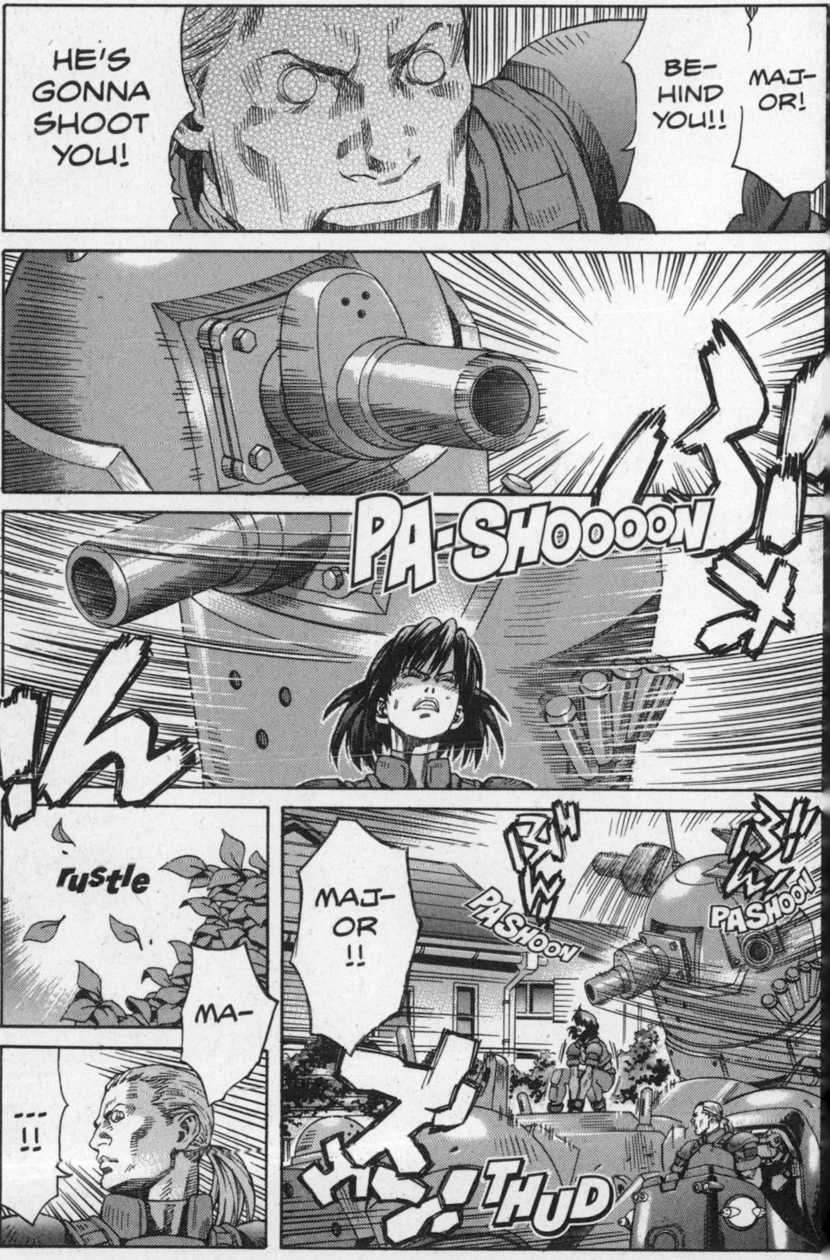
MAJ-OR!
BE-HIND YOU!!
HE'S GONNA SHOOT YOU!
PA-SHOOOON
PASHOON
MAJ-OR!!
PASHOON
THUD
rustle
MA-
...!!

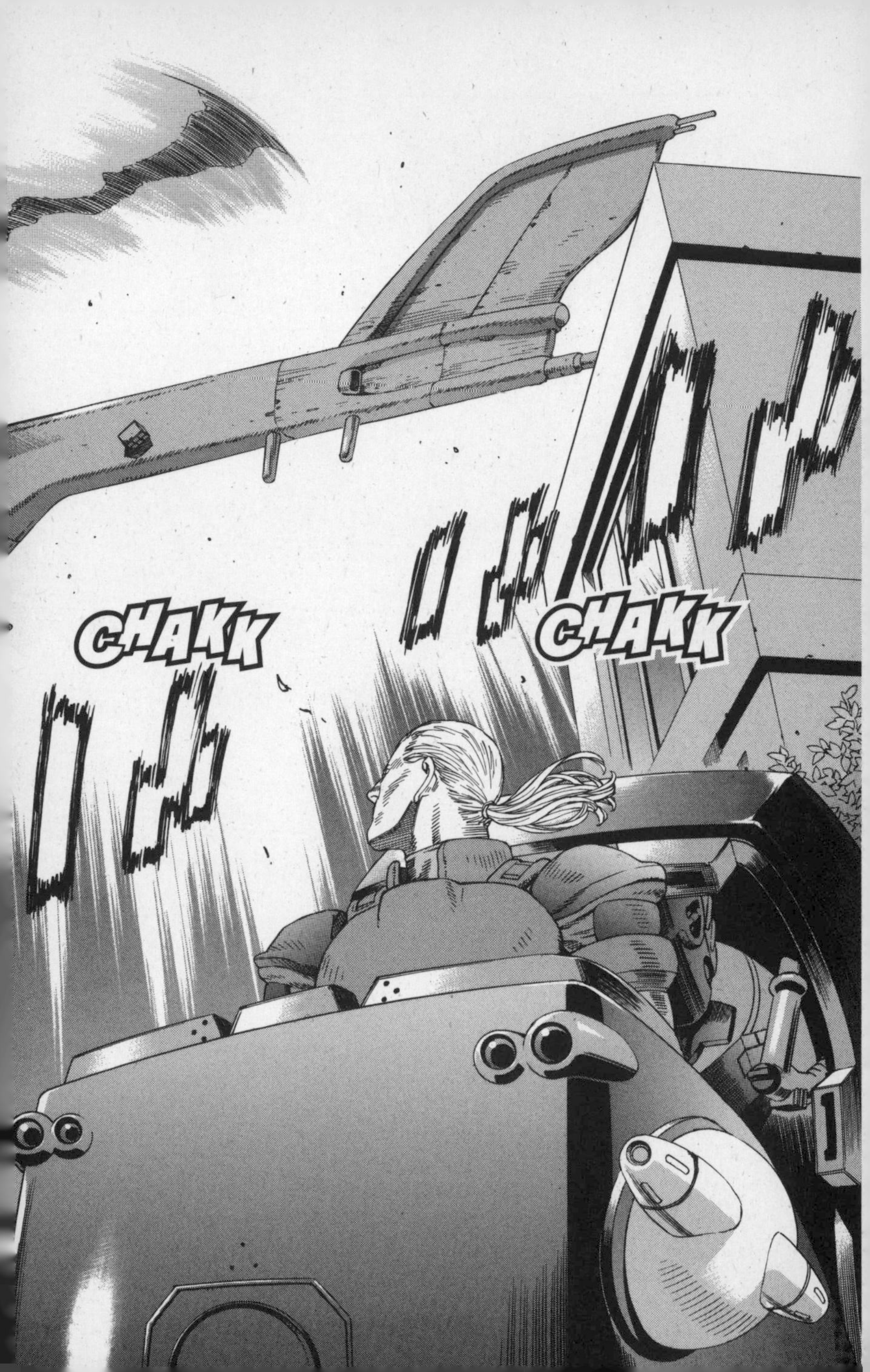
CHAKK
CHAKK

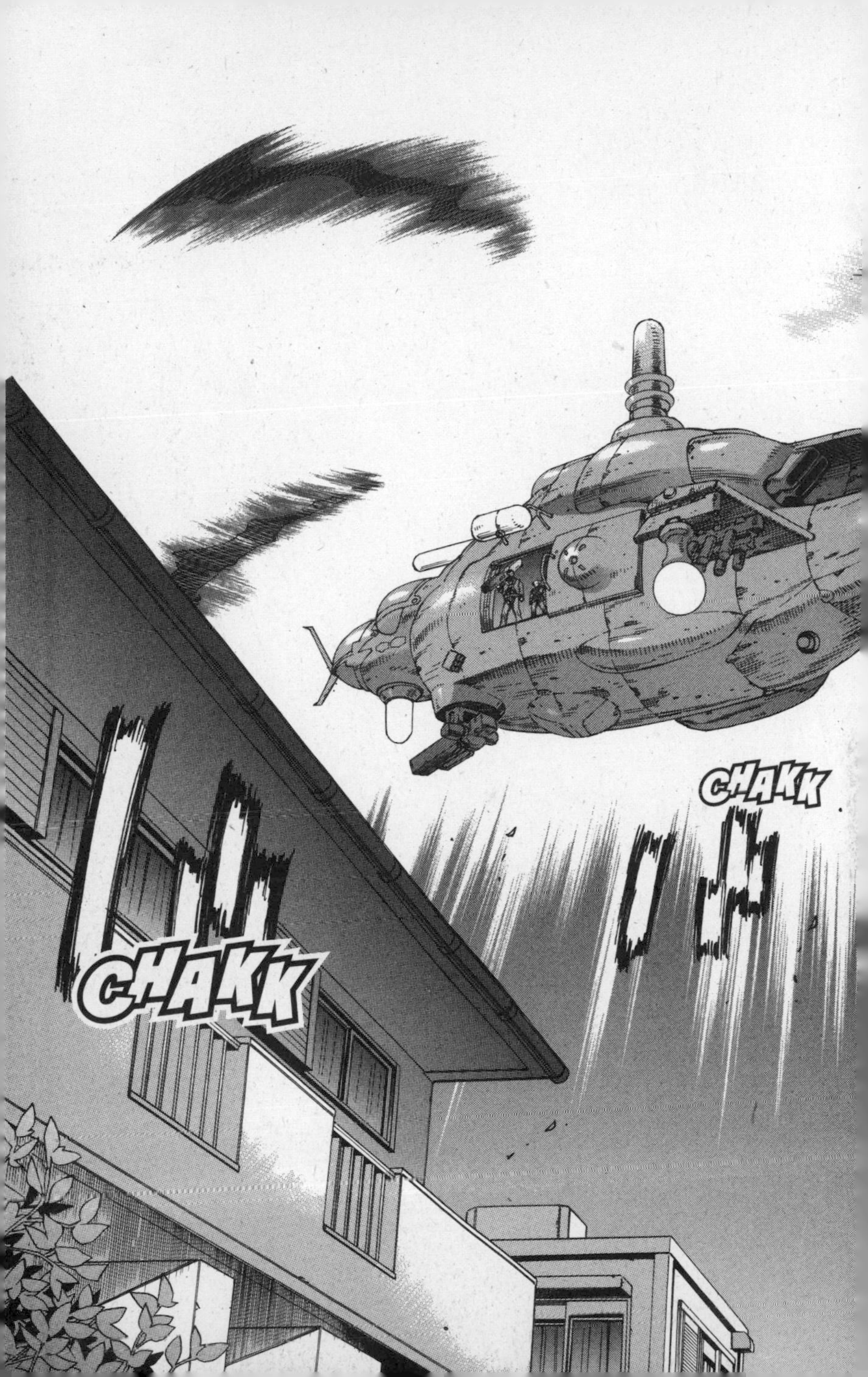
CHAKK
CHAKK

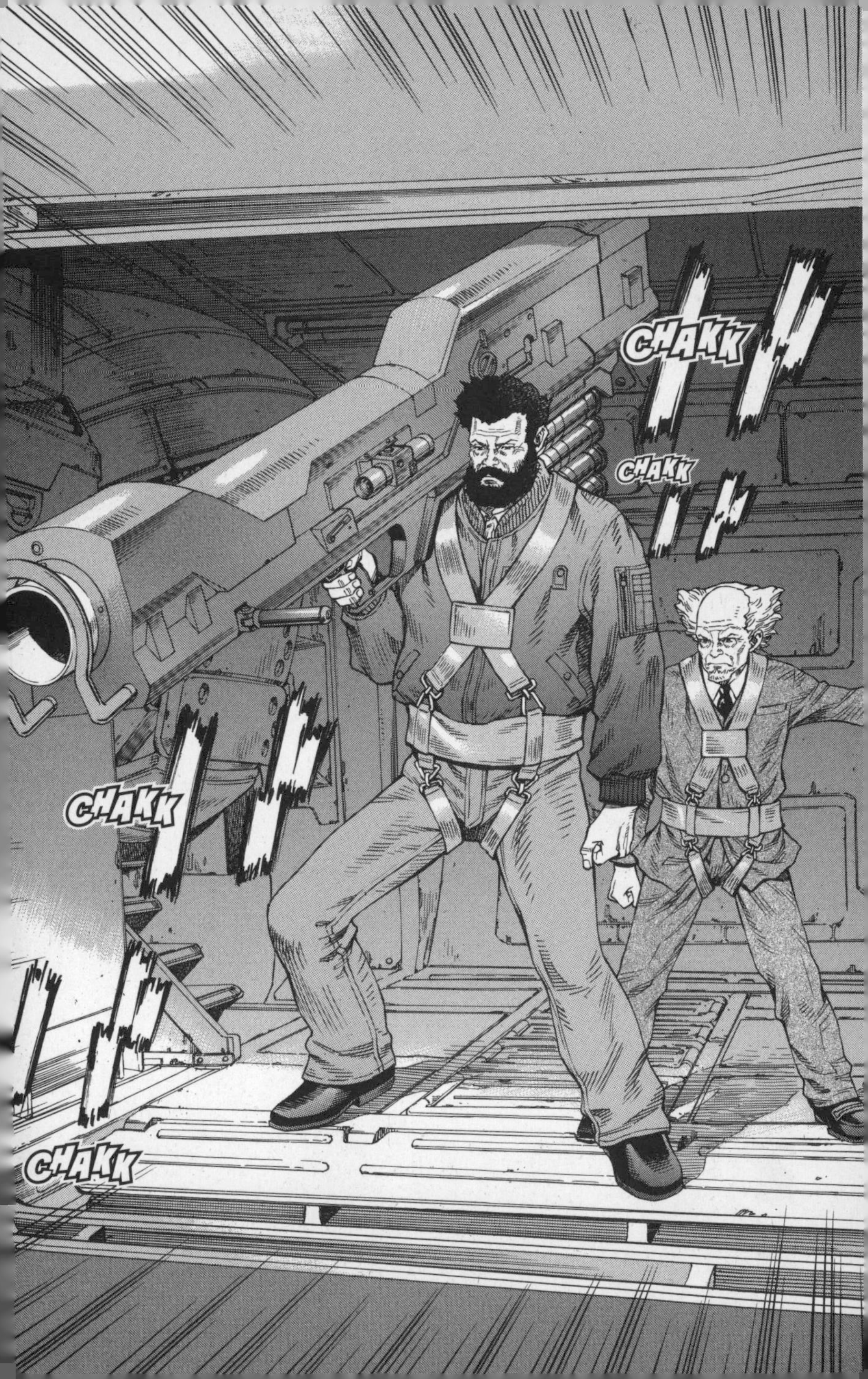
CHAKK
CHAKK
CHAKK
CHAKK

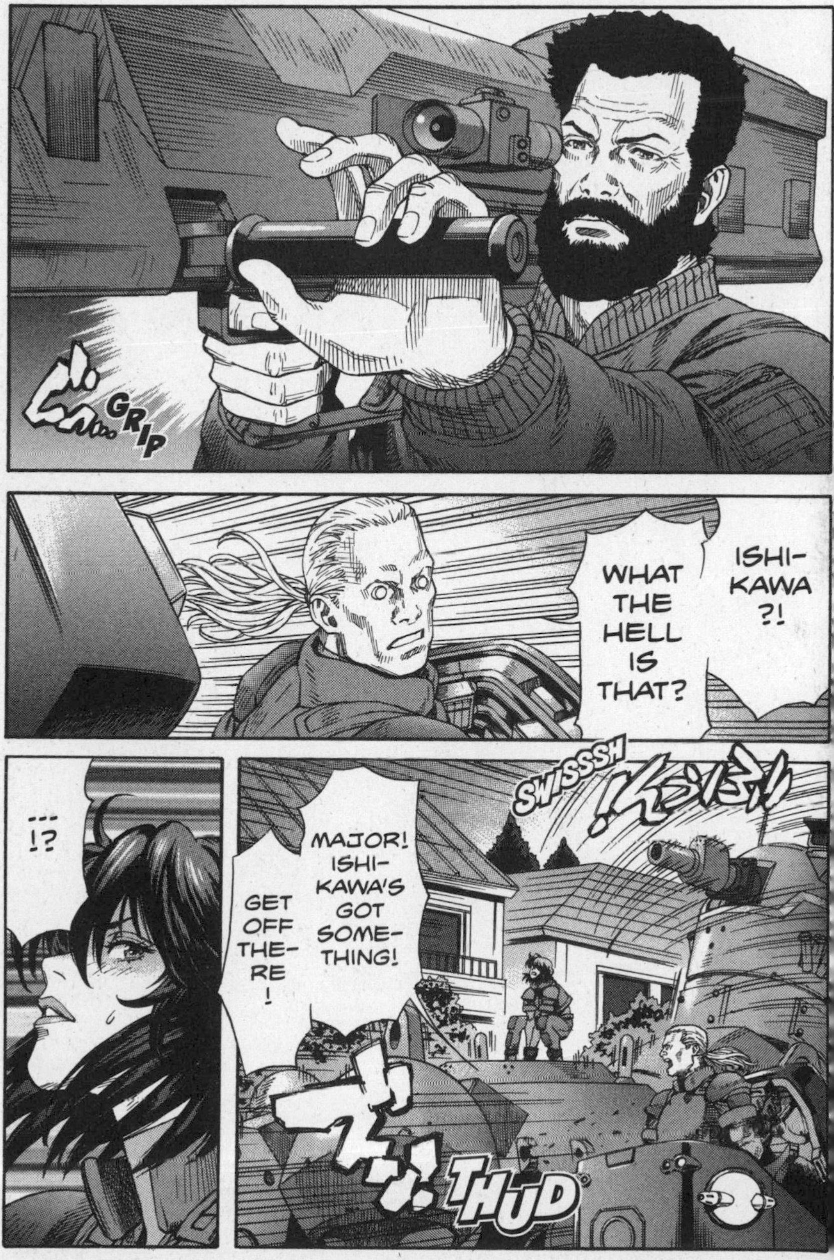
GRIP
ISHI-KAWA ?!
WHAT THE HELL IS THAT?
SWISSSH
MAJOR! ISHI-KAWA'S GOT SOME-THING!
GET OFF THE-RE!
THUD
...!?

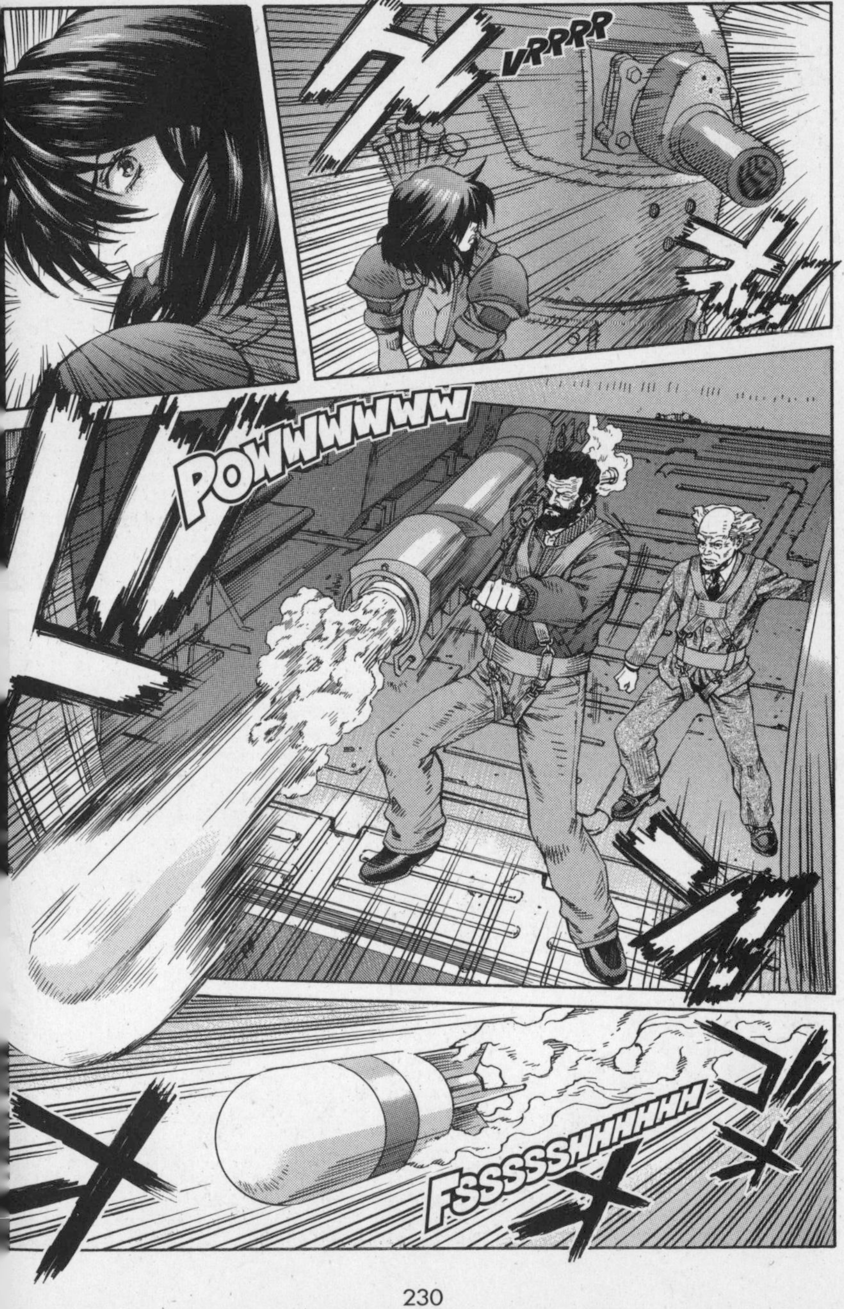
VRRRR
POWWWWWWW
FSSSSSHHHHHH

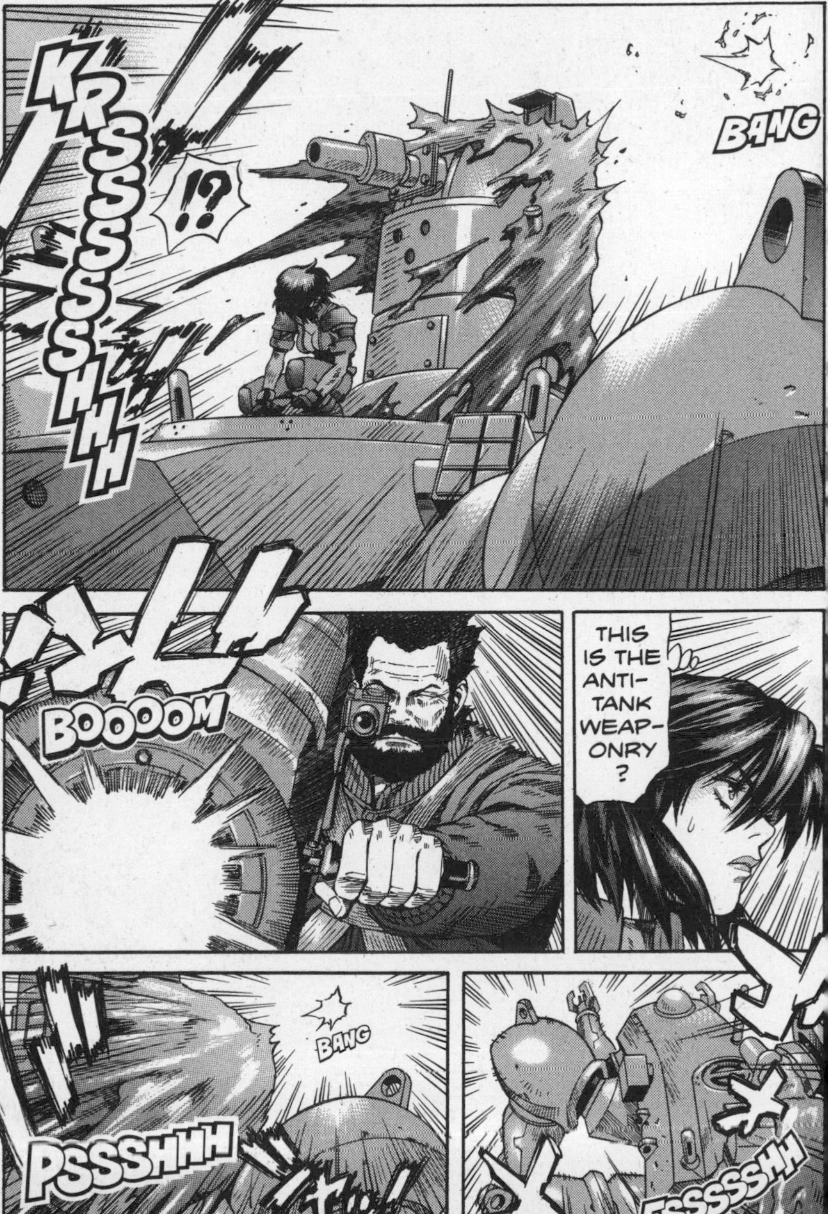
BANG
!?!!
KRSSSSSHHH
THIS IS THE ANTI-TANK WEAPONRY?
BOOOOM
FSSSSSHH
BANG
PSSSHHH

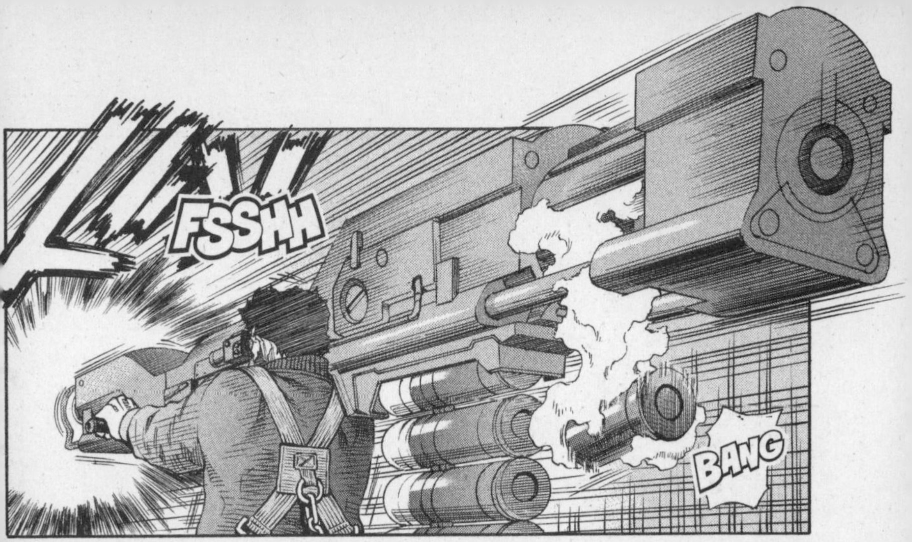
BANG
FSSHH
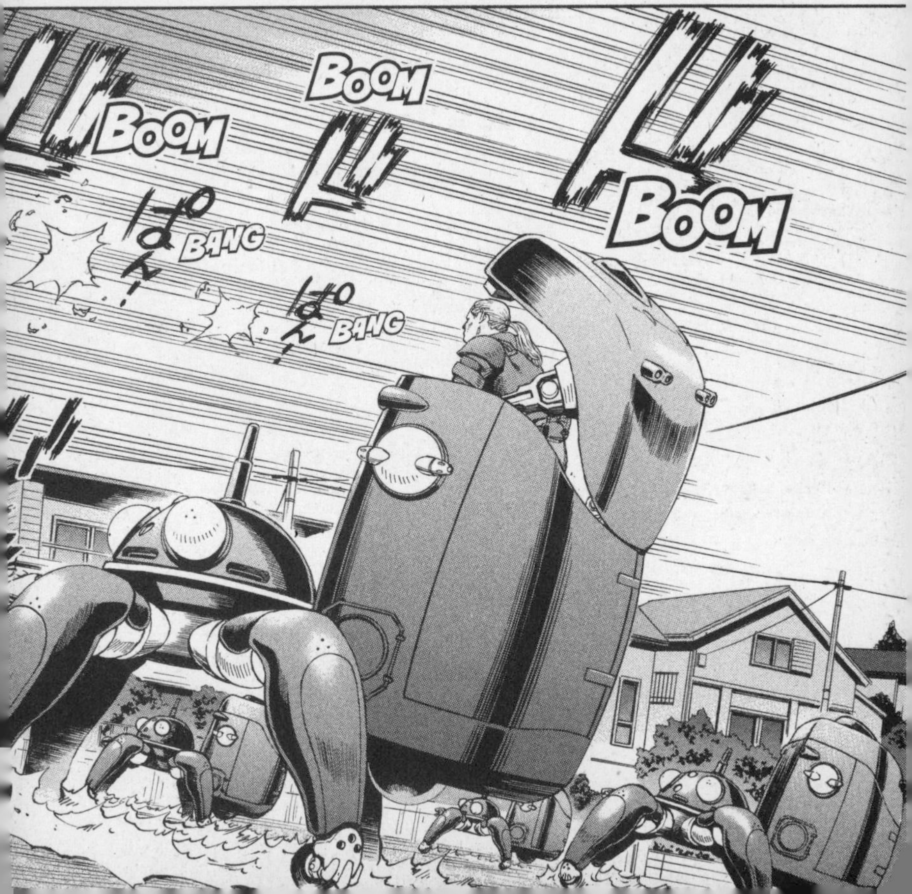
BOOM
BOOM
ぱん!
BANG
BOOM
ぱん!
BANG

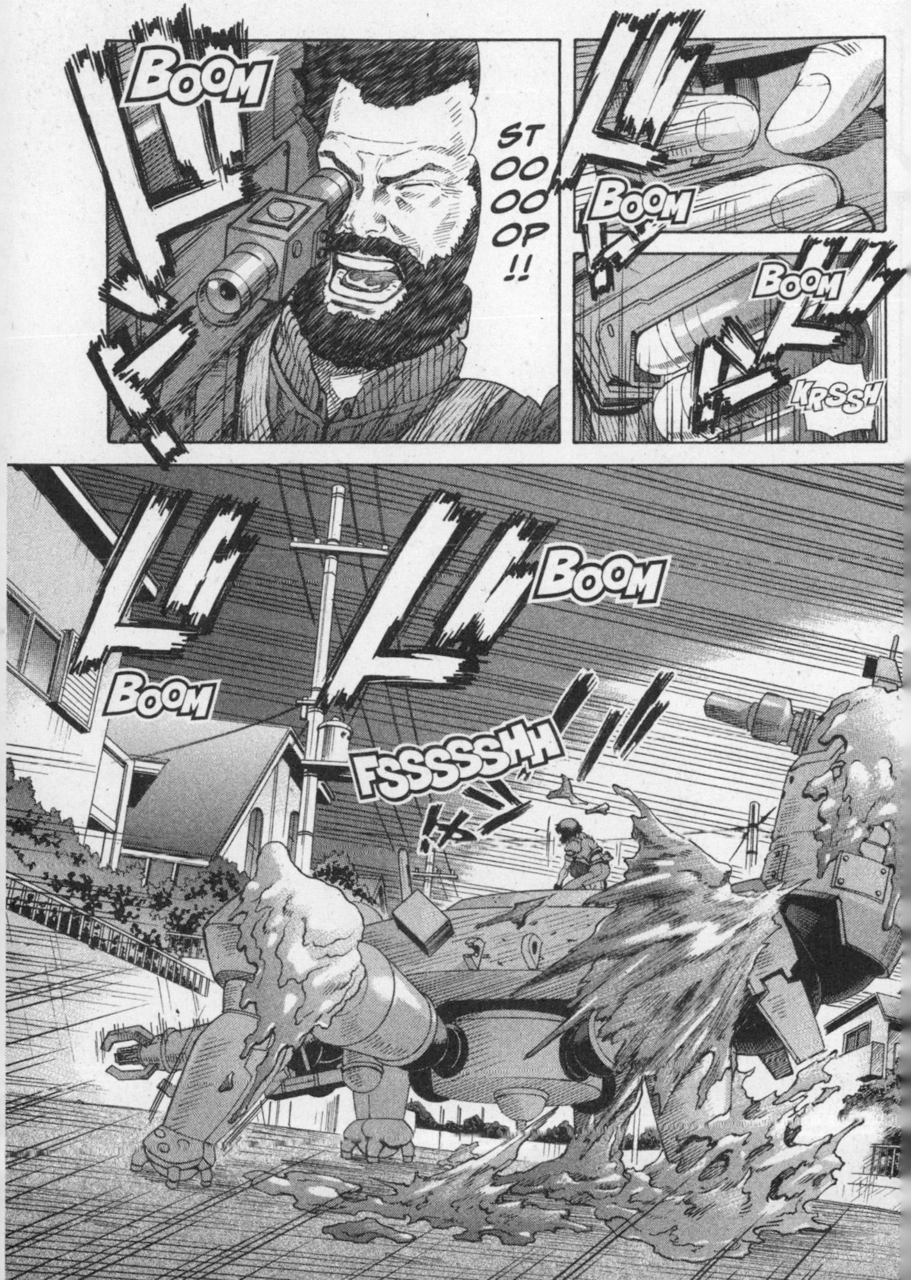
BOOM
BOOM
KRSSH
BOOM
STOOOOOOP!!
BOOM
BOOM
FSSSSSHH

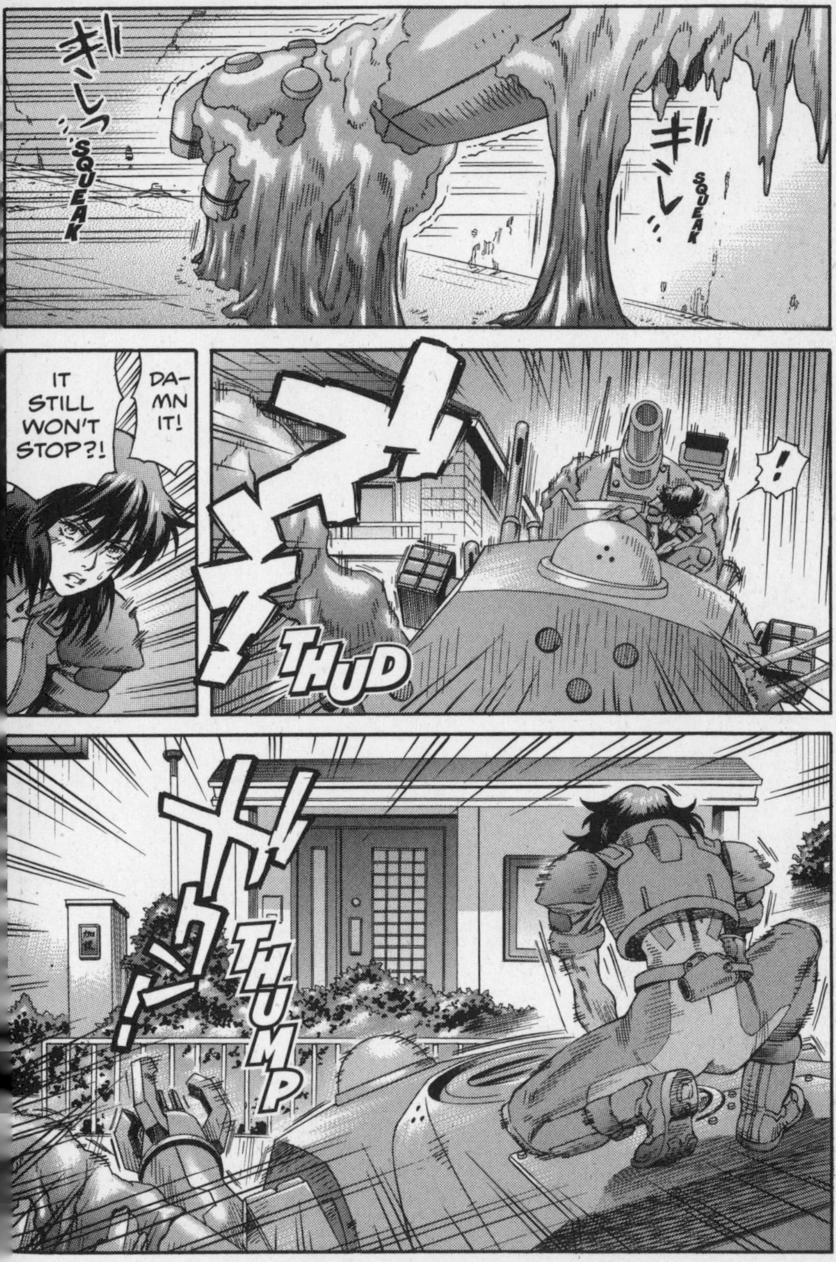
SQUEAK
SQUEAK
!
THUD
DA-MN IT!
IT STILL WON'T STOP?!
THUMP

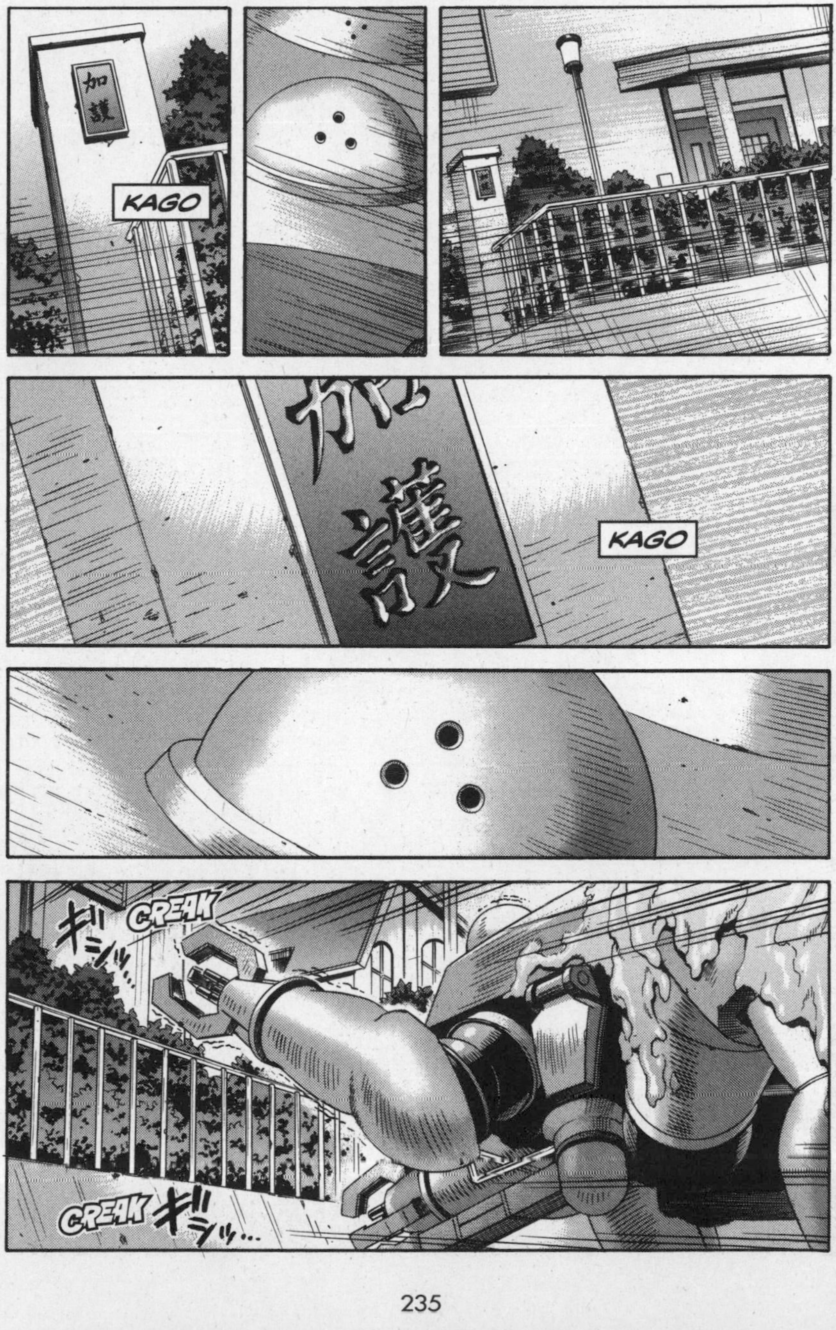
加護
KAGO
加護
KAGO
CREAK
CREAK

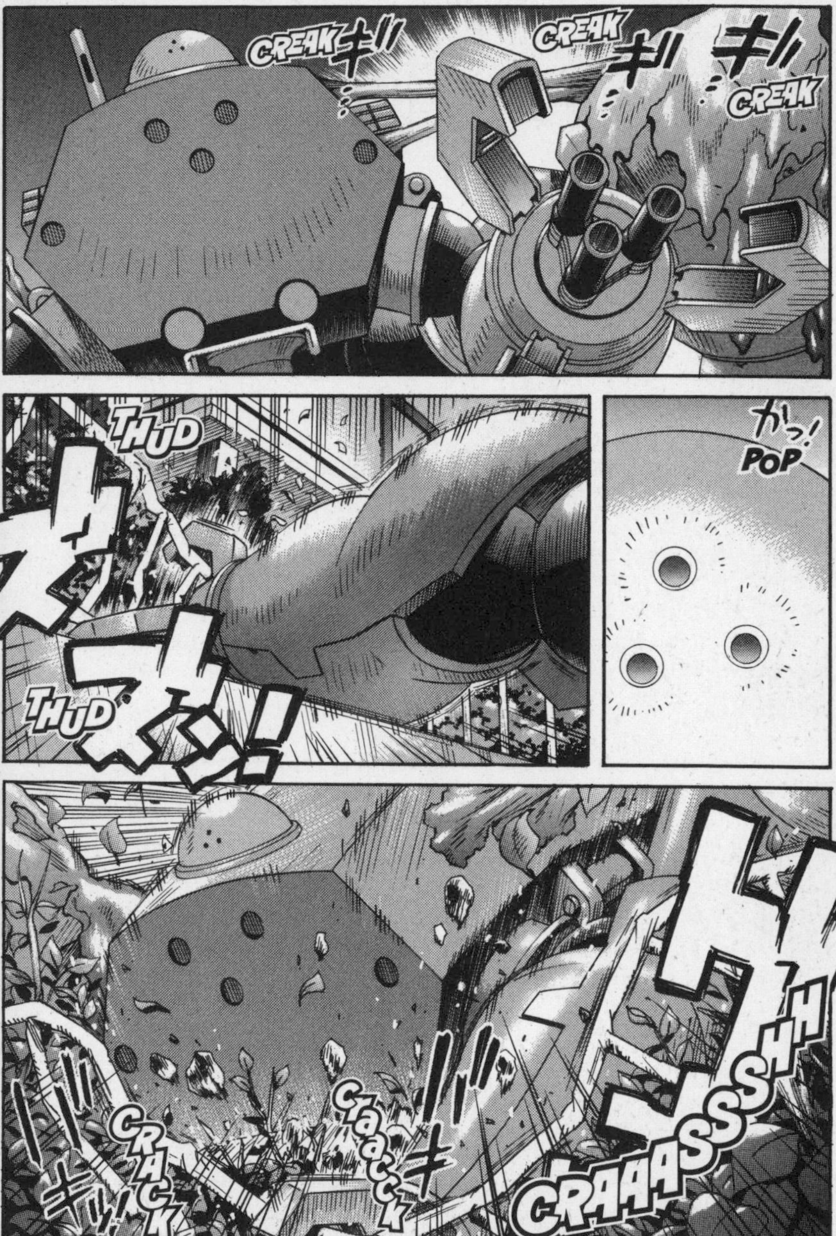
CREAK
キッ
キッ
CREAK
CREAK
キッ
かっ!
POP
THUD
THUD
CRAAASSSHH
craack
キ
CRACK
キッ!

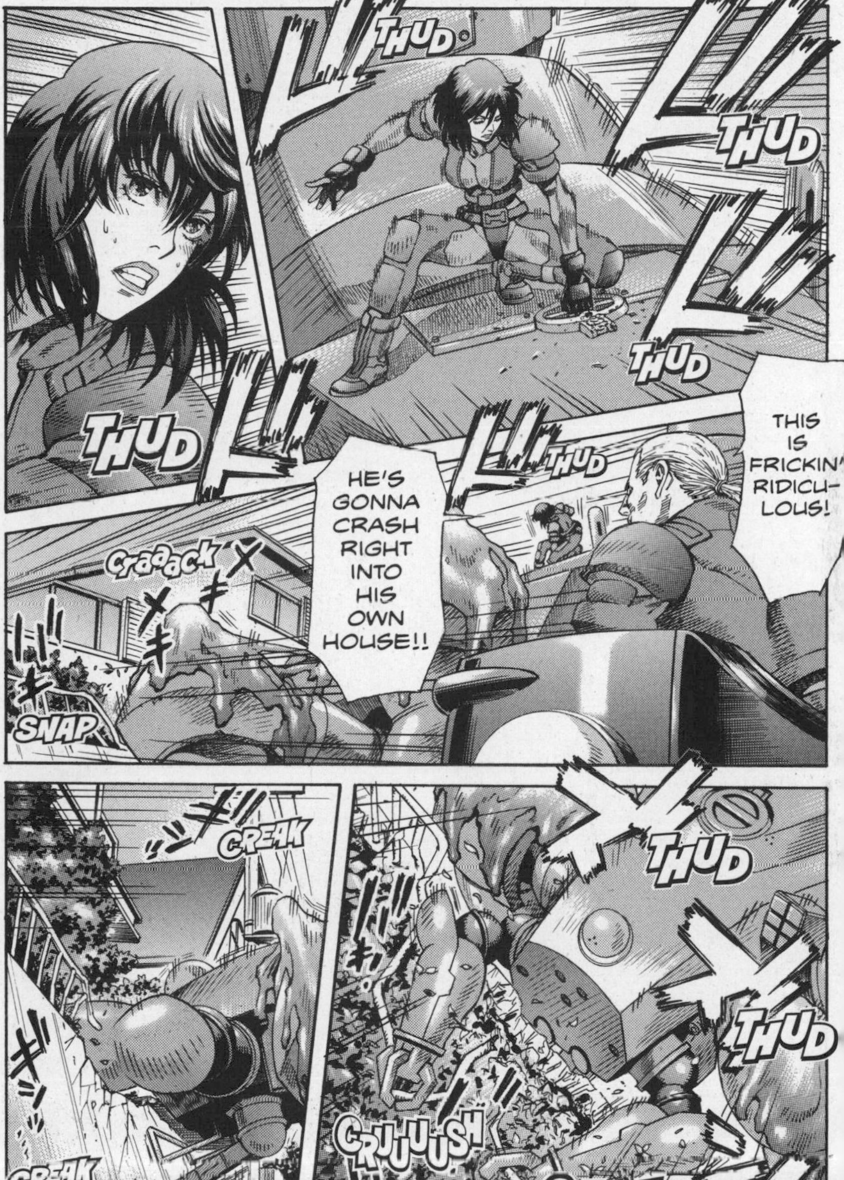
THUD
THUD
THUD
THUD
THIS IS FRICKIN' RIDICULOUS!
THUD
HE'S GONNA CRASH RIGHT INTO HIS OWN HOUSE!!
Craaack
SNAP
THUD
THUD
CRUUUUSH
CRUUUSH
SNAAAAAAP
CREAK
CREAK

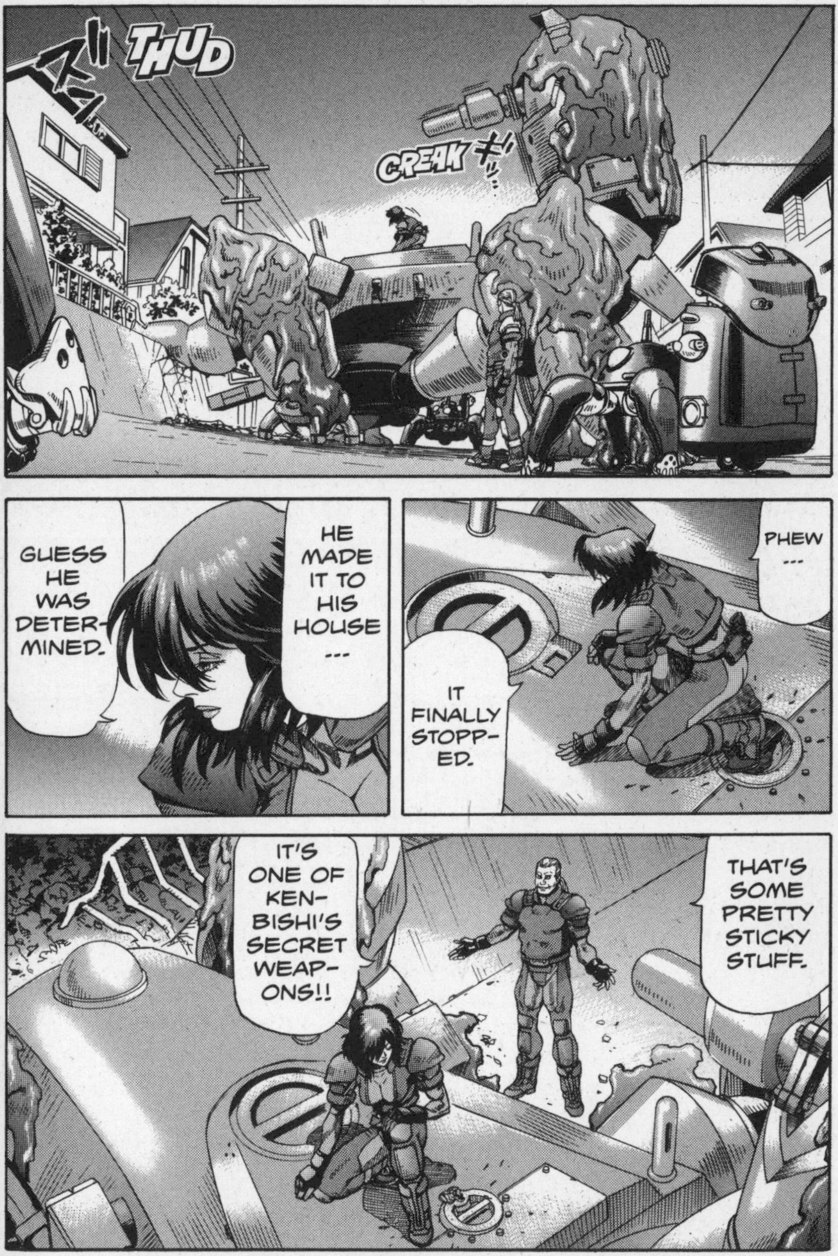
THUD
CREAK
PHEW ---
IT FINALLY STOPP-ED.
HE MADE IT TO HIS HOUSE ---
GUESS HE WAS DETER-MINED.
THAT'S SOME PRETTY STICKY STUFF.
IT'S ONE OF KEN-BISHI'S SECRET WEAP-ONS!!

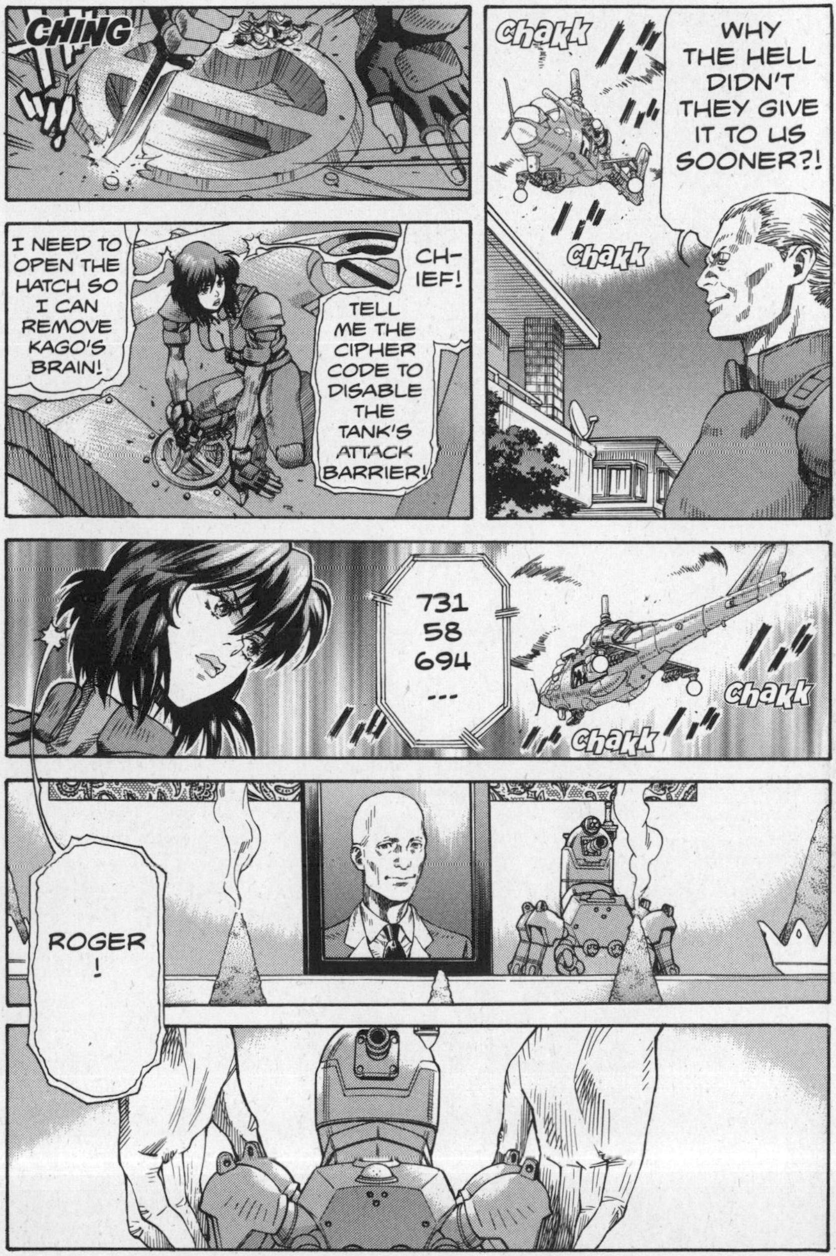
Chakk
WHY THE HELL DIDN'T THEY GIVE IT TO US SOONER?!
Chakk
CHING
CH-IEF!
TELL ME THE CIPHER CODE TO DISABLE THE TANK'S ATTACK BARRIER!
I NEED TO OPEN THE HATCH SO I CAN REMOVE KAGO'S BRAIN!
Chakk
Chakk
731 58 694 ---
ROGER!

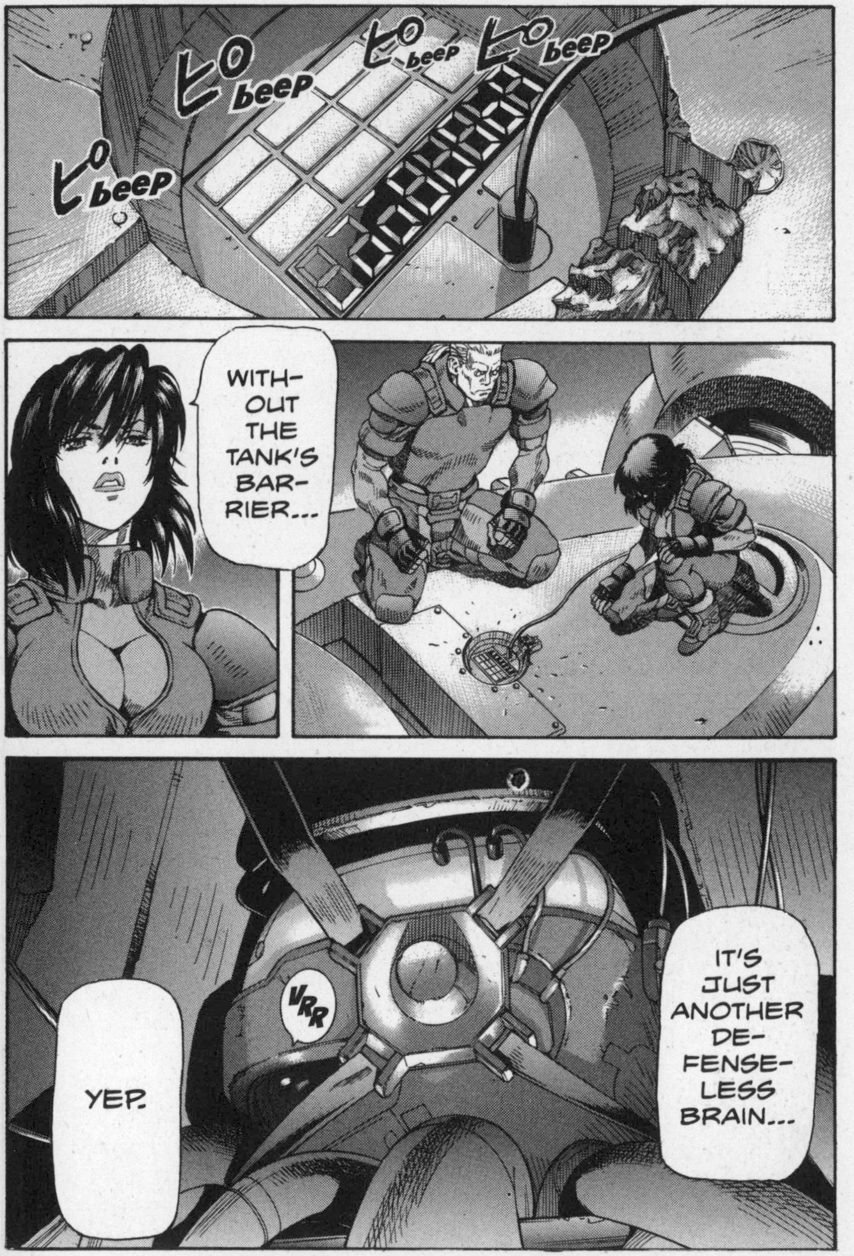
ピ beep
ピ beep
ピ beep
ピ beep
WITHOUT THE TANK'S BARRIER...
IT'S JUST ANOTHER DEFENSELESS BRAIN...
VRR
YEP.

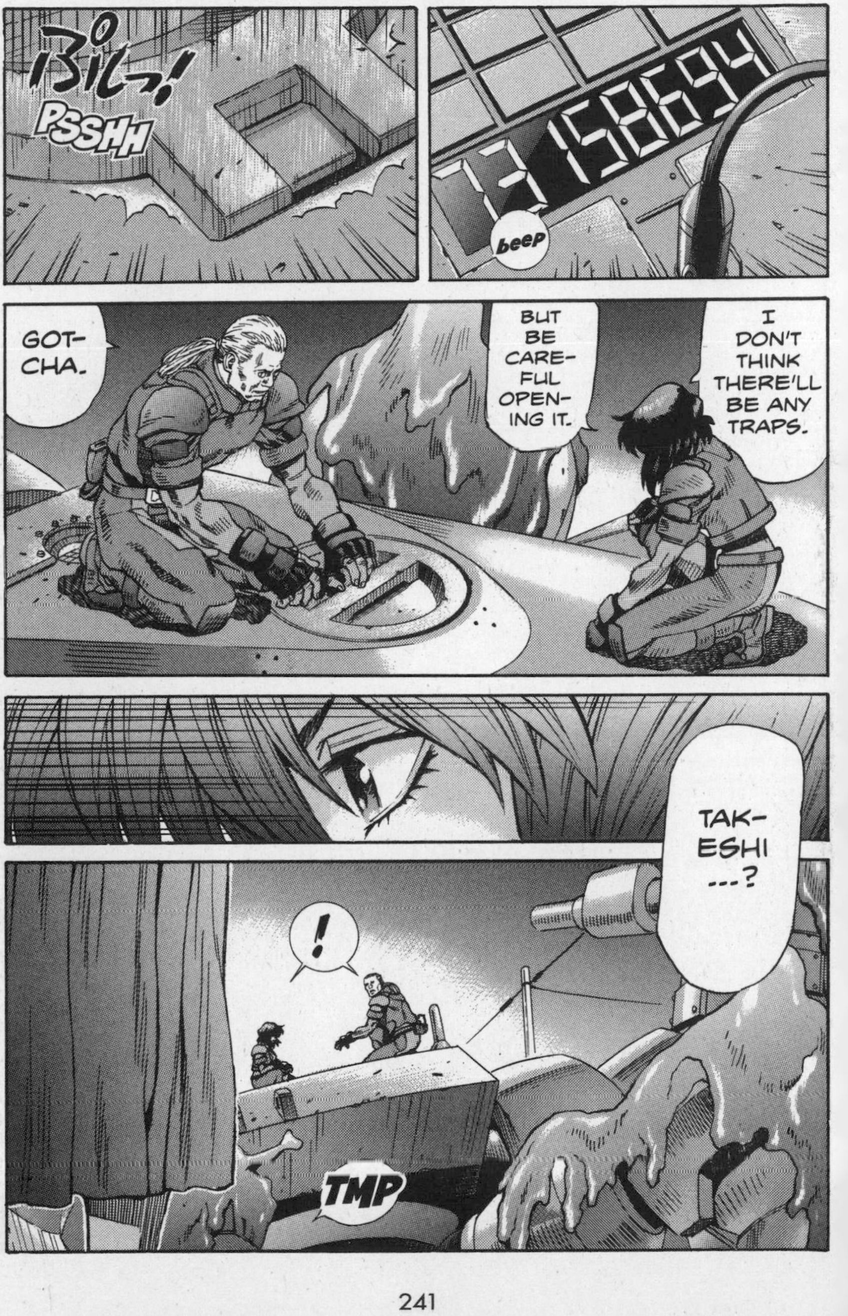

beep
ぷしゅっ!
PSSHH
I DON'T THINK THERE'LL BE ANY TRAPS.
BUT BE CARE-FUL OPEN-ING IT.
GOT-CHA.
TAK-ESHI ---?
!
TMP

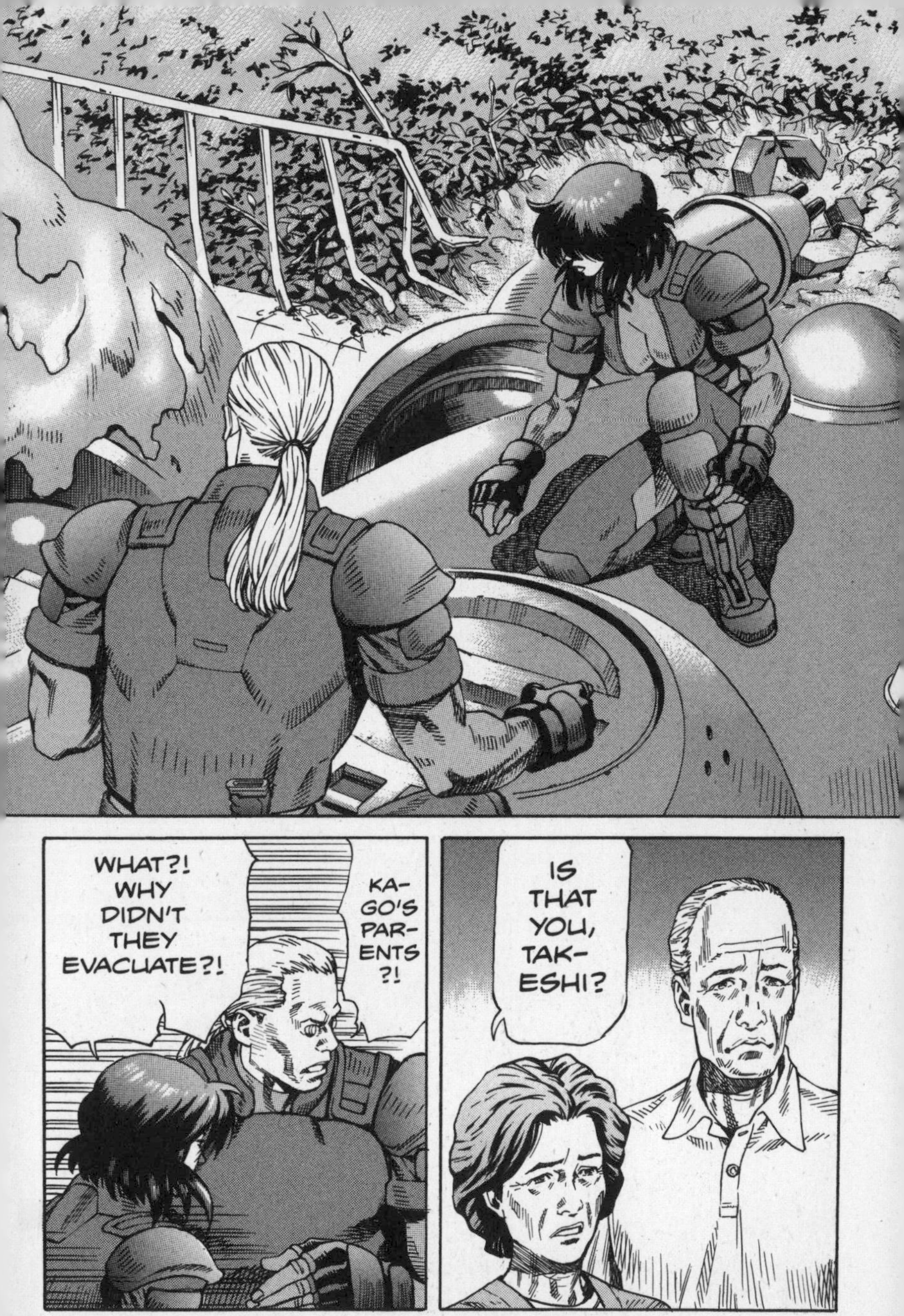
IS THAT YOU, TAK-ESHI?
KA-GO'S PAR-ENTS?!
WHAT?! WHY DIDN'T THEY EVACUATE?!

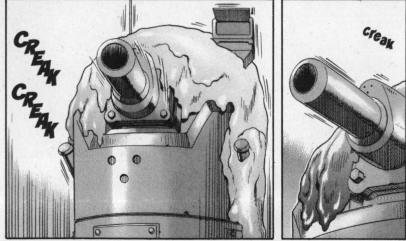

CREAK
CREAK

creak

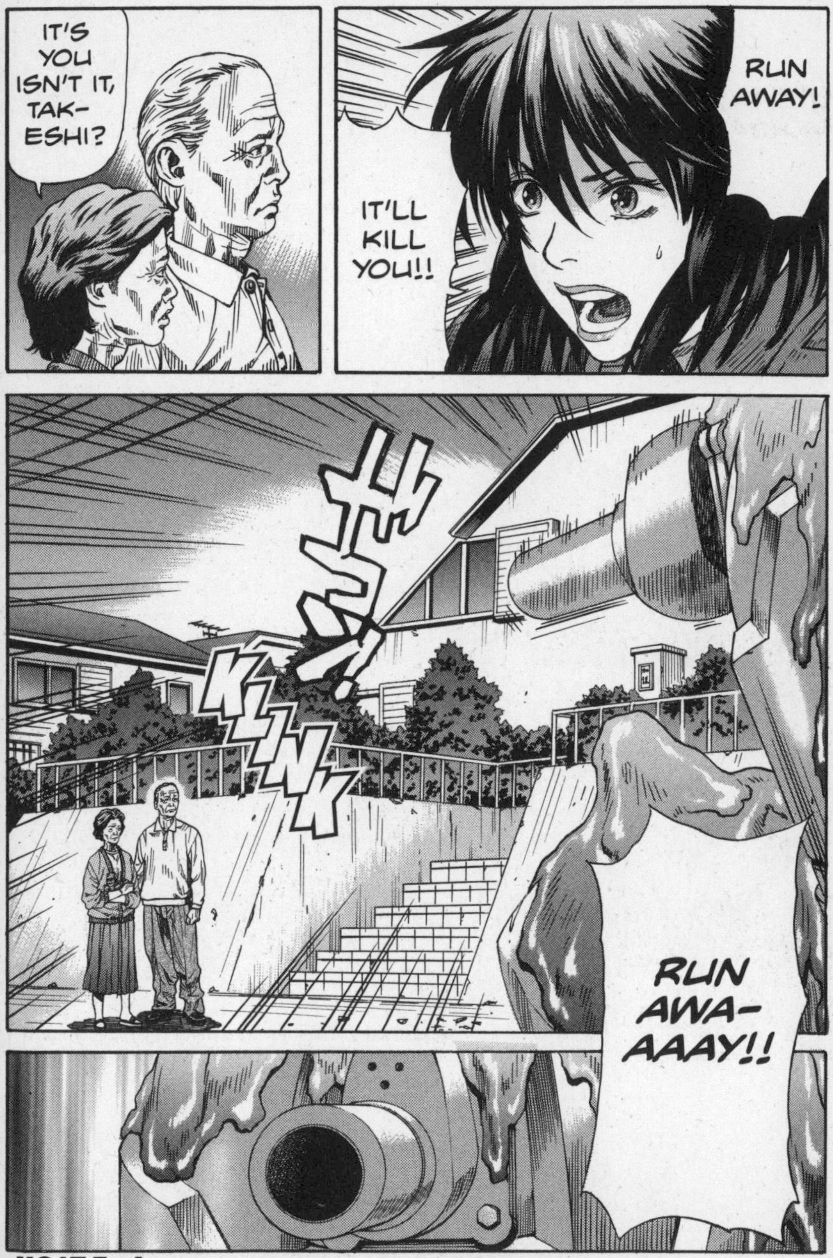
RUN AWAY!
IT'LL KILL YOU!!
IT'S YOU ISN'T IT, TAK-ESHI?
KLINK
RUN AWA-AAAY!!

#017 End

#018 Last Feeling

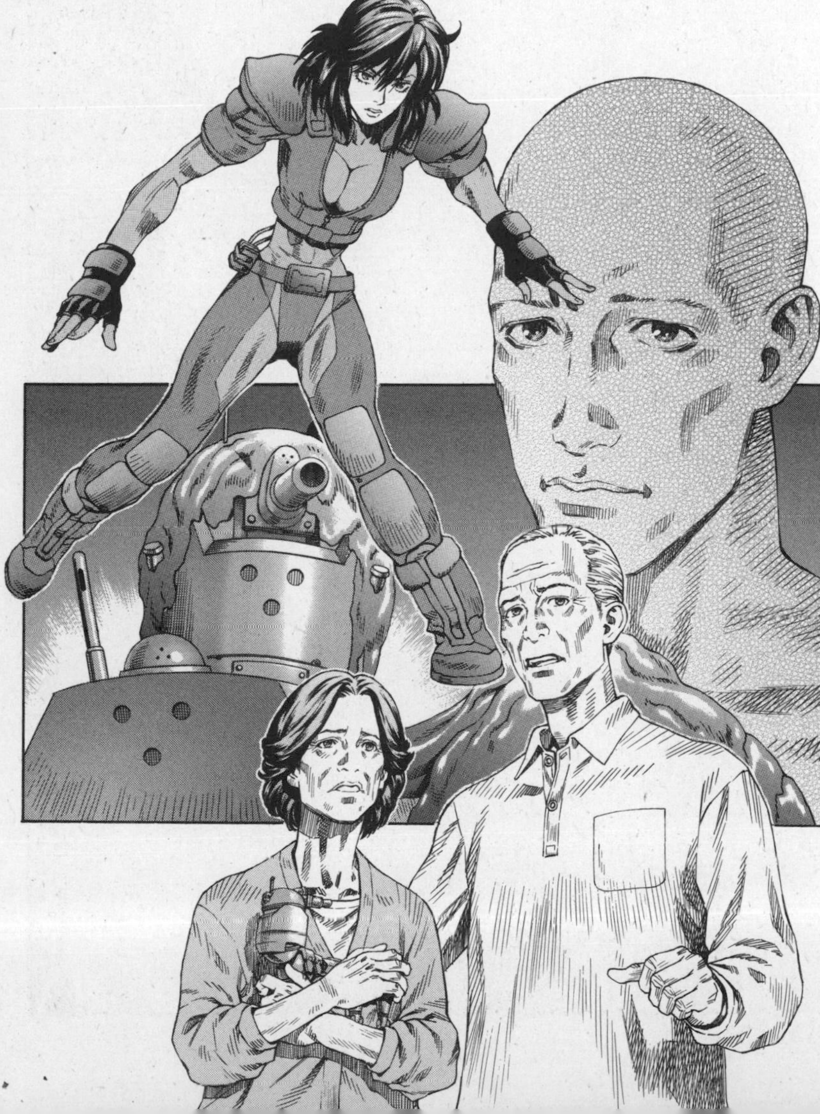

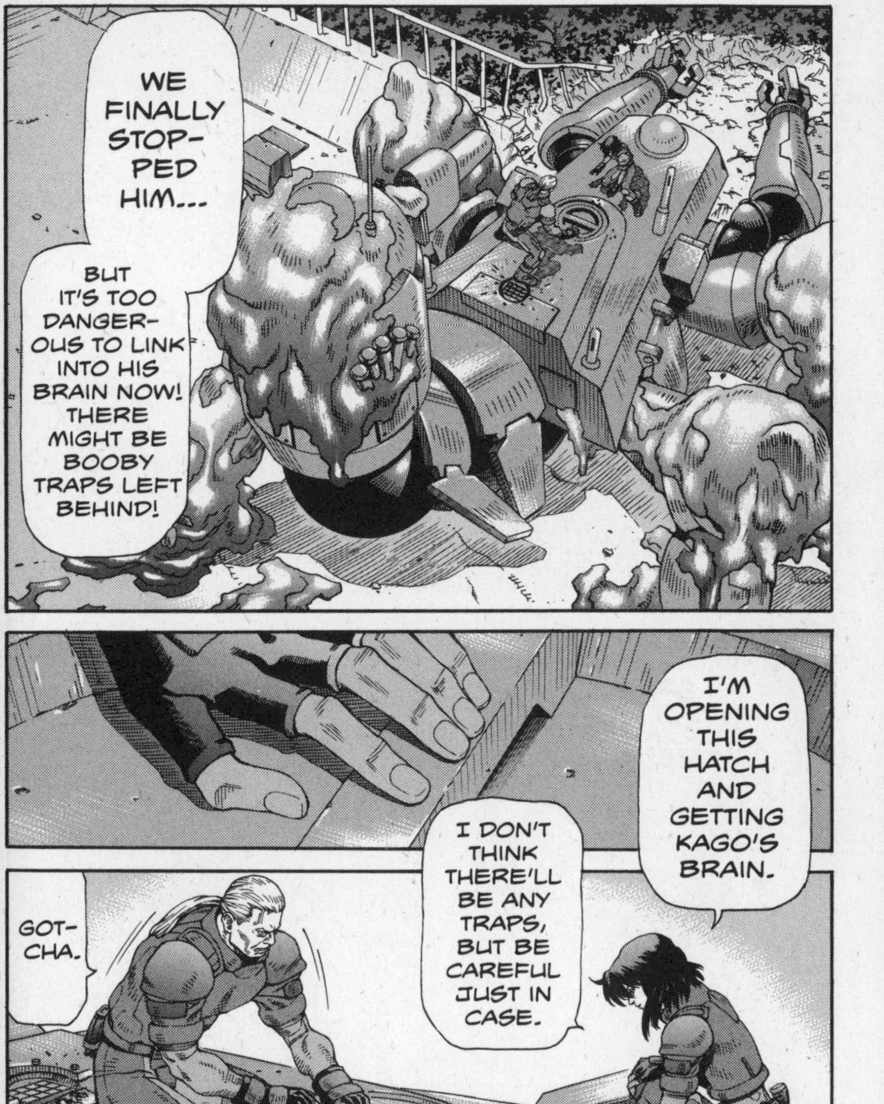
WE FINALLY STOP-PED HIM...
BUT IT'S TOO DANGER-OUS TO LINK INTO HIS BRAIN NOW! THERE MIGHT BE BOOBY TRAPS LEFT BEHIND!
I'M OPENING THIS HATCH AND GETTING KAGO'S BRAIN.
I DON'T THINK THERE'LL BE ANY TRAPS, BUT BE CAREFUL JUST IN CASE.
GOT-CHA.

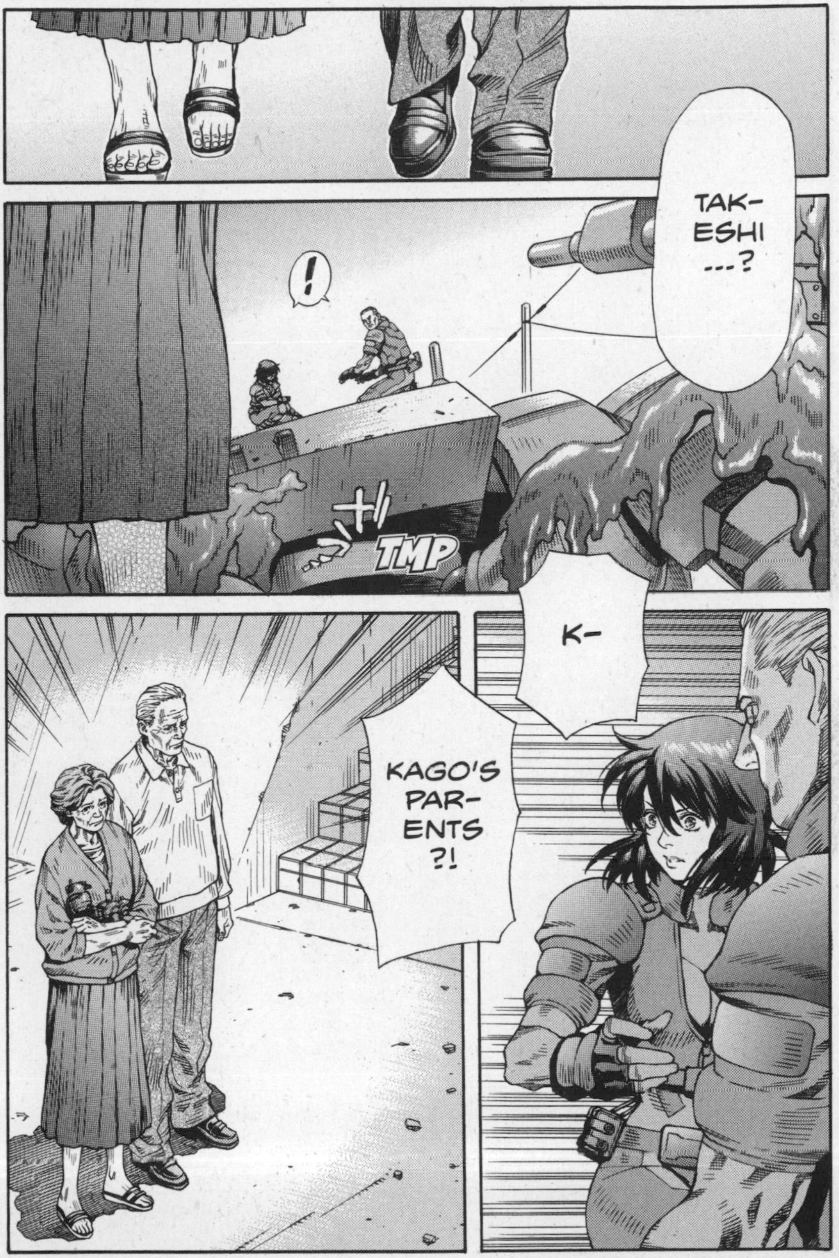
TAK-ESHI ...?
!
TMP
K-
KAGO'S PAR-ENTS ?!

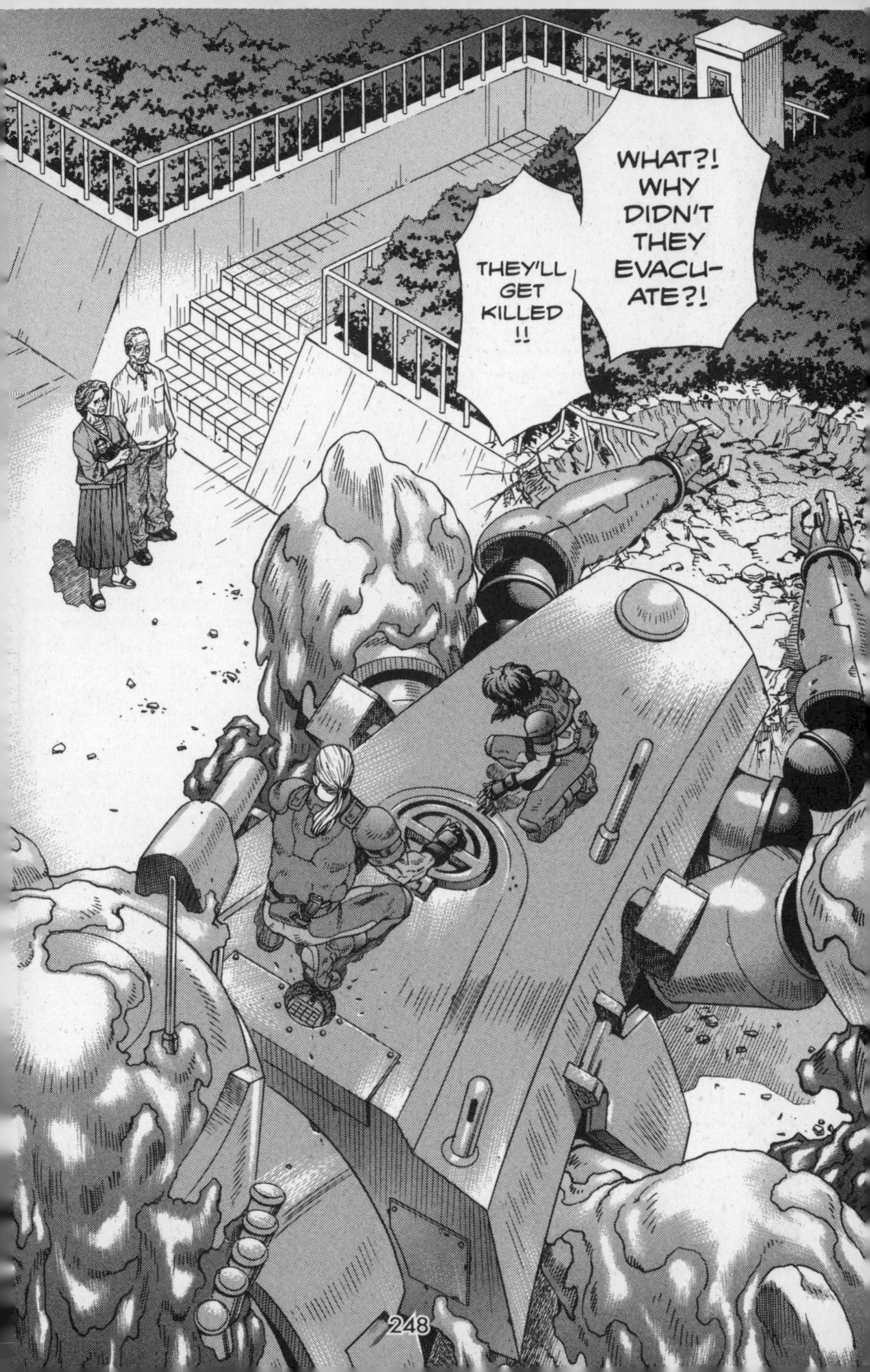
WHAT?! WHY DIDN'T THEY EVACU-ATE?!
THEY'LL GET KILLED !!

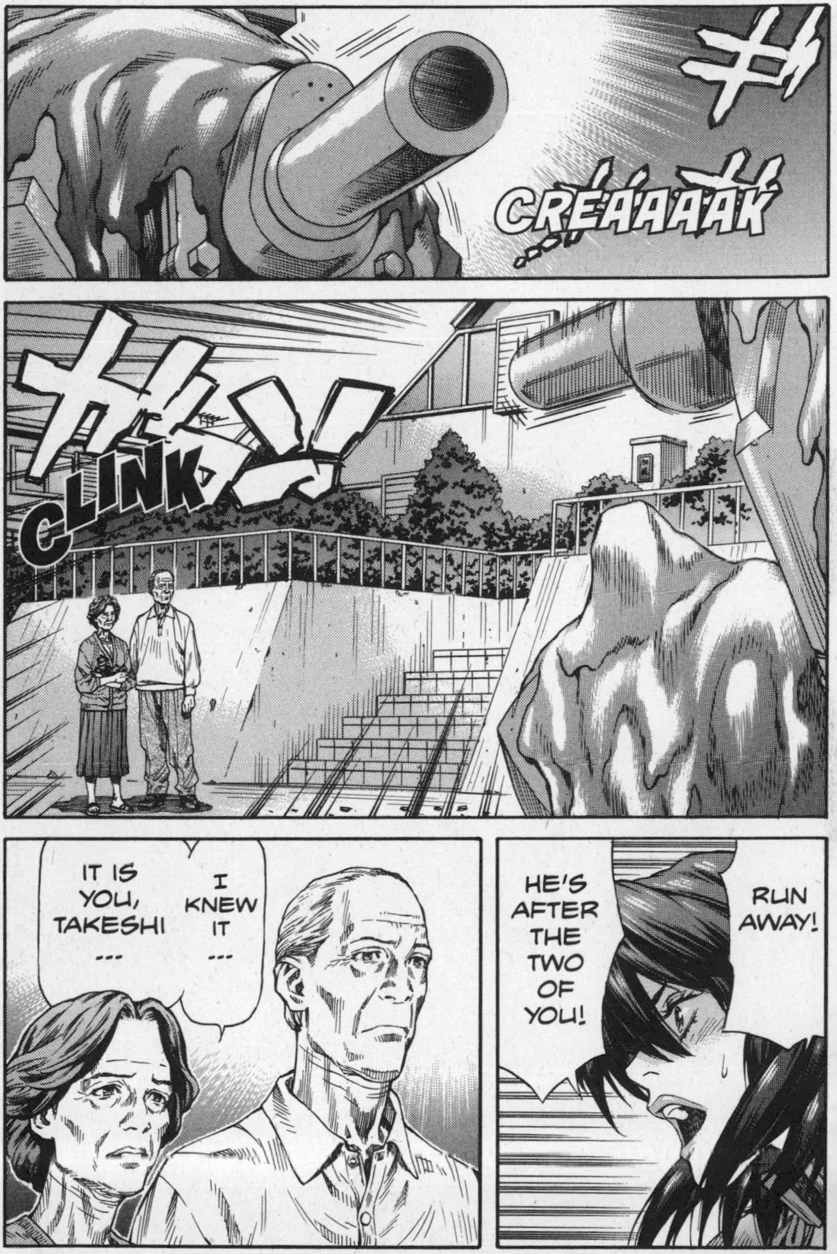
CREAAAAK
CLINK
RUN AWAY!
HE'S AFTER THE TWO OF YOU!
I KNEW IT ---
IT IS YOU, TAKESHI ---

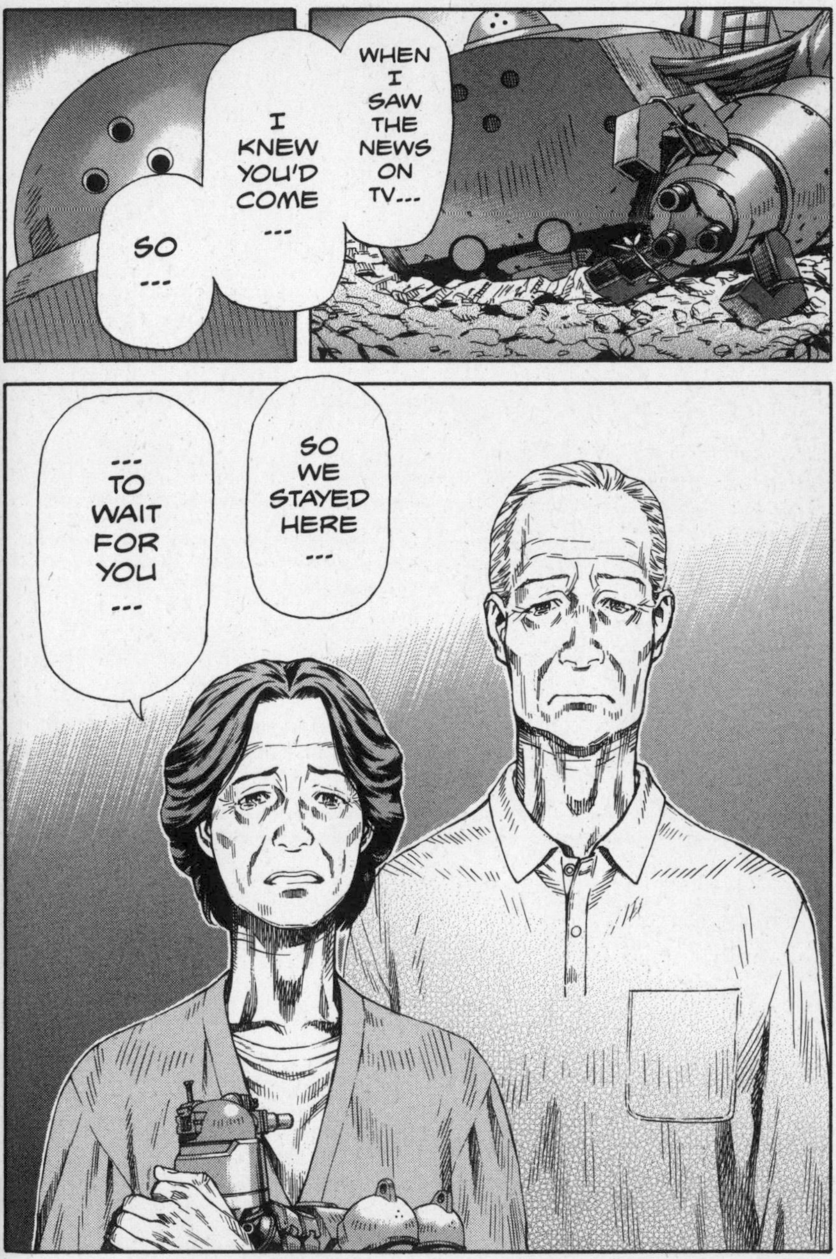
WHEN I SAW THE NEWS ON TV...
I KNEW YOU'D COME ...
SO ...
SO WE STAYED HERE ...
... TO WAIT FOR YOU ...

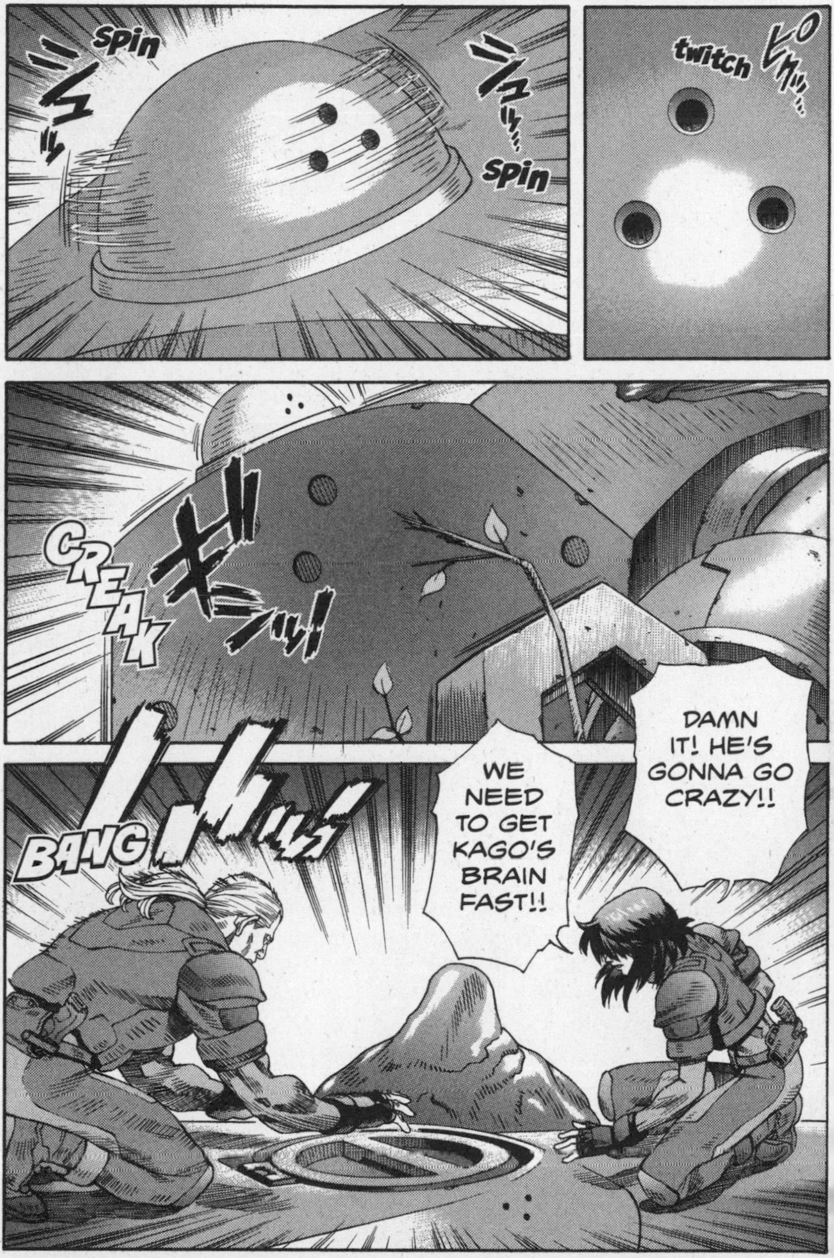
twitch
spin
spin
CREAK
DAMN IT! HE'S GONNA GO CRAZY!!
WE NEED TO GET KAGO'S BRAIN FAST!!
BANG

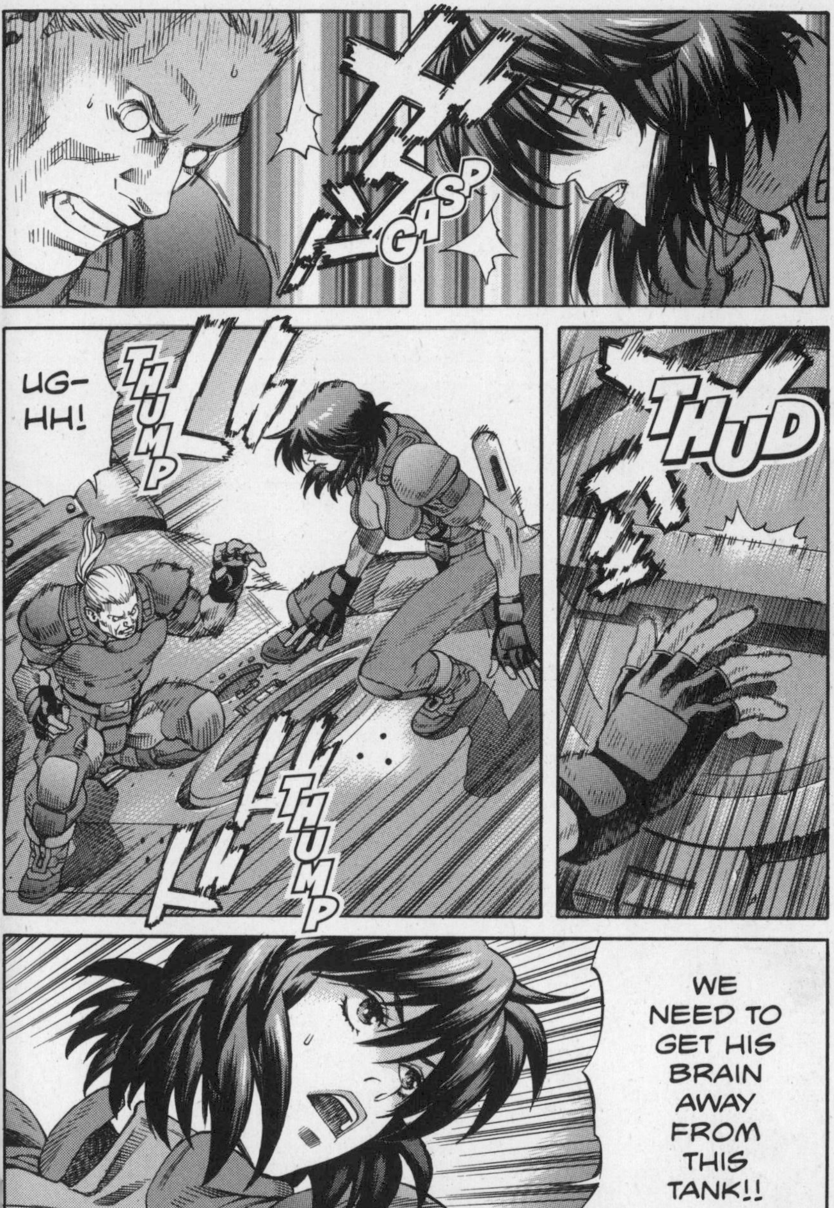
GASP
THUD
THUMP
UG-HH!
THUMP
WE NEED TO GET HIS BRAIN AWAY FROM THIS TANK!!

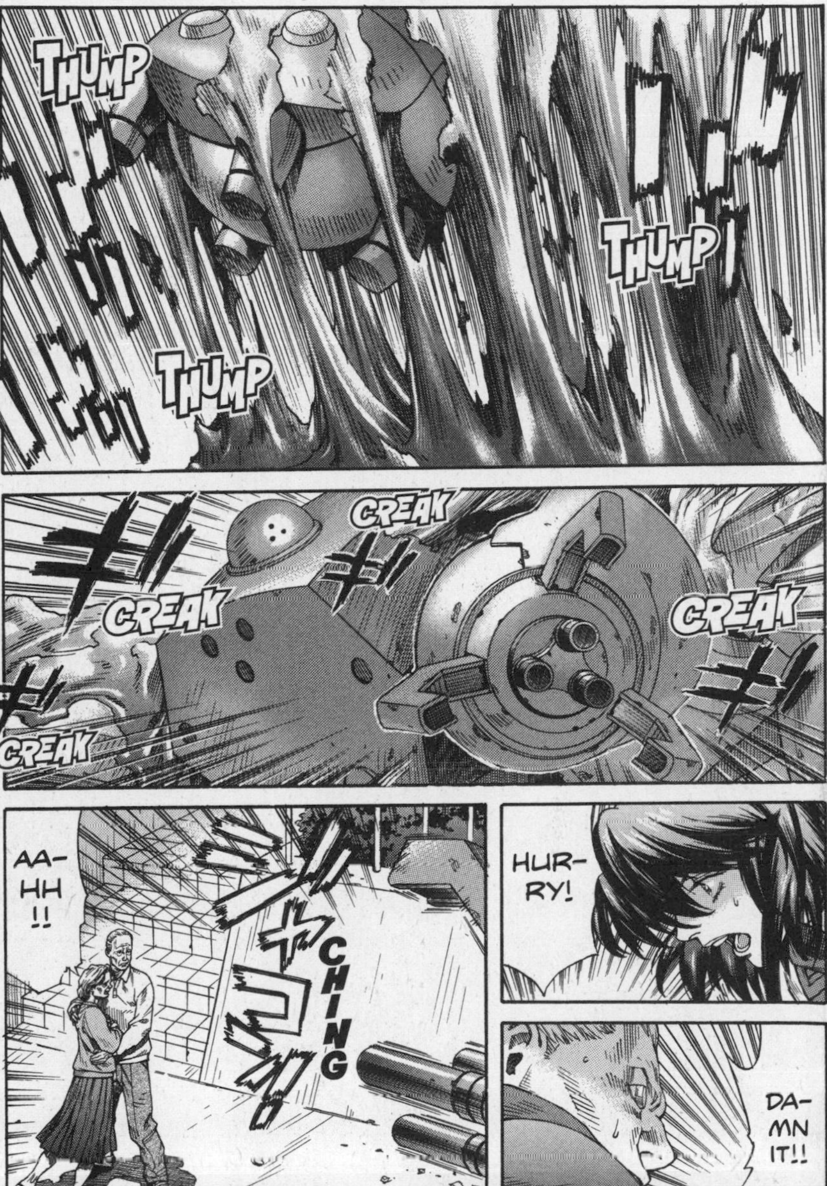
THUMP
THUMP
THUMP
CREAK
CREAK
CREAK
CREAK
HURRY!
DAMN IT!!
AAHH!!
CHING

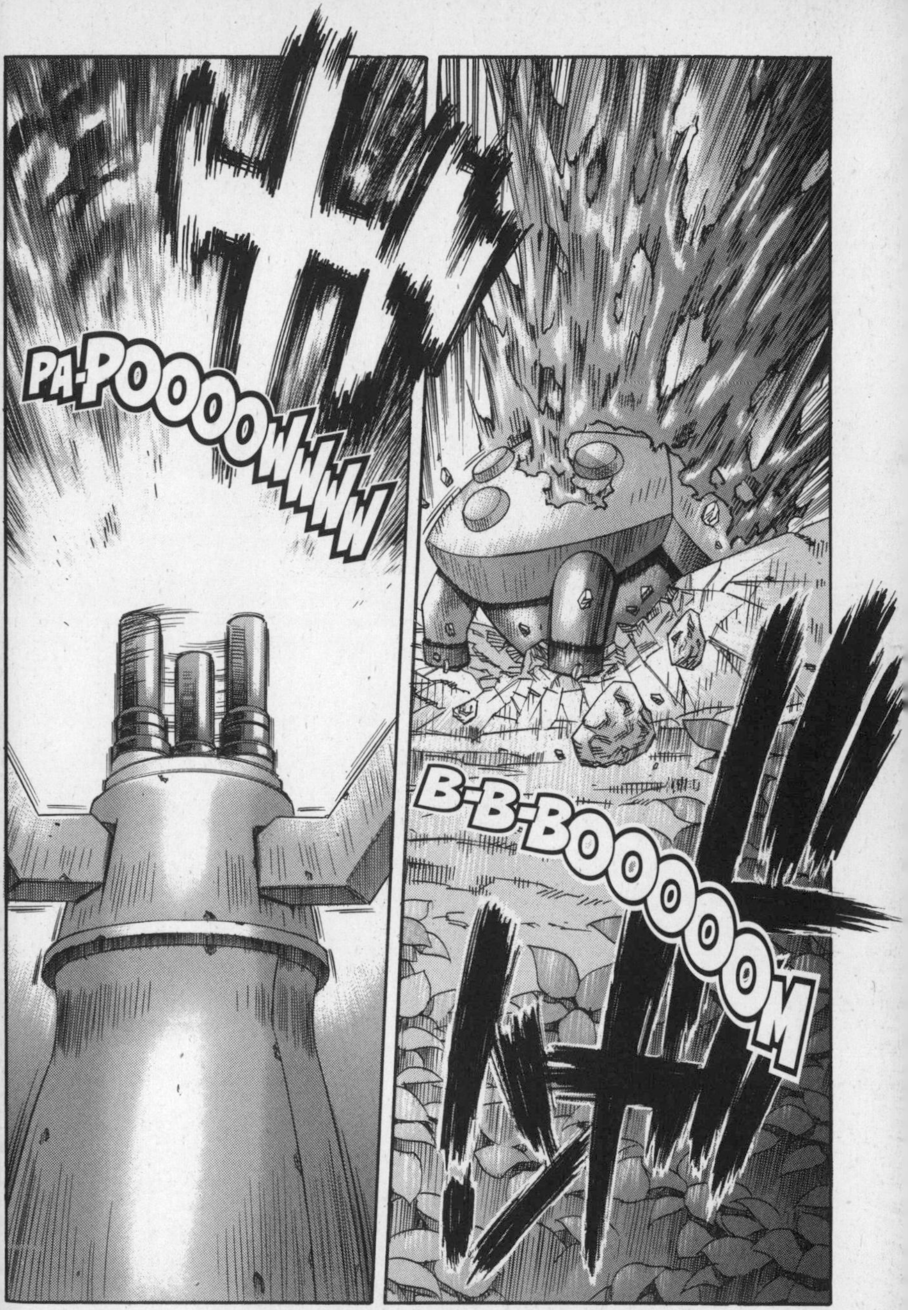
B-B-BOOOOOOM
PA-POOOOWWWW

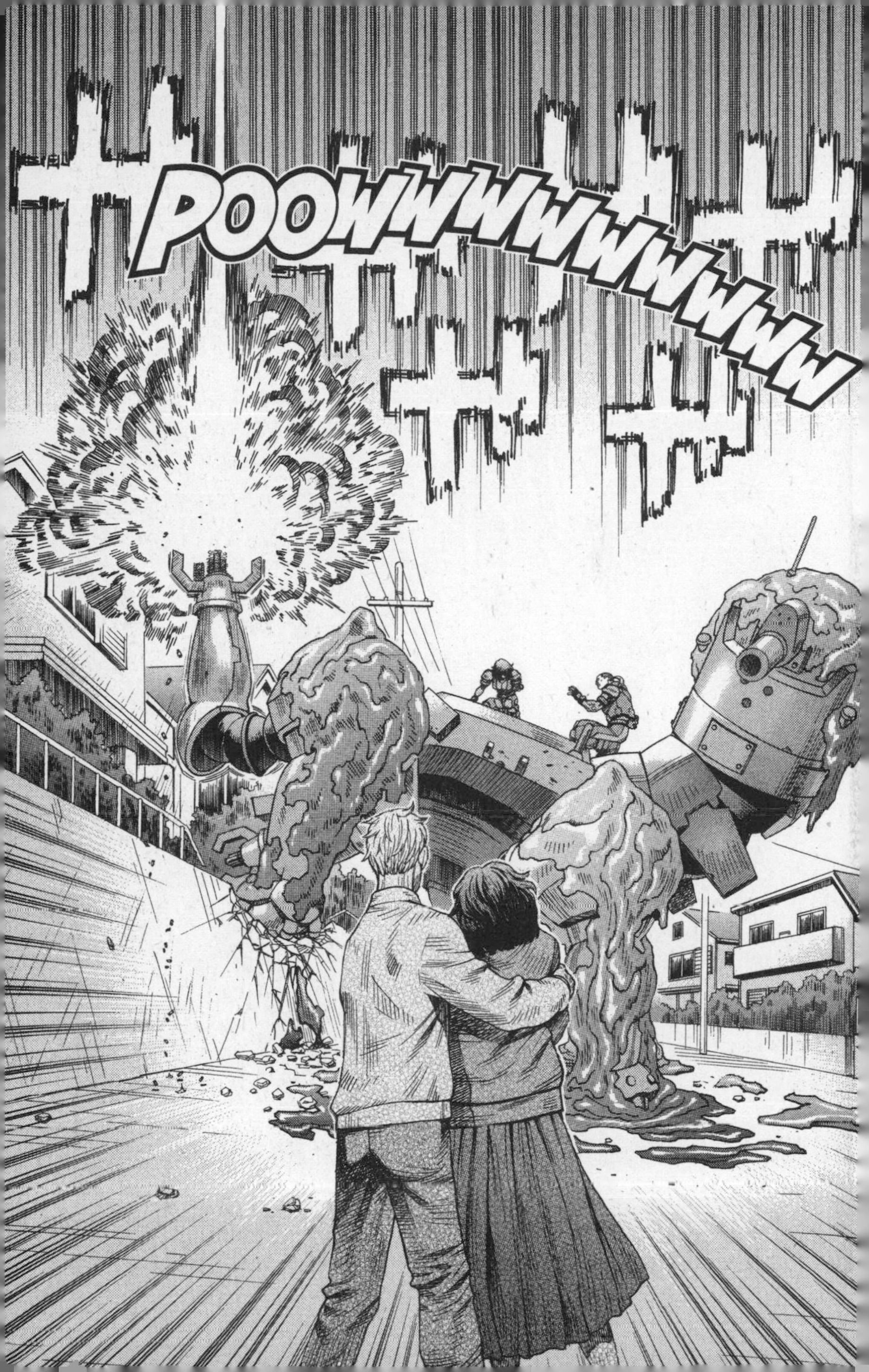
POOWWWWWWWWWW

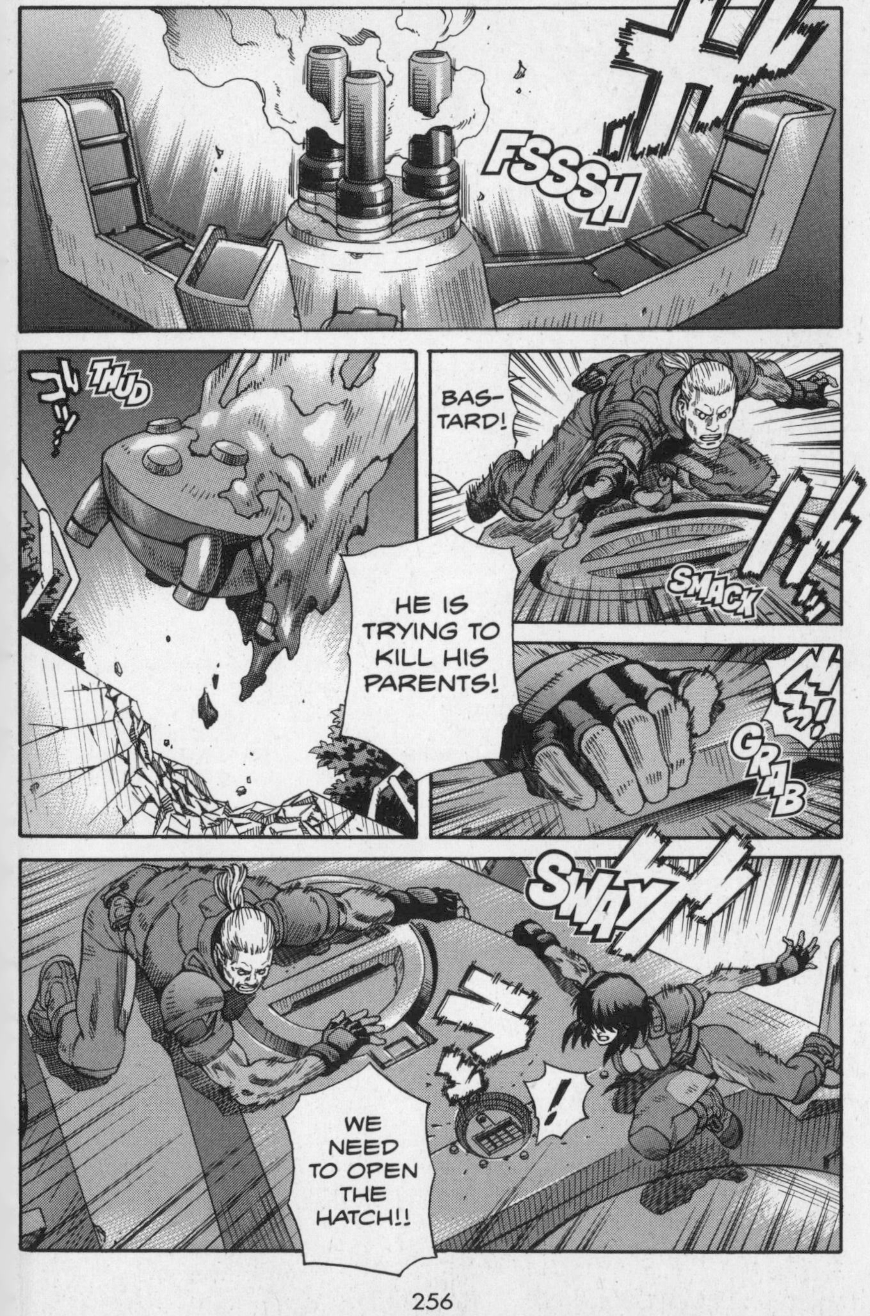
FSSSH
BAS-TARD!
SMACK
GRAB
THUD
HE IS TRYING TO KILL HIS PARENTS!
SWAY
!
WE NEED TO OPEN THE HATCH!!

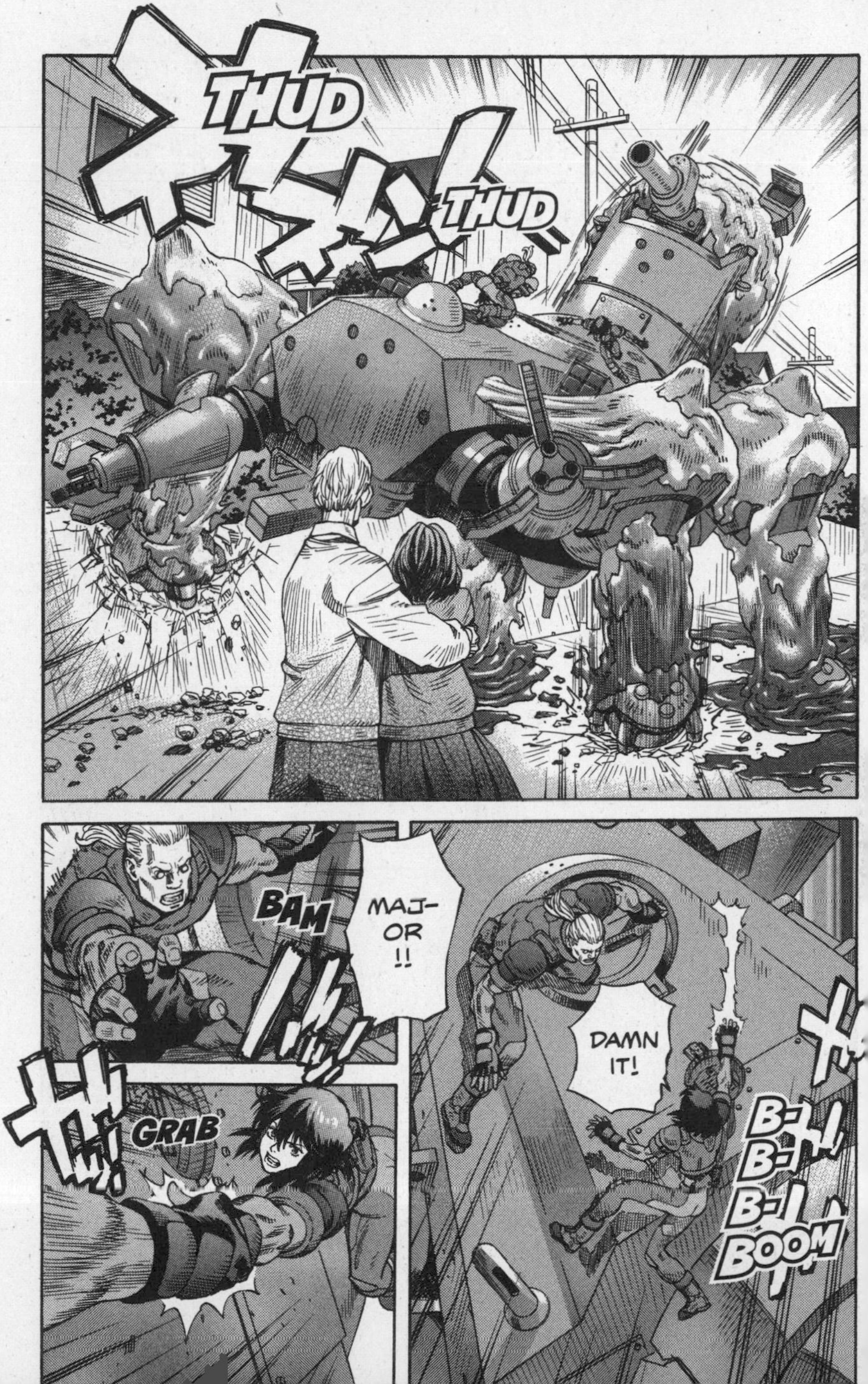
THUD
THUD
DAMN IT!
B-B-B-BOOM
MAJ-OR !!
BAM
GRAB

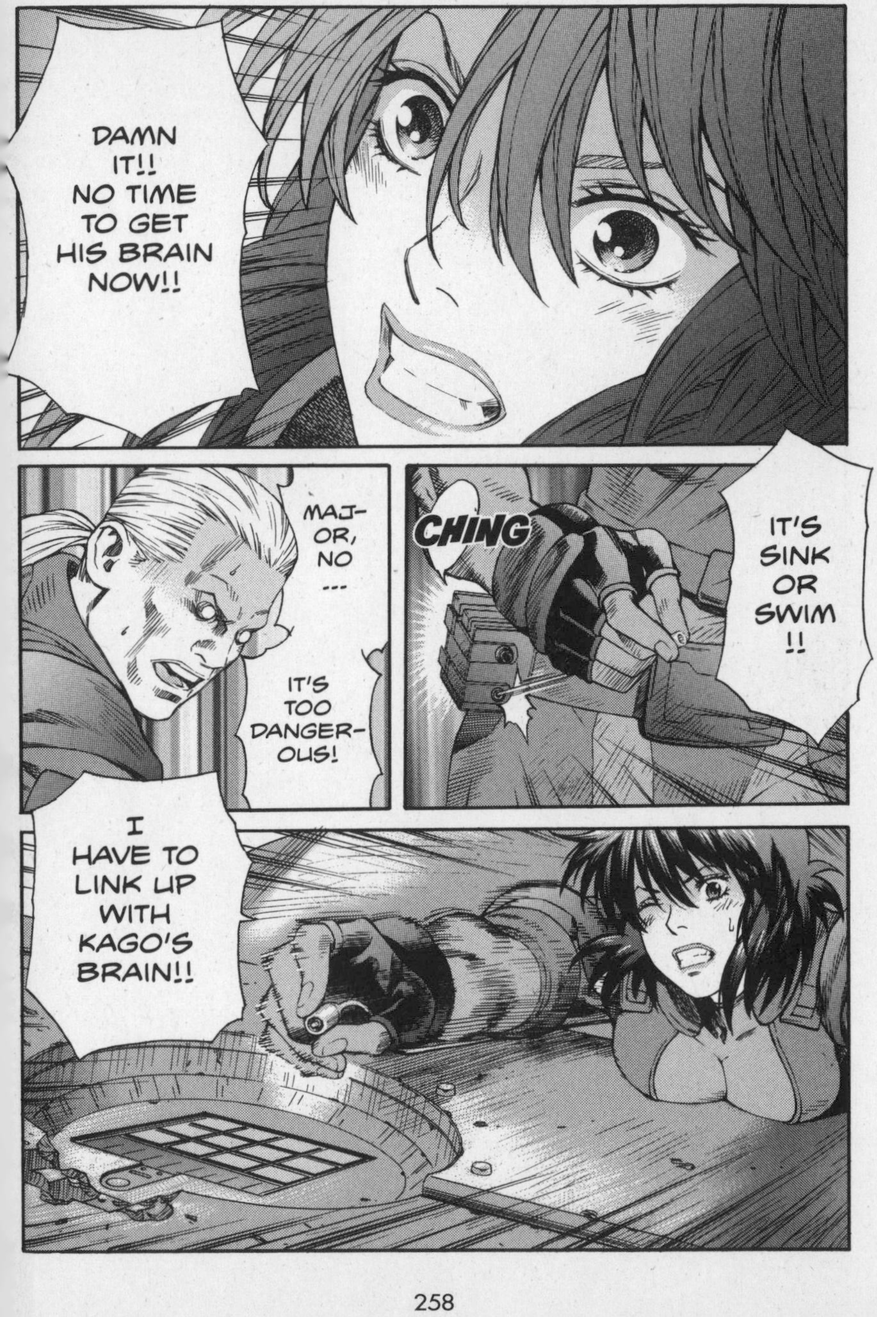
DAMN IT!! NO TIME TO GET HIS BRAIN NOW!!
IT'S SINK OR SWIM !!
CHING
MAJ-OR, NO ---
IT'S TOO DANGER-OUS!
I HAVE TO LINK UP WITH KAGO'S BRAIN!!

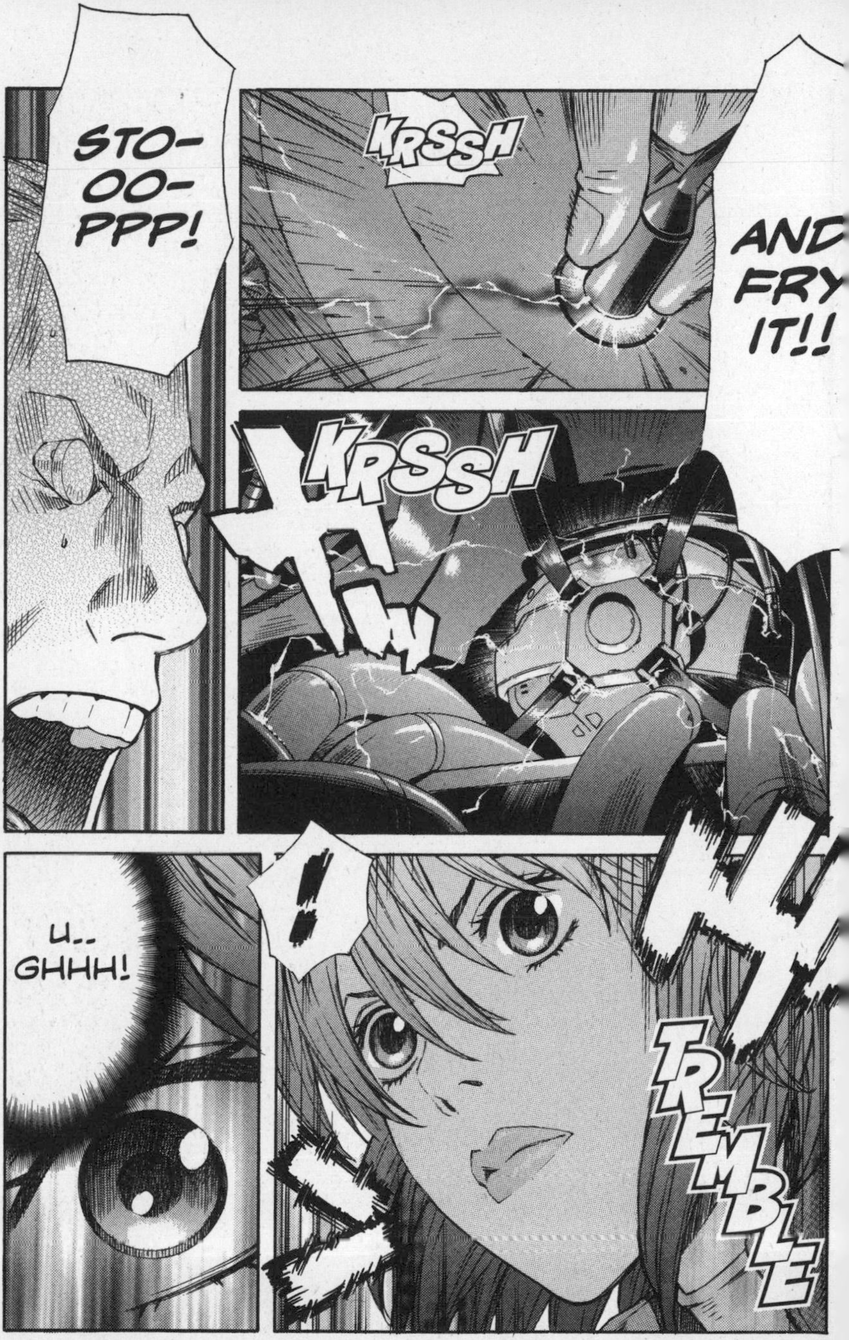
AND FRY IT!!
KRSSH
KRSSH
STO-OO-PPP!
!
TREMBLE
U.. GHHH!

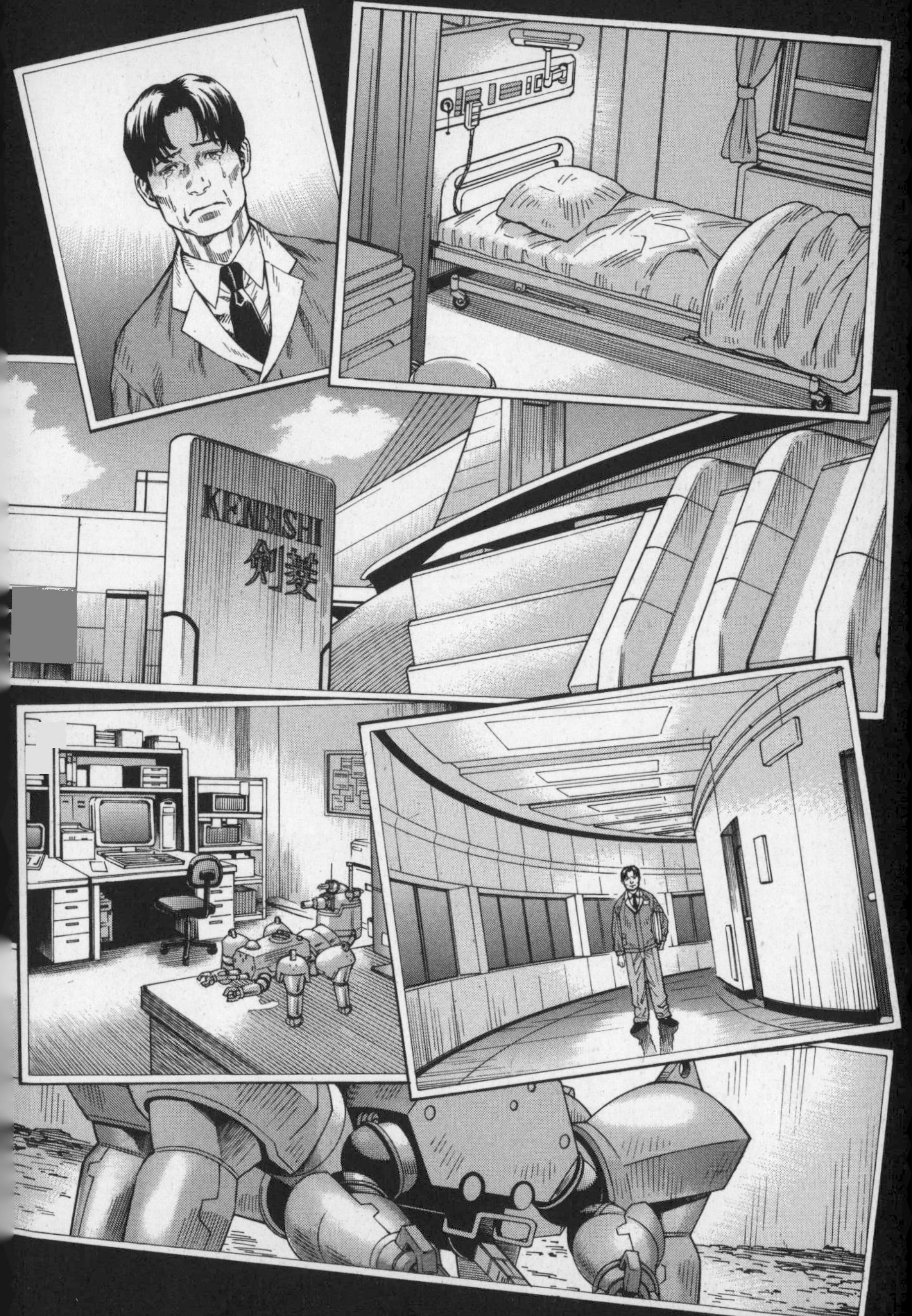
KENBISHI
剣菱

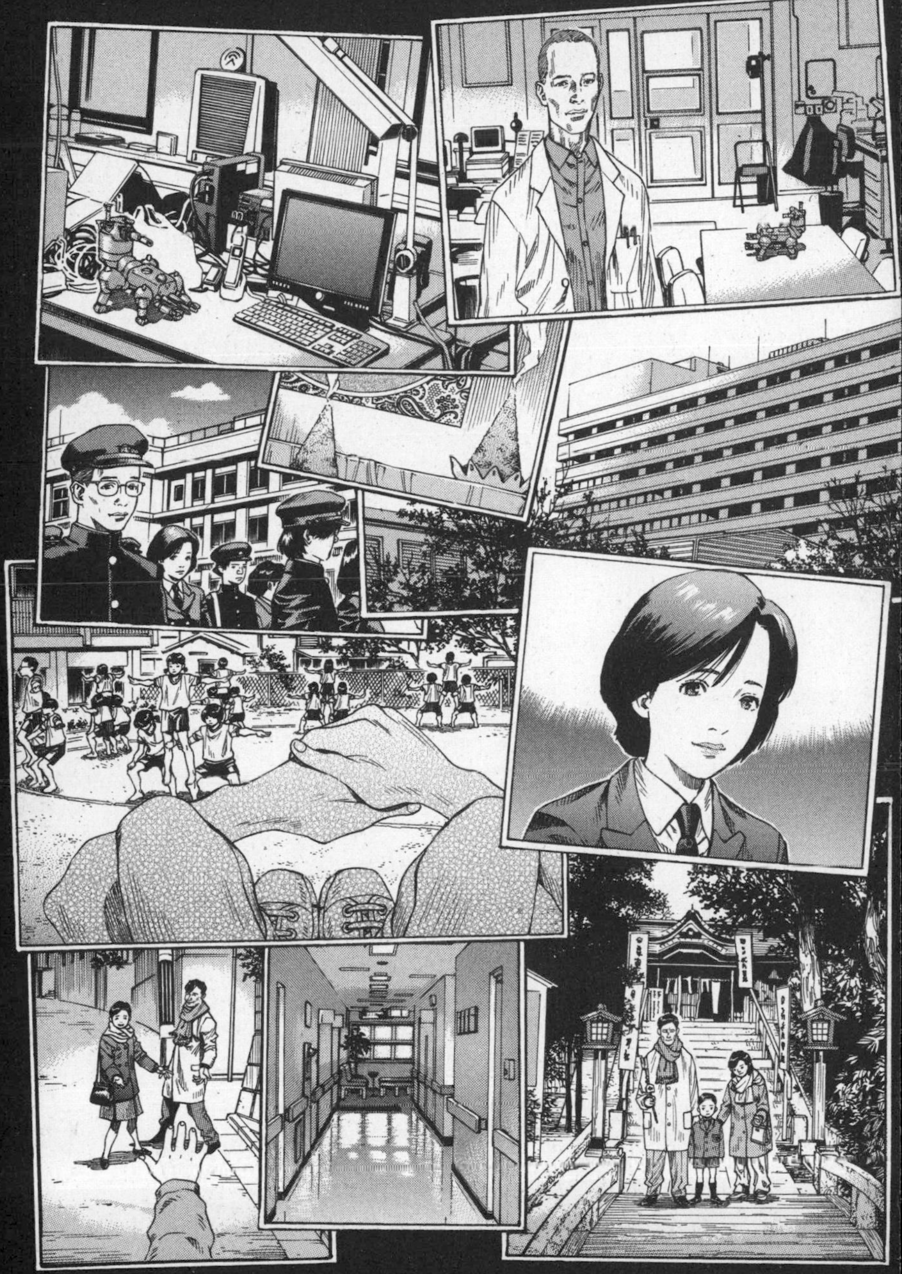

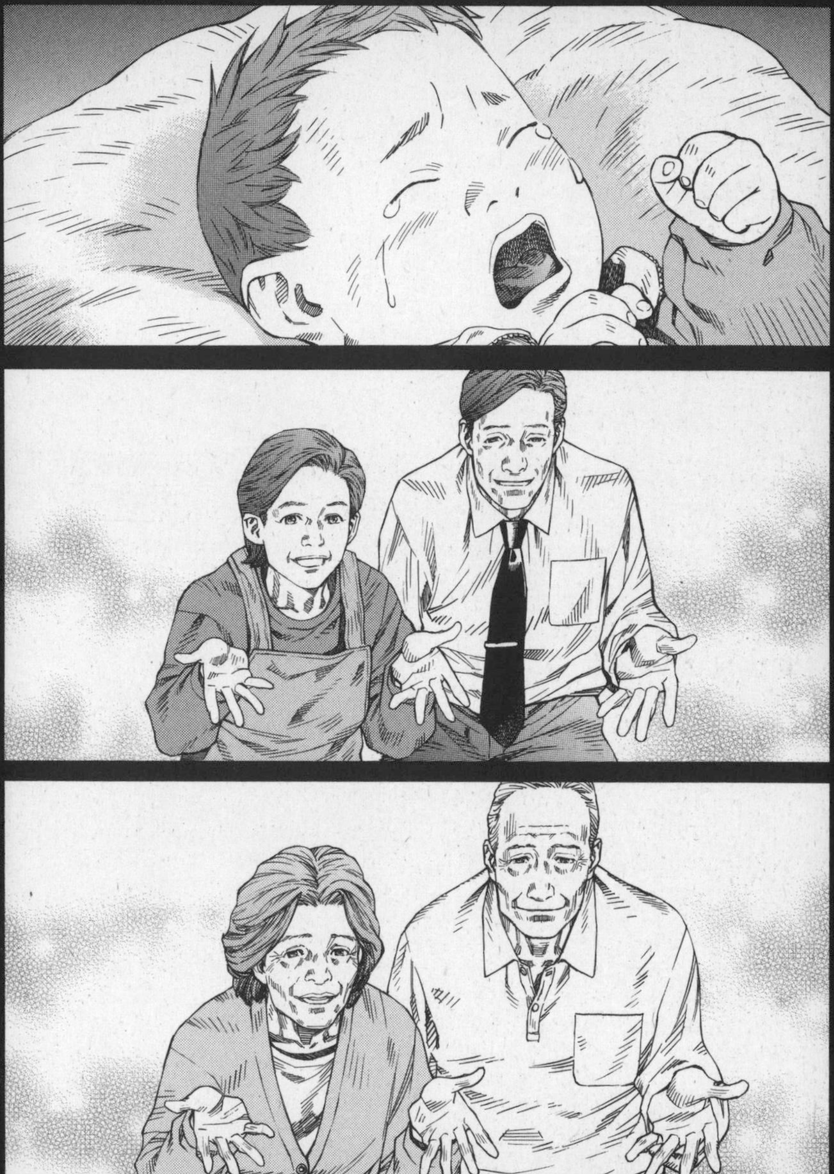

I'M HOME.

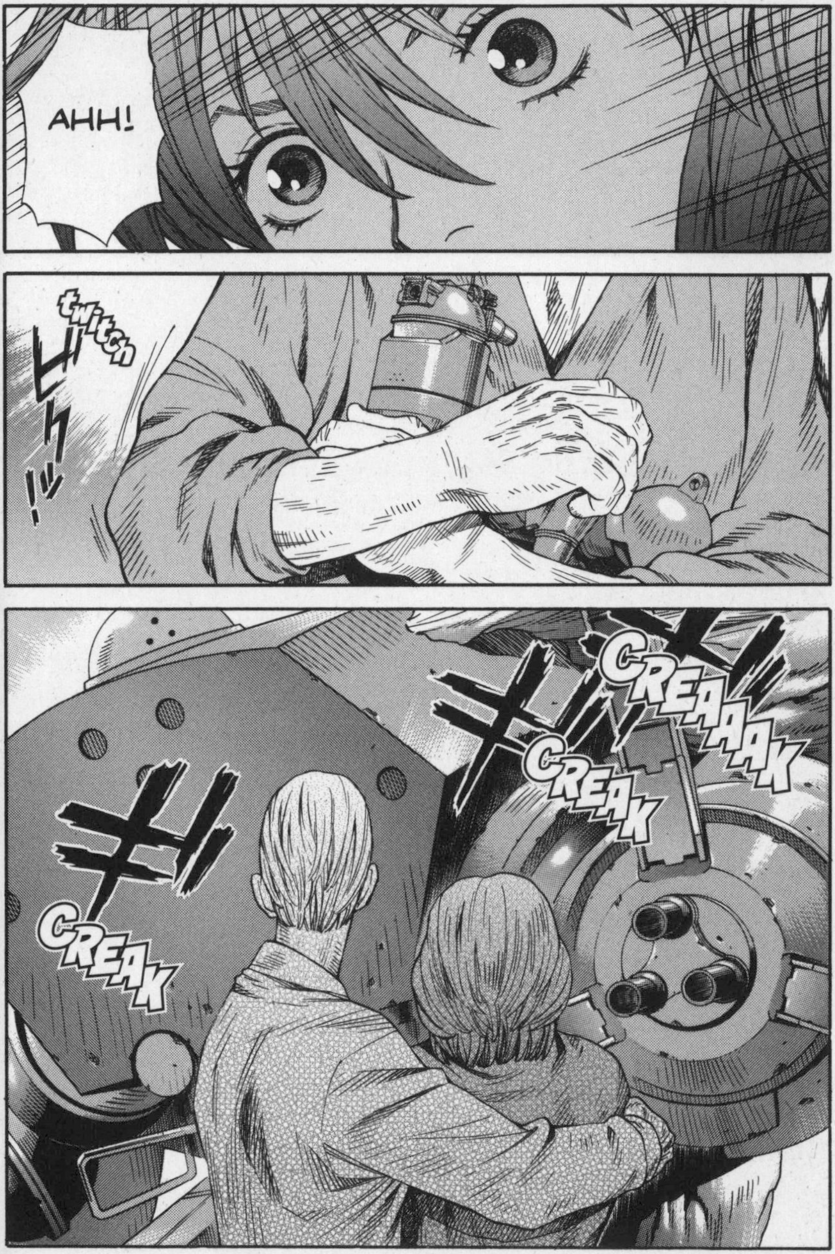
AHH!
twitch
ビクッ!!
CREAAAAK
CREAK
CREAK

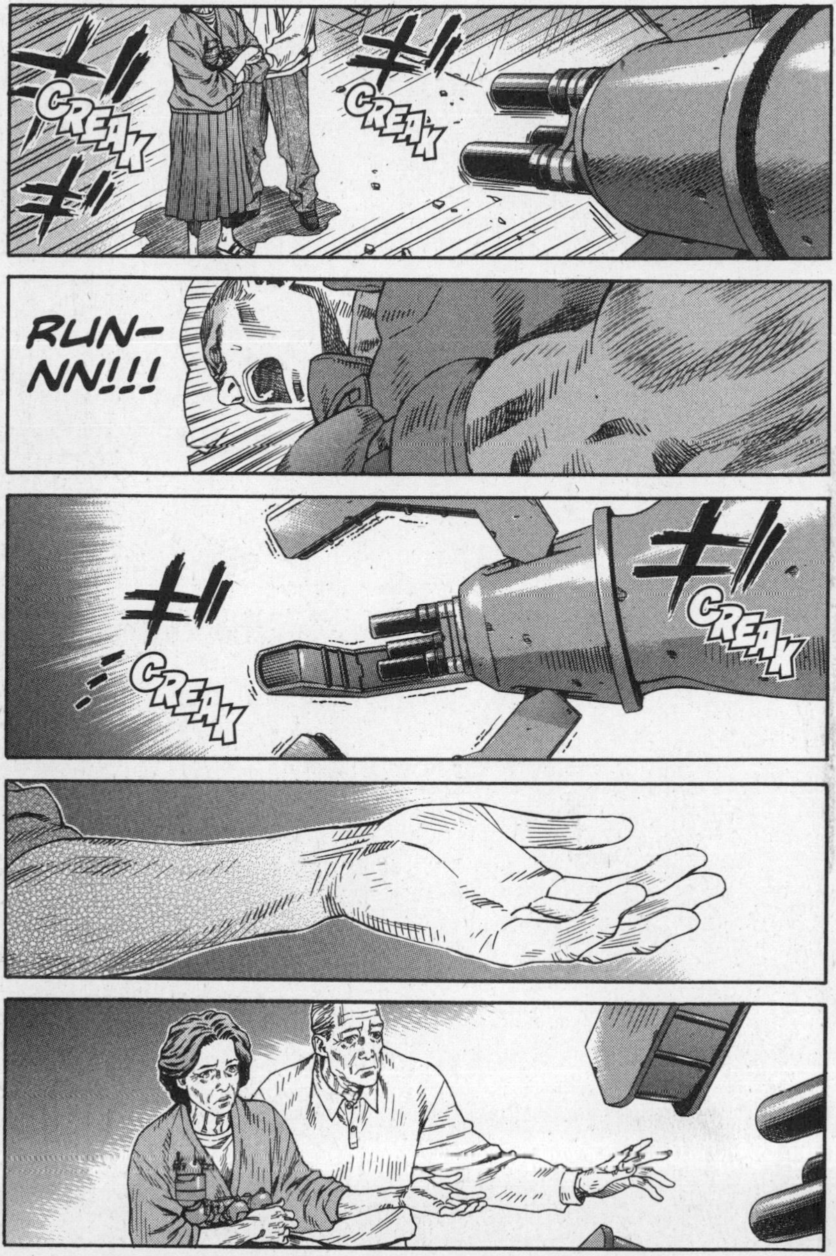
CREAK
CREAK
RUN-NN!!!
CREAK
CREAK

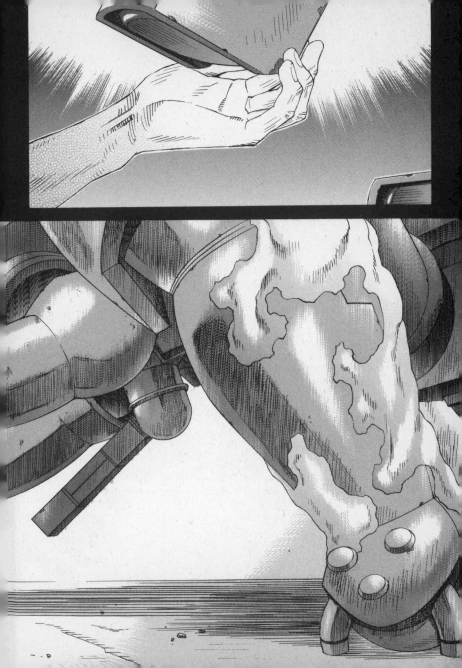

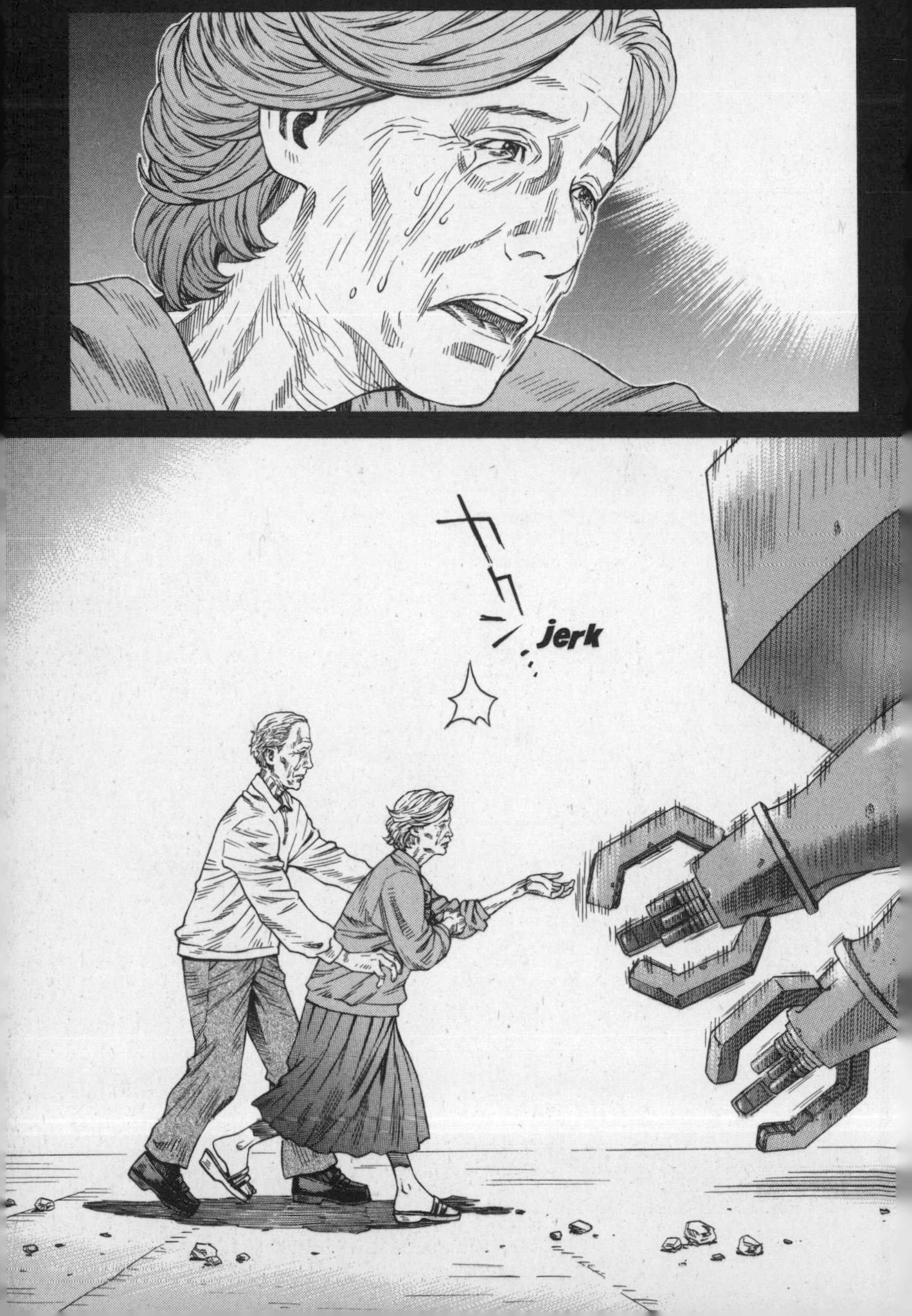
jerk

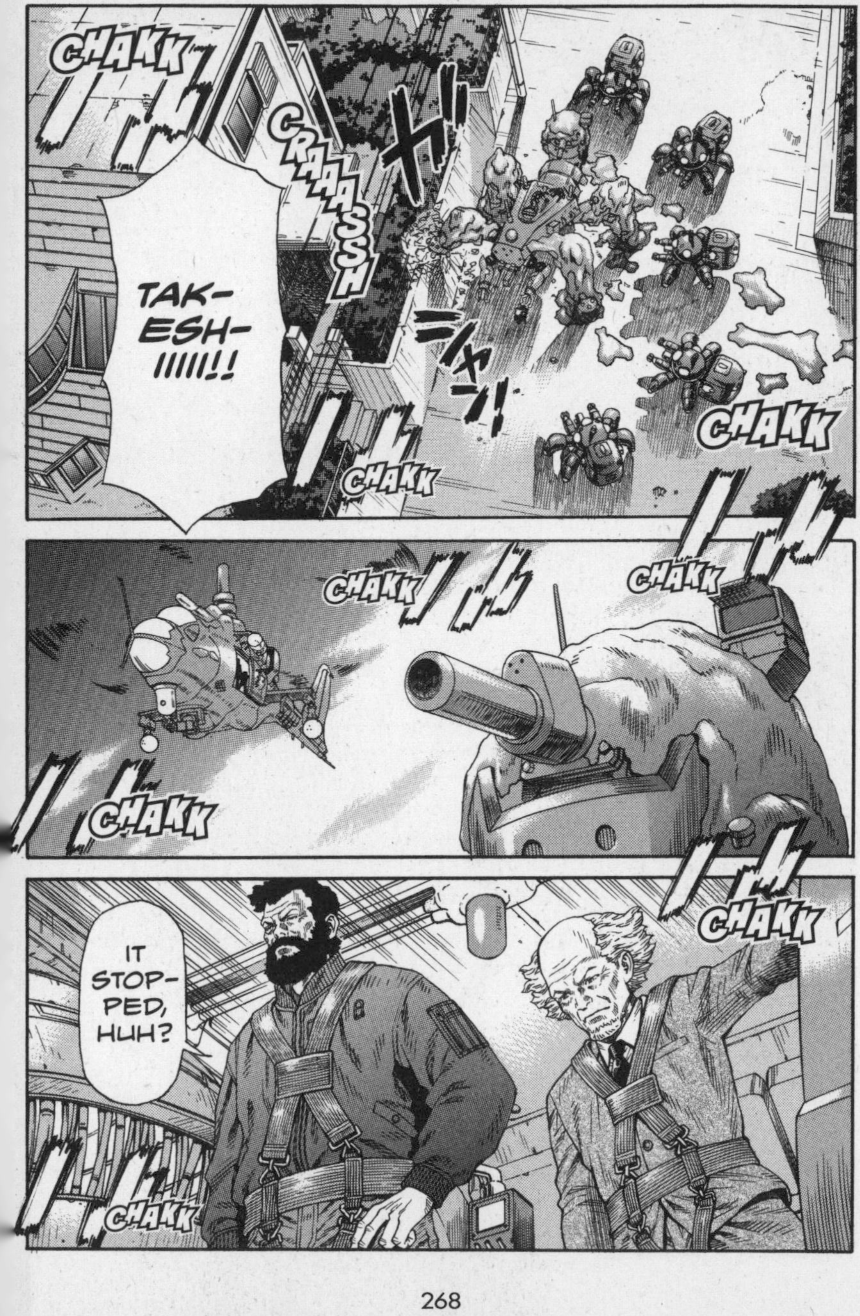
CHAKK
CRAAAASSH
CHAKK
TAK-
ESH-
IIIIII!!
CHAKK
CHAKK
CHAKK
CHAKK
CHAKK
IT STOP-
PED,
HUH?
CHAKK

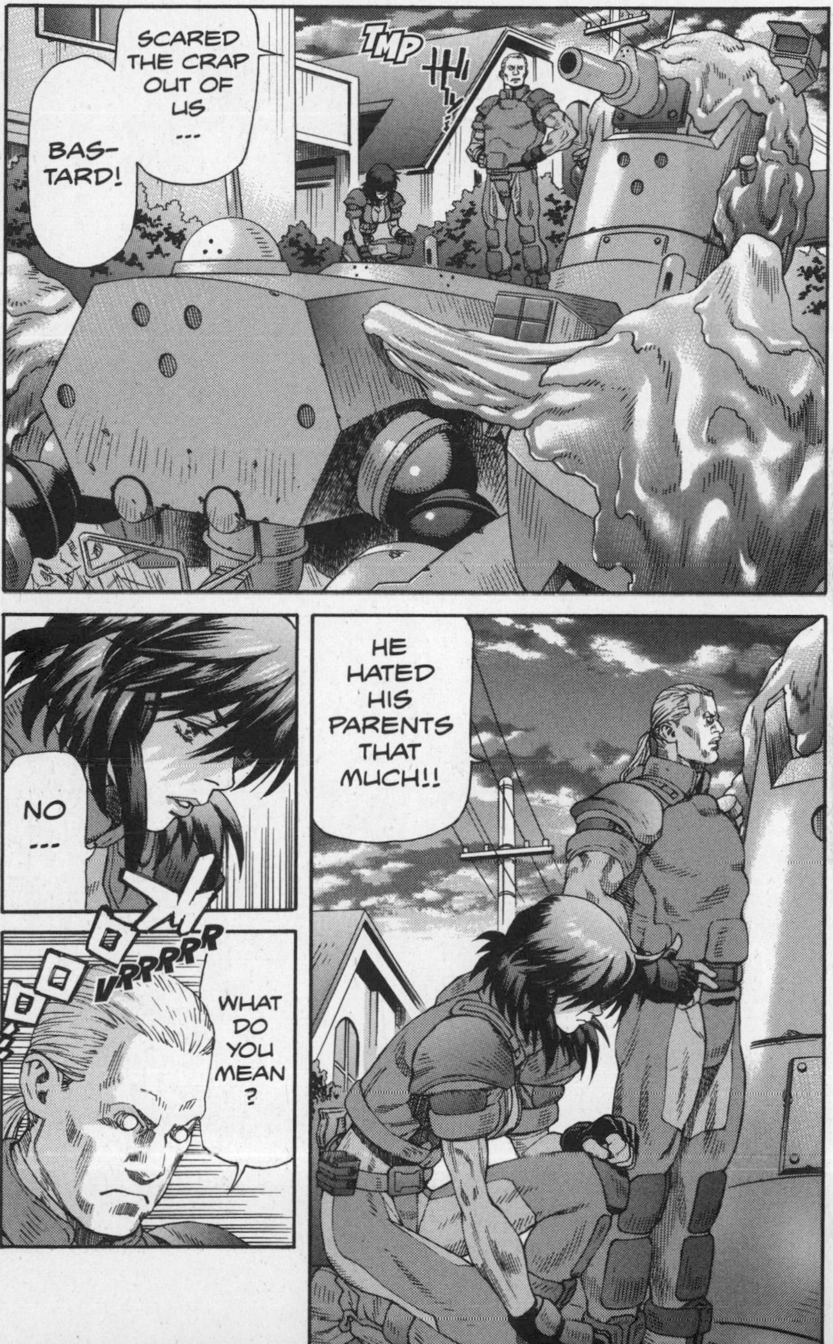
TMP
SCARED THE CRAP OUT OF US --- BAS-TARD!
HE HATED HIS PARENTS THAT MUCH!!
NO ---
VRRRRR
WHAT DO YOU MEAN ?

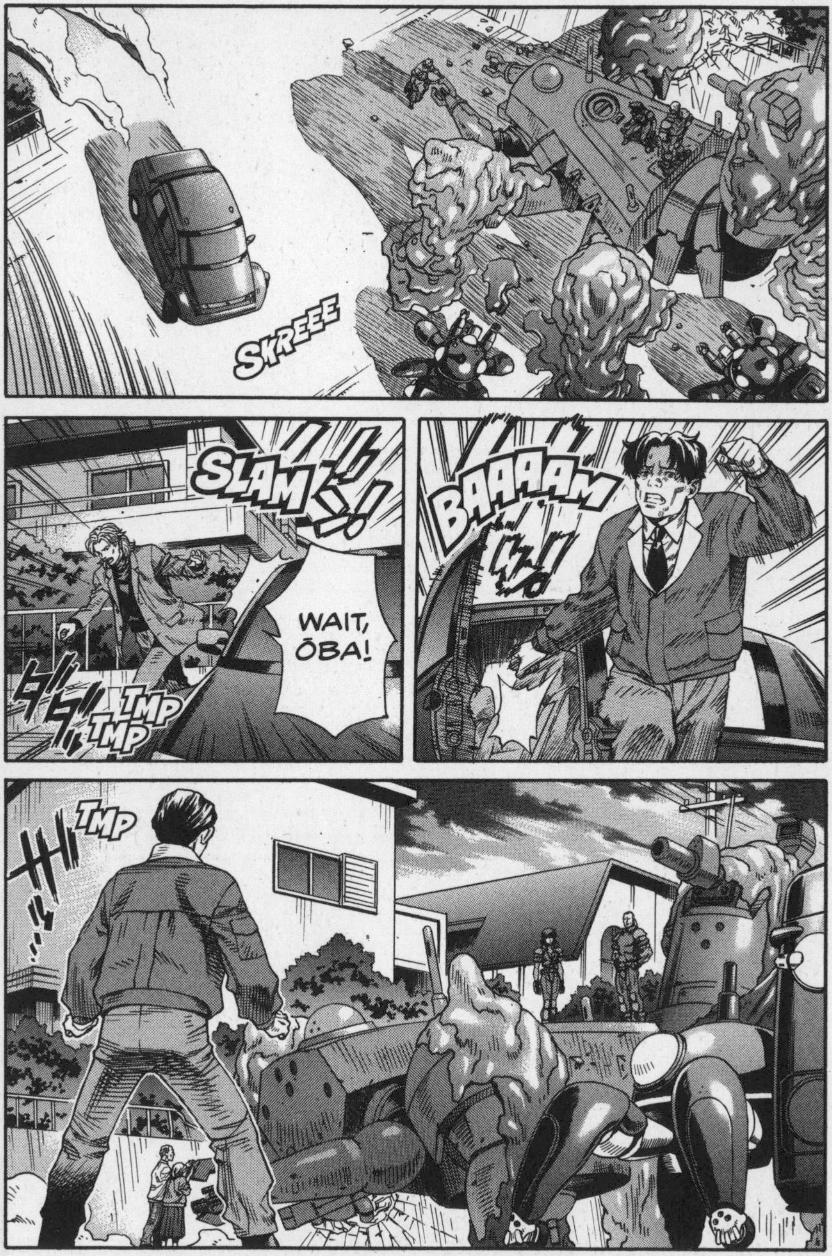
SKREEE
BAAAAAM
SLAM
WAIT, ŌBA!
TMP
TMP
TMP

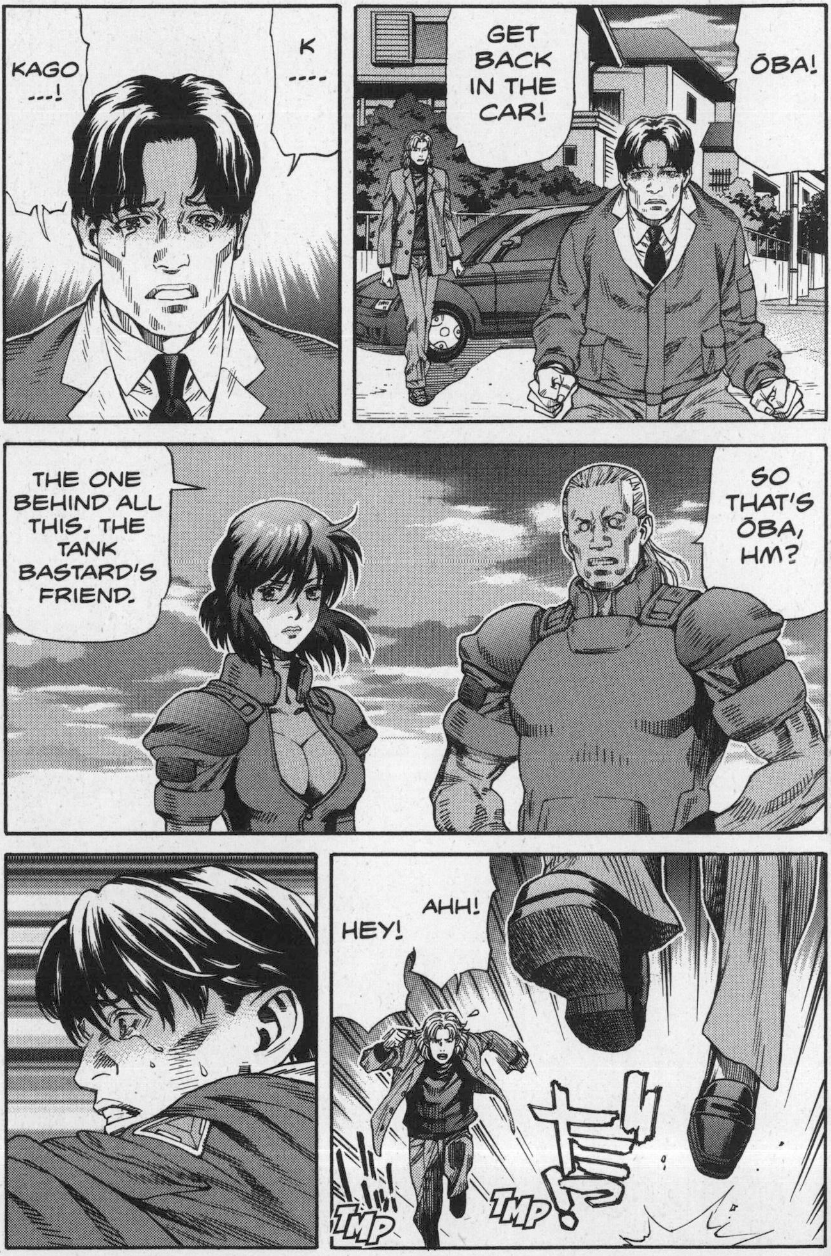
ŌBA!
GET BACK IN THE CAR!
K ----
KAGO ---!
SO THAT'S ŌBA, HM?
THE ONE BEHIND ALL THIS. THE TANK BASTARD'S FRIEND.
AHH!
HEY!
TMP
TMP

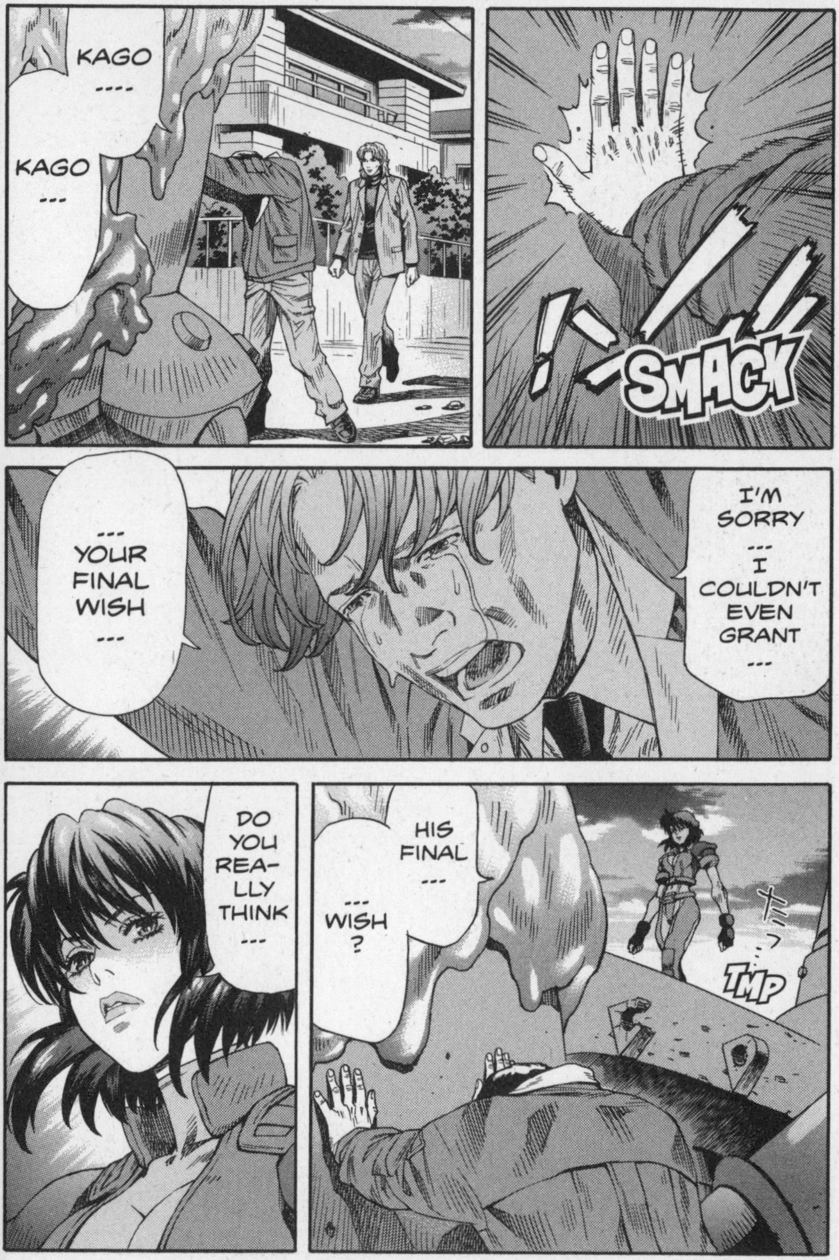
SMACK
KAGO ----
KAGO ---
I'M SORRY --- I COULDN'T EVEN GRANT ---
--- YOUR FINAL WISH ---
HIS FINAL --- --- WISH ?
TMP
DO YOU REA-LLY THINK ---

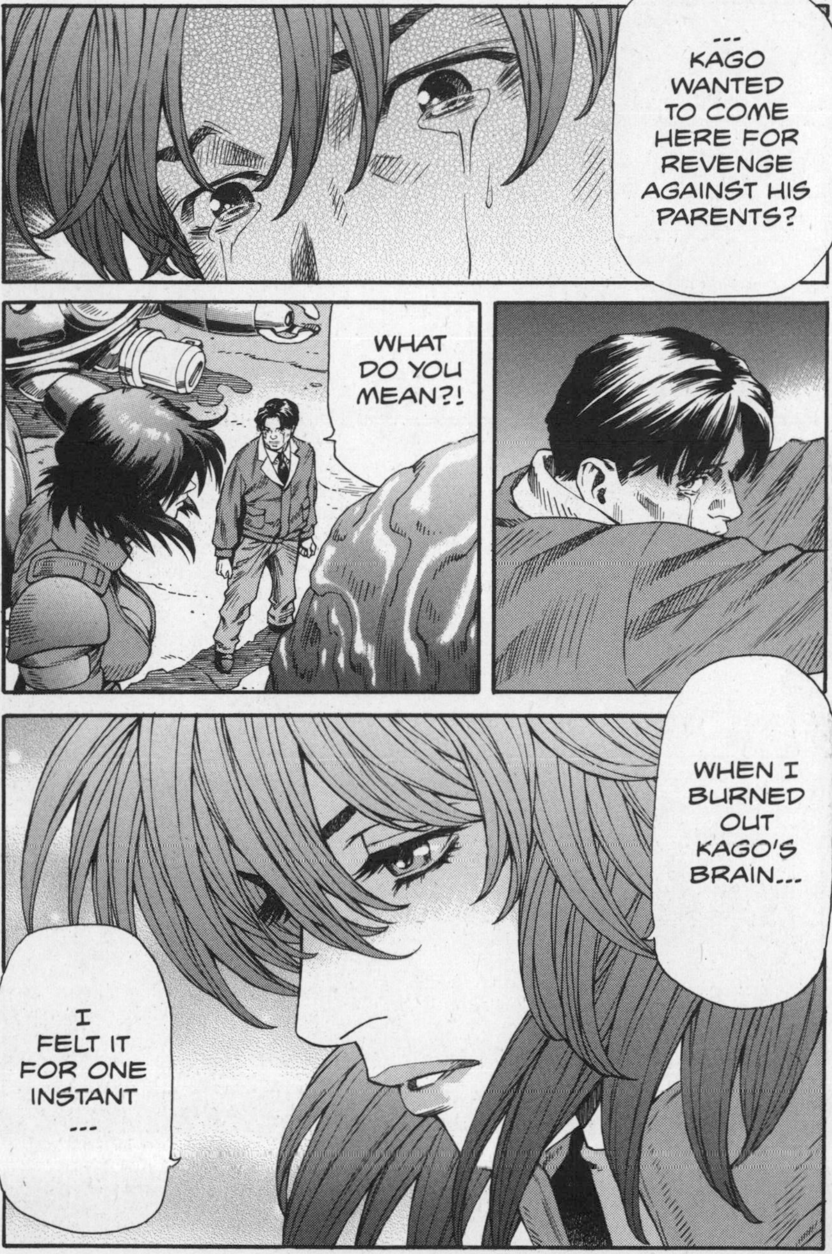
... KAGO WANTED TO COME HERE FOR REVENGE AGAINST HIS PARENTS?
WHAT DO YOU MEAN?!
WHEN I BURNED OUT KAGO'S BRAIN...
I FELT IT FOR ONE INSTANT ...

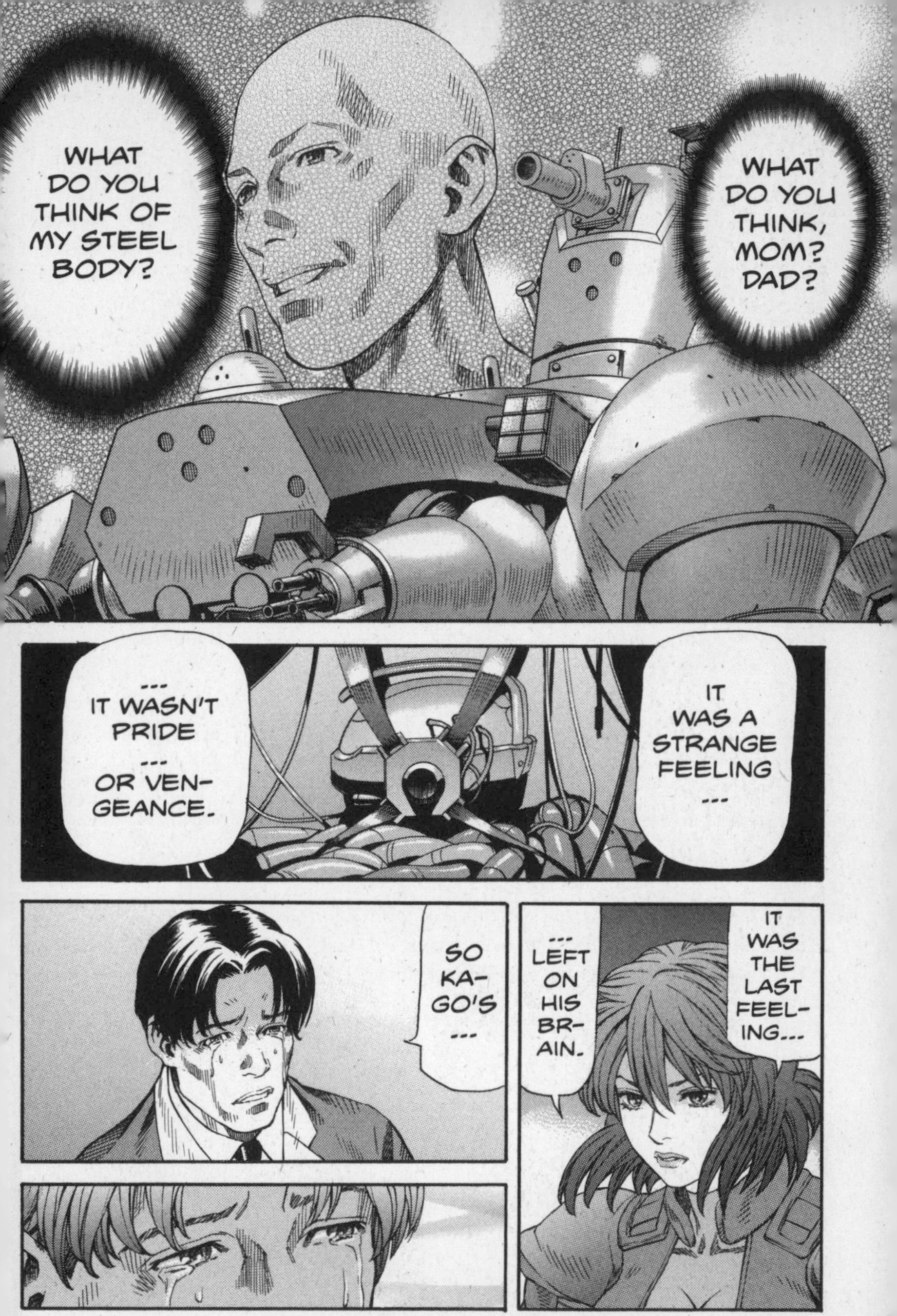
WHAT DO YOU THINK, MOM? DAD?
WHAT DO YOU THINK OF MY STEEL BODY?
IT WAS A STRANGE FEELING ---
--- IT WASN'T PRIDE --- OR VEN-GEANCE.
IT WAS THE LAST FEEL-ING...
--- LEFT ON HIS BR-AIN.
SO KA-GO'S ---

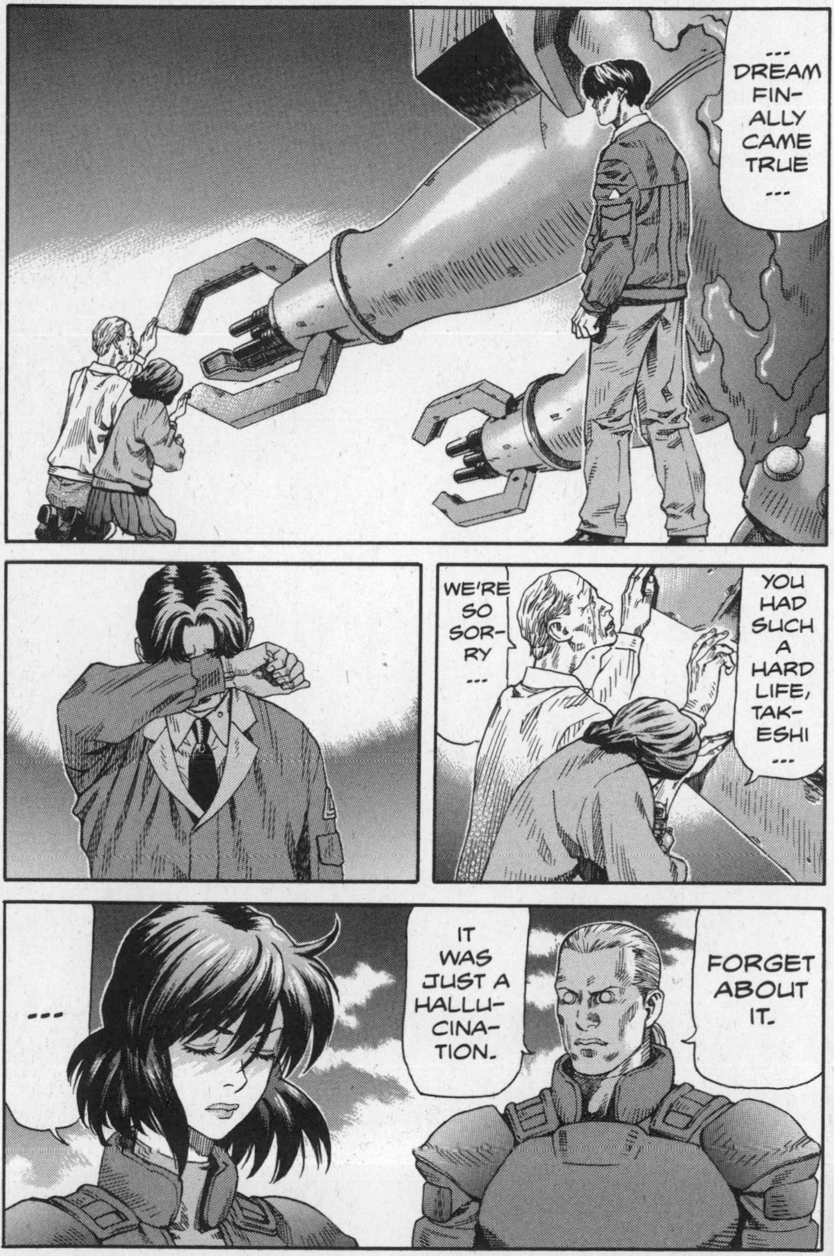
...DREAM FINALLY CAME TRUE...
YOU HAD SUCH A HARD LIFE, TAKESHI...
WE'RE SO SORRY...
FORGET ABOUT IT.
IT WAS JUST A HALLUCINATION.
...

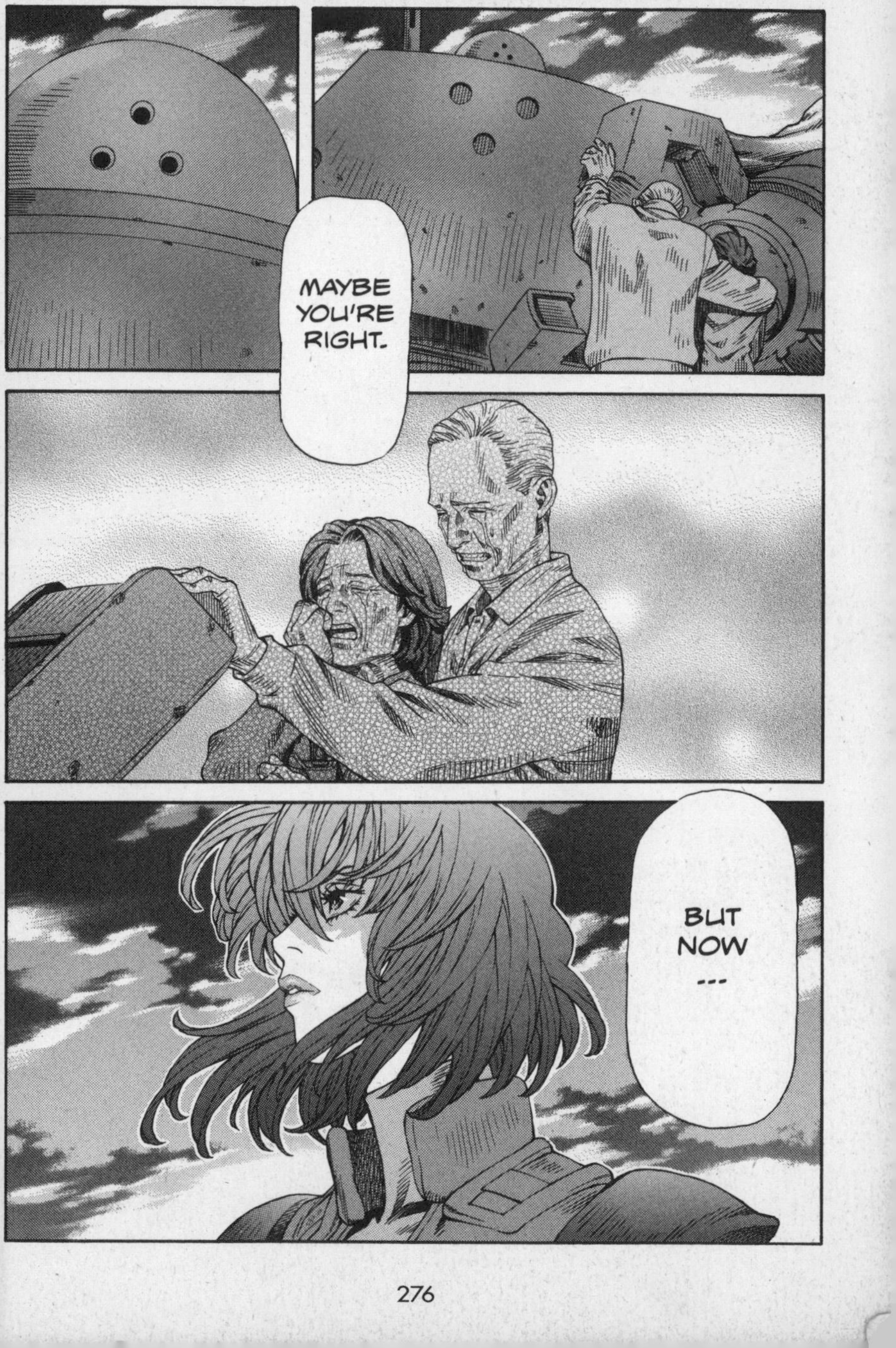
MAYBE YOU'RE RIGHT.
BUT NOW ...

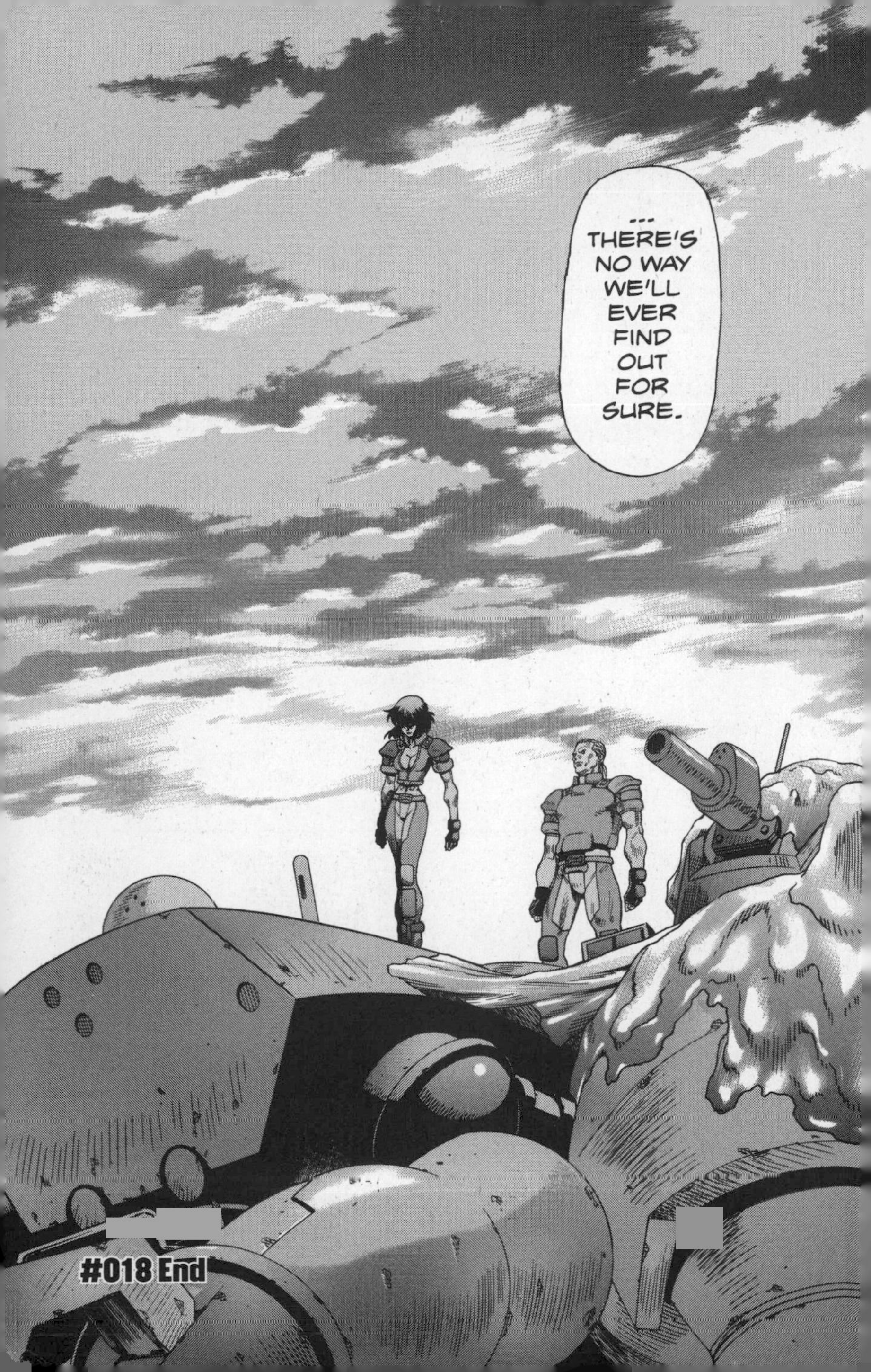
... THERE'S NO WAY WE'LL EVER FIND OUT FOR SURE.
#018 End

MARDOCK

マルドゥック・スクランブル

SCRAMBLE

**Created by
Tow Ubukata** ✕ **Manga by
Yoshitoki Oima**

"I'd rather be dead."

Rune Balot was a lost girl with
nothing to live for. A man
named Shell took her in and
cared for her...until he tried
to murder her. Standing at
the precipice of death Rune is
saved by Dr. Easter, a private
investigator, who uses an
experimental procedure known
as "Mardock Scramble 09."
The procedure grants Balot
extraordinary abilities. Now,
Rune must decide whether to
use her new powers to help Dr.

Ages: 16+

Easter bring Shell to justice, or if she even has the will to keep
living a life that's been broken so badly.

**KC
KODANSHA
COMICS**

VISIT KODANSHACOMICS.COM TO:
• View release date calendars for upcoming volumes
• Find out the latest about upcoming Kodansha Comics series

© Tow Ubukata / Yoshitoki Oima / KODANSHA LTD. All rights reserved.

BY **OH!GREAT**

Itsuki Minami needs no introduction—everybody's heard of the "Babyface" of the Eastside. He's the strongest kid at Higashi Junior High School, easy on the eyes but dangerously tough when he needs to be. Plus, Itsuki lives with the mysterious and sexy Noyamano sisters. Life's never dull, but it becomes downright dangerous when Itsuki leads his school to victory over vindictive Westside punks with gangster connections. Now he stands to lose his school, his friends, and everything he cares about. But in his darkest hour, the Noyamano girls give him an amazing gift, one that just might help him save his school: a pair of Air Trecks. These high-tech skates are more than just supercool. They'll enable Itsuki to execute the wildest, most aggressive moves ever seen—and introduce him to a thrilling and terrifying new world.

Ages: 16 +

Special extras in each volume! Read them all!

VISIT WWW.KODANSHACOMICS.COM TO:
- View release date calendars for upcoming volumes
- Find out the latest about new Kodansha Comics series

Air Gear © 2003 Oh!great / KODANSHA LTD. All rights reserved.

GHOST IN THE SHELL
STAND ALONE COMPLEX
EPISODE TESTATION·